Cancer-Leading Proteases

Cancer-Leading Proteases

Structures, Functions, and Inhibition

Edited by

Satya P. Gupta

ELSEVIER

ACADEMIC PRESS

An imprint of Elsevier

Academic Press is an imprint of Elsevier
125 London Wall, London EC2Y 5AS, United Kingdom
525 B Street, Suite 1650, San Diego, CA 92101, United States
50 Hampshire Street, 5th Floor, Cambridge, MA 02139, United States
The Boulevard, Langford Lane, Kidlington, Oxford OX5 1GB, United Kingdom

Library of Congress Cataloging-in-Publication Data
A catalog record for this book is available from the Library of Congress

British Library Cataloguing-in-Publication Data
A catalogue record for this book is available from the British Library

ISBN 978-0-12-818168-3

For information on all Academic Press publications
visit our website at https://www.elsevier.com/books-and-journals

Publisher: Andre Gerhard Wolff
Acquisition Editor: Erin Hill-Parks
Editorial Project Manager: Tracy Tufaga
Production Project Manager: Kiruthika Govindaraju
Cover Designer: Victoria Pearson

Typeset by SPi Global, India

Contents

Contributors

Numbers in parentheses indicate the pages on which the authors' contributions begin.

Nilanjan Adhikari (265), Natural Science Laboratory, Division of Medicinal and Pharmaceutical Chemistry, Department of Pharmaceutical Technology, Jadavpur University, Kolkata, India

Gouri Ahir (295), RASA Life science Informatics, Pune, India

Hanan A. Al-Dossary (417), Institute for Research and Medical Consultations (IRMC), Imam Abdulrahman Bin Faisal University, Dammam, Saudi Arabia

Meneerah Abdurhman Aljafary (417), Department of Biology, College of Science, Imam Abdulrahman Bin Faisal University, Dammam, Saudi Arabia

Khulood Mohammed Al-Khater (417), Department of Anatomy, College of Medicine, Imam Abdulrahman Bin Faisal University, Dammam, Saudi Arabia

Ebtesam Abdullah Al-Suhaimi (417), Department of Biology, College of Science, Imam Abdulrahman Bin Faisal University, Dammam, Saudi Arabia

Sk. Abdul Amin (265), Natural Science Laboratory, Division of Medicinal and Pharmaceutical Chemistry, Department of Pharmaceutical Technology, Jadavpur University, Kolkata, India

Ghulam Md Ashraf (295), King Fahd Medical Research Center; Department of Medical Laboratory Technology, Faculty of Applied Medical Sciences, King Abdulaziz University, Jeddah, Saudi Arabia

Reem A. Assuhaimi (417), Institute for Research and Medical Consultations (IRMC), Imam Abdulrahman Bin Faisal University, Dammam, Saudi Arabia

Himani Balutia (243), National Institute of Pharmaceutical Education and Research (NIPER), Kolkata, India

Anwar L. Bilgrami (295), Deanship of Scientific Research, King Abdulaziz University, Jeddah, Saudi Arabia

Diana Campos-Iglesias (73), Department of Biochemistry and Molecular Biology, University Institute of Oncology (IUOPA), University of Oviedo, Oviedo, Spain

Sapana Sameer Chaudhary (295), RASA Life science Informatics, Pune, India

Sameer Choudhary (295), RASA Life science Informatics, Pune, India

V. Cicaloni (13), Department of Biotechnology, Chemistry and Pharmacy (Department of Excellence 2018-2022), University of Siena; Toscana Life Sciences, Siena, Italy

Rohit Dutt (51), School of Medical and Allied Sciences, GD Goenka University, Gurugram, India

Sayan Dutta Gupta (1), Department of Pharmaceutical Chemistry, Gokaraju Rangaraju College of Pharmacy, Hyderabad, India

Abdelhamid Elaissari (417,449), Univ Lyon, University Claude Bernard Lyon-1, CNRS, LAGEP-UMR 5007, Lyon, France

I. Fotopoulos (165), Department of Pharmaceutical Chemistry, School of Pharmacy, Aristotle University of Thessaloniki, Thessaloniki, Greece

José M.P. Freije (73), Department of Biochemistry and Molecular Biology, University Institute of Oncology (IUOPA), University of Oviedo, Oviedo, Spain

Ankit Ganeshpurkar (121), Pharmaceutical Chemistry Research Laboratory, Department of Pharmaceutical Engineering & Technology, Indian Institute of Technology (Banaras Hindu University), Varanasi, India

Vandana Garg (51), MD University, Rohtak, India

Rishitha Gundala (243), National Institute of Pharmaceutical Education and Research (NIPER), Kolkata, India

Satya P. Gupta (1), Department of Pharmaceutical Technology, Meerut Institute of Engineering and Technology, Meerut, India

Nahor Haddish-Berhane (359), Janssen Research & Development, LLC, Spring House, PA, United States

D. Hadjipavlou-Litina (165), Department of Pharmaceutical Chemistry, School of Pharmacy, Aristotle University of Thessaloniki, Thessaloniki, Greece

B.S. Harish (215), Bioprospecting Laboratory, Department of Biotechnology, School of Chemical and Biotechnology, SASTRA Deemed University, Thanjavur, India

Srabanti Jana (121), Pharmaceutical Chemistry Research Laboratory, Department of Pharmaceutical Engineering & Technology, Indian Institute of Technology (Banaras Hindu University), Varanasi, India

Tarun Jha (265), Natural Science Laboratory, Division of Medicinal and Pharmaceutical Chemistry, Department of Pharmaceutical Technology, Jadavpur University, Kolkata, India

Deepak Kumar (391), Organic & Medicinal Chemistry, Council of Scientific and Industrial Research-Indian Institute of Chemical Biology, Kolkata, India

Devendra Kumar (121), Pharmaceutical Chemistry Research Laboratory, Department of Pharmaceutical Engineering & Technology, Indian Institute of Technology (Banaras Hindu University), Varanasi, India

Sanjay Kumar (391), Division of Biology, Indian Institute of Science Education & Research Tirupati, Tirupati, India

R. Lavanya (243), National Institute of Pharmaceutical Education and Research (NIPER), Kolkata, India

Carlos López-Otín (73), Department of Biochemistry and Molecular Biology, University Institute of Oncology (IUOPA), University of Oviedo, Oviedo, Spain

A.K. Madan (51), Pt. BD Sharma University of Health Sciences, Rohtak, India

Ayesha Mahmood (449), Faculty of Pharmacy, The University of Lahore, Lahore, Pakistan

Subhajit Makar (121), Pharmaceutical Chemistry Research Laboratory, Department of Pharmaceutical Engineering & Technology, Indian Institute of Technology (Banaras Hindu University), Varanasi, India

Tanima Mandal (391), Cancer Biology & Inflammatory Disorder Division, Council of Scientific and Industrial Research-Indian Institute of Chemical Biology, Kolkata, India

Ashima Nagpal (51), School of Medical and Allied Sciences, GD Goenka University, Gurugram, India

Dolly A. Parasrampuria (359), Janssen Research & Development, LLC, Spring House, PA, United States

A. Peperidou (165), Department of Pharmaceutical Chemistry, School of Pharmacy, Aristotle University of Thessaloniki, Thessaloniki, Greece

F. Pettini (13), Department of Biotechnology, Chemistry and Pharmacy (Department of Excellence 2018-2022), University of Siena, Siena, Italy

Nitesh Kumar Poddar (183), Department of Biosciences, Manipal University Jaipur, Jaipur, Rajasthan, India

E. Pontiki (165), Department of Pharmaceutical Chemistry, School of Pharmacy, Aristotle University of Thessaloniki, Thessaloniki, Greece

Pankaj Kumar Rai (183), Department of Biotechnology, Invertis University, Bareilly, India

Vijaya Ravinayagam (417), Nanomedicine Research Department, Institute for Research and Medical Consultations (IRMC), Deanship of Scientific Research, Imam Abdulrahman Bin Faisal University, Dammam, Saudi Arabia

Sakshi Rawat (295), RASA Life science Informatics, Pune, India

Kuldeep K. Roy (243), National Institute of Pharmaceutical Education and Research (NIPER), Kolkata, India

Priyanka Saha (391), Cancer Biology & Inflammatory Disorder Division, Council of Scientific and Industrial Research-Indian Institute of Chemical Biology, Kolkata, India

Adeeb Shehzad (417), Department of Clinical Pharmacy, Institute for Research and Medical Consultations (IRMC), Imam Abdulrahman Bin Faisal University, Dammam, Saudi Arabia

Devendra Shukla (391), Cancer Biology & Inflammatory Disorder Division, Council of Scientific and Industrial Research-Indian Institute of Chemical Biology, Kolkata, India

Sushil Kumar Singh (121), Pharmaceutical Chemistry Research Laboratory, Department of Pharmaceutical Engineering & Technology, Indian Institute of Technology (Banaras Hindu University), Varanasi, India

O. Spiga (13), Department of Biotechnology, Chemistry and Pharmacy (Department of Excellence 2018-2022), University of Siena, Siena, Italy

Amit Kumar Srivastava (391), Cancer Biology & Inflammatory Disorder Division, Council of Scientific and Industrial Research-Indian Institute of Chemical Biology, Kolkata, India

Mohamad Tarhini (417,449), Univ Lyon, University Claude Bernard Lyon-1, CNRS, LAGEP-UMR 5007, Lyon, France

Rajiv Kumar Tonk (327), Department of Pharmaceutical Chemistry, Delhi Pharmaceutical Sciences and Research University, New Delhi, India

A. Trezza (13), Department of Biotechnology, Chemistry and Pharmacy (Department of Excellence 2018-2022), University of Siena, Siena, Italy

Kiran Babu Uppuluri (215), Bioprospecting Laboratory, Department of Biotechnology, School of Chemical and Biotechnology, SASTRA Deemed University, Thanjavur, India

Ravichandiran Velayutham (243), National Institute of Pharmaceutical Education and Research (NIPER), Kolkata, India

Saroj Verma (327), Department of Pharmaceutical Chemistry, Delhi Pharmaceutical Sciences and Research University, New Delhi, India

Alex Yu (359), Janssen Research & Development, LLC, Spring House, PA, United States

Nadiah Zafar (449), Faculty of Pharmacy, The University of Lahore, Lahore, Pakistan

About the Editor

Satya P. Gupta is presently a Professor Emeritus at Meerut Institute of Engineering and Technology (MIET), Meerut, India, after retiring as Professor in the Department of Applied Sciences at National Institute of Technical Teachers' Training and Research (NITTTR), Bhopal. Earlier he served at Tata Institute of Fundamental Research (TIFR), Mumbai, a world renowned Institution of India, Birla Institute of Technology and Science (BITS), Pilani, and then at MIET as its Director-cum Distinguished Professor in the Department of Pharmacy. Professor Gupta has a very long standing of teaching various courses such as Physical Chemistry, Quantum Chemistry, Pharmaceutical Chemistry, Biophysics, and Drug Design. He had obtained his M.Sc. and D.Phil. degrees from University of Allahabad, Allahabad, in 1967 and 1971, respectively. He is a world renowned scientist. For his work in Drug Design, he has bagged several honors and awards. To his credit, Gupta has more than 200 research publications in highly reputed national and international journals and several reviews in highly prestigious periodicals such as Chemical Reviews (American Chemical Society), Progress in Drug Research (Birkhäuser Verlag, Basel, Switzerland), and Current Medicinal Chemistry (Bentham Science, the Netherlands), and has been on editorial board of several international journals. Dr. Gupta himself has been editor of several scientific journals and books of international repute published by Springer-Verlag, Berlin; Heidelberg, Germany; CRC Press, Taylor and Francis Group; Nova Science Publishers, NY, USA; and Elsevier (Academic Press), USA. He has delivered several invited plenary/key-note lectures in various national and international conferences on Drug Design as well as chaired various scientific sessions in these conferences. His scientific activity has brought him on the forefront of scientific community of the world.

Preface

Proteases that are also known as proteinases or peptidases regulate diverse biochemical processes in humans, such as gene expression, differentiation, and cell death. A few of them are selectively found in cancer cells. The set of proteases involved in cancer progression is collectively known as the "cancer degradome." There are five classes of proteases: cysteine proteases, serine proteases, aspartic proteases, threonine proteases, and metalloproteases, all of which are involved in cancer initiation, growth, metastasis, and invasion. This book presents a detailed account of the structures and functions of these proteases and the mechanism by which they can be involved in cancer progression and how they can be inhibited. Some introductory remarks on all these aspects of proteases are presented by Gupta and Duttagupta in the very first chapter entitled "Cancer-Leading Proteases: An Introduction" to arouse the curiosity among the readers to go through the whole book. These proteases, as obvious, constitute good targets to develop anticancer drugs. Chapter 2, written by Trezza et al. and entitled as "Potential Roles of Protease Inhibitors as Anticancer Drugs," focuses attention on protease inhibitors, describing their structure and mechanism of action. Shifting to the roles of individual families of proteases and their inhibitors, Dutt et al. presented in Chapter 3 a detail of studies on cysteine proteases and their inhibitors for anticancer drug design. In Chapter 4 entitled "Ubiquitin-specific Proteases as Targets for Anti-cancer Drug Therapies," Campos-Iglesias et al. discuss the growing relevance of using ubiquitin-specific proteases (USPs) as targets in cancer therapy and the current status of small inhibitory molecules against USP functions. USPs are involved in a plethora of cellular processes, several of which are frequently altered in cancer. Chapter 5 authored by Ganeshpurkar et al. and entitled as "Aspartic Proteases: Potential Drug Targets for Anticancer Drug Development" presents the structural aspects of various aspartic proteases (APs) and a collective view on the structure and ligand-based drug design for the inhibition of this class of proteases.

It has been found that human immunodeficiency virus (HIV) protease, one of the enzymes crucial to the life cycle of HIV, could be important to serve as a target to develop anticancer agents for HIV-induced cancer types. In fact, many cancers have been found to be related to HIV infection, such as Kaposi's sarcoma, B-cell lymphomas (Hodgkin/Non-Hodgkin Lymphoma), leukemia, and breast, prostate, and cervical cancers, which become the main cause of death in HIV-infected persons. Therefore, Pontiki et al. presented in Chapter 6 entitled

"Inhibitors of HIV Protease in Cancer Therapy" the detail of design and discovery of inhibitors of HIV protease and their importance in cancer therapy. More recently, it was reported that the serine proteases such as hepsin, maspin, kallikreins, and matriptase-2 are overexpressed in ovarian cancer (OC) and they may contribute to tumor progression by promoting the extracellular lytic activity of tumor cells. Therefore, Rai and Poddar presented in Chapter 7 entitled "Serine Proteases in Ovarian Cancer" an insight into the roles of these serine proteases and their inhibitors in ovarian cancer. In continuation to this, Harish and Uppuluri presented a detail of some serine proteases that are specific to prostate cancer in Chapter 8 entitled as "Serine Proteases Leading to Prostate Cancer: Structures, Functions, and Development of Anticancer Drugs." In this chapter, authors present a detail of structures and functions of serine proteases specific to prostate cancer and their inhibitors. Not only HIV protease but also hepatitis C virus (HCV) NS3/4A serine protease is also associated with cancer. It leads to hepatocellular carcinoma (HCC) or liver cancer, which is the second leading cause of cancer-related death worldwide. Therefore, Gundala et al. presented in Chapter 9 entitled "HCV NS4 Serine Protease as a Drug Target for Development of Drugs against Hepatocellular Carcinoma (Liver Cancer)" a wide variety of HCV NS3/4A protease inhibitors that have been approved or are under clinical investigation for the treatment of various HCV genotypes and thus for the prevention of HCV-induced HCC. The two subgroups of matrix metalloproteases (MMPs), collagenases (MMP-1, MMP-8, and MMP-13) and gelatinases (MMP-2 and MMP-9), have been found to play crucial role in progression, metastasis, and angiogenic events related to cancer. Therefore, their inhibitors may be an effective remedy for cancer prevention and treatment and thus a number of compounds with different zinc-binding groups and nonzinc-binding features have been discussed in detail in Chapter 10 authored by Adhikari et al. and entitled as "Collagenases and Gelatinases and Their Inhibitors as Anti-cancer Agents."

c-Met, also known as hepatocyte growth factor receptor (HGFR), is a protein encoded by c-MET gene. In all breast cancers, c-Met is overexpressed in 20%–30% of the cases, and around 52% in triple negative breast cancer (TNBC), which is the most aggressive subgroup of breast cancers. c-Met targeting drugs have potential role in targeting many cancers including TNBC, but to maximize the efficacy proper selection and study is required. This aspect of c-Met has been very well presented by Chaudhary et al. in Chapter 11 entitled "c-Met as a Potential Therapeutic Target in Triple Negative Breast Cancer." In Chapter 12 entitled "Rhomboid Proteases Leading to Cancer: Structures, Functions and Inhibition," Verma and Tonk discuss about rhomboid proteases and their inhibitors. Rhomboids are most conserved family of intramembrane cleaving proteases and are implicated in the progression of cancer cells. The chapter reviews biological functions and structures of rhomboid proteases to advance the understanding of the topic in the exploration of potential anticancer drugs. The RAS oncogenes are the focus of intense research since they are mutated in a wide range of cancers and make these malignancies particularly intractable to current therapies. The KRAS isoform of RAS is found to be mutated in 84% of all RAS-mutant cancers making it a high value target for drug therapy. Therefore, Parasrampuria et al. have presented in Chapter 13 entitled "KRAS: Structure, Function and Development of Anticancer Drugs" the detail of structure and function of this oncogene and how it can be exploited to develop anticancer drugs.

Though majority of studies have been related to the role of proteases in initiating the cancer, a large number of studies have shown that dozens of proteases have firm tumor suppressive activity. In Chapter 14 entitled "Tumor Suppressive Proteases Revisited: Role in Inhibiting Tumor Progression and Metastasis," Shukla et al. have discussed current knowledge on the multidimensional impact of tumor-suppressive proteases in various types of cancer. Additionally, these authors have highlighted known mechanisms through which tumor-suppressive proteases display antitumor properties. Thus, cancer therapy has not been solely based on synthetic drugs inhibiting proteases, but some other means also have been found to treat cancer. Nowadays, a huge research is directed to the role of vitamin D in treating the cancer. Vitamin D has been found to downregulate serine proteases and matrix metalloproteases and upregulate the angiogenesis inhibitors in tumors. Thus in Chapter 15 entitled "Vitamin D as Therapeutic Agent Acting against Cancers Caused by Proteases," AL-Suhaimi et al. present comprehensive, up-to-date descriptive roles of vitamin D in the regulation of cell functions through modulation of proteases and protease inhibitors. Conclusively, vitamin D supplement alone or in combination with cancer therapy may help to prevent or reduce cancer incidence and mortality. Mahmood et al., however, have presented in the last chapter entitled "Molecular Imaging of Proteases in Cancer" how molecular imaging has been of great help to treat cancer. Molecular imaging has made possible the accurate and early disease detection, phenotyping, and staging by gathering information about the molecular mechanisms underlying physiological cellular processes in diseased tissues. Molecular Imaging for proteases in cancer includes Nuclear Imaging (SPECT, PET, MRI, hyperpolarize MRI), Optical Imaging, and Ultrasound Imaging modalities. I greatly enjoyed reading all these chapters and hope so will do the readers. I thank all the authors for their excellent contributions.

Satya P. Gupta
Meerut Institute of Engineering and Technology, Meerut, India

Chapter 1

Cancer-leading proteases: An introduction

Satya P. Gupta[a], Sayan Dutta Gupta[b]

[a]*Department of Pharmaceutical Technology, Meerut Institute of Engineering and Technology, Meerut, India,* [b]*Department of Pharmaceutical Chemistry, Gokaraju Rangaraju College of Pharmacy, Hyderabad, India*

1.1 Introduction

Proteases are ubiquitously expressed enzymes that hydrolyze the peptide bond between amino acid residues in a protein. They are also known as proteinases or peptidases. In normal cells, 2% of proteins are proteases, wherein they regulate diverse biochemical process like gene expression, differentiation, cell death, etc. A few of the proteases are selectively found in cancer cells. However, they are not exclusively expressed by cancer cells. In many instances, cancer cells induce the expression of proteases in neighboring normal cells, thereby favoring invasion. The set of proteases involved in cancer progression is collectively known as the "cancer degradome." From the standpoint of anticancer targets, proteases are classified depending on the amino acid residue of the catalytic site. Thus they have been classified as cysteine proteases, serine proteases, aspartic proteases, threonine proteases, and metalloproteases (Rakashanda et al., 2012). All the five classes of proteases are involved in cancer initiation, growth, metastasis, and invasion (Herszényi et al., 2014). Fig. 1.1 presents a general model to show how proteases play roles in dissemination and colonization of tumor cells by direct and indirect activation of other proteinase cascades and related factors (Rakashanda et al., 2012).

In normal cells proteases are required to carry out biological processes, but a balance between them and their antiproteases is required for healthy cells; otherwise any disturbance to this balance leads to many diseases such as cancer. Steps starting from tumor initiation, growth, metastasis, and finally invasion into some other site involve all five classes of proteases as mentioned above.

Cancer-Leading Proteases. https://doi.org/10.1016/B978-0-12-818168-3.00001-2

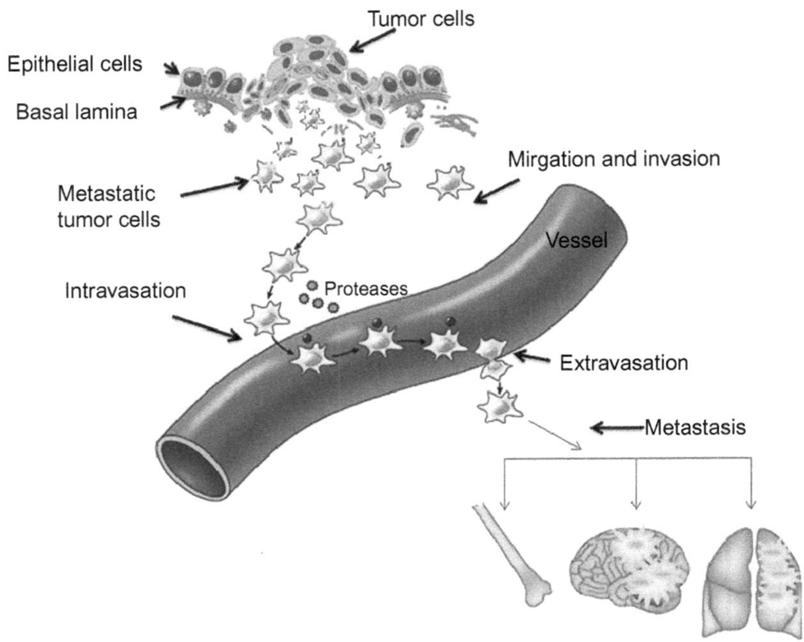

FIG. 1.1 Presenting a general model to show how proteases play roles in dissemination and colonization of tumor cells by direct and indirect activation of other proteinase cascades and related factors. *(Reprinted from Rakashanda, S., Rana, F., Rafiq, S., Masood, A., Amin, S., 2012. Role of proteases in cancer: a review. Biotechnol. Mol. Biol. Rev. 74, 90–101 (Open Access publication).)*

Proteases found in some viruses also lead to cancer (Gupta, 2017). This chapter presents a brief introductory description of all five classes of proteases, their roles in progression of some cancers, and their inhibitors. An introductory remark is also presented on the roles of anticancer on some of these proteases.

1.2 Different classes of proteases

1.2.1 Cysteine proteases

Cysteine proteases are characterized by an active site cysteine residue and are secreted in some cell types under pathological conditions. These proteases mediate general functions such as intracellular protein catabolism and specialized functions, e.g., selective activation of signaling molecules like interleukin, enkephalin, protein kinase C, or extracellular protein degradation. Several studies have shown that there exists a correlation between the activity of lysosomal cysteine proteases and tumor progression. Cysteine proteases can be localized in the lysosome (cathepsins B, L, H, and S), or cytosol (calpains), and are secreted in some cell types under pathological conditions. Cathepsin cysteine proteases have been shown to function intracellularly as well as extracellularly and thus can degrade both intracellular and extracellular matrix (ECM) proteins (Jedeszko and Sloane, 2004; Joyce et al., 2004; Mohamed and Sloane, 2006; Gocheva and Joyce, 2007). Since extracellular activity of cathepsins allows cancer cells to attack nearby tissues, blood, and lymph vessels and metastasize to outlying tissues (Vasiljeva and Turk, 2008; Matarrese et al., 2010), they are considered to be promising targets for anticancer therapy (Jedeszko and Sloane, 2004; Gocheva and Joyce, 2007). Cathepsin B was the first lysosomal protease to be associated with breast carcinoma (Poole et al., 1978).

1.2.2 Serine proteases

In serine proteases the active site is serine residue. This class of proteases is closely related to cell growth and differentiation. The normal regulation of their activities is essential for physiological activities of the cell, and abnormal regulation can lead to pathological conditions.

A number of studies have shown that the expression of serine proteases and their enzyme activity regulation are closely related to malignant phenotype of tumors. Trypsin is one of the best characterized serine proteases that have been found to play crucial roles in a wide range of important pathological processes, e.g., atherosclerosis, inflammation, and cancer, while being important for many physiological processes such as food digestion, blood coagulation, fibrinolysis, and control of blood pressure (Borg, 2004). Trypsin has been found to be involved in colorectal carcinogenesis and in promoting proliferation, invasion, and metastasis (Yamamoto et al., 2003; Soreide et al., 2006). However, the understanding as to how trypsin causes cancer is in progress, but it is known that trypsin activates and is coexpressed with matrix metalloproteases (MMPs), another class of proteases as mentioned above, which are known to facilitate invasion and metastasis (Nyberg et al., 2002).

1.2.3 Aspartic proteases

Aspartic proteases contain two highly conserved aspartates in the active site and are optimally active at acidic pH. They use an activated water molecule bound to one or more aspartate residues for catalysis of their peptide substrate. Nearly all known aspartic proteases are inhibited by pepstatin. Eukaryotic aspartic proteases include pepsins, cathepsins, and renins. They have a two-domain structure, arising from ancestral duplication. With reference to cancer, the most crucial member of this family of proteases has been cathepsin-D (Cath-D). It is an aspartic endo-protease that is ubiquitously distributed in lysosomes (Barrett and Cathepsin, 1970) and has been extensively studied for its role in cancer development and as a suggested independent tumor marker. Studies have shown that Cath-D stimulates cancer cell proliferation, fibroblast outgrowth, angiogenesis, and metastasis (Vashishta et al., 2007; Hu et al., 2008; Ohri et al., 2008).

1.2.4 Threonine proteases

Threonine proteases are a family of proteolytic enzymes harboring a threonine (Thr) residue within the active site. The prototype members of this class of enzymes are the catalytic subunits of the proteasome. Aberrant proteasome-dependent proteolysis is assumed to be associated with the pathophysiology of some malignancies. Therefore, the study on the inhibition of proteasome function is thought to be useful to design a novel class of anticancer drugs. It has been observed that proteasome inhibition leads to the accumulation of pro-apoptotic proteins in tumorigenic cells but not normal tissue (Berenson et al., 2006; Kane et al., 2006).

1.2.5 Matrix metalloproteases

Matrix metalloproteases (MMPs), also known as matrixins, are calcium-dependent zinc-containing endopeptidases. They belong to a larger family of proteases known as the metzincin superfamily and are capable of degrading all kinds of extracellular matrix proteins. They are also thought to play a major role in cell behaviors such as cell proliferation, migration (adhesion/dispersion), differentiation, angiogenesis, apoptosis, and host defense. The overactivation of these enzymes results in tissue degradation, leading to a wide array of disease processes such as rheumatoid arthritis, osteoarthritis, tumor metastasis, multiple sclerosis, congestive heart failure, and a host of others (Gupta, 2012). MMPs have drawn great attention due to their ability to cleave virtually any component of the ECM and basement membranes, thereby allowing cancer cells to penetrate and infiltrate the subjacent stromal matrix (Brinckerhoff and Matrisian, 2002; Bertucci and Birnbaum, 2009; Jemal et al., 2010). Thus MMPs have established their relevance in cancer research, and for the last several years they are being exploited for the investigation of useful anticancer drugs. The secretion and activation of MMPs result from a specific interaction between tumor and stromal cells (Nielsen et al., 2001; De Wever and Mareel, 2003) as shown in Fig. 1.2. Thus the relevance of MMPs in cancer research has grown considerably, and particularly two subfamilies, collagenases (MMP-1, MMP-8, and MMP-13) and gelatinases (MMP-2 and MMP-9), have been well studied for their roles in cancer development and to be exploited for the investigation of anticancer drugs.

1.3 Mechanism of cancerous roles of proteases

Living beings contain an extracellular matrix (ECM), which is a three-dimensional network of extracellular macromolecules, such as collagen, enzymes, and glycoproteins, that give structural and biochemical support to surrounding cells. Components of the ECM are produced intracellularly by resident cells and secreted into the ECM via exocytosis (Plopper, 2007). The common functions of this ECM are cell adhesion, cell-to-cell communication,

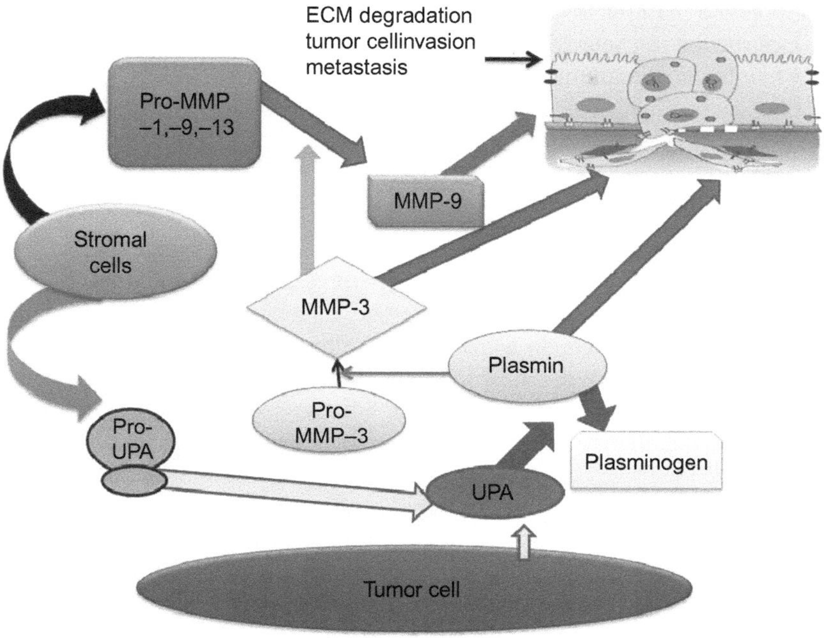

FIG. 1.2 A schematic representation of the role of matrix metalloproteinases in extracellular matrix (ECM) degradation, invasion, and metastasis. *(Reprinted from Rakashanda, S., Rana, F., Rafiq, S., Masood, A., Amin, S., 2012. Role of proteases in cancer: a review. Biotechnol. Mol. Biol. Rev. 74, 90–101 (Open Access publication).)*

and differentiation (Abedin and King, 2010). Proteolytic enzymes degrade or disrupt ECM and basement membranes (BMs) that are highly specialized extracellular matrices viewed as dynamic and versatile environments which modulate cellular behaviors to regulate tissue development, function, and repair. This act of proteolytic enzymes allows the in situ cancer cells to migrate into the adjacent stroma or to disseminate to distant organ, and it is commonly accepted that progression from in situ to invasive or metastatic cancer is caused by proteases produced by tumor cells that increase linearly in concentration with tumor progression (Herszényi et al., 2000, 2012; Man et al., 2013; Mignatti and Rifkin, 1993; Liotta and Stetler-Stevenson, 1991; Sun, 2010). As summarized by Herszényi et al. (2014), general roles of proteases in cancer progression can be as follows:

1. Degradation or disruption of basement membrane and extracellular matrix
2. Produce components which allow the in situ cancer cells to disseminate to distant organ
3. Formation of a complex microenvironment that promotes malignant transformation
4. Activation of growth factors, adhesion molecules

5. Suppression of tumor cell apoptosis
6. Destruction of chemokine gradients
7. Modulation of antitumor immune reactions
8. Dual and complex role in angiogenesis

1.4 Protease specificity

Proteases typically bind to a single amino acid on the substrate and so only have specificity for that residue. Also some proteases are highly specific and only cleave substrates with a certain sequence. Endoproteases that break peptide bonds of nonterminal amino acids within the molecule specifically recognize certain amino acids or types of amino acids, and for them not only are the amino acids forming the peptide bond important, but also neighboring residues play a role in their specificity. This specificity is mediated by specificity pockets, regions within the protease around the active site that bind some amino acid side chains more favorably than others. Some of the most common protease specificities may be mentioned, e.g., trypsin-like proteases predominantly cleave proteins at the carboxyl side of arginine or lysine, chymotrypsin-like proteases prefer to cleave on the carboxyl side of large aromatic residues (tryptophan, tyrosine, or phenylalanine), caspase-like proteases predominantly cleave on the carboxyl side of aspartate, but one caspase in Drosophila has been shown to also cleave on the carboxyl side of glutamate, and elastase-like proteases predominantly cleave on the carboxyl side of small, aliphatic amino acids (glycine, alanine, or valine) (Ritchie, 2013).

1.5 Protease inhibitors

Protease inhibitors can be derived from proteins, peptides, or small molecules. Proteins or peptides are usually naturally occurring inhibitors, but synthetic peptide-like or small molecule inhibitors are developed in laboratories. Fig. 1.3 shows examples of all three types of protease inhibitors, where compound **1** (Aprotinin) refers to a small protein that acts as bovine pancreatic trypsin inhibitor (BPTI), **2** (E-64) refers to a peptide-like molecule that can irreversibly inhibit a wide range of cysteine proteases, and **3** (phenylmethylsulfonyl fluoride) refers to a small molecule which acts as a serine protease inhibitor. MMPs have their own specific endogenous tissue inhibitors (TIMPs), which comprise a family of four protease inhibitors: TIMP-1, TIMP-2, TIMP-3, and TIMP-4 (Brew et al., 2000).

For developing protease inhibitors for therapeutic applications, however, one should have complete understanding of the mechanism by which inhibitors inhibit the proteases. Inhibitors can involve reversible inhibition or irreversible inhibition, where in the case of the former inhibitors usually bind to the protease with multiple noncovalent interactions and after the reaction is complete the inhibitors are removed from the protease and in the case of the latter, inhibitors

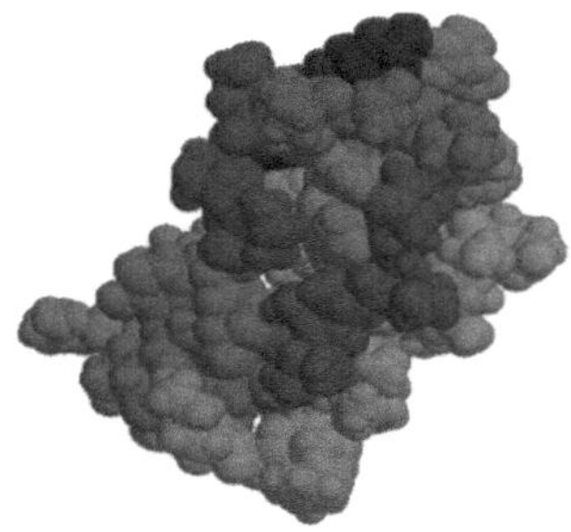

1, Aprotinin (a small protein bovine pancreatic trypsin inhibitor, BPTI)

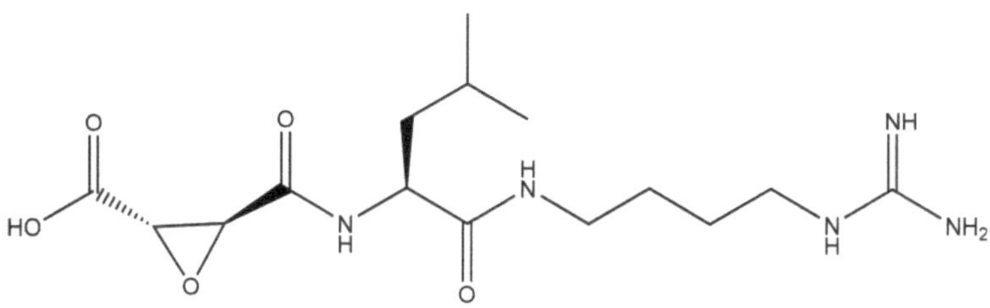

2, E-64 (an epoxide)

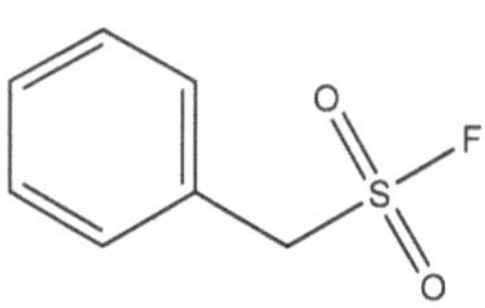

3, Phenylmethylsulfonyl fluoride (PMSF)

FIG. 1.3 Examples of three different types of protease inhibitors: **1**, a naturally occurring peptide (BPTI); **2**, a peptide-like molecule (E-64, an epoxide); and **3**, a small molecule (PMSF).

function by specifically altering the active site of its specific target through the covalent bond formation. Reversible inhibition can be of three types: competitive, uncompetitive, and noncompetitive. In competitive inhibition, inhibitors bind to the active site of the protease, competing with substrates for access to the active site residues. In uncompetitive inhibition, inhibitors bind only to the protease when it is already attached to a substrate and in noncompetitive inhibition, inhibitors bind to the protease with or without bound substrate with similar affinities and inhibit protease activity through an allosteric mechanism. In addition to these three types of common inhibitors, there is one more type of inhibitors known as suicide inhibitors, which are typically analogs of the substrate and are a type of irreversible inhibitors that covalently bind to the protease.

However, in addition to protease inhibitors derived from proteins, peptides, or small molecules, vitamin D also has been found to play anticancer role (Álvarez-Díaz et al., 2010). The active vitamin D metabolite, 1α,25-dihydroxyvitamin D3 (1,25$(OH)_2D_3$, calcitriol), is a major regulator of gene expression in higher organisms. It has been recently shown that calcitriol strongly induces the expression of cystatin D, an inhibitor of several cysteine proteases of the cathepsin family, which may contribute to its antitumor effect against colon cancer by mechanisms that are both dependent and independent of cathepsin inhibition (Álvarez-Díaz et al., 2010). Vitamin D modulates the activity of MMPs and serine proteases. It has been shown that $1,25(OH)_2D_3$ inhibits invasion of prostate cancer cells via modulation of selective proteases (Bao et al., 2006) and that it and its analogues downregulate cell invasion-associated proteases in cultured malignant cells (Koli and Keski-Oja, 2000).

1.6 Anticancer activity of proteases

Notwithstanding the roles of proteases in the development and spread of cancer, they also have been studied for their anticancer roles (Dudani et al., 2018). There have been studies on their diverse roles in posttranslational modification and signaling in a complex microenvironment that exploit protease activity for anticancer effect. Protease activity may be measured as a biomarker of cancer, with wide-ranging utility from early detection to monitoring therapeutic response. Attempts are being made to exploit protease activity to improve cancer management on diagnostic and therapeutic fronts. Protease-activated therapeutics have been found to incorporate more sophisticated activation strategies in the tumor microenvironment, which is particularly useful for therapeutics with dose-limiting off-target toxicity (Choi et al., 2012). Proteases have been found to modulate immune function and mediate therapeutic resistance, and therefore investigations have been made for combination therapies to thwart resistance or potentiate existing treatment. Proteolytic pathways that elicit therapeutic resistance are enhanced in doxorubicin-treated cancer cells, e.g., MMP-7 cleaved Fas ligand off the cell surface, resulting in decreased cell death (Mitsiades et al., 2001). MMP-9 has been found to have a tumor-protective effect (Nakasone et al., 2012). However, the complexity of protease function in cancer suggests that it is important to target them in combination with other therapies; for example, inhibiting proteases to potentiate therapies that target another aspect of cancer biology could improve outcomes.

1.7 Conclusions

There are five different families of proteases. All these proteases play major roles in cancer invasion and metastasis as well as in malignant transformation of precancerous lesions into cancer. Thus they have been found as good targets for the development of anticancer agents. Protease inhibitors can be derived from proteins, peptides, or small molecules. Additionally, vitamin D also has been found to play anticancer role. It has been shown that $1,25(OH)_2D_3$, an active vitamin D metabolite, inhibits prostate cancer cells invasion via modulation of selective proteases. However, proteases have also been studied for their anticancer roles.

Nonetheless, the complexity of protease function in cancer suggests that it is important to target them in combination with other therapies.

References

Abedin, M., King, N., 2010. Diverse evolutionary paths to cell adhesion. Trends Cell Biol. 20 (12), 734–742.

Álvarez-Díaz, S., Larriba, M.J., López-Otín, C., Muñoz, A., 2010. Vitamin D: proteases, protease inhibitors and cancer. Cell Cycle 9, 32–37.

Bao, B.Y., Yeh, S.D., Lee, Y.F., 2006. 1alpha, 25-Dihydroxyvitamin D_3 inhibits prostate cancer cell invasion via modulation of selective proteases. Carcinogenesis 27, 32–42.

Barrett, A.J., Cathepsin, D., 1970. Purification of isoenzymes from human and chicken liver. Biochem. J. 117, 601–607.

Berenson, J.R., Yang, H.H., Sadler, K., Jarutirasarn, S.G., Vescio, R.A., Mapes, R., et al., 2006. Phase I/II trial assessing bortezomib and melphalan combination therapy for the treatment of patients with relapsed or refractory multiple myeloma. J. Clin. Oncol. 24, 937–944.

Bertucci, F., Birnbaum, D., 2009. Distant metastasis: not out of reach any more. J. Biol. 8, 28. https://doi.org/10.1186/jbiol128.

Borg, T.K., 2004. It's the matrix! ECM, proteases, and cancer. Am. J. Pathol. 164, 1141–1142.

Brew, K., Dinakarpandian, D., Nagase, H., 2000. Tissue inhibitors of metalloproteinases: evolution, structure and function. Biochim. Biophys. Acta 1477, 267–283.

Brinckerhoff, C.E., Matrisian, L.M., 2002. Matrix metalloproteinases: a tail of a frog that became a prince. Nat. Rev. Mol. Cell Biol. 3, 207–214.

Choi, K.Y., Swierczewska, M., Lee, S., Chen, X., 2012. Protease-activated drug development. Theranostics 2, 156–178.

De Wever, O., Mareel, M., 2003. Role of tissue stroma in cancer cell invasion. J. Pathol. 200, 429–447.

Dudani, J.S., Warren, A.D., Bhatia, S.N., 2018. Harnessing protease activity to cancer care. Annu. Rev. Cancer Biol. 2, 353–376.

Gocheva, V., Joyce, J.A., 2007. Cysteine cathepsins and the cutting edge of cancer invasion. Cell Cycle 1, 60–64.

Gupta, S.P. (Ed.), 2012. Matrix Metalloproteinase Inhibitors: Specificity of Binding and Structure-Activity Relationships. Springer Basel AG.

Gupta, S.P. (Ed.), 2017. Viral Proteases and Their Inhibitors. Academic Press (Elsevier), London (UK)/San Diego (US).

Herszényi, L., Plebani, M., Carraro, P., De Paoli, M., Roveroni, G., Cardin, R., et al., 2000. Proteases in gastrointestinal neoplastic diseases. Clin. Chim. Acta 291, 171–187.

Herszényi, L., Lakatos, G., Hritz, I., Varga, M.Z., Cierny, G., Tulassay, Z., 2012. The role of inflammation and proteinases in tumor progression. Dig. Dis. 30, 249–254.

Herszényi, L., Barabás, L., Hritz, I., István, G., Tulassay, I., 2014. Impact of proteolytic enzymes in colorectal cancer development and progression. World J. Gastroenterol. 20, 13246–13257.

Hu, L., Roth, J.M., Brooks, P., Luty, J., Karpatkin, S., 2008. Thrombin up-regulates cathepsin D which enhances angiogenesis, growth, and metastasis. Cancer Res. 68, 4666–4673.

Jedeszko, C., Sloane, B.F., 2004. Cysteine cathepsins in human cancer. Biol. Chem. 385, 1017–1027.

Jemal, A., Siegel, R., Xu, J., Ward, E., 2010. Cancer statistics, 2010. CA Cancer J. Clin. 60, 277–300.

Joyce, J.A., Baruch, A., Chehade, K., Meyer-Morse, N., Giraudo, E., 2004. Cathepsin cysteine proteases are effectors of invasive growth and angiogenesis during multistage tumorigenesis. Cancer Cell 5, 409–410.

Kane, R.C., Farrell, A.T., Sridhara, R., Pazdur, R., 2006. United States Food and Drug Administration approval summary: bortezomib for the treatment of progressive multiple myeloma after one prior therapy. Clin. Cancer Res. 12, 2955–2960.

Koli, K., Keski-Oja, J., 2000. 1alpha,25-Dihydroxyvitamin D_3 and its analogues downregulate cell invasion associated proteases in cultured malignant cells. Cell Growth Differ. 11, 221–229.

Liotta, L.A., Stetler-Stevenson, W.G., 1991. Tumor invasion and metastasis: an imbalance of positive and negative regulation. Cancer Res. 51, 5054s–5059s.

Man, Y.G., Stojadinovic, A., Mason, J., Avital, I., Bilchik, A., Bruecher, B., et al., 2013. Tumor-infiltrating immune cells promoting tumor invasion and metastasis: existing theories. J. Cancer 4, 84–95.

Matarrese, P., Barbara, A., Laura, C., Rosa, V., Carlo, L., Marco, S., et al., 2010. Cathepsin B inhibition interferes with metastatic potential of human melanoma: an *in vitro* and *in vivo* study. Mol. Cancer 9, 207.

Mignatti, P., Rifkin, D.B., 1993. Biology and biochemistry of proteinases in tumor invasion. Physiol. Rev. 73, 161–195.

Mitsiades, N., Yu, W., Poulaki, V., Tsokos, M., Stamenkovic, I., 2001. Matrix metalloproteinase-7-mediated cleavage of Fas ligand protects tumor cells from chemotherapeutic drug cytotoxicity. Cancer Res. 61, 577–581.

Mohamed, M.M., Sloane, B.F., 2006. Cysteine cathepsins: multifunctional enzymes in cancer. Nat. Rev. Cancer 6, 764–775.

Nakasone, E.S., Askautrud, H.A., Kees, T., Park, J.-H., Plaks, V., et al., 2012. Imaging tumor-stroma interactions during chemotherapy reveals contributions of the microenvironment to resistance. Cancer Cell 21, 488–503.

Nielsen, B.S., Rank, F., Lopez, J.M., Balbin, M., Vizoso, F., Lund, L.R., et al., 2001. Collagenase-3 expression in breast myofibroblasts as a molecular marker of transition of ductal carcinoma in situ lesions to invasive ductal carcinomas. Cancer Res. 61, 7091–7100.

Nyberg, P., Moilanen, M., Paju, A., Sarin, A., Stenman, U.H., Sorsa, T., et al., 2002. MMP-9 activation by tumor trypsin-2 enhances in vivo invasion of human tongue carcinoma cells. J. Dent. Res. 81, 831–835.

Ohri, S.S., Vashishta, A., Proctor, M., Fusek, M., Vetvicka, V., 2008. The propeptide of cathepsin D increases proliferation, invasion and metastasis of breast cancer cells. Int. J. Oncol. 32, 491–498.

Plopper, G., 2007. The extracellular matrix and cell adhesion. In: Lewin, B., Cassimeris, L., Lingappa, V., Plopper, G. (Eds.), Cells. Jones and Bartlett, Sudbury, MA, pp. 3905–3908.

Poole, A.R., Tiltman, K.J., Recklies, A.D., Stoker, T.A.M., 1978. Differences in secretion of the proteinases cathepsin B at the edges of human breast carcinomas and fibroadenomas. Nature 273, 545–547.

Rakashanda, S., Rana, F., Rafiq, S., Masood, A., Amin, S., 2012. Role of proteases in cancer: a review. Biotechnol. Mol. Biol. Rev. 74, 90–101.

Ritchie, C., 2013. Protease inhibitors. Mater. Methods 3, 169. https://doi.org/10.13070/mm.en.3.169.

Soreide, K., Jansse, E.A., Korner, H., Baak, J.P.A., 2006. Trypsin in colorectal cancer: molecular biological mechanisms of proliferation, invasion and metastasis. J. Pathol. 209, 145–156.

Sun, J., 2010. Matrix metalloproteinases and tissue inhibitor of metalloproteinases are essential for the inflammatory response in cancer cells. J. Signal Transduct. https://doi.org/10.1155/2010/985132.

Vashishta, A., Ohri, S.S., Proctor, M., Fusek, M., Vetvicka, V., 2007. Ribozyme-targeting procathepsin D and its effect on invasion and growth of breast cancer cells: an implication in breast cancer therapy. Int. J. Oncol. 30, 1223–1230.

Vasiljeva, O., Turk, B., 2008. Dual contrasting roles of cysteine cathepsins in cancer progression: apoptosis versus tumour invasion. Biochimie 90, 380–386.

Yamamoto, H., Ikv, S., Adachi, Y., Imsumran, A., Taniguchi, H., Nosho, K., et al., 2003. Association of trypsin expression with tumor progression and matrilysin expression in human colorectal cancer. J. Pathol. 199, 176–184.

Further reading

Koblinski, J.E., Mamoun, A., Bonnie, F.S., 2000. Unraveling the role of proteases in cancer. Clin. Chim. Acta 291, 113–135.

Chapter 2

Potential roles of protease inhibitors in anticancer therapy

A. Trezza[a], V. Cicaloni[a,b], F. Pettini[a], O. Spiga[a]
[a]*Department of Biotechnology, Chemistry and Pharmacy (Department of Excellence 2018-2022), University of Siena, Siena, Italy,* [b]*Toscana Life Sciences, Siena, Italy*

2.1 Introduction

Peptide bonds make proteins the most stable biological polymers (Drag and Salvesen, 2010). In every organism, one of the most essential catalytic reactions is proteolysis, also known as proteolytic activity, which has been ascribed to a class of enzymes called proteases. Proteolysis is the hydrolysis of a peptide bond by attacking the carbonyl group of a peptide chain (Eatemadi et al., 2017). Peptide bonds can endure hours in hostile conditions such as in boiling concentrated acid environment, but they persist less than a few of microseconds in the presence of a particular protease (Drag and Salvesen, 2010).

The study of proteolysis goes back to the first half of the nineteenth century with the description of pepsin by Schwann in 1836 and, successively, of trypsin by Corvisart in 1856. Since then, proteases have been identified in almost every organism. In fact they are a various group of enzymes present from 2% to 4% in the genomes of human, chimpanzee, mouse, rat, and other species (Drag and Salvesen, 2010; Perez-Silva et al., 2016). Proteases are enzymes that are broadly distributed distribution and that have been discovered to play crucial roles in most biological pathways and to be implicated in almost every disease (Drag and Salvesen, 2010).

In particular, the importance of proteases is confirmed by the existence of more than one hundred diverse hereditary diseases caused by mutations in protease genes (Perez-Silva et al., 2016). Additionally, proteases have also been involved in multiple human pathologies like cancer. Due to the relevance of proteolytic enzymes in both human physiology and pathology, a concept of degradome, defined as the complete set of proteases expressed by a tissue or organism, has been recently introduced. The degradome has been shown to affect many crucial biochemical pathways. Thus, a lot of proteases play key roles in several biological processes, such as cell cycle progression, tissue remodeling,

Cancer-Leading Proteases. https://doi.org/10.1016/B978-0-12-818168-3.00002-4

neuronal outgrowth, haemostasis, wound healing, angiogenesis, digestion, blood clotting, immunity, host defense, pathogenic infection, viral replication, disease progression, and apoptosis (Farady and Craik, 2010; Perez-Silva et al., 2016). Because proteases trigger the cleavage of a polypeptide chain, which is an irreversible process, their activity must be tightly controlled. Dysregulated proteolytic activity could be responsible for the disruption in the homeostatic balance of a biological system and can result in any number of poor biological outcomes. As a result, organisms have developed different strategies to control proteolysis including spatial and temporal regulation, e.g., zymogen activation, degradation of proteases, and the inhibition of proteases by macromolecular inhibitors (Farady and Craik, 2010). Conversely, degradome misregulation is implicated in a broad range of pathological conditions including arthritis, vascular diseases, progeria, neurodegenerative processes, neurological diseases, and cancer. Nowadays, the degradome database (Perez-Silva et al., 2016) encompasses 82 protease families in four species (*Homo sapiens*, *Pan troglodytes*, *Mus musculus,* and *Rattus norvegicus*). Specifically, the human degradome, which makes up a complete list of proteases synthesized by human cells, is made up of at least 990 known protease genes and, moreover, more than 1600 protease inhibitor genes are known (Eatemadi et al., 2017; Lopez-Otin and Matrisian, 2007). In the recent years, degradomics has experienced a remarkable growth, not only in terms of number of known proteases but also in terms of biological and pathological roles played by the degradome. Thus, almost all the progress in terms of number of known proteases has been through the inclusion of new protein families which were not previously known to display proteolytic activity (Perez-Silva et al., 2016). Also, the number of known diseases caused by mutations in protease genes has increased from 77 to 119. Such increase reflects the rising interest on the roles of the degradome in multiple diseases, expecially in cancer (Perez-Silva et al., 2016)

2.2 Role of proteases in cancer development and metastasis

The growth of malignant tumors is described by five main steps: proliferation, apoptosis, angiogenesis, invasion, and finally, migration of cells. In healthy tissue, there is a regular balance between cell division and programmed cell death. In contrast, in malignant tumors, such balance is interrupted by increased cell division, decreased apoptosis, or both (Gupta et al., 2010).

One of the primary features of tumor cells is their ability to attack normal tissues (Hanahan and Weinberg, 2011). Various methods are involved in invasion and migration processes, for instance the loss of cell-cell and cell-matrix adhesion or the degradation of extracellular matrix (ECM) components (Revach and Geiger, 2014). When the expression of cell-cell and cell-matrix adhesion molecules is reduced or missing, cells lose the contact with their microenvironment and are inclined to invade adjacent tissues. In fact, endothelial cells, fibroblasts, myoepithelial cells, pericytes, and inflammatory cells, present within the tumor stroma and at the invasive edge of tumors, constitute a microenvironment that can significantly affect the behavior of malignant cells (DeClerck et al., 2004). Thus, after shedding themselves off from the primary tumor, malignant cells start to migrate into ECM, a dense network composed of laminin, fibronectin, and other glycoproteins, collagens, and proteoglycans (Lu et al., 2012; Yang et al., 2015). The role of ECM in the tumor microenvironment is not limited to being a barrier against tumor invasion but it is also a reservoir of cell binding proteins and growth factors that affect tumor cell behavior (DeClerck et al., 2004).

Malignant cells show increased proteolytic activity, which helps them to digest the ECM. Such cells can adhere to some molecules of intercellular substance, and activate cells for the synthesis of different degrading enzymes in order to assist the tumor cells entrance into the blood vessel through the ECM (Lu et al., 2012; van Horssen et al., 2013). This digestion is required for cancer cells to invade and migrate through the basal lamina, which is the hallmark of malignancy (Yang et al., 2015). Invasion and migration of cancer cells may lead to the development of metastases at distant sites (Yang et al., 2015). Proteases in normal cells are essential in carrying out biological processes and can regulate a diversity of different cellular processes such as gene expression, differentiation, and cell death (Eatemadi et al., 2017). However, because of proteases' ability to degrade extracellular matrices and proteins, they are strongly associated with cancer progression (Choi et al., 2012) both at primary and metastatic sites (Yang et al., 2009a).

ECM-degrading proteases also play a critical role in angiogenesis, where they can act as positive as well as negative regulators of endothelial cell proliferation and vascular morphogenesis. In fact, when a tumor is large enough in size, it becomes dependent on the development of new blood vessels for a continuous supply of oxygen and nutrients and elimination of waste products. New blood vessels are vital for the proliferation of primary tumor and for the creation of a metastatic colony (DeClerck et al., 2004). Metastases and tumor progression are highly dependent on nutrient and oxygen supply, which are motivated by various proteases in the tumor and surrounding tissues and organs (Yang et al., 2009a).

In this context, it is possible to assert that proteases play a crucial role in the proteolytic degradation of ECM tumor and in angiogenesis (Alitalo and Detmar, 2012). A lot of proteases have been linked with increasing tumor metastasis in different human cancers, suggesting their central functions in the metastatic process for their capacity to degrade the ECM barrier. Metastases are the major cause of death in cancer patients. Therefore, reduction of metastatic progression is the greatest challenge in the development of effective anticancer therapies (Yang et al., 2015). Proteins of the ECM form a noncellular compartment to the tumor microenvironment that is extensively modified and remodeled by proteases either secreted by neoplastic and nonneoplastic cells or localized at the surface of cells. As a result of the activity of these proteases, important changes in cell-cell and cell-ECM interactions occur, and new signals are generated from the cell surface. These signals affect gene expression and ultimately influence critical cell behaviors such as proliferation, survival, differentiation, and motility (DeClerck et al., 2004).

Several tumors have shown to have increased levels of proteases at an early stage that are now indicated to be involved in many aspects of cancer, such as proliferation, immune responses, inflammatory cell recruitment, tumor invasion, angiogenesis, metastasis, apoptosis, epithelial to mesenchymal transition (EMT), the mobilization of normal cells from their tissue compartments to metastasis, as well as response to therapy such as in resistance to chemotherapy (Kim et al., 1998; Mason and Joyce, 2011). The understanding of the proteolytic network in the tumor microenvironment is rapidly increasing as a result of raised interest both in protease and in new techniques that allow for comprehensive analysis of protease activity in physiologically relevant conditions. It is possible to gain insights into tumor biology by examining their interconnectivity, as illustrated by several recognizable cascades of proteolytic interactions. Generally, well-established proteolytic networks consist of multiple steps of activation, several key nodes through which a majority of signals pass, and inhibitors that can regulate activity of different points in such networks. Some representative examples of protease cascades and networks of recently discovered interactions that may be important in cancer will be next illustrated (Mason and Joyce, 2011). Every described example features proteases as principal nodes that can serve as main regulatory core for the entire cascade. Smaller cascades centered on these nodes can then be connected to form a network of proteolytic activity:

2.2.1 Caspases and apoptosis

In every organism, all the tumors avoid apoptotic process in order to progress toward malignancy. One of the main important proteolytic cascades involving in apoptotic pathways includes caspases, a family of protease enzymes playing essential roles in programmed cell death and inflammation. Their name is due to their specific cysteine protease activity. At the beginning of programmed cell death cascade, the initiator caspases (2, 8, 9, and 10) are involved (Li and Yuan, 2008; Siegel, 2006). These initiator caspases trigger the effector caspases 3, 6, and 7 in a direct or indirect way through the cleavage of their pro-domains. Once trigged, these effector caspases cleave a large variety of biochemical compounds, with the final result to activate apoptotic pathways. They can be divided into two:

- Intrinsic pathway: It involves cytochrome c release from the mitochondria.
- Extrinsic pathway: It involves activation of death domain receptors on the cell surface.

Recent studies demonstrate that the loss of one initiator caspase (in particular caspase 8) leads to cell survival and promotes metastasis in neuroblastoma (Stupack et al., 2006) confirming its crucial role in cancer.

A way to bypass the loss of caspase 8 and to induce apoptosis is the indirect activation of another initiator caspase, caspase 3, through the release of granzyme B into the cell via cytotoxic T lymphocyte-mediated (Lord et al., 2003). Granzyme B itself is the downstream product of two other proteases: cathepsin C and cathepsin H that are responsible for its activation. This fact demonstrates that regulation of apoptosis occurs at many levels (D'Angelo et al., 2010) in which proteases are often involved. Moreover, also inhibition process of caspases is regulated by several endogenous protease inhibitors such as XIAP, which can be inactivated by different proteases, including several cysteine cathepsins (Droga-Mazovec et al., 2008). These interactions allow a link between the caspase cascade and other proteolytic networks. Thus, positive and negative regulation of the effector caspases highlights the importance of proteases as critical nodes in the caspase cascade (Mason and Joyce, 2011).

2.2.2 Cathepsin B

As opposed to the caspase cascade having a mono-directional trend, the proteolytic network stimulating tumor growth includes a large variety of multidirectional interactions that affect a large number of tumor-promoting processes, for example, the cascade of cathepsin B. Cathepsin B belongs to a family of cysteine proteases and plays an important role in intracellular proteolysis (Sloane, 1990); Cathepsin B levels are upregulated in many different tumor microenvironments (Sloane et al., 2005). Cathepsin B may enhance the activity of other proteases, including matrix metalloproteinase, urokinase, and cathepsin D (Alapati et al., 2014; Vigneswaran et al., 2000, Fig. 2.1). Moreover, it has a crucial position in the proteolytic process of extracellular matrix components, in interruption of intercellular communication and in inhibition of another proteases expression (Yang et al., 2016). Thus, it is implicated in the remodeling and dissolution of basement membrane and connective tissue in the processes of tumor growth, invasion, and metastasis (van der Stappen et al., 1996), which may result in ECM degradation and invasion via secreted lysosomes (Abboud-Jarrous et al., 2008).

Cathepsin B is also involved in autophagy and catabolism, which are beneficial processes in tumor malignancy (Fais, 2007). Cathepsin D is one of the proteases responsible for the conversion of pro-cathepsin B in active cathepsin B. Cathepsin D is an aspartic protease which also activates cathepsin L (van der Stappen et al., 1996, Fig. 1), a key cysteine protease that is fundamental to the stimulation of heparanase, an enzyme involved in matrix degradation (Abboud-Jarrous et al., 2008). Moreover, cathepsin B is triggered by different proteases like cathepsin G, urokinase-type plasminogen activator (uPA), tissue-type plasminogen activator (tPA), and elastase (Skrzydlewska et al., 2005). In particular, elastase and cathepsin G are activated by another protease, cathepsin C (Methot et al., 2007). The interaction between cathepsin B and uPA is not unique; in fact cathepsin B can also activate uPA (Kobayashi et al., 1991). Such case of reciprocity underlines the assessment that proteolytic interactions are not a simpler mono-directional cascade but they are part of a complex network. Cathepsin B

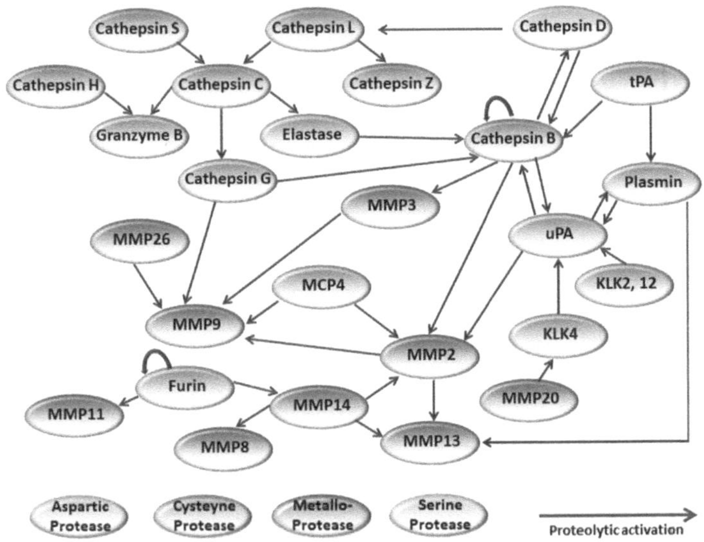

FIG. 2.1 Ensemble of interactions within a proteolytic network. Proteolytic interactions could be described as a network of coordinated cascades revealing multiple entry points, multidirectional interactions, and signals. Examining protease-protease interactions specifically shows that similar to the cascade view, several proteases occupy nodes in the network and function as key regulators of proteolytic activity. Additionally, interactions involve proteases of different families and can proceed in multiple different pathways, allowing for some proteases to compensate for the absence of others. For instance, cathepsin D activates cathepsin L, cathepsin B activates cathepsin D, MMP2, and MMP3, tissue-type plasminogen activator (tPA) activates cathepsin B and plasmin. *(Modified from Mason, S.D., Joyce, J.A., 2011. Proteolytic networks in cancer. Trends Cell Biol. 21, 228–237. Elsevier. Copyright 2011 Elsevier. Licence Number: 4583081161935.)*

cleaves a large variety of targets depending on its subcellular localization in the tumor microenvironment (Cavallo-Medved et al., 2003; Gocheva et al., 2010b; Mohamed et al., 2010).

2.2.3 Urokinase-type plasminogen activator

The association between stromal and tumor cells modulates two protease systems that are involved in proteolysis outside the cell: the MMPs and urokinase plasminogen activator (uPA)/uPA receptor network (Eatemadi et al., 2017).

Urokinase-type plasminogen activator (uPA), more simply urokinase, is a serine protease ubiquitous in humans and in other organisms (Degryse, 2011). The name urokinase is because it was originally isolated from urine, but it is also included in blood and the extracellular matrix. uPA has a wide range of targets and a prominent position in the proteolytic network but it is principally known because it is responsible for the activation of the enzyme plasminogen, which is a zymogen of plasmin, another serine protease. Subsequently, plasmin triggers a proteolytic cascade that participates not only in thrombolysis, involving in vascular diseases, but also in extracellular matrix degradation, related to cancer progression (Tang and Han, 2013).

Activation of uPA can be carried out by plasmin (Behrendt et al., 1995; Skrzydlewska et al., 2005). In this way, a feedback loop by which plasmin and uPA can activate each other is created. Alternatively, it can activate by cathepsin B (Fig. 1). Beyond plasmin and cathepsin B, other direct or indirect targets of uPA are matrix metalloproteinases (MMPs), in particular MMP2. uPA is involved in the triggering of MMP2 through a mechanism dependent on contributions from stromal fibroblasts (He et al., 2007). Stromal MMP-2 and uPA are synthesized as inactive compounds and then activated on the tumor cells' surface, thereby causing cancer cells to disrupt basement membranes (Eatemadi et al., 2017). Moreover, the enzymes stimulate blood vessels developing to feed the increasing tumor. This finding highlights the complexity of proteolytic interconnections in the tumor microenvironment, which are dependent not only on proteases provided by tumor cells but also on proteolytic contributions from various stromal cells.

Existing antitumor therapies, having as target these stromal contributions to metastasis, migration, and angiogenesis, attack a genetically constant cell population, so they may not attack the resistance related to the use of traditional chemotherapeutic drugs (Eatemadi et al., 2017).

2.2.4 Matrix metalloproteinases (MMPs)

In biology, and especially in cancer research, MMPs are the most widely studied proteases for their recurrent overexpression in several malignant tumors and for their capacity to degrade many substrates (Kessenbrock et al., 2010). Nevertheless, clinical trials using inhibitors of MMPs to treat pancreatic, brain, lung, or renal cancer were often unsatisfactory, generally as a consequence of the large number of MMPs with potentially opposing functions (Overall and Kleifeld, 2006). There are 25 types of MMPs, each one characterized by conserved peptide, catalytic domains, and a zinc ion in their active site (Overall and Kleifeld, 2006). It is not easy to classify these genes as MMPs, because it is important to consider the large variety in substrates and interactions for this family. In fact, multiple mechanisms exist for the activation of MMPs. MMPs can degrade all kinds of extracellular matrix proteins and process different bioactive molecules. They are involved in the cleavage of cell surface receptors, the release of apoptotic ligands, and chemokine inactivation (Van Lint and Libert, 2007).

Moreover, they play an important role in cell proliferation, migration, differentiation, angiogenesis, and apoptosis and in tissue remodeling associated with various physiological or pathological processes such as arthritis, cancer, and metastasis. In particular, MMP-2 and MMP-9 are crucial in metastasis.

A recent proteomic study has found novel substrates for MMP2, including cystatin C (resulting in decreased inhibition of cathepsin L) (Dean et al., 2007), and proteases such as cathepsins B and L (Kleifeld et al., 2010; Fig. 2.1). Expanding such proteomic approaches to the investigation of other proteases, the wealth of obtained information allows to gain a more exhaustive picture of the proteolytic interaction network placed in the tumor microenvironment. These approaches are extremely important to monitor the dynamics nature of proteases linked with tumor progression (Doucet et al., 2008).

In summary, several proteases, including for example cathepsins B, H, L, S, uPA (or its receptor), MMP2, MMP14, and MMP26, have been implicated in tumor angiogenesis and invasion (Deng et al., 2010; Devy et al., 2009; Gocheva et al., 2006, 2010a; Woenne et al., 2010), indicating the importance of discovering methods to concurrently target multiple proteases and underscoring the potential of blocking multiple nodes in the proteolytic interaction network. Joining in vivo experiments with in vitro data, representing the abundance of the identified proteolytic connections, it is possible to observe that proteases function in a coordinated cascade in cancer biology (Affara et al., 2009; Ovaere et al., 2009; Skrzydlewska et al., 2005). As opposed to a comprehensive network view, depicting proteolytic interactions exclusively as cascades needs to place some proteases earlier in the cascade than others; this is a challenging issue due to the plethora of possible interactions.

2.3 Classification of proteases and their specific role in cancer

Proteases are a various class of enzymes involved in many key physiological or pathological processes. Protease signaling pathways are strictly controlled, and disorders in protease activity can result in pathological changes such as cardiovascular and inflammatory diseases, cancer, and neurological disorders (Yang et al., 2015). Such variety in structure and function needs a classification of proteases into several subgroups. Proteases could be classified on the basis of different criteria as mentioned below.

2.3.1 Optimal pH in which they are active

- Acid proteases, using a catalytic aspartic or glutamic acid in the active site. For example, pepsin works well at pH 2.
- Neutral proteases generally released by mast cells and causes activation of complement and kinins.
- Alkaline or basic proteases that work optimally at a pH range from 8 to 11. For example, trypsin and chymotrypsin work well at pH 8.

2.3.2 The catalyzed reaction

- Endopeptidases cleave the target protein internally. In fact, they break peptide bonds of nonterminal amino acids; this is the reason why they cannot break down peptides into monomers. A specific example of endopeptidase is oligopeptidase, whose substrates are not proteins but oligopeptides.

- Exopeptidases remove single amino acids from either the amino- or carboxy-terminal ends of a protein releasing a single amino acid or dipeptide from the peptide chain. Exopeptidases are divided into carboxypeptidases or aminopeptidases depending on whether they digest proteins from the carboxy- or amino-terminus, respectively. Generally, aminopeptidases are zinc-dependent enzyme secreted by glands of the small intestine with the role of helping the enzymatic digestion of proteins (Ansorge and Langner, 1997). One of the first studied carboxypeptidases was pancreatic carboxypeptidase involved in the digestion of food. The identified carboxypeptidases have a large range of functions from to catabolism to posttranslational modification. Carboxypeptidases are usually classified into one of several families based on their active site mechanism; for example, all the proteases using a metal in the active site are called metallo-carboxypeptidases, those using serine residues in the active site are serine carboxypeptidases, those using an active site cysteine are called cysteine carboxypeptidase.

2.3.3 Chemical nature of the catalytic site

Based on the nature of the key amino acid in the active site of the protease and the mechanism of the peptide bond cleavage, proteases can be classified into six groups: matrix metalloproteases (MMPs), cysteine proteases, serine proteases, aspartic proteases, threonine proteases, and glutamic proteases (less common) (Sanman and Bogyo, 2014; Turk et al., 2012; Verbovšek et al., 2015; Yang et al., 2009a). The main classes of proteases that contribute to the lytic processes around tumors are MMPs, cathepsins (cysteine proteases), and plasminogen activators (serine proteases) (Yang et al., 2015). Specifically, matrix metalloproteases are involved in cancer progression, growth, invasion, and angiogenesis; cysteine cathepsin proteases are implicated in cancer invasion, angiogenesis, tumor of bone and breast cancer metastases; plasminogens are involved in migration of tumor cells and tumor diffusion (Yang et al., 2015). The mechanism underlying the cleavage of a peptide bond with a protease typically occurs in the presence of water molecule (especially in aspartate, metallo proteases) or a cysteine, serine, or threonine residue as the nucleophile in the active site (Boy et al., 2008).

Proteases are involved in different phases of cancer; this is the reason why it is important to gather evidences in how every class of proteases influence tumor progression.

2.3.3.1 Cysteine proteases

Cysteine proteases, also called calpains, are generally ubiquitous in the cytosol or in the lysosome, like cathepsins. In pathological processes, they are synthetized in several types of cells having a role in common functions, for example in intracellular protein catabolism, or specific functions such as stimulation of extracellular protein catabolism, macrophage activation, and in diverse signaling pathways (Zucker et al., 2001). The family of cathepsin, that are classified as cysteine proteases, are involved in both intracellular and extracellular functions such as the degradation of intracellular and extracellular matrix (Gocheva and Joyce, 2007; Mohamed and Sloane, 2006). This is the reason why cathepsins are considered effective targets for chemotherapy in cancer (Gocheva and Joyce, 2007; Jedeszko and Sloane, 2004): their extracellular activities are aimed at stimulating tumor cells growth to adjacent tissues, blood vessels, and in metastasis formation in outlying tissues (Matarrese et al., 2010; Vasiljeva and Turk, 2008). They are also considered, in particular cathepsin B, as suitable prognostic biomarkers for identifying patients who are suffering from various types of tumors such as colorectal cancer (Hirai et al., 1999), breast cancer (Kandalaft et al., 1993), pancreatic cancer (Michl, 2012), and tongue carcinoma (Saleh et al., 2006). Other lysosomal proteases, such as cathepsins D, H, or L, are useful in monitoring other malignant conditions (Fujise et al., 2000), for instance cathepsin L2 (CTSL2) is upregulated in in lung, breast, gastric, colon, head and neck carcinomas, gliomas, melanomas (Lankelma et al., 2010), and endometrial cancer (Skrzypczak et al., 2012).

2.3.3.2 Serine proteases

Serine protease group is one of the most populated in the entire peptidase ensemble: about one third of all proteases can be classified as serine proteases characterizing for the presence of a nucleophilic serine residue in the active site (Hedstrom, 2002). From the structural point of view, serine proteases were noted for the presence of the so called "catalytic triad" composed of Asp-His-Ser amino acids (Dodson and Wlodawer, 1998) implicated in at least four diverse structural contexts, for example subtilisin, chymotrypsin, carboxypeptidase Y, and Clp protease (Dodson and Wlodawer, 1998; Rawlings and Barrett, 2000). Their activity is finely regulated because it could be very critical for physiological functions of cells and tissues. In fact, an abnormal regulation can easily lead to pathological situations such as cancer (DeClerck et al., 2004). One of the well-characterized serine proteases is trypsin which plays a critical role in a wide spectrum of pathological conditions such as inflammation, atherosclerosis, and cancer (DeClerck et al., 2004).

2.3.3.3 Aspartate proteases

Aspartate proteases are noted for having two highly conserved aspartates in their active site and are optimally active at acidic pH. The most well-known proteases of such group are Cathepsin-D (Cath-D), renin, pepsinogen, and chymosin (also known as rennin) and all are characterized by a bilobed structure (Liaudet-Coopman et al., 2006). Cath-D is an endoprotease commonly found in lysosomes (Barrett, 1970). It has two central roles: on the one hand it is responsible for the precursor's activation of biologically active proteins in prelysosomal compartments of specialized cells, and on the other hand it is considered as a major protein-degrading enzyme in lysosomes and phagosomes (Diment et al., 1989). Generally, aspartate proteases are overexpressed and synthetized at high levels by epithelial breast cancer cells (Masson et al., 2011; Nicotra et al., 2010; Radisky and Radisky, 2010; Vashishta et al., 2009) as it stimulates cancer cell proliferation, angiogenesis, and metastasis (Huang et al., 2008; Ohri et al., 2008; Vashishta et al., 2007). This is the reason why it is considered a reliable prognostic marker in breast cancer (Rodríguez et al., 2005).

2.3.3.4 *Threonine proteases*

Threonine proteases are a family of proteolytic enzymes containing a threonine residue within their active site. The members of this class of enzymes are the catalytic subunits of the proteasome. In fact, the protein's expression and degradation is controlled by the activity of such ubiquitin-proteasome (Weathington and Mallampalli, 2014). Threonine proteases participate in removing cellular proteins, which are marked for degradation through a complex modification known as poly-ubiquitination which is a process of adding a sequence of ubiquitin molecules to another protein, targeted for degradation (Mitchell, 2003). Anomalous proteasome-dependent proteolysis seems to be related with the pathophysiology of several malignant tumors (Chen et al., 2011).

2.3.3.5 *Matrix metalloproteinases (MMPs)*

Matrix metalloproteinases (MMPs), also known as matrixins, are a class of more than nine highly homologous Zn^{2+} endopeptidases that together are responsible for the cleavage of several constituents of the ECM and are also involved in degradation of many bioactive molecules. Increased level of MMPs has been reported in numerous cancer types (Anastasov et al., 2013; Evrosimovska Andonovska et al., 2011). MMPs are responsible for the remodeling process of ECM proteins (Rakashanda et al., 2012) and their increased expression is related with the pathophysiology of cancer.

2.3.3.6 *Glutamic proteases*

Glutamic proteases are a class of proteolytic enzymes including a glutamic acid residue in their active site. Such category of enzymes was recently described for the first time (in 2004) becoming the sixth catalytic group of proteases (Fujinaga et al., 2004). Formerly, components of this class had been supposed to be an aspartate protease, but a more detailed structural determination showed it to belong to a novel family of proteolytic enzymes. These enzymes are acid proteases and, in most cases, work well at pH 2.0.

2.4 Importance of inhibitors of proteases in cancer

Proteases have a central role in various signaling pathways; thus they represent potential drug targets for a large set of diseases, from cardiovascular disorders to cancer, as well as for eradicating many types of parasites and viruses. Since inhibitors of known protease targets such as angiotensin-converting enzyme and HIV protease have shown considerable success for therapeutic point of view, developing drugs for new protease targets, especially in the treatment of cancer, has proved one of the most challenging and interesting task in recent years (Drag and Salvesen, 2010). As a matter of fact, in the last ten years, there have been enormous strides in the elucidation of proteases mechanisms of action, their biology, and their structure. However, protease inhibitor design is a complex issue since different types of cancers use different proteases at the fluctuating stages of cancer development and no single inhibitor can be used in all classes of proteases. In this context, proteases and their inhibitors are widespread experimental models for structural biologists, for protein engineers, and in studies of protein folding (Drag and Salvesen, 2010). Substantial engineering efforts have gone into altering and improving potency and specificity of novel inhibitors, following the same design principles that work efficiently in nature (Farady and Craik, 2010). The number of known proteases has also increased substantially and the MEROPS database has been regularly updated. The MEROPS database (Rawlings et al., 2018) is a manually curated integrated source of information about peptidases, their substrates, and inhibitors located in EMBL-EBI (European Molecular Biology Laboratory-European Bioinformatics Institute) during 2017. The hierarchical classification is: protein-species, family, clan, with an identifier at each level. A first hierarchical classification in MEROPS was established for peptidases in 1993 (Rawlings and Barrett, 1993) and for peptidase inhibitors in 2004 (Rawlings et al., 2004). Such classification includes the clustering of homologous sets of both peptidase and protein inhibitor sequences into different peptidase and inhibitor categorizes, characterized by a unique identifier ID, which are in turn clustered into families, which are clustered into clans. A family contains related sequences whereas a clan contains related tertiary structures. Sequence analysis is focused on the portion of the protease directly responsible for the activity of peptidase or inhibitor; such portion is called as "peptidase unit" or the "inhibitor unit." The peptidase unit includes primary substrate binding sites and the catalytic residues whereas the inhibitor unit is a domain that interacts with a peptidase domain and will include the residues that provide the reactive bond that occupies the active site. A peptidase or inhibitor unit normally corresponds to a structural domain, and some proteins contain more than one peptidase or inhibitor domain (Rawlings et al., 2004). In addition, since MEROPS classification of inhibitors can only be applied to inhibitors that are proteins, a second collection of small molecule inhibitors was established (Rawlings et al., 2008). The strong evidence of protease involvement in diseases makes proteases a crucial target of inhibitors design and gives them a central role in drug development.

2.5 Inhibitors of proteases

Several disorders are present in cancer pathology (Harter et al., 2006; Holland et al., 2013; Stark et al., 2002). However, in recent years, particular attention has been focused on deregulation of protease and proteasome processes (Mofers et al., 2017; Rastogi and Mishra, 2012), and some therapeutic approaches have been proposed (Chen and Dou, 2010; Grigoreva et al., 2015; Schmidt and Finley, 2014; Weathington and Mallampalli, 2014; Yang et al., 2009b). Notable success has been obtained in the treatment of hematological malignancies, where proteasome inhibitors have been tested as therapeutic strategies in medicine field for over 10 years (Lopez-Otin and Matrisian, 2007). The first treatment for relapsed multiple myeloma and mantle cell lymphoma was carried out using Bortezomib, a protease inhibitor (Field-Smith et al., 2006; Korubo et al., 2018; Scott et al., 2016). Unfortunately, its high cost, as well as of other inhibitors in this class, had caused a lack of success and overall interest (Chen et al., 2011). Due to this, further attempts were made, where more specific protease targets were investigated, such as the design of recombinant forms of proteases, but in this method large doses were required to achieve desired effects (Burden et al., 2008; Craik et al., 2011). A second approach was the gene therapy in which protease genes were targeted. In this approach protease activity was observed to have remarkable improvement (Kuriyama et al., 2001). Important results were observed in prostate cancer, where the transfer of the gene in lentiviral-mediated neprilysin was found to block the process of prostate cancer growth (Horiguchi et al., 2007). Another approach, that may be called an indirect approach, is to block protease inhibitors in order to reduce the inhibition of protective proteases involved in antitumor processes. As reported in an interesting work of Karikari et al. (2007), the inhibition of caspase inhibitors increased and induced the apoptosis process in pancreatic cancer. Preventing the inhibition of proteases may sensitize cancer cells to drug therapies or induce the cellular apoptosis. Finally, a fourth method, probably more interesting, was to use a biomarker for the diagnosis or the prognosis of tumors. This approach is based on detecting the concentration of protective proteases. It may provide a good prediction of a clinical prognosis. It may entail a different therapeutic approach even in the absence of protective proteases. However, the activities and the regulation of the proteolytic process may remarkably increase the progression of diseases (Choi et al., 2012). The biological regulation of proteases is severely and finely regulated by complicated signaling pathway, as their deregulation, or anomalies in their function or activity may lead to a dramatic consequences, since various pathologies, including cancer (DeClerck et al., 2004; Sevenich and Joyce, 2014; Skrzydlewska et al., 2005). A large overview on protease processes in their metabolic context is crucial for the design and development of protease inhibitors to act against tumor and metastasis progression. Unfortunately, in accordance to the cancer type, different proteases play different key roles at different stages of the cancer development. This feature makes the design and development of protease inhibitors further difficult and complicated (Mason and Joyce, 2011). During the evolution process, proteases assume different features, adapting their structure and function in wide range of conditions into human organism, such as change of pH, reductive/ oxidative environment, substrate concentration, using numerous and different mechanism of actions in order to be able to hydrolyze the substrate (Kawaguchi et al., 2013). Recently, very important goals have been achieved in medicine field, where the use of protease inhibitors as therapeutic approach aimed to reduce the invasion and metastasis progression of cancer cells has shown excellent results (DeClerck and Imren, 1994; Eatemadi et al., 2017). We thus focused here our attention on protease inhibitors to describe their structure and mechanism of action. Protease inhibitors (PIs) are compounds that act on proteases to block their function and thus play a key role in cancer therapies. There are several pharmaceutical strategies aimed to interfere with proteases using different inhibitors. They may be classified based on their mechanism of action and molecular class (Rawlings et al., 2004). PIs may be proteins, peptides, or small molecules, although, usually, they are often synthetic peptide-like or small molecules (Ritchie, 2013; Schneider and Balskus, 2018).

2.5.1 Classification of protease inhibitors by mechanism of action

PIs may be divided into three main classes as shown in Fig. 2.2, namely reversible class, irreversible class, and engineering class, which are described in detail as follows:

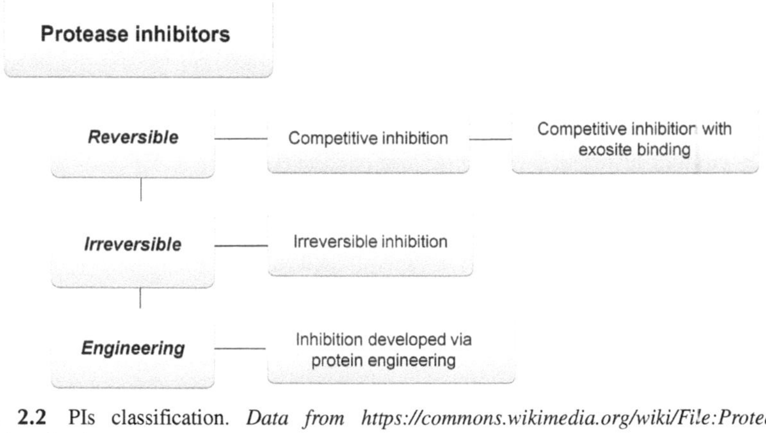

FIG. 2.2 PIs classification. *Data from https://commons.wikimedia.org/wiki/File:Protease_inibhitors.jpg.)*

2.5.2 Reversible class

Reversible inhibitors of proteases bind in the active site of the proteases but also may have a secondary binding sites outside the active site (exosite binding), which are crucial to inhibition. Exosite binding sites provide two major benefits: the increased surface area for the protein-protein interaction and the specificity of the inhibitor binding (Farady and Craik, 2010). Reversible PIs constitute a major class of clinically useful drugs (Farady and Craik, 2010). Despite different targets and dissimilar mechanisms of inhibition, most PIs bind at a common binding pocket of the protease active site in a substrate-like manner (Fig. 2.3; Kromann-Hansen et al., 2016). Although PIs binding on protease active site show a high efficacy and potency, they face some problems due to high degree of homology with other families of proteases, as the latter may also be inhibited. To date, 612 human proteases are known with 115 PIs released, achieving a ratio of one PI to five proteases (Hong et al., 2018). Reversible PIs may be classified in three different classes, such as small molecules, peptide-like molecules, and small proteins (Fig. 2.4).

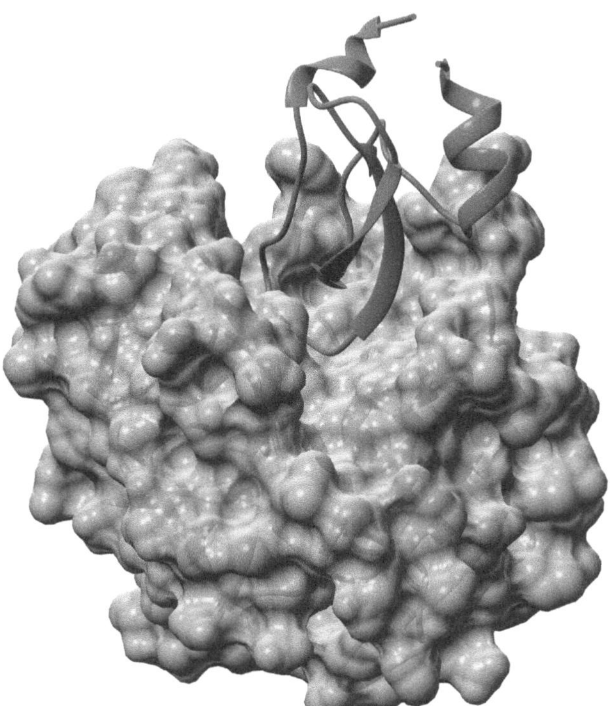

FIG. 2.3 Competitive active site inhibition of a protease represented by crystal structure of a matripase [MTSP1, in *blue surface (light gray in print version)*] with a bovine pancreatic trypsin inhibitor [aprotinin, in *purple cartoon (dark gray in print version)*]. *(Data from https://commons.wikimedia.org/wiki/File:1eaw.jpg. Molecular graphics and analyses performed with UCSF Chimera.)*

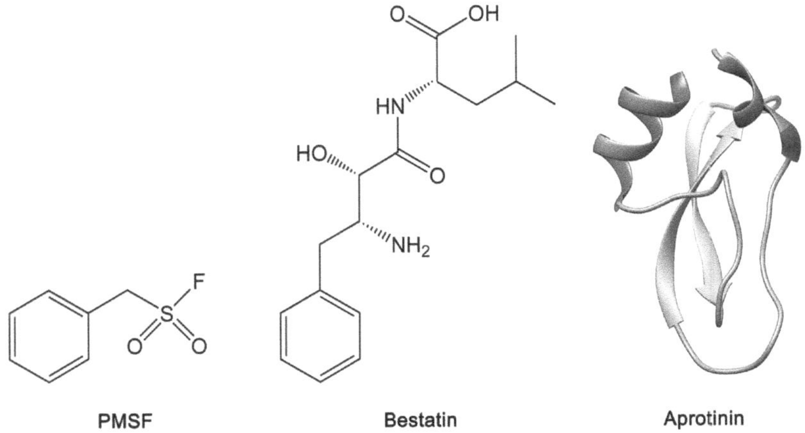

FIG. 2.4 Three different commercially available protease inhibitors. PMSF (phenylmethylsulfonyl) is a small molecule, bestatin is a peptide-like molecule, and aprotinin is a small protein. *(Data from https://commons.wikimedia.org/wiki/File:Commercial_PI.jpg.)*

Reversible inhibitors usually bind to the protease with multiple noncovalent interactions, such as hydrophobic interactions, hydrogen bonding, π-stacking, and salt-bridges (Beck et al., 2012). Given their nonpermanent bond on proteases, such inhibitors may be displaced from other ligands or removed by other processes like dilution or dialysis. Reversible inhibitors include protease competitive inhibitors (PCIs) (Fig. 2.5A), uncompetitive inhibitors (PUIs), and non-

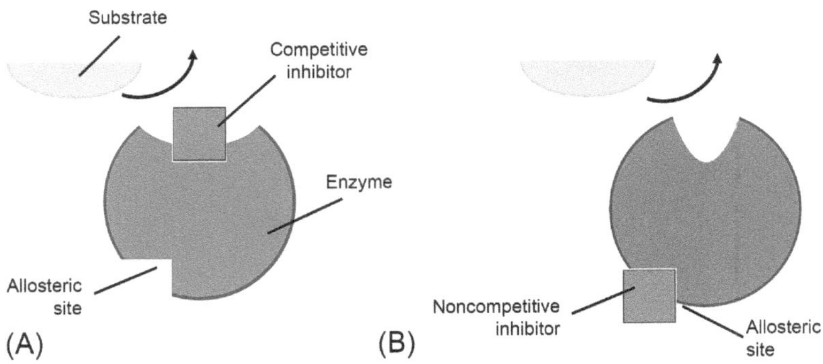

FIG. 2.5 A schematic representation of competitive (A) and noncompetitive inhibition (B). A competitive inhibitor *[blue quadrate (gray in print version)]*, similar to the natural substrate *[yellow segment (light gray in print version)]* of the enzyme *[red circle (gray in print version)]*, competing for the active site (A). A competitive inhibitor binding to the active site prevents further reactions. A noncompetitive inhibitor *[blue quadrate (gray in print version)]* binds to a site on the enzyme which is not the active one (allosteric site). This causes a conformational change of the protein, altering the active site and thus making it unable to bind with the substrate *[yellow segment (light gray in print version)]*. Till the noncompetitive inhibitor is bound with the enzyme, the enzyme *[green circle (dark gray in print version)]* remains inactive (B). *(Data from https://commons.wikimedia.org/wiki/File:Fig 5_inhibitors.jpg.)*

competitive inhibitors (PNCIs) (Fig. 2.5B). The first category competes with the protease substrate for binding to the active site. A peculiar feature of competitive inhibitors is their transition state, which is structurally similar to the natural substrate. The ability of PCIs to mimic the structure of the substrate transition state confers on them a high strength of binding on proteases, blocking the normal enzyme reaction. PUIs compete with the substrate; in fact, they bind to proteases when they are complexed with the substrate, and finally, PNCIs bind to proteases both in complexed and free form with the substrate.

2.5.2.1 *Irreversible class*

Notwithstanding the reversible class of inhibitors, the irreversible class of inhibitors of proteases binds to the target through a covalent bond, altering permanently the enzyme active site and its function. This class of inhibitors are also called as *suicide substrates* due to being analogous in structure and function with the protease substrate (Bhagavan and Ha, 2015). These suicide substrates or inhibitors also bind like irreversible inhibitors to the protease with a covalent bond, inhibiting irreversibly the enzyme.

2.5.2.2 *Engineering class*

This class of inhibitors constitutes a new generation of PIs, having increased potency as well as specificity and possessing diverse mechanisms of actions (Storer, 1991). High homology of proteases leads to different problems, such as their localization and nonspecific action of individual proteases. Engineering approach has resolved this problem by structural modifications in them or their scaffolds so that they could have very high potency and specificity for their individual targets. Another approach consists in development of polypeptide-based inhibitors of proteases (PIPs). Usually, PIPs are formed by 10–20 residues and may have disulfide bonds or components of their scaffolds that may confer rigidity to them, thus helping in the binding with proteases. The mechanisms of action of these inhibitors are to mime known biological mechanisms or adopt a completely novel one. Unfortunately, this strategy has disadvantage, due to vulnerability to the proteolysis process, but the "small size" of inhibitors lets them to perform with several combinations and create libraries of extremely diverse nature (Farady and Craik, 2010).

2.5.3 Classification of protease inhibitors by target

Protease inhibitors have also been classified based on targets or the class of proteases they inhibit (Oda, 2012), i.e., they may be called as aspartic protease inhibitors (APIs), cysteine protease inhibitors (CPIs), matrix metalloproteinase inhibitors (MMPIs), serine protease inhibitors (SPIs), threonine protease inhibitors (TPIs), etc. These inhibitors inhibit the catalytic mechanism of related proteases. Different proteases follow the mechanism of actions as briefly described below.

2.5.3.1 Aspartic proteases

Aspartic proteases (APs) use two extremely conserved aspartic acid residues located within active site for catalytic cleavage of peptide substrate. Two aspartate residues, coordinating a water molecule, through an intermediate state, start their mechanism of action on the substrate (Fig. 2.6). AP inhibitors bound inside the active site of an AP, involving their hydroxyl group to form a hydrogen bond with any of the acid aspartic residues, and thus simulating the intermediate state of the reaction and forbidding the protease to give its product. Pepstatin, a hexa-peptide, is one of the potent APIs containing the unusual amino acid statin. Because of its specific structure it can penetrate and bind to the active site of APs and inhibit them.

2.5.3.2 Cysteine proteases

Cysteine and thiol proteases have a common catalytic moiety, a nucleophilic cysteine thiol in a catalytic triad or dyad. CPs' catalytic mechanism involves hydrolysis of peptide bond performed by deprotonation of a thiol group present in the active site of the enzyme carried out by an adjacent residue having a basic side chain, usually a histidine. Deprotonation of a thiol group may start nucleophilic attack by deprotonated cysteine on its substrate (Fig. 2.7). Cysteine protease inhibitors are able to bind closely to the active site of the enzyme, where the presence of a ketone group allows the inhibitors to inhibit the function of the enzyme (Tarnowska et al., 1992).

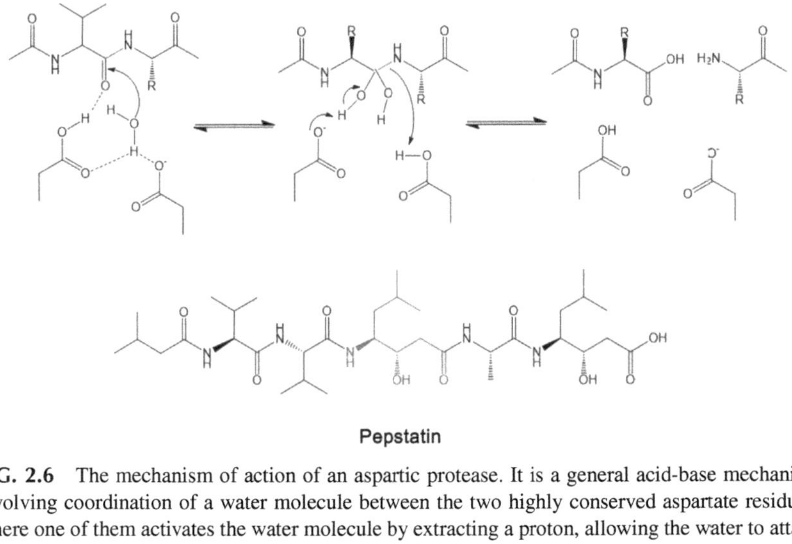

Pepstatin

FIG. 2.6 The mechanism of action of an aspartic protease. It is a general acid-base mechanism involving coordination of a water molecule between the two highly conserved aspartate residues, where one of them activates the water molecule by extracting a proton, allowing the water to attack the carbonyl carbon of the substrate scissile bond, generating a tetrahedral oxyanion intermediate. Rearrangement of this intermediate leads to protonation of the scissile amide.

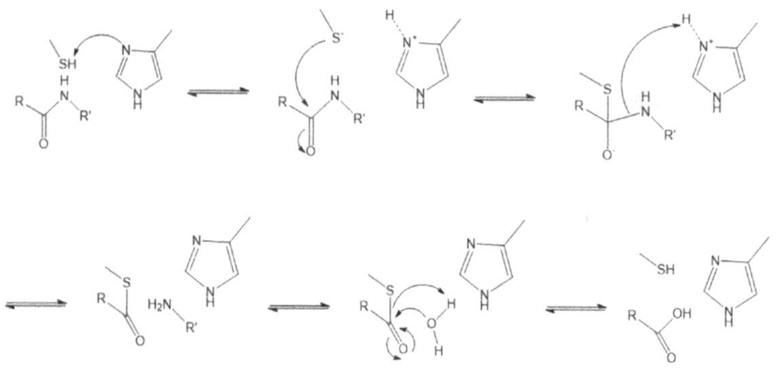

FIG. 2.7 Mechanism of action of a cysteine protease. The first step is deprotonation of a thiol by a histidine residue. The second step is nucleophilic attack by the deprotonated cysteine's anionic sulfur, releasing an amine terminus of a substrate fragment. The histidine residue in the protease is reestablished to its deprotonated form, forming a thioester intermediate. The thioester bond is hydrolyzed to generate a carboxylic acid moiety on the remaining substrate fragment, regenerating the free enzyme.

2.5.3.3 Matrix metalloproteinases

Matrix metalloproteinases (MMPs) are calcium-dependent zinc-containing endopeptidases which belong to the family of proteases. As shown from MMP X-ray crystallographic structures, their catalytic domain is an oblate sphere containing many components to form the active site (Baumann, 1994). MMP's active site contains a Zn^{2+} crucial for catalysis. This Zn^{2+} is bound to three histidine residues, highly conserved and located in HExxHxxGxxH zinc-binding motif. In this zinc-binding motif is present an highly conserved glutamate acid, which belongs to the active site (Bode et al., 1993). Different mechanisms of action have been suggested for MMPs, where one of the mechanisms is the Manzetti mechanism. It suggests that the histidine present in zinc-binding motif can displace the Zn^{2+} ion from its initial state to bind to the substrate, leading to the formation of a transient state which results in peptide bond cleavage of the substrate (Frederick Woessner Jr, 1999; Fig. 2.8).

2.5.3.4 Serine proteases

Serine proteases have a catalytic triad formed of three highly conserved residues, His57, Ser195, and Asp102, where Serine195 acts as a nucleophile. It binds to the carbonyl carbon of substrate peptide bond and His57 accepts the hydrogen bond from the Serine-OH group coordinating the attack of peptide bond. Finally, Asp102 forms a hydrogen bond with His57 and the C-terminus of the peptide is ejected (Fig. 2.9). Serpins having similar structure to proteins act as SPIs and inhibit SPs with an irreversible mechanism of action. In fact, on binding to the active site of SPs, they cause a large conformational change in them, disrupting the active site (Hedstrom, 2002).

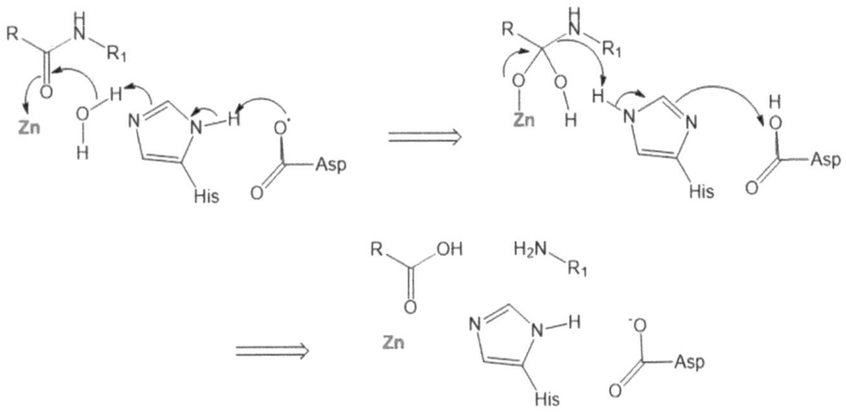

FIG. 2.8 Manzetti mechanism of MMP action. A water molecule is activated by a histidine residue attacking the carbonyl of the scissile amide bond. The carbonyl of the amide coordinates to the zinc stabilizing the oxyanion. It starts elimination of the amine of the amide which then is protonated by histidine. The protonation and deprotonation of the histidine are assisted by a neighboring acid.

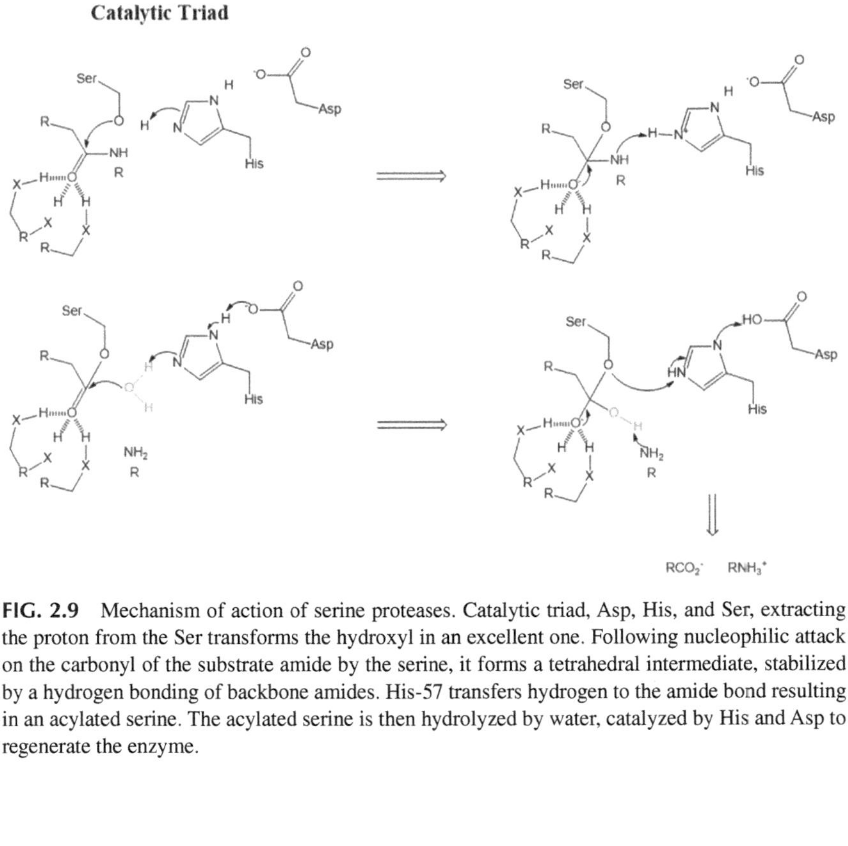

FIG. 2.9 Mechanism of action of serine proteases. Catalytic triad, Asp, His, and Ser, extracting the proton from the Ser transforms the hydroxyl in an excellent one. Following nucleophilic attack on the carbonyl of the substrate amide by the serine, it forms a tetrahedral intermediate, stabilized by a hydrogen bonding of backbone amides. His-57 transfers hydrogen to the amide bond resulting in an acylated serine. The acylated serine is then hydrolyzed by water, catalyzed by His and Asp to regenerate the enzyme.

2.5.3.5 *Threonine proteases*

The active site residues of threonine, serine, and cysteine proteases share many catalytic features. As previously described for serine and cysteine proteases, threonine proteases (TPs), in order to perform their mechanism of action first, form a covalent intermediate with the substrate, which in the second step is hydrolyzed by a water molecule, giving free enzyme as a final product (Fig. 2.10). Bortezomib, a TPI, is an N-protected dipeptide, which stands for pyrazinoic acid, phenylalanine, and leucine with a boronic acid instead of a carboxylic acid. Once Bortezomib penetrates the TP active site, it forms a covalent interaction between its boron atom and TP active site Thr-Oγ, forming a tetrahedral boronate, which is further stabilized by other interactions. These structure-function similarities between Bortezomib and TP substrate lead to inhibition of the enzyme (Brannigan et al., 1995; Cheng and Grishin, 2005).

Below (Table 2.1) are reported some examples of important inhibitors of each family of proteases acting as anticancer drugs with their chemical structures.

2.5.4 Plant products as protease inhibitors

Plant products are well known as one of best candidates to have numerous applications and to be used in both biotechnology and medicine field. Various plant products have been extracted for the control of pathologic processes and many diseases (Lingaraju and Gowda, 2008). To date, about more than half of the world's population still depends completely on plants and their medicinal products. The application of natural compounds as therapeutic strategies is widely used in different fields, such as Ayurvedic, Homeopathy, Unani, and even in allopathic systems. Compounds inhibited from plants have been found to act as the inhibitors of many classes of enzymes. It has been reported that the occurrence

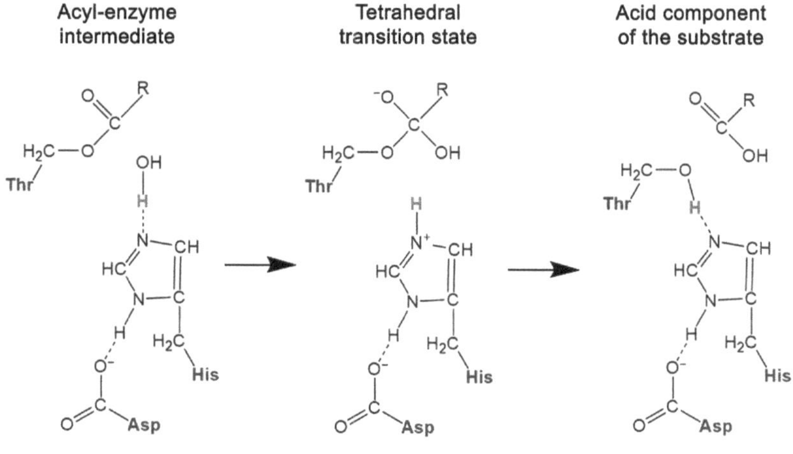

FIG. 2.10 TP mechanism of action. An acyl-enzyme intermediate is formed through TP-substrate reaction. It will be hydrolyzed by a water molecule, forming the free enzyme.

TABLE 2.1 Some examples of important inhibitors of each family of proteases acting as anticancer drugs with their chemical structures.

Protease family	Inhibitor	Chemical structure
Aspartic protease	Cathepsin D	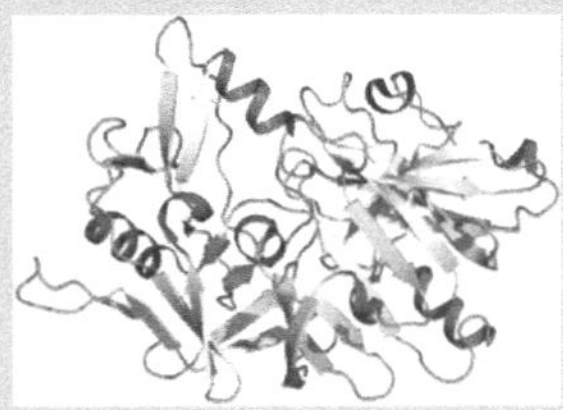
	Pepstatin	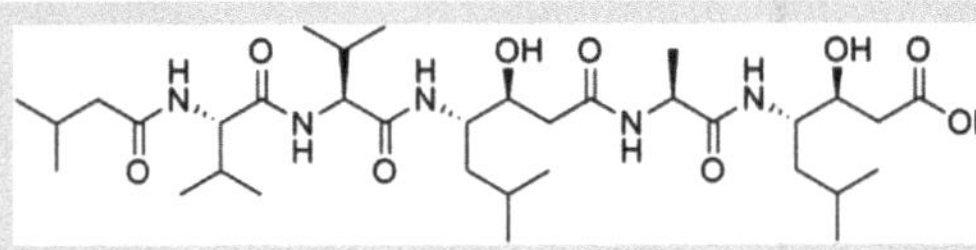
Cysteine protease	Stefin A	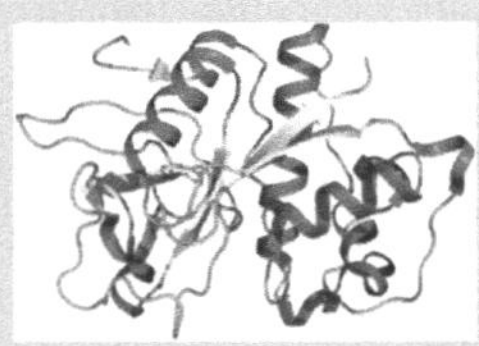
	Cystatin D	
Matrix metalloprotease	Batimastat	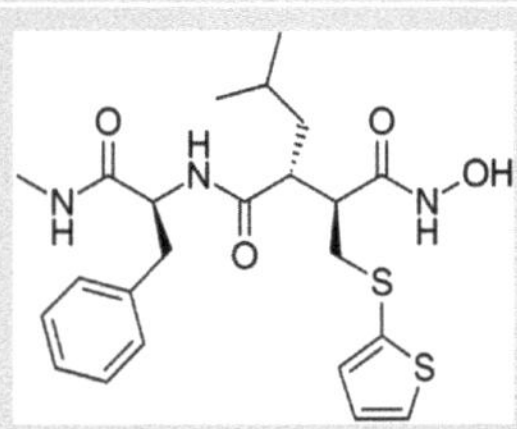
	Marimastat	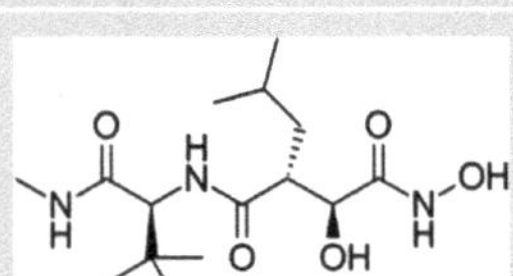

TABLE 2.1 Some examples of important inhibitors of each family of proteases acting as anticancer drugs with their chemical structures—cont'd

Protease family	Inhibitor	Chemical structure
Serine protease	Serpin 1	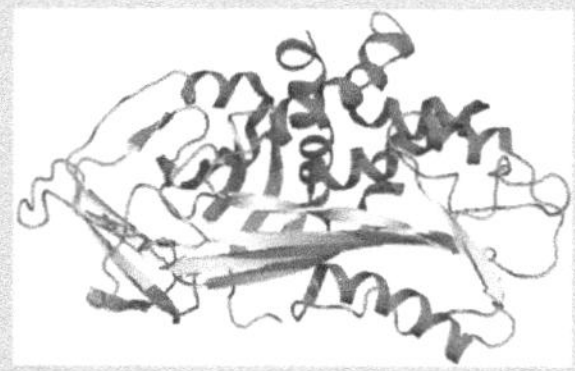
	Serpin 8	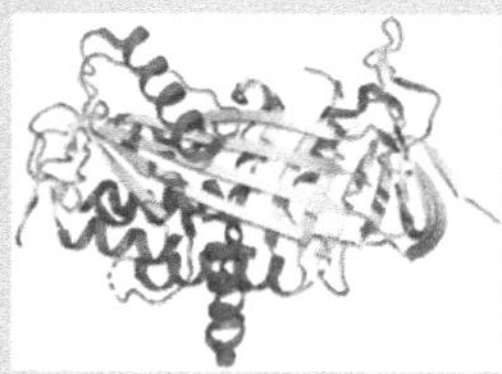
Threonine protease	Epoxomicin	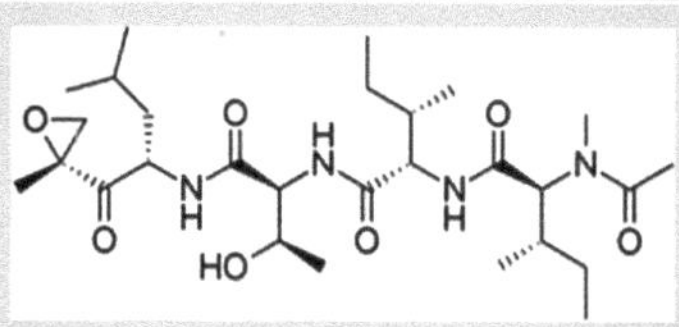
	Bortezomib	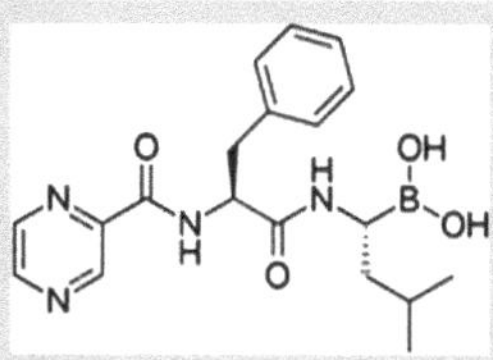

Data from Eatemadi, A., Aiyelabegan, H.T., Negahdari, B., Mazlomi, M.A., Daraee, H., Daraee, N., Eatemadi, R., Sadroddiny, E., 2017. Role of protease and protease inhibitors in cancer pathogenesis and treatment. Biomed. Pharmacother. 86, 221–231. Open Access Review.

rates of breast, colon, and prostate cancer are low in populations that usually consume a higher amount of seeds like beans, maize, and rice (Correa, 1981). It has also been demonstrated that a plant-based diet decreases remarkably the risk of chronic diseases as well as cancer (Hasler, 1998). Block et al. (1992) described that risk of cancer in people who adopted a vegetarian diet, with a high consumption of fruits and vegetables, was half of that in people who did not adopt vegetarian diet. It has been shown that food intake has the ability to influence the initiation or progression of different diseases (Dirsch and Vollmar, 2001; Losso, 2008). Nowadays, dietary factors have also attracted attention as therapy and prevention agents of cancer disease, due to their pharmacological safety. Several plants contain bioactive components like flavonoids and phenolic acids that possess powerful antioxidant activities (Lizcano et al., 2010; Pietta, 2000). Likewise, plants also contain components that may act as protease inhibitors. These plant components may be called as plant protease inhibitors (PPIs) and have been classified into several families, such as Bowman-Birk, Kunitz, Potato I, Potato II, Serpin, Cereal, Rapeseed, Mustard, and Squash (Laskowski and Qasim, 2000). Most of these PPIs inhibit mostly serine proteases. Some of these PPIs are exemplified in Fig. 2.11 and are described below.

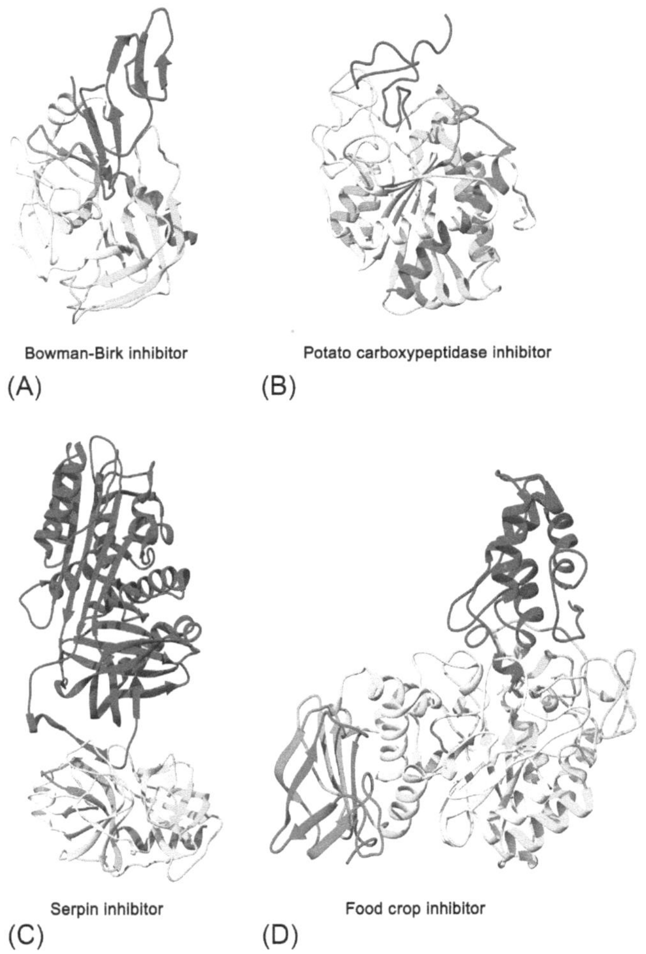

FIG. 2.11 Examples of some plant protease inhibitors [represented by *purple ribbon (dark gray in print version)]* complexed with a protease (represented in *multicolor ribbon*). (A) Bowmin-Birk inhibitor-trypsin complex (PDB code 2G81); (B) A PCI-carboxypeptidase A complex (PDB code 4CPA); (C) Michaelis complex between SERPINA1 and inactive trypsin (PDB code 1OPH); (D) A Ragi bifunctional protease inhibitor complexed with Tenebrio molitor larval alpha-amylase (PDB code 1TMQ). *(Data from https://commons.wikimedia.org/wiki/File:PI_families.jpg. Molecular graphics and analyses performed with UCSF Chimera.)*

2.5.4.1 Bowman-Birk inhibitors

Bowman-Birk Inhibitors (Fig. 2.11A) mainly inhibit serine peptidases of the S1 family but can also inhibit S3 peptidases. Members of this family have a duplicated structure and generally possess two distinct inhibitory sites. They are generally found in plants, and particularly in the seeds of legumes, and in cereal grains. An interesting feature of the Bowman-Birk inhibitors is the structure of the interacting loop, which is particularly well-defined, with disulfide-linked and a short beta-sheet region (Brauer et al., 2003; McBride and Leatherbarrow, 2001; McBride et al., 2002).

2.5.4.2 Potato I and II or potato carboxypeptidase inhibitors (PCIs)

Potato carboxypeptidase inhibitors (PCIs) (Fig. 2.11B) are usually present in potatoes. These PCIs can bind, with a strong and competitive interaction, to several metal carboxypeptidases, forming a transient complex. The structure of PCIs is made up of 39 amino acids forming a 27-residue globular domain, that is stabilized by three disulfide bridges, and a C-terminal tail formed by 4 residues (Michael Hass and Ryan, 1981). A crucial structural feature of PCIs is present in its pattern, known as T-knot scaffold that consists of a small cysteine-rich array (Sun and Davies, 1995). T-knot scaffold is essential for the mechanism of action of PCIs because it shares several similarities with several protein families, such as epidermal growth factor (EGF) family. Given such structural similarity as with EGF, PCIs are able to block the tumor cell growth process. The mechanism of action of PCIs involves the inhibition of the dimerization between the receptor and the receptor trans-auto phosphorylation carried out by EGF. The blockage of this dimerization causes the loss of the formation and then the activation of ErbB1/ErbB-2 (EGFR and HER2) complexes, which is involved in the onset of carcinoma pathologies (Sitja-Arnau et al., 2005).

2.5.4.3 Serpins

Serpins (Fig. 2.11C) are moderately large molecules formed of 330 to 500 residues. This class of PPIs is widely studied to reveal that they are "suicide" or "single use" inhibitors that undergo a unique and extensive conformational change in order to carry out their action. Structural mobility and the high flexibility of serpins cause several problems to their structure. Due to their structural features, they are heat-labile and susceptible to mutations and thus are susceptible misfolding, spontaneous conformational change, formation of inactive serpin polymers, and serpin deficiency (Carrell and Lomas, 1997). In humans several diseases (serpinopapthies) have been found to be associated with serpin polymerization. Such diseases may be named as emphysema (SERPINA1 (antitrypsin) deficiency) (Lomas et al., 1992), thrombosis (SERPINC1 (antithrombin) deficiency) (Bruce et al., 1994), angio-edema (SERPING1 (C1 esterase inhibitor) deficiency) (Aulak et al., 1988), and cancer (Heit et al., 2013).

The mechanism of action of serpins is very complicated as one can see in Fig. 2.12. This particular mechanism of action of serpins, that involves the cleavage of reactive center loop, led to call serpins as irreversible and suicide inhibitors (Law et al., 2006). Accumulation of serpin polymers in the endoplasmic reticulum of serpin-secreting cells can also result in diseases, such as the most notably cirrhosis (SERPINA1 polymerization) and familial dementia (SERPINI1 (neuroserpin) polymerization) (Davis et al., 1999). However,

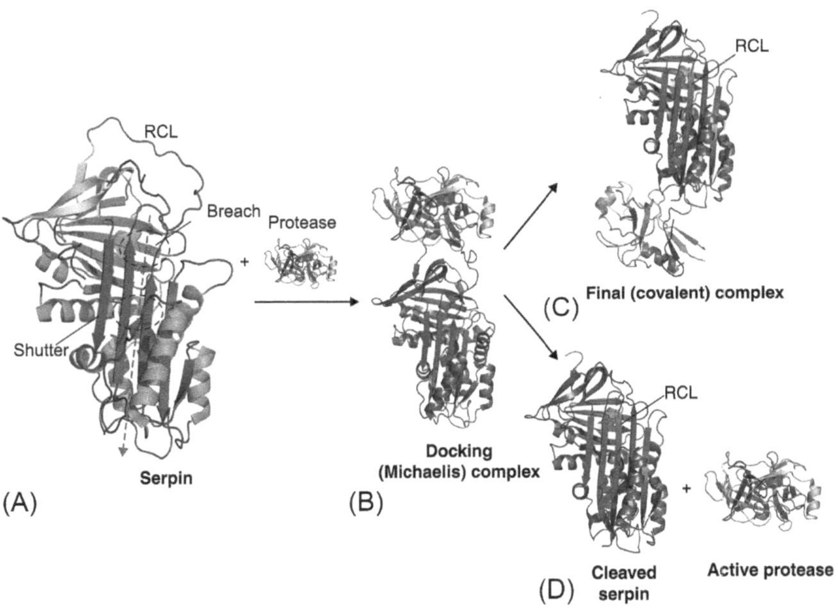

FIG. 2.12 Structure and mechanism of inhibitory serpins. (a) The structure of native SERPINA1 (PDB code 1QLP). The A, B, and C sheets are in *red cartoon (dark gray in print version), green cartoon (gray in print version)*, and *yellow cartoon (light gray in print version)*, respectively; helices (hA-hI) are in *blue cartoon (dark gray in print version)*. The reactive center loop (RCL) is at the top of the molecule, in *magenta cartoon (gray in print version)*. The positions of the breach and the shutter are labeled and the path of the RCL insertion is indicated *[magenta (gray in print version) dashed line]*. Both of these regions contain several highly conserved residues, many of which are mutated in various serpinopathies. (b) The Michaelis or docking complex between SERPINA1 and inactive trypsin (PDB code 1OPH), with the protease (multicolor cartoon) docked onto the RCL *[magenta sheet (gray in print version)]*. Upon docking with an active protease (b), two possible pathways are apparent. (c) The final serpin enzyme complex (PDB code 1EZX). The serpin has undergone the S to R transition, and the protease hangs distorted at the base of the molecule. (d) The structure of cleaved SERPINA1 is shown (PDB code 7API) with the RCL *[magenta sheet (gray in print version)]* forming the fourth strand of β-sheet A. The result of serpin substrate-like behavior can be seen where the protease has escaped the conformational trap, leaving active protease and inactive, cleaved serpin. Certain serpin mutations, particularly nonconservative substitutions within the hinge region of the RCL, result in substrate-like, rather than inhibitory, behavior. *(From Law, R.H.P., Zhang, Q., McGowan, S., Buckle, A.M., Silverman, G.A., Wong, W., Rosado, C.J., Langendorf, C.G., Pike, R.N., Bird, P.I., Whisstock, J.C., 2006. An overview of the serpin superfamily. Genome Biol. 7, 216. Open Access publication.)*

serpins are protease inhibitors, targeting extracellular, chymotrypsin-like serine proteases. Some serpins inhibit proteases of other classes also, such as cysteine proteases in particular, and are termed as "cross-class inhibitors."

2.5.4.4 Food crop

Food crop is considered an excellent diet for its nutritional qualities, long storage capability, and medicinal properties. As reported by some authors (Sen and Dutta, 2012), *Ragi (Elusine coracana)*, a cereal crop, is a small bifunctional inhibitor (RBI), that can simultaneously inhibit α-amylase and trypsin forming a ternary complex (Maskos et al., 1996). Its structure is constituted of 122 amino acids, forming a monomeric protein. In addition, it contains five intramolecular disulfide bonds (Campos and Richardson, 1983). This bifunctional inhibitor can reduce cellular proliferation and induce apoptosis of chronic myeloid leukemia cell. A Ragi bifunctional protease inhibitor complexed with Tenebrio molitor larval alpha-amylase is shown in Fig. 2.11C.

2.5.5 HIV protease inhibitors

HIV PIs are established as broad-spectrum anticancer agents that work through pleiotropic mechanisms in cancer cells (Bernstein and Dennis, 2008; Maksimovic-Ivanic et al., 2017). HIV-1 protease belongs to aspartyl protease family and is a homodimer. It is formed of 99 residues and its active site is represented by an aspartic acid at position 25 (Davies, 1990). The main function of HIV protease is the cleavage of a precursor Gag and Gag-pol polyprotein, which is essential to produce mature active protein. The biological process aimed to activate the mature protein of HIV involves several steps. First, Gag and Gag-pol polyproteins are cleaved by HIV protease and digested by other enzymes (reverse transcriptase, RNase, and integrase). Differently from other proteases, the active site of HIV protease is not completely exposed, but it is hidden by two β-hairpin flaps, as shown in Fig. 2.13. HIV protease, in order to perform the biological function, must open the β-hairpin flaps allowing the access of the substrate into active site. Strategy to inhibit HIV protease is to block its active site. The mechanism of action of HIV protease is carried out mainly by two Asp25 residues of the active site of homodimer. The catalytic activity of HIV protease consists of hydrolysis of peptide bond of the substrate, for which the Asp25 residues are present in two different states, protonated and not protonated states. Once substrate binds into HIV protease active site, deprotonated Asp25 residue and a water molecule allow the formation of a hydrogen bond between the Asp25 hydroxyl ion and the carbonyl carbon of the substrate peptide bond, forming an intermediate state, stabilized by protonated Asp-25 residue. Intermediate state is processed by further chemical reaction and it will be cleaved. HIV protease inhibitors block the protease enzyme function, which is crucial to cleave polyproteins and to form proteins biologically active, fundamental for the assembly of the new viral components. Hence, HIV inhibitors,

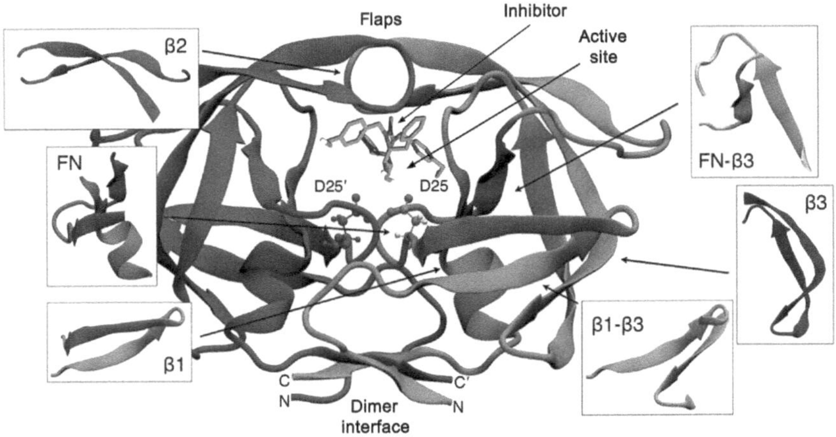

FIG. 2.13 Structure of the HIV-1-PR dimer (PDB code 1BVG) complexed with its inhibitor (orchid). The active site is situated at the interface between the two identical subunits of the homodimer. It is characterized by the sequence Asp-Thr-Gly (Asp25, Thr26, and Gly27), common to aspartic proteases. The two Asp25 residues act as the catalytic residues. At the top are the flexible flaps. In the *small boxes* are shown the six main motifs. *(From Bonomi, M., Barducci, A., Gervasio, F.L., Parrinello, M., 2010. Multiple routes and milestones in the folding of HIV-1 protease monomer. PLoS One 5(10), e13208. Open Access publication.)*

blocking the formation of active proteins, cause virions to remain immature and unable to infect other cells (Pettit et al., 2004). Out of several protease inhibitors that were approved by FDA for the treatment of HIV infection, the three inhibitors, ritonavir, saquinavir, nelfinavir (Fig. 2.14), were found to inhibit proliferation of nonsmall-cell lung carcinoma (NSCLC) cells, as well as every cell line in the NCI-60 cell line panel. The NCI-60 cancer cell line panel is a group of 60 human cancer cell lines used by the National Cancer Institute (NCI) for the screening of compounds to detect potential anticancer activity. Out of these three compounds, nelfinavir was found to be the most potent and thus to be a lead compound with pleiotropic effects in cancer cells, which is likely to be

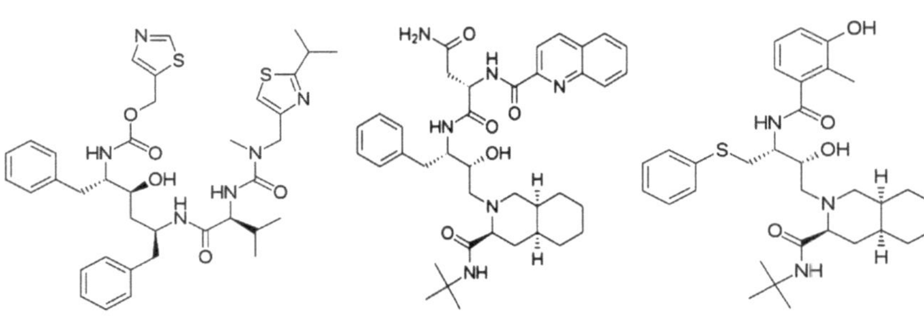

FIG. 2.14 Some HIV Protease inhibitors possessing anticancer potency, in which Nelfinavir has been found to have great promise.

repositioned by FDA as a cancer therapeutic. Nelfinavir in fact has wide spectrum of activity and good bioavailability. Nelfinavir caused two types of cell death, caspase-dependent apoptosis and caspase independent death, that was characterized by induction of endoplasmic reticulum (ER) stress and autophagy (Gills et al., 2007).

2.6 Conclusions

In this chapter, we have provided an insight into the role of the proteases and their inhibitors in cancer. Proteases are functionally implicated in different processes of cancer progression, from benign to malignancy. In the case of cancers, these proteases were initially considered to stimulate cancer cells to escape through tissue barriers. However, proteolytic activity in cancers is complicated by the involvement of inflammatory cells, immune responses, proliferation, and apoptosis. Activity of proteases is regulated by their interactions with their endogenous inhibitors. In the last ten years, there have been huge attempts to elucidate the mechanism of action of proteases and their biology and structures. However, the design and development of their inhibitors has been a complex issue, since different types of cancers use different proteases at the mutable stages of cancer growth and no single inhibitor can be used on all classes of proteases. But now the techniques of inhibitor design are developing significantly with the use of in silico approaches. Today's strategy in inhibitor design is to provide compounds complementary to active sites of proteins to be inhibited. Another solution is to develop allosteric inhibitors altering proteinase activity by binding outside the enzyme active site, most likely in the cavity lacking any physiological role. The advancement in computer-based methods for drug design (particularly docking techniques) might be very helpful in this respect. The studies of the role of proteases and their inhibitors in cancer progression and regression extend the therapeutic window for cancer treatment. Further insight into the roles of proteases in tumor progression and metastasis will guide the development of novel therapeutic strategies against cancer.

References

Abboud-Jarrous, G., Atzmon, R., Peretz, T., Palermo, C., Gadea, B.B., Joyce, J.A., Vlodavsky, I., 2008. Cathepsin L is responsible for processing and activation of proheparanase through multiple cleavages of a linker segment. J. Biol. Chem. 283, 18167–18176.

Affara, N.I., Andreu, P., Coussens, L.M., 2009. Delineating protease functions during cancer development. Methods Mol. Biol. 539, 1–32.

Alapati, K., Kesanakurti, D., Rao, J.S., Dasari, V.R., 2014. uPAR and cathepsin B-mediated compartmentalization of JNK regulates the migration of glioma-initiating cells. Stem Cell Res. 12, 716–729.

Alitalo, A., Detmar, M., 2012. Interaction of tumor cells and lymphatic vessels in cancer progression. Oncogene 31, 4499–4508.

Anastasov, A., Vihinen, P., Nikkola, J., Pyrhönen, S., Vlaykova, T., 2013. Matrix metalloproteinses in development and progression of skin malignant melanoma. Sci. Technol. Med. 1, 1.

Ansorge, S., Langner, J., 1997. Cellular peptidases in immune functions and diseases. In: Advances in Experimental Medicine and Biology. vol. 421.

Aulak, K.S., Pemberton, P.A., Rosen, F.S., Carrell, R.W., Lachmann, P.J., Harrison, R.A., 1988. Dysfunctional C1-inhibitor(At), isolated from a type II hereditary-angio-oedema plasma, contains a P1 'reactive centre' (Arg444----His) mutation. Biochem. J. 253, 615–618.

Barrett, A.J., 1970. Cathepsin D. Purification of isoenzymes from human and chicken liver. Biochem. J. 117, 601–607.

Baumann, U., 1994. Crystal structure of the 50 kDa metallo protease from Serratia marcescens. J. Mol. Biol. 242, 244–251.

Beck, P., Dubiella, C., Groll, M., 2012. Covalent and non-covalent reversible proteasome inhibition. Biol. Chem. 393, 1101–1120.

Behrendt, N., Ronne, E., Dano, K., 1995. The structure and function of the urokinase receptor, a membrane protein governing plasminogen activation on the cell surface. Biol. Chem. Hoppe Seyler 376, 269–279.

Bernstein, W.B., Dennis, P.A., 2008. Repositioning HIV protease inhibitors as cancer therapeutics. Curr. Opin. HIV AIDS 3, 666–675.

Bhagavan, N.V., Ha, C.-E., 2015. Biochemistry of hemostasis. In: Essentials of Medical Biochemistry. first ed., pp. 637–660.

Block, G., Patterson, B., Subar, A., 1992. Fruit, vegetables, and cancer prevention: a review of the epidemiological evidence. Nutr. Cancer 18, 1–29.

Bode, W., Gomis-Rüth, F.-X., Stöckler, W., 1993. Astacins, serralysins, snake venom and matrix metalloproteinases exhibit identical zinc-binding environments (HEXXHXXGXXH and Met-turn) and topologies and should be grouped into a common family, the 'metzincins'. FEBS Lett. 331, 134–140.

Boy, R.G., Knapp, E.-M., Eisenhut, M., Haberkorn, U., Mier, W., 2008. Enzymes/Transporters. In: Molecular Imaging II. pp. 131–143.

Brannigan, J.A., Dodson, G., Duggleby, H.J., Moody, P.C., Smith, J.L., Tomchick, D.R., Murzin, A.G., 1995. A protein catalytic framework with an N-terminal nucleophile is capable of self-activation. Nature 378, 416–419.

Brauer, A.B., Nievo, M., McBride, J.D., Leatherbarrow, R.J., 2003. The structural basis of a conserved P2 threonine in canonical serine proteinase inhibitors. J. Biomol. Struct. Dyn. 20, 645–656.

Bruce, D., Perry, D.J., Borg, J.Y., Carrell, R.W., Wardell, M.R., 1994. Thromboembolic disease due to thermolabile conformational changes of antithrombin Rouen-VI (187 Asn-->Asp). J. Clin. Invest. 94, 2265–2274.

Burden, R.E., Snoddy, P., Buick, R.J., Johnston, J.A., Walker, B., Scott, C.J., 2008. Recombinant cathepsin S propeptide attenuates cell invasion by inhibition of cathepsin L-like proteases in tumor microenvironment. Mol. Cancer Ther. 7, 538–547.

Campos, F.A.P., Richardson, M., 1983. The complete amino acid sequence of the bifunctional α-amylase/trypsin inhibitor from seeds of ragi (Indian finger millet, Eleusine coracana Gaertn). FEBS Lett. 152, 300–304.

Carrell, R.W., Lomas, D.A., 1997. Conformational disease. Lancet 350, 134–138.

Cavallo-Medved, D., Dosescu, J., Linebaugh, B.E., Sameni, M., Rudy, D., Sloane, B.F., 2003. Mutant K-ras regulates cathepsin B localization on the surface of human colorectal carcinoma cells. Neoplasia 5, 507–519.

Chen, D., Dou, Q.P., 2010. The ubiquitin-proteasome system as a prospective molecular target for cancer treatment and prevention. Curr. Protein Pept. Sci. 11, 459–470.

Chen, D., Frezza, M., Schmitt, S., Kanwar, J., Dou, Q.P., 2011. Bortezomib as the first proteasome inhibitor anticancer drug: current status and future perspectives. Curr. Cancer Drug Targets 11, 239–253.

Cheng, H., Grishin, N.V., 2005. DOM-fold: a structure with crossing loops found in DmpA, ornithine acetyltransferase, and molybdenum cofactor-binding domain. Protein Sci. 14, 1902–1910.

Choi, K.Y., Swierczewska, M., Lee, S., Chen, X., 2012. Protease-activated drug development. Theranostics 2, 156–179.

Correa, P., 1981. Epidemiological correlations between diet and cancer frequency. Cancer Res. 41, 3685–3690.

Craik, C.S., Page, M.J., Madison, E.L., 2011. Proteases as therapeutics. Biochem. J. 435, 1–16.

D'Angelo, M.E., Bird, P.I., Peters, C., Reinheckel, T., Trapani, J.A., Sutton, V.R., 2010. Cathepsin H is an additional convertase of pro-granzyme B. J. Biol. Chem. 285, 20514–20519.

Davies, D.R., 1990. The structure and function of the aspartic proteinases. Annu. Rev. Biophys. Biophys. Chem. 19, 189–215.

Davis, R.L., Shrimpton, A.E., Holohan, P.D., Bradshaw, C., Feiglin, D., Collins, G.H., Sonderegger, P., Kinter, J., Becker, L.M., Lacbawan, F., Krasnewich, D., Muenke, M., Lawrence, D.A., Yerby, M.S., Shaw, C.M., Gooptu, B., Elliott, P.R., Finch, J.T., Carrell, R.W., Lomas, D.A., 1999. Familial dementia caused by polymerization of mutant neuroserpin. Nature 401, 376–379.

Dean, R.A., Butler, G.S., Hamma-Kourbali, Y., Delbe, J., Brigstock, D.R., Courty, J., Overall, C.M., 2007. Identification of candidate angiogenic inhibitors processed by matrix metalloproteinase 2 (MMP-2) in cell-based proteomic screens: disruption of vascular endothelial growth factor (VEGF)/heparin affin regulatory peptide (pleiotrophin) and VEGF/Connective tissue growth factor angiogenic inhibitory complexes by MMP-2 proteolysis. Mol. Cell. Biol. 27, 8454–8465.

DeClerck, Y.A., Imren, S., 1994. Protease inhibitors: role and potential therapeutic use in human cancer. Eur. J. Cancer 30A, 2170–2180.

DeClerck, Y.A., Mercurio, A.M., Stack, M.S., Chapman, H.A., Zutter, M.M., Muschel, R.J., Raz, A., Matrisian, L.M., Sloane, B.F., Noel, A., Hendrix, M.J., Coussens, L., Padarathsingh, M., 2004. Proteases, extracellular matrix, and cancer: a workshop of the path B study section. Am. J. Pathol. 164, 1131–1139.

Degryse, B., 2011. The urokinase receptor system as strategic therapeutic target: challenges for the 21st century. Curr. Pharm. Des. 17, 1872–1873.

Deng, Y., Li, W., Li, Y., Yang, H., Xu, H., Liang, S., Zhang, L., Li, Y., 2010. Expression of matrix metalloproteinase-26 promotes human glioma U251 cell invasion in vitro and in vivo. Oncol. Rep. 23, 69–78.

Devy, L., Huang, L., Naa, L., Yanamandra, N., Pieters, H., Frans, N., Chang, E., Tao, Q., Vanhove, M., Lejeune, A., van Gool, R., Sexton, D.J., Kuang, G., Rank, D., Hogan, S., Pazmany, C., Ma, Y.L., Schoonbroodt, S., Nixon, A.E., Ladner, R.C., Hoet, R., Henderikx, P., Tenhoor, C., Rabbani, S.A., Valentino, M.L., Wood, C.R., Dransfield, D.T., 2009. Selective inhibition of matrix metalloproteinase-14 blocks tumor growth, invasion, and angiogenesis. Cancer Res. 69, 1517–1526.

Diment, S., Martin, K.J., Stahl, P.D., 1989. Cleavage of parathyroid hormone in macrophage endosomes illustrates a novel pathway for intracellular processing of proteins. J. Biol. Chem. 264, 13403–13406.

Dirsch, V.M., Vollmar, A.M., 2001. Ajoene, a natural product with non-steroidal anti-inflammatory drug (NSAID)-like properties? Biochem. Pharmacol. 61, 587–593.

Dodson, G., Wlodawer, A., 1998. Catalytic triads and their relatives. Trends Biochem. Sci. 23, 347–352.

Doucet, A., Butler, G.S., Rodriguez, D., Prudova, A., Overall, C.M., 2008. Metadegradomics: toward in vivo quantitative degradomics of proteolytic post-translational modifications of the cancer proteome. Mol. Cell. Proteomics 7, 1925–1951.

Drag, M., Salvesen, G.S., 2010. Emerging principles in protease-based drug discovery. Nat. Rev. Drug Discov. 9, 690–701.

Droga-Mazovec, G., Bojic, L., Petelin, A., Ivanova, S., Romih, R., Repnik, U., Salvesen, G.S., Stoka, V., Turk, V., Turk, B., 2008. Cysteine cathepsins trigger caspase-dependent cell death through cleavage of bid and antiapoptotic Bcl-2 homologues. J. Biol. Chem. 283, 19140–19150.

Eatemadi, A., Aiyelabegan, H.T., Negahdari, B., Mazlomi, M.A., Daraee, H., Daraee, N., Eatemadi, R., Sadroddiny, E., 2017. Role of protease and protease inhibitors in cancer pathogenesis and treatment. Biomed. Pharmacother. 86, 221–231.

Evrosimovska Andonovska, B., Boris, V., Dimova, C., Veleska, D., 2011. Matrix Metalloproteinases (With Accent to Collagenases). J. Cell Anim. Biol. 5, 113–120.

Fais, S., 2007. Cannibalism: a way to feed on metastatic tumors. Cancer Lett. 258, 155–164.

Farady, C.J., Craik, C.S., 2010. Mechanisms of macromolecular protease inhibitors. ChemBioChem 11, 2341–2346.

Field-Smith, A., Morgan, G.J., Davies, F.E., 2006. Bortezomib (Velcadetrade mark) in the treatment of multiple myeloma. Ther. Clin. Risk Manag. 2, 271–279.

Frederick Woessner Jr, J., 1999. Matrix Metalloproteinase Inhibition: From the Jurassic to the Third Millennium. Ann. N. Y. Acad. Sci..

Fujinaga, M., Cherney, M.M., Oyama, H., Oda, K., James, M.N., 2004. The molecular structure and catalytic mechanism of a novel carboxyl peptidase from Scytalidium lignicolum. Proc. Natl. Acad. Sci. USA 101, 3364–3369.

Fujise, N., Nanashima, A., Taniguchi, Y., Matsuo, S., Hatano, K., Matsumoto, Y., Tagawa, Y., Ayabe, H., 2000. Prognostic impact of cathepsin B and matrix metalloproteinase-9 in pulmonary adenocarcinomas by immunohistochemical study. Lung Cancer 27, 19–26.

Gills, J.J., LoPiccolo, J., Tsurutani, J., Shoemaker, R.H., Best, C.J.M., Abu-Asab, M.S., et al., 2007. Nelfinavir, a lead HIV protease inhibitor, is a broad-spectrum, anticancer agent that induces endoplasmic reticulum stress, autophagy, and apoptosis in vitro and in vivo. Clin. Cancer Res. 13, 5183–5194.

Gocheva, V., Joyce, J.A., 2007. Cysteine cathepsins and the cutting edge of cancer invasion. Cell Cycle 6, 60–64.

Gocheva, V., Zeng, W., Ke, D., Klimstra, D., Reinheckel, T., Peters, C., Hanahan, D., Joyce, J.A., 2006. Distinct roles for cysteine cathepsin genes in multistage tumorigenesis. Genes Dev. 20, 543–556.

Gocheva, V., Chen, X., Peters, C., Reinheckel, T., Joyce, J.A., 2010a. Deletion of cathepsin H perturbs angiogenic switching, vascularization and growth of tumors in a mouse model of pancreatic islet cell cancer. Biol. Chem. 391, 937–945.

Gocheva, V., Wang, H.W., Gadea, B.B., Shree, T., Hunter, K.E., Garfall, A.L., Berman, T., Joyce, J.A., 2010b. IL-4 induces cathepsin protease activity in tumor-associated macrophages to promote cancer growth and invasion. Genes Dev. 24, 241–255.

Grigoreva, T.A., Tribulovich, V.G., Garabadzhiu, A.V., Melino, G., Barlev, N.A., 2015. The 26S proteasome is a multifaceted target for anti-cancer therapies. Oncotarget 6, 24733–24749.

Gupta, S.C., Hye Kim, J., Prasad, S., Aggarwal, B., 2010. Regulation of survival, proliferation, invasion, angiogenesis, and metastasis of tumor cells through modulation of inflammatory pathways by nutraceuticals. Cancer Metastasis Rev. 29, 405–434.

Hanahan, D., Weinberg, R.A., 2011. Hallmarks of cancer: the next generation. Cell 144, 646–674.

Harter, M., Woll, S., Wunsch, A., Bengel, J., Reuter, K., 2006. Screening for mental disorders in cancer, cardiovascular and musculoskeletal diseases. Comparison of HADS and GHQ-12. Soc. Psychiatry Psychiatr. Epidemiol. 41, 56–62.

Hasler, W.L., 1998. Visceral analgesia: an emerging concept for managing functional gastrointestinal disease. Gastroenterology 115, 1023–1024.

He, Y., Liu, X.D., Chen, Z.Y., Zhu, J., Xiong, Y., Li, K., Dong, J.H., Li, X., 2007. Interaction between cancer cells and stromal fibroblasts is required for activation of the uPAR-uPA-MMP-2 cascade in pancreatic cancer metastasis. Clin. Cancer Res. 13, 3115–3124.

Hedstrom, L., 2002. Serine protease mechanism and specificity. Chem. Rev. 102, 4501–4524.

Heit, C., Jackson, B.C., McAndrews, M., Wright, M.W., Thompson, D.C., Silverman, G.A., Nebert, D.W., Vasiliou, V., 2013. Update of the human and mouse SERPIN gene superfamily. Hum. Genomics 7, 22.

Hirai, K., Yokoyama, M., Asano, G., Tanaka, S., 1999. Expression of cathepsin B and cystatin C in human colorectal cancer. Hum. Pathol. 30, 680–686.

Holland, J.C., Andersen, B., Breitbart, W.S., Buchmann, L.O., Compas, B., Deshields, T.L., Dudley, M.M., Fleishman, S., Fulcher, C.D., Greenberg, D.B., Greiner, C.B., Handzo, G.F., Hoofring, L., Hoover, C., Jacobsen, P.B., Kvale, E., Levy, M.H., Loscalzo, M.J., McAllister-Black, R., Mechanic, K.Y., Palesh, O., Pazar, J.P., Riba, M.B., Roper, K., Valentine, A.D., Wagner, L.I., Zevon, M.A., McMillian, N.R., Freedman-Cass, D.A., 2013. Distress management. J. Natl. Compr. Cancer Netw. 11, 190–209.

Hong, T.T., Dat, T.T.H., Cuc, N.T.K., Cuong, P.V., 2018. Mini-review protease inhibitor (PI) and PIs from sponge-associated microorganisms. Vietnam J. Sci.Technol. 56, 409–410.

Horiguchi, A., Zheng, R., Goodman Jr., O.B., Shen, R., Guan, H., Hersh, L.B., Nanus, D.M., 2007. Lentiviral vector neutral endopeptidase gene transfer suppresses prostate cancer tumor growth. Cancer Gene Ther. 14, 583–589.

Huang, H., Pierstorff, E., Osawa, E., Ho, D., 2008. Protein-mediated assembly of nanodiamond hydrogels into a biocompatible and biofunctional multilayer nanofilm. ACS Nano 2, 203–212.

Jedeszko, C., Sloane, B.F., 2004. Cysteine cathepsins in human cancer. Biol. Chem. 385, 1017–1027.

Kandalaft, P.L., Chang, K.L., Ahn, C.W., Traweek, S.T., Mehta, P., Battifora, H., 1993. Prognostic significance of immunohistochemical analysis of cathepsin D in low-stage breast cancer. Cancer 71, 2756–2763.

Karikari, C.A., Roy, I., Tryggestad, E., Feldmann, G., Pinilla, C., Welsh, K., Reed, J.C., Armour, E.P., Wong, J., Herman, J., Rakheja, D., Maitra, A., 2007. Targeting the apoptotic machinery in pancreatic cancers using small-molecule antagonists of the X-linked inhibitor of apoptosis protein. Mol. Cancer Ther. 6, 957–966.

Kawaguchi, M., Inoue, K., Iuchi, I., Nishida, M., Yasumasu, S., 2013. Molecular co-evolution of a protease and its substrate elucidated by analysis of the activity of predicted ancestral hatching enzyme. BMC Evol. Biol. 13, 231.

Kessenbrock, K., Plaks, V., Werb, Z., 2010. Matrix metalloproteinases: regulators of the tumor microenvironment. Cell 141, 52–67.

Kim, J., Yu, W., Kovalski, K., Ossowski, L., 1998. Requirement for specific proteases in cancer cell intravasation as revealed by a novel semiquantitative PCR-based assay. Cell 94, 353–362.

Kleifeld, O., Doucet, A., auf dem Keller, U., Prudova, A., Schilling, O., Kainthan, R.K., Starr, A.E., Foster, L.J., Kizhakkedathu, J.N., Overall, C.M., 2010. Isotopic labeling of terminal amines in complex samples identifies protein N-termini and protease cleavage products. Nat. Biotechnol. 28, 281–288.

Kobayashi, H., Schmitt, M., Goretzki, L., Chucholowski, N., Calvete, J., Kramer, M., Gunzler, W.A., Janicke, F., Graeff, H., 1991. Cathepsin B efficiently activates the soluble and the tumor cell receptor-bound form of the proenzyme urokinase-type plasminogen activator (Pro-uPA). J. Biol. Chem. 266, 5147–5152.

Korubo, K.I., Madu, A.J., Okoye, H.C., Nwogoh, B., 2018. Bortezomib prescription pattern for the treatment of multiple myeloma by hematologists in Nigeria. J. Glob. Oncol., 4, 1–7.

Kromann-Hansen, T., Oldenburg, E., Yung, K.W., Ghassabeh, G.H., Muyldermans, S., Declerck, P.J., Huang, M., Andreasen, P.A., Ngo, J.C., 2016. A camelid-derived antibody fragment targeting the active site of a serine protease balances between inhibitor and substrate behavior. J. Biol. Chem. 291, 15156–15168.

Kuriyama, N., Kuriyama, H., Julin, C.M., Lamborn, K.R., Israel, M.A., 2001. Protease pretreatment increases the efficacy of adenovirus-mediated gene therapy for the treatment of an experimental glioblastoma model. Cancer Res. 61, 1805–1809.

Lankelma, J.M., Voorend, D.M., Barwari, T., Koetsveld, J., Van der Spek, A.H., De Porto, A.P.N.A., Van Rooijen, G., Van Noorden, C.J.F., 2010. Cathepsin L, target in cancer treatment? Life Sci. 86, 225–233.

Laskowski, M., Qasim, M.A., 2000. What can the structures of enzyme-inhibitor complexes tell us about the structures of enzyme substrate complexes? Biochim. Biophys. Acta 1477, 324–337.

Law, R.H., Zhang, Q., McGowan, S., Buckle, A.M., Silverman, G.A., Wong, W., Rosado, C.J., Langendorf, C.G., Pike, R.N., Bird, P.I., Whisstock, J.C., 2006. An overview of the serpin superfamily. Genome Biol. 7, 216.

Li, J., Yuan, J., 2008. Caspases in apoptosis and beyond. Oncogene 27, 6194–6206.

Liaudet-Coopman, E., Beaujouin, M., Derocq, D., Garcia, M., Glondu-Lassis, M., Laurent-Matha, V., Prébois, C., Rochefort, H., Vignon, F., 2006. Cathepsin D: newly discovered functions of a long-standing aspartic protease in cancer and apoptosis. Cancer Lett. 237, 167–179.

Lingaraju, M.H., Gowda, L.R., 2008. A Kunitz trypsin inhibitor of Entada scandens seeds: another member with single disulfide bridge. Biochim. Biophys. Acta 1784, 850–855.

Lizcano, A., Chin, T., Sauer, K., Tuomanen, E.I., Orihuela, C.J., 2010. Early biofilm formation on microtiter plates is not correlated with the invasive disease potential of Streptococcus pneumoniae. Microb. Pathog. 48, 124–130.

Lomas, D.A., Evans, D.L., Finch, J.T., Carrell, R.W., 1992. The mechanism of Z alpha 1-antitrypsin accumulation in the liver. Nature 357, 605–607.

Lopez-Otin, C., Matrisian, L.M., 2007. Emerging roles of proteases in tumour suppression. Nat. Rev. Cancer 7, 800–808.

Lord, S.J., Rajotte, R.V., Korbutt, G.S., Bleackley, R.C., 2003. Granzyme B: a natural born killer. Immunol. Rev. 193, 31–38.

Losso, J.N., 2008. The biochemical and functional food properties of the bowman-birk inhibitor. Crit. Rev. Food Sci. Nutr. 48, 94–118.

Lu, P., Weaver, V.M., Werb, Z., 2012. The extracellular matrix: a dynamic niche in cancer progression. J. Cell Biol. 196, 395–406.

Maksimovic-Ivanic, D., Fagone, P., McCubrey, J., Bendtzen, K., Mijatovic, S., Nicoletti, F., 2017. HIV-protease inhibitors for the treatment of cancer: Repositioning HIV protease inhibitors while developing more potent NO-hybridized derivatives? Int. J. Cancer 140, 1713–1726.

Maskos, K., Huber-Wunderlich, M., Glockshuber, R., 1996. RBI, a one-domain alpha-amylase/trypsin inhibitor with completely independent binding sites. FEBS Lett. 397, 11–16.

Mason, S.D., Joyce, J.A., 2011. Proteolytic networks in cancer. Trends Cell Biol. 21, 228–237.

Masson, O., Prebois, C., Derocq, D., Meulle, A., Dray, C., Daviaud, D., Quilliot, D., Valet, P., Muller, C., Liaudet-Coopman, E., 2011. Cathepsin-D, a key protease in breast cancer, is upregulated in obese mouse and human adipose tissue, and controls adipogenesis. PLoS One 6, e16452.

Matarrese, P., Ascione, B., Ciarlo, L., Vona, R., Leonetti, C., Scarsella, M., Mileo, A.M., Catricalà, C., Paggi, M.G., Malorni, W., 2010. Cathepsin B inhibition interferes with metastatic potential of human melanoma: an in vitro and in vivo study. Mol. Cancer 9, 1–2.

McBride, J.D., Leatherbarrow, R.J., 2001. Synthetic peptide mimics of the Bowman-Birk inhibitor protein. Curr. Med. Chem. 8, 909–917.

McBride, J.D., Watson, E.M., Brauer, A.B., Jaulent, A.M., Leatherbarrow, R.J., 2002. Peptide mimics of the Bowman-Birk inhibitor reactive site loop. Biopolymers 66, 79–92.

Methot, N., Rubin, J., Guay, D., Beaulieu, C., Ethier, D., Reddy, T.J., Riendeau, D., Percival, M.D., 2007. Inhibition of the activation of multiple serine proteases with a cathepsin C inhibitor requires sustained exposure to prevent pro-enzyme processing. J. Biol. Chem. 282, 20836–20846.

Michael Hass, G., Ryan, C.A., 1981. Carboxypeptidase inhibitor from potatoes. In: Methods in Enzymology. Academic Press, pp. 778–791.

Michl, P., 2012. Targeting cathepsins: a new glimmer of hope for pancreatic cancer therapy? Gut 61, 790.

Mitchell, B.S., 2003. The proteasome—an emerging therapeutic target in cancer. N. Engl. J. Med. 348, 2597–2598.

Mofers, A., Pellegrini, P., Linder, S., D'Arcy, P., 2017. Proteasome-associated deubiquitinases and cancer. Cancer Metastasis Rev. 36, 635–653.

Mohamed, M.M., Sloane, B.F., 2006. Multifunctional enzymes in cancer. Nat. Rev. Cancer 6, 764.

Mohamed, M.M., Cavallo-Medved, D., Rudy, D., Anbalagan, A., Moin, K., Sloane, B.F., 2010. Interleukin-6 increases expression and secretion of cathepsin B by breast tumor-associated monocytes. Cell. Physiol. Biochem. 25, 315–324.

Nicotra, G., Castino, R., Follo, C., Peracchio, C., Valente, G., Isidoro, C., 2010. The dilemma: does tissue expression of cathepsin D reflect tumor malignancy? The question: does the assay truly mirror cathepsin D mis-function in the tumor? Cancer Biomark. 7, 47–64.

Oda, K., 2012. New families of carboxyl peptidases: serine-carboxyl peptidases and glutamic peptidases. J. Biochem. 151, 13–25.

Ohri, S.S., Vashishta, A., Proctor, M., Fusek, M., Vetvicka, V., 2008. The propeptide of cathepsin D increases proliferation, invasion and metastasis of breast cancer cells. Int. J. Oncol. 32, 491–498.

Ovaere, P., Lippens, S., Vandenabeele, P., Declercq, W., 2009. The emerging roles of serine protease cascades in the epidermis. Trends Biochem. Sci. 34, 453–463.

Overall, C.M., Kleifeld, O., 2006. Tumour microenvironment—opinion: validating matrix metalloproteinases as drug targets and anti-targets for cancer therapy. Nat. Rev. Cancer 6, 227–239.

Perez-Silva, J.G., Espanol, Y., Velasco, G., Quesada, V., 2016. The degradome database: expanding roles of mammalian proteases in life and disease. Nucleic Acids Res. 44, D351–D355.

Pettit, S.C., Everitt, L.E., Choudhury, S., Dunn, B.M., Kaplan, A.H., 2004. Initial cleavage of the human immunodeficiency virus type 1 GagPol precursor by its activated protease occurs by an intramolecular mechanism. J. Virol. 78, 8477–8485.

Pietta, P.G., 2000. Flavonoids as antioxidants. J. Nat. Prod. 63, 1035–1042.

Radisky, E.S., Radisky, D.C., 2010. Matrix metalloproteinase-induced epithelial-mesenchymal transition in breast cancer. J. Mammary Gland Biol. Neoplasia 15, 201–212.

Rakashanda, S., Rana, F., Rafiq, S., Masood, A., Amin, S., 2012. Role of proteases in cancer: a review. Biotechnol. Mol. Biol. Rev. 7, 90–101.

Rastogi, N., Mishra, D.P., 2012. Therapeutic targeting of cancer cell cycle using proteasome inhibitors. Cell Div 7, 26.

Rawlings, N.D., Barrett, A.J., 1993. Evolutionary families of peptidases. Biochem. J. 290 (Pt 1), 205–218.

Rawlings, N.D., Barrett, A.J., 2000. MEROPS: the peptidase database. Nucleic Acids Res. 28, 323–325.

Rawlings, N.D., Tolle, D.P., Barrett, A.J., 2004. Evolutionary families of peptidase inhibitors. Biochem. J. 378, 705–716.

Rawlings, N.D., Morton, F.R., Kok, C.Y., Kong, J., Barrett, A.J., 2008. MEROPS: the peptidase database. Nucleic Acids Res. 36, D320–D325.

Rawlings, N.D., Barrett, A.J., Thomas, P.D., Huang, X., Bateman, A., Finn, R.D., 2018. The MEROPS database of proteolytic enzymes, their substrates and inhibitors in 2017 and a comparison with peptidases in the PANTHER database. Nucleic Acids Res. 46, D624–D632.

Revach, O.Y., Geiger, B., 2014. The interplay between the proteolytic, invasive, and adhesive domains of invadopodia and their roles in cancer invasion. Cell Adhes. Migr. 8, 215–225.

Ritchie, C., 2013. Protease Inhibitors, Mater. Methods 3.

Rodríguez, J., Vízquez, J., Corte, M.D., Lamelas, M., Bongera, M., Corte, M.G., Alvarez, A., Allende, M., Gonzalez, L., Sínchez, M., Vijande, M., Muñiz, J.G., Vizoso, F., 2005. Clinical significance of cathepsin D concentration in tumor cytosol of primary breast cancer. Int. J. Biol. Markers 20, 103–111.

Saleh, Y., Wnukiewicz, J., Andrzejak, R., Trziszka, T., Siewinski, M., Ziolkowski, P., Kopec, W., 2006. Cathepsin B and cysteine protease inhibitors in human tongue cancer: correlation with tumor staging and in vitro inhibition of cathepsin B by chicken cystatin. J. Cancer Mol. 2, 67–72.

Sanman, L.E., Bogyo, M., 2014. Activity-based profiling of proteases. Annu. Rev. Biochem. 83, 249–273.

Schmidt, M., Finley, D., 2014. Regulation of proteasome activity in health and disease. Biochim. Biophys. Acta 1843, 13–25.

Schneider, B.A., Balskus, E.P., 2018. Discovery of small molecule protease inhibitors by investigating a widespread human gut bacterial biosynthetic pathway. Tetrahedron 74, 3215–3230.

Scott, K., Hayden, P.J., Will, A., Wheatley, K., Coyne, I., 2016. Bortezomib for the treatment of multiple myeloma. Cochrane Database Syst. Rev. 4. CD010816.

Sen, S., Dutta, S.K., 2012. Cloning, expression and characterization of biotic stress inducible Ragi bifunctional inhibitor (RBI) gene from Eleusine coracana Gaertn. J. Plant Biochem. Biotechnol. 21, 66–76.

Sevenich, L., Joyce, J.A., 2014. Pericellular proteolysis in cancer. Genes Dev. 28, 2331–2347.

Siegel, R.M., 2006. Caspases at the crossroads of immune-cell life and death. Nat. Rev. Immunol. 6, 308–317.

Sitja-Arnau, M., Molina, M.A., Blanco-Aparicio, C., Ferrer-Soler, L., Lorenzo, J., Aviles, F.X., Querol, E., de Llorens, R., 2005. Mechanism of action of potato carboxypeptidase inhibitor (PCI) as an EGF blocker. Cancer Lett. 226, 169–184.

Skrzydlewska, E., Sulkowska, M., Koda, M., Sulkowski, S., 2005. Proteolytic-antiproteolytic balance and its regulation in carcinogenesis. World J. Gastroenterol. 11, 1251–1266.

Skrzypczak, M., Springwald, A., Lattrich, C., Häring, J., Schüler, S., Ortmann, O., Treeck, O., 2012. Expression of cysteine protease cathepsin L is increased in endometrial cancer and correlates with expression of growth regulatory genes. Cancer Investig. 30, 398–403.

Sloane, B.F., 1990. Cathepsin B and cystatins: evidence for a role in cancer progression. Semin. Cancer Biol. 1, 137–152.

Sloane, B.F., Yan, S., Podgorski, I., Linebaugh, B.E., Cher, M.L., Mai, J., Cavallo-Medved, D., Sameni, M., Dosescu, J., Moin, K., 2005. Cathepsin B and tumor proteolysis: contribution of the tumor microenvironment. Semin. Cancer Biol. 15, 149–157.

Stark, D., Kiely, M., Smith, A., Velikova, G., House, A., Selby, P., 2002. Anxiety disorders in cancer patients: their nature, associations, and relation to quality of life. J. Clin. Oncol. 20, 3137–3148.

Storer, A.C., 1991. Engineering of proteases and protease inhibition. Curr. Opin. Biotechnol. 2, 606–613.

Stupack, D.G., Teitz, T., Potter, M.D., Mikolon, D., Houghton, P.J., Kidd, V.J., Lahti, J.M., Cheresh, D.A., 2006. Potentiation of neuroblastoma metastasis by loss of caspase-8. Nature 439, 95–99.

Sun, P.D., Davies, D.R., 1995. The cystine-knot growth-factor superfamily. Annu. Rev. Biophys. Biomol. Struct. 24, 269–291.

Tang, L., Han, X., 2013. The urokinase plasminogen activator system in breast cancer invasion and metastasis. Biomed. Pharmacother. 67, 179–182.

Tarnowska, M., Oldziej, S., Liwo, A., Kania, P., Kasprzykowski, F., Grzonka, Z., 1992. MNDO study of the mechanism of the inhibition of cysteine proteinases by diazomethyl ketones. Eur. Biophys. J. 21, 217–222.

Turk, B., Turk, D., Turk, V., 2012. Protease signalling: the cutting edge. EMBO J. 31, 1630–1643.

van der Stappen, J.W., Williams, A.C., Maciewicz, R.A., Paraskeva, C., 1996. Activation of cathepsin B, secreted by a colorectal cancer cell line requires low pH and is mediated by cathepsin D. Int. J. Cancer 67, 547–554.

van Horssen, R., Buccione, R., Willemse, M., Cingir, S., Wieringa, B., Attanasio, F., 2013. Cancer cell metabolism regulates extracellular matrix degradation by invadopodia. Eur. J. Cell Biol. 92, 113–121.

Van Lint, P., Libert, C., 2007. Chemokine and cytokine processing by matrix metalloproteinases and its effect on leukocyte migration and inflammation. J. Leukoc. Biol. 82, 1375–1381.

Vashishta, A., Ohri, S.S., Proctor, M., Fusek, M., Vetvicka, V., 2007. Ribozyme-targeting procathepsin D and its effect on invasion and growth of breast cancer cells: an implication in breast cancer therapy. Int. J. Oncol. 30, 1223–1230.

Vashishta, A., Ohri, S., Vetvicka, V., 2009. Pleiotropic effects of cathepsin D. Endocr. Metab. Immune Disord. Drug Targets 9, 385–391.

Vasiljeva, O., Turk, B., 2008. Dual contrasting roles of cysteine cathepsins in cancer progression: apoptosis versus tumour invasion. Biochimie 90, 380–386.

Verbovšek, U., Van Noorden, C.J.F., Lah, T.T., 2015. Complexity of cancer protease biology: cathepsin K expression and function in cancer progression. Semin. Cancer Biol. 35, 71–84.

Vigneswaran, N., Zhao, W., Dassanayake, A., Muller, S., Miller, D.M., Zacharias, W., 2000. Variable expression of cathepsin B and D correlates with highly invasive and metastatic phenotype of oral cancer. Hum. Pathol. 31, 931–937.

Weathington, N.M., Mallampalli, R.K., 2014. Emerging therapies targeting the ubiquitin proteasome system in cancer. J. Clin. Invest. 124, 6–12.

Woenne, E.C., Lederle, W., Zwick, S., Palmowski, M., Krell, H., Semmler, W., Mueller, M.M., Kiessling, F., 2010. MMP inhibition blocks fibroblast-dependent skin cancer invasion, reduces vascularization and alters VEGF-A and PDGF-BB expression. Anticancer Res. 30, 703–711.

Yang, Y.-G., Wei, J.Y., Nakajima, K., 2009a. On period variations of the K-type eclipsing binary BM ursae majoris. Publ. Astron. Soc. Jpn 61, 13–18.

Yang, Y., Kitagaki, J., Wang, H., Hou, D.X., Perantoni, A.O., 2009b. Targeting the ubiquitin-proteasome system for cancer therapy. Cancer Sci. 100, 24–28.

Yang, P., Li, Z.-Y., Li, H.-Q., 2015. Potential roles of protease inhibitors in cancer progression. Asian Pac. J. Cancer Prev. 16, 8047–8052.

Yang, W.E., Ho, C.C., Yang, S.F., Lin, S.H., Yeh, K.T., Lin, C.W., Chen, M.K., 2016b. Cathepsin B expression and the correlation with clinical aspects of oral squamous cell carcinoma. PLoS One 11, e0152165.

Zucker, S., Cao, J., Chen, W.-T., 2001. Critical appraisal of the use of matrix metalloproteinase inhibitors in cancer treatment. Oncogene 19, 6642.

Further reading

Multum, C., Atazanavir Uses, Side Effects & Warnings. From https://www.drugs.com/mtm/atazanavir.html

Chapter 3

Studies on cysteine proteases and their inhibitors for anticancer drug design

Rohit Dutt[a], Ashima Nagpal[a], Vandana Garg[b], A.K. Madan[c]
[a]School of Medical and Allied Sciences, GD Goenka University, Gurugram, India, [b]MD University, Rohtak, India, [c]Pt. BD Sharma University of Health Sciences, Rohtak, India

3.1 Introduction

Cancer is a catastrophic disease, primarily characterized by abnormal out-of-control growth of cells. It is an accumulation of more than 100 diseases that predominantly share the customary characteristic of abnormal cell growth. However, there is a substantial difference among these diseases that has been a matter of concern pertaining to their cure through chemotherapy. It has now become conspicuous that there are multifarious pathways through which cancer can develop in a human being. The involvement of multiple pathways in cell growth has been attributed to this rise in uncontrolled cell growth. Manifold studies have unearthed a direct correlation between the complexity of a tumor and the release of various proteases. Advances in diverse bioinformatic technologies have simply enabled researchers to find approximately 600 proteases in human and mouse genomes, many of which are orthologous, but only few of them are responsible for progression and growth of tumor at both the primary and metastatic sites (Puente et al., 2003). As tumor advances toward malignancy, it passes through various crucial stages that involve the action of proteases (Duffy, 1992; Mignati and Rifkin, 1993). In the first stage, angiogenesis requires the release of matrix-bound preangiogenic growth factors and degradation of the vascular basement membrane. In the second stage, for cancer cells to invade the surrounding tissue, the junctions between the cells must dissolve along with degradation of epithelial membrane and remodeling of extracellular matrix to facilitate release of cancer cells from the primary tumor mass. In the third stage, minimum of two crucial steps in metastasis need proteolysis: intravasation of cancer cells into the blood or lymphatic circulation at the primary site and then extravasation at the secondary site, where proteases can play

Cancer-Leading Proteases. https://doi.org/10.1016/B978-0-12-818168-3.00003-6

role in encouraging the colonization and further growth of cancer. Proteases may cooperate in regulating/controlling these steps with individual ones playing different roles. Therefore, inhibition of their activity can naturally prove to be highly beneficial in subduing the growth of cancer. A plethora of oncology research in the last decade has unveiled the potential roles of protein assessment in the development of tumors. For instance, they are now contemplated as extremely important signaling molecule playing key roles in diverse vital processes (Kolkhorst et al., 1998). Protease signaling pathways are among the most rigorously modulated pathways. Hence, deregulation of their activities can tremendously result in various pathologies, including cancer. Thus, development of an inhibitor, capable of inhibitory action on progression of tumor growth and metastasis, is not possible without placing specific protein as important in the proper metabolic context. Design of an appropriate inhibitor is further complicated because varied types of cancers utilize diverse proteases at different stages of cancer growth (Castro-Guillén and Chapter, 2010; Lee et al., 2004; Magdolen et al., 2002; Pandey et al., 2007; Puxbaum and Mach, 2009).

Depending upon their action mechanism, human proteases may be classified as aspartic acid, cysteine, threonine, serine, and metalloproteinases (Rakashanda et al., 2012; Zucker et al., 2000; Joyce et al., 2004). Most of these proteases possess unique characteristic of being competent of carrying out proteolysis commonly known as proteolytic activity i.e., hydrolysis of peptide bond that occurs as a result of an attack on the carbonyl functional group of the peptide. The cleaving action of a peptide bond by a protease usually takes place in the presence of water molecule (in glutamic acid, aspartate, and metalloproteases) or a serine, cysteine, or threonine residue (typically a histidine residue activation) acting as the nucleophile in the binding site (Joyce and Hanahan, 2004). The link between tumor and stromal cells controls two protease systems that are known to have their role in proteolysis outside the cell. These are the urokinase plasminogen activator (uPA)/uPA receptor (uPAR)/plasminogen network and matrix metalloproteases (MMPs). Stromal MMP-2 and uPA are primarily released as inactive precursors that get activated on the surface of tumor cells. This causes malignant cells to rupture the basement membranes (Eatemadia et al., 2017). In addition, proteases are also known to promote sprouting of blood vessels to provide nourishment to the growing cancer. Anticancer treatments targeting these stromal contributions to invasion, metastasis, and angiogenesis attack a cell population that is genetically constant, so they may not get resistant to the use of conventional chemotherapeutic agent (Kim et al., 1998). In the present review, a staunch need for development of cysteine protease inhibitors as anticancer agents has been accentuated.

3.2 The role of cysteine proteases in tumor growth and progession

Proteases in noncancerous cells play key roles in performing vital biological processes, such as regulating an array of diverse cellular processes such as differentiation, gene expression, and cell death (Gocheva et al., 2006). Cysteine proteases are named because of the importance of a cysteine thiol group as the key nucleophile in the active site of the enzyme. The thiol group acts as a nucleophile in the initial steps of catalytic cleavage of the peptide bond. However, classification of cysteine proteases into distinct families is dependent both on sequence homology and on the specificity of the protease for amino acid sidechains in the "P1" position of the substrate. Remember, "cysteine" proteases are not named because they cleave a peptide bond next to a cysteine (McKerrow, 2018).

Despite a vast pool of evidence depicting the key role of lysosomal cysteine proteases in expression, localization, and activation of tumor cells, this class of proteases has gained immense attention in oncology research. In mammalian cells, cysteine proteases are restricted mainly to the cytoplasm (caspase and calpain families) and lysosomal compartments (legumain and cathepsin families).

3.2.1 Caspases and calpains

The caspases are considered to play an important function in apoptosis, whereas calpains are considered the best characterized duo factor in both apoptosis and necrosis (Wang, 2000). By cleaving essential proteins, caspases modulate the apoptosis process both morphologically and biochemically, such as cytoplasmic and chromatin condensation, cell shrinkage, membrane blebbing, nuclear fragmentation, and finally formation of membrane bound apoptotic bodies, which catalyze their own engulfment by phagocytes (Jäger and Zwacka, 2010). There is a third group of caspases, which combine a role in apoptosis initiation with an inflammatory function. There are two major signaling pathways of caspase activation, the death receptor (extrinsic) pathway and the stress (intrinsic or mitochondria-mediated) pathway (Harwood et al., 2005).

Calpains are primarily neutral, cytosolic cysteine proteases. Broadly, calpains are reported to have 15 isoforms among which 11 have been identified in human tissues (Huang and Wang, 2001; Sorimachi et al., 2011). These enzymes manifest a unique behavior when compared with other cysteine proteases in that the cytosolic proenzyme is stimulated by Ca^{2+} ions, that in-turn induces a change in its conformation. The two majorly studied isoforms of calpain, calpains 1 and 2, or μ- and m-calpain show wide distribution and require 5 and 30 mmol/L Ca^{2+} for stimulation, respectively (Goll et al., 2003). The presence of phosphoinositides or phospholipids decrease the concentration of Ca^{2+} required to activate calpain 2 (Arthur and Crawford, 1996; Shao et al., 2006). Due to the high homogeneity in the substrates and active site of calpain 1 and 2, development of specific inhibitors has not yet been achieved. Cathepsins and calpains, through restricted proteolytic cleavage at certain sites, modulate the activity of other biomolecules. Since functional proteins are mostly derived through these enzyme catalyzed reactions, these cysteine proteases are among the crucial regulatory enzymes. In few cases, mutations in the regulatory domain of β-catenin mark the main characteristic of cancer. The result of these mutations is the stabilization of β-catenin and enhanced TCF-dependent transcriptional activity. A study revealed that calpain cleaved β-catenin proteolytically resulted in the deletion of the N-terminal regulatory domain (Rios-Doria et al., 2004). Additionally, expression analysis of in a prostate cancer microarray showed significant increase in m-calpain cDNA levels in 19 metastatic and 49 localized and prostate cancer in comparison to 26 normal prostate samples. Therefore, calpain can be considered as a potential target for cancer therapy and development of inhibitors of calpain may prove to be of profound benefit (Rios-Doria (II) et al., 2004).

3.2.2 Cysteine cathepsins

Cysteine cathepsins constitute a family of lysosomal proteases that show enhanced expression in several human cancers. These have been involved in diverse tumorigenic pathways such as invasion angiogenesis, apoptosis, and proliferation (Overall and Kleifeld, 2006; Laufs et al., 2006; Turk and Guncar, 2003; Turk et al., 2001; Gocheva and Joyce, 2007). The name cathepsin, basically derived from the Greek word kathepsein (to digest), was primarily proposed for the proteases that were active particularly in a faintly acidic environment (Jäger and Zwacka, 2010). The family of human cysteine cathepsin is comprised of 11 members (Cat B, C, F, H, L, K, O, S, V, W, X/Z). Later on, the lysosomal cysteine cathepsins (the serine proteases cathepsins A and G) and the aspartic proteases (cathepsins D and E) also came under this class. All of these share a conserved binding site formed by cysteine and histidine residues (Bell-McGuinn et al., 2007). The proteases can belong to the category of endopeptidases, exopeptidases, or can possess both types of enzymatic activities leading to significantly distinct preferences for the substrate for different cathepsins (Koblinski et al., 2000). Primarily, the cathepsins are released as inactive precursors, which get stimulated in the lysosomes that provide them with acidic environment favorable for their activation. Earlier, the main function of cathepsins was believed to be limited to lysosomal terminal protein degradation, which is not an exclusive property of any one cathepsin (Berdowska, 2004). Most of the cathepsins show wide expression in mammalian tissues. Their location in diverse tissues implies their involvement in a normal cellular protein turnover and degradation. Whereas, cathepsins K, S, and W are restricted to the specific cells or tissues, clearly suggesting their specific roles. However, many studies have been reported depicting the localization of active cathepsins in various cellular compartments, such as the cytoplasm, nucleus, and plasma membrane. Through this evidence, the role of catalytically active cathepsin L in the regulation of cell-cycle progression (Turk and Guncar, 2003) and the proteolytic processing of the N-terminus of the histone H3 tail can be justified (Duncan et al., 2008; Santos-Rosa et al., 2009). Additionally, many studies have provided sufficient evidence indicating that the specific physiological functions of the cathepsins are somewhat due to their differences in expression inside and outside the cells (Barrett and Rawlings, 2004; Zavašnik-Bergant and Turk, 2006; Brix et al., 2008).

As the cancer progresses, cathepsins translocate to the surface of tumor cells, or are released into the extracellular milieu, where they play key role in promoting tumor invasion through varied possible mechanisms (Joyce et al., 2004). First, by directly cleaving components of the basement membrane and extracellular matrix, cadherins thereby clear a path for the tumor cell migration away from the primary tumor mass. Second, at the cell surface, cathepsins direct a proteolytic cascade, thereby activating other proteases such as matrix metalloproteinases and urokinase plasminogen activator, eventually promoting invasion. Finally, cell adhesion protein cleavage, E-cadherin, at the surface of the cell can disrupt adherens junctions and thus promote cancer cell migration and invasion. Therefore, cathepsins have emerged as key players in progression of tumor cells, making them important drug targets for a wide range of human cancers (Joyce et al., 2004; Joyce and Hanahan, 2004).

Increased expression of cathepsins B and L is normally witnessed in several types of tumors (Mason and Joyce, 2011; Fong et al., 1991). Additionally, the predominant manifestation of cathepsin K in osteoclasts has obviously rendered this enzyme as a crucial target for the design of novel drugs for the therapy of bone tumors (Frlan and Gobec, 2006). The common belief is that cathepsin-mediated degradation of the extracellular matrix is primarily extracellular at the invasive front of tumor cells. This proteolytic pathway is connected both with early tumor progression, affecting tumor cell development and angiogenesis, and with diffusion of malignant cells from primary tumors (Mohamed and Sloane, 2006). Due to this reason, inhibitors of cathepsins are among the most intensively studied ones. In particular cathepsins B and L have been implicated in tumor invasion and are thought to be important mediators of metastasis. An aspartic enzyme, cathepsin D, is known to convert pro-cathepsin B into cathepsin B. A number of other proteases, along with cathepsins C and G, tissue-type plasminogen activator, and urokinase-type plasminogen activator, can also activate cathepsin B. Finally, cathepsin B may undergo auto-activation under certain conditions. Cathepsin B, upon activation, cleaves an assortment of targets based on its subcellular localization in the tumor microenvironment (Mort, 1997; Cygler et al., 1996). This complex pathway of activity focuses on the dominant role of cathepsins in progression of tumor cells that in another way explains why design of its inhibitors is the need of current oncology research.

3.2.2.1 Cathepsin substrate (E-cadherin)

This cathepsin substrate, E-cadherin, was identified a decade ago. It is known to get cleaved by cathepsin B, L and S, thus unraveling another pathway through which invasion could be attained (Turk and Guncar, 2003). E-cadherin is the major constituent of adherens junctions and facilitates cell-cell adhesion especially in epithelial cells (Bell-McGuinn et al., 2007; Noe et al., 2001). Its significance in causing cancer has now been well defined, as most epithelial cancers lose E-cadherin function as soon as they turn malignant, resulting in abrogation of its adhesive properties, thus facilitating invasiveness in cell along with metastasis. In the RIP1-Tag2 model it has been explained that loss of E-cadherin controls the transition from adenoma to carcinoma and further supports an invasive phenotype (Bell-McGuinn et al., 2007; Maretzky et al., 2005). General pathways of E-cadherin downregulation are comprised of gene mutations, transcriptional repression, proteolytic cleavage (Koblinski et al., 2000; Noe et al., 2001) and epigenetic silencing of the ectodomain by proteases like ADAM10-7 and MMP-3 among others (Lindeman et al., 2004; Turk et al., 2004). It has been shown that tumors from cathepsin B, L or S null RT2 mice exhibited a constant E-cadherin levels, as opposite to the typical protein down regulation usually witnessed in invasive tumors from cathepsin C null or wild-type RT2 mice. In addition, in vitro assays to study cleavage, by employing recombinant proteins, reported that upon incubation, cathepsin B, L or S with the adherens junction component lead to cleavage of E-cadherin in the extracellular portion of the enzyme, which suggests that cell-cell adhesion will be lost that would eventually lead to tumor invasion (Turk and Guncar, 2003).

3.2.2.2 Cathepsin B

The human cathepsin B gene is known to be positioned on chromosome 8p22 and comprises of 12 exons (Mohamed and Sloane, 2006). Cysteine cathepsins are primarily released as inactive precursors. Pro-cathepsin B possesses an N-terminal fragment to cover the binding site and active sites. Pro-cathepsins are essentially stimulated in lysosomes where the acidic environment, favorable for their activation is provided and it is believed that it is there that they initially begin to function as intracellular proteases and control proteolysis (Koblinski et al., 2000). Fully developed cathepsin B consists of a light chain of 5 kDa and a heavy chain of 25–26 kDa (Mohamed and Sloane, 2006). Cathepsin B is very distinct from other cathepsins possessing unique enzyme features. Majority of cysteine cathepsins are endopeptidases, but cathepsin B exhibits an additional carboxyopeptidase activity (Koblinski et al., 2000).

Cathepsin B, like other cysteine cathepsins, possesses a conserved active site that is constituted by histidine (His199) and cysteine (Cys29) residues. The substrate binding cleft is located next to the binding site, and is mediated by the occluding loop, which is an 18 residue long insertion. Additionally, the occluding loop consists of two His residues (His110 and His111) that have ability to show interaction with the C-terminus carboxylic group of the substrate peptide and assist in the entry of substrate into the binding domain (Mort, 1997). The interaction between the carboxylate group and the two His residues describes the action of cathepsin B as carboxy dipeptidase at an acidic pH (Mohamed and Sloane, 2006). The flexibility of the occluding loop permits cathepsin B to function as an endopeptidase, during the movement of occluding loop from the active site cleft to cleave the internal peptide bonds (Mort, 1997). Cathepsin B, though, is less effective as an endopeptidase when compared to other proteases of the papain family due to the requirement of large amount of energy to modify the conformation of the occluding loop (Cygler et al., 1996).

3.2.2.3 Cathepsin S

Cathepsin S is a single-chain, nonglycosylated potent enzyme which has a unique characteristic of exhibiting proteolytic activity at neutral pH whereas all other cathepsins get activated at acidic pH. Cathepsin S has the highest homogeneity or sequence similarity (73.3% and 75.5%, respectively) and identity (57.8% and 55.4%, respectively) to Cathepsin K and Cathepsin L. Cathepsin S, K, and L share a conserved active site comprised of histidine and cysteine residues (Burden et al., 2009). Cathepsin S has been shown to be crucial for MHC class II-associated antigen processing and exhibition (Frizler et al., 2010). The defective development of micro-vessel during wound repair and the abnormal angiogenesis in micro-vascular endothelial cells was witnessed in the mice deficient of Cathepsin S. These outcomes clearly suggested the crucial role of Cathepsin S in different aspects of angiogenesis both in vivo and in vitro (Fernandez et al., 2001). In addition, enhanced expression of Cathepsin S has also been witnessed in a wide range of tumors such as astrocytomas, prostate, pancreatic and hepatocellular carcinomas (Flannery et al., 2003, 2006; Ryschich et al., 2006; Irie et al., 2008). The expression of Cathepsin S as well as Cathepsin B has been found to be increased in neoplastic prostatic cells from preinvasive to invasive and clinically diagnosable stage (Palermo and Joyce, 2008). Cathepsin S is witnessed to have enhanced expression in astrocytoma obtained from brain tumor cell cultures, but not in from normal astrocytes derived cells, neurons, oligodendrocytes and endothelial cells (Chang et al., 2007). The highest level of Cat S activity has also been seen in grade IV tumors among 59 astrocytoma biopsies (Keppler, 2006). In murine model of hepatocellular carcinoma, Cathepsin S was found to be the most overexpressed protease at the time of vessel spouting (Perl et al., 1998). On one hand, activity of cysteine cathepsin has been functionally indicated in pancreatic islets of a mouse model of carcinogenesis (Saleh et al., 2006). On the contrary, Cathepsin S activity was found to be controlled by endogenous inhibitors like cystatin C (Saleh et al., 2006), various exogenous inhibitors like E-64, and nonpeptide and peptide synthetic compounds (Turk et al., 2001). Diminished angiogenesis and tumor growth were witnessed in Cathepsin S knockout mice, whereas opposite phenotypes were exhibited in mice deficient in the endogenous inhibitor cystatin C (Mussap and Plebani, 2004). The invasive and proangiogenic effects of in preclinical and clinical evaluation were obstructed by antibody Fsn0503 against Cathepsin S6. The invasive behavior in U251MG glioblastoma cells was interrupted by a peptidic, irreversible Cathepsin S inhibitor, 4-morpholineurea-Leu-HomoPhe-vinylsulphone (Chang et al., 2007). These studies suggested that Cathepsin S possesses correlation with cancer migration and invasion and can be a possible target for antimigration and antiinvasive therapy (Mussap and Plebani, 2004; Wieczerzak et al., 2002). Design of selective and potent cathepsin S inhibitors is, therefore, of immense significance in cancer therapy.

3.3 Inhibitors of cysteine proteases

As discussed above, cysteine proteases may be involved in initiation and progression of different types of cancer and hence the attention has been focused on the studies of their inhibitors. Inhibitors of cysteine proteases can be endogenous, natural, and synthetic. Further, all inhibitors can be put in two categories: reversible or irreversible inhibitors. Inhibitors bind to enzymes noncovalently and involve weak interactions such as hydrogen bondings, hydrophobic interaction, or van der Waals interactions. On the other hand, irreversible inhibitors involve covalent strong binding that is permanent. Let us describe here cysteine protease inhibitors based on their sources.

3.3.1 Endogenous inhibitors

Things that are produced within a cell or organ are called endogenous and things that affect cell or organ are called exogenous. The most prominent endogenous inhibitors of cysteine proteases are cystatins. Cystatins constitute a super family of inhibitors that encompass proteins which contain multiple cystatin-like sequences. This super family has 3 subfamilies of inhibitors: type 1 cystatins (stefins), type 2 cystatins, and kininogens (Folgueras et al., 2004). Type 1 cystatins (stefins) are single domain proteins of about 100 amino acids, having no disulfide bonds, while type 2 cystatins are somewhat longer, about 120 amino acids, and have two internal disulfide bonds, kininogens are high molecular mass and multidomain glycoproteins (Pavlova et al., 2000). Stefins have been proposed as prognostic and diagnostic tools for cancer. There are two types of human stefins, stefins A and stefins B. Despite possessing diverse biochemical characters, cystatins share a sequence homology and a common tertiary structure of an α-helix lying on top of an antiparallel β-sheet as shown in Fig. 3.1.

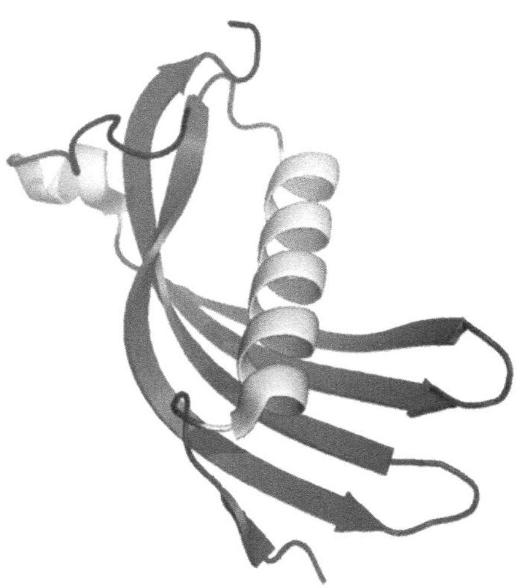

FIG. 3.1 General structure of cystatins. *(From Wikipedia: https://en.wikipedia.org/wiki/Cystatin.)*

Their inhibitory site is constituted by the juxtaposition of three regions of the molecule, forming a wedge shaped edge that is complementary to the binding site of papain family of proteases. Since the cystatins can inhibit cathepsin activity, many reports have suggested their potential use as anticancer agents (Palermo and Joyce, 2008). Fig. 3.2 depicts a high resolution crystal structure of cathepsin B complexed with type 1 cystatin, stefin A.

Cystatins of other subfamilies, however, have not been found so useful as anticancer agents and this failure is attributed to their low bioavailability, small circulation time, and high cost (140 $ USA per milligram) (Mussap and Plebani, 2004; Wieczerzak et al., 2002). Imitating the section of cystatin that interacts with the cathepsin binding domain can be the technique of choice and this approach led to design a highly active inhibitor of cathepsin B, N-1845 (**I**) (Ki = 0.088 nM), that contains azaglycine residue in place of evolutionary conserved glycine residue in the N terminal part of cystatin (Wieczerzak et al., 2007). Further modification of this molecule with the help of molecular dynamics and NMR techniques led to design another potent and selective inhibitor (**II,** Ki = 0.48 nM) of cathepsin B. Among 11 human cysteine cathepsins, cathepsin B is reported to be upregulated in many types of cancer just because of its role in tumor growth, invasion, angiogenesis, and metastasis.

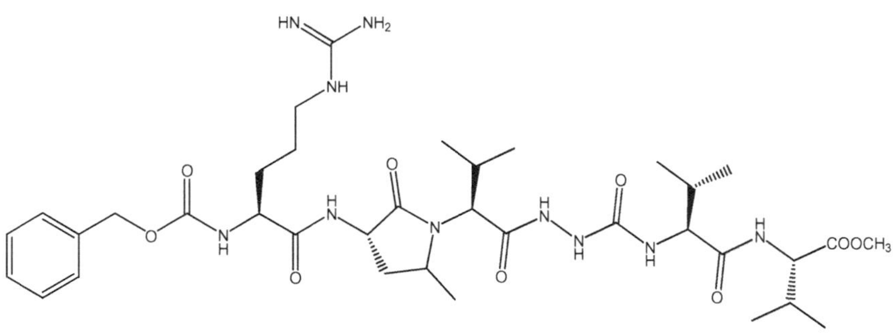

I, N-1845 (Ki = 0.88 nM)

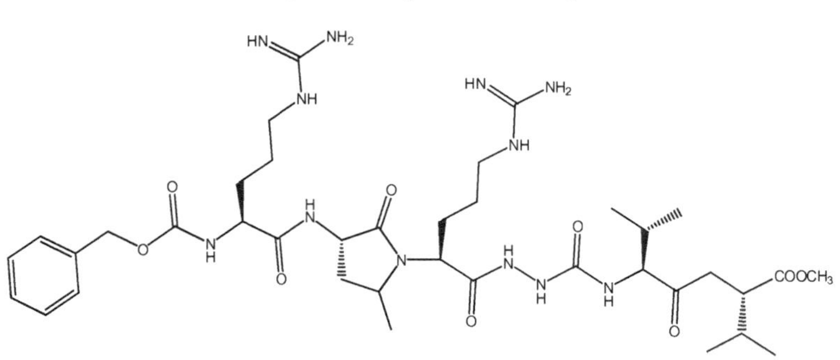

II (Ki = 0.48 nM)

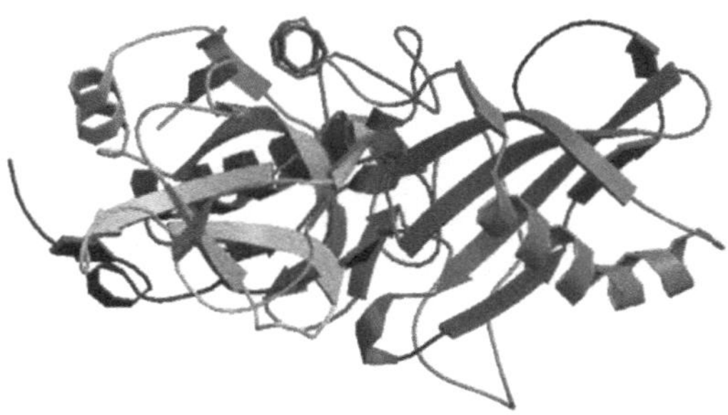

FIG. 3.2 Stefin A (*black*) complexed with cathepsin B (PDB entry 3K9M). *(From https://www.rcsb.org/structure/3K9M.)*

3.3.2 From natural sources

Natural sources have been exploited since ages in the search of potential lead substances with therapeutic properties. Anticancer potential of curcumin is well known. Surprisingly, curcumin (Fig. 3.3) has also been reported to possess inhibitory activity against cathepsin B (Ravish and Raghav, 2014). Additionally, studies have shown that bacteria are also capable of producing inhibitors against cysteine proteases that exhibit far broader specificity. The molecular nature of cysteine protease inhibitors obtained from bacterial sources is not restricted to protein-like compounds. Bacteria are also shown to produce a number of small-molecule inhibitors; leupeptin being one of those that is reported to be secreted extracellularly by variety of species belonging to the class of actinomycetes. Leupeptin (Fig. 3.3) is a tripeptidyl aldehyde, which occurs in the form of acetyl- or propionyl L-leucyl-L-leucylargininal (Kuramochi et al., 1979). It shows covalent bonding with the catalytic cysteine and serine residues of cysteine and serine proteases, respectively, and thereby inhibiting them competitively and reversibly (Kim and Lee, 1995).

Typically, secondary metabolites obtained from *Streptomyces* show a great difference when their biological activity and physicochemical nature are compared. Therefore, due to obvious reasons their secondary metabolites emerged as potential lead compounds. In a reported study, the combination of two peptide

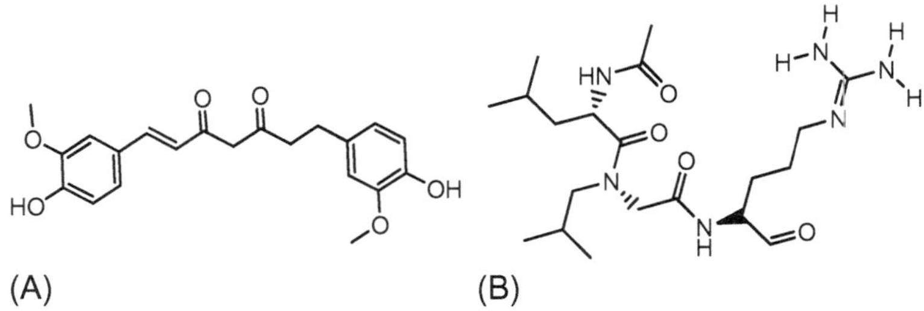

FIG. 3.3 Structure of curcumin (A) and leupeptin (B). *(Reproduced with the permission from McConnell, M.R., Barnes, G.E., Hoyng, C.F., Gunn, J.M., 1990. New leupeptin analogs: synthesis and inhibition data. J. Med. Chem. 33, 86–93. Copyright 1990 American Chemical Society.)*

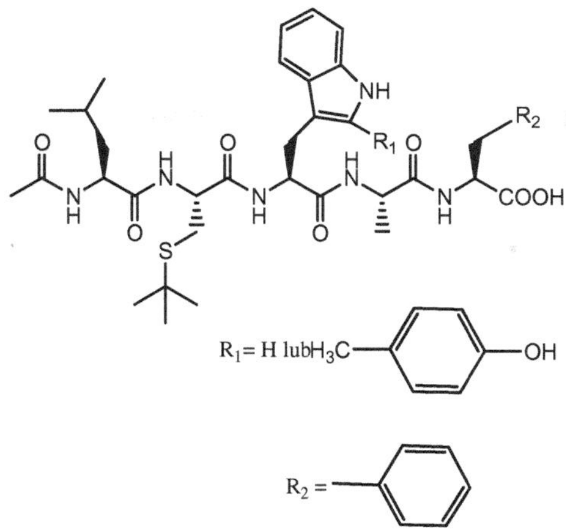

FIG. 3.4 Anticancer peptide produced by *Streptomyces* NCIM 2081:CPI-2081. *(Reproduced with the permission from Singh, J.P., Tamang, S., Rajamohanan, P.R., Jima, N.C., Chakraborty, G., Kundu, G.C., Gaikwad, S.M., Khan, M.I., 2010. Isolation, structure and functional elucidation of modified pentapeptide, cysteine protease inhibitor (CPI-2081) from Streptomyces species 2081 that exhibit inhibitory effect on cancer cell migration. J. Med. Chem. 53, 5121–5128. Copyright 2010 American Chemical Society.)*

metabolites obtained from *Streptomyces* resulted in a potent inhibitor, CPI-2081, that exhibited strong inhibitory activity against papain (Fig. 3.4). This inhibitor showed considerable suppression in tumor cell migration at subcytotoxic concentration, clearly suggesting its excellent potential to be an antimetastatic agent (Singh et al., 2010).

3.3.3 Reversible and irreversible inhibitors

A broad difference between reversible and irreversible inhibitors has already been pointed out. The basic point is that electrophilic functionality in reversible inhibitors is reversible vis-à-vis irreversible inhibitors. A methylketone, an aldehyde, a nitrile, or α-ketoamide groups are representative examples of some of the reactive electrophiles as included in some of the reported reversible inhibitors. Some of them are presently being studied in animal models to investigate their inhibitory affect in the progression of cancer. A large number of these inhibitors were retrieved using computer-aided design. Literature reveals the discovery of one of the most potent inhibitors of cathepsin B (Ki = 7 nM), dipeptide nitrile, as an outcome of molecular modeling and high-resolution X-ray crystallographic analysis (Stroup et al., 2001).

Most of the synthetic cysteine protease inhibitors comprised of a peptide fragment for recognition by the target enzyme and an electrophilic moiety capable of reacting with the thiolate functionality present at cysteine binding domain. Mostly, this leads to the covalent modification of the protease, thereby resulting in its irreversible inhibition. A vast assortment of such reactive functional groups has been utilized. These include vinyl sulfone, acyloxymethyl ketone, azomethyl- or halomethyl ketone, acylhydroxamate, and chloromethylsulfoxide. It is also worth mentioning that epoxysuccinates, explained earlier, are also a part of this class of inhibitors (Elie et al., 2010; Ward et al., 2002; Ovat et al., 2010; Niestroj et al., 2002).

The strength of electrophilicity of the attached group is one of the most crucial determinants of the selectivity and rate with which the inhibitor reacts and forms the covalent enzyme-inhibitor complex. For an instance, halomethyl ketones exhibit nonselectivity by reacting with cysteine as well as serine proteinases (Niestroj et al., 2002). Despite high selectivity and potency, anticancer potential of irreversible inhibitors is limited due to side effects produced as a result of prolonged action with other cysteine proteases (Kumar et al., 2010; Otto and Schirmeister, 1997). X-ray studies of cysteine protease complexed with inhibitor are a reliable tool for rational design of the peptidomimetic or peptidyl part of inhibitor. This not only facilitates the design of the selective inhibitors but also provides clear insight into the binding domain and active site of the target enzyme. The precise knowledge of the amino acid sequence at the active site of cathepsin B combined with molecular docking studies was demonstrated in one study for the design of dual action mechanism-based inhibitor (Ravish and Raghav, 2014). First, active site Cys-29 gets acylated by the inhibitor, followed by transfer of acetyloxy moiety of the inhibitor, catalyzed by His-199, thus, causing irreversible blocking of two vital binding domain amino acids.

In a study, E-64 (Fig. 3.5), which is a specific and irreversible inhibitor of cysteine proteases, was isolated from *Aspergillus japonicus* in the year 1978. The epoxysuccinate part of this molecule has been shown to interact with binding domain of cysteine, forming a covalent bond with the enzyme. By using the structural framework of this molecule as a template, specific inhibitors of cathepsin B and L were designed using their X-ray crystal structures (Fong et al., 1991), which upon evaluation showed promising anticancer activity in animals (Hanada et al., 1978). An ethyl ester of E-64 was tested in clinical trials in Japanese individuals with muscular dystrophy, but the trials were stopped at phase III of development due to suboptimal activity profile. Another derivative of E-64 with less hydrophilic character was designed to target muscular dystrophy and was developed to overcome the problem of poor absorption

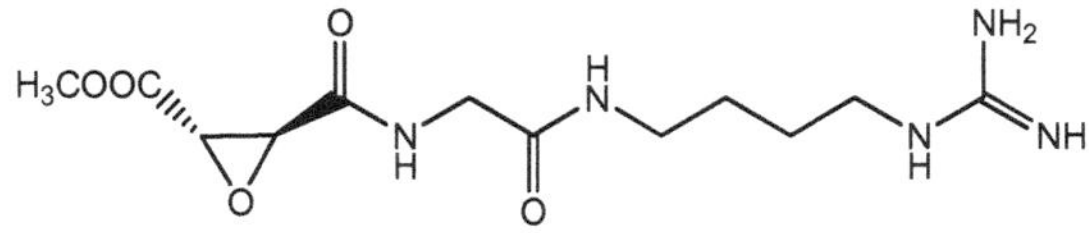

E-64

FIG. 3.5 Specific inhibitor of cathepsins B and L (E-64). *(Reproduced with the permission from Hanada, K., Tamai, M., Yamagishi, M., Ohmura, S., Sawada, J., Tanaka, I., 1978. Isolation and identification of E-64, a new thiol protease inhibitor. Agric. Biol. Chem. Tokyo. 42, 523–528. Agric. Biol. Chem. Taylor and Francis Publisher).*

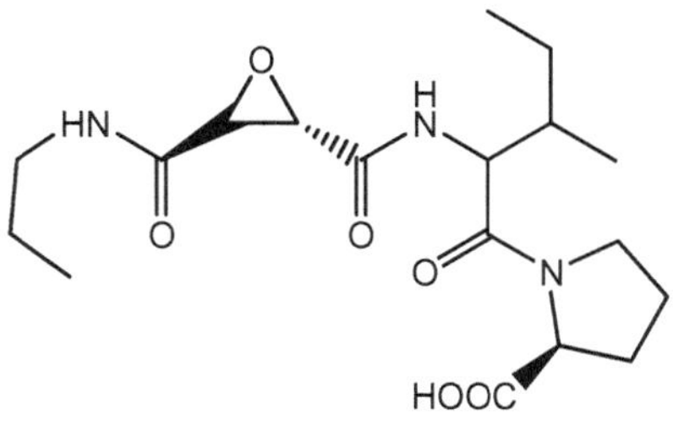

CA-074

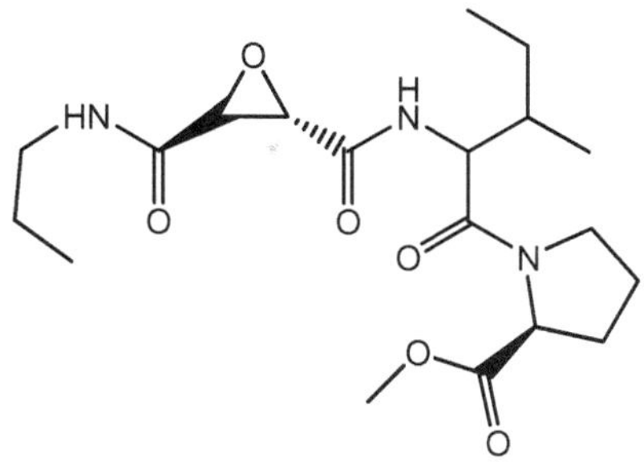

CA-074Me

FIG. 3.6 Specific inhibitors of cathepsins B and L (CA-074 and CA-074Me). *(Reproduced with the permission from Mashamba-Thompson, T., Soliman, M.E.S., 2015. Insight into the binding theme of CA-074Me to cathepsin B: molecular dynamics simulations and scaffold hopping to identify potential analogues as anti-neurodegenerative diseases. Med. Chem. Res. 24, 701–713. Copyright 2014, Springer Science Business Media New York.)*

(McGowan et al., 1989; Satoyoshi, 1992). E-64 also showed covalent bonding with proteases other than cysteine cathepsins, such as the related calpains (Satoyoshi, 1992); because of which, more recent biological evaluation studies led to develop another epoxide-based inhibitor known as JPM-OEt (Joyce et al., 2004; Tamai et al., 1986).

JPM-OEt shows structural similarity to E-64 but does not exhibit wide reactivity, and also is not an inhibitor of calpain in vivo (Tamai et al., 1986). Besides epoxysuccinyl-cysteine cathepsin inhibitors, vinyl sulfones have exhibited good efficacy when tested in vivo. One of the irreversible inhibitors of this class, *N*-methyl-piperazine-phenylalanyl-homophenylalanylvinyl sulfone phenyl (K11777), has manifested significant potency in animal models of the parasitic disease schistosomiasis (Onishi et al., 2004). The selective inhibitor of cathepsin B, CA-074 (Fig. 3.6), was reported to be the first cathepsin B inhibitor to show selective inhibition. Further studies showed that this inhibitor exploits the exopeptidase activity of cathepsin B, which is unique among the other cathepsin members. Its inactive methyl ester CA-074Me (Fig. 3.6) was developed to surmount the barrier of poor cell permeability exhibited by the parent compound, CA-074 (Montaser et al., 2002; Steverding, 2011). All important inhibitors of cathepsins categorized as reversible and irreversible inhibitors are shown in Table 3.1.

3.3.4 Metalloinhibitors

The class of metallodrugs comprises of those compounds that cause damage to DNA through direct interaction with it. Although various researches have provided enough evidence establishing their ability to exert cytotoxic effect on certain enzymes, derivatives of Ruthenium (II)-arene show considerable selectivity toward solid tumors, probably by inhibiting two crucial enzymes involved

TABLE 3.1 Cathepsin reversible and irreversible inhibitors and their inhibitory profiles.

Reversible inhibitors	Inhibitory profile	References
Panduration A and nicolaioidesin natural aromatic ketones (chalcones)	Cathepsins B and L (not defined)	Kim et al. (2013)
Nicotinamide antimicrobial, cathepsin B like inhibitor	Cathepsin B	Unciti-Broceta et al. (2013)
Curcumin natural (turmeric root)	Cathepsins B and H	Ravish and Raghav (2014)
Dipeptidyl nitriles (odanacatib)	Cathepsin K	Pérez-Castrillón et al. (2010)
VBY-825 (potent and reversible)	Cathepsins B, L, S, and V	Elie et al. (2010)
Irreversible inhibitors	**Inhibitory profile**	**References**
E-64	Cathepsins B, L, H, K, S, F, O, V, W, X	Hanada et al. (1978)
E-64D	Cathepsins B, L, H, K, S, F, O, V, W, X	McGowan et al. (1989)
E-64C	Cathepsins B, L, H, K, S, F, O, V, W, X	Tamai et al. (1986)
CA-074	Cathepsin B (specific)	Montaser et al. (2002)
CA-074Me	Cathepsins B and L	Montaser et al. (2002)
Morpholinourea-leucyl-homophenolalaninyl-phenyl-vinyl-sulfone (LHVS)	Cathepsins S, B, and L	Thurmond et al. (2003)
Benzyloxycarbonyl-Phe-Ala-fluoromethylketone (Z-FA-FMK)	Cathepsins S, B, and L	Schotte et al. (2001)
K11777	Cathepsins B and L	Cartledge et al. (2013)
NC-2300	Cathepsins B, K, and S	Asagiri et al. (2008)
CIPB-4 inhibiting domain found on insulin like growth factor-binding protein 4 (IGFBP-4)	Cathepsins B and L	Baek et al. (2013)
Nitroxoline	Quinolone antibiotic, reversible inhibitor	Mirkoviä et al. (2011)

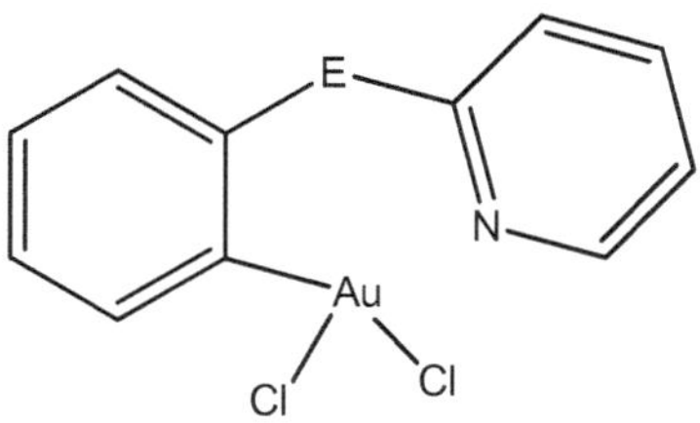

FIG. 3.7 Basic structure of square-planar cycloaurated gold (III) compounds as anticancer agents. *(Reproduced with the permission of Zhu, Y., Cameron, B.R., Mosi, R., Anastassov, V., Cox, J., Qin, L., Santucci, Z., Metz, M., Skerlj, R.T., Fricker, S.P., 2011. Inhibition of the cathepsin cysteine proteases B and K by square-planar cycloaurated gold (III) compounds and investigation of their anticancer activity. J. Inorg. Biochem. 105, 754–762. Copyright © 2011 Elsevier Inc.)*

in tumor development, cathepsin B, and thioredoxin reductase. The most active cathepsin B inhibitor reported so far shows reversible binding with the binding site amino acids of the enzyme. Docking studies have unveiled that the most significant interactions, accountable for its activity (Casini et al., 2008), are those with the residues flanking the active site.

On the contrary, recently discovered organotelluranes class of cathepsin V and S inhibitors have been shown to have irreversible inhibitory effect on the enzyme (Piovan et al., 2011). Tellurium atom is an electrophilic center, which gets attacked by a nucleophilic functionality (cysteine thiol) present at the binding site of the protease. In this reaction, cleavage of tellurium-halogen bond takes place and tellurium sulfur bond is formed. On comparing the electrophilic strength of the chalcogen, it has been found that tellurium is a weak nucleophile than selenium. Additionally, owing to the capacity to stabilize negative charge, bromide is a better leaving group than the chloride. This can explain the highest reaction ability of the dibromo-organotelluranes toward cysteine cathepsins. In another study, square-planar six-membered cycloaurated Au (III) compounds have been examined for potential anticancer activity. The interaction of thiophilic gold with a cysteine at the active site was found responsible for catalytic mechanism of the cathepsin cysteine proteases (Zhu et al., 2011; Fig. 3.7).

3.4 Conclusions

The scientific viewpoint about proteases has now dramatically shifted from protein degrading enzyme to that of extremely important signaling pathways involved in cancer pathogenesis. In comparison to other proteases, cysteine proteases have got relatively less attention as potential targets in anticancer drug design and discovery. Identification and validation of endogenous substrates and other physiological ligands is a key issue for better understanding of cysteine protease signaling pathways. Development of a bioavailable and nontoxic inhibitors against cysteine proteases with excellent selectivity may prove to be an ideal approach for *war against cancer*. Therapeutic inhibition of validated protease targets could be achieved through exploring natural resources and drug repurposing. Systematic exploration of plants growing in diverse hostile environments could provide new avenues for the development of specific inhibitors of cysteine proteases as anticancer agents (Dutt et al., 2014). Simultaneous use of natural therapies with chemotherapeutic drugs holds a huge potential for the development of novel therapeutic strategies against cancer.

References

Arthur, J.S.C., Crawford, C., 1996. Investigation of the interaction of m-calpain with phospholipids: calpain-phospholipid interactions. Biochim. Biophys. Acta 1293, 201–206.

Asagiri, M., Hirai, T., Kunigami, T., Kamano, S., Gober, H.J., Okamoto, K., Nishikawa, K., Latz, E., Golenbock, D.T., Aoki, K., Ohya, K., Imai, Y., Morishita, Y., Miyazono, K., Kato, S., Saftig, P., Takayanagi, H., 2008. Cathepsin K dependent toll-like receptor 9 signaling revealed in experimental arthritis. Science 319, 624–627.

Baek, K.H., Karki, R., Lee, E.S., Na, Y., Kwon, Y., 2013. Synthesis and investigation of dihydroxychalcones as calpain and cathepsin inhibitors. Bioorg. Chem. 51, 24–30.

Barrett, A.J., Rawlings, N.D., 2004. In: Woessner, J.F. (Ed.), Handbook of Proteolytic Enzymes, second ed. Elsevier, Amsterdam.

Bell-McGuinn, K.M., Garfall, A.L., Bogyo, M., Hanahan, D., Joyce, J.A., 2007. Inhibition of cysteine cathepsin protease activity enhances chemotherapy regimens by decreasing tumor growth and invasiveness in a mouse model of multistage cancer. Cancer Res. 67, 7378–7385.

Berdowska, I., 2004. Cysteine proteases as disease markers. Clin. Chim. Acta 342, 41–69.

Brix, K., Dunkhorst, A., Mayer, K., Jordans, S., 2008. Cysteine cathepsins: cellular roadmap to different functions. Biochimie 90, 194–207.

Burden, R.E., Gormley, J.A., Jaquin, T.J., Small, D.M., Quinn, D.J., Hegarty, S.M., Ward, C., Walker, B., Johnston, J.A., Olwill, S.A., Scott, C.J., 2009. Antibody-mediated inhibition of cathepsin S blocks colorectal tumor invasion and angiogenesis. Clin. Cancer Res. 15, 6042–6051.

Cartledge, D.M., Colella, R., Glazewski, L., Lu, G., Mason, R.W., 2013. Inhibitors of cathepsins B and L induce autophagy and cell death in neuroblastoma cells. Investig. New Drugs 31, 20–29.

Casini, A., Gabbiani, C., Sorrentino, F., Rigobello, M.P., Bindoli, A., Geldbach, T.J., Marrone, A., Re, N., Hartinger, C.G., Dyson, P.J., Messori, L., 2008. Emerging protein targets for anticancer metallodrugs: inhibition of thioredoxin reductase and cathepsin B by antitumor ruthenium (II)–arene compounds. J. Med. Chem. 51, 6773–6781.

Castro-Guillén, J.L., Chapter, V., 2010. Protease inhibitors as anticancer agents. In: Mejia Vazquez, V.C., Navarro, S. (Eds.), New Approaches in the Treatment of Cancer. Nova Science Publishers, New York, United States, pp. 91–124.

Chang, W.S.W., Wu, H.R., Yeh, C.T., Wu, C.W., Chang, J.Y., 2007. Lysosomal cysteine proteinase cathepsin S as potential target for anti-cancer therapy. J. Cancer Mol. 3, 5–14.

Cygler, M., Sivaraman, J., Grochulski, P., Coulombe, R., Storer, A.C., Mort, J.S., 1996. Structure of rat procathepsin B: model for inhibition of cysteine protease activity by the pro region. Structure 4, 405–416.

Duffy, M.J., 1992. The role of proteolytic enzymes in cancer invasion and metastasis. Clin. Exp. Metastasis 10, 145–155.

Duncan, E.M., Muratore-Schroeder, T.L., Cook, R.G., Garcia, B.A., Shabanowitz, J., Hunt, D.F., Allis, C.D., 2008. Cathepsin L proteolytically processes histone H3 during mouse embryonic stem cell differentiation. Cell 2008 (135), 284–294.

Dutt, R., Garg, V., Madan, A., 2014. Can plants growing in diverse hostile environments provide a vital source of anticancer drugs? Cancer Ther. 10, 13–37.

Eatemadia, A., Aiyelabegan, H.T., Negahdari, B., Mazlom, M.A., Daraee, H., Daraee, N., Eatemadi, R., Sadroddiny, E., 2017. Role of protease and protease inhibitors in cancer pathogenesis and treatment. Biomed. Pharmacother. 86, 221–231.

Elie, B.T., Gocheva, V., Shree, T., Dalrymple, S.A., Holsinger, L.J., Joyce, J.A., 2010. Identification and pre-clinical testing of a reversible cathepsin protease inhibitor reveals anti-tumor efficacy in a pancreatic cancer model. Biochimie 92, 1618–1624.

Fernandez, P.L., Farré, X., Nadal, A., Fernández, E., Peiró, N., Sloane, B.F., Shi, G.P., Chapman, H.A., Campo, E., Cardesa, A., 2001. Expression of cathepsins B and S in the progression of prostate carcinoma. Int. J. Cancer 95, 51–55.

Flannery, T., Gibson, D., Mirakhur, M., McQuaid, S., Greenan, C., Trimble, A., Walker, B., Patrick, D.M., Johnston, G., 2003. The clinical significance of cathepsin S expression in human astrocytomas. Am. J. Pathol. 163, 175–182.

Flannery, T., McQuaid, S., McGoohan, C., McConnell, R.S., McGregor, G., Mirakhur, M., Hamilton, P., Diamond, J., Cran, G., Walker, B., Scott, C., Martin, L., Ellison, D., Patel, C., Nicholson, C., Mendelow, D., McCormick, D., Johnston, P.G., 2006. Cathepsin S expression: an independent prognostic factor in glioblastoma tumours—a pilot study. Int. J. Cancer 119, 854–860.

Folgueras, A.R., Pendas, A.M., Sanchez, L.M., López-Otín, C., 2004. Matrix metalloproteinases in cancer: from new functions to improved inhibition strategies. Int. J. Dev. Biol. 48, 411–424.

Fong, D., Chan, M.M., Hsieh, W.T., 1991. Gene mapping of human cathepsins and cystatins. Biomed. Biochim. Acta 50, 595–598.

Frizler, M., Stirnberg, M., Sisay, M.T., Michael, G., 2010. Development of nitrile-based peptidic inhibitors of cysteine cathepsins. Curr. Top. Med. Chem. 10, 294–322.

Frlan, R., Gobec, S., 2006. Inhibitors of cathepsin B. Curr. Med. Chem. 13, 2309–2327.

Gocheva, V., Joyce, J.A., 2007. Cysteine cathepsins and the cutting edge of cancer invasion. Cell Cycle 6, 60–64.

Gocheva, V., Zeng, W., Ke, D., Klimstra, D., Reinhecke, T., Peters, C., Hanahan, D., Joyce, J.A., 2006. Distinct roles for cysteine cathepsin genes in multistage tumorigenesis. Genes Dev. 20, 543–556.

Goll, D.E., Thompson, V.F., Li, H., Wei, W., Cong, J., 2003. The calpain system. Physiol. Rev. 83, 731–801.

Hanada, K., Tamai, M., Yamagishi, M., Ohmura, S., Sawada, J., Tanaka, I., 1978. Isolation and identification of E-64, a new thiol protease inhibitor. Agric. Biol. Chem. Tokyo 42, 523–528.

Harwood, S.M., Yaqoob, M.M., Allen, D.A., 2005. Caspase and calpain function in cell death: bridging the gap between apoptosis and necrosis. Ann. Clin. Biochem. 42, 415–431. https://www.rcsb.org/structure/3K9M/IGD3.

Huang, Y., Wang, K.K.W., 2001. The calpain family and human disease. Trends Mol. Med. 7, 355–362.

Irie, O., Ehara, T., Iwasaki, A., Yokokawa, F., Sakaki, J., Hirao, H., Kanazawa, T., Teno, N., Horiuchi, M., Umemura, I., Gunji, H., Masuya, K., Hitomi, Y., Iwasaki, G., Nonomura, K., Tanabe, K., Fukaya, H., Kosaka, T., Snell, C.R., Hallett, A., 2008. Discovery of selective and nonpeptidic cathepsin S inhibitors. Bioorg. Med. Chem. Lett. 18, 3959–3962.

Jäger, R., Zwacka, R.M., 2010. The enigmatic roles of caspases in tumor development. Cancer 2, 1952–1979.

Joyce, J.A., Hanahan, D., 2004. Multiple roles for cysteine cathepsins in cancer. Cell Cycle 3, 1516–1519.

Joyce, J.A., Baruch, A., Chehade, K., Morse, N.M., Giraudo, E., Tsai, F.Y., Greenbaum, D.C., Hager, J.H., Bogyo, M., Hanahan, D., 2004. Cathepsin cysteine proteases are effectors of invasive growth and angiogenesis during multistage tumorigenesis. Cancer Cell 5, 443–453.

Keppler, D., 2006. Towards novel anti-cancer strategies based on cystatin function. Cancer Lett. 235, 159–175.
Kim, I.S., Lee, K.J., 1995. Physiological roles of leupeptin and extracellular proteases in mycelium development of *Streptomyces exfoliatus* SMF13. Microbiology 141, 1017–1025.
Kim, J., Yu, W., Kovalski, K., Ossowski, L., 1998. Requirement for specific proteases in cancer cell intravasation as revealed by a novel semiquantitative PCR-based assay. Cell 94, 353–362.
Kim, S.H., Lee, E., Baek, K.H., Kwon, H.B., Woo, H., Lee, E.S., Kwon, Y., Na, Y., 2013. Chalcones, inhibitors for topoisomerase I and cathepsin B and L, as potential anti-cancer agents. Bioorg. Med. Chem. Lett. 23, 3320–3324.
Koblinski, J.E., Ahram, M., Sloane, B.F., 2000. Unraveling the role of proteases in cancer. Clin. Chim. Acta 291, 113–135.
Kolkhorst, V., Sturzebecher, J., Wiederanders, B., 1998. Inhibition of tumour cell invasion by protease inhibitors: correlation with the protease profile. J. Cancer Res. Clin. Oncol. 124, 598–606.
Kumar, G.D.K., Chavarria, G.E., Charlton-Sevcik, A.K., Arispe, W.M., Macdonough, M.T., Strecker, T.E., Chen, S.E., Siim, B.G., Chaplin, D.J., Trawick, M.L., Pinney, K.G., 2010. Design, synthesis and biological evaluation of potent thiosemicarbazone based cathepsin L inhibitors. Bioorg. Med. Chem. Lett. 2, 1415–1419.
Kuramochi, H., Nakata, H., Ishii, S., 1979. Mechanism of association of a specific aldehyde inhibitor, leupeptin, with bovine trypsin. J. Biochem. 86, 1403–1410.
Laufs, S., Schumacher, J., Allgayer, H., 2006. Urokinase-receptor (u-PAR): an essential player in multiple games of cancer: a review on its role in tumor progression, invasion, metastasis, proliferation/dormancy, clinical outcome and minimal residual disease. Cell Cycle 5, 1760–1771.
Lee, M., Fridman, R., Mobashery, S., 2004. Extracellular proteases as targets for treatment of cancer metastases. Chem. Soc. Rev. 33, 401–409.
Lindeman, J.H., Hanemaaijer, R., Mulder, A., Dijkstra, P.D.S., Szuhai, K., Bromme, D., Verheijen, J.H., Hogendoorn, P.C.W., 2004. Cathepsin K is principal protease in giant cell tumor of bone. Am. J. Pathol. 165, 593–600.
Magdolen, U., Krol, J., Sato, S., Mueller, M.M., Sperl, S., Krüger, A., Schmitt, M., Magdolen, V., 2002. Natural inhibitors of tumor-associated proteases. Radiol. Oncol. 36, 131–143.
Maretzky, T., Reiss, K., Ludwig, A., Buchholz, J., Scholz, F., Proksch, E., Strooper, B.D., Hartmann, D., Saftig, P., 2005. ADAM10 mediates E-cadherin shedding and regulates epithelial cell-cell adhesion, migration, and beta-catenin translocation. Proc. Natl. Acad. Sci. USA 102, 9182–9187.
Mason, S.D., Joyce, J.A., 2011. Proteolytic networks in cancer. Trends Cell Biol. 21, 228–237.
McConnell, M.R., Barnes, G.E., Hoyng, C.F., Gunn, J.M., 1990. New leupeptin analogs: synthesis and inhibition data. J. Med. Chem. 33, 86–93.
McGowan, E.B., Becker, E., Detwiler, T.C., 1989. Inhibition of calpain in intact platelets by the thiol protease inhibitor E-64d. Biochem. Biophys. Res. Commun. 158, 432–435.
McKerrow, J.H., 2018. The diverse roles of cysteine proteases in parasites and their suitability as drug targets. PLoS Negl. Trop. Dis. 12, e0005639.
Mignati, P., Rifkin, D.B., 1993. Biology and biochemistry of proteinases in tumor invasion. Physiol. Rev. 73, 161–195.
Mirkoviä, B., Renko, M., Turk, S., Sosič, I., Jevnikar, Z., Obermajer, N., Turk, D., Gobec, S., Kos, J., 2011. Novel mechanism of cathepsin B inhibition by antibiotic nitroxoline and related compounds. Chem. Med. Chem. 6, 1351–1356.
Mohamed, M.M., Sloane, B.F., 2006. Cysteine cathepsins: multifunctional enzymes in cancer. Nat. Rev. Cancer 6, 764–775.
Montaser, M., Lalmanach, G., Mach, L., 2002. CA-074, but not its methyl ester CA-074Me is a selective inhibitor of cathepsin B within living cells. Biol. Chem. 383, 1305–1308.

Mort, J.S., 1997. Cathepsin B. Int. J. Biochem. Cell Biol. 29, 715–720.

Mussap, M., Plebani, M., 2004. Biochemistry and clinical role of human cystatin C. Crit. Rev. Clin. Lab. Sci. 41, 467–550.

Niestroj, A.J., Feussner, K., Heiser, U., Dando, P.M., Barrett, A., Gerhartz, B., Demuth, H.U., 2002. Inhibition of mammalian legumain by Michaels acceptors and AzaAsn-halomethylketones. Biol. Chem. 383, 1205–1214.

Noe, V., Fingleton, B., Jacobs, K., Crawford, H.C., Vermeulen, S., Steelant, W., Bruyneel, E., Matrisian, L.M., Mareel, M., 2001. Release of an invasion promoter E-cadherin fragment by matrilysin and stromelysin-1. J. Cell Sci. 114, 111–118.

Onishi, K., Li, Y., Ishii, K., Hisaeda, H., Tang, L., Duan, X., Dainichi, T., Maekawa, Y., Katunuma, N., Himeno, K., 2004. Cathepsin L is crucial for a Th1-type immune response during Leishmania major infection. Microbes Infect. 6, 468–474.

Otto, H.H., Schirmeister, T., 1997. Cysteine proteases and their inhibitors. Chem. Rev. 97, 133–172.

Ovat, A., Li, Z.Z., Hampton, C.Y., Asress, S.A., Fernández, F.M., Glass, J.D., Power, J.C., 2010. Peptidyl α-ketoamides with nucleobases, methylpiperazine and dimethylaminoalkyl substituents as calpain inhibitors. J. Med. Chem. 53, 6326–6336.

Overall, C.M., Kleifeld, O., 2006. Validating matrix metalloproteinases as drug targets and anti-targets for cancer therapy. Nat. Rev. Cancer 6, 227–239.

Palermo, C., Joyce, J.A., 2008. Cysteine cathepsin proteases as pharmacological targets in cancer. Trends Pharmacol. Sci. 29, 22–28.

Pandey, R., Patil, N., Rao, M., 2007. Proteases and protease inhibitors: implications in antitumorigenesis and drug development. Int. J. Hum. Genet. 17, 67–82.

Pavlova, A., Krupa, J.C., Mort, J.S., Abrahamson, M., Björk, I., 2000. Cystatin inhibition of cathepsin B requires dislocation of the proteinase occluding loop. Demonstration by release of loop anchoring through mutation of his110. FEBS Lett. 487, 156–160.

Pérez-Castrillón, J.L., Pinacho, F., Luis, D.D., Lopez-Menendez, M., Laita, A.D., 2010. Odanacatib, a new drug for the treatment of osteoporosis: review of the results in postmenopausal women. J. Osteoporos. 2010, 401581. https://doi.org/10.4061/2010/401581.

Perl, A.K., Wilgenbus, P., Dahl, U., Semb, H., Christofori, G., 1998. A causal role for E-cadherin in the transition from adenoma to carcinoma. Nature 392, 190–193.

Piovan, L., Alves, M.F., Juliano, L., Brömme, D., Cunha, R.L., Andrade, L.H., 2011. Structure-activity relationship of hyper valent organo chalcogenanes as inhibitors of cysteine cathepsins V and S. Bioorg. Med. Chem. 19, 2009–2014.

Puente, X.S., Sánchez, L.M., Overall, C.M., López-Otín, C., 2003. Human and mouse proteases: a comparative genomic approach. Nat. Rev. Genet. 4, 544–558.

Puxbaum, V., Mach, L., 2009. Proteinases and their inhibitors in liver cancer. World J. Hepatol. 31, 28–34.

Rakashanda, S., Rana, F., Rafiq, S., Masood, A., Amin, S., 2012. Role of proteases in cancer: a review. Biotechnol. Mol. Biol. Rev. 7, 90–101.

Ravish, I., Raghav, N., 2014. Curcumin as inhibitor of mammalian cathepsin B, cathepsin H, acid phosphatase and alkaline phosphatase: a correlation with pharmacological activities. Med. Chem. Res. 23, 2847–2855.

Rios-Doria (II), J., Chinnaiyan, A.M., Rubin, M.A., Day, M.L., 2004. Proteolytic regulation of β-catenin by calpain and potential role in cancer. Proc. Am. Assoc. Cancer Res. 64, 331–339.

Rios-Doria, J., Kuefer, R., Ethier, S.P., Day, M.L., 2004. Cleavage of beta-catenin by calpain in prostate and mammary tumor cells. Cancer Res. 64, 7237–7240.

Ryschich, E., Lizdenis, P., Ittrich, C., Benner, A., Stahl, S., Hamann, A., Schmidt, J., Knolle, P., Arnold, B., Hämmerling, G.J., Ganss, R., 2006. Molecular fingerprinting and autocrine growth regulation of endothelial cells in a murine model of hepatocellular carcinoma. Cancer Res. 66, 198–211.
Saleh, Y., Wnukiewicz, J., Trziszka, T., Siewinski, M., Ziolkowski, P., Kopec, W., 2006. Cathepsin B and cysteine protease inhibitors in human tongue cancer: correlation with tumor staging and in vitro inhibition of cathepsin B by chicken cystatin. J. Cancer Mol. 2, 67–72.
Santos-Rosa, H., Kirmizis, A., Nelson, C., Bartke, T., Saksouk, N., Cote, J., Kouzarides, T., 2009. Histone H3 tail clipping regulates gene expression. Nat. Struct. Mol. Biol. 16, 17–22.
Satoyoshi, E., 1992. Therapeutic trials on progressive muscular dystrophy. J. Intern. Med. 31, 841–846.
Schotte, P., Schauvliege, R., Janssens, S., Beyaert, R., 2001. The cathepsin B inhibitor z-FA-FMK, inhibits cytokine production in macrophages stimulated by lipopolysaccharide. J. Biol. Chem. 276, 21153–21157.
Shao, H., Chou, J., Baty, C.J., Burke, N.A., Watkins, S.C., Stolz, D.B., Wells, A., 2006. Spatial localization of m-calpain to the plasma membrane by phosphoinositide biphosphate binding during epidermal growth factor receptor-mediated activation. Mol. Cell. Biol. 26, 5481–5496.
Singh, J.P., Tamang, S., Rajamohanan, P.R., Jima, N.C., Chakraborty, G., Kundu, G.C., Gaikwad, S.M., Khan, M.I., 2010. Isolation, structure and functional elucidation of modified pentapeptide, cysteine protease inhibitor (CPI-2081) from *Streptomyces* species 2081 that exhibit inhibitory effect on cancer cell migration. J. Med. Chem. 53, 5121–5128.
Sorimachi, H., Hata, S., Ono, Y., 2011. Impact of genetic insights into calpain biology. J. Biochem. 150, 23–37.
Steverding, D., 2011. The cathepsin B-selective inhibitors CA-074 and CA-074Me inactivate cathepsin L under reducing conditions. Open Enzym. Inhib. J. 4, 11–16.
Stroup, G.B., Lark, M.W., Veber, D.F., Bhattacharyya, A., Blake, S., Dare, L.C., Erhard, K.F., Hoffman, S.J., James, I.E., Marquis, R.W., Ru, Y., Vasko-Moser, J.A., Smith, B.R., Tomaszek, T., Gowen, M., 2001. Potent and selective inhibition of human cathepsin K lead to inhibition of bone resorption in vivo in a non-human primate. J. Bone Miner. Res. 16, 1739–1746.
Tamai, M., Matsumoto, K., Omura, S., Koyama, I., Ozawa, Y., Hanada, K., 1986. In vitro and in vivo inhibition of cysteine proteinases by EST, a new analog of E-64. J. Pharmacobiodyn. 9, 672–677.
Thurmond, R.L., Sun, S., Sehon, C.A., Baker, S.M., Cai, H., Gu, Y., Jiang, W., Riley, J.P., Williams, K.N., Edwards, J.P., Karlsson, L., 2003. Identification of a potent and selective noncovalent cathepsin S inhibitor. J. Pharmacol. Exp. Ther. 308, 268–276.
Turk, D., Guncar, G., 2003. Lysosomal cysteine proteases (cathepsins): promising drug targets. Acta Crystallogr. D Biol. Crystallogr. 59, 203–213.
Turk, V., Turk, B., Turk, D., 2001. Lysosomal cysteine proteases: facts and opportunities. EMBO J. 20, 4629–4633.
Turk, V., Kos, J., Turk, B., 2004. Cysteine cathepsins (proteases)—on the main stage of cancer? Cancer Cell 5, 409–410.
Unciti-Broceta, J.D., Maceira, J., Morales, S., García-Pérez, A., Muñóz-Torres, M.E., Garcia-Salcedo, J.A., 2013. Nicotinamide inhibits the lysosomal cathepsin B-like protease and kills African trypanosomes. J. Biol. Chem. 288, 10548–10557.
Wang, K.K.W., 2000. Calpain and caspases: can you tell the difference? Trends Neurosci. 23, 20–26.
Ward, Y.D., Thomson, D.S., Frye, L.L., Cywin, C.L., Morwick, T., Emmanuel, M.J., Zindell, R., McNeil, D., Bekkali, Y., Hrapchak, M., DeTuri, M., Crane, K., White, D., Pav, S., Wang, Y., Hao, M.H., Grygon, C.A., Labadia, M.E., Freeman, D.M., Davidson, W., Hopkins, J.L., Brown, M.L., Spero, D.M., 2002. Design and synthesis of dipeptide nitriles as reversible and potent cathepsin S inhibitors. J. Med. Chem. 45, 5471–5482.

Wieczerzak, E., Drabik, P., Łankiewicz, L., Ołdziej, S., Grzonka, Z., Abrahamson, M., Grubb, A., Brömme, D., 2002. Azapeptides structurally based upon inhibitory sites of cystatins as potent and selective inhibitors of cysteine proteases. J. Med. Chem. 45, 4202–4211.
Wieczerzak, E., Rodziewicz-Motowidło, S., Jankowska, E., Giełdoń, A., Ciarkowski, J., 2007. An enormously active and selective azapeptide inhibitors of cathepsin B. J. Pept. Sci. 13, 536–543.
Zavašnik-Bergant, T., Turk, B., 2006. Cysteine cathepsins in the immune response. Tissue Antigens 67, 349–355.
Zhu, Y., Cameron, B.R., Mosi, R., Anastassov, V., Cox, J., Qin, L., Santucci, Z., Metz, M., Skerlj, R.T., Fricker, S.P., 2011. Inhibition of the cathepsin cysteine proteases B and K by square-planar cycloauratedgold(III) compounds and investigation of their anti-cancer activity. J. Inorg. Biochem. 105, 754–762.
Zucker, S., Cao, J., Chen, W.T., 2000. Critical appraisal of the use of matrix metalloproteinase inhibitors in cancer treatment. Oncogene 19, 6642–6650.

Further reading

Mashamba-Thompson, T., Soliman, M.E.S., 2015. Insight into the binding theme of CA-074Me to cathepsin B: molecular dynamics simulations and scaffold hopping to identify potential analogues as anti-neurodegenerative diseases. Med. Chem. Res. 24, 701–713.

Chapter 4

Ubiquitin-specific proteases as targets for anticancer drug therapies

Diana Campos-Iglesias, Carlos López-Otín, José M.P. Freije
Department of Biochemistry and Molecular Biology, University Institute of Oncology (IUOPA), University of Oviedo, Oviedo, Spain

4.1 Introduction

Ubiquitination is an essential posttranslational modification (PTM) responsible for regulating the stability, activity, conformation, and localization of target proteins. The attachment of ubiquitin (Ub), a 76 amino acid polypeptide, is a dynamic and reversible process coordinated by the action of ubiquitinating and deubiquitinating enzymes that add or remove ubiquitin molecules, respectively (Fraile et al., 2012). Mechanistically, the ubiquitination process is a multistep reaction catalyzed by, at least, three different enzymes: Ub-activating (E1), Ub-conjugating (E2), and Ub-ligating (E3) (Fig. 4.1). In the first step, ubiquitin is activated by the E1 enzyme, which links a cysteine residue to the C-terminal glycine of ubiquitin through a thioester linkage, in an ATP-dependent manner (Clague et al., 2015). Activated ubiquitin is then transferred to a cysteine residue of E2 conjugating enzyme, which carries out the transfer of ubiquitin to the ε-amino group of a lysine residue or the α-amino group of the N-terminal residue on the target protein, which is bound to an Ub-ligase E3 enzyme (Ye and Rape, 2009; Buetow and Huang, 2016). If only a single ubiquitin moiety is attached, we referred to this process as monoubiquitination. However, additional ubiquitin molecules can be added to the target protein, forming polyubiquitin chains that vary in length and linkage type (Akutsu et al., 2016).

Ubiquitin itself possesses eight sites that enable the attachment of another ubiquitin moiety, including its N-terminus and seven different lysine residues (Lys6, Lys11, Lys27, Lys29, Lys33, Lys48, and Lys63) (Clague et al., 2015). Depending on the lysine residue involved in the formation of the polyubiquitin chain, there are different consequences for the targeted protein. Thus, proteins tagged with Lys-11, Lys-29, and especially Lys48-linked polyubiquitin chains are committed to proteasomal degradation, whereas Lys63-linked polyubiquitin

Cancer-Leading Proteases. https://doi.org/10.1016/B978-0-12-818168-3.00004-8

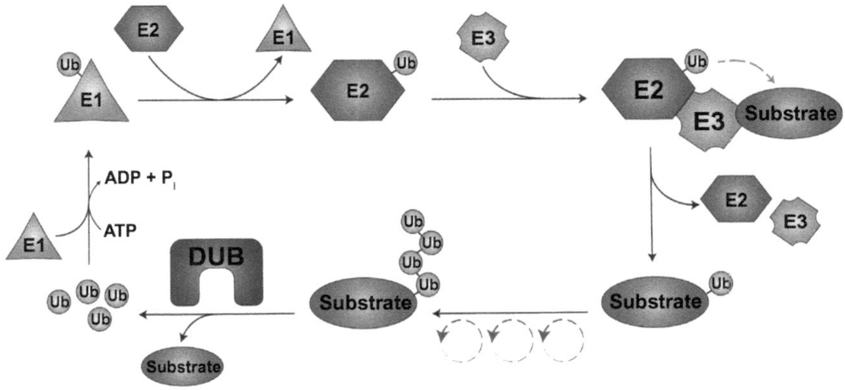

FIG. 4.1 The ubiquitination cascade. Schematic representation of key events in the ubiquitination and deubiquitination process. Ubiquitin (Ub) is conjugated by the action of three consecutive enzymes: ubiquitin-activating enzymes E1, ubiquitin-conjugating enzymes E2, and ubiquitin ligases E3. In subsequent rounds, ubiquitin molecules can be conjugated to the N-terminal amino group or lysine residues on the ubiquitin itself, forming polyubiquitin chains. Deubiquitinases or DUBs can remove ubiquitin molecules from substrates, generating free ubiquitin pools and therefore maintaining the ubiquitin homeostasis. *(Source: Prepared for this publication.)*

chains are associated with the autophagy-lysosome degradation pathway, as well as other cellular roles, such as signal transduction, DNA repair, and replication (Komander and Rape, 2012; Jacq et al., 2013). Likewise, some studies have shown that linear and Lys-11-linked polyubiquitination are important in immunity processes and cell division, respectively (Lill and Wertz, 2014).

The ubiquitination process can be reversed by the action of a specific group of proteases, known as deubiquitinases or deubiquitinating enzymes (DUBs), which specifically cleave the isopeptide bond that links the C-terminal group of ubiquitin to the ε-amino group of lysine residues of target proteins, or the peptide bond that links the C-terminal group of ubiquitin to the α-amino group of the N-terminal group of the target protein (Wilkinson, 1997). Three different mechanisms of action have been described for this group of proteases (Komander et al., 2009). The first one is based on the generation of free ubiquitin molecules, a process that can occur simultaneously with translation (Farshi et al., 2015). The second is based on the release of specific ubiquitin moieties of polyubiquitin chains, inversely regulating the action of E3 Ub-ligases (Lill and Wertz, 2014), similar to the regulatory processes mediated by kinases and phosphatases (Millard and Wood, 2006; Nguyen et al., 2013). Therefore, DUB cleavage in different parts of a specific polyubiquitin chain could have different effects on the destiny of the target proteins (Farshi et al., 2015). The third mechanism of DUB action is the complete cleavage of the polyubiquitin chain, stabilizing the target protein and thus, blocking its proteasomal or lysosomal degradation, or changing its subcellular localization (Komander et al., 2009).

The human genome encodes at least 100 DUBs that, according to sequence and structural properties, are classified into seven different families (Fig. 4.2): ubiquitin-specific proteases (USPs), ubiquitin carboxy-terminal hydrolases

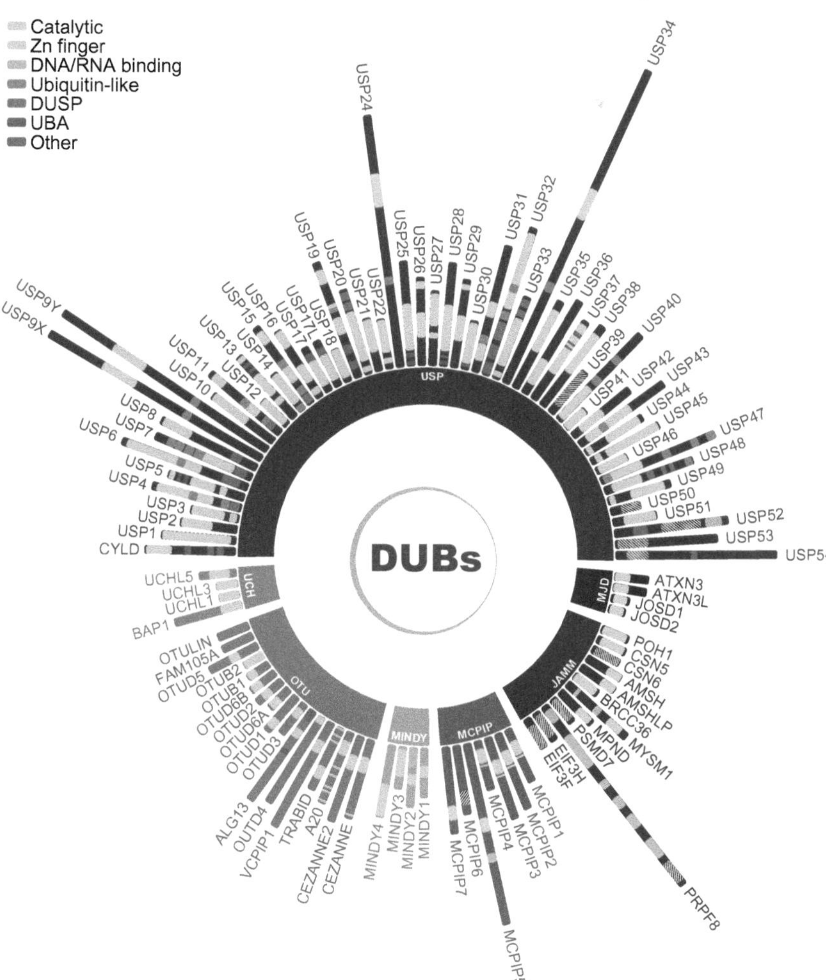

FIG. 4.2 Classification of human deubiquitinases. Human DUBs are classified into seven families represented by different colors: USPs (*dark blue; dark gray* in print version), UCHs (*light blue; light gray* in print version), OTUs (*green; dark gray* in print version), MINDYs (*yellow; light gray* in print version), MCPIPs (*orange; light gray* in print version), JAMMs (*maroon; light gray* in print version), and MJDs (*purple; light gray* in print version). Proteins are represented with their N termini oriented toward the center of the circle and the length of each DUB corresponds to the size of the protein in amino acids. The catalytic domains are represented in beige and are stripped in "nonprotease" DUBs. Additional domains are represented with different colors. *USPs*, ubiquitin-specific proteases; *UCHs*, ubiquitin carboxy-terminal hydrolases; *OTUs*, ovarian tumor proteases; *MJDs*, Machado-Joseph disease protein domain proteases; *MCPIPs*, monocyte chemotactic protein-induced proteins; *JAMMs*, JAMM/MPN domain-associated metallopeptidases; *MINDYs*, motif-interacting with ubiquitin-containing novel DUB family. *(Source: Prepared for this publication.)*

(UCHs), ovarian tumor proteases (OTUs), Machado-Joseph disease protein domain proteases (MJDs), monocyte chemotactic protein-induced proteins (MCPIPs), and JAMM/MPN domain-associated metallopeptidases (JAMMs) (Fraile et al., 2012; Clague et al., 2015). Recently, a new family of DUBs called Motif-Interacting with ubiquitin-containing Novel DUB family (MINDY) has been proposed (Abdul Rehman et al., 2016; Maurer and Wertz, 2016). Among DUBs, the USPs comprise the largest and most diverse family, with more than 50 members (Quesada et al., 2004). Most of them exhibit a conserved catalytic site within the USP domain, characterized by a catalytic triad composed of Cys, His, and Asp (or Asn) residues, although some USPs (USP39, USP50, USP52, USP53, and USP54) have been described as "nonproteases" due to the lack of functional catalytic sites. The additional noncatalytic domains are highly diverse at the amino acid level, conferring the substrate specificity of USPs, including the B-box domain present in CYLD; the zinc finger ubiquitin-binding domain (ZnF-UBP domain) located in USP3, USP5, USP39, USP44, USP45, USP49, and USP51; the ubiquitin interacting motif (UIM) shared by USP25 and USP37; the ubiquitin-associated domain (UBA) in USP5 and USP13; the exonuclease III domain present in USP52; and the ubiquitin-like domain of USP4, USP7, USP14, USP32, USP47, and USP48 (Quesada et al., 2004).

4.2 Roles of ubiquitin-specific proteases

The wide functional diversity of USPs has a critical influence on the regulation of multiple biological processes and cellular pathways, such as cell cycle, chromatin remodeling, DNA damage repair, RNA maturation and protein synthesis, and signaling pathways, among others. Thus, studying in-depth the roles of USPs in these pathways, which are frequently altered in cancer, could provide new strategies for developing anticancer therapies.

4.2.1 Cell cycle regulation

Several members of the USP family are key components in the regulatory pathways of cell cycle progression, acting either directly or indirectly through different factors. Controlling the G2/M checkpoint is essential for a correct cell division, and it has been described that USP50, despite being catalytically inactive, is involved in the regulation of this process. This USP acts as a main regulator of HSP90-dependent Wee1 stabilization, thus repressing the cell entrance in mitosis (Aressy et al., 2010). Other USPs are also essential modulators of cell division. In this sense, CYLD regulates polo-like kinase 1 (PLK1) and controls mitotic spindle orientation (Stegmeier et al., 2007b; Yang et al., 2014). USP13 counteracts anaphase-promoting complex (APC/C)-Cdh1 function by inhibiting the ubiquitination of SKP2, causing the accumulation of p27, a cyclin-dependent kinase inhibitor, and thus a cell-cycle delay (Chen et al., 2011b). Similarly to the USP13 role in this context, USP37 also antagonizes APC/C-Cdh1 function, inhibiting the ubiquitination of Cyclin A after being activated by CDK2, thus promoting S-phase entry (Huang et al., 2011). USP37 positively regulates the stability of WAPL, facilitating sister chromatid resolution during mitosis (Yeh et al., 2015). USP35 and USP39 are essential for mitotic spindle checkpoint, controlling levels of Aurora B kinase, therefore impeding its APC/C-Cdh1-induced proteasomal degradation (van Leuken et al., 2008; Park et al., 2018). Likewise, USP44 has been reported to be critical for controlling APC function, preventing its premature activation by deubiquitinating and stabilizing the APC/C-inhibitory Mad2-Cdc20 complex (Stegmeier et al., 2007a). Independently of its role in the mitotic checkpoint, USP44 inhibits chromosome segregation errors by regulating centrosome separation, positioning, and mitotic spindle geometry (Zhang et al., 2012d). Together with USP1's role in the regulation of centrosome duplication (Jung et al., 2016), USP33 has also been related to centrosome regulation, stabilizing CP110, a centriolar protein that positively regulates centriole duplication (Li et al., 2013a). Recently, the X-linked USP9 (USP9X) has also been related to centrosome biogenesis and stabilization, through its association with PCM1 and CEP55 proteins (Wang et al., 2017b). Furthermore, USP11 is critical for bipolar spindle formation by regulating the ubiquitination levels of RAE1, likely modulating the functional interaction with the mitotic spindle associated protein NuMA (Stockum et al., 2018).

USP2a impairs ubiquitination and stabilizes Cyclin A1, an important cell cycle regulator (Kim et al., 2012). In addition, it has been described that USP2 also stabilizes the G1 Cyclin D1, a crucial regulator in cell-cycle progression (Shan et al., 2009), whereas USP19 regulates cell proliferation through both E3-ligase KPC1-dependent and independent mechanisms (Lu et al., 2009, 2011). Moreover, USP7 (also known as HAUSP) interacts with and deubiquitinates FOXO, and also regulates the localization of phosphatase and tensin homolog (PTEN), thus having an essential role in cell growth and metabolism (van der Horst et al., 2006; Song et al., 2008). Likewise, USP10 and USP13 also regulate PTEN protein levels by deubiquitination (Zhang et al., 2013a; Sun et al., 2018). Another ubiquitin-specific protease, USP4, is also involved in the regulation of cell metabolism and proliferation, by regulating the mono-ubiquitination status of PDK1, a master growth factor signaling kinase (Uras et al., 2012). Finally, USP22 has been recently related to cell cycle regulation, by deubiquitinating and stabilizing cyclin D1 (Gennaro et al., 2018).

Functional analyses have revealed that different USPs are involved in the stability of c-Myc, the master regulator of cell growth, proliferation, and apoptosis. c-Myc can be ubiquitinated by TRIM32 and SCF(Fbw7), among other ubiquitin ligases, whereas it can be deubiquitinated and stabilized by USP7, USP13, USP22, USP28, USP36, and USP37 (Popov et al., 2007; Pan et al., 2015; Sun et al., 2015; Fang et al., 2017; Kim et al., 2017; Nicklas et al., 2019). By contrast, USP10 antagonizes the transcriptional activity of c-Myc, through SIRT6 stabilization, thus inhibiting cell-cycle progression (Lin et al., 2013).

4.2.2 Chromatin remodeling

Histone PTMs are highly dynamic and control chromatin structure and gene transcription, processes frequently altered in cancer. In this regard, several USPs have been described as regulators of histone PTMs, directly acting on H2A and H2B ubiquitination status. Thus, USP22 functions as a subunit of the SAGA (Spt-Ada-Gcn5-acetyltransferase) histone acetyltransferase (HAT) complex, catalyzing H2A and H2B deubiquitination (Zhang et al., 2008b). Besides USP22, other USPs, such as USP12 and USP46, can deubiquitinate both H2A and H2B (Zhang et al., 2008a; Joo et al., 2011). USP10 can regulate the ubiquitination status of mono-ubiquitinated H2A.Z variant of H2A, resulting in androgen receptor (AR) increased activity (Draker et al., 2011). Moreover, USP16 (known also as UbpM) specifically deubiquitinates H2A, but no H2B, and is required for dephosphorylation of histone H3 and chromosome segregation before mitosis (Joo et al., 2007).

Ubiquitination of H2B is also important in maintaining cellular homeostasis; thus different USPs have been related to target specifically this histone. In this sense, USP42 directly influences transcription by deubiquitinating H2B (Hock et al., 2014). Similarly, USP49 also deubiquitinates this histone and therefore regulates the cotranscriptional pre-mRNA splicing through the formation of a complex with RuvB-like 1 (RVB1) and SUG1 (Zhang et al., 2013b). H2B ubiquitination can also be reverted by the action of USP15, which associates with SART3, a component of the splicing machinery, facilitating deubiquitination of H2B in free histones (Long et al., 2014). Moreover, USP44 interacts with several components of the nuclear receptor co-repressor (N-CoR) complex, deubiquitinating H2B and contributing to the repression of target genes (Lan et al., 2016). Recently, it has been reported that USP36 also participates in the H2B deubiquitination process (DeVine et al., 2018).

Ubiquitination of histones also plays an important role in the DNA damage response and repair pathways. During DNA damage sensing, a fraction of the H2AX variant of H2A, known as γH2AX, is phosphorylated by the action of DNA-PK, ATM, and ATR kinases (Sharma and Hendzel, 2019). The E3 ligase RNF168 catalyzes the monoubiquitination of H2A and γH2AX after DNA damage; this action is being required for 53BP1 recruitment at DNA damage sites (Mattiroli et al., 2012). In this sense, RNF168-mediated ubiquitination can be counteracted by the action of USP3 (Sharma et al., 2014). USP44 is also recruited after DNA damage in a RNF168-dependent manner (Mosbech et al., 2013). USP51 also influences H2A deubiquitination, being recruited to chromatin after DNA damage. Accordingly, its depletion results in impaired DNA damage repair (Wang et al., 2016c).

Besides histone deubiquitination, USPs can regulate gene expression by acting on other chromatin-related substrates. This is the case of USP7, which has been reported to deubiquitinate PHF8, a histone demethylase involved in multiple pathological disorders (Wang et al., 2016a). Moreover, besides acting directly on H2A ubiquitination status, USP21 can also associate with the nucleolar-remodeling complex NoRC in order to stabilize TIP5, thus establishing an inhibitory heterochromatic state at rDNA promoters (Nakagawa et al., 2008; Khan et al., 2015). Additionally, USP22 participates in telomere maintenance by controlling the stability of telomeric repeat binding factor 1 (TRF1) (Atanassov et al., 2009), being also involved in the regulation of (FUSE)-binding protein 1 (FBP1) (Atanassov and Dent, 2011). USP7 and USP11 have been shown to associate with chromatin and to bind to several Polycomb repressive complex 1 (PRC1) components, including BMI1 and MEL18, affecting the transcriptional regulation of $p16^{INK4a}$. USP7 seems to deubiquitinate also H2A and H2B (Maertens et al., 2010).

4.2.3 DNA damage repair and p53 signaling

Genomic DNA is under permanent risk of damage by both endogenous and environmental factors, and consequently, an improper response to DNA damage can lead to genome instability, a key hallmark of cancer (Hanahan and Weinberg, 2011). DNA repair and DNA-damage response (DDR) mechanisms are tightly regulated by PTMs such as ubiquitination (Brinkmann et al., 2015). One example is USP1, which deubiquitinates Fanconi anemia group D2 protein (FANCD2), essential in the Fanconi anemia (FA) pathway of DNA crosslink repair (Nijman et al., 2005; van Twest et al., 2017). Deubiquitination of FANCI by USP1 is required for FA core complex formation and recruitment at sites of DNA damage (Castella et al., 2015). USP1 also maintains both total and phosphorylated CHK1 protein levels, controlling a feedback loop that limits CHK1 activity to rescue DNA-damaged cells (Guervilly et al., 2011). Moreover, USP1 regulates the ubiquitination status of proliferating cell nuclear antigen (PCNA), a safeguard against error-prone translesion synthesis of DNA (Huang et al., 2006). The USP1 association with its WD40 binding partner, USP1-associated factor 1 (UAF1), is crucial to promote double-strand break (DSB) repair through homologous recombination (Murai et al., 2011).

Another USP linked to DNA repair is USP11, which interacts with the DDR tumor suppressor breast cancer type 2 susceptibility protein (BRCA2) to resolve mitomycin C-induced DNA damage, participating in the BRCA2 repair pathway independently of BRCA2 ubiquitination (Schoenfeld et al., 2004). Moreover, depletion of USP11 sensitizes cells to the DDR enzyme poly(ADP-ribose) polymerase 1 (PARP1) inhibitor AZD2281 (Olaparib) (Wiltshire et al., 2010). Recently, it has been reported that USP11 catalytic activity is necessary to counteract PALB2 ubiquitination, which suppresses its interaction with BRCA1. Thus, USP11 is required for the formation of a stable BRCA1-PALB2-BRCA2 complex upon DNA damage (Orthwein et al., 2015). USP28 was shown to bind and stabilize 53BP1, Claspin, and CHK2, promoting the ATM-53BP1-Chk2-p53-PUMA pathway, important in DNA damage response and also in p53 mediated-transcriptional responses (Zhang et al., 2006; Cuella-Martin et al., 2016).

However, it has been subsequently demonstrated that USP28 depletion did not cause significant DDR defects, suggesting that its role in DNA repair responses is limited (Knobel et al., 2014).

During S phase, USP9X, USP20, and USP29 also regulate the stability of the protein Claspin, an adaptor protein activated by CHK1 in the ATR-CHK1 pathway, maintaining DNA damage checkpoint responses and DNA replication fork stability (Zhu et al., 2014; Martin et al., 2015; McGarry et al., 2016). Depletion of USP51 has been associated with an increase in spontaneous DDR, thus raising USP51 as a novel regulator of this process, through the control of H2A ubiquitination levels (Wang et al., 2016c). Another USP with critical functions in DNA damage repair is USP7, which is essential for maintaining RAD18 stability, necessary for the integrity of translesion synthesis (TLS) pathway, in which the replicative DNA polymerase is temporarily replaced by a specialized enzyme that can act across DNA lesions (Bi, 2015; Zlatanou et al., 2016). Moreover, USP7 also regulates the stability of DNA polymerase eta (Polη) through direct and indirect mechanisms (Qian et al., 2015). Like USP1, USP7 also regulates directly the mono-ubiquitination status of PCNA, crucial for avoiding the accumulation of mutations in the genome. USP1 suppresses UV-induced mutations involving DNA replication, whereas USP7 acts in a cell-cycle independent fashion suppressing oxidative stress-induced mutagenesis (Kashiwaba et al., 2015). Similarly to USP1, USP7 also controls CHK1 protein levels by direct deubiquitination (Alonso-de Vega et al., 2014). Other USPs, such as USP3, USP5, USP16, USP26, USP37, and USP44, have also been related to DSB repair (Kee and Huang, 2016).

USP7, USP24, and USP45 have been related to nucleotide excision repair (NER). NER can be divided into two pathways: global genome NER (GG-NER), which acts throughout the entire genome, and transcription-coupled NER (TC-NER), which acts specifically on the newly transcribed DNA strand at transcriptionally active genes (Zhang and Gong, 2016). USP7 has an important role in UV-damage response pathway by regulating both GG-NER and TC-NER. This USP deubiquitinates XPC, a damage recognition factor in GG-NER pathway, and its inhibition leads to a decreased efficiency in the repair of UV-induced DNA lesions (He et al., 2014). TC-NER is also regulated in part by USP7, which interacts and cooperates with the UV-stimulated scaffold protein A (UVSSA), subsequently controlling the stability of CSB/ERCC6 and RNA pol II to ensure efficient repair after UV irradiation (Zhang et al., 2012c). Moreover, USP24 has been connected to NER by controlling the stability of damage-specific DNA-binding protein 2 (DDB2), a protein involved in the DDR (Zhang et al., 2012a). Finally, USP45 is also involved in UV-induced damage repair, by controlling the NER factor ERCC1 endonuclease (Perez-Oliva et al., 2015).

Another DDR mechanism in which the ubiquitin system is important is the base excision repair (BER) pathway, that actively repairs simple DNA base lesions such as apurinic/apyrimidinic (AP) sites and oxidations (Edmonds and Parsons, 2014). USP47 plays an important role in this process, controlling the ubiquitination levels of DNA polymerase β (Polβ), thus being essential for maintaining genome integrity (Parsons et al., 2011).

The tumor suppressor p53, which is altered in multiple tumor types, plays a critical role in the regulation of DNA damage response, coordinating the repair pathways with DNA replication and also controlling apoptosis initiation in the case of excessive DNA damage (Kastenhuber and Lowe, 2017). Several USPs deubiquitinate p53 directly, or regulate its levels indirectly, by targeting E3 ligases (Kwon et al., 2017b). Among the USPs that regulate directly p53, USP7 has a dual role in regulating the stability of this tumor suppressor, since it can deubiquitinate both p53 and the ubiquitin ligase MDM2, which targets p53 for proteasomal degradation (Brooks et al., 2007; Kon et al., 2010). Thus, depending on whether USP7 deubiquitinates p53 or MDM2, it can be considered an anti- or pro-tumoral deubiquitinase, respectively. In this regard, it has been reported that the downregulation of USP7 by the ATM-dependent phosphatase PPMIG1 leads to a p53-dependent DDR (Khoronenkova et al., 2012). Although USP2a do not act on p53 stability in a direct manner, it regulates protein levels of both MDM2 and MDMX (Stevenson et al., 2007; Allende-Vega et al., 2010). USP15 also controls MDM2 stability (Zou et al., 2014) and was recently described as a regulator of the p53-R175H mutant isoform, present in various types of cancer (Padmanabhan et al., 2018). Moreover, USP10 deubiquitinates both wild-type and mutated p53 isoforms, thus having pro- or antitumoral roles depending on p53 status (Yuan et al., 2010). Similarly, USP24 and USP29 can deubiquitinate p53, regulating UV-induced and oxidative stress damage, respectively (Liu et al., 2011a; Zhang et al., 2015). USP42 has also been identified as a p53 deubiquitinase, contributing to its stabilization during early phases of DDR (Hock et al., 2011). USP4 promotes p53 degradation by deubiquitination of ARF-BP1 ubiquitin ligase and the histone deacetylase HDAC2, thus arising as a potential oncogene (Zhang et al., 2011b; Li et al., 2016). USP22 regulates p53 activity by inhibiting its acetylation and transcriptional activation through the control of SIRT1 ubiquitination levels (Lin et al., 2012) and the regulation of MDMX stability (Ding et al., 2014). Moreover, USP49 has been recently reported to act as a p53 deubiquitinase, possibly forming a positive feedback loop with this tumor suppressor (Tu et al., 2018). Finally, USP5 has also been proposed to indirectly regulate p53 activity (Dayal et al., 2009).

4.2.4 Regulation of RNA maturation and protein synthesis

Several USPs have emerged as essential regulators of RNA maturation and protein synthesis, fundamental processes in controlling cellular biology. In this regard, RNA splicing is a key event in eukaryotic cells that removes noncoding intronic sequences from pre-mRNAs, thus allowing RNA maturation. This reaction is catalyzed by the spliceosome, a complex of five small nuclear RNAs and more than 200 proteins (Lee and Abdel-Wahab, 2016). For the correct progression of the splicing cycle, the tri-snRNP ubiquitinated proteins PRP3 and

PRP31 present in the spliceosome get deubiquitinated through the action of USP4 and USP15, respectively (Chanarat and Mishra, 2018). Both USP4 and USP15 are recruited to the spliceosome by SART3 factor (Zhang et al., 2016c). Furthermore, USP49 also regulates cotranscriptional pre-mRNA splicing through H2B deubiquitination (Zhang et al., 2013b). Additionally, promoted by SART3, USP4 also interacts with RNPS1, which activates constitutive and alternative splicing (Kwon et al., 2017a). Finally, USP39 has also been described as a regulator of global pre-mRNA splicing efficiency (Fraile et al., 2017).

Ribosome biogenesis is a crucial process for normal cell growth and proliferation; therefore, its dysregulation is associated with a variety of human pathologies, including cancer. It is a spatially organized process that occurs in the nucleolus, and comprises transcription of rDNA genes, processing of the 47S pre-rRNA to mature 18S, 5.8S, and 28S rRNAs and modification and assembly of preribosomal molecules (Pelletier et al., 2018). Different USPs have been related to ribosome biogenesis, such as USP21 and USP36. USP21 can be stabilized by the SUMOylated protein BEND3, therefore stabilizing the Tip5/NoRC complex and repressing rDNA transcription (Khan et al., 2015). Moreover, it has been shown that USP36 plays a critical role in the regulation of rRNA synthesis, having also an important impact on mRNA translation process mediated, at least in part, by the regulation of DEAH-box RNA helicase DHX33 stability (Fraile et al., 2018).

4.2.5 Other cancer-related signaling pathways

During the last decades, reversible ubiquitination has emerged as an important downstream element of signaling cascades, such as NF-κB, TGF-β, receptor tyrosine kinases (RTKs), and Wnt pathways, which are frequently altered in cancer.

The NF-κB pathway is constitutively activated in several types of cancer, being also implicated in metastasis formation (Xia et al., 2014). Different USPs act as negative regulators of NF-κB signaling, such as CYLD, which is an NEMO-interacting protein that inhibits IKK and NF-κB by deubiquitinating TGF-β-activated kinase 1 (TAK1), TRAF2, TRAF6, and NEMO (Reiley et al., 2007; Harhaj and Dixit, 2012). Additionally, CYLD also regulates RIPK1 ubiquitination levels in the TNFα-induced necrosome complex (Moquin et al., 2013). Moreover, USP25 inhibits IL-17-induced activation of NF-κB by modulating TRAF5 and TRAF6 ubiquitination (Zhong et al., 2012). MCPIP1 deubiquitinates TRAF2, TRAF3, and TRAF6 and mediates USP10-dependent ubiquitination of NEMO, thus inhibiting NF-κB signaling and promoting apoptosis (Niu et al., 2013). Moreover, the deubiquitination of TRAF6 by USP10 prevents genotoxic NF-κB activation (Wang et al., 2015).

USP4 also removes ubiquitin from TRAF2, TRAF6, and TAK1, thus inhibiting TNFα-induced NF-κB signaling (Fan et al., 2011; Xiao et al., 2012). Other USPs, such as USP2, USP4, USP7, USP11, and USP21, also participate in the

NF-κB activation in response to TNFα. USP11 has been shown to deubiquitinate IκBα, thus inhibiting NF-κB activation (Sun et al., 2010). In the case of USP2, USP4, USP7, and USP21, they act by regulating the ubiquitination levels of RIPK1 (Xu et al., 2010; Mahul-Mellier et al., 2012; Hou et al., 2013; Zaman et al., 2013). However, USP2 has also been described as a positively regulator of NF-κB signaling (Metzig et al., 2011).

Furthermore, the COP9 signalosome (CSN), a regulator of cullin-RING-ubiquitin ligases activity, associates with USP15 and promotes the deubiquitination and stabilization of IκBα (Schweitzer et al., 2007). USP48 is also associated with CSN, and confers stability to nuclear NF-κB/RelA by deubiquitination (Schweitzer and Naumann, 2015). USP18 regulates NF-κB signaling by targeting TAK1-TAB1 complex and NEMO for deubiquitination (Liu et al., 2013a; Yang et al., 2015). Furthermore, USP7 deubiquitinates NF-κB, promoting its transcriptional activity (Colleran et al., 2013), whereas USP6 activates classical NF-κB in an atypical manner characterized by the absence of IκB degradation (Pringle et al., 2012).

Several USPs are implicated in the regulation of TGF-β signaling, which has a dual role in the context of cancer, acting as both a tumor suppressor in premalignant cells and as a tumor promoter in later stages (David and Massague, 2018). In this sense, CYLD, USP4, USP9X, USP11, and USP15 have emerged as regulators of this pathway. USP4 and USP11 regulate the ubiquitination levels of type I TGF-β receptor (TβR-I), strongly inducing TGF-β signaling (Al-Salihi et al., 2012; Zhang et al., 2012b). In a similar way, USP15 deubiquitinates and stabilizes TβR-I and SMURF2, the E3 Ub-ligase that targets TβR complexes for proteasomal-mediated degradation (Eichhorn et al., 2012; Iyengar et al., 2015). Moreover, USP15 also deubiquitinates BMP receptors and receptor-activated SMADs (Herhaus and Sapkota, 2014). CYLD was shown to target K63-linked ubiquitination of SMAD7, thereby inhibiting TGF-β signaling and controlling the development of Tregs (Zhao et al., 2011b), and also decreases the stability of SMAD3 acting on K63-polyubiquitinated AKT (Lim et al., 2012). Furthermore, USP9X positively regulates TGF-β signaling by countering monoubiquitination of SMAD4, thus allowing its interaction with SMAD2/3 (Dupont et al., 2009).

Dysregulation of receptor tyrosine kinases (RTKs) signaling has been found in different types of human cancer (Du and Lovly, 2018). Some USPs, like USP2, USP8, USP18, and USP22 can interfere in the trafficking of several RTKs. In this context, USP2a prevents endocytosis-mediated EGFR degradation, resulting in constitutive EGFR activation (Liu et al., 2013b) and USP22 sustains the trafficking of EGFR back to the plasma membrane (Zhang et al., 2018a). Moreover, USP18 modulates EGFR translation (Duex and Sorkin, 2009). The specific role of USP8 in this context is not well established yet, as some studies support a role of this protease in the stabilization of RTKs (Berlin et al., 2010), while others have suggested its implication in RTK degradation (Alwan and van Leeuwen, 2007).

The Wnt signaling pathway plays a key role in embryonic development and tissue homeostasis, and its dysregulation is frequently associated with cancer (Zhan et al., 2017b). Several USPs have been shown to impinge on this pathway, including CYLD, USP2a, USP4, USP5, USP6, USP7, USP9X, USP15, USP22, USP25, USP34, and USP47. Thus, CYLD has been raised as a negative regulator of Wnt/β-catenin signaling, through the deubiquitination of the cytoplasmic effector protein Dishevelled (Dvl) (Tauriello et al., 2010). Moreover, USP4 and USP15 negatively modulate Wnt signaling by interacting with Nemo-like kinase and promoting β-catenin degradation, respectively (Huang et al., 2009; Zhao et al., 2009). Ubiquitination and degradation of β-catenin is a key event in this pathway, and different USPs, such as USP2a, USP4, USP9X, and USP47, are involved in its deubiquitination and stabilization, thereby acting as positive regulators of Wnt/β-catenin signaling (Shi et al., 2015; Yun et al., 2015; Yang et al., 2016; Kim et al., 2018). Furthermore, USP5 and USP22 act on FOXM1, an essential protein for β-catenin transactivation and recruitment to Wnt-target gene promoters, deubiquitinating this factor and upregulating its levels (Ning et al., 2014; Chen et al., 2016). USP6 also acts as a potent activator of this pathway, enhancing Wnt signaling by deubiquitinating the Wnt receptors Frizzleds (Fzds) (Madan et al., 2016). Moreover, USP25 and USP34 are also positive regulators of Wnt signaling. Of note, USP25 directly interacts with and stabilizes tankyrases (Xu et al., 2017a), whereas USP34 controls the stability of axin, opposing its tankyrase-dependent ubiquitination (Lui et al., 2011). Finally, a recent study has shown that USP7 is crucial in sustaining pathological, but not physiological, Wnt activation in APC-mutated colorectal cancer by mediating β-catenin deubiquitination (Novellasdemunt et al., 2017).

4.3 Alterations of USPs in human cancer

Several studies have assessed the presence of specific gene mutations and changes in the expression levels of USPs in different cancer types, showing that these proteases can exhibit oncogenic or tumor suppressing functions. Moreover, some USPs have pro- or antitumorigenic potential depending on the target affected or the cellular context, having a dual role (Fraile et al., 2016). A list of different roles played by USPs in cancer is summarized in Table 4.1.

Although recurrent mutations of USPs in cancer are not very frequent, there are some examples of different tumor types that exhibit specific mutations in these proteases. Mutations in *CYLD* gene underlie different tumor disorders of the skin appendages that are associated with hereditary diseases including familial cylindromatosis, Brooke-Spiegler syndrome, and multiple familial trichoepitelioma (Dubois et al., 2017) and different disrupting and inactivating mutations of *USP9X* have been described in MSI-H colorectal cancers (Jo et al., 2017). Moreover, chromosomal translocations leading to the fusion of *CHD11*, *TRAP150*, *ZNF9*, *OMD*, *COL1A1*, or *PPP6R3* promoters to the full-length *USP6* gene result in overexpression of this deubiquitinase in aneurismal

TABLE 4.1 Ubiquitin-specific proteases involved in human cancers.

USP	Type of cancer associated	Type of Change	Clinicopathological features/additional information	References
CYLD	Skin tumors	Specific mutations ✗	Mutations typically cause CYLD protein truncation; associated with hereditary diseases such as familial cylindromatosis, Brooke-Spiegler syndrome and multiple familial trichoepitelioma	Dubois et al. (2017)
	Melanoma	Downregulation ↓	CYLD is reduced, while pJNK and β1-integrin are increased in melanoma cell lines and tissues	Ke et al. (2013)
	Hepatocellular carcinoma		*CYLD* expression is reduced or lost in all tumor cell lines and most tumorous tissues analyzed	Hellerbrand et al. (2007)
	Colorectal cancer			
USP1	Gastric cancer	Downregulation ↓	Expression of *USP1* is lost in the transition from the normal to the metaplastic state	Luise et al. (2011)
USP2	Breast cancer	Downregulation ↓	*USP2* expression is significantly reduced in the different types of mammary carcinoma	Metzig et al. (2011)
	Advanced cutaneous T-cell lymphoma		*USP2* shows a decreased expression in advanced CTCL compared with the early stage disease and blocks apoptosis in malignant p53wt T-lymphocytes	Wei et al. (2016)
	Ovarian carcinoma	Upregulation ↑	*USP2* is overexpressed (>3-fold) in ovarian serous cystadenocarcinoma tissues	Yang et al. (2007)

Continued

TABLE 4.1 Ubiquitin-specific proteases involved in human cancers—cont'd

USP	Type of cancer associated	Type of Change	Clinicopathological features/additional information	References
	Prostate carcinoma		Genes that have been described as targets of p53-mediated suppression are also upregulated The proliferative and invasive properties of *USP2a*-overexpressing cells are MYC-dependent	Priolo et al. (2006) Benassi et al. (2012)
	Glioma		Levels of USP2 and its substrate FASN are higher in high-grade than in low-grade gliomas	Tao et al. (2013)
	Bladder cancer*		Overexpression of *USP2a* in T24 human bladder cancer cells enhances oncogenic properties	Kim et al. (2012)
USP3	Gastric cancer	Upregulation ↑	Overexpression of *USP3* correlates with poor disease-free survival of patients	Fang et al. (2018)
USP4	Lung adenocarcinoma	Downregulation ↓	The high *USP4* expression group has better overall survival and recurrence-free survival	Zhong et al. (2018)
	Colorectal cancer	Upregulation ↑	*USP4* overexpression is associated with tumor size, differentiation, metastasis, and poor survival	Xing et al. (2016)
	Human neck squamous cell carcinoma		USP4 regulates RIP1-mediated NF-κB activation and promotes TNF-α-induced apoptosis	Hou et al. (2013)
	Bladder cancer		USP4 levels seem to be elevated in other tumor types to a lesser extent	Zhang et al. (2011b)
	Prostate cancer		USP4 inhibits p53 through deubiquitinating and stabilizing ARF-BP1	

	Melanoma		USP4 plays an oncogenic role by inhibiting stress-induced apoptosis and promoting metastasis	Guo et al. (2018)
USP5	Pancreatic ductal adenocarcinoma	Upregulation ↑	USP5 loss leads to accumulation of DNA damage in pancreatic cancer cells	Kaistha et al. (2017)
USP6	Nodular fasciitis	Upregulation ↑	*MYH9-* or *PPPR6R3-USP6* gene fusion leads to *USP6* overexpression	Guo et al. (2016)
	Aneurysmal bone cyst		*CDH11-*, *TRAP150-*, *ZNF9-*, *OMD-* or *COL1A1-USP6* gene fusion leads to *USP6* overexpression	Oliveira and Chou (2014)
USP7	Colorectal cancer	Downregulation ↓	STAT3 activation downregulates *USP7* expression, leading to the degradation of p53	Yang et al. (2012)
	Breast cancer	Upregulation ↑	Levels of USP7 and its substrate PHF8 are correlated with the different histological grades	Wang et al. (2016a)
	Non-small-cell lung cancer		USP7 stabilizes Ki-67 and their expression levels increase from high to low differentiate tumors	Zhang et al. (2016a)
	Epithelial ovarian cancer		Expression levels of *USP7* are correlated with lymph node metastasis and poor prognosis	Zhang et al. (2016b)
USP7	Esophageal squamous cell carcinoma	Upregulation ↑	The higher expression of *USP7* is positively correlated with lymph node metastasis	Hu et al. (2019)
	T-cell leukemia		USP7 is transcriptionally regulated by NOTCH1 and in turn, USP7 controls NOTCH1 levels	Jin et al. (2019)

Continued

TABLE 4.1 Ubiquitin-specific proteases involved in human cancers—cont'd

USP	Type of cancer associated	Type of Change	Clinicopathological features/additional information	References
	Cervical cancer		*USP7* is amplified in cervical cancer and its expression levels correlate with worse survival rates	Su et al. (2018)
	Hepatocellular carcinoma		High expression of *USP7* is correlated with advanced tumor stage and poor overall survival	Wang et al. (2018b)
	Prostate cancer		High levels of *USP7* are associated with nuclear exclusion of PTEN and more aggressive disease	Song et al. (2008)
	Glioma		*USP7* expression levels are associated with disease progression and survival rate	Cheng et al. (2013)
	Melanoma		USP7 plays a central role in mediating melanoma tumor cells residence in the bone marrow	Vishnoi et al. (2018)
	Neuroblastoma		USP7 levels are increased in patients with high-risk compared to patients with low-risk	Tavana et al. (2016)
	Medulloblastoma*		Enforced expression of *USP7* enhances cell proliferation and migration in medulloblastoma cells	Zhan et al. (2017a)
USP8	Corticotroph adenomas of the pituitary	Somatic mutations ✕	*USP8* mutations cause Cushing's disease via activation of EGF receptor signaling	Reincke et al. (2015)
	Melanoma Cervical cancer	Upregulation ↑	USP8 directly deubiquitylates and stabilizes FLIPL (not the short isoform)	Jeong et al. (2017)

USP9X	Colorectal cancer	Somatic mutations ✗	*USP9X* is inactivated in some colorectal cancers with high microsatellite instability (MSI-H)	Jo et al. (2017)
	Pancreatic ductal adenocarcinoma	Downregulation ↓	USP9X levels are inversely associated with metastatic burden in advanced disease	Perez-Mancera et al. (2012)
	Melanoma	Upregulation ↑	USP9X and ETS-1 were detected in metastatic tumors versus normal skin or benign lesions	Potu et al. (2017)
	Non-small-cell lung cancer		*USP9X* expression directly correlates with Ki67 expression	Luise et al. (2011)
USP10	Lung cancer	Downregulation ↓	USP10 directly interacts with and stabilizes PTEN via deubiquitination	Sun et al. (2018)
	Hepatocellular carcinoma		*USP10* expression correlates with tumor size, disease-free survival and overall survival	Lu et al. (2018)
	Prostate cancer	Upregulation ↑	USP10 levels are associated with G3BP2 levels and with poor outcome	Takayama et al. (2018)
	Melanoma		USP10 levels are higher in metastatic melanoma compared with benign nevi and primitive tumors	Luise et al. (2011)
USP11	Hepatocellular carcinoma	Upregulation ↑	High *USP11* expression correlates with recurrence and a shorter overall survival	Zhang et al. (2018b)
	Breast cancer		Patients with high expression of *USP11* have decreased overall survival	Garcia et al. (2018)
	Melanoma		USP11 levels are higher in metastatic melanoma compared with benign nevi and primitive tumors	Luise et al. (2011)

Continued

TABLE 4.1 Ubiquitin-specific proteases involved in human cancers—cont'd

USP	Type of cancer associated	Type of Change	Clinicopathological features/additional information	References
USP13	Ovarian cancer	Upregulation ↑	*USP13* is often co-amplified with *PIK3CA* and its overexpression is associated with poor outcome	Han et al. (2016)
	Melanoma*		USP13 stabilizes and upregulates MITF, an essential factor for melanoma progression	Zhao et al. (2011a)
USP14	Pancreatic ductal adenocarcinoma	Upregulation ↑	*USP14* levels are higher in various cancer tissues. Moreover, in vitro experiments using different cancer cell lines showed that *USP14* overexpression promotes cell proliferation and migration whereas *USP14* silencing has the opposite effects	Zhu et al. (2016)
	Lung cancer			
	Breast cancer			
USP14	Gastric cancer	Upregulation ↑	Increased *USP14* expression positively correlates with poor overall survival	Fu et al. (2018)
	Melanoma		High *USP14* expression associates with lower survival in patients with metastatic melanoma	Didier et al. (2018)
	Multiple myeloma*		Enforced expression of *USP14* enhances cell adhesion and its loss induces apoptosis	Xu et al. (2017b)
USP15	Ovarian cancer	Downregulation ↓	*USP15* is downregulated in paclitaxel-resistant ovarian cancer samples	Xu et al. (2009)
	Melanoma*	Upregulation ↑	USP15 stabilizes MDM2, mediating cancer cell survival and inhibiting antitumor T-cell responses	Zou et al. (2014)

USP17	Glioma	Downregulation ⬇	*USP17* was more highly expressed in low grade (I + II) glioma than high-grade (III + IV) glioma	Hu et al. (2016)
	Osteosarcoma	Upregulation ⬆	High expression of *USP17* is correlated with tumor size, metastasis, and poor prognosis	Song et al. (2017)
	Colon adenocarcinoma		*USP17* expression may be modulated during cell division in a similar manner to core components of the cell cycle machinery. Its expression is necessary to coordinate cell cycle progression	McFarlane et al. (2010)
	Lung squamous cell carcinoma			
	Esophageal squamous cell carcinoma			
	Cervix squamous cell carcinoma			
USP18	Leiomyosarcoma	Downregulation ⬇	Patients with reduced *USP18* expression tumor levels have an unfavorable outcome	Chinyengetere et al. (2015)
	Breast cancer	Upregulation ⬆	Increased USP18 levels are associated with less disease-free survival and HER2-positive patients	Tan et al. (2018)
	Lung adenocarcinoma		*USP18* expression is augmented in KRAS-mutated lung cancers	Mustachio et al. (2017)
	Acute promyelocytic leukemia (APL)*	In this study, the knockdown of *USP18* repressed PML/RARα and reduced APL cell growth by promoting apoptosis		Guo et al. (2010)
	Glioblastoma*	In this study, the downregulation of *USP18* enhanced IFN-induced apoptosis in glioblastoma cells		Sgorbissa et al. (2011)

Continued

TABLE 4.1 Ubiquitin-specific proteases involved in human cancers—cont'd

USP	Type of cancer associated	Type of Change	Clinicopathological features/additional information	References
USP22	Invasive breast cancer	Upregulation ⬆	High *USP22* expression is related to metastasis, Her-2, Ki67, recurrence, and poorer outcome	Zhang et al. (2011d)
	Melanoma		USP22 levels are higher in metastatic melanoma compared with benign nevi and primitive tumors	Luise et al. (2011)
	Chemoresistant hepatocellular carcinoma		*USP22* expression correlates with tumor size, differentiation, TNM stage, and overall survival time	Zhang et al. (2017)
	Recurrent colorectal cancer		USP22 levels are significantly increased in recurrent colorectal cancer tissues	Jiang et al. (2018)
	Lung adenocarcinoma		USP22 levels positively correlate with poorer overall survival and disease-free survival	Zhang et al. (2018a)
	Glioma		High expression of *USP22* is associated with poor survival	Liang et al. (2018)
USP24	Lung cancer	Upregulation ⬆	Lung cancer patients with higher *USP24* expression levels have a poor prognosis	Wang et al. (2016b)
USP28	Lobular breast cancer	Somatic mutations ✗	Somatic mutations were found in metastasis and primary tumor (with low frequency)	Shah et al. (2009)
	Gastric cancer	Upregulation ⬆	USP28 levels are significantly correlated with the presence of distant metastases	Zhao et al. (2018)

	Non-small-cell lung cancer		High levels of USP28 are correlated with poor survival in patients	Wang et al. (2018a)
	Breast cancer		In clinical tumor samples, *USP28* overexpression is correlated with LSD1 upregulation	
	Colorectal cancer		USP28 can stabilize FBW7-targeted proteins, exhibiting oncogenic activities	
	Glioma		USP28 levels are directly correlated with glioma grade and inversely correlated with survival	
USP28	Bladder cancer	Upregulation ↑	USP28 levels are correlated with histopathological grade, clinical stage, and recurrence	Wang et al. (2018a)
USP32	Breast cancer	Upregulation ↑	In vitro silencing of *USP32* causes a decrease in the proliferation and migration rate of cells	Akhavantabasi et al. (2010)
	Human small cell lung cancer		High *USP32* expression is significantly correlated with disease stage and invasion	Hu et al. (2017)
USP33	Gastric adenocarcinoma	Downregulation ↓	Lower USP33 levels indicate severe invasion depth, advanced TNM stage, and poorer outcome	Chen et al. (2018b)
USP36	Ovarian cancer	Upregulation ↑	*USP36* transcripts were identified in ascites and serum of ovarian cancer patients	Li et al. (2008)
USP37	Lung adenocarcinoma	Upregulation ↑	Overexpression of *USP37* is positively correlated with c-Myc levels and inversely correlated with *USP37* gene methylation	Pan et al. (2015)
	Lung squamous cell carcinoma			

Continued

TABLE 4.1 Ubiquitin-specific proteases involved in human cancers—cont'd

USP	Type of cancer associated	Type of Change	Clinicopathological features/additional information	References
	Breast cancer		Higher expression of *USP37* is associated with metastasis and elevated rates of mortality	Qin et al. (2018)
USP39	Hepatocellular carcinoma	Upregulation ↑	The expression of *USP39* is strongly associated with the pathological grade of HCC	Yuan et al. (2015)
	Prostate cancer		USP39 levels are positively correlated with a poor outcome	Huang et al. (2016)
	Pancreatic cancer		Overexpression of *USP39* is closely correlated with tumor progression and poor survival	Cai et al. (2017)
	Colorectal carcinoma Lung adenocarcinoma		*USP39* expression correlates with KRAS levels and poor clinical outcome	Fraile et al. (2017)
USP42	Acute myeloid leukemia Myeloid neoplasms	Chromosomal rearrangement ✕	The t(7;21)(p22;q22) rearrangement generating a 5′*RUNX1*-3′*USP42* fusion transcript has been reported in some cases of acute myeloid leukemia and further in myeloid neoplasms	Zagaria et al. (2014)
	Gastric cancer	Upregulation ↑	USP42 levels are associated with tumor size, TNM stage, lymph node metastasis, and survival	Hou et al. (2016)
USP44	Colorectal adenoma	Downregulation ↓	*USP44* is transcriptionally silenced by CpG island promoter methylation	Sloane et al. (2014)

	Lung adenocarcinoma		USP44 reduction is associated with a more aggressive tumor biology and poor clinical outcome	Zhang et al. (2012d)
	T-cell acute lymphoblastic leukemia	Upregulation ↑	USP44 may contribute to the pathogenesis of T-ALL through a mechanism involving aneuploidy	Zhang et al. (2011c)
USP46	Colorectal cancer	Downregulation ↓	USP46 deubiquitinates PHLPP, and both function together to suppress tumorigenesis	Li et al. (2013b)
	Papilloma-virus transformed cancer*	USP46 is essential for proliferation and tumor growth of HPV-transformed cancer cells		Kiran et al. (2018)
USP48	Corticotroph adenomas of the pituitary	Somatic mutations ✕	*USP48* mutations cause Cushing's disease via enhancing the promoter activity of the *POMC* gene	Chen et al. (2018a)
USP49	Pancreatic ductal adenocarcinoma	Downregulation ↓	Low *USP49* and low *FKBP51* expression have significantly decreased overall survival	Luo et al. (2017)
USP54	Acute lymphoblastic leukemia	Somatic mutations ✕	These discovered mutations seem to be relapse-associated	Xiao et al. (2016)
	Colorectal cancer	Upregulation ↑	There is a positive correlation between high *USP54* expression and lower survival	Fraile et al. (2016)

Boxes marked with an asterisk (*) refer to those human cancer types in which USP involvement has been assessed without using human tumor biopsies (using instead different cell lines).

bone cysts, whereas the fusion of *MYH9* promoter to *USP6* leads to its overexpression in nodular fasciitis (Oliveira and Chou, 2014; Guo et al., 2016). Additionally, a fusion involving *RUNX1* and *USP42* was reported in some cases of acute myeloid leukemia (AML) and in myeloid neoplasms (Zagaria et al., 2014). Furthermore, mutations found in *USP54* and *USP28* genes have been associated with relapsed acute lymphoblastic leukemia (ALL) and lobular breast cancer, respectively (Shah et al., 2009; Xiao et al., 2016). Finally, *USP8* and *USP48* somatic mutations were found in corticotroph adenomas of the pituitary, being the major cause of Cushing's disease (Reincke et al., 2015; Chen et al., 2018a).

Many USPs are associated with different types of human cancer by alterations in their protein expression levels. This is the case of *USP4*, overexpressed in colorectal cancer and associated with tumor size, differentiation status, metastasis, and survival (Xing et al., 2016). Another USP involved in this type of cancer is *USP54*, which is overexpressed in colorectal cancer stem cells, promoting intestinal tumorigenesis (Fraile et al., 2016). *USP22* has also emerged as a cancer marker, being overexpressed in recurrent and chemoresistant colorectal cancer and hepatocellular carcinoma (HCC) (Zhang et al., 2017; Jiang et al., 2018). This USP also promotes the proliferation, migration, and invasion of glioma cells (Liang et al., 2018) and the resistance to EGFR-TKIs (epidermal growth factor tyrosine kinase inhibitors) in mutant lung adenocarcinoma cells (Zhang et al., 2018a). The overexpression of *USP22* has also been correlated with poor prognosis in invasive breast cancer (Zhang et al., 2011d), while *USP2* was reported to be downregulated in this tumor type (Metzig et al., 2011). Moreover, a recent study has shown that *USP2* levels are decreased in advanced cutaneous T-cell lymphoma (CTCL) compared with the early stage disease, blocking apoptosis in malignant lymphocytes (Wei et al., 2016). By contrast, this USP is upregulated in prostate and ovarian carcinomas (Priolo et al., 2006; Yang et al., 2007). In agreement, *USP2* overexpression protects human prostate cancer cells from chemotherapeutic-induced apoptosis (Priolo et al., 2006) and elevates MYC protein levels, leading to MYC-driven oncogenic transformation (Benassi et al., 2012). *USP2* also enhances tumor progression in bladder cancer cells (Kim et al., 2012) and its upregulation strongly correlates with glioma tumor grade (Tao et al., 2013). Therefore, *USP2* may have pro- or antitumor effects in a time- or tissue-specific-dependent manner.

Increased levels of *USP7* have been reported in cervical cancer, epithelial ovarian carcinoma (EOC), breast carcinoma, HCC, nonsmall cell lung cancer (NSCLC), esophageal squamous cell carcinoma (ESCC) and T-cell leukemia, promoting cell proliferation (Wang et al., 2016a; Zhang et al., 2016b; Hu et al., 2019; Jin et al., 2019; Su et al., 2018; Wang et al., 2018b), whereas its expression and activity are repressed by STAT3 in colon cancer (Yang et al., 2012). Additionally, *USP7* is also overexpressed in prostate cancer, being associated with tumor aggressiveness, and its expression levels correlate with disease progression and survival in patients with glioma (Song et al., 2008; Cheng et al., 2013).

A recent study has shown that higher expression of *USP7* in melanoma is associated with a decreased patient survival, indicating that this protease plays a central role in mediating melanoma cancer tumor cells residence in the bone marrow (Vishnoi et al., 2018). Moreover, *USP7* is more abundant in neuroblastoma patients with poor prognosis and its expression substantially correlates with N-Myc transcriptional activity, thus rising as a potential target for *MYCN*-amplified tumors (Tavana et al., 2016). Finally, it was found that knockdown of *USP7* inhibits the proliferation and migration of medulloblastoma cells (Zhan et al., 2017a).

Besides *USP7*, other USPs are involved in malignant melanoma. Thus, *USP4*, *USP8*, *USP10*, *USP11*, *USP14*, *USP15*, and *USP22* are overexpressed in this cancer type (Luise et al., 2011; Zou et al., 2014; Jeong et al., 2017; Didier et al., 2018; Guo et al., 2018), whereas *CYLD* expression levels are decreased (Ke et al., 2013). Furthermore, it has been described that USP9X and USP13 impinge on melanoma progression by regulating ETS-1 and MITF protein levels, respectively (Zhao et al., 2011a; Potu et al., 2017). Moreover, *USP9X* expression is lost focally in human pancreatic ductal adenocarcinoma (PDAC) (Perez-Mancera et al., 2012) and the *USP13* gene is co-amplified with *PIK3CA* in some high-grade serous ovarian cancer, being associated with poor clinical outcome (Han et al., 2016). Besides its implication in melanoma, *USP10* has been found to play tumor suppressing functions in HCC and lung cancer, being downregulated in both tumor types (Lu et al., 2018; Sun et al., 2018), while it seems to have oncogenic roles in prostate cancer (Takayama et al., 2018). A recent work suggests that *USP11* is a promoter of HCC metastasis, showing higher expression levels in tumor than in nontumor tissue (Zhang et al., 2018b). Moreover, it also seems to regulate TGFβ-induced epithelial-mesenchymal plasticity and metastasis in breast cancer (Garcia et al., 2018).

Overexpression of *USP17* has been found in osteosarcoma, lung, colon, esophagus, and cervix tumor biopsies (McFarlane et al., 2010; Song et al., 2017), while it was found downregulated in glioma samples (Hu et al., 2016). Similarly, *USP4* is overexpressed in various human tumors, including human neck squamous cell carcinoma, bladder and prostate cancer, among others (Zhang et al., 2011b; Hou et al., 2013), but is downregulated in lung adenocarcinoma (Zhong et al., 2018). Expression levels of *USP44* are also diminished in lung adenocarcinomas, where low expression is associated with poor prognosis (Zhang et al., 2012d), whereas *USP9X* seems to be overexpressed in NSCLC (Luise et al., 2011). *USP32* was also reported to be overexpressed in lung cancer, specifically in human small cell lung cancer (HSCLC), as well as in breast cancer (Akhavantabasi et al., 2010; Hu et al., 2017). Likewise, a recent study has shown that *USP24* expression is upregulated in most late-stage lung cancer patients due to increased mRNA stability caused by SNPs or RNA editing (Wang et al., 2016b). Overexpression of *USP37* in lung cancer has also been reported, correlating inversely with *USP37* gene methylation (Pan et al., 2015). This protease is also upregulated in breast cancer tissues, and its overexpression seems to be associated with poor prognosis (Qin et al., 2018). Moreover, *USP44* epigenetic inactivation is an early event in colorectal adenomas (Sloane et al., 2014), but its expression is elevated in human T-cell ALL, being associated with chromosomal instability (Zhang et al., 2011c). Expression levels of *USP28* have been also related with some types of human cancer. In this regard, *USP28* was found upregulated in NSCLC, colorectal carcinoma, bladder, breast, and gastric cancer and glioma (Wang et al., 2018a; Zhao et al., 2018).

Likewise, *USP36* is upregulated in ovarian cancer (Li et al., 2008) and *USP39* overexpression correlates with poor prognosis in prostate cancer patients (Huang et al., 2016) and is upregulated in HCC and pancreatic, colon and lung tumors, raising as an essential USP for KRAS-driven cancer (Yuan et al., 2015; Cai et al., 2017; Fraile et al., 2017). Moreover, *USP1* expression levels are correlated with early steps of transformation in gastric cancer (Luise et al., 2011), whereas *USP3* and *USP42* overexpression promotes gastric carcinogenesis, being associated with poor prognosis (Hou et al., 2016; Fang et al., 2018). Another USP with implication in this tumor type is *USP33*, whose expression is diminished in gastric adenocarcinoma (Chen et al., 2018b).

An aberrant expression of *USP14* has been shown in various cancers, including myeloma, PDAC, gastric, lung and breast cancer, among others (Zhu et al., 2016; Xu et al., 2017b; Fu et al., 2018). Furthermore, *USP15* is downregulated in paclitaxel-resistant ovarian cancer samples (Xu et al., 2009) and, besides melanoma, *CYLD* expression levels are also reduced in colon and hepatocellular carcinomas (Hellerbrand et al., 2007).

Similarly, leiomyosarcoma patients with reduced *USP18* expression tumor levels have an unfavorable outcome (Chinyengetere et al., 2015), whereas in breast cancer *USP18* promotes cell growth by upregulating EGFR and activating the AKT/Skp2 pathway (Tan et al., 2018). Moreover, *USP18* is overexpressed in *KRAS*-mutant lung adenocarcinomas and seems to affect KRAS stability in lung cancer cells (Mustachio et al., 2017). Additionally, downregulation of *USP18* reduces acute promyelocytic leukemia (APL) cell growth (Guo et al., 2010), while silencing *USP18* in glioblastoma cells was shown to enhance IFN-induced apoptosis (Sgorbissa et al., 2011). *USP46* is downregulated in colorectal cancer, leading to AKT signaling pathway inhibition (Li et al., 2013b) and was recently described as an essential deubiquitinase for proliferation and tumor growth of herpes papilloma virus-transformed cancers (Kiran et al., 2018). Finally, loss of *USP49* expression has been found in PDAC samples (Luo et al., 2017), whereas *USP5* seems to be overexpressed in this tumor type (Kaistha et al., 2017).

4.4 Targeting USPs in cancer

The important implication of USPs in cancer, together with their special structure, converts these proteases into attractive targets for anticancer therapies, and as a consequence, the interest in developing new USP-specific inhibitors is growing rapidly. There are a large number of small-molecule USP inhibitors as summarized in Table 4.2.

TABLE 4.2 Reported inhibitors targeting ubiquitin-specific proteases.

USP	Inhibitor	References	USP	Inhibitor	References
USP1	Pimozide	Chen et al. (2011a) Mistry et al. (2013) Liang et al. (2014)		HBX90659	
	ML323			ML364	
	C527			9-oxo-9-*H*-indeno[1,2-b] pyrazine-2,3-dicarbonitrile and analogs	
	SJB2-043				
	SJB3-019A		USP9X	WP1130	Kapuria et al. (2010) Peterson et al. (2015) Lawson et al. (2017)
	GW7647			G9 (EOAI3402143)	
	PEITC			PEITC	
USP2	ML363	Nicholson et al. (2008) Issaenko and Amerik (2012) Davis et al. (2016) Chuang et al. (2018)	USP10	P22077	Liu et al. (2011b) Weisberg et al. (2017) Lawson et al. (2017) Li et al. (2019)
	AM146			HBX19818	
	RA-9			Spautin-1	
	RA-14			PEITC	
	F6 (NSC632839)			Gold(I)complex-Au(PPh3)PT	
	6TG (6-thioguanine)		USP11	Mitoxantrone	Burkhart et al. (2013) Lawson et al. (2017)
	2-Cyano-pyrimidine and triazine derivatives			PEITC	

Continued

TABLE 4.2 Reported inhibitors targeting ubiquitin-specific proteases—cont'd

USP	Inhibitor	References	USP	Inhibitor	References
USP3	PEITC	Lawson et al. (2017)	USP13	Spautin-1	Liu et al. (2011b)
USP4	Vialinin A	Issaenko and Amerik (2012) Okada et al. (2013)	USP14	WP1130	Kapuria et al. (2010) Coughlin et al. (2014) Chen et al. (2017) Li et al. (2019)
				AC17	
USP5	Vialinin A	Kapuria et al. (2010) Okada et al. (2013) Peterson et al. (2015) Yeasmin Khusbu et al. (2018)		RA-9	
	AM146			b-AP15	
	RA-9			VLX1570	
	RA-14			IU1	
	WP1130			Auranofin	
	HBX41108			CuPT	
	G9 (EOAI3402143)			ZnPT	
USP7	HBX41108	Reverdy et al. (2012) Qin et al. (2016)Pozhidaeva et al. (2017) Wang et al. (2017a) Lamberto et al. (2017) Turnbull et al. (2017) Kategaya et al. (2017) Yeasmin Khusbu et al. (2018) Zhou et al. (2018) Li et al. (2019)		PtPT	
	HBX19818			NiPT	
	HBX28258			Gold(I)complex-Au(PPh3)PT	
	P5091		USP15	Gold(I)complex-Au(PPh3)PT	Li et al. (2019)
	P22077		USP16	PEITC	Lawson et al. (2017)
	P50429		USP22	PEITC	Lawson et al. (2017)
	P217564		USP24	G9 (EOAI3402143)	Peterson et al. (2015)

	XL188		USP25	AZ1; AZ2; AZ3; AZ4	Wrigley et al. (2017) Li et al. (2019)
	FT827			Gold(I)complex-Au(PPh3)PT	
	FT671		USP28	AZ1; AZ2; AZ3; AZ4	Wrigley et al. (2017)
	GNE-6640		USP30	MF-094	Yue et al. (2014) Kluge et al. (2018)
	GNE-677			MF-095	
	CDDO-Me			15-Oxospiramilactone (S3)	
	Spongiacidin C		USP40	PEITC	Lawson et al. (2017)
	Sulawesins A-C(1-3)		USP44	P5091	Pozhidaeva et al. (2017) Wang et al. (2017a)
	Gold(I)complex-Au(PPh3)PT			P22077	
	1′-(2-Phenylethylene)-ditryptophena-line			P50429	
	Furanosesterterpene tetronic acids (three)			P217564	
USP8	AM146	Daviet and Colland (2008) Kapuria et al. (2010) Colombo et al. (2010) Okada et al. (2013) Davis et al. (2016) Yeasmin Khusbu et al. (2018)	USP48	PEITC	Lawson et al. (2017)
	RA-9		Broad range molecules		
	RA-14		Betulinic and Gambogic acids PR-619 J-series prostaglandins and punaglandins Diarylcarbonates		Love et al. (2007) D'Arcy et al. (2015) Long et al. (2019)
	WP1130				
	HBX41108				
	HBX90397				

As previously discussed, USP1 forms a complex with UAF1 in order to regulate the DDR pathway and also promotes stabilization of ID proteins. The study of these USP1 functions has allowed to develop specific USP1 inhibitors, such as Pimozide, ML323, C527, SJB2-043, SJB3-019A, and GW7647 (Chen et al., 2011a; Mistry et al., 2013; Liang et al., 2014). Regarding USP2, different inhibitors have been reported, including 2-cyano-pyrimidine and triazine derivatives, F6 (also known as NSC632839), ML364 and the chalcone-based inhibitors AM146, RA-9, and RA-14 (Nicholson et al., 2008; Issaenko and Amerik, 2012; Davis et al., 2016). Recently, an old drug still clinically used to treat leukemia, 6-thioguanine (6TG), was described as a potent inhibitor of USP2 (Chuang et al., 2018). It has been shown that Vialinin A effectively inhibits the enzymatic activities of USP4 and USP5 (Okada et al., 2013). Furthermore, the activity of USP5 and USP8 is also blocked by AM146, RA-9, RA-14 (Issaenko and Amerik, 2012), and by WP1130, a small molecule with antiproliferative and apoptotic effects in several cancer types, which also inhibits USP9X and USP14 (Kapuria et al., 2010). In the case of USP7, a wide range of inhibitors have been developed. In this context, the cyano-indenopyrazine derivative HBX41108 was the first identified inhibitor of this protease, and it is also capable of blocking USP5 and USP8 functions (Yeasmin Khusbu et al., 2018). A high-throughput screening allowed the identification of two irreversible USP7 inhibitors, known as HBX19818 and HBX28258 (Reverdy et al., 2012). Moreover, a pharmaceutical company reported the USP7 inhibitory molecules P5091, P22077, and P50429, which have shown antitumor properties (Pozhidaeva et al., 2017). Due to their capacity of blocking both USP7 and USP47 activity, these compounds are considered as dual inhibitors. Furthermore, the second-generation USP7 inhibitor P217564 was recently reported, showing an increased potency but blocking also USP47 activity (Wang et al., 2017a). In contrast to the previously described compounds, which target the invariant catalytic cysteine of USP7, the small molecule XL188 is a noncovalent active-site inhibitor (Lamberto et al., 2017). Recently, novel potent and selective USP7 inhibitors have been developed, FT827 and FT671, which bind covalently and noncovalently to USP7 catalytic domain, respectively (Turnbull et al., 2017). The selective inhibitory compounds GNE-6640 and GNE-6776 were also developed recently, targeting USP7 noncovalently 12Å distant from the catalytic cysteine, and thereby attenuating ubiquitin binding and inhibiting USP7 activity (Kategaya et al., 2017). Moreover, the synthetic triterpenoid C-28 methyl ester of 2-cyano-3, 12-dioxoolen-1, 9-dien-28-oic acid (CDDO-Me) was also identified as an inhibitor of USP7 but not of other cysteine proteases, such as cathepsin B and cathepsin D (Qin et al., 2016). Additionally, some natural molecules have been also recognized as a USP7 inhibitors, including Spongiacidin C, three furanosesterterpene tetronic acids, sulawesins A-C (1-3), and several diketopiperazine alkaloids, among which 1′-(2-phenylethylene)-ditryptophena-line strongly inhibits USP7 enzymatic activity (Yeasmin Khusbu et al., 2018;

Zhou et al., 2018). Different compounds have been reported as USP8 inhibitors, including HBX90397, HBX90659, and 9-oxo-9-H-indeno [1,2-b] pyrazine-2,3-dicarbonitrile, and analogs (Daviet and Colland, 2008; Colombo et al., 2010). Additionally, the USP2 inhibitor ML364 can also block USP8 activity (Davis et al., 2016). In the case of USP9X, it has been reported a new compound, known as EOAI3402143 or G9, with greater solubility and inhibitory activity against this protease than WP1130. This compound also inhibits USP5 and USP24 (Peterson et al., 2015). Besides USP7 and USP47 inhibition, the aforementioned molecules P22077 and HBX19818 are also capable of blocking the activity of a previously unreported target, USP10 (Weisberg et al., 2017). Moreover, USP10 activity is also inhibited by the small molecule Spautin-1, which also targets USP13 (Liu et al., 2011b). A systematic high-throughput screen of Food and Drug Administration (FDA)-approved compounds identified mitoxantrone as the most potent inhibitor of USP11. Importantly, an in vitro drug sensitivity assay has demonstrated that the use of mitoxantrone can impact on PDAC cell survival (Burkhart et al., 2013).

USP14 is a direct component of the proteasome; therefore its pharmacological targeting may have a profound impact on cancer treatment. Different compounds have been described as USP14 inhibitors, including 4-arylidene curcumin analog (AC17), RA-9, b-AP15, VLX1570, IU1, and some metal-based compounds, such as auranofin, copper pyrithione (CuPT), zinc pyrithione (ZnPT), platinum pyrithione (PtPT), and nickel pyrithione (NiPT) (Coughlin et al., 2014; Chen et al., 2017). Recently, it has been reported the generation of the first USP28 inhibitors, known as AZ1, AZ2, AZ3, and AZ4, which possess an equivalent potency against USP25 (Wrigley et al., 2017). The mitochondria-localized deubiquitinase USP30 is target of various inhibitors, including the structurally similar compounds MF-094 and MF-095 and the small natural compound, 15-oxospiramilactone (S3), derived from spiramine A of *Spiraea japonica* (Yue et al., 2014; Kluge et al., 2018). Also, a gold(I) complex, Au(PPh3)PT, was reported to exhibit potent antitumor activities both in vitro and in vivo, targeting 19S proteasome-associated DUBs (UCHL5 and USP14) as well as other nonproteasome DUBs (USP7, USP10, USP15, and USP25) (Li et al., 2019).

Moreover, it was described that phenethyl isothiocyanate (PEITC), an isothiocyanate with anticancer activity, is capable of inhibiting various USPs, such as USP1, USP3, USP9X, USP10, USP11, USP16, USP22, USP40, and USP48 (Lawson et al., 2017). Finally, different molecules have been described as a broad DUB inhibitors, including betulinic acid (BA), gambogic acid, PR-619 (D'Arcy et al., 2015), diarylcarbonates (Long et al., 2019), and also J-series prostaglandins and punaglandins, which show ubiquitin isopeptidase inhibitory capacity (Love et al., 2007).

Because of the oncogenic transformation, tumor cells are subjected to different and enhanced cellular stresses that might lead to an exacerbated dependence on the normal function of certain USPs (Freije et al., 2011). In this sense, these proteolytic enzymes can be essential for human malignancies, even without presenting any mutation or change in expression patterns, a concept known as *non-oncogene addiction*. Therefore, the identification of those USPs involved in this process might be essential for developing new treatment strategies. In this regard, the inhibition of USP1-UAF1 complex potentiates cisplatin toxicity, overcoming the resistance of cancer cells to this drug (Liang et al., 2014). Additionally, USP2 blockage has been described as an effective approach to suppress growth in those cancer cells addicted to cyclin D1 (Shan et al., 2009). Moreover, USP4 depletion was shown to mitigate TGF-β-induced epithelial to mesenchymal transition and metastasis (Zhang et al., 2012b) and USP15 depletion decreases TGF-β signaling and oncogenesis (Eichhorn et al., 2012). Furthermore, USP6 has oncogenic properties by positively regulating NF-κB signaling (Pringle et al., 2012). The interaction between USP9X and MCL1 can be disrupted by gemcitabine, sensitizing cells to ABT-737 treatment and inducing caspase-dependent apoptosis (Zhang et al., 2011a). In addition, depletion of USP11 leads to spontaneous DNA damage response activation and hypersensitivity to PARP inhibition and other stresses (Wiltshire et al., 2010). USP37 blockage impairs the proliferation of lung cancer cells by reducing c-Myc levels (Pan et al., 2015) and USP39 downregulation selectively abrogates the growth and tumorigenic potential of lung and colorectal cancer cells dependent on KRAS (Fraile et al., 2017).

4.5 Concluding remarks

During the past decade, the understanding of DUB functions in both physiological and pathological processes has dramatically increased. In this sense, several members of the USP family have raised as essential regulators of central cellular processes frequently dysregulated in human malignancies, including cell cycle progression, chromatin remodeling, DNA damage repair, RNA maturation and protein synthesis, and various signaling pathways. In this context, the number of USPs altered in human cancer, behaving like oncogenes or tumor suppressors, has kept growing over the last years. On this basis, USPs emerge as attractive targets for the development of new cancer therapies, although some USP functions need to be further investigated. Work carried out in this field has led to the identification of many inhibitors with selective action against various USPs, pointing out the feasibility of targeting these proteases as an anticancer therapy. However, many challenges still have to be overcome, and great efforts are needed to clarify the functional complexity of these proteolytic enzymes, as well as their clinical validation as drug targets. Hopefully, the research in this field will continue growing, providing new therapeutic opportunities based on USP-targeting drugs.

Acknowledgments

We thank Dr. Víctor Quesada and Dr. Julia M. Fraile for helpful assistance. Our work is supported by grants from Ministerio de Economía y Competitividad, Instituto de Salud Carlos III (RTICC) and Principado de Asturias, Spain. The Instituto Universitario de Oncología is supported by Fundación Bancaria Caja de Ahorros de Asturias.

Conflicts of interest

The authors declare no competing interests.

References

Abdul Rehman, S.A., Kristariyanto, Y.A., Choi, S.Y., Nkosi, P.J., Weidlich, S., Labib, K., Hofmann, K., Kulathu, Y., 2016. MINDY-1 is a member of an evolutionarily conserved and structurally distinct new family of deubiquitinating enzymes. Mol. Cell 63, 146–155.

Akhavantabasi, S., Akman, H.B., Sapmaz, A., Keller, J., Petty, E.M., Erson, A.E., 2010. USP32 is an active, membrane-bound ubiquitin protease overexpressed in breast cancers. Mamm. Genome 21, 388–397.

Akutsu, M., Dikic, I., Bremm, A., 2016. Ubiquitin chain diversity at a glance. J. Cell Sci. 129, 875–880.

Allende-Vega, N., Sparks, A., Lane, D.P., Saville, M.K., 2010. MdmX is a substrate for the deubiquitinating enzyme USP2a. Oncogene 29, 432–441.

Alonso-de Vega, I., Martin, Y., Smits, V.A., 2014. USP7 controls Chk1 protein stability by direct deubiquitination. Cell Cycle 13, 3921–3926.

Al-Salihi, M.A., Herhaus, L., Macartney, T., Sapkota, G.P., 2012. USP11 augments TGFbeta signalling by deubiquitylating ALK5. Open Biol. 2, 120063.

Alwan, H.A., van Leeuwen, J.E., 2007. UBPY-mediated epidermal growth factor receptor (EGFR) de-ubiquitination promotes EGFR degradation. J. Biol. Chem. 282, 1658–1669.

Aressy, B., Jullien, D., Cazales, M., Marcellin, M., Bugler, B., Burlet-Schiltz, O., Ducommun, B., 2010. A screen for deubiquitinating enzymes involved in the G(2)/M checkpoint identifies USP50 as a regulator of HSP90-dependent Wee1 stability. Cell Cycle 9, 3815–3822.

Atanassov, B.S., Dent, S.Y., 2011. USP22 regulates cell proliferation by deubiquitinating the transcriptional regulator FBP1. EMBO Rep. 12, 924–930.

Atanassov, B.S., Evrard, Y.A., Multani, A.S., Zhang, Z., Tora, L., Devys, D., Chang, S., Dent, S.Y., 2009. Gcn5 and SAGA regulate shelterin protein turnover and telomere maintenance. Mol. Cell 35, 352–364.

Benassi, B., Flavin, R., Marchionni, L., Zanata, S., Pan, Y., Chowdhury, D., Marani, M., Strano, S., Muti, P., Blandino, G., Loda, M., 2012. MYC is activated by USP2a-mediated modulation of microRNAs in prostate cancer. Cancer Discov. 2, 236–247.

Berlin, I., Schwartz, H., Nash, P.D., 2010. Regulation of epidermal growth factor receptor ubiquitination and trafficking by the USP8.STAM complex. J. Biol. Chem. 285, 34909–34921.

Bi, X., 2015. Mechanism of DNA damage tolerance. World J. Biol. Chem. 6, 48–56.

Brinkmann, K., Schell, M., Hoppe, T., Kashkar, H., 2015. Regulation of the DNA damage response by ubiquitin conjugation. Front. Genet. 6, 98.

Brooks, C.L., Li, M., Hu, M., Shi, Y., Gu, W., 2007. The p53--Mdm2--HAUSP complex is involved in p53 stabilization by HAUSP. Oncogene 26, 7262–7266.

Buetow, L., Huang, D.T., 2016. Structural insights into the catalysis and regulation of E3 ubiquitin ligases. Nat. Rev. Mol. Cell Biol. 17, 626–642.

Burkhart, R.A., Peng, Y., Norris, Z.A., Tholey, R.M., Talbott, V.A., Liang, Q., Ai, Y., Miller, K., Lal, S., Cozzitorto, J.A., Witkiewicz, A.K., Yeo, C.J., Gehrmann, M., Napper, A., Winter, J.M., Sawicki, J.A., Zhuang, Z., Brody, J.R., 2013. Mitoxantrone targets human ubiquitin-specific peptidase 11 (USP11) and is a potent inhibitor of pancreatic cancer cell survival. Mol. Cancer Res. 11, 901–911.

Cai, J., Liu, T., Huang, P., Yan, W., Guo, C., Xiong, L., Liu, A., 2017. USP39, a direct target of microRNA-133a, promotes progression of pancreatic cancer via the AKT pathway. Biochem. Biophys. Res. Commun. 486, 184–190.

Castella, M., Jacquemont, C., Thompson, E.L., Yeo, J.E., Cheung, R.S., Huang, J.W., Sobeck, A., Hendrickson, E.A., Taniguchi, T., 2015. FANCI regulates recruitment of the FA core complex at sites of DNA damage independently of FANCD2. PLoS Genet. 11, e1005563.

Chanarat, S., Mishra, S.K., 2018. Emerging roles of ubiquitin-like proteins in pre-mRNA splicing. Trends Biochem. Sci. 43, 896–907.

Chen, J., Dexheimer, T.S., Ai, Y., Liang, Q., Villamil, M.A., Inglese, J., Maloney, D.J., Jadhav, A., Simeonov, A., Zhuang, Z., 2011a. Selective and cell-active inhibitors of the USP1/UAF1 deubiquitinase complex reverse cisplatin resistance in non-small cell lung cancer cells. Chem. Biol. 18, 1390–1400.

Chen, M., Gutierrez, G.J., Ronai, Z.A., 2011b. Ubiquitin-recognition protein Ufd1 couples the endoplasmic reticulum (ER) stress response to cell cycle control. Proc. Natl. Acad. Sci. U. S. A. 108, 9119–9124.

Chen, Y., Li, Y., Xue, J., Gong, A., Yu, G., Zhou, A., et al., 2016. Wnt-induced deubiquitination FoxM1 ensures nucleus beta-catenin transactivation. EMBO J. 35, 668–684.

Chen, X., Yang, Q., Xiao, L., Tang, D., Dou, Q.P., Liu, J., 2017. Metal-based proteasomal deubiquitinase inhibitors as potential anticancer agents. Cancer Metastasis Rev. 36, 655–668.

Chen, J., Jian, X., Deng, S., Ma, Z., Shou, X., Shen, Y., et al., 2018a. Identification of recurrent USP48 and BRAF mutations in Cushing's disease. Nat. Commun. 9, 3171.

Chen, Y., Pang, X., Ji, L., Sun, Y., Ji, Y., 2018b. Reduced expression of deubiquitinase USP33 is associated with tumor progression and poor prognosis of gastric adenocarcinoma. Med. Sci. Monit. 24, 3496–3505.

Cheng, C., Niu, C., Yang, Y., Wang, Y., Lu, M., 2013. Expression of HAUSP in gliomas correlates with disease progression and survival of patients. Oncol. Rep. 29, 1730–1736.

Chinyengetere, F., Sekula, D.J., Lu, Y., Giustini, A.J., Sanglikar, A., Kawakami, M., et al., 2015. Mice null for the deubiquitinase USP18 spontaneously develop leiomyosarcomas. BMC Cancer 15, 886.

Chuang, S.J., Cheng, S.C., Tang, H.C., Sun, C.Y., Chou, C.Y., 2018. 6-Thioguanine is a noncompetitive and slow binding inhibitor of human deubiquitinating protease USP2. Sci. Rep. 8, 3102.

Clague, M.J., Heride, C., Urbe, S., 2015. The demographics of the ubiquitin system. Trends Cell Biol. 25, 417–426.

Colleran, A., Collins, P.E., O'Carroll, C., Ahmed, A., Mao, X., McManus, B., Kiely, P.A., Burstein, E., Carmody, R.J., 2013. Deubiquitination of NF-kappaB by ubiquitin-specific protease-7 promotes transcription. Proc. Natl. Acad. Sci. U. S. A. 110, 618–623.

Colombo, M., Vallese, S., Peretto, I., Jacq, X., Rain, J.C., Colland, F., Guedat, P., 2010. Synthesis and biological evaluation of 9-oxo-9H-indeno[1,2-b]pyrazine-2,3-dicarbonitrile analogues as potential inhibitors of deubiquitinating enzymes. ChemMedChem 5, 552–558.

Coughlin, K., Anchoori, R., Iizuka, Y., Meints, J., MacNeill, L., Vogel, R.I., Orlowski, R.Z., Lee, M.K., Roden, R.B., Bazzaro, M., 2014. Small-molecule RA-9 inhibits proteasome-associated DUBs and ovarian cancer in vitro and in vivo via exacerbating unfolded protein responses. Clin. Cancer Res. 20, 3174–3186.

Cuella-Martin, R., Oliveira, C., Lockstone, H.E., Snellenberg, S., Grolmusova, N., Chapman, J.R., 2016. 53BP1 integrates DNA repair and p53-dependent cell fate decisions via distinct mechanisms. Mol. Cell 64, 51–64.

D'Arcy, P., Wang, X., Linder, S., 2015. Deubiquitinase inhibition as a cancer therapeutic strategy. Pharmacol. Ther. 147, 32–54.

David, C.J., Massague, J., 2018. Contextual determinants of TGFbeta action in development, immunity and cancer. Nat. Rev. Mol. Cell Biol. 19, 419–435.

Daviet, L., Colland, F., 2008. Targeting ubiquitin specific proteases for drug discovery. Biochimie 90, 270–283.

Davis, M.I., Pragani, R., Fox, J.T., Shen, M., Parmar, K., Gaudiano, E.F., et al., 2016. Small molecule inhibition of the ubiquitin-specific protease USP2 accelerates cyclin D1 degradation and leads to cell cycle arrest in colorectal cancer and mantle cell lymphoma models. J. Biol. Chem. 291, 24628–24640.

Dayal, S., Sparks, A., Jacob, J., Allende-Vega, N., Lane, D.P., Saville, M.K., 2009. Suppression of the deubiquitinating enzyme USP5 causes the accumulation of unanchored polyubiquitin and the activation of p53. J. Biol. Chem. 284, 5030–5041.

DeVine, T., Sears, R.C., Dai, M.S., 2018. The ubiquitin-specific protease USP36 is a conserved histone H2B deubiquitinase. Biochem. Biophys. Res. Commun. 495, 2363–2368.

Didier, R., Mallavialle, A., Ben Jouira, R., Domdom, M.A., Tichet, M., Auberger, P., et al., 2018. Targeting the proteasome-associated deubiquitinating enzyme USP14 impairs melanoma cell survival and overcomes resistance to MAPK-targeting therapies. Mol. Cancer Ther. 17, 1416–1429.

Ding, F., Bao, C., Tian, Y., Xiao, H., Wang, M., Xie, X., et al., 2014. USP22 promotes NSCLC tumorigenesis via MDMX up-regulation and subsequent p53 inhibition. Int. J. Mol. Sci. 16, 307–320.

Draker, R., Sarcinella, E., Cheung, P., 2011. USP10 deubiquitylates the histone variant H2A.Z and both are required for androgen receptor-mediated gene activation. Nucleic Acids Res. 39, 3529–3542.

Du, Z., Lovly, C.M., 2018. Mechanisms of receptor tyrosine kinase activation in cancer. Mol. Cancer 17, 58.

Dubois, A., Hodgson, K., Rajan, N., 2017. Understanding inherited cylindromas: clinical implications of gene discovery. Dermatol. Clin. 35, 61–71.

Duex, J.E., Sorkin, A., 2009. RNA interference screen identifies Usp18 as a regulator of epidermal growth factor receptor synthesis. Mol. Biol. Cell 20, 1833–1844.

Dupont, S., Mamidi, A., Cordenonsi, M., Montagner, M., Zacchigna, L., Adorno, M., et al., 2009. FAM/USP9x, a deubiquitinating enzyme essential for TGFbeta signaling, controls Smad4 monoubiquitination. Cell 136, 123–135.

Edmonds, M.J., Parsons, J.L., 2014. Regulation of base excision repair proteins by ubiquitylation. Exp. Cell Res. 329, 132–138.

Eichhorn, P.J., Rodon, L., Gonzalez-Junca, A., Dirac, A., Gili, M., Martinez-Saez, E., et al., 2012. USP15 stabilizes TGF-beta receptor I and promotes oncogenesis through the activation of TGF-beta signaling in glioblastoma. Nat. Med. 18, 429–435.

Fan, Y.H., Yu, Y., Mao, R.F., Tan, X.J., Xu, G.F., Zhang, H., et al., 2011. USP4 targets TAK1 to downregulate TNFalpha-induced NF-kappaB activation. Cell Death Differ. 18, 1547–1560.

Fang, X., Zhou, W., Wu, Q., Huang, Z., Shi, Y., Yang, K., et al., 2017. Deubiquitinase USP13 maintains glioblastoma stem cells by antagonizing FBXL14-mediated Myc ubiquitination. J. Exp. Med. 214, 245–267.

Fang, C.L., Lin, C.C., Chen, H.K., Hseu, Y.C., Hung, S.T., Sun, D.P., et al., 2018. Ubiquitin-specific protease 3 overexpression promotes gastric carcinogenesis and is predictive of poor patient prognosis. Cancer Sci. 109, 3438–3449.

Farshi, P., Deshmukh, R.R., Nwankwo, J.O., Arkwright, R.T., Cvek, B., Liu, J., Dou, Q.P., 2015. Deubiquitinases (DUBs) and DUB inhibitors: a patent review. Expert. Opin. Ther. Pat. 25, 1191–1208.

Fraile, J.M., Quesada, V., Rodriguez, D., Freije, J.M., Lopez-Otin, C., 2012. Deubiquitinases in cancer: new functions and therapeutic options. Oncogene 31, 2373–2388.

Fraile, J.M., Campos-Iglesias, D., Rodriguez, F., Espanol, Y., Freije, J.M., 2016. The deubiquitinase USP54 is overexpressed in colorectal cancer stem cells and promotes intestinal tumorigenesis. Oncotarget 7, 74427–74434.

Fraile, J.M., Manchado, E., Lujambio, A., Quesada, V., Campos-Iglesias, D., Webb, T.R., et al., 2017. USP39 deubiquitinase is essential for KRAS oncogene-driven cancer. J. Biol. Chem. 292, 4164–4175.

Fraile, J.M., Campos-Iglesias, D., Rodriguez, F., Astudillo, A., Vilarrasa-Blasi, R., Verdaguer-Dot, N., et al., 2018. Loss of the deubiquitinase USP36 destabilizes the RNA helicase DHX33 and causes preimplantation lethality in mice. J. Biol. Chem. 293, 2183–2194.

Freije, J.M., Fraile, J.M., Lopez-Otin, C., 2011. Protease addiction and synthetic lethality in cancer. Front. Oncol. 1, 25.

Fu, Y., Ma, G., Liu, G., Li, B., Li, H., Hao, X., Liu, L., 2018. USP14 as a novel prognostic marker promotes cisplatin resistance via Akt/ERK signaling pathways in gastric cancer. Cancer Med. 7, 5577–5588.

Garcia, D.A., Baek, C., Estrada, M.V., Tysl, T., Bennett, E.J., Yang, J., et al., 2018. USP11 enhances TGFbeta-induced epithelial-mesenchymal plasticity and human breast cancer metastasis. Mol. Cancer Res. 16, 1172–1184.

Gennaro, V.J., Stanek, T.J., Peck, A.R., Sun, Y., Wang, F., Qie, S., et al., 2018. Control of CCND1 ubiquitylation by the catalytic SAGA subunit USP22 is essential for cell cycle progression through G1 in cancer cells. Proc. Natl. Acad. Sci. U. S. A. 115, E9298–E9307.

Guervilly, J.H., Renaud, E., Takata, M., Rosselli, F., 2011. USP1 deubiquitinase maintains phosphorylated CHK1 by limiting its DDB1-dependent degradation. Hum. Mol. Genet. 20, 2171–2181.

Guo, Y., Dolinko, A.V., Chinyengetere, F., Stanton, B., Bomberger, J.M., Demidenko, E., et al., 2010. Blockade of the ubiquitin protease UBP43 destabilizes transcription factor PML/RARalpha and inhibits the growth of acute promyelocytic leukemia. Cancer Res. 70, 9875–9885.

Guo, R., Wang, X., Chou, M.M., Asmann, Y., Wenger, D.E., Al-Ibraheemi, A., et al., 2016. PPP6R3-USP6 amplification: Novel oncogenic mechanism in malignant nodular fasciitis. Genes Chromosomes Cancer 55, 640–649.

Guo, W., Ma, J., Pei, T., Zhao, T., Guo, S., Yi, X., et al., 2018. Up-regulated deubiquitinase USP4 plays an oncogenic role in melanoma. J. Cell. Mol. Med. 22, 2944–2954.

Han, C., Yang, L., Choi, H.H., Baddour, J., Achreja, A., Liu, Y., et al., 2016. Amplification of USP13 drives ovarian cancer metabolism. Nat. Commun. 7, 13525.

Hanahan, D., Weinberg, R.A., 2011. Hallmarks of cancer: the next generation. Cell 144, 646–674.

Harhaj, E.W., Dixit, V.M., 2012. Regulation of NF-kappaB by deubiquitinases. Immunol. Rev. 246, 107–124.

He, J., Zhu, Q., Wani, G., Sharma, N., Han, C., Qian, J., et al., 2014. Ubiquitin-specific protease 7 regulates nucleotide excision repair through deubiquitinating XPC protein and preventing XPC protein from undergoing ultraviolet light-induced and VCP/p97 protein-regulated proteolysis. J. Biol. Chem. 289, 27278–27289.

Hellerbrand, C., Bumes, E., Bataille, F., Dietmaier, W., Massoumi, R., Bosserhoff, A.K., 2007. Reduced expression of CYLD in human colon and hepatocellular carcinomas. Carcinogenesis 28, 21–27.

Herhaus, L., Sapkota, G.P., 2014. The emerging roles of deubiquitylating enzymes (DUBs) in the TGFbeta and BMP pathways. Cell. Signal. 26, 2186–2192.

Hock, A.K., Vigneron, A.M., Carter, S., Ludwig, R.L., Vousden, K.H., 2011. Regulation of p53 stability and function by the deubiquitinating enzyme USP42. EMBO J. 30, 4921–4930.

Hock, A.K., Vigneron, A.M., Vousden, K.H., 2014. Ubiquitin-specific peptidase 42 (USP42) functions to deubiquitylate histones and regulate transcriptional activity. J. Biol. Chem. 289, 34862–34870.

Hou, X., Wang, L., Zhang, L., Pan, X., Zhao, W., 2013. Ubiquitin-specific protease 4 promotes TNF-alpha-induced apoptosis by deubiquitination of RIP1 in head and neck squamous cell carcinoma. FEBS Lett. 587, 311–316.

Hou, K., Zhu, Z., Wang, Y., Zhang, C., Yu, S., Zhu, Q., et al., 2016. Overexpression and biological function of ubiquitin-specific protease 42 in gastric cancer. PLoS One 11, e0152997.

Hu, M., Chen, H., Han, C., Lan, J., Xu, Y., Li, C., Xue, Y., Lou, M., 2016. Expression and functional implications of USP17 in glioma. Neurosci. Lett. 616, 125–131.

Hu, W., Wei, H., Li, K., Li, P., Lin, J., Feng, R., 2017. Downregulation of USP32 inhibits cell proliferation, migration and invasion in human small cell lung cancer. Cell Prolif. 50, e12343.

Hu, T., Zhang, J., Sha, B., Li, M., Wang, L., Zhang, Y., et al., 2019. Targeting the overexpressed USP7 inhibits esophageal squamous cell carcinoma cell growth by inducing NOXA-mediated apoptosis. Mol. Carcinog. 58, 42–54.

Huang, T.T., Nijman, S.M., Mirchandani, K.D., Galardy, P.J., Cohn, M.A., Haas, W., et al., 2006. Regulation of monoubiquitinated PCNA by DUB autocleavage. Nat. Cell Biol. 8, 339–347.

Huang, X., Langelotz, C., Hetfeld-Pechoc, B.K., Schwenk, W., Dubiel, W., 2009. The COP9 signalosome mediates beta-catenin degradation by deneddylation and blocks adenomatous polyposis coli destruction via USP15. J. Mol. Biol. 391, 691–702.

Huang, X., Summers, M.K., Pham, V., Lill, J.R., Liu, J., Lee, G., et al., 2011. Deubiquitinase USP37 is activated by CDK2 to antagonize APC(CDH1) and promote S phase entry. Mol. Cell 42, 511–523.

Huang, Y., Pan, X.W., Li, L., Chen, L., Liu, X., Lu, J.L., et al., 2016. Overexpression of USP39 predicts poor prognosis and promotes tumorigenesis of prostate cancer via promoting EGFR mRNA maturation and transcription elongation. Oncotarget 7, 22016–22030.

Issaenko, O.A., Amerik, A.Y., 2012. Chalcone-based small-molecule inhibitors attenuate malignant phenotype via targeting deubiquitinating enzymes. Cell Cycle 11, 1804–1817.

Iyengar, P.V., Jaynes, P., Rodon, L., Lama, D., Law, K.P., Lim, Y.P., et al., 2015. USP15 regulates SMURF2 kinetics through C-lobe mediated deubiquitination. Sci. Rep. 5, 14733.

Jacq, X., Kemp, M., Martin, N.M., Jackson, S.P., 2013. Deubiquitylating enzymes and DNA damage response pathways. Cell Biochem. Biophys. 67, 25–43.

Jeong, M., Lee, E.W., Seong, D., Seo, J., Kim, J.H., Grootjans, S., et al., 2017. USP8 suppresses death receptor-mediated apoptosis by enhancing FLIPL stability. Oncogene 36, 458–470.

Jiang, S., Song, C., Gu, X., Wang, M., Miao, D., Lv, J., Liu, Y., 2018. Ubiquitin-specific peptidase 22 contributes to colorectal cancer stemness and chemoresistance via Wnt/beta-catenin pathway. Cell. Physiol. Biochem. 46, 1412–1422.

Jin, Q., Martinez, C.A., Arcipowski, K.M., Zhu, Y., Gutierrez-Diaz, B.T., Wang, K.K., et al., 2019. USP7 cooperates with NOTCH1 to drive the oncogenic transcriptional program in T cell leukemia. Clin. Cancer Res. 25, 222–239.

Jo, Y.S., Kim, M.S., Yoo, N.J., Lee, S.H., 2017. USP9X, a putative tumor suppressor gene, exhibits frameshift mutations in colorectal cancers. Pathol. Oncol. Res. 23, 219–220.

Joo, H.Y., Zhai, L., Yang, C., Nie, S., Erdjument-Bromage, H., Tempst, P., et al., 2007. Regulation of cell cycle progression and gene expression by H2A deubiquitination. Nature 449, 1068–1072.

Joo, H.Y., Jones, A., Yang, C., Zhai, L., Smith, A.D.T., Zhang, Z., et al., 2011. Regulation of histone H2A and H2B deubiquitination and Xenopus development by USP12 and USP46. J. Biol. Chem. 286, 7190–7201.

Jung, J.K., Jang, S.W., Kim, J.M., 2016. A novel role for the deubiquitinase USP1 in the control of centrosome duplication. Cell Cycle 15, 584–592.

Kaistha, B.P., Krattenmacher, A., Fredebohm, J., Schmidt, H., Behrens, D., Widder, M., et al., 2017. The deubiquitinating enzyme USP5 promotes pancreatic cancer via modulating cell cycle regulators. Oncotarget 8, 66215–66225.

Kapuria, V., Peterson, L.F., Fang, D., Bornmann, W.G., Talpaz, M., Donato, N.J., 2010. Deubiquitinase inhibition by small-molecule WP1130 triggers aggresome formation and tumor cell apoptosis. Cancer Res. 70, 9265–9276.

Kashiwaba, S., Kanao, R., Masuda, Y., Kusumoto-Matsuo, R., Hanaoka, F., Masutani, C., 2015. USP7 is a suppressor of PCNA ubiquitination and oxidative-stress-induced mutagenesis in human cells. Cell Rep. 13, 2072–2080.

Kastenhuber, E.R., Lowe, S.W., 2017. Putting p53 in context. Cell 170, 1062–1078.

Kategaya, L., Di Lello, P., Rouge, L., Pastor, R., Clark, K.R., Drummond, J., et al., 2017. USP7 small-molecule inhibitors interfere with ubiquitin binding. Nature 550, 534–538.

Ke, H., Augustine, C.K., Gandham, V.D., Jin, J.Y., Tyler, D.S., Akiyama, S.K., et al., 2013. CYLD inhibits melanoma growth and progression through suppression of the JNK/AP-1 and beta1-integrin signaling pathways. J. Invest. Dermatol. 133, 221–229.

Kee, Y., Huang, T.T., 2016. Role of deubiquitinating enzymes in DNA repair. Mol. Cell. Biol. 36, 524–544.

Khan, A., Giri, S., Wang, Y., Chakraborty, A., Ghosh, A.K., Anantharaman, A., et al., 2015. BEND3 represses rDNA transcription by stabilizing a NoRC component via USP21 deubiquitinase. Proc. Natl. Acad. Sci. U. S. A. 112, 8338–8343.

Khoronenkova, S.V., Dianova, I.I., Ternette, N., Kessler, B.M., Parsons, J.L., Dianov, G.L., 2012. ATM-dependent downregulation of USP7/HAUSP by PPM1G activates, response to DNA damage. Mol. Cell 45, 801–813.

Kim, J., Kim, W.J., Liu, Z., Loda, M., Freeman, M.R., 2012. The ubiquitin-specific protease USP2a enhances tumor progression by targeting cyclin A1 in bladder cancer. Cell Cycle 11, 1123–1130.

Kim, D., Hong, A., Park, H.I., Shin, W.H., Yoo, L., Jeon, S.J., et al., 2017. Deubiquitinating enzyme USP22 positively regulates c-Myc stability and tumorigenic activity in mammalian and breast cancer cells. J. Cell. Physiol. 232, 3664–3676.

Kim, J., Alavi Naini, F., Sun, Y., Ma, L., 2018. Ubiquitin-specific peptidase 2a (USP2a) deubiquitinates and stabilizes beta-catenin. Am. J. Cancer Res. 8, 1823–1836.

Kiran, S., Dar, A., Singh, S.K., Lee, K.Y., Dutta, A., 2018. The deubiquitinase USP46 is essential for proliferation and tumor growth of HPV-transformed cancers. Mol. Cell 72, 823–835. e5.

Kluge, A.F., Lagu, B.R., Maiti, P., Jaleel, M., Webb, M., Malhotra, J., et al., 2018. Novel highly selective inhibitors of ubiquitin specific protease 30 (USP30) accelerate mitophagy. Bioorg. Med. Chem. Lett. 28, 2655–2659.

Knobel, P.A., Belotserkovskaya, R., Galanty, Y., Schmidt, C.K., Jackson, S.P., Stracker, T.H., 2014. USP28 is recruited to sites of DNA damage by the tandem BRCT domains of 53BP1 but plays a minor role in double-strand break metabolism. Mol. Cell. Biol. 34, 2062–2074.

Komander, D., Rape, M., 2012. The ubiquitin code. Annu. Rev. Biochem. 81, 203–229.

Komander, D., Clague, M.J., Urbe, S., 2009. Breaking the chains: structure and function of the deubiquitinases. Nat. Rev. Mol Cell Biol. 10, 550–563.

Kon, N., Kobayashi, Y., Li, M., Brooks, C.L., Ludwig, T., Gu, W., 2010. Inactivation of HAUSP in vivo modulates p53 function. Oncogene 29, 1270–1279.

Kwon, S.K., Kim, E.H., Baek, K.H., 2017a. RNPS1 is modulated by ubiquitin-specific protease 4. FEBS Lett. 591, 369–381.

Kwon, S.K., Saindane, M., Baek, K.H., 2017b. p53 stability is regulated by diverse deubiquitinating enzymes. Biochim. Biophys. Acta Rev. Cancer 1868, 404–411.

Lamberto, I., Liu, X., Seo, H.S., Schauer, N.J., Iacob, R.E., Hu, W., et al., 2017. Structure-guided development of a potent and selective non-covalent active-site inhibitor of USP7. Cell Chem. Biol. 24, 1490–1500. e1411.

Lan, X., Atanassov, B.S., Li, W., Zhang, Y., Florens, L., Mohan, R.D., et al., 2016. USP44 is an integral component of N-CoR that contributes to gene repression by deubiquitinating histone H2B. Cell Rep. 17, 2382–2393.

Lawson, A.P., Bak, D.W., Shannon, D.A., Long, M.J.C., Vijaykumar, T., Yu, R., et al., 2017. Identification of deubiquitinase targets of isothiocyanates using SILAC-assisted quantitative mass spectrometry. Oncotarget 8, 51296–51316.

Lee, S.C., Abdel-Wahab, O., 2016. Therapeutic targeting of splicing in cancer. Nat. Med. 22, 976–986.

Li, J., Olson, L.M., Zhang, Z., Li, L., Bidder, M., Nguyen, L., et al., 2008. Differential display identifies overexpression of the USP36 gene, encoding a deubiquitinating enzyme, in ovarian cancer. Int. J. Med. Sci. 5, 133–142.

Li, J., D'Angiolella, V., Seeley, E.S., Kim, S., Kobayashi, T., Fu, W., et al., 2013a. USP33 regulates centrosome biogenesis via deubiquitination of the centriolar protein CP110. Nature 495, 255–259.

Li, X., Stevens, P.D., Yang, H., Gulhati, P., Wang, W., Evers, B.M., et al., 2013b. The deubiquitination enzyme USP46 functions as a tumor suppressor by controlling PHLPP-dependent attenuation of Akt signaling in colon cancer. Oncogene 32, 471–478.

Li, Z., Hao, Q., Luo, J., Xiong, J., Zhang, S., Wang, T., et al., 2016. USP4 inhibits p53 and NF-kappaB through deubiquitinating and stabilizing HDAC2. Oncogene 35, 2902–2912.

Li, X., Huang, Q., Long, H., Zhang, P., Su, H., Liu, J., 2019. A new gold(I) complex-Au(PPh3)PT is a deubiquitinase inhibitor and inhibits tumor growth. EBioMedicine 39, 159–172.

Liang, Q., Dexheimer, T.S., Zhang, P., Rosenthal, A.S., Villamil, M.A., You, C., et al., 2014. A selective USP1-UAF1 inhibitor links deubiquitination to DNA damage responses. Nat. Chem. Biol. 10, 298–304.

Liang, J., Zhang, X.L., Li, S., Xie, S., Wang, W.F., Yu, R.T., 2018. Ubiquitin-specific protease 22 promotes the proliferation, migration and invasion of glioma cells. Cancer Biomark. 23, 381–389.

Lill, J.R., Wertz, I.E., 2014. Toward understanding ubiquitin-modifying enzymes: from pharmacological targeting to proteomics. Trends Pharmacol. Sci. 35, 187–207.

Lim, J.H., Jono, H., Komatsu, K., Woo, C.H., Lee, J., Miyata, M., et al., 2012. CYLD negatively regulates transforming growth factor-beta-signalling via deubiquitinating Akt. Nat. Commun. 3, 771. https://doi.org/10.1038/ncomms1776.

Lin, Z., Yang, H., Kong, Q., Li, J., Lee, S.M., Gao, B., et al., 2012. USP22 antagonizes p53 transcriptional activation by deubiquitinating Sirt1 to suppress cell apoptosis and is required for mouse embryonic development. Mol. Cell 46, 484–494.

Lin, Z., Yang, H., Tan, C., Li, J., Liu, Z., Quan, Q., et al., 2013. USP10 antagonizes c-Myc transcriptional activation through SIRT6 stabilization to suppress tumor formation. Cell Rep. 5, 1639–1649.

Liu, J., Chung, H.J., Vogt, M., Jin, Y., Malide, D., He, L., et al., 2011a. JTV1 co-activates FBP to induce USP29 transcription and stabilize p53 in response to oxidative stress. EMBO J. 30, 846–858.

Liu, J., Xia, H., Kim, M., Xu, L., Li, Y., Zhang, L., et al., 2011b. Beclin1 controls the levels of p53 by regulating the deubiquitination activity of USP10 and USP13. Cell 147, 223–234.

Liu, X., Li, H., Zhong, B., Blonska, M., Gorjestani, S., Yan, M., et al., 2013a. USP18 inhibits NF-kappaB and NFAT activation during Th17 differentiation by deubiquitinating the TAK1-TAB1 complex. J. Exp. Med. 210, 1575–1590.

Liu, Z., Zanata, S.M., Kim, J., Peterson, M.A., Di Vizio, D., Chirieac, L.R., et al., 2013b. The ubiquitin-specific protease USP2a prevents endocytosis-mediated EGFR degradation. Oncogene 32, 1660–1669.

Long, L., Thelen, J.P., Furgason, M., Haj-Yahya, M., Brik, A., Cheng, D., et al., 2014. The U4/U6 recycling factor SART3 has histone chaperone activity and associates with USP15 to regulate H2B deubiquitination. J. Biol. Chem. 289, 8916–8930.

Long, M.J.C., Lawson, A.P., Baggio, R., Qian, Y., Rozhansky, L., Fasci, D., et al., 2019. Diarylcarbonates are a new class of deubiquitinating enzyme inhibitor. Bioorg. Med. Chem. Lett. 29, 204–211.

Love, K.R., Catic, A., Schlieker, C., Ploegh, H.L., 2007. Mechanisms, biology and inhibitors of deubiquitinating enzymes. Nat. Chem. Biol. 3, 697–705.

Lu, Y., Adegoke, O.A., Nepveu, A., Nakayama, K.I., Bedard, N., Cheng, D., et al., 2009. USP19 deubiquitinating enzyme supports cell proliferation by stabilizing KPC1, a ubiquitin ligase for p27Kip1. Mol. Cell. Biol. 29, 547–558.

Lu, Y., Bedard, N., Chevalier, S., Wing, S.S., 2011. Identification of distinctive patterns of USP19-mediated growth regulation in normal and malignant cells. PLoS One 6, e15936.

Lu, C., Ning, Z., Wang, A., Chen, D., Liu, X., Xia, T., et al., 2018. USP10 suppresses tumor progression by inhibiting mTOR activation in hepatocellular carcinoma. Cancer Lett. 436, 139–148.

Lui, T.T., Lacroix, C., Ahmed, S.M., Goldenberg, S.J., Leach, C.A., Daulat, A.M., et al., 2011. The ubiquitin-specific protease USP34 regulates axin stability and Wnt/beta-catenin signaling. Mol. Cell. Biol. 31, 2053–2065.

Luise, C., Capra, M., Donzelli, M., Mazzarol, G., Jodice, M.G., Nuciforo, P., et al., 2011. An atlas of altered expression of deubiquitinating enzymes in human cancer. PLoS One 6, e15891.

Luo, K., Li, Y., Yin, Y., Li, L., Wu, C., Chen, Y., et al., 2017. USP49 negatively regulates tumorigenesis and chemoresistance through FKBP51-AKT signaling. EMBO J. 36, 1434–1446.

Madan, B., Walker, M.P., Young, R., Quick, L., Orgel, K.A., Ryan, M., et al., 2016. USP6 oncogene promotes Wnt signaling by deubiquitylating Frizzleds. Proc. Natl. Acad. Sci. U. S. A. 113, E2945–E2954.

Maertens, G.N., El Messaoudi-Aubert, S., Elderkin, S., Hiom, K., Peters, G., 2010. Ubiquitin-specific proteases 7 and 11 modulate Polycomb regulation of the INK4a tumour suppressor. EMBO J. 29, 2553–2565.

Mahul-Mellier, A.L., Pazarentzos, E., Datler, C., Iwasawa, R., AbuAli, G., Lin, B., et al., 2012. De-ubiquitinating protease USP2a targets RIP1 and TRAF2 to mediate cell death by TNF. Cell Death Differ. 19, 891–899.

Martin, Y., Cabrera, E., Amoedo, H., Hernandez-Perez, S., Dominguez-Kelly, R., Freire, R., 2015. USP29 controls the stability of checkpoint adaptor Claspin by deubiquitination. Oncogene 34, 1058–1063.

Mattiroli, F., Vissers, J.H., van Dijk, W.J., Ikpa, P., Citterio, E., Vermeulen, W., et al., 2012. RNF168 ubiquitinates K13-15 on H2A/H2AX to drive DNA damage signaling. Cell 150, 1182–1195.

Maurer, T., Wertz, I.E., 2016. Length matters: MINDY is a new deubiquitinase family that preferentially cleaves long polyubiquitin chains. Mol. Cell 63, 4–6.

McFarlane, C., Kelvin, A.A., de la Vega, M., Govender, U., Scott, C.J., Burrows, J.F., et al., 2010. The deubiquitinating enzyme USP17 is highly expressed in tumor biopsies, is cell cycle regulated, and is required for G1-S progression. Cancer Res. 70, 3329–3339.

McGarry, E., Gaboriau, D., Rainey, M.D., Restuccia, U., Bachi, A., Santocanale, C., 2016. The deubiquitinase USP9X maintains DNA replication fork stability and DNA damage checkpoint responses by regulating CLASPIN during S-phase. Cancer Res. 76, 2384–2393.

Metzig, M., Nickles, D., Falschlehner, C., Lehmann-Koch, J., Straub, B.K., Roth, W., et al., 2011. An RNAi screen identifies USP2 as a factor required for TNF-alpha-induced NF-kappaB signaling. Int. J. Cancer 129, 607–618.

Millard, S.M., Wood, S.A., 2006. Riding the DUBway: regulation of protein trafficking by deubiquitylating enzymes. J. Cell Biol. 173, 463–468.

Mistry, H., Hsieh, G., Buhrlage, S.J., Huang, M., Park, E., Cuny, G.D., et al., 2013. Small-molecule inhibitors of USP1 target ID1 degradation in leukemic cells. Mol. Cancer Ther. 12, 2651–2662.

Moquin, D.M., McQuade, T., Chan, F.K., 2013. CYLD deubiquitinates RIP1 in the TNFalpha-induced necrosome to facilitate kinase activation and programmed necrosis. PLoS One 8, e76841.

Mosbech, A., Lukas, C., Bekker-Jensen, S., Mailand, N., 2013. The deubiquitylating enzyme USP44 counteracts the DNA double-strand break response mediated by the RNF8 and RNF168 ubiquitin ligases. J. Biol. Chem. 288, 16579–16587.

Murai, J., Yang, K., Dejsuphong, D., Hirota, K., Takeda, S., D'Andrea, A.D., 2011. The USP1/UAF1 complex promotes double-strand break repair through homologous recombination. Mol. Cell. Biol. 31, 2462–2469.

Mustachio, L.M., Lu, Y., Tafe, L.J., Memoli, V., Rodriguez-Canales, J., Mino, B., et al., 2017. Deubiquitinase USP18 loss mislocalizes and destabilizes KRAS in lung cancer. Mol. Cancer Res. 15, 905–914.

Nakagawa, T., Kajitani, T., Togo, S., Masuko, N., Ohdan, H., Hishikawa, Y., et al., 2008. Deubiquitylation of histone H2A activates transcriptional initiation via trans-histone cross-talk with H3K4 di- and trimethylation. Genes Dev. 22, 37–49.

Nguyen, L.K., Kolch, W., Kholodenko, B.N., 2013. When ubiquitination meets phosphorylation: a systems biology perspective of EGFR/MAPK signalling. Cell Commun. Signal. 11, 52.

Nicholson, B., Leach, C.A., Goldenberg, S.J., Francis, D.M., Kodrasov, M.P., Tian, X., et al., 2008. Characterization of ubiquitin and ubiquitin-like-protein isopeptidase activities. Protein Sci. 17, 1035–1043.

Nicklas, S., Hillje, A.L., Okawa, S., Rudolph, I.M., Collmann, F.M., van Wuellen, T., et al., 2019. A complex of the ubiquitin ligase TRIM32 and the deubiquitinase USP7 balances the level of c-Myc ubiquitination and thereby determines neural stem cell fate specification. Cell Death Differ. 26, 728–740.

Nijman, S.M., Huang, T.T., Dirac, A.M., Brummelkamp, T.R., Kerkhoven, R.M., D'Andrea, A.D., et al., 2005. The deubiquitinating enzyme USP1 regulates the Fanconi anemia pathway. Mol. Cell 17, 331–339.

Ning, Z., Wang, A., Liang, J., Xie, Y., Liu, J., Feng, L., et al., 2014. USP22 promotes the G1/S phase transition by upregulating FoxM1 expression via beta-catenin nuclear localization and is associated with poor prognosis in stage II pancreatic ductal adenocarcinoma. Int. J. Oncol. 45, 1594–1608.

Niu, J., Shi, Y., Xue, J., Miao, R., Huang, S., Wang, T., et al., 2013. USP10 inhibits genotoxic NF-kappaB activation by MCPIP1-facilitated deubiquitination of NEMO. EMBO J. 32, 3206–3219.

Novellasdemunt, L., Foglizzo, V., Cuadrado, L., Antas, P., Kucharska, A., Encheva, V., et al., 2017. USP7 is a tumor-specific WNT activator for APC-mutated colorectal cancer by mediating beta-catenin deubiquitination. Cell Rep. 21, 612–627.

Okada, K., Ye, Y.Q., Taniguchi, K., Yoshida, A., Akiyama, T., Yoshioka, Y., et al., 2013. Vialinin A is a ubiquitin-specific peptidase inhibitor. Bioorg. Med. Chem. Lett. 23, 4328–4331.

Oliveira, A.M., Chou, M.M., 2014. USP6-induced neoplasms: the biologic spectrum of aneurysmal bone cyst and nodular fasciitis. Hum. Pathol. 45, 1–11.

Orthwein, A., Noordermeer, S.M., Wilson, M.D., Landry, S., Enchev, R.I., Sherker, A., et al., 2015. A mechanism for the suppression of homologous recombination in G1 cells. Nature 528, 422–426.

Padmanabhan, A., Candelaria, N., Wong, K.K., Nikolai, B.C., Lonard, D.M., O'Malley, B.W., et al., 2018. USP15-dependent lysosomal pathway controls p53-R175H turnover in ovarian cancer cells. Nat. Commun. 9. Article No. 1270.

Pan, J., Deng, Q., Jiang, C., Wang, X., Niu, T., Li, H., et al., 2015. USP37 directly deubiquitinates and stabilizes c-Myc in lung cancer. Oncogene 34, 3957–3967.

Park, J., Kwon, M.S., Kim, E.E., Lee, H., Song, E.J., 2018. USP35 regulates mitotic progression by modulating the stability of Aurora B. Nat. Commun. 9. Article No. 688.

Parsons, J.L., Dianova, I.I., Khoronenkova, S.V., Edelmann, M.J., Kessler, B.M., Dianov, G.L., 2011. USP47 is a deubiquitylating enzyme that regulates base excision repair by controlling steady-state levels of DNA polymerase beta. Mol. Cell 41, 609–615.

Pelletier, J., Thomas, G., Volarevic, S., 2018. Ribosome biogenesis in cancer: new players and therapeutic avenues. Nat. Rev. Cancer 18, 51–63.

Perez-Mancera, P.A., Rust, A.G., van der Weyden, L., Kristiansen, G., Li, A., Sarver, A.L., et al., 2012. The deubiquitinase USP9X suppresses pancreatic ductal adenocarcinoma. Nature 486, 266–270.

Perez-Oliva, A.B., Lachaud, C., Szyniarowski, P., Munoz, I., Macartney, T., Hickson, I., et al., 2015. USP45 deubiquitylase controls ERCC1-XPF endonuclease-mediated DNA damage responses. EMBO J. 34, 326–343.

Peterson, L.F., Sun, H., Liu, Y., Potu, H., Kandarpa, M., Ermann, M., et al., 2015. Targeting deubiquitinase activity with a novel small-molecule inhibitor as therapy for B-cell malignancies. Blood 125, 3588–3597.

Popov, N., Wanzel, M., Madiredjo, M., Zhang, D., Beijersbergen, R., Bernards, R., et al., 2007. The ubiquitin-specific protease USP28 is required for MYC stability. Nat. Cell Biol. 9, 765–774.

Potu, H., Peterson, L.F., Kandarpa, M., Pal, A., Sun, H., Durham, A., et al., 2017. Usp9x regulates Ets-1 ubiquitination and stability to control NRAS expression and tumorigenicity in melanoma. Nat. Commun. 8, 14449.

Pozhidaeva, A., Valles, G., Wang, F., Wu, J., Sterner, D.E., Nguyen, P., et al., 2017. USP7-specific inhibitors target and modify the enzyme's active site via distinct chemical mechanisms. Cell Chem. Biol. 24, 1501–1512. e1505.

Pringle, L.M., Young, R., Quick, L., Riquelme, D.N., Oliveira, A.M., May, M.J., et al., 2012. Atypical mechanism of NF-kappaB activation by TRE17/ubiquitin-specific protease 6 (USP6) oncogene and its requirement in tumorigenesis. Oncogene 31, 3525–3535.

Priolo, C., Tang, D., Brahamandan, M., Benassi, B., Sicinska, E., Ogino, S., et al., 2006. The isopeptidase USP2a protects human prostate cancer from apoptosis. Cancer Res. 66, 8625–8632.

Qian, J., Pentz, K., Zhu, Q., Wang, Q., He, J., Srivastava, A.K., et al., 2015. USP7 modulates UV-induced PCNA monoubiquitination by regulating DNA polymerase eta stability. Oncogene 34, 4791–4796.

Qin, D., Wang, W., Lei, H., Luo, H., Cai, H., Tang, C., et al., 2016. CDDO-Me reveals USP7 as a novel target in ovarian cancer cells. Oncotarget 7, 77096–77109.

Qin, T., Li, B., Feng, X., Fan, S., Liu, L., Liu, D., et al., 2018. Abnormally elevated USP37 expression in breast cancer stem cells regulates stemness, epithelial-mesenchymal transition and cisplatin sensitivity. J. Exp. Clin. Cancer Res. 37, 287.

Quesada, V., Diaz-Perales, A., Gutierrez-Fernandez, A., Garabaya, C., Cal, S., Lopez-Otin, C., 2004. Cloning and enzymatic analysis of 22 novel human ubiquitin-specific proteases. Biochem. Biophys. Res. Commun. 314, 54–62.

Reiley, W.W., Jin, W., Lee, A.J., Wright, A., Wu, X., Tewalt, E.F., et al., 2007. Deubiquitinating enzyme CYLD negatively regulates the ubiquitin-dependent kinase Tak1 and prevents abnormal T cell responses. J. Exp. Med. 204, 1475–1485.

Reincke, M., Sbiera, S., Hayakawa, A., Theodoropoulou, M., Osswald, A., Beuschlein, F., et al., 2015. Mutations in the deubiquitinase gene USP8 cause Cushing's disease. Nat. Genet. 47, 31–38.

Reverdy, C., Conrath, S., Lopez, R., Planquette, C., Atmanene, C., Collura, V., et al., 2012. Discovery of specific inhibitors of human USP7/HAUSP deubiquitinating enzyme. Chem. Biol. 19, 467–477.

Schoenfeld, A.R., Apgar, S., Dolios, G., Wang, R., Aaronson, S.A., 2004. BRCA2 is ubiquitinated in vivo and interacts with USP11, a deubiquitinating enzyme that exhibits prosurvival function in the cellular response to DNA damage. Mol. Cell. Biol. 24, 7444–7455.

Schweitzer, K., Naumann, M., 2015. CSN-associated USP48 confers stability to nuclear NF-kappaB/RelA by trimming K48-linked Ub-chains. Biochim. Biophys. Acta 1853, 453–469.

Schweitzer, K., Bozko, P.M., Dubiel, W., Naumann, M., 2007. CSN controls NF-kappaB by deubiquitinylation of IkappaBalpha. EMBO J. 26, 1532–1541.

Sgorbissa, A., Tomasella, A., Potu, H., Manini, I., Brancolini, C., 2011. Type I IFNs signaling and apoptosis resistance in glioblastoma cells. Apoptosis 16, 1229–1244.

Shah, S.P., Morin, R.D., Khattra, J., Prentice, L., Pugh, T., Burleigh, A., et al., 2009. Mutational evolution in a lobular breast tumour profiled at single nucleotide resolution. Nature 461, 809–813.

Shan, J., Zhao, W., Gu, W., 2009. Suppression of cancer cell growth by promoting cyclin D1 degradation. Mol. Cell 36, 469–476.

Sharma, A.K., Hendzel, M.J., 2019. The relationship between histone posttranslational modification and DNA damage signaling and repair. Int. J. Radiat. Biol. 95, 382–393.

Sharma, N., Zhu, Q., Wani, G., He, J., Wang, Q.E., Wani, A.A., 2014. USP3 counteracts RNF168 via deubiquitinating H2A and gammaH2AX at lysine 13 and 15. Cell Cycle 13, 106–114.

Shi, J., Liu, Y., Xu, X., Zhang, W., Yu, T., Jia, J., et al., 2015. Deubiquitinase USP47/UBP64E regulates beta-catenin ubiquitination and degradation and plays a positive role in Wnt signaling. Mol. Cell. Biol. 35, 3301–3311.

Sloane, M.A., Wong, J.W., Perera, D., Nunez, A.C., Pimanda, J.E., Hawkins, N.J., et al., 2014. Epigenetic inactivation of the candidate tumor suppressor USP44 is a frequent and early event in colorectal neoplasia. Epigenetics 9, 1092–1100.

Song, M.S., Salmena, L., Carracedo, A., Egia, A., Lo-Coco, F., Teruya-Feldstein, J., et al., 2008. The deubiquitinylation and localization of PTEN are regulated by a HAUSP-PML network. Nature 455, 813–817.

Song, C., Liu, W., Li, J., 2017. USP17 is upregulated in osteosarcoma and promotes cell proliferation, metastasis, and epithelial-mesenchymal transition through stabilizing SMAD4. Tumour Biol. 39. 1010428317717138.

Stegmeier, F., Rape, M., Draviam, V.M., Nalepa, G., Sowa, M.E., Ang, X.L., et al., 2007a. Anaphase initiation is regulated by antagonistic ubiquitination and deubiquitination activities. Nature 446, 876–881.

Stegmeier, F., Sowa, M.E., Nalepa, G., Gygi, S.P., Harper, J.W., Elledge, S.J., 2007b. The tumor suppressor CYLD regulates entry into mitosis. Proc. Natl. Acad. Sci. U. S. A. 104, 8869–8874.

Stevenson, L.F., Sparks, A., Allende-Vega, N., Xirodimas, D.P., Lane, D.P., Saville, M.K., 2007. The deubiquitinating enzyme USP2a regulates the p53 pathway by targeting Mdm2. EMBO J. 26, 976–986.

Stockum, A., Snijders, A.P., Maertens, G.N., 2018. USP11 deubiquitinates RAE1 and plays a key role in bipolar spindle formation. PLoS One 13, e0190513.

Su, D., Ma, S., Shan, L., Wang, Y., Wang, Y., Cao, C., et al., 2018. Ubiquitin-specific protease 7 sustains DNA damage response and promotes cervical carcinogenesis. J. Clin. Invest. 128, 4280–4296.

Sun, W., Tan, X., Shi, Y., Xu, G., Mao, R., Gu, X., et al., 2010. USP11 negatively regulates TNFalpha-induced NF-kappaB activation by targeting on IkappaBalpha. Cell. Signal. 22, 386–394.

Sun, X.X., He, X., Yin, L., Komada, M., Sears, R.C., Dai, M.S., 2015. The nucleolar ubiquitin-specific protease USP36 deubiquitinates and stabilizes c-Myc. Proc. Natl. Acad. Sci. U. S. A. 112, 3734–3739.

Sun, J., Li, T., Zhao, Y., Huang, L., Sun, H., Wu, H., et al., 2018. USP10 inhibits lung cancer cell growth and invasion by upregulating PTEN. Mol. Cell. Biochem. 441, 1–7.

Takayama, K.I., Suzuki, T., Fujimura, T., Takahashi, S., Inoue, S., 2018. Association of USP10 with G3BP2 inhibits p53 signaling and contributes to poor outcome in prostate cancer. Mol. Cancer Res. 16, 846–856.

Tan, Y., Zhou, G., Wang, X., Chen, W., Gao, H., 2018. USP18 promotes breast cancer growth by upregulating EGFR and activating the AKT/Skp2 pathway. Int. J. Oncol. 53, 371–383.

Tao, B.B., He, H., Shi, X.H., Wang, C.L., Li, W.Q., Li, B., et al., 2013. Up-regulation of USP2a and FASN in gliomas correlates strongly with glioma grade. J. Clin. Neurosci. 20, 717–720.

Tauriello, D.V., Haegebarth, A., Kuper, I., Edelmann, M.J., Henraat, M., Canninga-van Dijk, M.R., et al., 2010. Loss of the tumor suppressor CYLD enhances Wnt/beta-catenin signaling through K63-linked ubiquitination of Dvl. Mol. Cell 37, 607–619.

Tavana, O., Li, D., Dai, C., Lopez, G., Banerjee, D., Kon, N., et al., 2016. HAUSP deubiquitinates and stabilizes N-Myc in neuroblastoma. Nat. Med. 22, 1180–1186.

Tu, R., Kang, W., Yang, X., Zhang, Q., Xie, X., Liu, W., et al., 2018. USP49 participates in the DNA damage response by forming a positive feedback loop with p53. Cell. Death Dis. 9, 553.

Turnbull, A.P., Ioannidis, S., Krajewski, W.W., Pinto-Fernandez, A., Heride, C., Martin, A.C.L., et al., 2017. Molecular basis of USP7 inhibition by selective small-molecule inhibitors. Nature 550, 481–486.

Uras, I.Z., List, T., Nijman, S.M., 2012. Ubiquitin-specific protease 4 inhibits mono-ubiquitination of the master growth factor signaling kinase PDK1. PLoS One 7, e31003.

van der Horst, A., de Vries-Smits, A.M., Brenkman, A.B., van Triest, M.H., van den Broek, N., Colland, F., et al., 2006. FOXO4 transcriptional activity is regulated by monoubiquitination and USP7/HAUSP. Nat. Cell Biol. 8, 1064–1073.

van Leuken, R.J., Luna-Vargas, M.P., Sixma, T.K., Wolthuis, R.M., Medema, R.H., 2008. Usp39 is essential for mitotic spindle checkpoint integrity and controls mRNA-levels of aurora B. Cell Cycle 7, 2710–2719.

van Twest, S., Murphy, V.J., Hodson, C., Tan, W., Swuec, P., O'Rourke, J.J., et al., 2017. Mechanism of ubiquitination and deubiquitination in the Fanconi anemia pathway. Mol. Cell 65, 247–259.

Vishnoi, M., Boral, D., Liu, H., Sprouse, M.L., Yin, W., Goswami-Sewell, D., et al., 2018. Targeting USP7 identifies a metastasis-competent state within bone marrow-resident melanoma CTCs. Cancer Res. 78, 5349–5362.

Wang, W., Huang, X., Xin, H.B., Fu, M., Xue, A., Wu, Z.H., 2015. TRAF family member-associated NF-kappaB activator (TANK) inhibits genotoxic nuclear factor kappaB activation by facilitating deubiquitinase USP10-dependent deubiquitination of TRAF6 ligase. J. Biol. Chem. 290, 13372–13385.

Wang, Q., Ma, S., Song, N., Li, X., Liu, L., Yang, S., et al., 2016a. Stabilization of histone demethylase PHF8 by USP7 promotes breast carcinogenesis. J. Clin. Invest. 126, 2205–2220.

Wang, Y.C., Wang, S.A., Chen, P.H., Hsu, T.I., Yang, W.B., Chuang, Y.P., et al., 2016b. Variants of ubiquitin-specific peptidase 24 play a crucial role in lung cancer malignancy. Oncogene 35, 3669–3680.

Wang, Z., Zhang, H., Liu, J., Cheruiyot, A., Lee, J.H., Ordog, T., et al., 2016c. USP51 deubiquitylates H2AK13,15ub and regulates DNA damage response. Genes Dev. 30, 946–959.

Wang, F., Wang, L., Wu, J., Sokirniy, I., Nguyen, P., Bregnard, T., et al., 2017a. Active site-targeted covalent irreversible inhibitors of USP7 impair the functions of Foxp3+ T-regulatory cells by promoting ubiquitination of Tip60. PLoS One 12, e0189744.

Wang, Q., Tang, Y., Xu, Y., Xu, S., Jiang, Y., Dong, Q., et al., 2017b. The X-linked deubiquitinase USP9X is an integral component of centrosome. J. Biol. Chem. 292, 12874–12884.

Wang, X., Liu, Z., Zhang, L., Yang, Z., Chen, X., Luo, J., et al., 2018a. Targeting deubiquitinase USP28 for cancer therapy. Cell Death Dis. 9, 186.

Wang, X., Zhang, Q., Wang, Y., Zhuang, H., Chen, B., 2018b. Clinical significance of ubiquitin specific protease 7 (USP7) in predicting prognosis of hepatocellular carcinoma and its functional mechanisms. Med. Sci. Monit. 24, 1742–1750.

Wei, T., Biskup, E., Gjerdrum, L.M., Niazi, O., Odum, N., Gniadecki, R., 2016. Ubiquitin-specific protease 2 decreases p53-dependent apoptosis in cutaneous T-cell lymphoma. Oncotarget 7, 48391–48400.

Weisberg, E.L., Schauer, N.J., Yang, J., Lamberto, I., Doherty, L., Bhatt, S., et al., 2017. Inhibition of USP10 induces degradation of oncogenic FLT3. Nat. Chem. Biol. 13, 1207–1215.

Wilkinson, K.D., 1997. Regulation of ubiquitin-dependent processes by deubiquitinating enzymes. FASEB J. 11, 1245–1256.

Wiltshire, T.D., Lovejoy, C.A., Wang, T., Xia, F., O'Connor, M.J., Cortez, D., 2010. Sensitivity to poly(ADP-ribose) polymerase (PARP) inhibition identifies ubiquitin-specific peptidase 11 (USP11) as a regulator of DNA double-strand break repair. J. Biol. Chem. 285, 14565–14571.

Wrigley, J.D., Gavory, G., Simpson, I., Preston, M., Plant, H., Bradley, J., et al., 2017. Identification and characterization of dual inhibitors of the USP25/28 deubiquitinating enzyme subfamily. ACS Chem. Biol. 12, 3113–3125.

Xia, Y., Shen, S., Verma, I.M., 2014. NF-kappaB, an active player in human cancers. Cancer Immunol. Res. 2, 823–830.

Xiao, N., Li, H., Luo, J., Wang, R., Chen, H., Chen, J., et al., 2012. Ubiquitin-specific protease 4 (USP4) targets TRAF2 and TRAF6 for deubiquitination and inhibits TNFalpha-induced cancer cell migration. Biochem. J. 441, 979–986.

Xiao, H., Wang, L.M., Luo, Y., Lai, X., Li, C., Shi, J., et al., 2016. Mutations in epigenetic regulators are involved in acute lymphoblastic leukemia relapse following allogeneic hematopoietic stem cell transplantation. Oncotarget 7, 2696–2708.

Xing, C., Lu, X.X., Guo, P.D., Shen, T., Zhang, S., He, X.S., et al., 2016. Ubiquitin-specific protease 4-mediated deubiquitination and stabilization of PRL-3 is required for potentiating colorectal oncogenesis. Cancer Res. 76, 83–95.

Xu, M., Takanashi, M., Oikawa, K., Tanaka, M., Nishi, H., Isaka, K., et al., 2009. USP15 plays an essential role for caspase-3 activation during Paclitaxel-induced apoptosis. Biochem. Biophys. Res. Commun. 388, 366–371.

Xu, G., Tan, X., Wang, H., Sun, W., Shi, Y., Burlingame, S., et al., 2010. Ubiquitin-specific peptidase 21 inhibits tumor necrosis factor alpha-induced nuclear factor kappaB activation via binding to and deubiquitinating receptor-interacting protein 1. J. Biol. Chem. 285, 969–978.

Xu, D., Liu, J., Fu, T., Shan, B., Qian, L., Pan, L., et al., 2017a. USP25 regulates Wnt signaling by controlling the stability of tankyrases. Genes Dev. 31, 1024–1035.

Xu, X., Liu, J., Shen, C., Ding, L., Zhong, F., Ouyang, Y., et al., 2017b. The role of ubiquitin-specific protease 14 (USP14) in cell adhesion-mediated drug resistance (CAM-DR) of multiple myeloma cells. Eur. J. Haematol. 98, 4–12.

Yang, Y., Hou, J.Q., Qu, L.Y., Wang, G.Q., Ju, H.W., Zhao, Z.W., et al., 2007. Differential expression of USP2, USP14 and UBE4A between ovarian serous cystadenocarcinoma and adjacent normal tissues. Chin. J. Cell. Mol. Immunol. 23, 504–506.

Yang, Z., Huo, S., Shan, Y., Liu, H., Xu, Y., Yao, K., et al., 2012. STAT3 repressed USP7 expression is crucial for colon cancer development. FEBS Lett. 586, 3013–3017.

Yang, Y., Liu, M., Li, D., Ran, J., Gao, J., Suo, S., et al., 2014. CYLD regulates spindle orientation by stabilizing astral microtubules and promoting dishevelled-NuMA-dynein/dynactin complex formation. Proc. Natl. Acad. Sci. U. S. A. 111, 2158–2163.

Yang, Z., Xian, H., Hu, J., Tian, S., Qin, Y., Wang, R.F., et al., 2015. USP18 negatively regulates NF-kappaB signaling by targeting TAK1 and NEMO for deubiquitination through distinct mechanisms. Sci. Rep. 5, 12738. https://doi.org/10.1038/srep12738.

Yang, B., Zhang, S., Wang, Z., Yang, C., Ouyang, W., Zhou, F., et al., 2016. Deubiquitinase USP9X deubiquitinates beta-catenin and promotes high grade glioma cell growth. Oncotarget 7, 79515–79525.

Ye, Y., Rape, M., 2009. Building ubiquitin chains: E2 enzymes at work. Nat. Rev. Mol. Cell. Biol. 10, 755–764.

Yeasmin Khusbu, F., Chen, F.Z., Chen, H.C., 2018. Targeting ubiquitin specific protease 7 in cancer: a deubiquitinase with great prospects. Cell Biochem. Funct. 36, 244–254.

Yeh, C., Coyaud, E., Bashkurov, M., van der Lelij, P., Cheung, S.W., Peters, J.M., et al., 2015. The deubiquitinase USP37 regulates chromosome cohesion and mitotic progression. Curr. Biol. 25, 2290–2299.

Yuan, J., Luo, K., Zhang, L., Cheville, J.C., Lou, Z., 2010. USP10 regulates p53 localization and stability by deubiquitinating p53. Cell 140, 384–396.

Yuan, X., Sun, X., Shi, X., Jiang, C., Yu, D., Zhang, W., et al., 2015. USP39 promotes the growth of human hepatocellular carcinoma in vitro and in vivo. Oncol. Rep. 34, 823–832.

Yue, W., Chen, Z., Liu, H., Yan, C., Chen, M., Feng, D., et al., 2014. A small natural molecule promotes mitochondrial fusion through inhibition of the deubiquitinase USP30. Cell Res. 24, 482–496.

Yun, S.I., Kim, H.H., Yoon, J.H., Park, W.S., Hahn, M.J., Kim, H.C., et al., 2015. Ubiquitin specific protease 4 positively regulates the WNT/beta-catenin signaling in colorectal cancer. Mol. Oncol. 9, 1834–1851.

Zagaria, A., Anelli, L., Coccaro, N., Tota, G., Casieri, P., Cellamare, et al.., 2014. 5′RUNX1-3′USP42 chimeric gene in acute myeloid leukemia can occur through an insertion mechanism rather than translocation and may be mediated by genomic segmental duplications. Mol. Cytogenet. 7, 66, https://doi.org/10.1186/s13039-014-0066-7.

Zaman, M.M., Nomura, T., Takagi, T., Okamura, T., Jin, W., Shinagawa, T., et al., 2013. Ubiquitination-deubiquitination by the TRIM27-USP7 complex regulates tumor necrosis factor alpha-induced apoptosis. Mol. Cell. Biol. 33, 4971–4984.

Zhan, M., Sun, X., Liu, J., Li, Y., Li, Y., He, X., et al., 2017a. Usp7 promotes medulloblastoma cell survival and metastasis by activating Shh pathway. Biochem. Biophys. Res. Commun. 484, 429–434.

Zhan, T., Rindtorff, N., Boutros, M., 2017b. Wnt signaling in cancer. Oncogene 36, 1461–1473.

Zhang, L., Gong, F., 2016. The emerging role of deubiquitination in nucleotide excision repair. DNA Repair (Amst) 44, 118–122.

Zhang, D., Zaugg, K., Mak, T.W., Elledge, S.J., 2006. A role for the deubiquitinating enzyme USP28 in control of the DNA-damage response. Cell 126, 529–542.

Zhang, X.Y., Pfeiffer, H.K., Thorne, A.W., McMahon, S.B., 2008a. USP22, an hSAGA subunit and potential cancer stem cell marker, reverses the polycomb-catalyzed ubiquitylation of histone H2A. Cell Cycle 7, 1522–1524.

Zhang, X.Y., Varthi, M., Sykes, S.M., Phillips, C., Warzecha, C., Zhu, W., et al., 2008b. The putative cancer stem cell marker USP22 is a subunit of the human SAGA complex required for activated transcription and cell-cycle progression. Mol. Cell 29, 102–111.

Zhang, C., Cai, T.Y., Zhu, H., Yang, L.Q., Jiang, H., Dong, X.W., et al., 2011a. Synergistic antitumor activity of gemcitabine and ABT-737 in vitro and in vivo through disrupting the interaction of USP9X and Mcl-1. Mol. Cancer Ther. 10, 1264–1275.

Zhang, X., Berger, F.G., Yang, J., Lu, X., 2011b. USP4 inhibits p53 through deubiquitinating and stabilizing ARF-BP1. EMBO J. 30, 2177–2189.

Zhang, Y., van Deursen, J., Galardy, P.J., 2011c. Overexpression of ubiquitin specific protease 44 (USP44) induces chromosomal instability and is frequently observed in human T-cell leukemia. PLoS One 6, e23389.

Zhang, Y., Yao, L., Zhang, X., Ji, H., Wang, L., Sun, S., et al., 2011d. Elevated expression of USP22 in correlation with poor prognosis in patients with invasive breast cancer. J. Cancer Res. Clin. Oncol. 137, 1245–1253.

Zhang, L., Lubin, A., Chen, H., Sun, Z., Gong, F., 2012a. The deubiquitinating protein USP24 interacts with DDB2 and regulates DDB2 stability. Cell Cycle 11, 4378–4384.

Zhang, L., Zhou, F., Drabsch, Y., Gao, R., Snaar-Jagalska, B.E., Mickanin, C., et al., 2012b. USP4 is regulated by AKT phosphorylation and directly deubiquitylates TGF-beta type I receptor. Nat. Cell Biol. 14, 717–726.

Zhang, X., Horibata, K., Saijo, M., Ishigami, C., Ukai, A., Kanno, S., et al., 2012c. Mutations in UVSSA cause UV-sensitive syndrome and destabilize ERCC6 in transcription-coupled DNA repair. Nat. Genet. 44, 593–597.

Zhang, Y., Foreman, O., Wigle, D.A., Kosari, F., Vasmatzis, G., Salisbury, J.L., et al., 2012d. USP44 regulates centrosome positioning to prevent aneuploidy and suppress tumorigenesis. J. Clin. Invest. 122, 4362–4374.

Zhang, J., Zhang, P., Wei, Y., Piao, H.L., Wang, W., Maddika, S., et al., 2013a. Deubiquitylation and stabilization of PTEN by USP13. Nat. Cell Biol. 15, 1486–1494.

Zhang, Z., Jones, A., Joo, H.Y., Zhou, D., Cao, Y., Chen, S., et al., 2013b. USP49 deubiquitinates histone H2B and regulates cotranscriptional pre-mRNA splicing. Genes Dev. 27, 1581–1595.

Zhang, L., Nemzow, L., Chen, H., Lubin, A., Rong, X., Sun, Z., et al., 2015. The deubiquitinating enzyme USP24 is a regulator of the UV damage response. Cell Rep. 10, 140–147.

Zhang, C., Lu, J., Zhang, Q.W., Zhao, W., Guo, J.H., Liu, S.L., et al., 2016a. USP7 promotes cell proliferation through the stabilization of Ki-67 protein in non-small cell lung cancer cells. Int. J. Biochem. Cell Biol. 79, 209–221.

Zhang, L., Wang, H., Tian, L., Li, H., 2016b. Expression of USP7 and MARCH7 is correlated with poor prognosis in epithelial ovarian cancer. Tohoku J. Exp. Med. 239, 165–175.

Zhang, Q., Harding, R., Hou, F., Dong, A., Walker, J.R., Bteich, J., et al., 2016c. Structural basis of the recruitment of ubiquitin-specific protease USP15 by spliceosome recycling factor SART3. J. Biol. Chem. 291, 17283–17292.

Zhang, J., Luo, N., Tian, Y., Li, J., Yang, X., Yin, H., et al., 2017. USP22 knockdown enhanced chemosensitivity of hepatocellular carcinoma cells to 5-Fu by up-regulation of Smad4 and suppression of Akt. Oncotarget 8, 24728–24740.

Zhang, H., Han, B., Lu, H., Zhao, Y., Chen, X., Meng, Q., et al., 2018a. USP22 promotes resistance to EGFR-TKIs by preventing ubiquitination-mediated EGFR degradation in EGFR-mutant lung adenocarcinoma. Cancer Lett. 433, 186–198.

Zhang, S., Xie, C., Li, H., Zhang, K., Li, J., Wang, X., et al., 2018b. Ubiquitin-specific protease 11 serves as a marker of poor prognosis and promotes metastasis in hepatocellular carcinoma. Lab. Investig. 98, 883–894.

Zhao, B., Schlesiger, C., Masucci, M.G., Lindsten, K., 2009. The ubiquitin specific protease 4 (USP4) is a new player in the Wnt signalling pathway. J. Cell. Mol. Med. 13, 1886–1895.

Zhao, X., Fiske, B., Kawakami, A., Li, J., Fisher, D.E., 2011a. Regulation of MITF stability by the USP13 deubiquitinase. Nat. Commun. 2. Article No. 414.

Zhao, Y., Thornton, A.M., Kinney, M.C., Ma, C.A., Spinner, J.J., Fuss, I.J., et al., 2011b. The deubiquitinase CYLD targets Smad7 protein to regulate transforming growth factor beta (TGF-beta) signaling and the development of regulatory T cells. J. Biol. Chem. 286, 40520–40530.

Zhao, L.J., Zhang, T., Feng, X.J., Chang, J., Suo, F.Z., Ma, J.L., et al., 2018. USP28 contributes to the proliferation and metastasis of gastric cancer. J. Cell Biochem. https://doi.org/10.1002/jcb.28040. [Epub ahead of print].

Zhong, B., Liu, X., Wang, X., Chang, S.H., Liu, X., Wang, A., et al., 2012. Negative regulation of IL-17-mediated signaling and inflammation by the ubiquitin-specific protease USP25. Nat. Immunol. 13, 1110–1117.

Zhong, M., Jiang, Q., Jin, R., 2018. USP4 expression independently predicts favorable survival in lung adenocarcinoma. IUBMB Life 70, 670–677.

Zhou, J., Wang, J., Chen, C., Yuan, H., Wen, X., Sun, H., 2018. USP7: target validation and drug discovery for cancer therapy. Med. Chem. 14, 3–18.

Zhu, M., Zhao, H., Liao, J., Xu, X., 2014. HERC2/USP20 coordinates CHK1 activation by modulating CLASPIN stability. Nucleic Acids Res. 42, 13074–13081.

Zhu, Y., Zhang, C., Gu, C., Li, Q., Wu, N., 2016. Function of deubiquitinating enzyme USP14 as oncogene in different types of cancer. Cell. Physiol. Biochem. 38, 993–1002.

Zlatanou, A., Sabbioneda, S., Miller, E.S., Greenwalt, A., Aggathanggelou, A., Maurice, M.M., et al., 2016. USP7 is essential for maintaining Rad18 stability and DNA damage tolerance. Oncogene 35, 965–976.

Zou, Q., Jin, J., Hu, H., Li, H.S., Romano, S., Xiao, Y., et al., 2014. USP15 stabilizes MDM2 to mediate cancer-cell survival and inhibit antitumor T cell responses. Nat. Immunol. 15, 562–570.

Chapter 5

Aspartic proteases: Potential drug targets for anticancer drug development

Ankit Ganeshpurkar, Subhajit Makar, Devendra Kumar, Srabanti Jana, Sushil Kumar Singh

Pharmaceutical Chemistry Research Laboratory, Department of Pharmaceutical Engineering & Technology, Indian Institute of Technology (Banaras Hindu University), Varanasi, India

5.1 Introduction

Cancer is an uncontrolled proliferation of cells leading to the increase in metabolic demand of body and cell death due to starvation. It may be benign or malignant. The signs and symptoms of cancer depend much upon its place of origin. Environmental factors including chemicals, food, infection, and genetic cause, i.e., inherited or acquired mutation, are responsible for the development of cancer. Metastasis is one of the major complications which makes it fatal. Cancer is one of the major leading causes of death worldwide among all the noncommunicable diseases. According to GLOBOCAN, global statistics report 2018, it is the first or second leading cause of death in 91 out of 192 countries of the world (Bray et al., 2018). Around 18.1 million new cases of cancer along with 9.6 million death tolls were projected around the globe in the year 2018. South-central Asia, including India, shares about 25.1% morbidity due to cancer (Bray et al., 2018).

The developing countries are facing a new threat, where there is a paradigm shift leading to the replacement of "infection-related and poverty-related cancers" with cancers found in developed countries, may be due to westernization of their lifestyle (Maule and Merletti, 2012; Bernard et al., 2014). Lung cancer is leading cancer in both sexes followed by breast, colorectal, stomach and liver cancers. In the female population, breast cancer takes the lead over all others (Fig. 5.1). The prevalence of lung cancer is lower in women than men. South Asia seems to be the high-risk region for cancer of the oral cavity and lips. According to the WHO cancer fact sheet, 30%–50% of cancers can be prevented by cutting off the risk factors. The early diagnosis, effective healthcare strategies, and awareness among the people may help in combating the disease.

Cancer-Leading Proteases. https://doi.org/10.1016/B978-0-12-818168-3.00005-X

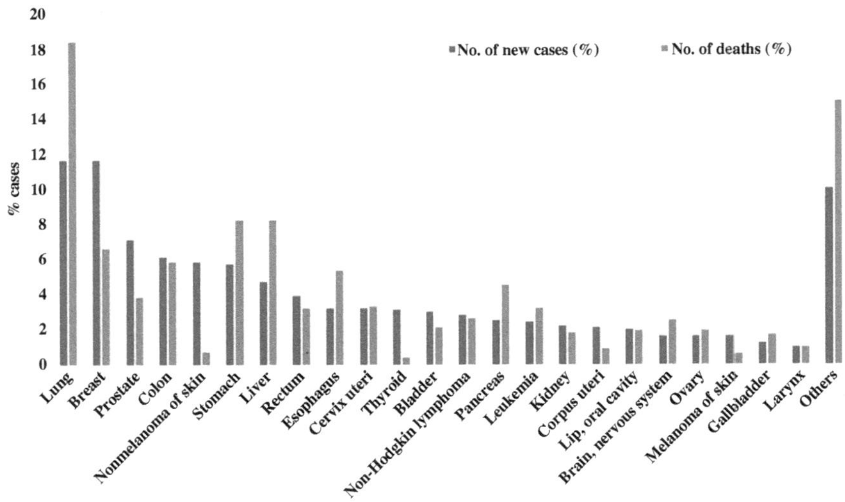

FIG. 5.1 Graphical representation of incidences (*blue; dark gray* in print version) and motility (*orange; light gray* in print version) due to common type of cancers prevalent across the globe. *(Data source: Global cancer statistics, 2018.)*

World Health Assembly aims to implement "Global Action Plan and 2030 UN agenda for Sustainable Development to reduce premature mortality from cancer" through governmental and WHO programs (Fig. 5.2).

The discovery of first therapeutic intervention for cancer began in the year 1846, which involved the use of surgery to treat cancer, whereby surgeons Billroth, Handley, and Halsted removed a tumor along with lymph node (Harvey, 1974). The advancement in surgery led to the use of miniature video camera-based endoscopy and cryosurgery in the treatment of cancer. The dawn of the 20th century also marked the first successful use of X-ray for treatment of basal cell carcinoma by S.W. Goldberg and Efim Semenovich London (Mould, 2007). Further, the mid-20th century unveiled use of chemotherapy and radiations along with surgery. Nitrogen mustard, also used in the last century, opened a new avenue for the treatment of cancer (Christakis, 2011). Hormonal and adjuvant therapy were also developed, which helped in destroying a few remaining cancer cells. The last decade of the 20th century evidenced development of antibodies, i.e., rituximab and trastuzumab, targeting lymphomas and breast cancer (Sudhakar, 2009).

Still, quest for the development of an efficacious anticancer drug with a minimal side effect is crucial challenge to be resolved. The contemporary era marked the search of small molecules that selectively focused on the emerging targets responsible for the pathogenesis of the disease. Various emerging molecular targets viz. kinases, proteases, metalloproteases, growth factor receptors, apoptosis proteins, glycolytic enzymes, nuclear factors, are overexpressed in cells causing disharmony in cell cycle and thus leading to various cancers.

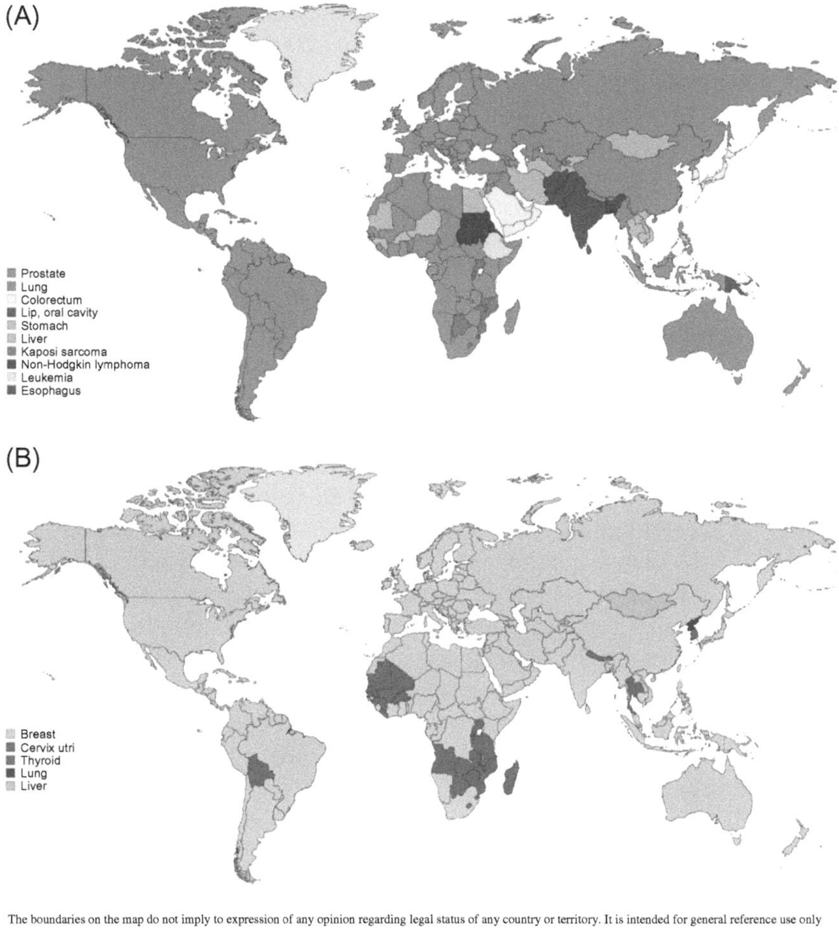

FIG. 5.2 Map representing (A) common type of cancers in male population prevalent across the globe, indicating higher prevalence of prostate and lung cancers (B) common type of cancers in female population prevalent across the globe, indicating higher prevalence of breast and cervical cancers. *(Data source: Global cancer statistics, 2018.)*

Proteases are a class of enzymes involved in proteolysis, i.e., hydrolysis of peptide bonds in proteins causing irreversible substrate cleavage. They constitute 2% of the human genome, and 990 genes are known to encode various proteases (Rawlings et al., 2014). There are about 565 members in this family (López-Otín and Overall, 2002). Proteases are classified into six classes, based upon their active site residues and mechanism of peptide cleavage. The clanes that include cysteine, serine, threonine, glutamic acid, aspartate proteases, and matrix metalloproteases (Taggart et al., 2017). They are tightly regulated by 1605 genes that produce protease inhibitors. Proteases play an essential role in regulatory processes, i.e., activation, inactivation, and modulation of various biochemical activities. These enzymes are involved in variety of processes including cell adhesion, cell motility (Wells et al., 2005), blood clotting (Walsh and Ahmad, 2002), activation of protein kinase (Schaap et al., 1990), tissue morphogenesis (Ortega et al., 2003; Tang, 2001) and remodeling (Chen, 1992), angiogenesis, vasculogenesis (Van Hinsbergh et al., 2006), ovulation (Curry et al., 1989), neurogenesis (Thiyagarajan et al., 2008), fertilization (Morales et al., 2003), and blood coagulation (Eaton et al., 1986; Kazama et al., 1995). These are also associated in a number of pathophysiological conditions viz. cancers (Nuttall et al., 2003; Sampson and Kakkar, 2002; Koblinski et al., 2000), neurodegenerative diseases (Steinfeld et al., 2006; Tao and Tong, 2003), arthritis (Tao and Tong, 2003; Spence Mccachren, 1991), cardiovascular (CVS) diseases (Lutgens et al., 2007), and inflammation (Yamasaki et al., 2007). Some of the proteases are critical prognostic markers and are useful in the diagnosis of diseases. Kallikrein-related peptidase 3 (KLK3) level in the blood has been found particularly useful in the detection of prostate cancer. Further, Kallikrein-related peptidase 2 (KLK2) present along with prostate-specific antigen (PSA) is also gaining diagnostic importance for the same (Hong, 2014). Other proteases such as plasminogen activators (PAs) are extracellular proteases responsible for activation of plasminogen into plasmin, and of various components leading to degradation of extracellular matrix into malignancies. FEMTELLE, a proprietary product and an ELISA-based detection kit, used to detect uPA/PAI-1, helps in the assessment of recurrence of breast cancer and effect of chemotherapy on it (Mengele et al., 2010; Mahmood et al., 2018). Pharmaceutical industry views proteases as a potentially druggable target. The angiotensin-converting enzyme inhibitors (ACEIs) are still one of the largest prescribed and sold drugs for managing hypertension and other CVS diseases since 1981. The other important class of protease inhibitors producing blood glucose lowering effect is dipeptidyl peptidase 4 (DPP4) inhibitors including sitagliptin, saxagliptin, and vildagliptin (Sheridan, 2012; Owens, 2007). However, one of the challenges in targeting proteases is their ability to cleave a vast variety of substrates including proteinase K, a protease of the subtilisin family, in the body. Of all the proteases, the role of aspartate proteases is conspicuous in diseases including cancer, neurodegenerative diseases, HIV-AIDS, etc. The chapter deals with the significance of aspartate proteases in cancer and the strategies to target them.

5.2 Aspartate proteases

Aspartate proteases (APs) are proteolytic enzymes having aspartic acid residues in their active site. They are also known as acid proteases, aspartyl proteinases, aspartic proteases, aspartic proteinases, aspartic-type endopeptidases, and carboxyl proteases. These are active below pH 6 and hence termed as acidic proteases. Pepsin was the first among APs to be discovered (Schwann, 1836). Pepsin family is one of the most characterized and explored APs by MEROPS.

5.2.1 Distribution and occurrence

APs are widely distributed in nature including various organisms. These are present in plants as extracellular digestive enzymes (Garg and Virupaksha, 1970). Cardosins, the abundant APs, provide a defense mechanism against insects and on the other hand, AP in barley helps in the germination of seeds. Similar enzymes are reported in microbes (Morihara, 1974) and fungi also (Ottesen and Rickert, 1970). Plasmepsin 2 is an AP responsible for digestion of hemoglobin in *Plasmodium falciferum's* vacuole (Silva et al., 1996). *Eutypella parasitica* produces endothiapepsin that leads to extracellular protein hydrolysis (Barkholt, 1987). Administration of pepstatin A, an inhibitor of AP, is reported to produce reduced motility in mice challenged with *Candida albicans* (Fallon et al., 1997). AP is also present in HIV-1 and hydrolyzes viral polyproteins in smaller one. Variety of APs is reported in humans that include pepsin, gastricsin, cathepsin D, E, napsin, BACE1, BACE2, renin, and presenilin. These are widely distributed in the stomach, brain, lungs, and kidneys in the body and are present in different subcellular locations, i.e., lysosome, subcellular vesicles, plasma membrane, etc.

5.2.2 Classification of aspartate proteases

The MEROPS database classifies APs into various families on the basis of their structures and functions which is summarized in Table 5.1 (Dunn, 2002). Family A1 of pepsin like enzymes includes maximum number of 202 APs, whereas families A9 and A12 have only one enzyme each.

TABLE 5.1 Classification of aspartate proteases based on MEROPS database.

Family	Description	Number of aspartate proteases
A1	Pepsin like enzymes	282
A2	Reteroviral peptidase	93
A3a	Cauliflower mosaic virus peptidase	16
A4b	Bacilliform virus putative endopeptidase	3
A4	Aspergillopepsin	4
A9	Human spumaretrovirus	1
A11a	Copia transposon	51
A12	Retrotransposons bs1 endopeptidase	1
A16	Tas retrotransposons endopeptidase	4

5.2.3 Structure of aspartate proteases

Superimposition of various human AP sequences evidenced that their structures are homologous. Predominantly, the tertiary structure of AP consists of two lobes or domains with two fold symmetry. Further, two domains have the same symmetry with identical secondary structure elements.

5.2.3.1 Zymogen and its activation

APs, such as pepsinogen, cathepsin D, renin, seminal plasmic acid proteases, are secreted as proenzymes or zymogens which are converted to their active form. Pepsin has two aspartate residues, Asp32 and Asp215, which are 3 Å close to the center of the enzyme. The inactivity of enzyme is due to the presence of pro-segment (p2-p44) of N-terminal region which completely occludes active site. Pro-segment consists of "one β-strand and three helices." After activation of the enzyme, p2-p9 strand becomes part of the active enzyme and forms a group of "six-stranded β-sheet," that results in hinging motion of 13–14 residues leading to the displacement of residues 1–13 to top of the enzyme (Fig. 5.3). The pro-segment residues p9-p44 form three helices and Lys36p-Tyr37p interact with the active site to provide inactive state to the enzyme (Šali et al., 1992; Sielecki et al., 1991; Cooper et al., 1990). The inactivity of enzyme is due to Lys36p residue, which forms hydrogen bonds with catalytic aspartate residues. Further, Tyr9 residue of the active segment also forms hydrogen bonding with aspartate residue (Asp32) (Koelsch et al., 1994).

5.2.3.2 Active site

The active site of pepsin and other APs consist of two aspartate residues. The two identical motifs "Asp-Thr-Gly" are present in both domains. Asp215 of pepsin was identified due to its ability to react and form an ester with "Diazoacetyl-DL-norleucine methyl ester (DAN)" in pepsin, and other APs also displayed similar chemical modification with different azo dyes (Rajagopalan et al., 1966; Bayliss et al., 1969). Further, another site-directed reagent 1,2-epoxy-3-(*p*-nitrophenoxy) propane (EPNP) was used to identify Asp32 of pepsin in the N-terminal domain (Tang et al., 1973). Both the modifications resulted in inactivation of the enzyme, which established the significance of the residues.

5.2.3.3 Flap

The flap, existing in the upper region of the substrate cavity, is formed by both N- and C-terminal lobes of APs. The flap present in pepsin is in close conformation making insufficient entry space for the substrate. It contains conserved Tyr75 residue present on a β-hairpin loop which is part of S_1 and S_3 subsites and plays a role in P1 side chain recognition of substrate. Replacement of Tyr75 with Asn and Phe did not produce any effect on the rate of catalysis, indicating that the residue may be necessary for the correct positioning of substrate and might be involved in substrate enzyme binding (Tang and Koelsch, 1995).

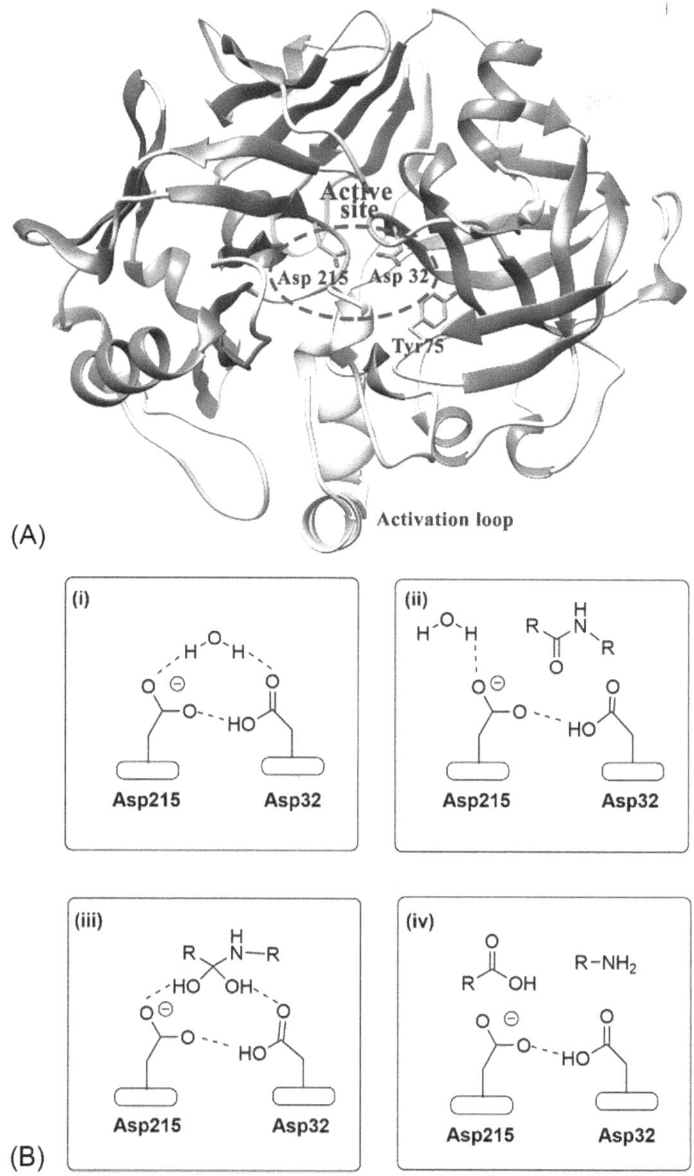

FIG. 5.3 Schematic representation of (A) structure of pepsinogen (PDB id—2PSG) highlighting active site residues i.e., Asp32 and Asp215 and (B) catalytic mechanism of peptide hydrolysis by aspartate proteases involving the role of aspartate residues.

5.2.4 Catalytic mechanism

The pK_a values of two aspartate residues were found to be 2 and 5. Asp32 residue has pK_a of 2.8, which helps the residue to form hydrogen bonding with Ser35. The other aspartate residue has pK_a of 5 and may be present in the ionized state. This residue may have a water molecule which is involved in attacking the peptide bond. The oxygen atom of water, through nucleophilic attack on the carbonyl carbon, causes the transition state to undergo addition of a proton to the departing nitrogen group, leading to completion of hydrolysis of the substrate (Davies, 1990).

5.2.5 Substrate specificity

The active site or primary binding site of pepsin can accommodate up to octapeptide substrate. Usually, the sessile bond or site of nucleophilic attack rests in the center of the peptide. The peptide substrate is hence divided into eight sites, i.e., P1′ to P4′ on the right side and P1 to P4 on the left side of the sessile bond. Further, corresponding active site regions, which accommodate these residues, are named S4 to S4′. The type of residues present in subsites of APs, provides substrate specificity that also helps in designing specific inhibitors. S3 pocket of pepsin consists of Phe111, which restricts the size of the pocket. While in other enzymes, this residue is substituted with Asn, Pro or Thr and allows binding with much larger substrate residues (Fujinaga et al., 1995).

5.2.6 Physiological role of aspartate proteases

APs play a wide variety of physiological functions in the body. Pepsin is released, as pepsinogen, from chief cells of the stomach wall and is responsible for digestion of proteins in the stomach upon activation in acidic medium. It has different types of commercial applications in molecular biology to dairy science (Nelson and Cox, 2017). Another digestive AP produced in the stomach is gastricsin, which also performs similar function as of pepsin. Renin, also known as angiotensinogenase secreted by kidneys, is responsible for the conversion of angiotensinogen to angiotensin. Angiotensin assists the regulation of falling blood pressure in the body by employing fluid retention and arterial vasoconstriction (Nguyen, 2011). Napsin A, responsible for normal alveolar functions, is another AP present in lungs and is involved in the processing of alveolar surfactant through proteolysis (Schauer-Vukasinovic et al., 1999). Presenilin-1 is the catalytic component of γ-secretase complex and is required in cleavage of amyloid precursor protein (APP), Notch receptors, and regulation of Notch and Wnt signaling cascades (Kumar et al., 2018). Cathepsin E is essential for many of the immune functions, i.e., processing of antigen, activation of lymphocytes and glial cells, etc. (Sealy et al., 1996).

5.3 Aspartate proteases involved in cancer

5.3.1 Cathepsin D

Cathepsin D (CatD) (Fig. 5.4A) is an aspartate protease found in lysosomes and occasionally in melanosomes (Didangelos et al., 2010). It is produced as prepropeptide of 412 amino acid residues, which is subsequently cleaved into propeptide (21–412). The enzyme is present in the form of zymogen which, on acidification, gets activated through multiple events involving cleavages and rearrangements. It has six β-sheets between the domains at pH 7.5, and if the structure is resolved at pH 5.1 then have only five β-sheets. At acidic pH, the enzyme consists of N-terminal flexible coil inserted near active site cleft leading to five β-sheets interdomain structure causing complete activation of the enzyme. Further, autolysis of the propeptide segment is observed upon activation. This delocalization is due to 180°rotation of Ala13 residue leading to disarrangement of β-hairpin. The ζ nitrogen atom of Lys8 residue interacts with water and forms a salt bridge with "Asp33 and Asp231". At neutral pH, the specificity of S1 pocket changes as Tyr10 forms hydrogen bonding with Asp33. The β-hairpin structure (flap) also gets displaced by 8 Å in neutral pH due to movement of Pro4 and Glu5 (Lee et al., 1998a). Interestingly, the structure includes a

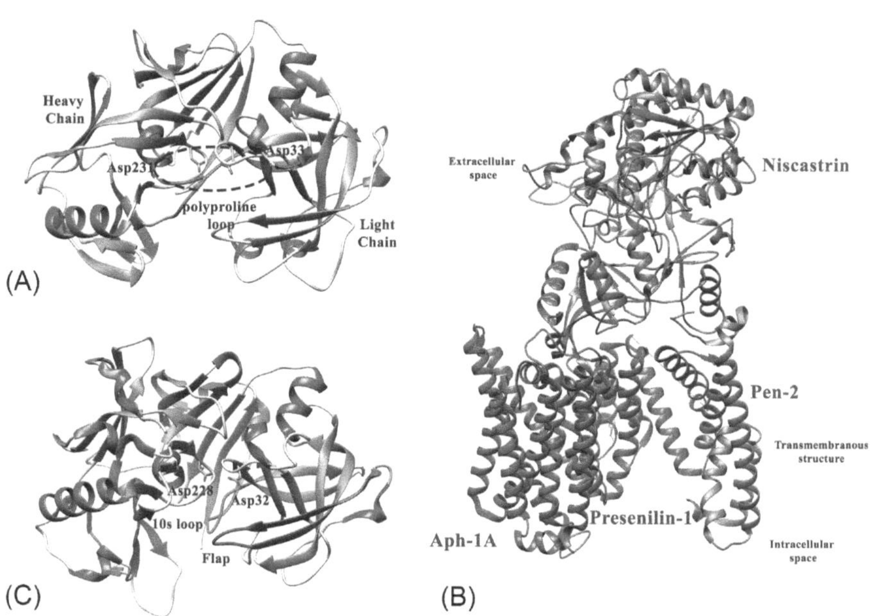

FIG. 5.4 Schematic representation of (A) structure of cathepsin D (PDB id—4OBZ) indicating heavy chain, light chain, polyproline loop, and active site aspartate residues i.e., Asp33 and Asp 231, (B) γ-secretase (PDB id—5A63) highlighting various domains i.e., Nicastrin (*purple; dark gray* in print version), Aph-1A (*blue; black* in print version), Pen-2 (*turquoise; light gray* in print version) and Presenilin-1 (*orange; gray* in print version) and (C) BACE-1(PDB id—6C2I) with characteristic 10s loop and flap.

poly-proline loop consisting of Pro312, 313 and 317, of which Pro313 and 317 consist of *cis*-peptide. Further, residues 98–106 of N-terminal are cleaved and produce two chains i.e., light and heavy chain in the CatD structure. The CatD also contains disulfide linkage between cystine residues 91–160, 110–117, 286–290, and 329–366. It also undergoes various posttranslational modifications including glycosylation at residues Thr63, Asn134, and Asn263 (Baldwin et al., 1993). CatD shows the presence of pH dependent ionizable switch. It consists of Asp33 and Asp231 and remains ionized at pH 7.5, but at pH 5.1 Lys8 residue moves in and neutralizes the additional charge of the active site. The other switches involve hydrogen bonding interactions between Glu180 and Asp187 and also Glu5 and Glu18, which on higher pH i.e., at pH 7.5 gets disrupted due to a repulsive force causing structural change.

The enzyme had no role in embryonic development in CD knock-out mice, but in adults it caused absence of intestinal mucosa, intestinal necrosis, decrease in lymphoid cells in spleen and thymus. Further, seizures, retinal atrophy, and blindness were also observed at the time of death in 4 weeks (Saftig et al., 1995; Guicciardi et al., 2004; Koike et al., 2003).

Various clinical investigations involving the measurement of the levels of pCatD/CatD (proCatD/CatD) and their effect on tumor grade, size, aggressiveness, and level of metastasis in different cancers have produced disconcerted results. However, several studies indicated that level of pCD/CD might be a prognostic marker for breast cancer (Ferrandina et al., 1997; Foekens et al., 1999; Billgren et al., 2000). It was also reported that pCatD acted as "autocrine growth factor" for lung, ovarian, breast, and prostate cancers (Vetvicka et al., 1994, 1998, 2004; Bazzett et al., 1999). Administration of anti-pCatD antibodies produced inhibition of tumor growth in both in vitro and in vivo experiments (Vetvicka et al., 1997, 1999). CatD suppresses the immune response against tumor growth through metabolism of chemokines and degrades MIP-1a, MIP-1b, and SLC chemokines (Wolf et al., 2003). MIP-1a and MIP-1b recruit and direct immature dendritic cells to tumor cells and cause expression of CCR7 on dendritic cells which binds to SLC to produce an antitumor immune response (Sallusto et al., 1998; Homey et al., 2002; Sozzani et al., 2000). The mutant pCatD, which is enzymatically inactive, has shown growth stimulation in cancer cells in both in vitro and in vivo models (Glondu et al., 2001; Berchem et al., 2002). C-terminal activated peptide (propeptide segment) is shown to stimulate cell growth in lung, breast, and prostate cancers (Vetvicka et al., 1997, 2004). The antisense gene therapy displayed a marked reduction in metastasis of MDA-MB-231 (breast cancer cell) in lungs of genetically nude mice (Glondu et al., 2002). The inhibition of specific cytokine by antibody reduced the mitogenic effect of pCatD or activation peptide in various cancer cell lines and inhibition of all the cytokines had almost abolished its mitogenic effect (Fusek et al., 2007). Further, pCatD secreted by cancer cells affects stromal cells which cause fibroblast proliferation, motility, and metastasis (Laurent-Matha et al., 1998). Therefore, it is evident that pCatD has a critical role in metastasis.

5.3.2 γ-Secretase

Haass and Selkoe first described cleavage of APP by an enzyme γ-secretase (Haass and Selkoe, 1993). It is widely expressed in the body including brain, liver, spleen, and lymph nodes (Sherrington et al., 1995; Mirinics et al., 2002). The enzyme consists of four subunits: presenilin (PS including PS1 and PS2), nicastrin, anterior pharynx defective 1 (Aph-1), and presenilin enhancer 2 (De Strooper, 2003; Kimberly et al., 2003; Kumar et al., 2018). It has molecular weight 170kDa along with an additional molecular weight of 30–70kDa due to glycosylation of nicastrin leading to a total molecular weight of 230kDa along with 19 transmembrane domains. PS1 and PS2 form the catalytic core of γ-secretase (Sogorb-Esteve et al., 2018). PS units are encoded by two genes that produce two isoforms PS1 and PS2. Aph-1 also has two isoforms viz. Aph-1a and Aph-1b (Fig. 5.4B). Thus, four possible subtypes of γ-secretase are available, of which nicastrin:Aph-1a:PS1:Pen-2 is expressed abundantly. Further, the heavily glycosylated nicastrin subunit of the enzyme is involved in substrate recognition and Aph-1 provides a supporting role (Shah et al., 2005; Lee et al., 2004). The structure of nicastrin is bi-lobed, larger lobe imparts substrate recognition site while smaller lobe provides hydrophobic pivot (Xie et al., 2014). Pen-2 helps in autoproteolysis of the loop between TM6 and TM7 of PS1, that is required for proteolytic activity of PS1 (Chen et al., 2006). PS1, an intramembranous AP, is a "single peptide peptidase" (Weihofen et al., 2002). The endolytic peptide cleavage of C- and N-terminals, near Met298 residue present in cytoplasmic side loop, facilitates its maturation. PS1 has nine transmembranous helical domains with its N-terminal present in the cytosol, while C-terminal is present towards the extracellular space (Friedmann et al., 2004; Fluhrer et al., 2009). Further, TM2 and TM6 are positioned near TM9. TM6 and TM7 have active site residues (Asp257 and Asp385 of PS1) as is established by the observation that proteolytic cleavage of two domains confer inactivity to the enzyme (Li et al., 2014). Residues Ser310 and Ser34 undergo posttranslational modifications, involving phosphorylation through protein kinase A and protein kinase C respectively, resulting in the reduction of apoptosis progression (Fluhrer et al., 2004). The mutations viz. Ile202Phe, Phe237Ile, Leu248Arg, Asp257Glu, Asp346Ala, and Asp385Glu lead to loss/abolition of APP processing activity, but the same in Leu226Phe increases APP proteolysis (Bai et al., 2015; Wrigley et al., 2004; Wolfe et al., 1999; Berezovska et al., 2000; Uemura et al., 2003). On the other hand, mutations such as Pro433Ala, Pro433Gly, and Ala434Asp affect both APP and Notch-1 processing (Wang et al., 2006a).

The enzyme γ-secretase is responsible for cleavage of intramembranous "type I proteins." It helps in the processing of various proteins i.e., E-cadherin, ErbB4, Alcadein, TREM2, CD44, tyrosinase, APP, and Notch (Marambaud et al., 2002; Ni et al., 2001; Hata et al., 2012; Wunderlich et al., 2013; Lammich et al., 2002; Wang et al., 2006b; De Strooper et al., 1998, 1999). The enzyme plays an important role in various cell signaling pathways including Notch and Wnt signaling, APP processing, and regulating cytosolic CTNNB1 levels (Murayama et al., 1998; Ray et al., 1999). Further, γ-secretase interacts with CDH-1 (E-cadherin) protein and promotes cell adhesion by stabilizing its interactions with β-catenin and γ-catenin (Marambaud et al., 2002). It also promotes angiogenesis, embryonic skeletal and brain development.

The "active Notch ICD" is released by γ-secretase from plasma membrane, which translocates in the nucleus, interacts with DNA and activates Notch genes (Kopan and Ilagan, 2009). Further, the treatment of Ras-transformed fibroblast with γ-secretase inhibitor has shown Notch1 mediated antineoplastic activity. Another tripeptide γ-secretase inhibitor has shown reduced tumor growth in mice grafted with melanoma and Kaposi sarcoma xenografts (Marambaud et al., 2002). It is also observed that Jagged 1 (a Notch ligand) activates Notch receptors and promotes metastasis of breast cancer cells in bone. Further, higher Notch activity stimulates interleukin 6 release in osteoblast and promotes the growth of metastatic cancer (Sethi et al., 2011). ErbB4 is an epidermal growth factor receptor (EGFR) which is processed by γ-secretase. Its intramembranous cleavage, by γ-secretase, produces free ErbB4 ICD leading to the growth of cancer cells in breast cancer (Ni et al., 2001). This is further established by expression of mutant ErbB4, which is not processed by γ-secretase leading abolition of pro-apoptotic activity (Vidal et al., 2005). The enzyme γ-secretase is responsible for processing/metabolism of E-cadherin, a potent tumor suppressor which leads to tumor progression and metastasis in breast cancer (Berx and Van Roy, 2001). Another γ-secretase substrate CD44 is responsible for cell proliferation, differentiation, and migration. The free ICD produced after γ-secretase processing of CD44 causes "neoplastic transformation of rat fibroblastic cells" (Pelletier et al., 2006).

5.3.3 β-Secretase-1 (BACE-1)

BACE-1 is class I transmembrane protein which consists of 434 amino acid residues long "ectodomain" anchored on membrane through "transmembrane domain" of 22 residues and short "cytoplasmic tail" of 24 residues. It is also called memapsin 2 and has a compact globular protein with two domains, i.e. "residues 47–146" and "residues 146–385." The active site of BACE-1 is present between N- and C-terminal domains (Hong et al., 2000). BACE-1 is also an AP with aspartic acid residues Asp32 and Asp228 present in active site cleft coordinated with water. The residues of the active site are present in ectodomain (Fig. 5.4C). The β-hairpin conformation near active site, formed by residues 67–77, represents the flap (Hong et al., 2002). Further, a 10s loop of residues 9–14 lies at the base of S3 pocket and is a flexible part of the enzyme (Patel et al., 2004). BACE-1 is widely distributed in endosomes, endoplasmic reticulum, cell surfaces, and Golgi complex (Huse et al., 2000; Capell et al., 2000). The enzyme is transported to the cell membrane through the endoplasmic reticulum and Golgi body. It undergoes N-glycosylation at four asparagine residues and disulfide bond formation between Cys216-Cys420, Cys278-Cys443, Cys330-Cys380 in the endoplasmic reticulum (Haniu et al., 2000). The residues Lys126, Lys275, Lys279, Lys-285, Lys299, Lys300, and Lys307 also undergo acetylation in the endoplasmic reticulum (Costantini et al., 2007; Ko and Puglielli, 2009).

BACE-1 is responsible for proteolytic cleavage of APP, which cleaves N-terminus at residue 671–672 (Lin et al., 2000) and plays a vital role in the process of angiogenesis. It is also observed that BACE-1 inhibitors restrain proliferation and differentiation of human brain endothelial cells in a dose-dependent manner and therefore their antiangiogenic effect may be useful in cancer. Further, they also inhibit human glioblastoma and human lung adenocarcinoma tumors in mice (Paris et al., 2005).

5.3.4 Pepsinogen C

Pepsinogen C or progastricsin (PGC) is an AP enzyme present in gastric secretion and seminal plasma protein. It is a zymogen having 374 residues, consisting of 331 residues gastracin moiety and 43 residues long activation segment, which is activated in acidic condition (Foltmann, 1988). The enzyme is expressed in stomach, pancreas, liver, prostate and Barrett epithelium (Tatematsu et al., 1990; Fukushima et al., 2004; Steele et al., 2007; Konishi et al., 1999; Pals et al., 1988). The PGC is expressed in two forms: pepsinogen A (adult animals) and pepsinogen F (fetus and infants) (Kageyama, 2002). It consists of 15% of α-helix and 44% β-strands. The active site is present in between the two lobes with two catalytic aspartate residues Asp32 and Asp215. S1 pocket contains Ile30, Tyr75, Thr77, and Phe111, which are located adjacent to Asp32 and helps in determining substrate specificity. It also has a loop called flap which is made up of Ley71-Gly82 (Hartsuck et al., 1992). The opposite pocket, i.e., S1′ pocket, is made up of Tyr189, Ile213, Val291, Thr293, Leu298, and Ile300 (Peerce et al., 1984). The activation segment or prosegment of PGC consists of a β-strand and three short helices in N-terminal of proteins. Lys36 of activation segment forms ionic interaction with active site aspartate residues (Fig. 5.5). The structure also contains three disulfide linkages between Cys45-Cys50, Cys208-Cys212, and Cys251-Cys284.

PCG is secreted by the stomach's chief cells and is stable under physiological pH, but gets activated below pH 5 due to the conformational changes and disruption of nonbonding interactions leading to exposure of active site. The enzyme is expressed after 23 weeks of gestational age of the fetus (Elabiad and Zhang, 2011). It plays a vital role in lung development through hydrolysis of pro-surfactant protein B (pro-SPB) produced by alveolar type 2 epithelial cells. The knockdown of PCG inhibits maturation of pro-SPB (Gerson et al., 2008; Foster et al., 2004). The other critical physiological roles of the enzyme are illustrated in Fig. 5.5 (Shen et al., 2017).

PGC is reported to be overexpressed in breast carcinoma as it is synthesized and secreted by cancer cells in significant quantity. The overexpression of enzyme causes proteolysis, invasion, and metastasis of breast cancer cells leading to lesions (Diez-Itza et al., 1993). Further clinical investigation has established

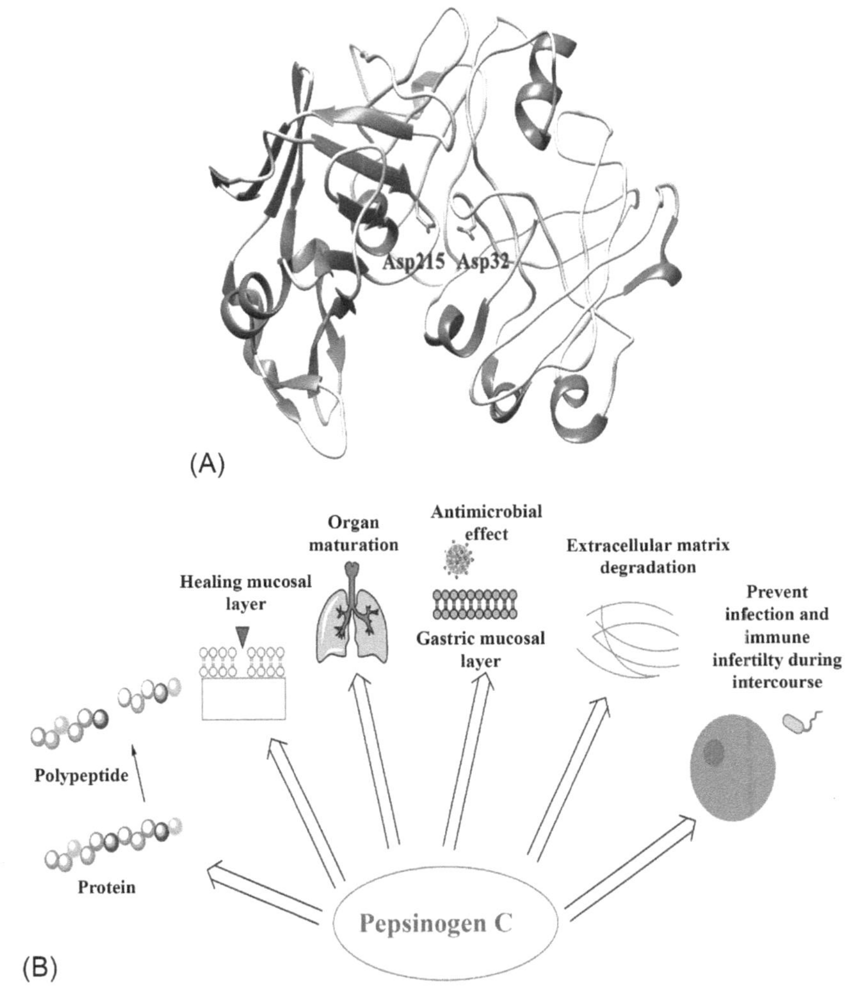

FIG. 5.5 Schematic representation of (A) structure of pepsinogen C (PDB id—1HTR) and (B) various physiological functions of pepsinogen C.

a significant relationship between tumor grade and PGC levels (Diez-Itza et al., 1993). The overexpression of PGC is also observed in "cancerous cells, basal cells, and squamous cell carcinomas of eyelids" (Alvarez et al., 2004). Its expression is also reported in malignant cutaneous, gall bladder, stomach, gastric, prostate, endometrial, and ovarian carcinomas (Hassan et al., 2010).

5.3.5 Napsin A

Napsin A, an AP having a molecular mass of 38 kDa, was first identified and isolated from rat kidney (Mori et al., 1997). It is expressed in type II pneumocytes, alveolar macrophages, kidney and also in the spleen at a low level (Gomes et al., 1997). The enzyme serves in the maturation of surfactant protein B (SP-B), a pulmonary surfactant (Ueno et al., 2004). It is highly expressed in primary lung adenocarcinomas but is missing in squamous cell carcinomas and small cell carcinomas of the lung (Turner et al., 2012; Mukhopadhyay and Katzenstein, 2011; Ueno et al., 2003).

5.4 Aspartic protease inhibitors

APs, a family of protease enzymes, contain highly conserved aspartic acid residues in the active site for catalytic cleavage of peptide substrates. Peptidase enzyme catalyzes the addition of water across amide or ester bonds for cleavage by nucleophilic attack on the electrophilic carbonyl carbon of the scissile bond (Menon and Goldberg, 1987; Northrop, 2001; Dunn, 2002). The associated mechanism of action depends upon an acid-base reaction involving coordination of a water molecule between the two highly conserved aspartate residues. One aspartate residue initiates the reaction by abstracting a proton to enable water to attack the carbonyl carbon of the peptide substrate and produces a tetrahedral oxyanion intermediate. Further, rearrangement of intermediate leads to protonation of a scissile amide bond. This intermediate acts as a crucial transition state and restabilization of the transition state makes the amino moiety of substrate a better leaving group resulting in cleavage into two peptide fragments (Baldwin et al., 1995). The chapter focuses on small molecule inhibitors of AP designed on the basis of the substrate sequence. The design of AP inhibitors depends on their ability to mimic the transition state formed during amide hydrolysis. Further insight indicated that the design strategies were based on analogous idea of peptidic substrates having a nonhydrolysable transition state isostere in place of normal hydrolyzable P1–P1′ amide bond. The introduction of an isosteric hydroxymethyl carbonyl function instead of amide, serves as an activating group that can mimic the tetrahedral transition state but cannot be hydrolyzed by protease (Vega et al., 2004; Clemente et al., 2006; Freedberg et al., 1998). The structural and kinetic studies also suggested that the mechanism involved was general acid-base catalysis with a water molecule that directly participated in the reaction. It was further supported by crystal structures of various AP-inhibitor complexes mimicking a tetrahedral intermediate, formed after the attack by a water molecule (Rao et al., 1998). Various crystal structures of AP inhibitors for viral proteases (HIV-1, HIV-2, SIV, FIV), CatD, CatL and CatE, renin, chymosin, pepsin, γ-secretase, β-secretase, endothelin converting enzyme (ECE), and napsin A are currently available on PDB. CatD and CatE have been mainly involved in cancer progression. The expression of CatD is associated with breast cancer, whereas the expression of CatE has been reported to be associated with tumor aggressiveness in patients with ovarian or endometrial cancers. It can also induce precursors of biologically potent proteins in prelysosomal compartments of specialized cells (Diment et al., 1989). CatD, a marker of poor prognosis in breast cancer (Rodriguez et al., 2005; Westley and May, 1999), is overexpressed and secreted at high levels by human epithelial breast cancer cells (Nicotra et al., 2010; Masson et al., 2011). It stimulates cancer cell proliferation, fibroblast outgrowth, angiogenesis, and metastasis (Ohri et al., 2008; Vashishta et al., 2007). The direct role of CatD in cancer metastasis was first demonstrated in rat tumor cells in which transfection induced CatD overexpression increased their metastatic potential in the in vivo study (Liaudet-Coopman et al., 2006). It is a rate-limiting factor in the outgrowth, tumorigenicity, and lung colonization of MDA-MB-231 breast cancer cells (Berchem et al., 2002). Procathepsin D (pCD), secreted from cancer cells, can act as a mitogen on both cancer and stromal cells and thus stimulates their proinvasive and prometastatic properties (Vetvicka and Fusek, 2012). Surprisingly, napsin A is expressed in lung cancer, where it is involved in the processing of surfactant protein B while it suppresses tumor growth in HEK-293 cells in a manner independent of its catalytic activity. Further insight into the mechanism may help in developing new drugs for renal and ovarian cancers (Ueno et al., 2008). APs are inhibited by pepstatin (**1**), which is one of the important HIV-1 protease inhibitors (Fig. 5.6). It is a natural reversible peptidomimetic inhibitor of several APs that consists of Iva-Val-Val-Sta-Ala-Statine (Umezawa et al., 1970). Pepstatin is a hexapeptide containing statine, i.e. (3*S*,4*S*)-4-amino-3-hydroxy-6-methylheptanoic acid. It was first identified and isolated from actinomycetes. The active site residues of APs are also sensitive to site directed affinity labels such as diazoacetyl norleucine methyl ester (DAN) and 1,2-epoxy-3-(*p*-nitrophenoxy)propane (EPNP) in presence of copper ions. Both DAN and EPNP react specifically with side-chain carboxyl of a distinct aspartic acid residue to inactivate the enzyme. Together, these residues contribute to the catalytic mechanism and provide the basis for nomenclature of this class of enzymes. In general, pepsins and other APs exhibit broad spectrum specificity toward cleavage in peptides of at least six hydrophobic amino acid residues at specific substrate positions (Umezawa et al., 1970; Dash et al., 2003).

5.4.1 HIV-1 protease inhibitors as anticancer agents

HIV-1 protease, an AP, is a homodimer consisting of identical, noncovalently bonded two subunits of 99 amino acid residues associated in a two fold C2 symmetric fashion. The active site is formed at the dimer interface and contains two conserved Asp 25 and Asp 125 catalytic residues (Ogden and Flexner, 2001; Van Ranst, 2001). Various HIV protease inhibitors, such as compounds (**2–9**) (Fig. 5.6), are available for clinical application. Kaposi sarcoma (KS) is a type of tumor, frequently associated with HIV infected patients. Treatment of such patients with HAART regimen, that includes at least one protease inhibitor leads to a dramatic reduction of KS (Boshoff and Weiss, 2002; Monini et al., 2004, 2003). Saquinavir (SQV, **2**) and Indinavir (IDV, **4**) block basic fibroblast growth factor (bFGF) and vascular endothelial growth factor (VEGF) induced

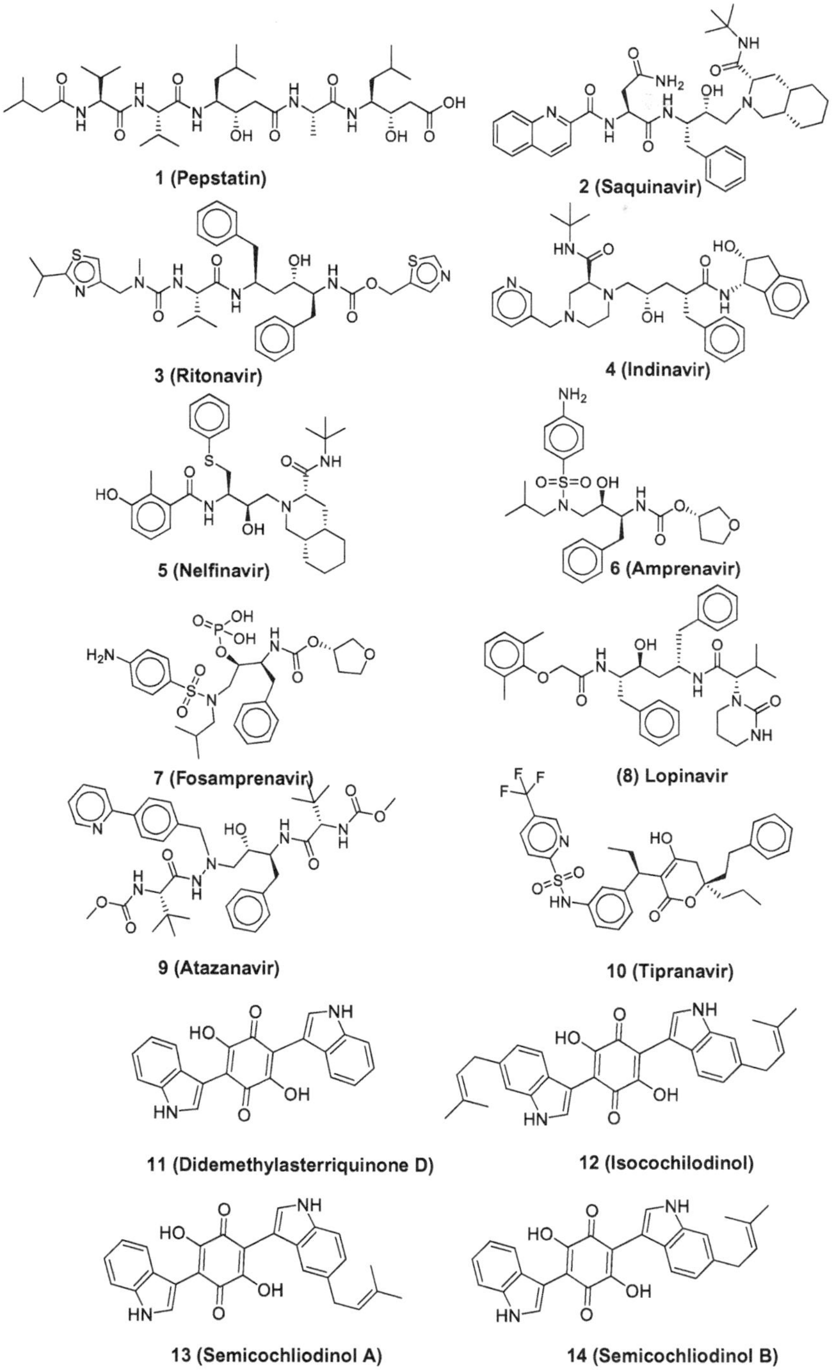

FIG. 5.6 Structures of HIV-1 protease inhibitors acting as anticancer agents.

angiogenesis in chorioallantoic membrane assay comparable to paclitaxel. HIV-1 protease inhibitors (HIV-1 PIs) also inhibited in vivo growth and invasion of angiogenic tumor cells. Thus, these are potent antiangiogenic and antitumor agents and can be used to treat non-HIV KS and other HIV-associated tumors due to their interference with several cellular pathways and inhibition of tumor proliferation (Sgadari et al., 2002; Monini et al., 2003). There was remission observed in other AIDS associated cancers, i.e., non-Hodgkin's lymphomas, diffuse large-cell lymphomas, primary nervous system lymphomas, and uterine cervical cancers after treatment with HAART regimen that included aspartate PIs. The mechanisms involved in anticancer activity of HIV-1 PIs include blockage of KS-cell apoptosis and endothelial cell activation by NFkβ inhibition, accumulation of the cyclin-dependent kinase inhibitor WAF1, inhibition of neoangiogenesis, and blocking of tumor cell invasion by extracellular matrix modification through MMP-2 inhibition (Monini et al., 2003; Maggiorella et al., 2005). The in vitro and in vivo studies evaluated the antitumor effect of RTV combined with ionizing radiation on the HEP-2 associated head and neck carcinoma model. They observed inhibition of tumor growth in mice treated with RTV, which was enhanced when it was combined with ionizing radiation. Further, western-blot analysis revealed that apoptosis was induced by an increased expression of Bax and decreased expression of Bcl-2 after combined treatment. These data suggested that RTV could clinically improve the tumor response to radiation therapy, especially in head and neck carcinomas (Maggiorella et al., 2005). The activation of phosphatidylinositol 3-kinase (PI3K)-Akt signaling pathway is common in human cancers, so it was hypothesized that HIV-1 PIs could inhibit Akt activity resulting in increased tumor cell sensitivity to ionizing radiation-induced cell death. Among the first-generation HIV-1 PIs tested, APV, NFV, and SQV inhibited Akt phosphorylation at Ser473 at serum concentrations routinely achieved in HIV patients (Gupta et al., 2005). Further, NFV induced growth arrest and apoptosis of human prostate cancer cells viz. LNCaP, DU145, and PC-3. It also blocked androgen receptor (AR) signaling with down-regulation of nuclear levels of AR in LNCaP cells. NFV disrupted STAT3 signaling by blocking interleukin 6-induced phosphorylation of DNA binding activity in LNCaP and DU145 cells. HIV PIs (NFV, RTV, and SQV) also blocked Toll-like receptor 4 (TLR4) and TLR2, TNF-α-mediated NF-κβ activation as well as e LPS induced IL-6 promoter transactivation in a dose-dependent manner (Equils et al., 2004). Pyrko et al. demonstrated anticancer activity of HIV-1 PIs in non-HIV-associated human cancer cells. The group observed that NFV and ATV cause cell death in an in vitro experiment on various malignant glioma cell lines. They established that stimulation of endoplasmic reticulum stress response (ESR), indicated by increased expression of two ESR markers i.e., GRP78 and CHOP and activation of ESR-associated caspase-4, may be the plausible mechanism for the activity. Furthermore, the treatment of cancer cells with aspartic HIV-1 PIs led to aggresomal formation and accumulation of polyubiquitinated proteins, implicated for proteasome inhibition (Pyrko et al., 2007). Lkezoe et al. evaluated the antiproliferative effect of HIV-1 PIs in human myeloid leukemia cells and their differentiation was enhanced in the presence of "all-trans-retinoic acid". Ritonavir inhibited CYP3A4 in liver microsome which was involved in drug metabolism and the acquisition of drug resistance. An in vitro study on DU145 cancer cells displayed that treatment of docetaxel either alone or in combination with ritonavir enhanced antiproliferative and proapoptotic effects of docetaxel in hormonally independent DU145 prostate cancer cells. The expression of induced CYP3A4 due to Docetaxel was examined by RT-PCR and it was observed that ritonavir (10^{-5} mol/L) completely inhibited the induction. Ritonavir also inhibited the DNA binding activity of nuclear factor κB (NFκB) in DU145 cells in ELISA study, which was a contributor to drug resistance. Furthermore, a combination treatment of docetaxel and ritonavir dramatically inhibited the growth of DU145 cells present as tumor xenografts in BNX nude mice as compared with either of the drugs (Ikezoe et al., 2004). Cancer cells represent overactivity of antiapoptotic transcription factor NF-κB. It was observed that specific proteasome inhibitors induced apoptosis in cancer cells at nonlethal concentrations. Pajnok et al. reported that protease coded by HIV-I virus share cleavage activities with the proteasome. It was shown that Saquinavir inhibited NF-κB activation, 26s proteasome activity in prostate cancer cells, and accelerated their apoptosis. Saquinavir treatment was observed to prevent LPS/IFN-γ-induced activation of NF-κB and stabilize expression of IκBα. It inhibited the 20s and 26s proteasome activity in lysates from LnCaP, DU-145, and PC-3 prostate cancer cells with an IC_{50} of 10 μM (Pajonk et al., 2002). Among the HIV-1 PIs compounds (**1–6**) [pepstatin, saquinavir (SQV), ritonavir (RTV), indinavir (IDV), nelfinavir (NFV), and amprenavir (APV)] are first-generation inhibitors and compounds (**7–10**) [fosamprenavir, lopinavir (LPV), atazanavir (ATV), and tipranavir (TPV)] are second-generation inhibitors (Fig. 5.6). The inhibitors also include bisalkylated 2,5-dihydroxybenzoquinones didemethylasterriquinone D (**11**), isocochliodinol (**12**), and semicochliodinol A and B (**13** and **14**), isolated from a culture of *Chrysosporium merdarium* P-5656 (Fredenhagen et al., 1997). Further, semicochliodinol A and B inhibited HIV-1 protease with an IC_{50} value as low as 0.17 μM, and EGFR protein tyrosine kinase in 15–60 μM range. The in silico studies of HIV-1-PI complexes showed hydrogen bonding between the dihydroxybenzoquinone moiety of didemethylasterriquinone D and isocochliodinol with active-site aspartic acids (Asp25/Asp25′) of the protease. The indole moiety of the inhibitors occupied P2 and P2′ pockets of the protease (Fredenhagen et al., 1997).

5.4.2 Cathepsin D inhibitors as anticancer agents

Cathepsin D (CatD), an aspartic endoprotease, is ubiquitously distributed in lysosomes. The primary function of the enzyme is to degrade lysosomal protein under acidic pH. It also activates the precursors of biologically active proteins in prelysosomal compartments of specialized cells (Barrett, 1970; Diment et al., 1989). It has a bilobed orientation similar to other APs i.e., renin, chymosin, and pepsinogen (Metcalf and Fusek, 1993). Pepstatin (**1**) (Fig. 5.6) has been used, not only in affinity chromatography for purification of CatD, but also produced inhibitory action on the enzyme (Umezawa et al., 1970). CatD is produced in the endoplasmic reticulum as pre-pro-enzyme that undergoes several proteolytic cleavages during the biosynthesis to produce a mature form. Estrogen and growth factors stimulate production of CatD protein and its mRNA accumulation in ER-positive breast cancer cell lines (Westley and May, 1987). CatD stimulates angiogenesis by releasing ECM-bound bFGF in breast cancer cells and prevents tumor apoptosis in an activity-dependent manner in CatD transfected 3Y1-Ad12 tumor xenografts model (Berchem et al., 2002; Fusek and Vetvicka, 1994). Lucanthone (**15**) (Fig. 5.7), a novel inhibitor of autophagy, stimulated CatD-mediated cell death, as observed by microarray analysis, qRT-PCR, and immunoblotting studies (Carew et al., 2011). Huo et al. investigated free binding energies of a set of CatD inhibitors obtained from combinatorial chemistry. The nonpeptide inhibitor complexes developed, on the basis of the crystal structure of a peptide-based inhibitor complexed with CatD, displayed less deviation during their molecular dynamic simulation. Further, the CatD-inhibitor complexes obtained from CombiBuild, displayed <1 Å mean Cα RMS deviation when compared to CatD-pepstatin complex. R configuration was also found unfavorable for binding of inhibitors. The hydroxyl group of compounds (**16–19**) displayed stable hydrogen bonding with CatD, but hydroxyl group of the R isomer of compound (**16**, compound **21**) did not form any hydrogen bond. The S epimer of compounds (**16–18** and **20**) produced hydrogen bonding between the oxygen atom of the carbonyl group of peptide bond and Gly81 or Ser82 backbone of CatD. The backbone oxygen atom of Gly233 displayed a hydrogen bond with the amino group of compound (**18**). Additionally, the hydroxyl group of Thr234 also formed a hydrogen bond with amino group of compounds (**16** and **20**). The study also reflected that the hydroxyl group of the scaffold should form a hydrogen bond with the active site aspartic acid residues of CatD which was absent in case of compound (**21**). Further, compound (**20**) produced additional intermolecular and electrostatic interactions which might be more favorable for CatD inhibition. The charge distribution on the R_2 substituent was altered due to incorporation of amino group on the ring, that resulted in enhanced hydrogen bonding between the ligand and CatD from the original (Huo et al., 2002). Lee et al. designed and synthesized statin-based inhibitors of CatD using a combinatorial chemistry approach. They identified compound (**22**) as a potent inhibitor of CatD with Ki of 0.7 nM. The study indicated that the P1 subsite of inhibitor supported larger hydrophobic side chains rather than smaller benzyl side chain (Lee et al., 1998b).

Eli Lilly reported nonpeptidomimetic, nonstatin-based CatD inhibitors (**23** and **24**) (Fig. 5.8) with submicromolar IC_{50} of 210 and 340 nM, respectively. Various substituents were added to allow additional hydrogen bond

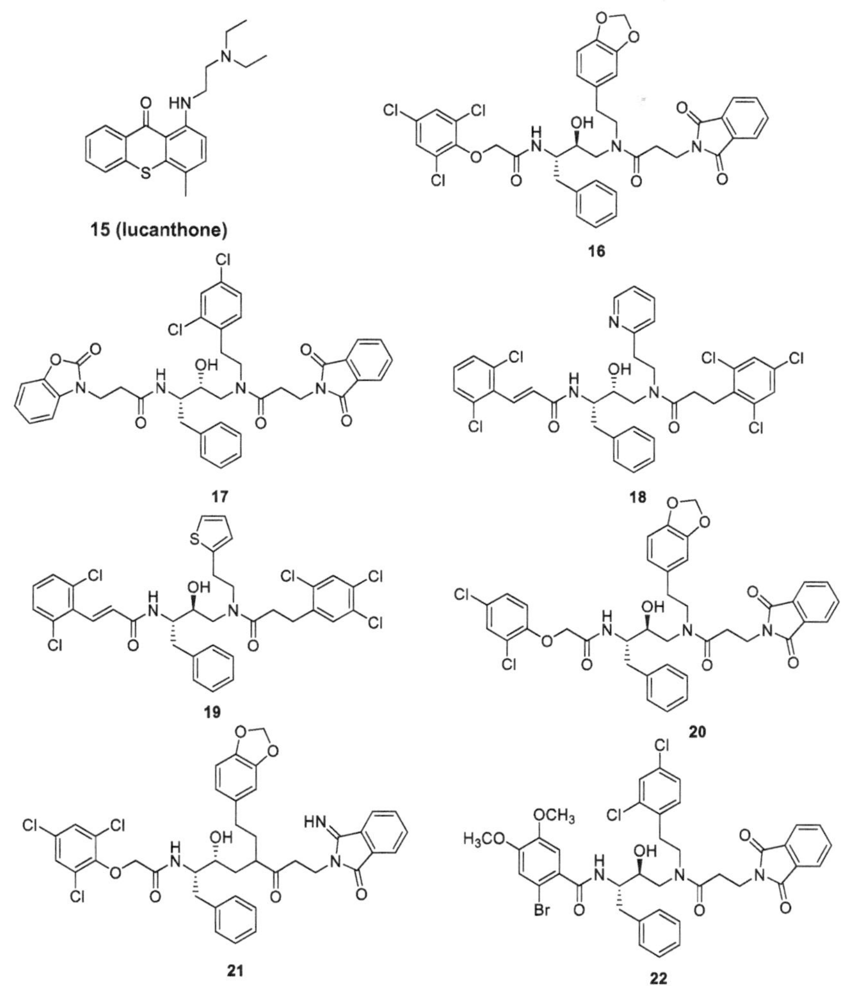

FIG. 5.7 Structure of cathepsin D inhibitors as anticancer agents.

interactions and improve the potency of CatD inhibitors. An additional *ortho* hydroxyl group introduced adjacent to the propyl chain was responsible for hydrogen bonding, and improved CatD potency (Whitesitt et al., 1996). Storey et al. screened human CatD and identified the primary hit molecule (**25,** $IC_{50} = 1.7\ \mu M$) as a reversible competitive CatD inhibitor. The hit molecule was modified further to improve potency by eliminating 2, 4-dichlorosalicylamide moiety responsible for mitochondrial uncoupling in the low micromolar range (Storey et al., 1975). The two aromatic entities of compound (**25**), i.e., benzothiazole and phenyl ring linked by a heteroatom were varied and keeping

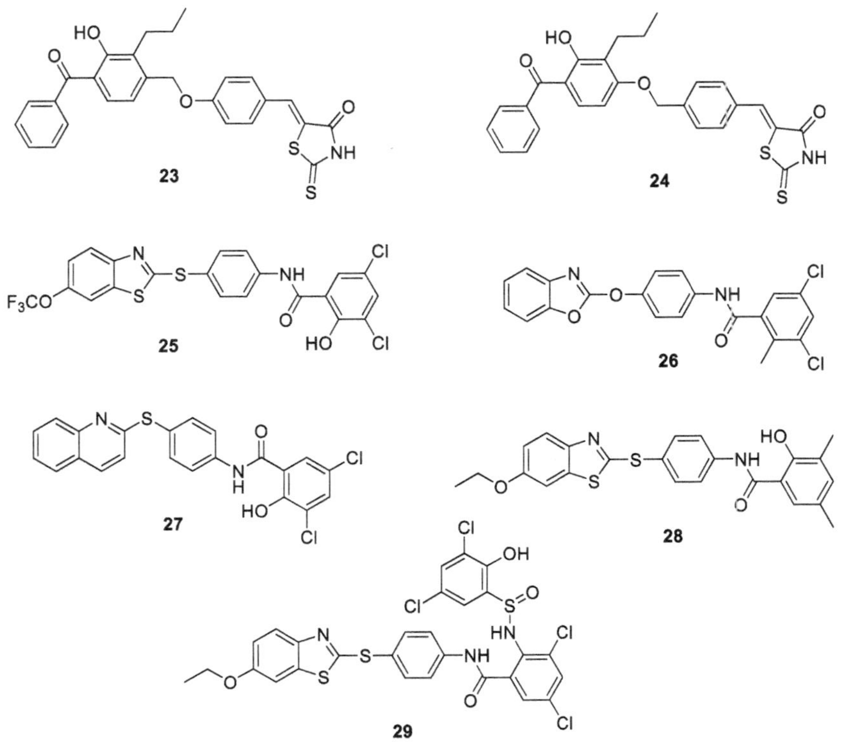

FIG. 5.8 Structures of nonpeptidomimetic, nonstatin-based cathepsin D inhibitors as anticancer agents.

the rest of the molecule unchanged. The benzothiazole substitution produced little effect on the activity but the heteroatom sulfur or oxygen linker between two rings was favorable for the activity (Dumas et al., 1999). Substitution with more hydrophilic benzoxazole, by replacing benzothiazole, produced diminished activity in compound (**26,** $IC_{50} = 5\,\mu M$) but replacement of benzothiazole with its quinoline isostere (**27**) showed improvement in activity ($IC_{50} = 2.5\,\mu M$). The alteration in phenyl bridge with lipophilic substituents like methyl, chloro, or trifluoromethyl at *ortho* position of heteroatom linker resulted in marginal increase in activity. Dichlorophenol group was found to be necessary for the activity and methylation of phenol produced an inactive compound. Removal of either or both chlorine atoms also resulted in a dramatic loss of activity. The pK_a of phenol might be necessary for activity as was established by the dimethyl analog (**28,** $IC_{50} = 10\,\mu M$) having similar lipophilicity, but different pK_a and was completely inactive. Replacement of hydroxyl by an amino group decreased activity. The most active compound of the series was amide-sulphonamide (**29,** $IC_{50} = 250\,nM$) which was stable to hydrolysis (Dumas et al., 1999).

5.4.3 Endothelin-converting enzyme inhibitors as anticancer agents

Peptide endothelin-1 (ET-1) was first identified in 1988 from culture media of porcine endothelial cells (Yanagisawa et al., 1988). It belongs to a family of multifunctional peptides (ET-1, 2 and 3) that are closely related to sarafotoxins. Among the isoforms, ET-1 has been extensively studied and is also implicated in cancer. ET-1 is formed via proteolytic cleavage of a large precursor molecule by endothelin converting enzyme (ECE). Increased plasma level of ET-1 have been detected in patients with various solid tumors including hepatocellular, gastric and prostate cancer (Sakamoto et al., 1991). Shankar et al. reported elevated plasma level of ET-1 in patients with primary colorectal cancer, with or without liver metastases (Shankar et al., 1998). Many human cancer cell lines including colonic, breast, stomach, prostate, and glioblastoma cells have been shown to produce ET-1 in vitro (Kusuhara et al., 1990; Ali et al., 2000). The elevated ET receptor expression in malignant colorectal, ovarian, and prostate tumor cells has been evaluated by using immunohistochemistry or autoradiography. ET-1 also contributed toward tumor growth by protecting cells from apoptosis. It protected rat fibroblasts and human endothelial cells from serum-deprivation-induced apoptosis in in vitro experiment (Bagnato et al., 1999). It was reported that ET-1 was a survival factor for rat colon carcinoma cells against FasL-mediated apoptosis. The peptide was a potent mitogen for both endothelial and vascular smooth muscle cells (VSMC) found in in vitro study and helped angiogenesis by indirect enhancement of endothelial cell proliferation through stimulation of vascular endothelial growth factor (VEGF) production by other cells (Bagnato et al., 1999). Yanagisawa et al. identified a biosynthetic pathway for the production of ET based on cDNA sequencing of cloned gene. Preproendothelin, a 203-amino acid precursor, initially cleaved adjacent to a pair of basic residues by normal hormone processing enzymes to form a 38-amino acid peptide prohormone. It was further cleaved between Trp-Val bond by endothelin converting enzyme (ECE) to release mature peptide (Inoue et al., 1989). The structures of inhibitors are included in figure (Fig. 5.9). Phosphoramidon (*N*-[(α-L-rhamnopyranosyloxy)hydroxyphosphenyl-L-leucyl-L-tryptophan, **30**) is a potent inhibitor of neutral ECE with IC_{50} value in 1–4 μM range. The activity of ECE was also inhibited by metal-chelating agents such as EDTA and *o*-phenanthroline; thus was established a metal-dependent enzyme. The presence of an acid-labile phosphorus-nitrogen bond makes it unsuitable to develop as an orally active drug (Jeng et al., 2002). Two structurally distinct series of potent and selective ECE inhibitors were developed by Shiosaki et al. as cancer therapeutics. Pepstatin-A and statine were basic skeletons for the first series of the key molecules, further modifications of structural core with various residues imparted potency and selectivity in rat lung ECE. The screening of existing in-house AP renin inhibitors exhibited a common dihydroxyethylene fragment that possessed moderate inhibition of rat lung ECE and subsequent modification

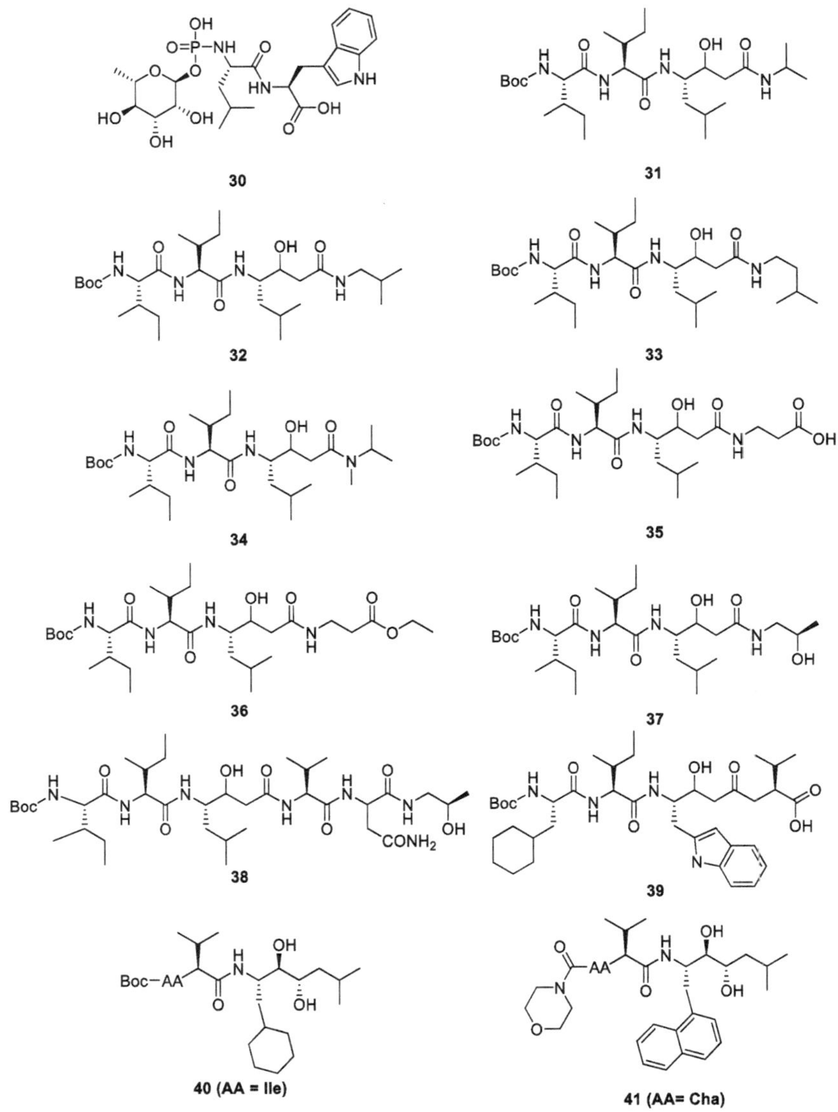

FIG. 5.9 Structure of ECE inhibitors as anticancer agents.

led to improvement in potency for ECE over renin. 3-Hydroxyl group of statine was expected to interact with two aspartic acid residues of the active site of the ECE and the isobutyl side chain of statine was to occupy S_1 binding pocket. Additional binding interactions was therefore expected upon appending two isoleucines in P2 and P3 positions of the substrate. Substitution of C-terminus of the amide by numerous branched alkyl groups exhibited significant improvement in potency. Isopropyl amide derivative (**31**) was better than primary amide

($IC_{50}=32\,nM$), while isobutyl (**32**) and isovaleryl (**33**) derivatives showed significant improvement in activity (IC_{50} 13 and 72 nM respectively). The substitution by *N*-methylisobutylamide (**34**) suggested that hydrogen in secondary amide was involved in the interaction and was vital for recognition/affinity toward ECE active site and increased 9-fold selectivity ($IC_{50}=6\,nM$) for the lung enzyme (Shiosaki et al., 1993). Incorporation of β-alanine (**35**) and β-alanine ethyl ester (**36**) to C-terminus improved anti-ECE potency over primary amide with IC_{50} 19 and 50 nM respectively. Threonine and valine are the P3′ and P1 residues in the substrate and therefore inclusion of 2-hydroxypropylamine, a threonine surrogate lacking α-carboxyl group (**37**) and valine (**38**) produced potent inhibition against ECE (IC_{50} 15 and 17 nM, respectively). The replacement of isopropyl side chain in statine with indol-3-yl group displayed interaction with tryptophan residues in P1 pocket of the substrate. Further, introduction of the P1 valine onto the C-terminus of indole-3-yl derivative (**39**) yielded a potent inhibitor of ECE with IC_{50} of 20 nM. A number of renin inhibitors representing a common dihydroxyethylene "hook" containing cyclohexylmethyl, demonstrated the ECE inhibitory activity with IC_{50} in the range of 50–100 nM, though they were very potent against renin ($IC_{50} < 1\,nM$). In order to increase ECE inhibitory potency over renin, compound (**40**) was synthesized with two isoleucines (P1 and P3 residues of ECE) attached to the N-terminus of cyclohexyl renin hook. The compound was one of the most potent inhibitors of lung ECE with an IC_{50} of 6 nM. The *N*-acetyl morpholine linked inhibitor (**41**), showed a good activity with IC_{50} of 2 nM (Shiosaki et al., 1993).

A series of azacyclic phosphonic acids as well as their enantiomers were synthesized from L-pyroglutamic acid, and 6-oxo-L-pipecolic acid, to study the effect of constraining acyclic inhibitors of ECE and to gain an insight into the functional and stereochemical requirements for inhibitory activity (Fig. 5.10). Proline was selected as azacyclic core unit to maintain the relative position of pharmacophores compared to the acyclic models. Since compounds (**42** and **43**) contained bulky aromatic groups as α-alkyl appendage, the cinnamyl, isobutyl, and *N*-(1,8-dicarboxynaphthalimido) ethyl were selected as potential predesigned hydrophobic pharmacophore (Jeng et al., 2002). Two compounds (**44** and **45**) of this series, from D-pyroglutamic and 6-oxo-D-pipecolic acids, respectively, showed 91% and 98% inhibition of ECE at 100 μM concentration (Hanessian et al., 2006). ECE-1 is present in significantly higher concentration in solid tumors as compared to effusions. Rayhman et al. studied the effect of RNA interference-induced knockdown of ECE1, a key enzyme in ET-1 production, on two ovarian carcinoma cell lines (ES2 and OVCAR3). Small interfering RNA (siRNA) targeted ECE-1 and markedly reduced ECE-1 mRNA protein levels, which subsequently led to 80%–90% inhibition of ET-1 peptide secretion in the ovarian cancer cells (Rayhman et al., 2008). Wallace et al. synthesized a series of potent and selective aryl acetylene derivatives as ECE-1 inhibitors. Compound (**46**), (*S*,*S*)-3-cyclohexyl-2-[[5-(2,4-difluorophenyl)-2-[(phosphonomethyl) amino]pent-4-ynoyl]amino]propionic acid, an aryl

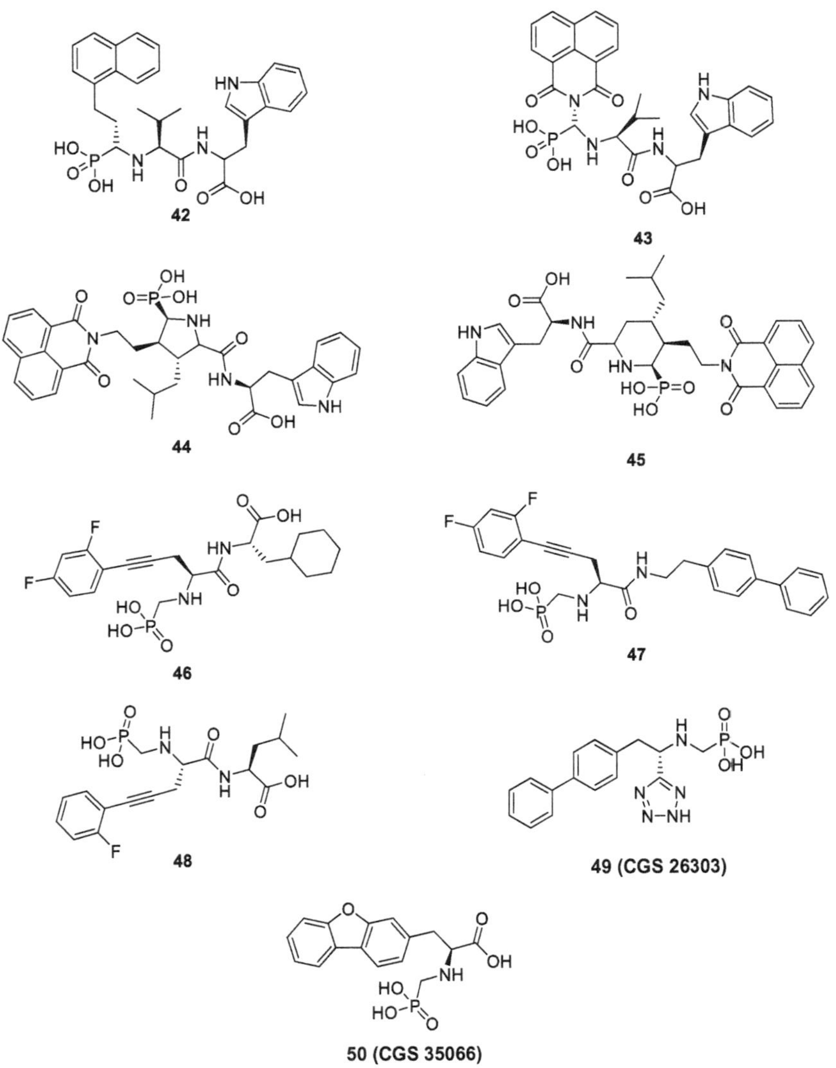

FIG. 5.10 Structures of azacyclic phosphonic acids and their enantiomers as ECE inhibitors.

acetylene amino phosphonate dipeptide, was found to be most active against ECE-1 with IC_{50} value of 14nM. Similarly, (*S*)-[[1-[(2-biphenyl-4-ylethyl)-carbamoyl]-4-(2-fluorophenyl)-3-but-ynyl]amino]methyl]phosphonic acid (**47**) showed marked inhibitory activity against ECE-1 (IC_{50} = 33 nM). A slight modification of the aryl moiety produced an extreme effect on ECE-1 selectivity. 2-Fluoro dipeptide analog, (*S*,*S*)-2-[[5-(2-fluorophenyl)-2-[(phosphonomethyl)-amino]pent-4-ynoyl]amino]-4-methylpentanoic acid (**48**), showed over 72-fold selectivity for ECE-1 (Wallace et al., 1998). Compound CGS 26303 (**49**) had already been reported to inhibit human endothelin converting enzyme-1

(ECE-1) with an IC_{50} value of 410nM and was efficacious in cancer therapeutics. But it was a more potent inhibitor of neutral endopeptidase (NEP) with an IC_{50} of 1 nM. The biphenyl and tetrazole moieties in CGS 26303 were replaced with dibenzofuran and carboxylic acid respectively, to afford CGS 35066 (**50**). This compound produced greater potency and selectivity toward ECE-1 inhibition and was a potent ECE-1 inhibitor with an IC_{50} of 22nM (Jeng et al., 2000).

Mckittrick et al. (1996) synthesized a series of phosphinic acid analogs as ECE inhibitors (Fig. 5.11). Compounds (**51** and **52**) of the series were identified to be quite potent with IC_{50} values of 2.5 and 1.5nM, respectively

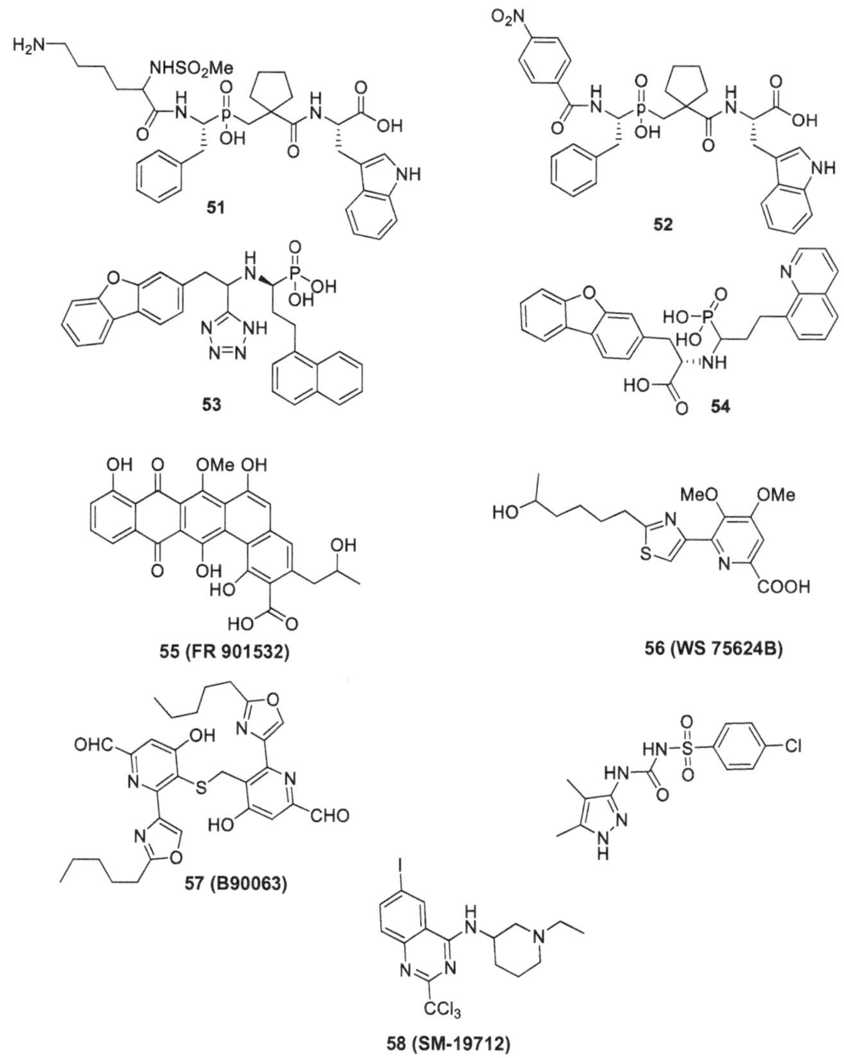

FIG. 5.11 Structures of miscellaneous ECE inhibitors as anticancer agents.

(Mckittrick et al., 1996). Compound (**53**) with a dipeptide aminophosphonic acid group, displayed ECE inhibition with IC_{50} value of 2 nM, while compound (**54**) showed marked inhibition against ECE with IC_{50} value of 14 nM (De Lombaert et al., 2000). Some of the natural products, viz., FR 901532 (**55**), WS 75624B (**56**), and B90063 (**57**), were isolated from fermentation of *Streptosporangium roseum*, *Saccharothrix* sp., and *Blastobacter* sp., respectively. These compounds exhibited excellent inhibition potencies against ECE with IC_{50} values of 140, 79, and 900 nM, respectively. Selective ECE inhibitors were identified from random screening of in-house compounds, where SM-19712 (**58**) and PD 069185 (**59**) were found to inhibit ECE with IC_{50} values of 42 and 900 nM, respectively (Jeng et al., 2002).

5.4.4 γ-Secretase inhibitor as anticancer agents

γ-Secretase is an integral membrane protein consisting of multisubunit protease complex. The complex constitutes presenilin-1 protein, an AP which is the catalytic site of γ-secretase (Wolfe, 2010). Aspartyl γ-secretase and its inhibitors control the production and release of Notch intracellular domain (NICD). The Notch pathway is disturbed in human breast carcinoma and overexpression of active Notch proteins induce mammary tumors in mice. Notch pathway has also been implicated in stem cell processes, including those of mammary epithelial stem cells. The potential of gamma (γ)-secretase inhibitor MRK-003 (**60**) in Notch pathway and tumor initiating cells (TIC) was investigated (Fig. 5.12). The compound inhibited the survival of tumorsphere-derived cells in vitro and eliminated TIC as assessed by cell transplantation into syngeneic mice. It also decreased the frequency of sphere-forming cells in established mammospheres ($P=1.2\times10^{-9}$) and tumor spheres ($P=2.4\times10^{-8}$) of breast carcinoma. MRK-003 monotherapy significantly blocked tumor growth (56%)

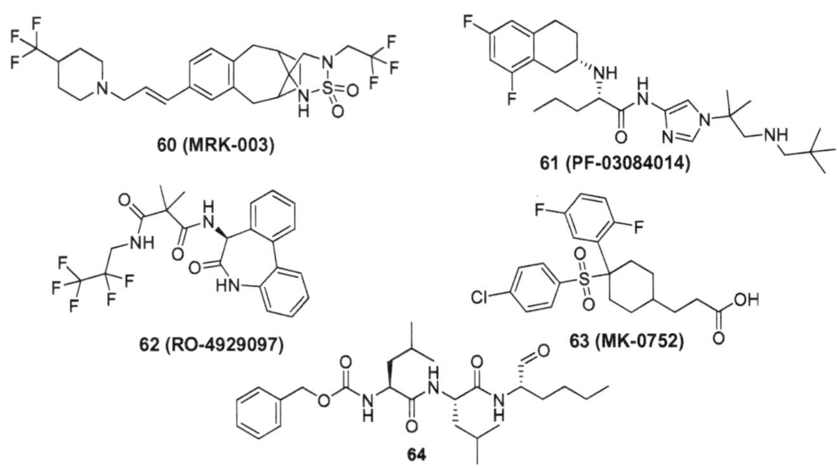

FIG. 5.12 Structures of γ-secretase inhibitors as anticancer agents.

in PDAC xenografts. A combination of MRK-003 and gemcitabine showed enhanced antitumor effect in 44% PDAC xenografts, reduced tumor cell proliferation, and induced apoptosis and intratumoral necrosis both (Kondratyev et al., 2012). T-cell acute lymphoblastic leukemia and lymphoma are aggressive hematologic cancers, associated with mutations in Notch. Notch1 has been established as an attractive therapeutic target of γ-secretase inhibitors for the treatment of lymphoblastic leukemia and lymphoma. The combination treatment of γ-secretase inhibitor PF-03084014 (**61**) and glucocorticoid exhibited a synergistic antileukemic effect in human T-ALL cell lines and primary human T-ALL patient samples. The treatment produced increased transcriptional upregulation of glucocorticoid receptor and glucocorticoid target genes (Samon et al., 2012). RO-4929097 (**62**), a potent and selective inhibitor of γ-secretase, produced inhibitory activity of Notch signaling in tumor cells. The preclinical studies monitored IL6 and IL8 serum levels of patients (prior to dosing with RO4929097 during phase I and in small group of patients deriving some clinical benefits), the drug presented with low baseline levels of IL6 and IL8 (Luistro et al., 2009). Schot et al. performed preclinical and clinical studies of γ-secretase inhibitor MK-0752 (**63**) in human breast tumor graft. MK-0752 in combination with docetaxel improved the efficacy of later in preclinical studies. Further, in clinical trial, 30 patients of advanced breast cancer were treated with escalating doses of MK-0752 and Docetaxel. The combination dose decreased CD44+, CD24−, ALDH+, and MSFE in tumors of patients undergoing serial biopsies with manageable toxicity and preliminary evidence of efficacy (Schott et al., 2013). Leupeptin derived γ-secretase inhibitor *N*-benzyloxycarbonyl-leu-leu-norleucine (**64**) (Z-Leu-Leu-Nle-CHO) induced apoptosis of tumor cells by inhibiting proteasome and Notch activity. Further, the challenging of two cell survival regulators contributed to apoptosis resistance of chronic lymphocytic leukemia (CLL) cells. Rosati et al. investigated the mechanism(s) through which GSI increased cell death of primary CLL cells. Time-course studies revealed that initial apoptotic events were due to inhibition of proteasome activity, concomitant with an increased endoplasmic reticulum (ER) stress apoptotic signaling and a consistent Noxa protein upregulation (Rosati et al., 2013).

5.4.5 β-Secretase inhibitors as anticancer agents

β-Secretase (BACE) is an essential AP for the formation of myelin sheaths in peripheral nerve cells. The transmembrane protein contains an active site made of two aspartate residues in its extracellular protein domain and may act as a dimer (Yan et al., 2001). The β-amyloid precursor protein, which is cleaved by β and γ-secretases to produce β-amyloid, is highly expressed in endothelium of neoforming vessels suggesting that it might play a role in angiogenesis. Both β and γ-secretase inhibitors were tested to reduce endothelial cell proliferation without inducing cellular toxicity and decreased the formation of capillary structures in in vitro and also suppressed sprouting of microvessel outgrowth in rat aortic ring model of angiogenesis. Two β-secretase inhibitors, i.e., *N*-benzyloxycarbonyl-Val-Leu-leucinal (**65,** *Z*-VLL-CHO) and OM99-2 (**66**) (Fig. 5.13), inhibited proliferation of human brain endothelial cells without affecting their viability. Z-VLL-CHO and γ-secretase inhibitor *N*-[*N*-(3,5-difluorophenacetyl-lalanyl)]-*S*-phenylglycine-*tert*-butyl-ester (**67,** DAPT) treatments ($P=0.12$) inhibited the growth of human glioblastoma xenografts. Paris et al. also evaluated the effect of DAPT and Z-VLL-CHO on proliferation of U87MG tumor cells and observed the dose dependent inhibition of the proliferation of lung adenocarcinoma cell line A549 without inducing tumor cell death (Paris et al., 2005). Novel *N,N*-dialkyl substituted chalcones (**68** and **69**) were synthesized by Nelson et al. as β-secretase-1 inhibitors.

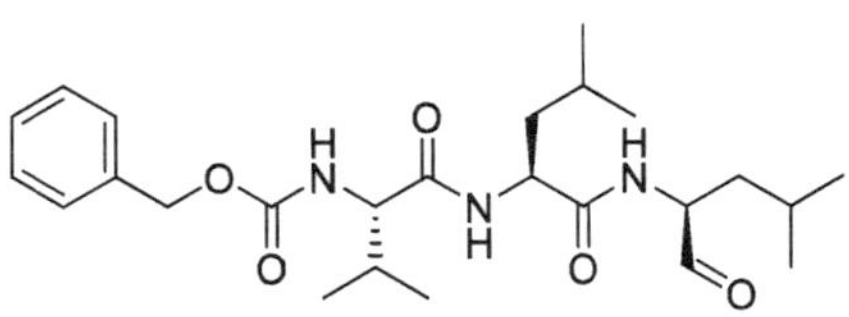

65

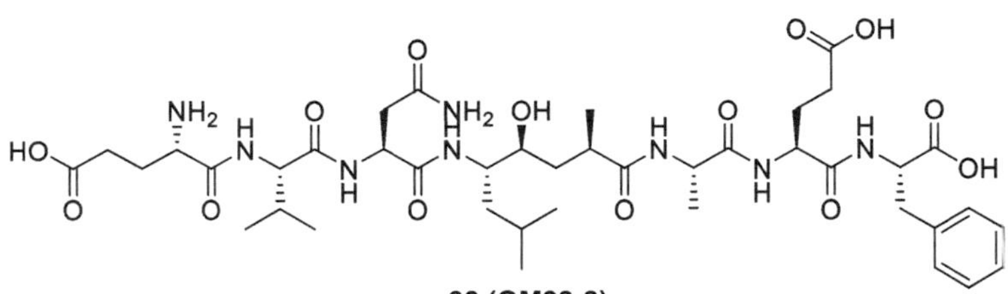

66 (OM99-2)

N-[*N*-(3,5-Difluorophenacetyl-lalanyl)]-*S*-phenylglycine-tert-butyl-ester

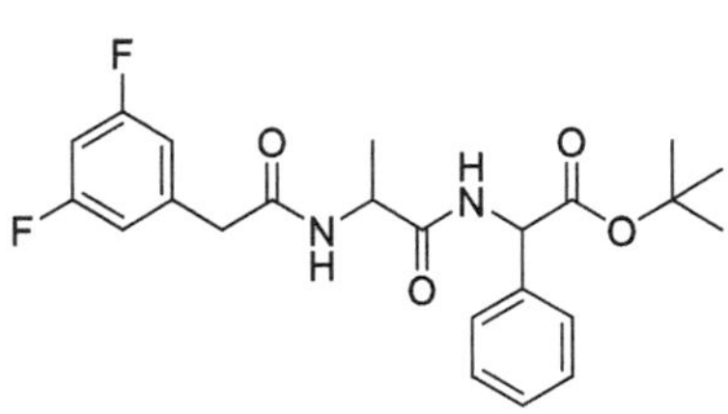

67(DAPT)

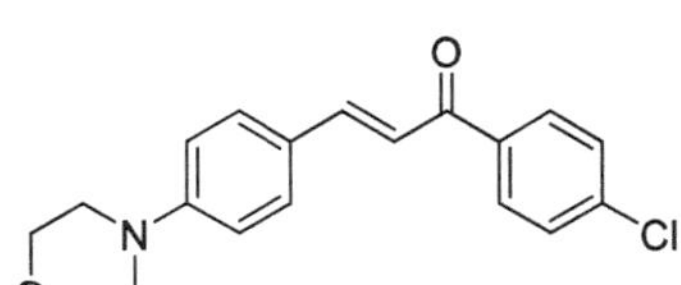

68

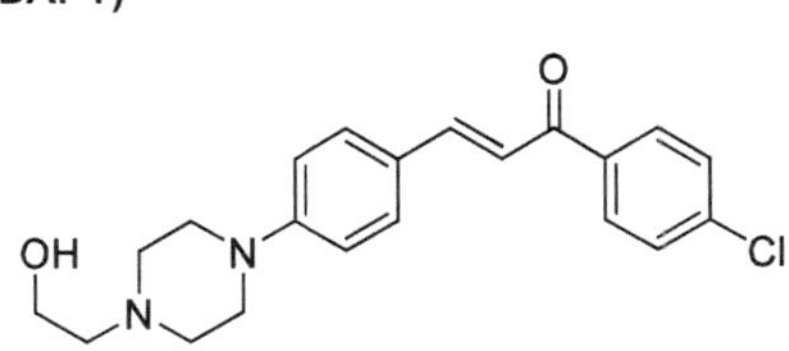

69

FIG. 5.13 Structures of β-secretase (BACE) inhibitors as anticancer agents.

Both the hydrophilic chalcones showed significant cytotoxicity with IC_{50} of 50 μM against MCF-7 breast cancer cell lines whereas compound (**68**) showed marked BACE-1 inhibitory activity with IC_{50} value of 50 μM (Nelson and Cox, 2017).

5.5 Conclusions

Cancer is the leading cause of death today, with an alarming surge in the incidences of morbidity and motility across the globe. Proteases appear to be a promising target and are being explored for drug development. These enzymes play a vital role in cellular development and processes. Their involvement in various cellular pathways expands the complexity of biological processes. The proteases are responsible for tumor growth, metastases, and angiogenesis in cancers. APs have been explored feebly. Profound understanding of structure and catalytic/mechanistic aspects of these are essential to gain insight into their role in various pathological conditions of cancer. With the advancement in crystallographic techniques, NMR, and cryo-electron microscopy, structural details of few APs including pepsinogen, β-secretase, γ-secretase, cathepsin D, etc. are now available. The designing of AP inhibitors involves mimicking of transition state formed during hydrolysis of the amide bond. Small molecules as well as peptidomimetics have been developed and evaluated as AP inhibitors with encouraging results. RO4929097, a γ-secretase inhibitor, has shown promising results in breast cancer patients in clinical trials. Compounds (**65** and **66**) displayed potential BACE-1 inhibition against human glioblastoma without affecting viability of human endothelial cells. Further structural and mechanistic understanding of this class of enzymes is an exigency for superior structure and ligand-based drug discovery and development.

References

Ali, H., Loizidou, M., Dashwood, M., Savage, F., Sheard, C., Taylor, I., 2000. Stimulation of colorectal cancer cell line growth by ET-1 and its inhibition by ETA antagonists. Gut 47, 685–688.

Alvarez, M.L., Barbon, J.J., Gonzalez, L.O., Lamelas, M.L., Vazquez, J., Vizoso, F.J., 2004. Expression of two androgen-induced proteins (pepsinogen C and apolipoprotein d) in epithelial skin cancers of the eyelids. Ophthalmologica 218, 115–119.

Bagnato, A., Salani, D., Di Castro, V., Wu-Wong, J.R., Tecce, R., Nicotra, M.R., Venuti, A., Natali, P.G., 1999. Expression of endothelin 1 and endothelin A receptor in ovarian carcinoma: evidence for an autocrine role in tumor growth. Cancer Res. 59, 720–727.

Bai, X.C., Yan, C., Yang, G., Lu, P., Ma, D., Sun, L., Zhou, R., Scheres, S.H.W., Shi, Y., 2015. An atomic structure of human gamma-secretase. Nature 525, 212–217.

Baldwin, E.T., Bhat, T.N., Gulnik, S., Hosur, M.V., Sowder 2nd, R.C., Cachau, R.E., Collins, J., Silva, A.M., Erickson, J.W., 1993. Crystal structures of native and inhibited forms of human cathepsin D: implications for lysosomal targeting and drug design. Proc. Natl. Acad. Sci. U. S. A. 90, 6796–6800.

Baldwin, E.T., Bhat, T.N., Gulnik, S., Liu, B., Topol, I.A., Kiso, Y., Mimoto, T., Mitsuya, H., Erickson, J.W., 1995. Structure of HIV-1 protease with KNI-272, a tight-binding transition-state analog containing allophenylnorstatine. Structure 3, 581–590.

Barkholt, V., 1987. Amino acid sequence of endothiapepsin: complete primary structure of the aspartic protease from Endothia parasitica. Eur. J. Biochem. 167, 327–331.

Barrett, A., 1970. Cathepsin D. Purification of isoenzymes from human and chicken liver. Biochem. J. 117, 601–607.

Bayliss, R., Knowles, J., Wybrandt, G.B., 1969. An aspartic acid residue at the active site of pepsin. The isolation and sequence of the heptapeptide. Biochem. J. 113, 377–386.

Bazzett, L.B., Watkins, C.S., Gercel-Taylor, C., Taylor, D.D., 1999. Modulation of proliferation and chemosensitivity by procathepsin D and its peptides in ovarian cancer. Gynecol. Oncol. 74, 181–187.

Berchem, G., Glondu, M., Gleizes, M., Brouillet, J.P., Vignon, F., Garcia, M., Liaudet-Coopman, E., 2002. Cathepsin-D affects multiple tumor progression steps in vivo: proliferation, angiogenesis and apoptosis. Oncogene 21, 5951–5955.

Berezovska, O., Jack, C., Mclean, P., Aster, J.C., Hicks, C., Xia, W., Wolfe, M.S., Kimberly, W.T., Weinmaster, G., Selkoe, D.J., Hyman, B.T., 2000. Aspartate mutations in presenilin and gamma-secretase inhibitors both impair notch1 proteolysis and nuclear translocation with relative preservation of notch1 signaling. J. Neurochem. 75, 583–593.

Bernard, W., Stewart, C., Freddie Bray, D.F., Hiroko Ohgaki, K.S., 2014. World Cancer Report 2014: International Agency for Research on Cancer (IARC). World Health Organization.

Berx, G., Van Roy, F., 2001. The E-cadherin/catenin complex: an important gatekeeper in breast cancer tumorigenesis and malignant progression. Breast Cancer Res. 3, 289–293.

Billgren, A.M., Rutqvist, L.E., Johansson, H., Hägerström, T., Skoog, L., 2000. The role of cathepsin D and PAI-1 in primary invasive breast cancer as prognosticators and predictors of treatment benefit with adjuvant tamoxifen. Eur. J. Cancer 36, 1374–1380.

Boshoff, C., Weiss, R., 2002. AIDS-related malignancies. Nat. Rev. Cancer 2, 373.

Bray, F., Ferlay, J., Soerjomataram, I., Siegel, R.L., Torre, L.A., Jemal, A., 2018. Global cancer statistics 2018: GLOBOCAN estimates of incidence and mortality worldwide for 36 cancers in 185 countries. CA Cancer J. Clin. 68, 394–424.

Capell, A., Steiner, H., Willem, M., Kaiser, H., Meyer, C., Walter, J., Lammich, S., Multhaup, G., Haass, C., 2000. Maturation and pro-peptide cleavage of beta-secretase. J. Biol. Chem. 275, 30849–30854.

Carew, J.S., Espitia, C.M., Esquivel, J.A., Mahalingam, D., Kelly, K.R., Reddy, G., Giles, F.J., Nawrocki, S.T., 2011. Lucanthone is a novel inhibitor of autophagy that induces cathepsin D-mediated apoptosis. J. Biol. Chem. 286, 6602–6613.

Chen, W.T., 1992. Membrane proteases: roles in tissue remodeling and tumour invasion. Curr. Opin. Cell Biol. 4, 802–809.

Chen, F., Hasegawa, H., Schmitt-Ulms, G., Kawarai, T., Bohm, C., Katayama, T., Gu, Y., Sanjo, N., Glista, M., Rogaeva, E., Wakutani, Y., Pardossi-Piquard, R., Ruan, X., Tandon, A., Checler, F., Marambaud, P., Hansen, K., Westaway, D., St George-Hyslop, P., Fraser, P., 2006. TMP21 is a presenilin complex component that modulates gamma-secretase but not epsilon-secretase activity. Nature 440, 1208–1212.

Christakis, P., 2011. The birth of chemotherapy at Yale. Bicentennial lecture series: Surgery Grand Round. Yale J. Biol. Med. 84, 169–172.

Clemente, J.C., Govindasamy, L., Madabushi, A., Fisher, S.Z., Moose, R.E., Yowell, C.A., Hidaka, K., Kimura, T., Hayashi, Y., Kiso, Y., 2006. Structure of the aspartic protease plasmepsin 4 from the malarial parasite Plasmodium malariae bound to an allophenylnorstatine-based inhibitor. Acta Crystallogr. Sect. D. Biol. Crystallogr. 62, 246–252.

Cooper, J., Khan, G., Taylor, G., Tickle, I., Blundell, T., 1990. X-ray analyses of aspartic proteinases: II. Three-dimensional structure of the hexagonal crystal form of porcine pepsin at 2.3 A resolution. J. Mol. Biol. 214, 199–222.

Costantini, C., Ko, M.H., Jonas, M.C., Puglielli, L., 2007. A reversible form of lysine acetylation in the ER and Golgi lumen controls the molecular stabilization of BACE1. Biochem. J. 407, 383–395.

Curry Jr., T.E., Dean, D.D., Sanders, S.L., Pedigo, N.G., Jones, P.B., 1989. The role of ovarian proteases and their inhibitors in ovulation. Steroids 54, 501–521.

Dash, C., Kulkarni, A., Dunn, B., Rao, M., 2003. Aspartic peptidase inhibitors: implications in drug development. Crit. Rev. Biochem. Mol. Biol. 38, 89–119.

Davies, D.R., 1990. The structure and function of the aspartic proteinases. Annu. Rev. Biophys. Biophys. Chem. 19, 189–215.

De Lombaert, S., Blanchard, L., Stamford, L.B., Tan, J., Wallace, E.M., Satoh, Y., Fitt, J., Hoyer, D., Simonsbergen, D., Moliterni, J., 2000. Potent and selective non-peptidic inhibitors of endothelin-converting enzyme-1 with sustained duration of action. J. Med. Chem. 43, 488–504.

De Strooper, B., 2003. Aph-1, Pen-2, and Nicastrin with Presenilin generate an active gamma-Secretase complex. Neuron 38, 9–12.

De Strooper, B., Saftig, P., Craessaerts, K., Vanderstichele, H., Guhde, G., Annaert, W., Von Figura, K., Van Leuven, F., 1998. Deficiency of presenilin-1 inhibits the normal cleavage of amyloid precursor protein. Nature 391, 387–390.

De Strooper, B., Annaert, W., Cupers, P., Saftig, P., Craessaerts, K., Mumm, J.S., Schroeter, E.H., Schrijvers, V., Wolfe, M.S., Ray, W.J., Goate, A., Kopan, R., 1999. A presenilin-1-dependent gamma-secretase-like protease mediates release of Notch intracellular domain. Nature 398, 518–522.

Didangelos, A., Yin, X., Mandal, K., Baumert, M., Jahangiri, M., Mayr, M., 2010. Proteomics characterization of extracellular space components in the human aorta. Mol. Cell. Proteomics 9, 2048–2062.

Diez-Itza, I., Merino, A.M., Tolivia, J., Vizoso, F., Sanchez, L.M., Lopez-Otin, C., 1993. Expression of pepsinogen C in human breast tumours and correlation with clinicopathologic parameters. Br. J. Cancer 68, 637–640.

Diment, S., Martin, K., Stahl, P., 1989. Cleavage of parathyroid hormone in macrophage endosomes illustrates a novel pathway for intracellular processing of proteins. J. Biol. Chem. 264, 13403–13406.

Dumas, J., Brittelli, D., Chen, J., Dixon, B., Hatoum-Mokdad, H., König, G., Sibley, R., Witowsky, J., Wong, S., 1999. Synthesis and structure activity relationships of novel small molecule cathepsin D inhibitors. Bioorg. Med. Chem. Lett. 9, 2531–2536.

Dunn, B.M., 2002. Structure and mechanism of the pepsin-like family of aspartic peptidases. Chem. Rev. 102, 4431–4458.

Eaton, D., Rodriguez, H., Vehar, G.A., 1986. Proteolytic processing of human factor VIII. Correlation of specific cleavages by thrombin, factor Xa, and activated protein C with activation and inactivation of factor VIII coagulant activity. Biochemistry 25, 505–512.

Elabiad, M.T., Zhang, J., 2011. Detection of pepsinogen in the neonatal lung and stomach by immunohistochemistry. J. Pediatr. Gastroenterol. Nutr. 53, 401–403.

Equils, O., Shapiro, A., Madak, Z., Liu, C., Lu, D., 2004. Human immunodeficiency virus type 1 protease inhibitors block toll-like receptor 2 (TLR2)-and TLR4-induced NF-κB activation. Antimicrob. Agents Chemother. 48, 3905–3911.

Fallon, K., Bausch, K., Noonan, J., Huguenel, E., Tamburini, P., 1997. Role of aspartic proteases in disseminated *Candida albicans* infection in mice. Infect. Immun. 65, 551–556.

Ferrandina, G., Scambia, G., Bardelli, F., Benedetti Panici, P., Mancuso, S., Messori, A., 1997. Relationship between cathepsin-D content and disease-free survival in node-negative breast cancer patients: a meta-analysis. Br. J. Cancer 76, 661–666.

Fluhrer, R., Friedlein, A., Haass, C., Walter, J., 2004. Phosphorylation of presenilin 1 at the caspase recognition site regulates its proteolytic processing and the progression of apoptosis. J. Biol. Chem. 279, 1585–1593.

Fluhrer, R., Steiner, H., Haass, C., 2009. Intramembrane proteolysis by signal peptide peptidases: a comparative discussion of GXGD-type aspartyl proteases. J. Biol. Chem. 284, 13975–13979.

Foekens, J.A., Look, M.P., Bolt-De Vries, J., Meijer-Van Gelder, M.E., Van Putten, W.L., Klijn, J.G., 1999. Cathepsin-D in primary breast cancer: prognostic evaluation involving 2810 patients. Br. J. Cancer 79, 300–307.

Foltmann, B., 1988. Structure and function of proparts in zymogens for aspartic proteinases. Biol. Chem. Hoppe Seyler 369 (Suppl), 311–314.

Foster, C., Aktar, A., Kopf, D., Zhang, P., Guttentag, S., 2004. Pepsinogen C: a type 2 cell-specific protease. Am. J. Physiol. Lung Cell Mol. Physiol. 286, L382–L387.

Fredenhagen, A., Petersen, F., Tintelnot-Blomley, M., Rösel, J., Mett, H., Hug, P., 1997. Semicochliodinol A and B: inhibitors of HIV-1 protease and EGF-R protein tyrosine kinase related to asterriquinones produced by the fungus Chrysosporium merdarium. J. Antibiot. 50, 395–401.

Freedberg, D.I., Wang, Y.-X., Stahl, S.J., Kaufman, J.D., Wingfield, P.T., Kiso, Y., Torchia, D., A., 1998. Flexibility and function in HIV protease: dynamics of the HIV-1 protease bound to the asymmetric inhibitor kynostatin 272 (KNI-272). J. Am. Chem. Soc. 120, 7916–7923.

Friedmann, E., Lemberg, M.K., Weihofen, A., Dev, K.K., Dengler, U., Rovelli, G., Martoglio, B., 2004. Consensus analysis of signal peptide peptidase and homologous human aspartic proteases reveals opposite topology of catalytic domains compared with presenilins. J. Biol. Chem. 279, 50790–50798.

Fujinaga, M., Chernaia, M.M., Tarasova, N.I., Mosimann, S.C., James, M.N., 1995. Crystal structure of human pepsin and its complex with pepstatin. Protein Sci. 4, 960–972.

Fukushima, N., Sato, N., Prasad, N., Leach, S.D., Hruban, R.H., Goggins, M., 2004. Characterization of gene expression in mucinous cystic neoplasms of the pancreas using oligonucleotide microarrays. Oncogene 23, 9042–9051.

Fusek, M., Vetvicka, V., 1994. Mitogenic function of human procathepsin D: the role of the propeptide. Biochem. J. 303, 775–780.

Fusek, M., Vetvickova, J., Vetvicka, V., 2007. Secretion of cytokines in breast cancer cells: the molecular mechanism of procathepsin D proliferative effects. J. Interf. Cytokine Res. 27, 191–199.

Garg, G.K., Virupaksha, T.K., 1970. Acid protease from germinated sorghum: 1. Purification and characterization of the enzyme. Eur. J. Biochem. 17, 4–12.

Gerson, K.D., Foster, C.D., Zhang, P., Zhang, Z., Rosenblatt, M.M., Guttentag, S.H., 2008. Pepsinogen C proteolytic processing of surfactant protein B. J. Biol. Chem. 283, 10330–10338.

Glondu, M., Coopman, P., Laurent-Matha, V., Garcia, M., Rochefort, H., Liaudet-Coopman, E., 2001. A mutated cathepsin-D devoid of its catalytic activity stimulates the growth of cancer cells. Oncogene 20, 6920–6929.

Glondu, M., Liaudet-Coopman, E., Derocq, D., Platet, N., Rochefort, H., Garcia, M., 2002. Down-regulation of cathepsin-D expression by antisense gene transfer inhibits tumor growth and experimental lung metastasis of human breast cancer cells. Oncogene 21, 5127–5134.

Gomes, R.A., Juliano, L., Chagas, J.R., Hial, V., 1997. Characterization of kininogenase activity of an acidic proteinase isolated from human kidney. Can. J. Physiol. Pharmacol. 75, 757–761.

Guicciardi, M.E., Leist, M., Gores, G.J., 2004. Lysosomes in cell death. Oncogene 23, 2881–2890.

Gupta, A.K., Cerniglia, G.J., Mick, R., Mckenna, W.G., Muschel, R.J., 2005. HIV protease inhibitors block Akt signaling and radiosensitize tumor cells both in vitro and in vivo. Cancer Res. 65, 8256–8265.

Haass, C., Selkoe, D.J., 1993. Cellular processing of beta-amyloid precursor protein and the genesis of amyloid beta-peptide. Cell 75, 1039–1042.

Hanessian, S., Gauchet, C., Charron, G., Marin, J., Nakache, P., 2006. Design and synthesis of diversely substituted azacyclic inhibitors of endothelin converting enzyme. J. Org. Chem. 71, 2760–2778.

Haniu, M., Denis, P., Young, Y., Mendiaz, E.A., Fuller, J., Hui, J.O., Bennett, B.D., Kahn, S., Ross, S., Burgess, T., Katta, V., Rogers, G., Vassar, R., Citron, M., 2000. Characterization of Alzheimer's beta -secretase protein BACE. A pepsin family member with unusual properties. J. Biol. Chem. 275, 21099–21106.

Hartsuck, J.A., Koelsch, G., Remington, S.J., 1992. The high-resolution crystal structure of porcine pepsinogen. Proteins 13, 1–25.

Harvey, A.M., 1974. Early contributions to the surgery of cancer: William S. Halsted, Hugh H. Young and John G. Clark. Johns Hopkins Med. J. 135, 399–417.

Hassan, M.I., Toor, A., Ahmad, F., 2010. Progastriscin: structure, function, and its role in tumor progression. J. Mol. Cell Biol. 2, 118–127.

Hata, S., Taniguchi, M., Piao, Y., Ikeuchi, T., Fagan, A.M., Holtzman, D.M., Bateman, R., Sohrabi, H.R., Martins, R.N., Gandy, S., Urakami, K., Suzuki, T., 2012. Multiple gamma-secretase product peptides are coordinately increased in concentration in the cerebrospinal fluid of a subpopulation of sporadic Alzheimer's disease subjects. Mol. Neurodegener. 7, 16.

Homey, B., Muller, A., Zlotnik, A., 2002. Chemokines: agents for the immunotherapy of cancer? Nat. Rev. Immunol. 2, 175–184.

Hong, S.K., 2014. Kallikreins as biomarkers for prostate cancer. Biomed. Res. Int. 2014, 10.

Hong, L., Koelsch, G., Lin, X., Wu, S., Terzyan, S., Ghosh, A.K., Zhang, X.C., Tang, J., 2000. Structure of the protease domain of memapsin 2 (beta-secretase) complexed with inhibitor. Science 290, 150–153.

Hong, L., Turner, R.T., Koelsch, G., Shin, D., Ghosh, A.K., Tang, J., 2002. Crystal structure of memapsin 2 (β-secretase) in complex with an inhibitor OM00-3. Biochemistry 41, 10963–10967.

Huo, S., Wang, J., Cieplak, P., Kollman, P.A., Kuntz, I.D., 2002. Molecular dynamics and free energy analyses of cathepsin D-inhibitor interactions: Insight into structure-based ligand design. J. Med. Chem. 45, 1412–1419.

Huse, J.T., Pijak, D.S., Leslie, G.J., Lee, V.M., Doms, R.W., 2000. Maturation and endosomal targeting of beta-site amyloid precursor protein-cleaving enzyme. The Alzheimer's disease beta-secretase. J. Biol. Chem. 275, 33729–33737.

Ikezoe, T., Hisatake, Y., Takeuchi, T., Ohtsuki, Y., Yang, Y., Said, J.W., Taguchi, H., Koeffler, H.P., 2004. HIV-1 protease inhibitor, ritonavir: a potent inhibitor of CYP3A4, enhanced the anti-cancer effects of docetaxel in androgen-independent prostate cancer cells in vitro and in vivo. Cancer Res. 64, 7426–7431.

Inoue, A., Yanagisawa, M., Kimura, S., Kasuya, Y., Miyauchi, T., Goto, K., Masaki, T., 1989. The human endothelin family: three structurally and pharmacologically distinct isopeptides predicted by three separate genes. Proc. Natl. Acad. Sci. U. S. A. 86, 2863–2867.

Jeng, A.Y., De, S.L., Beil, M.E., Bruseo, C.W., Savage, P., Chou, M., Trapani, A.J., 2000. Design and synthesis of a potent and selective endothelin-converting enzyme inhibitor, CGS 35066. J. Cardiovasc. Pharmacol. 36, S36–S39.

Jeng, A.Y., Mulder, P., Kwan, A.-L., Battistini, B., 2002. Nonpeptidic endothelin-converting enzyme inhibitors and their potential therapeutic applications. Can. J. Physiol. Pharmacol. 80, 440–449.

Kageyama, T., 2002. Pepsinogens, progastricsins, and prochymosins: structure, function, evolution, and development. Cell. Mol. Life Sci. 59, 288–306.

Kazama, Y., Hamamoto, T., Foster, D.C., Kisiel, W., 1995. Hepsin, a putative membrane-associated serine protease, activates human factor VII and initiates a pathway of blood coagulation on the cell surface leading to thrombin formation. J. Biol. Chem. 270, 66–72.

Kimberly, W.T., Lavoie, M.J., Ostaszewski, B.L., Ye, W., Wolfe, M.S., Selkoe, D.J., 2003. Gamma-secretase is a membrane protein complex comprised of presenilin, nicastrin, Aph-1, and Pen-2. Proc. Natl. Acad. Sci. U. S. A. 100, 6382–6387.

Ko, M.H., Puglielli, L., 2009. Two endoplasmic reticulum (ER)/ER Golgi intermediate compartment-based lysine acetyltransferases post-translationally regulate BACE1 levels. J. Biol. Chem. 284, 2482–2492.

Koblinski, J.E., Ahram, M., Sloane, B.F., 2000. Unraveling the role of proteases in cancer. Clin. Chim. Acta 291, 113–135.

Koelsch, G., Mareš, M., Metcalf, P., Fusek, M., 1994. Multiple functions of pro-parts of aspartic proteinase zymogens. FEBS Lett. 343, 6–10.

Koike, M., Shibata, M., Ohsawa, Y., Nakanishi, H., Koga, T., Kametaka, S., Waguri, S., Momoi, T., Kominami, E., Peters, C., Figura, K., Saftig, P., Uchiyama, Y., 2003. Involvement of two different cell death pathways in retinal atrophy of cathepsin D-deficient mice. Mol. Cell. Neurosci. 22, 146–161.

Kondratyev, M., Kreso, A., Hallett, R., Girgis-Gabardo, A., Barcelon, M., Ilieva, D., Ware, C., Majumder, P., Hassell, J., 2012. Gamma-secretase inhibitors target tumor-initiating cells in a mouse model of ERBB2 breast cancer. Oncogene 31, 93.

Konishi, N., Nakaoka, S., Matsumoto, K., Nakamura, M., Kuwashima, S., Hiasa, Y., Cho, M., Uemura, H., Hirao, Y., 1999. Expression of pepsinogen II with androgen and estrogen receptors in human prostate carcinoma. Pathol. Int. 49, 203–207.

Kopan, R., Ilagan, M.X., 2009. The canonical Notch signaling pathway: unfolding the activation mechanism. Cell 137, 216–233.

Kumar, D., Ganeshpurkar, A., Kumar, D., Modi, G., Gupta, S.K., Singh, S.K., 2018. Secretase inhibitors for the treatment of Alzheimer's disease: long road ahead. Eur. J. Med. Chem. 148, 436–452.

Kusuhara, M., Yamaguchi, K., Nagasaki, K., Hayashi, C., Suzaki, A., Hori, S., Handa, S., Nakamura, Y., Abe, K., 1990. Production of endothelin in human cancer cell lines. Cancer Res. 50, 3257–3261.

Lammich, S., Okochi, M., Takeda, M., Kaether, C., Capell, A., Zimmer, A.K., Edbauer, D., Walter, J., Steiner, H., Haass, C., 2002. Presenilin-dependent intramembrane proteolysis of CD44 leads to the liberation of its intracellular domain and the secretion of an Abeta-like peptide. J. Biol. Chem. 277, 44754–44759.

Laurent-Matha, V., Farnoud, M.R., Lucas, A., Rougeot, C., Garcia, M., Rochefort, H., 1998. Endocytosis of pro-cathepsin D into breast cancer cells is mostly independent of mannose-6-phosphate receptors. J. Cell Sci. 111, 2539–2549.

Lee, A.Y., Gulnik, S.V., Erickson, J.W., 1998a. Conformational switching in an aspartic proteinase. Nat. Struct. Biol. 5, 866–871.

Lee, C.E., Kick, E.K., Ellman, J.A., 1998b. General solid-phase synthesis approach to prepare mechanism-based aspartyl protease inhibitor libraries. Identification of potent cathepsin D inhibitors. J. Am. Chem. Soc. 120, 9735–9747.

Lee, S.F., Shah, S., Yu, C., Wigley, W.C., Li, H., Lim, M., Pedersen, K., Han, W., Thomas, P., Lundkvist, J., Hao, Y.H., Yu, G., 2004. A conserved GXXXG motif in APH-1 is critical for assembly and activity of the gamma-secretase complex. J. Biol. Chem. 279, 4144–4152.

Li, Y., Bohm, C., Dodd, R., Chen, F., Qamar, S., Schmitt-Ulms, G., Fraser, P.E., St George-Hyslop, P.H., 2014. Structural biology of presenilin 1 complexes. Mol. Neurodegener. 9, 59.

Liaudet-Coopman, E., Beaujouin, M., Derocq, D., Garcia, M., Glondu-Lassis, M., Laurent-Matha, V., Prébois, C., Rochefort, H., Vignon, F., 2006. Cathepsin D: newly discovered functions of a long-standing aspartic protease in cancer and apoptosis. Cancer Lett. 237, 167–179.

Lin, X., Koelsch, G., Wu, S., Downs, D., Dashti, A., Tang, J., 2000. Human aspartic protease memapsin 2 cleaves the beta-secretase site of beta-amyloid precursor protein. Proc. Natl. Acad. Sci. U. S. A. 97, 1456–1460.

López-Otín, C., Overall, C.M., 2002. Protease degradomics: a new challenge for proteomics. Nat. Rev. Mol. Cell Biol. 3, 509.

Luistro, L., He, W., Smith, M., Packman, K., Vilenchik, M., Carvajal, D., Roberts, J., Cai, J., Berkofsky-Fessler, W., Hilton, H., 2009. Preclinical profile of a potent γ-secretase inhibitor targeting notch signaling with in vivo efficacy and pharmacodynamic properties. Cancer Res. 69, 7672–7680.

Lutgens, S.P., Cleutjens, K.B., Daemen, M.J., Heeneman, S., 2007. Cathepsin cysteine proteases in cardiovascular disease. FASEB J. 21, 3029–3041.

Maggiorella, L., Wen, B., Frascogna, V., Opolon, P., Bourhis, J., Deutsch, E., 2005. Combined radiation sensitizing and anti-angiogenic effects of ionizing radiation and the protease inhibitor ritonavir in a head and neck carcinoma model. Anticancer Res. 25, 4357–4362.

Mahmood, N., Mihalcioiu, C., Rabbani, S.A., 2018. Multifaceted role of the urokinase-type plasminogen activator (uPA) and its receptor (uPAR): diagnostic, prognostic, and therapeutic applications. Front. Oncol. 8, 24.

Marambaud, P., Shioi, J., Serban, G., Georgakopoulos, A., Sarner, S., Nagy, V., Baki, L., Wen, P., Efthimiopoulos, S., Shao, Z., Wisniewski, T., Robakis, N.K., 2002. A presenilin-1/gamma-secretase cleavage releases the E-cadherin intracellular domain and regulates disassembly of adherens junctions. EMBO J. 21, 1948–1956.

Masson, O., Prébois, C., Derocq, D., Meulle, A., Dray, C., Daviaud, D., Quilliot, D., Valet, P., Muller, C., Liaudet-Coopman, E., 2011. Cathepsin-D, a key protease in breast cancer, is up-regulated in obese mouse and human adipose tissue, and controls adipogenesis. PLoS One 6, e16452.

Maule, M., Merletti, F., 2012. Cancer transition and priorities for cancer control. Lancet Oncol. 13, 745–746.

Mckittrick, B.A., Stamford, A.W., Weng, X., Ma, K., Chackalamannil, S., Czarniecki, M., Cleven, R., Fawzi, A.B., 1996. Design and synthesis of phosphinic acids that triply inhibit endothelin converting enzyme, angiotensin converting enzyme and neutral endopeptidase 24.11. Bioorg. Med. Chem. Lett. 6, 1629–1634.

Mengele, K., Napieralski, R., Magdolen, V., Reuning, U., Gkazepis, A., Sweep, F., Brünner, N., Foekens, J., Harbeck, N., Schmitt, M., 2010. Characteristics of the level-of-evidence-1 disease forecast cancer biomarkers uPA and its inhibitor PAI-1. Expert. Rev. Mol. Diagn. 10, 947–962.

Menon, A.S., Goldberg, A., 1987. Protein substrates activate the ATP-dependent protease La by promoting nucleotide binding and release of bound ADP. J. Biol. Chem. 262, 14929–14934.

Metcalf, P., Fusek, M., 1993. Two crystal structures for cathepsin D: the lysosomal targeting signal and active site. EMBO J. 12, 1293–1302.

Mirinics, Z.K., Calafat, J., Udby, L., Lovelock, J., Kjeldsen, L., Rothermund, K., Sisodia, S.S., Borregaard, N., Corey, S.J., 2002. Identification of the presenilins in hematopoietic cells with localization of presenilin 1 to neutrophil and platelet granules. Blood Cells Mol. Dis. 28, 28–38.

Monini, P., Sgadari, C., Barillari, G., Ensoli, B., 2003. HIV protease inhibitors: antiretroviral agents with anti-inflammatory, anti-angiogenic and anti-tumour activity. J. Antimicrob. Chemother. 51, 207–211.

Monini, P., Sgadari, C., Toschi, E., Barillari, G., Ensoli, B., 2004. Antitumour effects of antiretroviral therapy. Nat. Rev. Cancer 4, 861.

Morales, P., Kong, M., Pizarro, E., Pasten, C., 2003. Participation of the sperm proteasome in human fertilization. Hum. Reprod. 18, 1010–1017.

Mori, K., Ogawa, Y., Tamura, N., Ebihara, K., Aoki, T., Muro, S., Ozaki, S., Tanaka, I., Tashiro, K., Nakao, K., 1997. Molecular cloning of a novel mouse aspartic protease-like protein that is expressed abundantly in the kidney. FEBS Lett. 401, 218–222.

Morihara, K., 1974. Comparative specificity of microbial proteinases. Adv. Enzymol. Relat. Areas Mol. Biol. 41, 179–243.

Mould, R.F., 2007. Priority for radium therapy of benign conditions and cancer. Curr. Oncol. 14, 118–122.

Mukhopadhyay, S., Katzenstein, A.-L.A., 2011. Subclassification of non-small cell lung carcinomas lacking morphologic differentiation on biopsy specimens: utility of an immunohistochemical panel containing TTF-1, napsin A, p63, and CK5/6. Am. J. Surg. Pathol. 35, 15–25.

Murayama, M., Tanaka, S., Palacino, J., Murayama, O., Honda, T., Sun, X., Yasutake, K., Nihonmatsu, N., Wolozin, B., Takashima, A., 1998. Direct association of presenilin-1 with beta-catenin. FEBS Lett. 433, 73–77.

Nelson, D.L., Cox, M., 2017. Lehninger Principles of Biochemistry: International Edition. Macmillan Learning.

Nguyen, G., 2011. Renin, (pro)renin and receptor: an update. Clin. Sci. 120, 169–178.

Ni, C.Y., Murphy, M.P., Golde, T.E., Carpenter, G., 2001. gamma-Secretase cleavage and nuclear localization of ErbB-4 receptor tyrosine kinase. Science 294, 2179–2181.

Nicotra, G., Castino, R., Follo, C., Peracchio, C., Valente, G., Isidoro, C., 2010. The dilemma: does tissue expression of cathepsin D reflect tumor malignancy? The question: does the assay truly mirror cathepsin D mis-function in the tumor? Cancer Biomark. 7, 47–64.

Northrop, D.B., 2001. Follow the protons: a low-barrier hydrogen bond unifies the mechanisms of the aspartic proteases. Acc. Chem. Res. 34, 790–797.

Nuttall, R.K., Pennington, C.J., Taplin, J., Wheal, A., Yong, V.W., Forsyth, P.A., Edwards, D.R., 2003. Elevated membrane-type matrix metalloproteinases in gliomas revealed by profiling proteases and inhibitors in human cancer cells1 1 Norfolk and Norwich Big C Appeal; The Medical Research Council; The Canadian Institutes of Health Research; and The European Union Framework V (Contract no. QLG1-2000-00131). Mol. Cancer Res. 1, 333–345.

Ogden, R.C., Flexner, C.W., 2001. Protease Inhibitors in AIDS Therapy. Taylor & Francis.

Ohri, S.S., Vashishta, A., Proctor, M., Fusek, M., Vetvicka, V., 2008. The propeptide of cathepsin D increases proliferation, invasion and metastasis of breast cancer cells. Int. J. Oncol. 32, 491–498.

Ortega, N., Behonick, D., Stickens, D., Werb, Z., 2003. How proteases regulate bone morphogenesis. Ann. N. Y. Acad. Sci. 995, 109–116.

Ottesen, M., Rickert, W., 1970. The isolation and partial characterization of an acid protease produced by Mucor miehei. C. R. Trav. Lab. Carlsberg 37, 301–325.

Owens, J., 2007. 2006 Drug Approvals: Finding the Niche. Nature Publishing Group.

Pajonk, F., Himmelsbach, J., Riess, K., Sommer, A., Mcbride, W.H., 2002. The human immunodeficiency virus (HIV)-1 protease inhibitor saquinavir inhibits proteasome function and causes apoptosis and radiosensitization in non-HIV-associated human cancer cells. Cancer Res. 62, 5230–5235.

Pals, G., Eriksson, A.W., Pronk, J.C., Frants, R.R., Klinkenberg-Knol, E.C., Bosma, A., Westerveld, B.D., Taggart, R.T., Samloff, I.M., Meuwissen, S.G., 1988. Differential expression of pepsinogen isozymogens in a patient with Barrett esophagus. Clin. Genet. 34, 90–97.

Paris, D., Quadros, A., Patel, N., Delledonne, A., Humphrey, J., Mullan, M., 2005. Inhibition of angiogenesis and tumor growth by beta and gamma-secretase inhibitors. Eur. J. Pharmacol. 514, 1–15.

Patel, S., Vuillard, L., Cleasby, A., Murray, C.W., Yon, J., 2004. Apo and inhibitor complex structures of BACE (beta-secretase). J. Mol. Biol. 343, 407–416.

Peerce, B.E., Smolka, A., Sachs, G., 1984. Isolation of pepsinogen granules from rabbit gastric mucosa. J. Biol. Chem. 259, 9255–9262.

Pelletier, L., Guillaumot, P., Freche, B., Luquain, C., Christiansen, D., Brugiere, S., Garin, J., Manie, S.N., 2006. Gamma-secretase-dependent proteolysis of CD44 promotes neoplastic transformation of rat fibroblastic cells. Cancer Res. 66, 3681–3687.

Pyrko, P., Kardosh, A., Wang, W., Xiong, W., Schönthal, A.H., Chen, T.C., 2007. HIV-1 protease inhibitors nelfinavir and atazanavir induce malignant glioma death by triggering endoplasmic reticulum stress. Cancer Res. 67, 10920–10928.

Rajagopalan, T., Stein, W.H., Moore, S., 1966. The inactivation of pepsin by diazoacetylnorleucine methyl ester. J. Biol. Chem. 241, 4295–4297.

Rao, M.B., Tanksale, A.M., Ghatge, M.S., Deshpande, V.V., 1998. Molecular and biotechnological aspects of microbial proteases. Microbiol. Mol. Biol. Rev. 62, 597–635.

Rawlings, N.D., Barrett, A.J., Bateman, A., 2014. Using the MEROPS database for proteolytic enzymes and their inhibitors and substrates. Curr. Protoc. Bioinformatics 48. 1.25.21–21.25.33.

Ray, W.J., Yao, M., Mumm, J., Schroeter, E.H., Saftig, P., Wolfe, M., Selkoe, D.J., Kopan, R., Goate, A.M., 1999. Cell surface presenilin-1 participates in the gamma-secretase-like proteolysis of Notch. J. Biol. Chem. 274, 36801–36807.

Rayhman, O., Klipper, E., Muller, L., Davidson, B., Reich, R., Meidan, R., 2008. Small interfering RNA molecules targeting endothelin-converting enzyme-1 inhibit endothelin-1 synthesis and the invasive phenotype of ovarian carcinoma cells. Cancer Res. 68, 9265–9273.

Rodriguez, J., Vízquez, J., Corte, M., Lamelas, M., Bongera, M., Corte, M., Alvarez, A., Allende, M., Gonzalez, L., Sínchez, M., 2005. Clinical significance of cathepsin D concentration in tumor cytosol of primary breast cancer. Int. J. Biol. Marker 20, 103–111.

Rosati, E., Sabatini, R., De Falco, F., Del Papa, B., Falzetti, F., Di Ianni, M., Cavalli, L., Fettucciari, K., Bartoli, A., Screpanti, I., 2013. γ-Secretase inhibitor I induces apoptosis in chronic lymphocytic leukemia cells by proteasome inhibition, endoplasmic reticulum stress increase and notch down-regulation. Int. J. Cancer 132, 1940–1953.

Saftig, P., Hetman, M., Schmahl, W., Weber, K., Heine, L., Mossmann, H., Koster, A., Hess, B., Evers, M., Von Figura, K., 1995. Mice deficient for the lysosomal proteinase cathepsin D exhibit progressive atrophy of the intestinal mucosa and profound destruction of lymphoid cells. EMBO J. 14, 3599–3608.

Sakamoto, A., Yanagisawa, M., Sakurai, T., Takuwa, Y., Yanagisawa, H., Masaki, T., 1991. Cloning and functional expression of human cDNA for the ETB endothelin receptor. Biochem. Biophys. Res. Commun. 178, 656–663.

Šali, A., Veerapandian, B., Cooper, J.B., Moss, D.S., Hofmann, T., Blundell, T.L., 1992. Domain flexibility in aspartic proteinases. Proteins: Struct. Funct. Bioinf. 12, 158–170.

Sallusto, F., Schaerli, P., Loetscher, P., Schaniel, C., Lenig, D., Mackay, C.R., Qin, S., Lanzavecchia, A., 1998. Rapid and coordinated switch in chemokine receptor expression during dendritic cell maturation. Eur. J. Immunol. 28, 2760–2769.

Samon, J.B., Castillo-Martin, M., Hadler, M., Ambesi-Impiombato, A., Paietta, E., Racevskis, J., Wiernik, P.H., Rowe, J.M., Jakubczak, J.L., Randolph, S., 2012. Preclinical analysis of the gamma-secretase inhibitor PF-03084014 in combination with glucocorticoids in T-cell acute lymphoblastic leukemia. Mol. Cancer Ther. 11, 0938.2011.

Sampson, M., Kakkar, A., 2002. Coagulation Proteases and Human Cancer. Portland Press Limited.

Schaap, D., Hsuan, J., Totty, N., Parker, P.J., 1990. Proteolytic activation of protein kinase C-epsilon. Eur. J. Biochem. 191, 431–435.

Schauer-Vukasinovic, V., Bur, D., Kling, D., Grüninger, F., Giller, T., 1999. Human napsin A: expression, immunochemical detection, and tissue localization. FEBS Lett. 462, 135–139.

Schott, A.F., Landis, M.D., Dontu, G., Griffith, K.A., Layman, R.M., Krop, I., Paskett, L.A., Wong, H., Dobrolecki, L.E., Lewis, M.T., 2013. Preclinical and clinical studies of gamma secretase inhibitors with docetaxel on human breast tumors. Clin. Cancer Res. 1512–1524.

Schwann, T., 1836. Mullers Arch. Anat. Physiol. 1, 90–138.

Sealy, L., Mota, F., Rayment, N., Tatnell, P., Kay, J., Chain, B., 1996. Regulation of cathepsin E expression during human B cell differentiation in vitro. Eur. J. Immunol. 26, 1838–1843.

Sethi, N., Dai, X., Winter, C.G., Kang, Y., 2011. Tumor-derived JAGGED1 promotes osteolytic bone metastasis of breast cancer by engaging notch signaling in bone cells. Cancer Cell 19, 192–205.

Sgadari, C., Barillari, G., Toschi, E., Carlei, D., Bacigalupo, I., Baccarini, S., Palladino, C., Leone, P., Bugarini, R., Malavasi, L., 2002. HIV protease inhibitors are potent anti-angiogenic molecules and promote regression of Kaposi sarcoma. Nat. Med. 8, 225.

Shah, S., Lee, S.F., Tabuchi, K., Hao, Y.H., Yu, C., Laplant, Q., Ball, H., Dann 3rd, C.E., Sudhof, T., Yu, G., 2005. Nicastrin functions as a gamma-secretase-substrate receptor. Cell 122, 435–447.

Shankar, A., Loizidou, M., Aliev, G., Fredericks, S., Holt, D., Boulos, P., Burnstock, G., Taylor, I., 1998. Raised endothelin 1 levels in patients with colorectal liver metastases. Br. J. Surg. 85, 502–506.

Shen, S., Jiang, J., Yuan, Y., 2017. Pepsinogen C expression, regulation and its relationship with cancer. Cancer Cell Int. 17, 57.

Sheridan, C., 2012. SGLT2 Inhibitors Race to Enter Type-2 Diabetes Market. Nature Publishing Group.

Sherrington, R., Rogaev, E.I., Liang, Y., Rogaeva, E.A., Levesque, G., Ikeda, M., Chi, H., Lin, C., Li, G., Holman, K., Tsuda, T., Mar, L., Foncin, J.F., Bruni, A.C., Montesi, M.P., Sorbi, S., Rainero, I., Pinessi, L., Nee, L., Chumakov, I., Pollen, D., Brookes, A., Sanseau, P., Polinsky, R.J., Wasco, W., Da Silva, H.A., Haines, J.L., Perkicak-Vance, M.A., Tanzi, R.E., Roses, A.D., Fraser, P.E., Rommens, J.M., St George-Hyslop, P.H., 1995. Cloning of a gene bearing missense mutations in early-onset familial Alzheimer's disease. Nature 375, 754–760.

Shiosaki, K., Tasker, A.S., Sullivan, G.M., Sorensen, B.K., Von Geldern, T.W., Wu-Wong, J.R., Marselle, C.A., Opgenorth, T.J., 1993. Potent and selective inhibitors of an aspartyl protease-like endothelin converting enzyme identified in rat lung. J. Med. Chem. 36, 468–478.

Sielecki, A., Fujinaga, M., Read, R., James, M., 1991. Refined structure of porcine pepsinogen at 1.8 Å resolution. J. Mol. Biol. 219, 671–692.

Silva, A., Lee, A., Gulnik, S., Maier, P., Collins, J., Bhat, T., Collins, P., Cachau, R., Luker, K., Gluzman, I., 1996. Structure and inhibition of plasmepsin II, a hemoglobin-degrading enzyme from *Plasmodium falciparum*. Proc. Natl. Acad. Sci. U. S. A. 93, 10034–10039.

Sogorb-Esteve, A., Garcia-Ayllon, M.S., Llansola, M., Felipo, V., Blennow, K., Saez-Valero, J., 2018. Inhibition of gamma-secretase leads to an increase in presenilin-1. Mol. Neurobiol. 55, 5047–5058.

Sozzani, S., Allavena, P., Vecchi, A., Mantovani, A., 2000. Chemokines and dendritic cell traffic. J. Clin. Immunol. 20, 151–160.

Spence Mccachren, S., 1991. Expression of metalloproteinases and metalloproteinase inhibitor in human arthritic synovium. Arthritis Rheum. 34, 1085–1093.

Steele, I.A., Dimaline, R., Pritchard, D.M., Peek Jr., R.M., Wang, T.C., Dockray, G.J., Varro, A., 2007. Helicobacter and gastrin stimulate Reg1 expression in gastric epithelial cells through distinct promoter elements. Am. J. Physiol. Gastrointest. Liver Physiol. 293, G347–G354.

Steinfeld, R., Reinhardt, K., Schreiber, K., Hillebrand, M., Kraetzner, R., Brück, W., Saftig, P., Gärtner, J., 2006. Cathepsin D deficiency is associated with a human neurodegenerative disorder. Am. J. Hum. Genet. 78, 988–998.

Storey, B.T., Wilson, D.F., Bracey, A., Rosen, S.L., Stephenson, S., 1975. Steric and electronic effects on the uncoupling activity of substituted 3, 5 dichlorosalicylanilides. FEBS Lett. 49, 338–341.

Sudhakar, A., 2009. History of cancer, ancient and modern treatment methods. J. Cancer Sci. Ther. 1, 1–4.

Taggart, C., Mall, M.A., Lalmanach, G., Cataldo, D., Ludwig, A., Janciauskiene, S., Heath, N., Meiners, S., Overall, C.M., Schultz, C., Turk, B., Borensztajn, K.S., 2017. Protean proteases: at the cutting edge of lung diseases. Eur. Respir. J. 49, 1501200.

Tang, B.L., 2001. ADAMTS: a novel family of extracellular matrix proteases. Int. J. Biochem. Cell Biol. 33, 33–44.

Tang, J., Koelsch, G., 1995. A possible function of the flaps of aspartic proteases: the capture of substrate side chains determines the specificity of cleavage positions. Protein Peptide Lett. 2, 257–266.

Tang, J., Sepulveda, P., Marciniszyn, J., Chen, K., Huang, W., Tao, N., Liu, D., Lanier, J., 1973. Amino-acid sequence of porcine pepsin. Proc. Natl. Acad. Sci. U. S. A. 70, 3437–3439.

Tao, X., Tong, L., 2003. Crystal structure of human DJ-1, a protein associated with early onset Parkinson's disease. J. Biol. Chem. 278, 31372–31379.

Tatematsu, M., Ichinose, M., Miki, K., Hasegawa, R., Kato, T., Ito, N., 1990. Gastric and intestinal phenotypic expression of human stomach cancers as revealed by pepsinogen immunohistochemistry and mucin histochemistry. Acta Pathol. Jpn. 40, 494–504.

Thiyagarajan, M., Fernández, J.A., Lane, S.M., Griffin, J.H., Zlokovic, B.V., 2008. Activated protein C promotes neovascularization and neurogenesis in postischemic brain via protease-activated receptor. J. Neurosci. 28, 12788–12797.

Turner, B.M., Cagle, P.T., Sainz, I.M., Fukuoka, J., Shen, S.S., Jagirdar, J., 2012. Napsin A, a new marker for lung adenocarcinoma, is complementary and more sensitive and specific than thyroid transcription factor 1 in the differential diagnosis of primary pulmonary carcinoma: evaluation of 1674 cases by tissue microarray. Arch. Pathol. Lab. Med. 136, 163–171.

Uemura, K., Kitagawa, N., Kohno, R., Kuzuya, A., Kageyama, T., Chonabayashi, K., Shibasaki, H., Shimohama, S., 2003. Presenilin 1 is involved in maturation and trafficking of N-cadherin to the plasma membrane. J. Neurosci. Res. 74, 184–191.

Ueno, T., Linder, S., Elmberger, G., 2003. Aspartic proteinase napsin is a useful marker for diagnosis of primary lung adenocarcinoma. Br. J. Cancer 88, 1229–1233.

Ueno, T., Linder, S., Na, C.L., Rice, W.R., Johansson, J., Weaver, T.E., 2004. Processing of pulmonary surfactant protein B by napsin and cathepsin H. J. Biol. Chem. 279, 16178–16184.

Ueno, T., Elmberger, G., Weaver, T.E., Toi, M., Linder, S., 2008. The aspartic protease napsin A suppresses tumor growth independent of its catalytic activity. Lab. Investig. 88, 256.

Umezawa, H., Aoyagi, T., Morishima, H., Matsuzaki, M., Hamada, M., Takeuchi, T., 1970. Pepstatin, a new pepsin inhibitor produced by agtinomygetes. J. Antibiot. 23, 259–262.

Van Hinsbergh, V.W., Engelse, M.A., Quax, P.H., 2006. Pericellular proteases in angiogenesis and vasculogenesis. Arterioscler. Thromb. Vasc. Biol. 26, 716–728.

Van Ranst, M., 2001. Recensie: Protease Inhibitors in AIDS Therapy, vol. 57. Tijdschrift voor geneeskunde, New York.

Vashishta, A., Ohri, S.S., Proctor, M., Fusek, M., Vetvicka, V., 2007. Ribozyme-targeting procathepsin D and its effect on invasion and growth of breast cancer cells: an implication in breast cancer therapy. Int. J. Oncol. 30, 1223–1230.

Vega, S., Kang, L.W., Velazquez-Campoy, A., Kiso, Y., Amzel, L.M., Freire, E., 2004. A structural and thermodynamic escape mechanism from a drug resistant mutation of the HIV-1 protease. Proteins: Struct. Funct. Bioinf. 55, 594–602.

Vetvicka, V., Fusek, M., 2012. Procathepsin D as a tumor marker, anti-cancer drug or screening agent. Anti Cancer Agents Med. Chem. 12, 172–175.

Vetvicka, V., Vektvickova, J., Fusek, M., 1994. Effect of human procathepsin D on proliferation of human cell lines. Cancer Lett. 79, 131–135.

Vetvicka, V., Vetvickova, J., Hilgert, I., Voburka, Z., Fusek, M., 1997. Analysis of the interaction of procathepsin D activation peptide with breast cancer cells. Int. J. Cancer 73, 403–409.

Vetvicka, V., Vetvickova, J., Fusek, M., 1998. Effect of procathepsin D and its activation peptide on prostate cancer cells. Cancer Lett. 129, 55–59.

Vetvicka, V., Vetvickova, J., Fusek, M., 1999. Anti-human procathepsin D activation peptide antibodies inhibit breast cancer development. Breast Cancer Res. Treat. 57, 261–269.

Vetvicka, V., Vetvickova, J., Benes, P., 2004. Role of enzymatically inactive procathepsin D in lung cancer. Anticancer Res. 24, 2739–2743.

Vidal, G.A., Naresh, A., Marrero, L., Jones, F.E., 2005. Presenilin-dependent gamma-secretase processing regulates multiple ERBB4/HER4 activities. J. Biol. Chem. 280, 19777–19783.

Wallace, E.M., Moliterni, J.A., Moskal, M.A., Neubert, A.D., Marcopulos, N., Stamford, L.B., Trapani, A.J., Savage, P., Chou, M., Jeng, A.Y., 1998. Design and synthesis of potent, selective inhibitors of endothelin-converting enzyme. J. Med. Chem. 41, 1513–1523.

Walsh, P.N., Ahmad, S.S., 2002. Proteases in blood clotting. Essays Biochem. 38, 95–111.

Wang, J., Beher, D., Nyborg, A.C., Shearman, M.S., Golde, T.E., Goate, A., 2006a. C-terminal PAL motif of presenilin and presenilin homologues required for normal active site conformation. J. Neurochem. 96, 218–227.

Wang, R., Tang, P., Wang, P., Boissy, R.E., Zheng, H., 2006b. Regulation of tyrosinase trafficking and processing by presenilins: partial loss of function by familial Alzheimer's disease mutation. Proc. Natl. Acad. Sci. U. S. A. 103, 353–358.

Weihofen, A., Binns, K., Lemberg, M.K., Ashman, K., Martoglio, B., 2002. Identification of signal peptide peptidase, a presenilin-type aspartic protease. Science 296, 2215–2218.

Wells, A., Huttenlocher, A., Lauffenburger, D.A., 2005. Calpain proteases in cell adhesion and motility. Int. Rev. Cytol. 245, 1–16.

Westley, B.R., May, F.E., 1987. Oestrogen regulates cathepsin D mRNA levels in oestrogen responsive human breast cancer cells. Nucleic Acids Res. 15, 3773–3786.

Westley, B., May, F., 1999. Prognostic value of cathepsin D in breast cancer. Br. J. Cancer 79, 189.

Whitesitt, C.A., Simon, R.L., Reel, J.K., Sigmund, S.K., Phillips, M.L., Shadle, J.K., Heinz, L.J., Koppel, G.A., Hunden, D.C., Lifer, S.L., 1996. Synthesis and structure-activity relationships of benzophenones as inhibitors of cathepsin D. Bioorg. Med. Chem. Lett. 6, 2157–2162.

Wolf, M., Clark-Lewis, I., Buri, C., Langen, H., Lis, M., Mazzucchelli, L., 2003. Cathepsin D specifically cleaves the chemokines macrophage inflammatory protein-1 alpha, macrophage inflammatory protein-1 beta, and SLC that are expressed in human breast cancer. Am. J. Pathol. 162, 1183–1190.

Wolfe, M.S., 2010. Structure, mechanism and inhibition of γ-secretase and presenilin-like proteases. Biol. Chem. 391, 839–847.

Wolfe, M.S., Xia, W., Ostaszewski, B.L., Diehl, T.S., Kimberly, W.T., Selkoe, D.J., 1999. Two transmembrane aspartates in presenilin-1 required for presenilin endoproteolysis and gamma-secretase activity. Nature 398, 513–517.

Wrigley, J.D., Nunn, E.J., Nyabi, O., Clarke, E.E., Hunt, P., Nadin, A., De Strooper, B., Shearman, M.S., Beher, D., 2004. Conserved residues within the putative active site of gamma-secretase differentially influence enzyme activity and inhibitor binding. J. Neurochem. 90, 1312–1320.

Wunderlich, P., Glebov, K., Kemmerling, N., Tien, N.T., Neumann, H., Walter, J., 2013. Sequential proteolytic processing of the triggering receptor expressed on myeloid cells-2 (TREM2) protein by ectodomain shedding and gamma-secretase-dependent intramembranous cleavage. J. Biol. Chem. 288, 33027–33036.

Xie, T., Yan, C., Zhou, R., Zhao, Y., Sun, L., Yang, G., Lu, P., Ma, D., Shi, Y., 2014. Crystal structure of the gamma-secretase component nicastrin. Proc. Natl. Acad. Sci. U. S. A. 111, 13349–13354.

Yamasaki, K., Di Nardo, A., Bardan, A., Murakami, M., Ohtake, T., Coda, A., Dorschner, R.A., Bonnart, C., Descargues, P., Hovnanian, A., 2007. Increased serine protease activity and cathelicidin promotes skin inflammation in rosacea. Nat. Med. 13, 975.

Yan, R., Han, P., Miao, H., Greengard, P., Xu, H., 2001. The transmembrane domain of the Alzheimer's beta-secretase (BACE1) determines its late Golgi localization and access to APP substrate. J. Biol. Chem. 36788–36796.

Yanagisawa, M., Kurihara, H., Kimura, S., Tomobe, Y., Kobayashi, M., Mitsui, Y., Yazaki, Y., Goto, K., Masaki, T., 1988. A novel potent vasoconstrictor peptide produced by vascular endothelial cells. Nature 332, 411.

Chapter 6

Inhibitors of HIV protease in cancer therapy

E. Pontiki, A. Peperidou, I. Fotopoulos, D. Hadjipavlou-Litina
Department of Pharmaceutical Chemistry, School of Pharmacy, Aristotle University of Thessaloniki, Thessaloniki, Greece

Abbreviations

ADMET	pharmacokinetic properties
AIDS	acquired immune deficiency syndrome
AKT	protein kinase B
cdk	cyclin-dependent kinases
CDK2	protein kinase 2
cDNA	complementary DNA
EBV	Epstein-Barr virus
ER	endoplasmic reticulum
ESR	stress response
HAART	highly active antiretroviral therapies
HGG	high grade glioma
HIV	human immunodeficiency virus
Hsp90	heat shock protein 90
IDV	indinavir sulfate
IN	integrase
KP	Kaposi's sarcoma
KSHV	Kaposi's sarcoma associated herpesvirus
MMPs	metalloproteases
MTC	medullary thyroid carcinoma
NF-B	nuclear factor-B
NFV	nelfinavir mesylate
NRTIs	nucleoside reverse transcriptase inhibitors
PI	protease Inhibitors
PI3K/AKT	phosphatidylinositol 3-kinase
PI3K	phosphatidylinositol 3-kinase
PLWHAs	persons living with HIV/AIDS
PR	protease
RCC	renal cell carcinoma
RET	transmembrane receptor protein

Cancer-Leading Proteases. https://doi.org/10.1016/B978-0-12-818168-3.00006-1

ROS	reactive oxygen species
RT	reverse transcriptase
RTV	ritonavir
S2P	site-2 protease
SQV	saquinavir mesylate
UPR	unfolded protein response
VEGF	vascular endothelial growth factor

6.1 Introduction

The human immunodeficiency virus (HIV) is a retrovirus of the *Lentivirus* genus. It is regarded as an enveloped RNA virus, the genome of which is further enclosed in a capsid formed by many copies (approximately 2000 copies) of the p24 protein (Kuiken et al., 2008). The capsid contains several other proteins necessary for the development of the virus, e.g., protease (PR), reverse transcriptase (RT), and integrase (IN), each of which plays a distinct role in the maturation and development of the virus. The reverse transcriptase catalyzes the transcription of the viral RNA in a complementary DNA (cDNA) which is integrated in the host cell genome by the integrase. The HIV genome encodes some core precursor proteins. The three major proteins encoded within the retroviral genome are Gag, Pol, and Env, which are maturated into the active protein. Gag is a glycoprotein and is an acronym for group antigens (ag), Pol is the reverse transcriptase, whereas Env is an envelope protein that resides in lipid layer, which determines the viral tropism (Muesing et al., 1985; Ratner et al., 1985; Sanchez-Pescador et al., 1985; Wain-Hobson et al., 1985). The Gag precursor contains core structural proteins of the virus such as p24 and p7, while the Pol precursor contains three integral enzymes, i.e., PR, RT, and IN.

The HIV protease has been classified as an aspartic protease that functions as a homodimer (Roberts et al., 1990). The dimmer comprises of two catalytic domains, each containing a catalytic aspartate residue at position 25 within the sequence Asp-Thr-Gly (Agbowuro et al., 2018). The active site is covered by the flaps, a pair of antiparallel beta-hairpin loops (Eder et al., 2007). The catalytic process starts with the protonation of an aspartate residue that activates a water molecule, converting it into a nucleophile that attacks the carbonyl carbon of the amide bond. The result is the formation of a tetrahedral complex which is further cleaved by the aspartate residues into the corresponding carboxylic acid and amine (Fig. 6.1).

The HIV virus acts by infecting several cell types, especially $CD4^+$ T cells (a type of T cells that play an important role in the immune system, particularly in the adaptive immune system), via adsorption at the CD4 receptor which is located in the host cell surface. This process is mediated by the envelope (Env) protein (Cocchi et al., 1996). After adsorption, the viral genome is released into cytoplasm and transcripted into the cDNA by the reverse transcriptase. The viral cDNA is subsequently translocated in the nucleus and integrated into the cell's

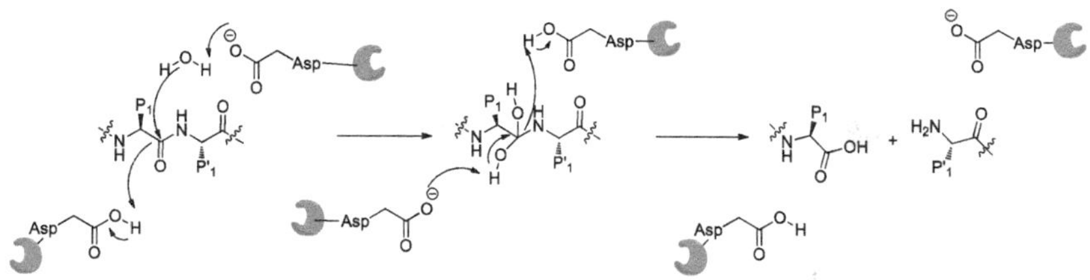

FIG. 6.1 A schematic representation of proteolytic activity of HIV protease.

genome by the integrase. Upon several stimuli, the viral genome is transcripted and translated into core proteins, i.e., Env, Gag, and Pol, which are enclosed in noninfectious virions and exert on the host cell. The virions become infectious only after the maturation process which is mediated by the protease. The protease cleaves the precursor Gag and Gag-Pol polypeptides into mature proteins. This step is crucial for the HIV life cycle (Monini et al., 2004).

Many cancers are related to HIV infection, making cancer a main cause of death in HIV-infected persons (Morlat et al., 2014). In its life cycle, the HIV virus infects $CD4^+$ cells and eventually leads to dysregulation of the immune system and the development of types of cancer (Yarchoan and Uldrick, 2018) such as Kaposi's sarcoma, Hodgkin's lymphoma, and cervical cancer. Kaposi's sarcoma is caused by a second infectious agent (Kaposi's sarcoma-associated herpesvirus—KSHV) (Beral et al., 1990); after the dysregulation of the immune system the infected cells permit the development of cancer types (Yarchoan and Uldrick, 2018). Kaposi's sarcoma is divided into four forms, i.e., classic, endemic, transplantation-associated, and epidemic, characterized by lesions of abnormal proliferation of endothelial-derived cells. Hodgkin's lymphoma is caused by EBV (Epstein-Barr virus) and is distinguished from the non-HIV-induced Hodgkin's lymphoma in terms of symptoms (mainly weight loss, fever, and night sweats) (Uldrick and Little, 2015) and histological features, since the Reed-Stenberg cells are infected by the EBV and the tumor microenvironment presents unique features.

From the above, it is clearly depicted that the development of several drugs that could act as HIV protease inhibitors could have a high potential to serve as anticancer agents for HIV-induced cancer types.

6.2 Protease inhibitors

The worldwide expansion of HIV and its poor prognosis forced the urgent need for novel and effective antiretroviral drugs. The discovery of protease inhibitors (PIs) offered a series of virologic and immunologic advantages compared to the previously used nucleoside reverse transcriptase inhibitors (NRTIs) (Sham et al., 1998). These compounds increased the life expectancy of persons living with HIV/AIDS (PLWHAs) (Sham et al., 1998; Rana and Dudley, 2012) significantly. However, the first PI drug presented several limitations, such as poor oral bioavailability, high protein binding, short plasma half-life, low blood levels requiring frequent dosing administration, and high doses in vivo.

In 1989 the optimization of crystal structure of HIV protease led to the design and synthesis of HIV protease inhibitors (Navia et al., 1989; Chow et al., 2009). Inhibitors of HIV protease consisted of a synthetic peptide bond between phenylalanine and proline amino-acids, which was the target of the HIV aspartyl protease (Flexner, 1998). Saquinavir was the first protease inhibitor that was approved by the FDA followed by ritonavir, indinavir, nelfinavir, and amprenavir (first-generation PIs). The next-generation PIs included lopinavir (in combination with ritonavir), atazanavir, fosamprenavir (a prodrug of amprenavir), tipranavir, and darunavir that were developed for antiretroviral therapy with or without the combination of any nucleoside or nonnucleoside reverse transcriptase inhibitors. As reported, two series of HIV protease inhibitors (first and second generation) were evaluated as anticancer agents to treat different types of tumors (Agbowuro et al., 2018). The mechanism of action for the first generation of PIs includes: (1) induction of apoptosis in cancer cells and (2) blockage of invasion, angiogenesis, growth of tumor, and inflammatory responses. However, they possess poor bioavailability and potency, hepatotoxicity, nephrotoxicity, dyslipidemia, and gastrointestinal toxicity (Pokorná et al., 2009; Brower et al., 2008; Cameron et al., 1999). PIs prevent angiogenesis through regulation of signaling pathways, such as phosphatidylinositol 3-kinase (PI3K)/AKT, associated with the expression of vascular endothelial growth factor (VEGF) and other factors involved in neovascularization (Sgadari et al., 2002).

Kaposi's sarcoma is an angioproliferative disease characterized by angiogenesis, endothelial cell growth (Kaposi's sarcoma cells), inflammatory-cell infiltration, and edema. People with HIV subjected to highly active antiretroviral therapies (HAART) were reported to have significant reductions in the incidence of Kaposi's sarcoma and in HIV-related non-Hodgkin lymphoma. Sgadari et al. (2002) were first to report that indinavir and saquinavir at low concentrations potently inhibited angiogenesis and tumor cell invasion. At higher concentrations, saquinavir inhibited 20S and 26S proteasome activity, increased apoptosis, and radiosensitized non-HIV-associated cancers, including prostate cancer, lymphoblastoid, leukemia, and glioblastoma (Pajonk et al., 2002). Indinavir at high concentration inhibited proteasome in Kaposi's sarcoma, while at low concentrations it inhibited MMP-2 and induced apoptosis in a murine model of hepatocellular carcinoma. MMP-2 has no similarities with the catalytic site of HIV protease which is an aspartyl protease (Esposito et al., 2006). Gupta et al. (2005) reported that SQN might target a serine kinase such as integrin-linked kinase at signaling pathway of PI3K/AKT with the ultimate goal of controlling cell growth and apoptosis. In continuation, Timeus et al. (2006) found that saquinavir influences the treatment of imatinib-resistant chronic myelogenous leukemia. This study showed a unique synergistic activity of saquinavir and of an inhibitor of tyrosine kinase.

It has been reported that ritonavir inhibited multiplication of endothelial cells and induced apoptosis in Kaposi's sarcoma cell lines by several mechanisms, including inhibition of production of cytokines that contribute to neovascularization (TNFα, interleukin 6, and vascular endothelial growth factor) and inhibition of transcriptional activation of NFkB. However, ritonavir has no chymotrypsin-like proteasome inhibitory activity at the concentrations studied in comparison to saquinavir and indinavir (Pati et al., 2002). Breast carcinoma was found similarly sensitive to ritonavir (Srirangam et al., 2006). Moreover, in breast cancer cell lines ritonavir was found to reduce expression of cyclin-dependent kinases (CDK) 2, 4, and 6 and cyclin D1, induce apoptosis, and inhibit Akt-phosphorylation and the chaperone function of heat shock protein 90 (Hsp90) (Srirangam et al., 2006).

Barillari et al. (2012) reported that ritonavir and saquinavir inhibit isoforms of MMP-2 and MMP-9 and block invasion of cervical intraepithelial neoplasia cells in vitro, whereas Esposito et al. (2013) reported that amprenavir inhibits MMP-2 in hepatocarcinoma cells and Jiang et al. (2017) reported that amprenavir inhibits an extracellular signal-regulated kinase-2 and induces apoptosis in MCF-7 human breast cancer cells.

6.2.1 First generation HIV protease inhibitors

Ritonavir, which was approved by the FDA in 1996, is a thiazole product, which was created by pharmacokinetic optimization of a lead molecule that presented good potency and poor bioavailability. The bioisosteric replacement of a phenyl moiety in the lead compound with a more hydrophilic thiazolyl group produced a new compound, ritonavir, a more soluble compound, and an inhibitor of cytochrome P450s. Indinavir possesses more lipophilic groups, a piperazinyl, and a pyridyl moiety. However, it has been totally replaced by second-generation protease inhibitors due to its high toxicity (Fig. 6.2).

Nelfinavir, another PI, entered the market in 1997. It has structural similarity to saquinavir, but it is more stable against hydrolytic enzymes and has significant higher oral bioavailability compared to other members of the first-generation drugs. It was the first protease inhibitor to be approved for use in the management of pediatric acquired immunodeficiency syndrome (AIDS) (Kempf et al., 1991; Wlodawer, 2002; Lv et al., 2015; Flexner, 1998; Floren et al., 2003). Another compound, nelfinavir (NLF) (Fig. 6.2), was found to be a promising inhibitor of not only HIV protease but also of phosphatidylinositol 3-kinase (PI3K) and protein kinase B (AKT) (Bardsley-Elliot and Plosker, 2000). Also, nelfinavir was reported to inhibit the growth of several types of cancer lines, including melanoma and non-small cell lung cancer (Yang et al., 2006; Jiang et al., 2007), due to the inhibition of the PI3K and AKT signaling pathway. Promising phase I results were reported for locally advanced pancreatic cancer, in which NLF exhibits the same mechanism of action (Brunner et al., 2008).

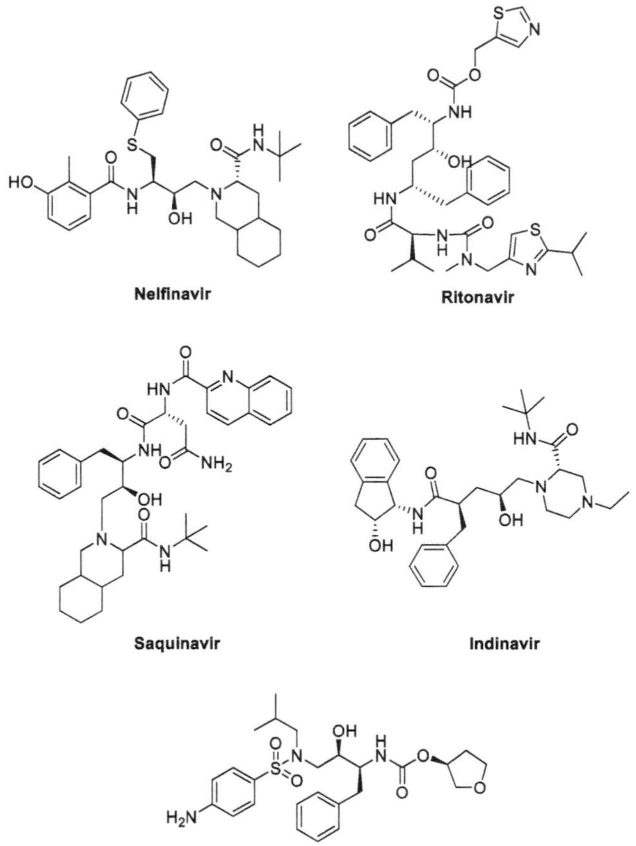

FIG. 6.2 First-generation protease inhibitors.

Pharmacological studies showed that nelfinavir selectively inhibited the growth of HER2-positive breast cancer cells in vitro and acted on a new heat shock protein 90 (Hsp90). Both are important implications to be seriously considered for the design of nelfinavir and its analogs as new anticancer agents against breast cancer. Although the molecular mechanism of antitumor action of nelfinavir against breast cancer is still unknown, Soprano et al. (2016) observed that its effects are related to its ability to inhibit protein kinase B (AKT), to increase reactive oxygen species (ROS) production selectively to cancer cells and to interact with ROS-related enzymes. Nelfinavir reduced breast cancer cell proliferation by inducing apoptosis and necrosis, without affecting primary normal breast cells. The antitumor activity of nelfinavir is due to an increase of intracellular ROS (reactive oxygen species) production strictly linked to the activation of flavoenzymes, which is limited to the cancer cells. Nelfinavir treated tumor cells also displayed a downregulation of the AKT pathway due to disruption of the AKT-Hsp90 complex, and subsequent degradation of AKT (Soprano et al.,

2016). It has been observed that HIV-1 protease inhibitors, such as saquinavir mesylate (SQV), ritonavir (RTV), indinavir sulfate (IDV), and nelfinavir mesylate (NFV) (Fig. 6.2), could induce growth arrest and apoptosis of both androgen-dependent and -independent prostate cancer cells (LNCaP) (in vitro and in vivo) in conjunction with a blockade of androgen receptor STAT3 and AKT signaling (Yang et al., 2005). Also SQV, RTV, and IDV were observed to induce the growth arrest and differentiation of NB4 and HL-60 human myeloid leukemia cells and to enhance the ability of all-trans retinoic acid to decrease proliferation and increase differentiation in these cells. It has also been reported that inhibitors of HIV protease can also decrease the proliferation of Kaposi sarcoma as well as prostate cancer cells via inhibition of nuclear factor-B (NF-B) activity (Sgadari et al., 2002; Pajonk et al., 2002; Ikezoe et al., 2000). Jiang et al. (2007) showed that nelfinavir might also inhibit growth of melanoma cells by inducing G1 cell-cycle arrest. However, in this example, the mechanism of nelfinavir's action followed the inhibition of protein kinase 2 (CDK2), associated with cell division and dephosphorylation of retinoblastoma protein. It inhibits CDK2 through activation of proteasome-dependent degradation of Cdc25A phosphatase. Nelfinavir and its analogs (Fig. 6.3) were shown to inhibit proliferation and induce apoptosis of castration-resistant prostate cancer through inhibition of site-2 protease (S2P) activity, which leads to suppression of regulated intramembrane proteolysis. Especially, they are more potent inhibitors of S2P

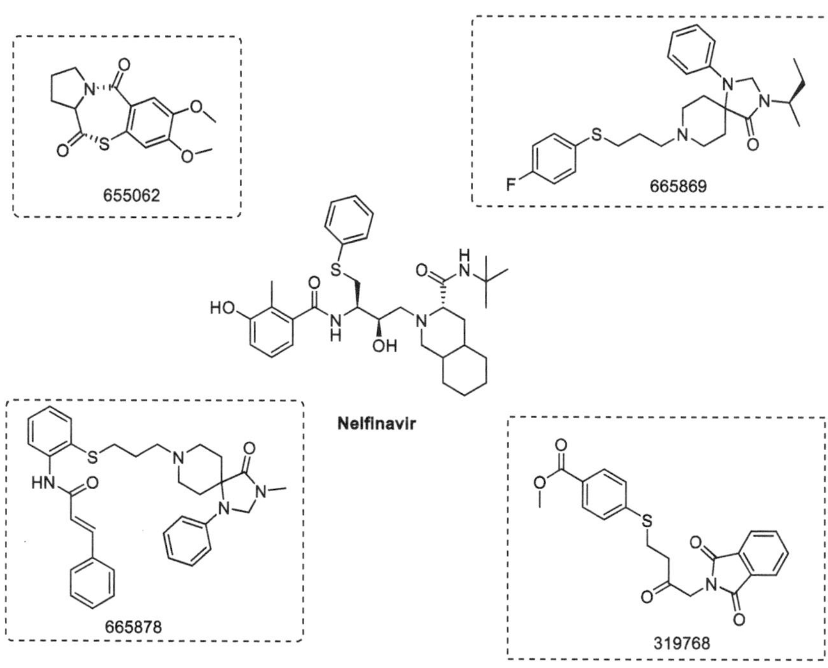

FIG. 6.3 Nelfinavir analogs.

cleavage activity than 1,10-phenanthroline, a metalloprotease-specific inhibitor (Guan et al., 2015).

Medullary thyroid carcinoma (MTC) is a known neuroendocrine tumor correlated with mutations of transmembrane receptor protein (RET) of tyrosine kinase gene. The stability of RET mutants is associated with the heat shock protein chaperone HSP90, which is a target for the HIV protease inhibitor nelfinavir (NFV). Kushchayeva et al. (2014) carried out cytotoxicity assays against MTC cells and studied the pharmacological mechanism of NFV. They realized that NFV has a wide spectrum of activity against medullary thyroid carcinoma cells, and its cytotoxicity can be increased by inhibiting autophagy.

Since the pediatric leukemia is one of the main causes of death in children, Meier-Stephenson et al. (2017) carried out cytotoxicity studies on pediatric leukemia cells using library of drugs against infections, including eight HIV protease inhibitors (FDA-approved, like amprenavir, atazanavir, darunavir, indinavir, lopinavir, nelfinavir, ritonavir, saquinavir). In particular, nelfinavir was found to exhibit the most potent antileukemic properties across all cell lines. Molecular mechanism studies showed that this agent leads to the induction of autophagy and apoptosis possibly through the induction of endoplasmic reticulum stress or through deactivation of signaling pathways, including AKT. Further, drug combination studies showed that NFV could be used in combination with known anticancer agents (e.g., sunitinib) to have better antileukemic activity.

Roche et al. (2008) reported a series of prodrugs of protease inhibitors, saquinavir, nelfinavir, and indinavir, containing valine separated by a spacer ($-C(O)(CH_2)_5NH-$), that improved pharmacological and pharmacokinetic properties, and evaluated their in vitro stability against hydrolysis and anti-HIV activity in several cancer cell lines. These authors also observed that these prodrugs were chemically more stable than the corresponding prodrugs containing no spacer. However, their stability was correlated with low in vitro anti-HIV activity. Whatsoever, derivatives with Rb groups were found to have better anti-HIV activity than those with Ra groups (Fig. 6.4). The antiviral activities were found to be lowest for the compounds where Ra = Rb, but PI-spacer-val prodrugs were less toxic than PI-valine.

6.2.2 Second-generation HIV protease inhibitors

Molla et al. (1996) had observed that although first-generation inhibitors, like ritonavir, reach high concentration in plasma, they do not manage to overcome HIV protease gene mutations of the valine at position 82 (Val82) as they do for alanine, threonine, or phenylalanine. This prompted to discover novel inhibitors effective against Val82 mutant HIV protease. The second-generation HIV protease inhibitors include lopinavir, atazanavir, tipranavir, darunavir, amprenavir, and the prodrug fosamprenavir (Fig. 6.5). In comparison to the

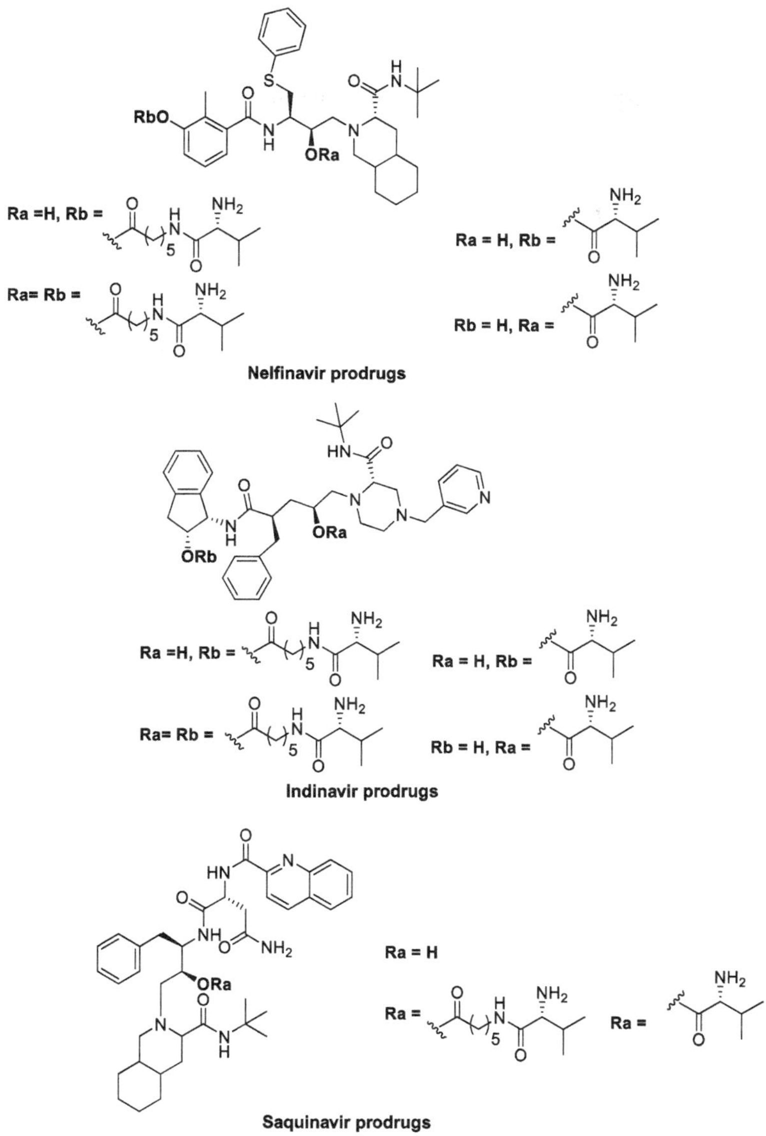

FIG. 6.4 Structures of the valine-containing protease inhibitors acting against adenocarcinoma.

first-generation drugs these agents were found to exhibit improved efficacy, safety, and resistance.

6.2.2.1 Lopinavir

Lopinavir belongs to the second-generation HIV protease inhibitors often used with ritonavir (first-generation PI) and other medications to treat HIV infection.

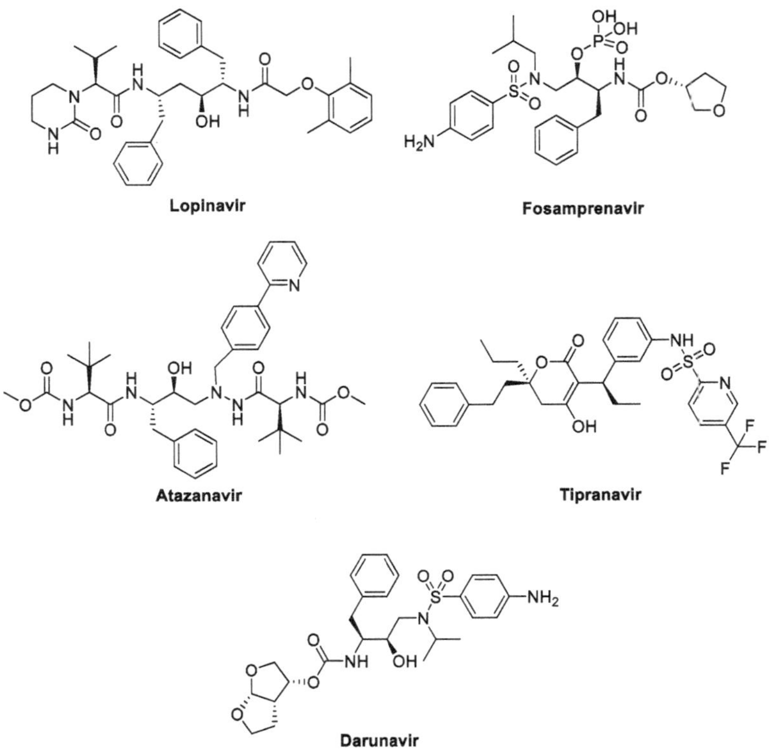

FIG. 6.5 Second-generation protease inhibitors.

Lopinavir was designed as a derivative of ritonavir (Fig. 6.5). A phenoxyacetyl group replaced the 5-thiazolyl group. The 2-isopropylthiazolyl group in ritonavir was replaced by a valine analog with a six-membered cyclic urea. In 1997, ABT-378, later to be named as lopinavir, was announced by Abbot at the 4th Conference on Retroviruses and Opportunistic Infections. Lopinavir retains its activity despite mutations and compared to ritonavir presents lower binding activity to serum proteins, though being 3–4 times more potent (Chandwani and Shuter, 2008). The main disadvantage of lopinavir is its poor bioavailability which seems to be ameliorated with coadministration with ritonavir, a potent inhibitor of cytochrome P450 3A4 (Walmsley et al., 2002). The combined drug, lopinavir/ritonavir, acts by inhibiting the formation of infectious virions, thus inhibiting consecutive waves of cellular contamination (Flexner, 1998). Lopinavir is not available separately but in coformulation with ritonavir, under the name of (Kaletra®). It was approved in September 2000 by the US Food and Drug Administration (FDA) and in April 2001 in Europe for the treatment of HIV infection. Additionally, it has been found that despite lopinavir being active against HIV infection, it is also effective against HIV-related illnesses such as cancer. Meningiomas are the most common type of brain tumors. Further, the antineoplastic implication of HIV protease inhibitors is well established but appears to vary widely. New-generation HIV protease inhibitors may offer valuable information as chemotherapeutics for meningiomas, the most common being intracranial tumors. Johnson et al. (2011) evaluated the effects of lopinavir, for its antitumor effects and mechanism of action on primary meningioma cell cultures. From this study it can be concluded that lopinavir reduces DNA synthesis/growth inhibition via cell cycle arrest. This mechanism alone, or in conjugation with others, can suppress meningioma cell growth. Additionally, it promotes apoptosis but not through Caspase 3 activation as other HIV protease inhibitors do. Based on these promising results further investigation should be done for defining the role of lopinavir as a potential chemotherapeutic agent. Lopinavir and nelfinavir were coadministered with carfilzomib, a second-generation proteasome inhibitor, in vitro for the treatment of renal cell carcinoma (RCC) (Abt et al., 2018). The results were very promising since lopinavir and nelfinavir significantly increased the cytotoxic effect of carfilzomib in all cell lines and primary cells, overcoming the resistance probably by induction of ROS (reactive oxygen species), activation of UPR (unfolded protein response, a cellular stress response related to the endoplasmic reticulum stress), and reduction of ABCB1 (ATP-binding cassette, major drug efflux pump that is upregulated in RCC activity). These interesting findings suggest that combined pharmaceutical therapy of carfilzomib with HIV protease inhibitors should be further investigated in a phase I/II clinical trial.

Kaposi's sarcoma (KS), a multicentric vascular tumor (Dittmer and Krown, 2007), remains the second most frequent tumor in HIV-infected patients. HIV protease inhibitors can be used in combination with doxorubicin for AIDS-Kaposi's sarcoma (KS) treatment. Lucia et al. (2011) reported that different HIV protease inhibitors (indinavir, nelfinavir, atazanavir, ritonavir, or lopinavir) in combination with doxorubicin were tested in KS cells in acute and chronic treatments. It has been found that Kaposi's cells treated with HIV protease inhibitors and doxorubicin resulted in an MDR phenotype based on ABCB1 protein expression in vitro.

6.2.2.2 *Atazanavir*

Atazanavir presents a better resistance as well as low toxicity compared to other protease inhibitors (Havlir and O'Marro, 2004). Based on the fact that HIV protease inhibitors present anticancer activity, Pyrko et al. (2007) tried to verify the role of nelfinavir and atazanavir on malignant glioma death and described their mechanism of action. In this study, the authors tried to define the role of the two drugs on three malignant glioma cell lines in vitro by using MTT assays. Both drugs presented very good activity on both assays with nelfinavir being more effective. Further studies defined the mechanism of action of these drugs via the stimulation of the endoplasmic reticulum (ER) stress response (ESR) or unfolded protein response (UPR). It has been found that both the drugs cause proteasome inhibition and accumulation of misfolded proteins. Additionally, the two drugs have been tested for their ability to affect cytoplasmic calcium levels in treated cells revealing that both of them manage to maintain steady calcium levels. The in vitro results have been verified with in vivo experiments based on the inhibition of growth on xenograft model of human malignant glioma.

6.2.2.3 Darunavir

Darunavir is structurally similar to amprenavir, although it has two condensed tetrahydrofuran rings (Fig. 6.5) (Tremblay, 2008; McCoy, 2007). Mahto et al. (2014) designed nine analogs of darunavir via modification on its reactive moiety and studied them in silico as anticancer agents. ChemBioOffice 2010 was used as a design tool while for minimization LigPrep tool of Schrödinger 2011 was used. This theoretical study using QikProp revealed that these derivatives possessed the required pharmacokinetic (ADMET) properties for being successful drugs, while docking studies showed that they were effective against five different cancer cell lines—bone, brain, breast, colon, and skin. Additionally, the active site amino acids were specified by Grid and the best model was selected based on *G*-scores and visualized via the XP tool. Darunavir proved to be more active (*G* score = −7.0 kcal/mol) than a few of its analogs (Fig. 6.6) against skin cancer, but the same activity (*G* score = −5.0 kcal/mol) as its analog **7** against bone cancer.

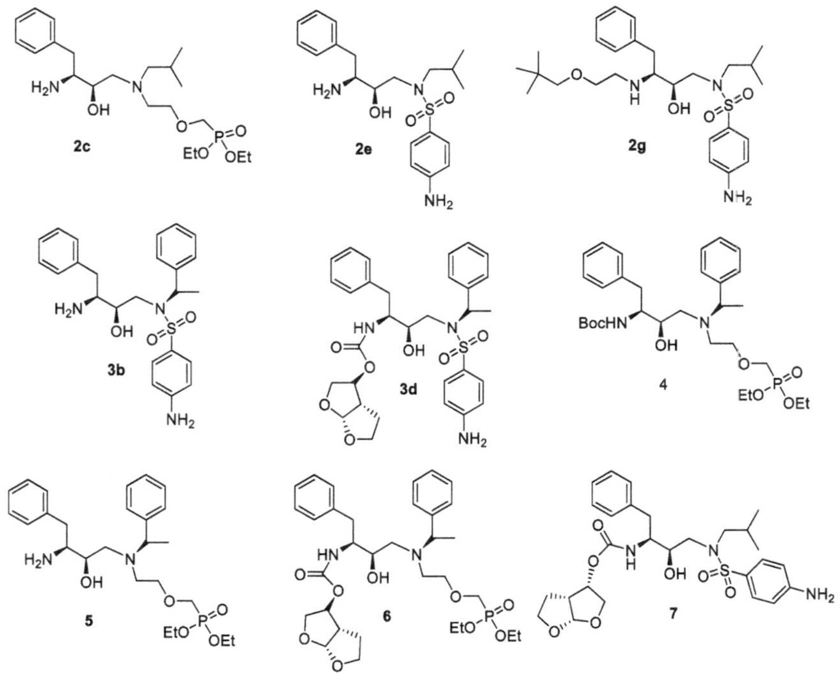

FIG. 6.6 Analogs of darunavir with potential anticancer activity.

6.2.2.4 Tipranavir

Tipranavir is the only nonpeptidic HIV protease inhibitor. It is an halogenated sulfonamide with substituted dihydropyrone groups (Fig. 6.5) (Orman and Perry, 2008).

6.2.2.5 Fosamprenavir

Fosamprenavir (Fig. 6.5) is a phosphoester prodrug of amprenavir which is converted to its active form in vivo (Wire et al., 2006). This modification was found to be necessary for the improvement of pharmacokinetic profile (solubility and bioavailability) of amprenavir.

Currently, the anticancer potential of tipranavir and fosamprenavir remain unreported.

6.3 HIV protease inhibitors and metalloproteases (MMPs)

It has been found that matrix metalloproteases (MMPs) are implicated in tumor cell migration and invasion by high grade glioma (HGG), promoting remodeling of the extracellular matrix (Anderson et al., 2008; Du et al., 2008). Studies have revealed that a number of HIV protease inhibitors are effective in decreasing the expression of MMPs in astrocytes and microglia, thus blocking endothelial and tumor cell invasion and angiogenesis (Liuzzi et al., 2004; Sgadari et al., 2002). Based on this fact, Ahluwalia et al. (2011) have evaluated the coadministration of ritonavir/lopinavir (400 mg/100 mg) twice daily in 19 patients with progressive or recurrent HGG in an open-label phase II trial until progression of disease or unacceptable toxicity. The results of this study were not promising although ritonavir/lopinavir was well tolerated in patients. This can be explained by the fact that a single target (proteases) was attacked or the bioavailability of the active drug was insufficient to reach the brain.

6.4 Conclusions

Patients infected with the human immunodeficiency virus (HIV) present an increased risk of developing several types of cancer. Many cancers are related to HIV infection, making cancer a main cause of death in HIV-infected persons. It is clearly depicted that the development of several drugs that could act as HIV protease inhibitors could have a high potential to serve as anticancer agents for HIV-induced cancer types. Nelfinavir, saquinavir, indinavir, and ritonavir belong to the first generation of PIs, whereas lopinavir, atazanavir, tipranavir, darunavir, amprenavir, and the prodrug fosamprenavir follow as second-generation PIs. Structurally, the inhibitors of HIV protease consisted of a synthetic peptide bond between phenylalanine and proline amino acids, which is the target of the HIV aspartyl protease. Synthetic attempts are made to solve the bioavailability problems, whereas computer-aided techniques are continuously used to investigate more selective PIs.

The PIs in combination with doxorubicin are used and are further investigated for better anticancer results. Studies on mechanism of antitumor activity of PIs of first and second generation have been carried out in the last decades in order to understand the relation between different types of cancer and PIs.

References

Abt, D., Besse, A., Sedlarikova, L., Kraus, M., Bader, J., Silzle, T., Vodinska, M., Slaby, O., Schmid, H.P., Engeler, D.S., Driessen, C., Besse, L., 2018. Improving the efficacy of proteasome inhibitors in the treatment of renal cell carcinoma by combination with the human immunodeficiency virus (HIV)-protease inhibitors lopinavir or nelfinavir. BJU Int. 121, 600–609.

Agbowuro, A.A., Huston, W.M., Gamble, A.B., Tyndall, J.D.A., 2018. Proteases and protease inhibitors in infectious diseases. Med. Res. Rev. 38, 1295–1331.

Ahluwalia, M.S., Patton, C., Stevens, G., Tekautz, T., Angelov, L., Vogelbaum, M.A., Weil, R.J., Chao, S., Elson, P., Suh, J.H., Barnett, G.H., Peereboom, D.M., 2011. Phase II trial of ritonavir/lopinavir in patients with progressive or recurrent high-grade gliomas. J. Neurooncol. 102, 317–321.

Anderson, J.C., Mcfarland, B.C., Gladson, C.L., 2008. New molecular targets in angiogenic vessels of glioblastoma tumours. Expert Rev. Mol. Med. 10, e23.

Bardsley-Elliot, A., Plosker, G.L., 2000. Nelfinavir: an update on its use in HIV infection. Drugs 59, 581–620.

Barillari, G., Iovane, A., Bacigalupo, I., Palladino, C., Bellino, S., Leone, P., Monini, P., Ensoli, B., 2012. Ritonavir or saquinavir impairs the invasion of cervical intraepithelial neoplasia cells via a reduction of MMP expression and activity. AIDS 26, 909–919.

Beral, V., Peterman, T.A., Berkelman, R.L., Jaffe, H.W., 1990. Kaposi's sarcoma among persons with AIDS: a sexually transmitted infection? Lancet 335, 123–128.

Brower, E.T., Bacha, U.M., Kawasaki, Y., Freire, E., 2008. Inhibition of HIV-2 protease by HIV-1 protease inhibitors in clinical use. Chem. Biol. Drug Des. 71, 298–305.

Brunner, T.B., Geiger, M., Grabenbauer, G.G., Lang-Welzenbach, M., Mantoni, T.S., Cavallaro, A., Sauer, R., Hohenberger, W., Mckenna, W.G., 2008. Phase I trial of the human immunodeficiency virus protease inhibitor nelfinavir and chemoradiation for locally advanced pancreatic cancer. J. Clin. Oncol. 26, 2699–2706.

Cameron, D.W., Japour, A.J., Xu, Y., Hsu, A., Mellors, J., Farthing, C., Cohen, C., Poretz, D., Markowitz, M., Follansbee, S., Angel, J.B., Mcmahon, D., Ho, D., Devanarayan, V., Rode, R., Salgo, M., Kempf, D.J., Granneman, R., Leonard, J.M., Sun, E., 1999. Ritonavir and saquinavir combination therapy for the treatment of HIV infection. AIDS 13, 213–224.

Chandwani, A., Shuter, J., 2008. Lopinavir/ritonavir in the treatment of HIV-1 infection: a review. Ther. Clin. Risk Manage. 4, 1023–1033.

Chow, W.A., Jiang, C., Guan, M., 2009. Anti-HIV drugs for cancer therapeutics: back to the future? Lancet Oncol. 10, 61–71.

Cocchi, F., Devico, A.L., Garzino-Demo, A., Cara, A., Gallo, R.C., Lusso, P., 1996. The V3 domain of the HIV-1 gp120 envelope glycoprotein is critical for chemokine-mediated blockade of infection. Nat. Med. 2, 1244–1247.

Dittmer, D.P., Krown, S.E., 2007. Targeted therapy for Kaposi's sarcoma and Kaposi's sarcoma-associated herpesvirus. Curr. Opin. Oncol. 19, 452–457.

Du, R., Petritsch, C., Lu, K., Liu, P., Haller, A., Ganss, R., Song, H., Vandenberg, S., Bergers, G., 2008. Matrix metalloproteinase-2 regulates vascular patterning and growth affecting tumor cell survival and invasion in GBM. Neuro Oncol. 10, 254–264.

Eder, J., Hommel, U., Cumin, F., Martoglio, B., Gerhartz, B., 2007. Aspartic proteases in drug discovery. Curr. Pharm. Des. 13, 271–285.

Esposito, V., Palescandolo, E., Spugnini, E.P., Montesarchio, V., De Luca, A., Cardillo, I., Cortese, G., Baldi, A., Chirianni, A., 2006. Evaluation of antitumoral properties of the protease inhibitor indinavir in a murine model of hepatocarcinoma. Clin. Cancer Res. 12, 2634–2639.

Esposito, V., Verdina, A., Manente, L., Spugnini, E.P., Viglietti, R., Parrella, R., Pagliano, P., Parrella, G., Galati, R., De Luca, A., Baldi, A., Montesarchio, V., Chirianni, A., 2013. Amprenavir inhibits the migration in human hepatocarcinoma cell and the growth of xenografts. J. Cell. Physiol. 228, 640–645.

Flexner, C., 1998. HIV-protease inhibitors. N. Engl. J. Med. 338, 1281–1292.

Floren, L.C., Wiznia, A., Hayashi, S., Jayewardene, A., Stanley, K., Johnson, G., Nachman, S., Krogstad, P., Aweeka, F.T., 2003. Nelfinavir pharmacokinetics in stable human immunodeficiency virus-positive children: Pediatric AIDS Clinical Trials Group Protocol 377. Pediatrics 112, e220–e227.

Guan, M., Su, L., Yuan, Y.C., Li, H., Chow, W.A., 2015. Nelfinavir and nelfinavir analogues block site-2 protease cleavage to inhibit castration-resistant prostate cancer. Sci. Rep. 5, 9698–9706.

Gupta, A.K., Cerniglia, G.J., Mick, R., Mckenna, W.G., Muschel, R.J., 2005. HIV protease inhibitors block Akt signaling and radiosensitize tumor cells both in vitro and in vivo. Cancer Res. 65, 8256–8265.

Havlir, D.V., O'Marro, S.D., 2004. Atazanavir: new option for treatment of HIV infection. Clin. Infect. Dis. 38, 1599–1604.

Ikezoe, T., Daar, E.S., Hisatake, J., Taguchi, H., Koeffler, H.P., 2000. HIV-1 protease inhibitors decrease proliferation and induce differentiation of human myelocytic leukemia cells. Blood 96, 3553–3559.

Jiang, W., Mikochik, P.J., Ra, J.H., Lei, H., Flaherty, K.T., Winkler, J.D., Spitz, F.R., 2007. HIV protease inhibitor nelfinavir inhibits growth of human melanoma cells by induction of cell cycle arrest. Cancer Res. 67, 1221–1227.

Jiang, W., Li, X., Li, T., Wang, H., Shi, W., Qi, P., Li, C., Chen, J., Bao, J., Huang, G., Wang, Y., 2017. Repositioning of amprenavir as a novel extracellular signal-regulated kinase-2 inhibitor and apoptosis inducer in MCF-7 human breast cancer. Int. J. Oncol. 50, 823–834.

Johnson, M.D., O'connell, M., Pilcher, W., 2011. Lopinavir inhibits meningioma cell proliferation by Akt independent mechanism. J. Neurooncol. 101, 441–448.

Kempf, D.J., Marsh, K.C., Paul, D.A., Knigge, M.F., Norbeck, D.W., Kohlbrenner, W.E., Codacovi, L., Vasavanonda, S., Bryant, P., Wang, X.C., 1991. Antiviral and pharmacokinetic properties of C2 symmetric inhibitors of the human immunodeficiency virus type 1 protease. Antimicrob. Agents Chemother. 35, 2209–2214.

Kuiken, C., Leitner, T., Foley, B., Hahn, B., Marx, P., Mccutchan, F., Wolinsky, S., Korber, B., 2008. HIV Sequence Compedium 2008. Theoretical Biology and Biophysics Group T-10. Los Alamos National Laboratory, Los Alamos, NM, USA.

Kushchayeva, Y., Jensen, K., Recupero, A., Costello, J., Patel, A., Klubo-Gwiezdzinska, J., Boyle, L., Burman, K., Vasko, V., 2014. The HIV protease inhibitor nelfinavir down-regulates RET signaling and induces apoptosis in medullary thyroid cancer cells. J. Clin. Endocrinol. Metabol. 99, E734–E745.

Liuzzi, G., Mastroianni, C., Latronico, T., Mengoni, F., Fasano, A., Lichtner, M., Vullo, V., Riccio, P., 2004. Anti-HIV drugs decrease the expression of matrix metalloproteinases in astrocytes and microglia. Brain 127, 398–407.

Lucia, M.B., Anu, R., Handley, M., Gillet, J.P., Wu, C.P., De Donatis, G.M., Cauda, R., Gottesman, M.M., 2011. Exposure to HIV-protease inhibitors selects for increased expression of P-glycoprotein (ABCB1) in Kaposi's sarcoma cells. Br. J. Cancer 105, 513–522.

Lv, Z., Chu, Y., Wang, Y., 2015. HIV protease inhibitors: a review of molecular selectivity and toxicity. HIV AIDS (Auckl.) 7, 95–104.

Mahto, M.K., Yellapu, N.K., Kilaru, R.B., Chamarthi, N.R., Bhaskar, M., 2014. Molecular designing and in silico evaluation of darunavir derivatives as anticancer agents. Bioinformation 10, 221–226.

McCoy, C., 2007. Darunavir: a nonpeptidic antiretroviral protease inhibitor. Clin. Ther. 29, 1559–1576.

Meier-Stephenson, V., Riemer, J., Narendran, A., 2017. The HIV protease inhibitor, nelfinavir, as a novel therapeutic approach for the treatment of refractory pediatric leukemia. Onco Targets Ther. 10, 2581–2593.

Molla, A., Korneyeva, M., Gao, Q., Vasavanonda, S., Schipper, P.J., Mo, H.M., Markowitz, M., Chernyavskiy, T., Niu, P., Lyons, N., Hsu, A., Granneman, G.R., Ho, D.D., Boucher, C.A., Leonard, J.M., Norbeck, D.W., Kempf, D.J., 1996. Ordered accumulation of mutations in HIV protease confers resistance to ritonavir. Nat. Med. 2, 760–766.

Monini, P., Sgadari, C., Toschi, E., Barillari, G., Ensoli, B., 2004. Antitumour effects of antiretroviral therapy. Nat. Rev. Cancer 4, 861–875.

Morlat, P., Roussillon, C., Henard, S., Salmon, D., Bonnet, F., Cacoub, P., Georget, A., Aouba, A., Rosenthal, E., May, T., Chauveau, M., Diallo, B., Costagliola, D., Chene, G., ANRS EN20 Mortalité 2010 Study Group, 2014. Causes of death among HIV-infected patients in France in 2010 (national survey): trends since 2000. AIDS 28, 1181–1191.

Muesing, M.A., Smith, D.H., Cabradilla, C.D., Benton, C.V., Lasky, L.A., Capon, D.J., 1985. Nucleic acid structure and expression of the human AIDS/lymphadenopathy retrovirus. Nature 313, 450–458.

Navia, M.A., Fitzgerald, P.M.D., Mckeever, B.M., Leu, C.-T., Heimbach, J.C., Herber, W.K., Sigal, I.S., Darke, P.L., Springer, J.P., 1989. Three-dimensional structure of aspartyl protease from human immunodeficiency virus HIV-1. Nature 337, 615–620.

Orman, J.S., Perry, C.M., 2008. Tipranavir: a review of its use in the management of HIV infection. Drugs 68, 1435–1463.

Pajonk, F., Himmelsbach, J., Riess, K., Sommer, A., Mcbride, W.H., 2002. The human immunodeficiency virus (HIV)-1 protease inhibitor saquinavir inhibits proteasome function and causes apoptosis and radiosensitization in non-HIV-associated human cancer cells. Cancer Res. 62, 5230–5235.

Pati, S., Pelser, C.B., Dufraine, J., Bryant, J.L., Reitz Jr., M.S., Weichold, F.F., 2002. Antitumorigenic effects of HIV protease inhibitor ritonavir: inhibition of Kaposi sarcoma. Blood 99, 3771–3779.

Pokorná, J., Machala, L., Rezáčová, P., Konvalinka, J., 2009. Current and novel inhibitors of HIV protease. Viruses 1, 1209–1239.

Pyrko, P., Kardosh, A., Wang, W., Xiong, W., Schonthal, A.H., Chen, T.C., 2007. HIV-1 protease inhibitors nelfinavir and atazanavir induce malignant glioma death by triggering endoplasmic reticulum stress. Cancer Res. 67, 10920–10928.

Rana, K.Z., Dudley, M.N., 2012. Human immunodeficiency virus protease inhibitors. Pharmacotherapy 19, 35–59.

Ratner, L., Haseltine, W., Patarca, R., Livak, K.J., Starcich, B., Josephs, S.F., Doran, E.R., Rafalski, J.A., Whitehom, E.A., Baumeister, K., Ivanoff, L., Petteway, S.R., Pearson, M.L., Lautenberger, J.A., Papas, T.S., Ghrayeb, J., Chang, N.T., Gallo, R.C., Wong-Staal, F., 1985. Complete nucleotide sequence of the AIDS virus, HTLV-III. Nature 313, 277–284.

Roberts, N.A., Martin, J.A., Kinchington, D., Broadhurst, A.V., Craig, J.C., Duncan, I.B., Galpin, S.A., Handa, B.K., Kay, J., Krohn, A., Lambert, R.W., Merret, J.H., Mills, J.S., Parkes, K.E.B., Redshaw, S., Ritchie, A.J., Taylor, D.L., Thomas, J.G., Machin, P.G., 1990. Rational design of peptide-based HIV proteinase inhibitors. Science 248, 358–361.

Roche, D., Greiner, J., Aubertin, A.M., Vierling, P., 2008. Synthesis and in vitro biological evaluation of valine-containing prodrugs derived from clinically used HIV-protease inhibitors. Eur. J. Med. Chem. 43, 1506–1518.

Sanchez-Pescador, R., Power, M.D., Barr, P.J., Steimer, K.S., Stempien, M.M., Brown-Shimer, S.L., Gee, W.W., Renard, A., Randolph, A., Levy, J.A., Dina, D., Luciw, P.A., 1985. Nucleotide sequence and expression of an AIDS-associated retrovirus (ARV-2). Science 227, 484–492.

Sgadari, C., Barillari, G., Toschi, E., Carlei, D., Bacigalupo, I., Baccarini, S., Palladino, C., Leone, P., Bugarini, R., Malavasi, L., Cafaro, A., Falchi, M., Valdembri, D., Rezza, G., Bussolino, F., Monini, P., Ensoli, B., 2002. HIV protease inhibitors are potent anti-angiogenic molecules and promote regression of Kaposi sarcoma. Nat. Med. 8, 225–232.

Sham, H.L., Kempf, D.J., Molla, A., Marsh, K.C., Kumar, G.N., Chen, C.-M., Kati, W., Stewart, K., Lal, R., Hsu, A., Betebenner, D., Korneyeva, M., Vasavanonda, S., Mcdonald, E., Saldivar, A., Wideburg, N., Chen, X., Niu, P., Park, C., Jayanti, V., Grabowski, B., Granneman, G.R., Sun, E., Japour, A.J., Leonard, J.M., Plattner, J.J., Norbeck, D.W., 1998. ABT-378, a highly potent inhibitor of the human immunodeficiency virus protease. Antimicrob. Agents Chemother. 42, 3218–3224.

Soprano, M., Sorriento, D., Rusciano, M.R., Maione, A.S., Limite, G., Forestieri, P., D'angelo, D., D'alessio, M., Campiglia, P., Formisano, P., Iaccarino, G., Bianco, R., Illario, M., 2016. Oxidative stress mediates the antiproliferative effects of nelfinavir in breast cancer cells. PLoS One 11, e0155970–e0155996.

Srirangam, A., Mitra, R., Wang, M., Gorski, J.C., Badve, S., Baldridge, L., Hamilton, J., Kishimoto, H., Hawes, J., Li, L., Orschell, C.M., Srour, E.F., Blum, J.S., Donner, D., Sledge, G.W., Nakshatri, H., Potter, D.A., 2006. Effects of HIV protease inhibitor ritonavir on Akt-regulated cell proliferation in breast cancer. Clin. Cancer Res. 12, 1883–1896.

Timeus, F., Crescenzio, N., Ricotti, E., Doria, A., Bertin, D., Saglio, G., Tovo, P.A., 2006. The effects of saquinavir on imatinib-resistant chronic myelogenous leukemia cell lines. Haematologica 91, 711–712.

Tremblay, C.L., 2008. Combating HIV resistance—focus on darunavir. Ther. Clin. Risk Manage. 4, 759–766.

Uldrick, T.S., Little, R.F., 2015. How I treat classical Hodgkin lymphoma in patients infected with human immunodeficiency virus. Blood 125, 1226–1235.

Wain-Hobson, S., Sonigo, P., Danos, O., Cole, S., Alizon, M., 1985. Nucleotide sequence of the AIDS virus, LAV. Cell 40, 9–17.

Walmsley, S., Bernstein, B., King, M., Arribas, J., Beall, G., Ruane, P., Johnson, M., Johnson, D., Lalonde, R., Japour, A., Brun, S., Sun, E., 2002. Lopinavir-ritonavir versus nelfinavir for the initial treatment of HIV infection. N. Engl. J. Med. 346, 2039–2046.

Wire, M.B., Shelton, M.J., Studenberg, S., 2006. Fosamprenavir: clinical pharmacokinetics and drug interactions of the amprenavir prodrug. Clin. Pharmacokinet. 45, 137–168.

Wlodawer, A., 2002. Rational approach to AIDS drug design through structural biology. Annu. Rev. Med. 53, 595–614.

Yang, Y., Ikezoe, T., Takeuchi, T., Adachi, Y., Ohtsuki, Y., Takeuchi, S., Koeffler, H.P., Taguchi, H., 2005. HIV-1 protease inhibitor induces growth arrest and apoptosis of human prostate cancer LNCaP cells in vitro and in vivo in conjunction with blockade of androgen receptor STAT3 and AKT signaling. Cancer Sci. 96, 425–433.

Yang, Y., Ikezoe, T., Nishioka, C., Bandobashi, K., Takeuchi, T., Adachi, Y., Kobayashi, M., Takeuchi, S., Koeffler, H.P., Taguchi, H., 2006. NFV, an HIV-1 protease inhibitor, induces growth arrest, reduced Akt signalling, apoptosis and docetaxel sensitisation in NSCLC cell lines. Br. J. Cancer 95, 1653–1662.

Yarchoan, R., Uldrick, T.S., 2018. HIV-associated cancers and related diseases. N. Engl. J. Med. 378, 1029–1041.

Chapter 7

Serine proteases in ovarian cancer

Pankaj Kumar Rai[a], Nitesh Kumar Poddar[b]
[a]*Department of Biotechnology, Invertis University, Bareilly, India,* [b]*Department of Biosciences, Manipal University Jaipur, Jaipur, Rajasthan, India*

7.1 Introduction

Cancer is considered as a leading cause of death along with the heart diseases. Ovarian cancer (OC) is the seventh most commonly diagnosed cancer among women in the world. Annually, it accounts nearly about 152,000 deaths worldwide (Zhang et al., 2011). A woman's lifetime risk of developing OC is 1 in 75, and her chance of dying of the disease is 1 in 100 (Reid et al., 2017). OC is often undetected until it spreads throughout the pelvis and abdomen. OC is more difficult to treat and often fatal in later stages. In earlier stages of OC, when disease is confined to the ovary, it is more likely to be successfully treated. The cell type in which cancer begins determines the type of OC. Epithelial tumors, for example, are one of the types of OCs that begins in the thin layer of tissue that covers the exterior part of the ovary. Epithelial type tumors account for about 90% of OCs (Reid et al., 2017), whereas, stromal tumors begin in the ovarian tissue that contains cells that produce hormones. Normally, these tumors are diagnosed earlier than other ovarian tumors. Approximately, 7% of ovarian tumors are reported to be stromal type tumor (Chen et al., 2003a). In addition, germ cell tumors occur in the stage of egg-producing cell phase. Younger women are more susceptible to such type of OCs. Studies have shown that proteases also contribute to tumor growth and progression, which depends heavily on the supply of nutrients and oxygen. The ability of solid tumors to invade and metastasize the surrounding tissue is linked with the formation and degradation of structural elements in the vicinity of tumor cells. Evidences have shown that proteases play a key role in the invasion and metastasis of tumor cells. On the basis of the key amino acids present in the active site and the type of mechanism involved in peptide bond cleavage: proteases can be classified into six groups: cysteine proteases, serine proteases, threonine proteases, glutamic acid proteases, aspartate proteases,

Cancer-Leading Proteases. https://doi.org/10.1016/B978-0-12-818168-3.00007-3

and matrix metalloproteases. Out of these six, serine proteases, metalloproteases (MMPs), cysteine proteases, and aspartyl proteases are reported to be involved in various types of cancers (Poddar et al., 2017). Serine proteases are considered to be the most important factor, which promotes the growth and spread of OC at an earlier stage of tumor formation and at the same time, if it is detected earlier, then it can be prevented from its formation by inhibiting the activity of serine proteases. In this chapter, we have focused on the role of serine proteases in OC.

7.2 Role of proteases in cancer

A standout among the most essential natural responses in the biological processes is proteolysis and this is known as proteolytic degradation, which is being carried out by enzymes called proteases. Proteases play an important role in various physiological processes such as homeostasis and inflammation. Proteolysis is the hydrolysis of peptide bond with the removal of the peptide carbonyl group. Proteases are a wide variety of enzymes found in the human body and approximately 990 protease genes and 1605 protease inhibitors were reported in human beings (Lin et al., 1995). The breakdown of a peptide bond with a protease usually occurs in the presence of water (in aspartate, metallo-, and glutamic proteases) and cysteine, serine, or threonine residue (generally, for the activation of histidine) act as a nucleophile in the active site (Bastians et al., 1999). The surrounding stromal and tumor cells modulate two type of protease systems involved in the proteolysis, namely matrix metalloproteases (MMPs) and urokinase plasminogen activator (uPA)/uPA receptor (uPAR)/plasminogen network. Stromal MMP-2 and uPA are synthesized as inactive precursors and then induce as active form at the surface of the tumor cells causing the malignant cells to rupture the basement membrane. Blood vessel proliferation is also promoted by these enzymes to feed the growing cancer (Poddar et al., 2017). In normal cells, proteases are very much required in carrying out various biological processes, and regulate a various cellular processes such as gene expression, differentiation, and cell death (Turk and Stoka, 2007). Recent studies have shown that proteases are also involved in the growth and progression of tumors at primary and metastatic sites (Borissenko and Groll, 2007) (Tables 7.1 and 7.2). Tumor cells have been shown to induce the expression of proteolytic enzymes in neighboring nonneoplastic cells and to control their activity to promote tumor growth (Rawlings et al., 2010). Metastasis and tumor progression mainly depends on the supply of nutrients and oxygen and is activated by proteases present in the tumor and/or in the surrounding tissues and organs (Borissenko and Groll, 2007). Several tumors have shown that increase in protease levels in the initial phase of the growth of cells can be associated with many facets of cancers, such as proliferation, immune response, inflammatory cell recruitment, tumor invasion, angiogenesis, metastasis, apoptosis, and epithelial to mesenchymal transition (EMT) (Poddar et al., 2017).

TABLE 7.1 Role of proteases in cancer.

Family (classes)	Protease	Location	Cancer	References
Cysteine Cathepsins	General	Intracellular, lysosome	Ubiquitously expressed in human tissues	Rawlings (2014) and Turk et al. (2012)
	Cathepsin K, Cathepsin B, Cathepsin L	Extracellular and pericellular under pathological conditions	Breast, cervix, colon, colorectal, gastric, Head and neck, liver, lung, melanoma, ovarian, pancreatic, prostate, thyroid	Yang et al. (2009), Verbovsek et al. (2015), Boy et al. (2008), Egeblad and Werb (2002), and Rakashanda et al.(2012)
Aspartatic Cathepsins	Cathepsin E Cathepsin D	Endosomal structures, ER, golgi, lysosome	Cervical, gastric, lung, pancreas adenocarcinomas, breast, colorectal, ovarian	Zucker et al. (2000)
Kallikreins (hK)	General	Intracellular, secreted	Ubiquitously expressed in human tissues and fluids	Kim et al. (1998) and Mason and Jyoce (2011)
	hk1, hk10, hk15	Tissue	Lungs adenocarcinoma, colon, ovarian, pancreatic, Head and neck, ovarian, prostate	Mohamed and Sloane (2006), Gocheva and Jyoce (2007), and Jedeszko and Sloane (2004)
	PSA (hk3)		Prostate, ovarian	Turk et al. (2012)
Serine Proteases	uPA, uPAR	Membrane, pericellular	Cervical, colorectal, gastric, prostate	Vasiljeva and Turk (2008)
Matrix metalloproteases (MMPs)	MMP-1,2,8,9, 13,14		Breast, colorectal, lung, malignant gliomas, ovarian	Matarrese et al. (2010), Joyce and Hanahan (2004), Tu et al. (2008), and Hirai et al. (1999)

Modified and adapted from Eatemadi, A., Aiyelabegan, H.T., Negahdari, B., Mazlomi, M.A., Daraee, H., Daraee, N., Sadroddiny, E., 2017. Role of protease and protease inhibitors in cancer pathogenesis and treatment. Biomed. Pharmacother. 86, 221–231.

TABLE 7.2 Serine proteases involved in different types of cancers (Cheng et al., 2006; Bugge et al., 2007; List, 2009; Webb et al., 2011; Poddar et al., 2017).

Serine proteases	Types of cancer						
	Breast	Cervical	Colon	Endometrial	Lung	Ovarian	Prostate
Hepsin	+	+		+	+	+	+
Matriptase	+	+	+	+	+	+	+
KLK6						+	+
KLK7	+	+	+			+	+
TMPRSS3	+					+	+

7.3 Roles of serine proteases in cancer

Regulation of serine proteases is crucial to the cell and various physiological functioning of tissues and its deregulation can lead to pathological conditions like cancer (Gondi et al., 2007). Pretty much, 33% of the proteases can be designated as serine proteases, known for the nucleophilic "Ser" residue at the active site (Andreasen et al., 1997). The active site of serine proteases was at first reported by the presence of three amino acids as Asp-His-Ser as a "charge relay" system or "catalytic triad" (Fisher et al., 2001). The Asp-His-Ser amino acids can be arranged in four different structural ways in proteases such as subtilisin, chymotrypsin, carboxypeptidase Y, and Clp protease on the basis of MEROPS nomenclature (Sidenius and Blasi, 2003), implying that this synergist machinery represents four different events or mechanisms (Fisher et al., 2001). There are other serine proteases with various reactant groups of triad and dyads, involving Ser-His-Glu, Ser-Lys/His, His-Ser-His, and N-terminal Ser (Fisher et al., 2001). Trypsin is one of the highly depicted serine proteases. These proteases play a key role in a variety of pathological conditions such as inflammation, atherosclerosis, and cancer (Gondi et al., 2007). Serine proteases (or serine endopeptidases) are used as serine in the active site for hydrolysis of peptide bond. More often than not, they are found to direct the enzyme activities as zymogens by controlling the specific activation of proteolysis. The basic division of serine proteases depends on the site where particular amino acids of the peptide bonds are cleaved. For example, trypsin, a serine peptidase, prefers to cleave the lysine and arginine peptide bonds in the cleavage site. Chymotrypsin prefers aromatic amino acids (phenylalanine, tyrosine, or tryptophan) to digest the peptide bond at the cleavage site. Elastase, a serine peptidase, prefers to cleave the amino acids with short lateral chains. Serine proteases perform various functions, such as protein digestion, blood coagulation, supplementation, differentiation, and advancement, in warm blood animals (Puente et al., 2005). Serine protease can be arranged into two broad classes depending on its location inside the extracellular space: secreted type and membrane anchored type. The secreted serine proteases are well-known individuals from S1 serine protease group. They are secreted from the secretory vesicles into the extracellular environment. The prototype members of the S1 family include chymotrypsin, trypsin, and thrombin. These secreted serine proteases show different biological events such as immunity and tissue repair (Puente et al., 2005). A subgroup of S1 serine proteases called the membrane anchored serine proteases has been reported and is simply anchored to the plasma layer via its amino or carboxyl terminal domain (Hooper et al., 2001). The membrane-anchored serine proteases are associated with a variety of physiological functions, such as epithelial barrier, fertilization, cell signaling, embryo development, and tissue morphogenesis (Puente et al., 2005). Based on their anchoring properties in different ways, they can be further divided into subgroups: (i) a carboxyl-terminal transmembrane domain through a GPI (glycosyl phosphatidylinositol) linkage which is involved in posttranslational processes, (ii) a carboxyl-terminal transmembrane domain (Type I), and (iii) an amino-terminal transmembrane domain with a cytoplasmic extension (type II transmembrane serine proteases-TTSPs) (Hooper et al., 2001). The type I serine proteases, tryptase γ1 and GPI-anchored serine proteases, prostasin, and testisin contain a hydrophobic carboxyl-terminal extension that serves as a transmembrane space (consisting of 310–370 amino acids). GPI anchors have been known to modify the prostatin and testisin posttranscriptionally (Hooper et al., 1999; Chen et al., 2001; Verghese et al., 2006). TTSPs are the membrane-anchored serine proteases (family S1) and can possibly be connected to cellular membrane by means of a hydrophobic stretch at their amino terminus. All the membrane-anchored serine proteases have conserved catalytic domain and they belong to S1 peptidase family. These serine proteases generally exist as zymogens (inactive form). For activation, they undergo auto-cleavage and form a two-chain form and ultimately separate the pro- and catalytic domain with the catalytic domain. A few precedents of TTSPs are TMPRSS2, matriptase, hepsin, and TMPRSS4 (Szabo and Bugge, 2008). Pericellular and extracellular proteolysis dysregulation by anchored membrane and secreted serine proteases are the characteristic features of various clinical disorders. Reports have shown that the extracellular matrix (ECM) proteolytic breakdown is the key step in metastasize of tumor cells (López-Otín and Matrisian, 2007; Lu et al., 2011). The series of activity of proteases engaged with tumor movement and progression is reported as the cancer "degredom." A positive cooperation has been identified between the aggressiveness of the tumor and the overexpression of numerous proteases (López-Otín and Matrisian, 2007). In the events of cancer development, serine proteases might be associated with any of the basic processes of tumorigenesis (Hooper et al., 2001) (Fig. 7.1). In normal conditions, an endogenous antiserine protease framework designated as serpins controls the activity of serine proteases and maintains the coordination between proteases and the inhibitors in the living being. An irregularity between the coordination of proteases and inhibitors might lead to the cancer development. For instance, in prostate cancer, hepsin, a cell surface serine protease, and maspin, a serine protease inhibitor, are reported to excessively upregulate and downregulate, respectively. This perturbs the cell homeostasis leading to tumor growth, invasion, and metastasis. This shows that serine protease helps in promoting cancer and there is a need of some check points in the activity of serine proteases to inhibit the progress and metastasis of tumors (Poddar et al., 2017). Serine proteases could be used as a tumor biomarker for detecting cancer at a beginning stage of tumor. Thrombotic and prostate cancer patients could be identified by screening of coagulation factor levels and serum prostate-particular antigen. Moreover, focusing on expression levels of proteases are the effectives methodologies for the advancement of antitumor therapy (Choi et al., 2012).

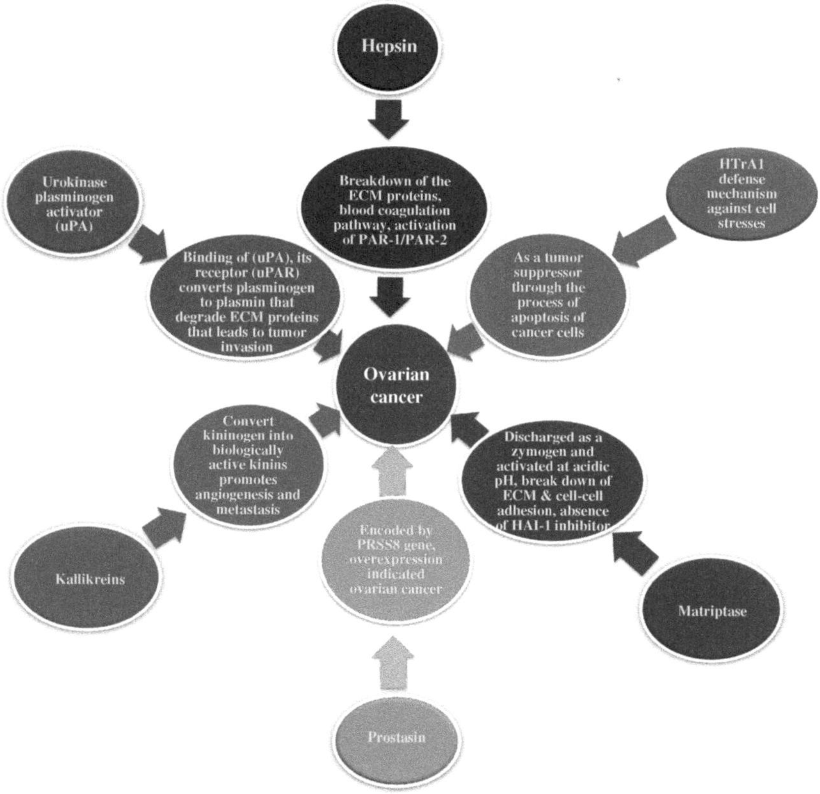

FIG. 7.1 Overview of role of serine proteases in ovarian cancer. Hepsin participates in blood coagulation pathway and remodeling of extracellular matrix, and promotes ovarian cancer by activation of transmembrane PAR-1/PAR-2 (protease-activated receptor). HtrA1 is a candidate of tumor suppressor protein involved in apoptosis of cells and downregulated in ovarian cancer. Overexpression of Matriptase degrades extracellular matrix proteins in the absence of hepatocyte growth factor activator inhibitor-1 results in the progression of ovarian cancer. Prostasin is used as a potential biomarker for the detection of ovarian cancer. Kallikreins convert kininogen to active kinin peptides and promote angiogenesis and metastasis through the activation of downstream signaling pathways. The binding of uPA with uPAR is involved in the activation of plasminogen to plasmin, which in turn initiates a series of proteolytic cascade to degrade the components of the extracellular matrix resulting in metastasis of cells.

Serine proteases in humans are well documented and around 175 are deciphered till date. A large portion of them are secretory in nature and have significant role in a numerous metabolic functions related to tissues homeostasis. The secretory serine protease uPA (urokinase plasminogen activator) and kallikrein play key roles in various physiological functions like cell growth, cell signaling, and tissue remodeling process. In any case, perturbation in the expression levels of serine proteases prompts tumor invasion and cancer.

7.3.1 Urokinase plasminogen activator

Urokinase was extracted from human urine and is also found in blood and extracellular matrix of tissues. Plasminogen (an inactive form of plasmin) is a primary substrate of urokinase. Activated plasmin provokes a proteolytic cascade that involves thrombolysis or extracellular degradation of the matrix based on the physiological environment. This proteolytic cascade is associated with vascular diseases and progression of cancer. The uPA framework is also linked to various tissue remodeling processes (Hildenbrand et al., 2008). The uPA system is a part of serine protease family and plays a crucial role in tumor invasion and cancer metastasis (Fig. 7.2) (Paschos et al., 2009). The two serine proteases, uPA and tissue plasminogen activator (tPA), two serpin inhibitors, plasminogen activator inhibitor-1 (PAI-1) and plasminogen activator inhibitor-2 (PAI-2), and the glycolipid-anchored uPA receptor (uPAR) are collectively form the plasminogen activator (PA) system. The plasminogen (an inactive form) is converted to plasmin (an active form) by the catalytic activity of uPA and tPA leading to the breakdown of the most extracellular proteins. The tPA follows fibrin-dependent pathway for blood clot dissolution mechanism (Collen and Lijnen, 1991). Whereas, uPA follows fibrin-independent pathway and generally acts on the plasminogen activator like uPAR which regulates the pericellular proteolysis including the degradation of ECM leading to invasion and cancer metastasis (Blasi, 1997). The uPA and uPAR are reported to express in different human cancers. The uPAR is a glycosylated cell surface protein attached to the cell membrane by a GPI anchor. The uPA catalyzes the conversion of plasminogen into plasmin that encourages the degradation of different ECM proteins resulting into loss of communication between cells, prompting the invasion of cancer cells (Gondi et al., 2007). It also activates the various inactive metalloproteases (MMPs) (Andreasen et al., 1997). The uPAR with

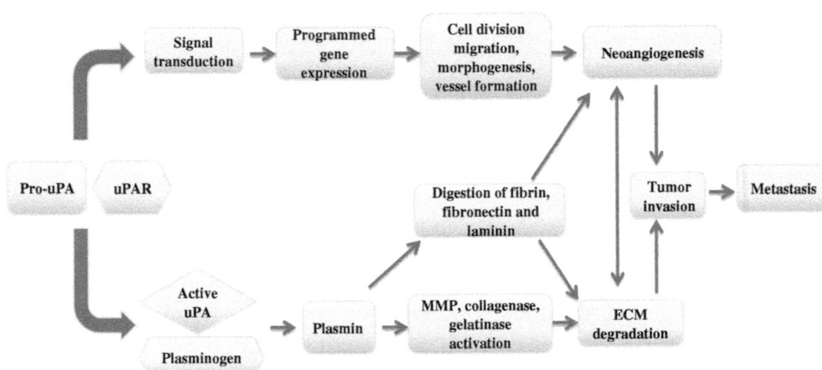

FIG. 7.2 Schematic representation of the role of urokinase plasminogen activator (uPA), uPA receptor (uPAR) and plasmin in the cancer.*(Modified and adapted from Paschos K.A., Canovas, D., Bird, N.C., 2009. The role of cell adhesion molecules in the progression of colorectal cancer and the development of liver metastasis. Cell. Signal. 21, 665–674.)*

uPA thus plays an important role in triggering a proteolytic cascade reaction that supports tumor growth by metastasis of cancer cells (Fisher et al., 2001). The significance of uPAR on cancer cell migration is deciphered on the basis of whether it is protease dependent or not. Since uPAR does not have a transmembrane structure, its nonprotease function relies on vitronectin (VN), integrin family, G-protein-coupled receptors, and growth factor receptors to relay its downstream signals (Sidenius and Blasi, 2003). Signaling via uPAR activates Tyr kinases, Src, the serine kinase Raf, FAK, and extracellular-signal controlled kinase (ERK)/mitogen-initiated protein kinase (MAPK) pathway leading to the activation of cell multiplication, metastasis, and cell-cell interaction (Aguirre Ghiso et al., 1999). The main objectives of uPAR are ECM degradation, angiogenesis, modulation of cAMP levels, and changes in cell association with integrins, tyrosine kinases, and serine/threonine kinases (Preissner et al., 2000). The uPA has been seen to be a predictive marker in numerous kinds of organ cancers, for example, cancers of lung (Oka et al., 1991), bladder (Hasui et al., 1992), stomach (Nekarda et al., 1994), and so on. Reports have suggested that uPA along with uPAR facilitates the migration of cell via various signaling pathways. Thus, integrins are vital uPAR signaling coreceptors and their activation induces the focal adhesion kinase (FAK). This step activates Src/MEK/ERK-subordinate signaling pathways, and ultimately transcriptional activation of the uPA promoter (Han et al., 2002). Various reports have suggested that uPA and plasminogen activator inhibitor (PAI)-1 assume an important role in the invasion and metastasis of tumors. However, the correlations between uPA and PAI-1 to epithelial OC have rarely reported. Cai et al. (2007) investigate the roles of uPA and PAI-1 in the invasion and metastasis of epithelial OC. Because of this, an immunohistochemistry technique was applied to decipher the protein expression pattern of uPA and PAI-1 in 80 specimens of epithelial OC and 20 specimens of benign ovarian tumor. It was reported that both uPA and PAI-1 are upregulated in epithelial OC, and might be used as markers to predict the prognosis of epithelial OC patients.

7.3.2 Kallikreins

The name "Kallikrein" was coined by Kraut and colleagues in 1930. It was derived from Greek word "kallikreas" meaning pancreas (Poddar et al., 2017). A type of secreted serine proteases, human tissue kallikreins (hKs), converts large molecular weight proteins into active small peptides (kinins). Kallikreins are classified into two families, the tissue and plasma kallikreins. Kallikrein I (hK1, pancreatic-renal kallikrein) is the only enzyme with decent activity among tissue kallikreins. Kallikreins genes are named as KLK1 to KLK15, a total of 15 in number and encode as hK1 to hK15 and are regulated by steroid hormones (Borgono et al., 2004). A large portion of the kallikreins is expressed in endocrine-related organs and is secreted by ECM for example, breast, ovary, prostrate, and testis. It is an established fact that the ECM degradation has an important role in tumor metastasis through extracellular proteolytic activity. Structural integrity of ECM is maintained by various growth factors and signaling molecules. The imbalance arisen due to the activity of extracellular proteases leads to change in the ECM microenvironment. This change affects the number of cell activity processes, for example, apoptosis, angiogenesis, and metastasis (Borgoño and Diamandis, 2004). ECM disruption results in the modification of cell-cell and cell-ECM interactions leading to the perturbation in the activity of growth factors and their receptors and is ultimately suggested to have either tumor promoting or tumor-suppressive effects (Borgoño and Diamandis, 2004). Schmitt et al. (2013) reported overexpression of KLK genes in ovarian carcinoma related to steroid-hormone-regulated cancer (Fig. 7.3). Aside from steroid-hormone-regulated cancer, kallikreins are de-regulated in different tumor types, for example, lung adenocarcinomas, pancreatic cancer, and acute lymphoblastic leukemia (Borgoño and Diamandis, 2004). hKs have potent angiogenic effects and catalyze the conversion of kininogen (inactive) to kinin peptides (active), which ultimately leads to activation of cAMP, Akt/PKB, and VEGF (vascular endothelial growth factor) pathways, thus promoting the angiogenesis (Milkiewicz et al., 2006). Likewise, KLKs may also take part in remodeling of ECM via the MMPs, uPA, and kinin signaling pathways (Desriviéres et al., 1993; Menashi et al., 1994; Saunders et al., 2005). The members of kallikrein family such as KLK2, 4, and 12 activate the uPA system which leads to plasmin formation and consequently activates plasmin and in turn resulting in the breakdown of numerous ECM proteins (Sidenius and Blasi, 2003; Takayama et al., 2001; Giusti et al., 2005; Frenette et al., 1997).

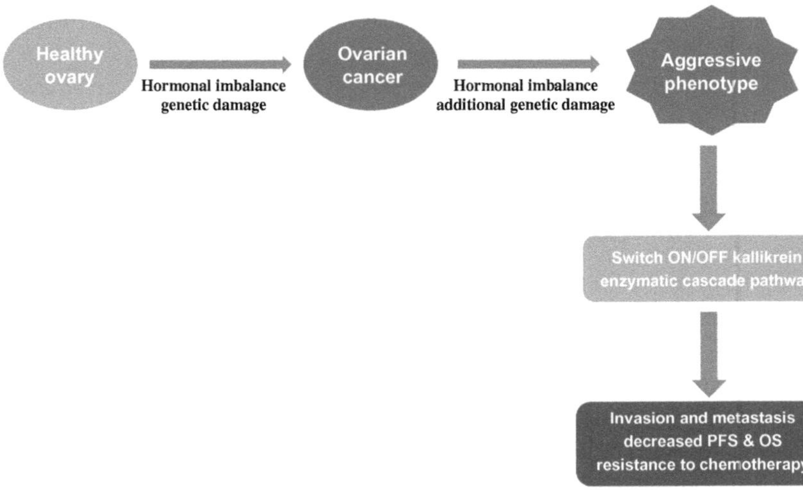

FIG. 7.3 Proposed model implicating multiple kallikrein overexpression during progression of OC by Diamandis and Yousef (2002). *PFS*, progression-free survival of OC patients; *OS*, overall survival of OC patients.

KLK1 and KLK12 convert kininogen to active kinin peptides and bradykinin, thus ultimately promoting angiogenesis and metastasis through the activation of downstream signaling pathways, for example, basic fibroblast growth factor (bFGF), cAMP, Akt/PKB, and VEGF pathways (Giusti et al., 2005; Colman, 2006; Emanueli and Madeddu, 2001).

7.3.3 HTRA1 (PRSS11 or IGFBP-5)

HtrA1 (otherwise called Prss11 or IGFBP-5 or DegP) is a member of high temperature requirement factor A (HtrA) of oxidative stress response serine proteases (Poddar et al., 2017). HtrA1 is a serine protease induced by heat shock and it operates as a chaperone, required for the survival of microscopic organisms at high temperature (Lipinska et al., 1990; Spiess et al., 1999). These serine proteases provide stability to the cells against various cell stresses like proteolysis of the misfolded proteins (Clausen et al., 2002). There are four human HtrAs: HtrA1 (Hu et al., 1998), HtrA2 (Gray et al., 2000), HtrA3 (pregnancy-related serine protease, PRSP) (Nie et al., 2006), and HtrA4 (Inagaki et al., 2012). They do various biological functions, for example, mitochondrial homeostasis, apoptosis, and cell signaling and their improper function prompts different clinical disorder (Zurawa-Janicka et al., 2013; Canfield et al., 2007). HtrA1 is one of the early reported members from the human HtrA family extracted from a normal fibroblast cell (Zumbrunn and Trueb, 1996). HtrA1 is downregulated in a variety of cancers, for example, melanoma (Baldi et al., 2002), glioma (Kotliarov et al., 2006), ovarian tumors (Chien et al., 2004; Narkiewicz et al., 2009), endometrial (Bowden et al., 2006; Narkiewicz et al., 2009), lung cancer (Esposito et al., 2006), and so forth. Several studies revealed that overexpression of HtrA1 plays a critical role as tumor suppressor through the apoptosis of cancer cells (Baldi et al., 2002). Likewise, it was demonstrated that HtrA1 and HtrA3 act as the inhibitors of growth factor system by transforming them (Oka et al., 2004). The best method for the discovery of a cancer drug is to rationalize the therapeutic agents which regulate the apoptotic process (Fesik, 2005). The process of apoptosis is regulated by pro-apoptotic and antiapoptotic proteins, a family of Bcl-2 antiapoptotic survival proteins, such as inhibitors of apoptosis proteins (IAPs), and caspases. Furthermore, HtrA2/Omi was reported to work as promoter in apoptotic cell death (Verhagen et al., 2002). The HtrA2/Omi induces apoptosis in human cells and functions as a caspase-independent system (proteolytic action) and in a caspase-dependent manner (degradation of IAPs) (Suzuki et al., 2001). A link between HtrA1, as found to be involved in resistance to chemotherapy in OC and X-linked inhibitor of apoptosis protein (XIAP), a member of the inhibitor of apoptosis proteins (IAPs) family as a potential substrate of HtrA1 and their relationships with chemoresistance in OC, was investigated by He et al. (2012). Results have indicated that purified wild-type HtrA1 degrades recombinant XIAP in vitro whereas, mutant HtrA1 was unable to do so. In addition, in vivo results have suggested the formation of a protein complex between HtrA1 and XIAP. Furthermore, overexpression of HtrA1 in OV202 cells promoted cell sensitivity to cisplatin-induced apoptosis which could be reversed by increased expression of XIAP. The cleavage of XIAP induced by HtrA1 was enhanced by cisplatin treatment. Moreover, XIAP was found as a novel substrate of HtrA1 and the degradation of XIAP by HtrA1 contributes to cell response to chemotherapy, suggesting that restoring expression of HtrA1 may be a promising treatment approach for OC. The identification of this new enzyme has capability to inactivate XIAP leading to a better understanding of the development of resistant phenotype in OC. The serine protease HtrA2/Omi localized in mitochondria is reported to be associated with a variety of malignancies. It is released into the cytosol after apoptotic stimuli. Wang et al. (2016) analyzed the expression of Omi/HtrA2 in 52 epithelial ovarian carcinoma (EOC) tissues and paired corresponding adjacent nontumor tissues to elaborate the clinical significance and antineoplastic efficacy of Omi/HtrA2 on subcutaneous transplanted tumor in a nude mice model. Collectively, the report concluded that overexpressed HtrA2/Omi could inhibit EOC cell growth in vitro as well as in vivo. HtrA1 and HtrA3 are reported to be downregulated in various types of cancers, leading to loss of these proteases in cancer. Singh et al. (2013) studied the downregulation of HtrA (HtrA1–3) in commonly used cancer cell lines and primary ovarian tumors. During the experiment, HtrA3 was found to be extensively downregulated in the cancer cell lines studied. In primary ovarian tumors, HtrA3 was significantly lower in serous cystadenocarcinoma and granulosa cell tumors. This study suggested that HtrA3 is likely to be more linked than HtrA associated with ovarian malignancy.

7.3.4 Type II transmembrane serine proteases (TTSPs)

Type II transmembrane serine proteases are considered to be an important part of the human degradome and are well known in conversion of precursor molecules (inactive) into active molecules and thus play an important role in tissues homeostasis and cancer (Antalis et al., 2010). The TTSPs family has diverse roles in mammalian system and their structure homology do not have a typical biochemical function. They usually participate in either the activation of hormones or growth factors or in the initiation of proteolytic cascades. This suggests that they play a key role in maintaining basic homeostasis by activating or deactivating the signaling molecules found in the biochemical reactions. Much attention has recently been paid, for example, to members of the TTSPs family, hepsin, matriptase-2, TMPRSS4 for their key physiological roles, their roles in tumorigenic action, and distinctive regulatory mechanisms.

7.3.5 Hepsin

Hepsin (TMPRSS1) is one of the members of type II transmembrane serine protease (Moran et al., 2006). Hepsin is found in liver and in trace amount in tissues of stomach, kidney, prostate, thyroid, and inner ear. It has one additional domain in its stem region, a group A scavenger receptor domain (SR) in addition to serine protease domain (SPD). Hepsin activates pro uPA, pro HGF, Laminin 332 and pro MSP (Moran et al., 2006), pro-hepatocyte growth factor and is inhibited by hepatocyte growth factor activator inhibitor-1B (HAI-1B) and hepatocyte growth factor activator inhibitor-2 (HAI-2) (Kirchhofer et al., 2005). It involves the activation of different proteolytic cascades, in particular the activation of nonactive proteases that promote the breakdown of ECM proteins. Furthermore, it also contributes to the blood coagulation pathway by catalyzing the conversion of factor VII to VIIa, which helps in the formation of thrombin, pericellular fibrin deposition, and PAR-1 activation (protease activated receptor) (Kazama et al., 1995). Hepsin is reported to be strongly expressed in OC by various groups (Tanimoto et al., 1997; Magee et al., 2001; Chen et al., 2003a,b). Tanimoto et al. (1997) reported overexpression of hepsin gene in ovarian carcinomas. They further deciphered the expression of hepsin gene in 44 ovarian tumors and 10 normal ovaries. The Northern blot analysis indicated the abundant hepsin transcript in carcinoma but was almost negligible in normal adult tissue, including normal ovary. The results projected hepsin as candidate protease in the invasive process and growth capacity of ovarian tumor cells.

7.3.6 Matriptase-2

Matriptase-2 or TMPRSS6 (80–90-kDa cell surface glycoprotein), a hepatic membrane serine protease expressed as zymogen on cell surface (Ramsay et al., 2009a,b), belongs to a type II transmembrane serine protease family (Velasco et al., 2002; Ramsay et al., 2008). Matriptase-2 involves a short N-terminal cytoplasmic tail, a transmembrane domain, an extracellular stem region containing a SEA domain (a single sea urchin sperm protein), two CUB domains (urchin embryonic growth factor), three LDLA repeats, and a C-terminal trypsin-like SPD domain (Velasco et al., 2002; Ramsay et al., 2008) and was found in most part in breast and prostate cancer (Webb et al., 2012; Shi et al., 1993). Matriptase-2 demonstrates high homology in terms of structure and functionality with matriptase-1 (Sanders et al., 2010) and is found to be overexpressed in epithelial cells, and in various types of cancers (Oberst et al., 2001). Matriptase is one of the most extensively studied type II transmembrane serine proteases with more than 350 published reports. Matriptase is reported to be upregulated in breast, cervical, colorectal prostate, endometrial, esophageal squamous cell carcinoma, gastric, head and neck, and pancreatic carcinoma; and in tumors of lung, liver, and kidney among others (Cheng et al., 2006; Bugge et al., 2007; List, 2009; Webb et al., 2011). Matriptase-2 is primarily found to be expressed in human liver and is found to be connected with the dissolution of ECM proteins (Velasco et al., 2002). The protease action can be controlled in different ways with its pericellular environment and it is reported that few proteases can be activated in acidic conditions, e.g., cathepsins in lysosomes and pepsinogen in the stomach (Tannock and Rotin, 1989; McQueney et al., 1997; Richter and Tanaka, 1998). It has also been observed that matriptase activity is firmly controlled by the cell's chemical environment (Tseng et al., 2010). Like other secreted or lysosomal proteases, matriptase is activated by an acidic pH with only difference lies in the sense that it is attached onto the cells surface (Lin et al., 1997). Matriptase is released as a zymogen and its auto-activation depends on the intrinsic activity of the zymogen matriptase, the noncatalytic enzyme domain, and posttranslational modification (Oberst et al., 2003; Xu et al., 2011). This protease is mainly expressed in normal tissue epithelial components along with the hepatocyte growth factor activator inhibitor-1 (HAI-1), suggesting that the function of matriptase is strictly regulated (Oberst et al., 2001; Lee et al., 2005; Szabo et al., 2007). Reports have proposed that an imbalance in the proportion of matriptase and HAI-1 is the key factor for the signature of cancer-related proteolytic events (Kang et al., 2003; Saleem et al., 2006). Although the proper mechanism of the deregulation of matriptase activity is as yet not known rather it might straight forwardly influence the cellular microenvironment via the activation or inactivation of downstream signaling molecules leading to the breakdown of ECM components and cell-cell adhesion (Bhatt et al., 2005). Matriptase, a type II transmembrane serine protease, expressed by epithelial ovarian tumor cells cleaves and activates proteins implicated in the advance of OC and represents a potential prognostic and therapeutic target. Oberst et al. (2002) study the expression of matriptase, and its inhibitor, hepatocyte growth factor activator inhibitor-1 (HAI-1), in epithelial OC. Total 54 tumors had been examined, out of which 39 (72%) and 11 (20%) were positive for matriptase and for HAI-1, respectively. It was interesting to found that all HAI-1-positive tumors were also matriptase positive. The researchers concluded that advanced-stage ovarian tumors expressing matriptase are more likely to do so in the absence of their inhibitor, HAI-1, indicating that an imbalance ratio of matriptase and HAI-1 may be important factor for advanced disease progression. These findings were again supported by Jin et al. (2006). They reported a significant elevation in matriptase immunostaining scores in various carcinomas indicating matriptase as a key player in the clinical aggressiveness of ovarian tumors. In order to confirm this, immunohistochemical matriptase analysis was carried out in tissue microarrays with 164 ovarian neoplasms. All ovarian tumors with the exception of fibromas and Brenner tumors showed a significant matriptase expression. The matriptase values in the tumors were considerably higher than in their nontumor counterparts. These findings show that matriptase is overexpressed in many malignant ovarian tumors and can be a new biomarker to diagnose and treat malignant ovarian tumors. Matriptase expression in ovarian serous adenocarcinoma, and its association with clinicopathological characteristics and patient prognosis was investigated by Ji et al. (2017). They examined the matriptase expression by immunohistochemistry technique and demonstrated the significant overexpression of matriptase protein in the ovarian serous adenocarcinoma tissues as compared with the normal ovarian tissues

($P=.0003$). The study shows that matriptase expression in early OC is high and common in comparison with normal ovarian tissue. Matriptase implication can contribute to the formation of ovarian tumors and can therefore serve as a marker for early diagnosis of this disease.

7.3.7 Prostasin

Ovarian cancer (OC) is detected at the final stage leading to poor survival rate. Mok et al. (2001) deciphered the overexpressed genes for secretory proteins and selected serine proteases prostasin (encoded by PRSS8 gene) by using microarray technology. Results indicated that the presence of prostasin is more strongly associated with cancerous ovarian epithelial cells and stroma than in normal ovarian tissue. Thus, the potential use of prostasin as a marker of OC has been suggested in this study. The serum prostasin levels were also reported to be significantly reduced after surgery in most of the cases. OC is generally diagnosed at advanced stages of the disease; therefore, its poor prognoses are very much typical. Costa et al. (2009) evaluate the expression of prostasin in OC samples and found its presence in all samples. Using quantitative PCR, prostasin was overexpressed in all samples and these findings indicated that prostasin was mainly overexpressed in many epithelial OCs. However, further studies are required to establish prostasin as a potential biomarker for OC. Tamir et al. (2016) identified potential OC biomarkers by bioinformatics analysis. The subjects were screened for differential expression in a library of OC cell lines. The gene expression results suggested 100-fold PRSS8 expression in OC in comparison to normal or benign ovarian lesions. Overexpression of PRSS8 was found in most of the ovarian cell lines tested. Interestingly, higher levels of prostasin were reported in early stage OC serum samples as compared to benign ovarian and normal donor samples. The secreted prostasin in early stage OC can potentially be used as a screening biomarker for early stage OC.

7.4 Biomarkers and protease inhibitors in cancer treatment

Serpins are a group of proteins with similar structures, which were first recognized as a set of proteins capable of inhibiting serine proteases (Esposito et al., 2006; Chien et al., 2006). The importance of regulated serine proteases in maintaining homeostasis and their relationship with cancer reflect the need of checkpoints of these enzymes under normal conditions. The enzymatic breakdown of serine proteases is therefore considered to be one of the important regulators for the maintenance of cell homeostasis. Excessive enzymatic activity often has a negative effect on cellular processes, which can also be linked to cancer. Protease regulators were also created in conjunction with the evolutionary development of proteases. These serine protease antiregulators are known as serpins. Specific serpins which are involved in OC and could be used for diagnosis and therapy in cancer are discussed here.

7.4.1 Serpin E1 (plasminogen activator inhibitor-1, PAI-1)

Serpin E1, or endothelial plasminogen activator inhibitor-1 (PAI-1), is 400 amino acids' residues long glycoprotein, with variable molecular weights from 38 to 70kDa (Declerck and Gils, 2013). Serpin E1 inhibits both uPA and tPA to prevent conversion of plasminogen into active plasmin and ultimately inhibited the outset of cancer (Dass et al., 2008). The binding of Serpin E1 to the uPA/uPAR complex triggers the internalization of the uPA/uPAR by means of endocytosis through low-density receptor-related protein-1 (LRP-1) and this results in the de-adhesion of plasma membrane matrix facilitating tumor growth and dissemination (Duffy, 2002). The interaction of Serpin E1 (activated, latent, and cleaved) with LRP1 enhanced the cell motility by activating the JAK/Stat1 pathway. Studies have shown that in many cancer patients, the positive association between high levels of Serpin E1 in tumors and blood with poor clinical results has been contradictory. This contradictory role of PAI-1 has been clarified by its pro-angiogenic activity [angiogenic activity (low concentration) and antiangiogenic activity (high concentration)] and its antiapoptotic cells. This activity of Serpin E1 is proposed to be related with preventing the apoptosis of the endothelial cells (Bajou et al., 2008). In addition, reports have shown that Serpin E1, which is absent in mice and cancer cells, can promote apoptosis and also inhibit angiogenesis (Bajou et al., 1998). Nishioka et al. (2012) have suggested that the deletion of Serpin E1 in gastric cancer cells lowers down the tumorigenicity. These outcomes revealed that PAI-1 can be used as a good agent for cancer treatment.

7.4.2 Serpin B5

SerpinB5, also called Maspin, was first described as a class II tumor suppressor in human breast cancer. This noninhibitory serpin promotes the tumor cell toward apoptosis and inhibits invasion and metastasis and thus plays a crucial role against tumor growth (Zou et al., 1994). Serpin B5 is found in cytoplasm and is also secreted to the cell surface. It is supposed to prevent angiogenesis and decrease the migration of numerous cells as reported in various studies (Sheng et al., 1994; Pemberton et al., 1997). Due to short hydrophobic loop, serpin B5 is incapable of conversion of stressed to relaxed transition form for inhibition and is therefore incapable to inhibit either tPA or uPA (Bass et al., 2002). However, serpin B5 has inhibitory impact against plasminogen activators uPA and tPA (McGowen et al., 2000; Biliran and Sheng, 2001; Sheng et al., 1998). Serpin B5 gene expression is reported to be downregulated with the malignancy, for example, serpinB5 is generally low in breast and prostate cancer cells as compared to normal cells (Zhang et al., 1997). SerpinB5 regulates adhesion-mediated cell signaling pathway through extracellular and cell-cell adhesion molecules. The enhancement of endothelial cell adhesion to FN, laminin, collagen, and vitronectin is mediated by this inhibitor. This adhesion prompts the activation of integrin family and FAK signal transduction pathway causing the modulation of focal adhesion and cytoskeleton reorganization and thus inhibiting the degradation of EC component and migration of tumorigenic cells (Qin and Zhang, 2010; Zhang et al., 2000). Various investigators have reported the induction of apoptosis by serpin B5 suppresses tumor cells, for example mammary carcinoma cells transfected with serpin B5 gene resulted into inhibition of invasion and metastasis (Wang et al., 2004). Consequently, such discoveries of molecular mechanisms for serpin B5-mediated apoptosis paved a new way for cancer treatment. Expressions of serpin B5 and ubiquitin-proteasome pathway are inversely related; serpinB5 expression reduces with the activity of the proteasome (Chen et al., 2005). Since the ubiquitin-proteasome pathway modulates several biochemical reactions through regulation of protein, the deregulation of proteasome function is proposed to be an important factor in the malignancy of tumors (Schwartz and Ciechanover, 1999). In recent studies, it has shown that either serpin B5 or in association with mammaglobin B (a secretoglobin) could be exploited as a biomarker for the identification of the breast cancer (Mercatali et al., 2006). In context with the epigenetic regulation of serpin B5, it was seen that the serpin B5 gene promoter was unmethylated in fetus for maternal blood cells and this opened a new avenue for developing further biomarkers for prenatal diagnosis (Chim et al., 2005). The established antitumorigenic/antimetastatic characteristic of serpin B5 in cancer provides valuable data with respect to the development of therapeutic agents (Shi et al., 2003; Li et al., 2005). It could be concluded that serpinB5 can be exploited as an antitumor agent in various cellular events for the inhibition of cell invasion and angiogenesis. Sood et al. (2002) have evaluated the serpin B5 expression and localization in ovarian cell lines and they found that ovarian surface epithelial cells had low levels of serpin B5. During this study, they also reported that serpin B5 was found to be overexpressed in a significant portion of ovarian tumors and could be used as an adverse prognostic factor. These paradoxical results may offer new insights regarding the role of serpin B5 in OC progression leading to better diagnosis and treatment. There were very few reports highlighting the role of serpinB5 in ovarian carcinoma. El Wahed (2005) evaluated serpin B5 expression in ovarian epithelial neoplasms and correlated its expression with some clinicopathologic parameters. A trend was established for serpin B5 expression with high grade, high stage, bilateral tumors and tumors with metastasis. Tumors that showed serpinB5 overexpression showed higher mitotic index (MI) ($P = .02$). These results can provide new insights into the role of serpin B5 in OC that can also have an impact on diagnosis and treatment policies. Further, Klasa-Mazurkiewicz et al. (2009) examined serpin B5 expression in human ovarian tumors and relation between serpin B5 expression and clinicopathological features as well as the role of serpin B5 in predicting clinical outcome in patients with OC. The study demonstrated the upregulation of serpin B5 in borderline tumors and the early stages of ovarian carcinoma and then significantly downregulated with malignant transformation. This study suggested that serpinB5 could be used in predicting the results of treatment of OC patients.

7.4.3 Serpin F1

Serpin F1, a pigment epithelium-derived factor (PEDF), was first described and purified from cultured human fetal retinal pigment epithelium cells (Poddar et al., 2017). It is classified as a noninhibitory member of the serpin superfamily (Steele et al., 1993) and is broadly present in fetal and adult tissues. This 50-kDa secreted glycoprotein plays a key role in many physiological and pathological processes (He et al., 2015). Serpin F1 possesses a tumor defensive system and acts as a biomarker for prostate cancer patients. The tumor growth could be reduced by SerpinF1 either indirectly by inhibiting angiogenesis or simply by activating cell apoptosis and/or differentiation processes that inhibit the invasion and metastasis. SerpinF1 is a highly selective angiogenesis inhibitor and produces new blood vessels while old cells have no such inhibitory effect and the process is reversible (Seruga et al., 2011). Dawson et al. (1999) were the first to propose SerpinF1 as a regulator of the growth of the blood vessel for angiogenesis in hypoxia, as found in tumors. Serpin F1 mediates antiangiogenesis by stopping the VEGF-driven vascular penetration in VEGF-stimulated endothelial cells by internalizing and degrading VEGF receptors, VEGFR-1 or VEGFR-2 (Johnston et al., 2015). This shows that SerpinF1 prevents the angiogenesis process by neutralizing the VEGF activity and prevents the growth of the tumor. With the increasing strength of metastatic melanoma, Serpin F1 regulation on cell proliferation and invasion is gradually lost. For instance, the Serpin F1 expression is diminished in numerous tumor grades of cancer, for example, prostate, pancreatic, and hepatocellular carcinoma (Belkacemi and Zhang, 2016). Recent reports have demonstrated that Serpin F1 shows its antiangiogenesis activity by specifically prompting the apoptosis of endothelial cells. In addition, some groups observed that apoptotic cells in prostate cancer have overexpressed Serpin F1 in comparison to control (Guan et al., 2007). Serpin F1 triggers the apoptosis of endothelial and tumor cell primarily through extrinsic and intrinsic pathways. The extrinsic pathway depends on the Fas/FasL activation and is a cell surface death receptor-mediated pathway. In the intrinsic pathway (mitochondrial pathway), the apoptosis of cells is administered by mitochondrial penetrability. Serpin F1 may exhibit antitumor activity by its capacity to promote tumor cell differentiation. This was well demonstrated by the intratumoral injection of rSerpinF1 in primitive neuroblastomas resulting in tumor cell differentiation (Crawford et al., 2001). Nowadays, Serpin F1 is in focus for developing a potential endogenous agent for treatment of cancer. Drug delivery system for example, gene therapy, in the form of a viral vector, systemic administration of naked SerpinF1 (free, unmodified) or the use of nanoparticles for controlled release of drugs are necessary for the efficient delivery of SerpinF1, to neoplastic sites that not only lead to tumor regression but also protect from side effect (Abramson et al., 2003). Recently, another methodology was utilized in improving PEDF expression through specific platinum-based chemotherapeutic phosphaplatin drugs (Mishur et al., 2008). Cheung et al. (2006) elucidate the role of PEDF in the tumorigenesis of OC. They demonstrated that SerpinF1 is an estrogen-responsive gene and represents the first direct implication of this protein in OC development and progression. The results indicated that PEDF plays an important role in regulating the normal ovarian surface epithelium (OSE) cell function. The decrease or loss of SerpinF1 could contribute to tumor development and progression. In addition, they demonstrated that SerpinF1 is consistently downregulated in OC. This highlights the potential of Serpin F1 as a tumor suppressor and may provide a target for therapeutic intervention in OC.

7.4.4 SPINK1 (Kazal type 1)

In 1948, the Kazal group first purified the serine protease inhibitor Kazal type 1 (SPINK1) from the bovine pancreas as a pancreatic secretory trypsin inhibitor (PSTI) (Kazal et al., 1948). After that, Stenman group isolated SPINK1 from the urine of OC patients and described it as a trypsin inhibitor (TATI) (Stenman et al., 1982). This inhibitor consists of 56 residues of amino acid containing three disulfide bonds and a Lys-Ile trypsin-specific binding site. The main function of SPINK1 is to suppress pancreatic and small intestinal serine proteases. SPINK1 is produced in pancreatic acinal cells where it prevents pancreatic cell autophagy by inhibiting trypsin activity in acinary cells. This inhibition in autophagy is due to the production of trypsinogen in similar cells and packed together with SPINK1 in zymogen granule (Kuwata et al., 2002). In general, the conversion of trypsinogen to trypsin is strictly regulated and a balanced level of trypsinogen and trypsin is maintained in acinar cells. In this way, it plays a key role in prevention of pancreatitis (Hirota et al., 2006). Various organ cancers like colon, breast, and liver are reported to have overexpressed SPINK1 (Gaber et al., 2009; Soon et al., 2011). SPINK1 is also reported to be overexpressed in the prostrate, and its expression is directly proportional to the tumor grade (Stenman et al., 1982). The tumor producing SPINK1 also synthesizes trypsin which ultimately activates MMPs of the matrix leading to the metastasis of cancer. Reports indicated that overexpression of SPINK1 leads to adverse prognosis in cancer (Ateeq et al., 2011). SPINK1 can act as a growth factor because epidermal growth factor (EGF) is found to be homology in structure. SPINK1 is also assumed to be a growth factor for tissue repair in inflammatory sites and to act as a booster for cancer cells if it has been prolonged (McKeehan et al., 1986). It was accounted that SPINK1 induces EMT by activating the epidermal growth factor receptor (EGFR) which causes pancreatic and breast cancer cell proliferation (Ozaki et al., 2009). For the specific therapy of patients, it is essential to focus on a specific or activated pathway relevant to target tumor. Small molecular inhibitors that interfere with the specific signaling network inside the cells should be discovered. This approach may prove SPINK1 as a relevant "druggable" target (Stenman, 2011). Human epididymis protein 4 (HE4) has been a target of keen interest due to its diagnostic and prognostic abilities for epithelial OC. Ribeiro et al. (2018) investigated the role of HE4 in invasion, haptotaxis, and adhesion of OC cells. The recombinant HE4 (rHE4) exposed OVCAR8 OC cells have promoted invasion and haptotaxis toward a fibronectin substrate. Further, a proteomic study revealed the activation of focal adhesion kinase signaling in OVCAR8 cells treated with conditioned media from HE4-overexpressing cells. These results indicate a direct role for HE4 in mediating malignant properties of OC cells.

7.5 Fibroblast activation protein

Song et al. (2016) investigated the expression of Fibroblast activation protein (FAP), a nonclassical serine protease, in ovarian cancer and its significance in clinical prognosis. For this, the expression of FAP in 102 formalin-fixed and paraffin-embedded OC tissues and the adjacent tissues were examined by immunohistochemistry (IHC). It was observed that the expression level of FAP in OC was higher than that in the adjacent tissues ($P < .05$). FAP expression was shown to be correlated with lymph node metastasis ($P < .05$), latent distant metastasis status ($P < .05$), and FIGO histology grade ($P < .05$). Furthermore, patients with a higher expression of FAP tended to have much shorter survival time than patients with lower FAP expression. The study concluded that high FAP expression indicated poor prognosis in OC and may serve as a novel prognostic marker in OC.

7.6 Serine proteases: A potential target for anticancer drugs

Serine proteases such as urokinase-type and tissue-type plasminogen activators and TTSPs are serving as important regulators of cancer development. The active site of serine proteases is exposed to their substrates or endogenous serine protease inhibitor and thus proteolytic activity of the enzyme is under strict control of endogenous inhibitor which prevents the progression of cancer development. Any imbalance or modification in the endogenous inhibitor leads to various diseases like cancer. So it is very necessary that anticancer drugs can be designed for normal functioning of serine proteases.

In this regard, Birk-Bowman inhibitor, an 8 kDa metalloprotein and Kunitz trypsin inhibitor, a 22 kDa protein isolated from soybeans (*Glycine max*), showed anticancerous activity against skin, lung, and ovarian tumors (Castro-Guillén et al., 2010; Kobayashi et al., 2004; Suzuki et al., 2005). On the contrary, the action of some protease inhibitors in some cases increases the potency of cancer development (Ozaki et al., 2009). These observations indicate that a careful study is needed for finding a good binding pocket for the inhibitor to bind with enzyme. On the basis of crystal structures and cyclic peptide model, chymotrypsin inhibitor, such as Symplocamine A, isolated from Marine Cyanobacterium shows promising results against cancer cells (Linington et al., 2008).

Among many irreversible classes of inhibitors, Diphenyl phosphonates is found to be more promising and act as competitive transition-state analogs, thus inhibiting the formation of enzyme-substrate acyl intermediate for further hydrolysis (Joossens et al., 2006). Based on the molecular modeling methods such as QSAR and crystal structure of enzyme-inhibitor complex, inhibitor like UK 122 can be developed against uPA inhibition (Zhu et al., 2007). Furthermore, inhibitors of urokinase family such as with aryl guanidines and aryl amidines can be designed in such a way that the positive charge of the inhibitors can bind with the negative negatively charged site chain of Asp189 (Lee et al., 2004). Therefore, it is not surprising that serine proteases are candidates for potential anticancer drugs and are already being tested in different laboratories.

7.7 Conclusions

Ovarian cancer is the leading cause of mortality. Several mechanisms are involved in OC pathogenesis. In addition to identifying potential therapeutic targets and prognostic markers, new therapies with higher success rates are urgently required to cure cancer. Studies have indicated the importance of proteases in tumor growth and progression. Serine proteases play an important role in various cancers and serve as biomarkers of progression of melanomas. There is strong evidence that protease inhibitors could be considered as a potent strategy in cancer therapy. With the development of advanced drug delivery systems, avenues for anticancer drug development and therapy is open for further exploration. Furthermore, a better understanding of the roles of serine proteases in OC development will guide the development of novel therapeutic strategies.

Acknowledgment

"Support by Enhanced Seed grants EF/2019-20/QE04-02 (to NKP) from Manipal University Jaipur, Rajasthan, India is gratefully acknowledged".

References

Abramson, L.P., Stellmach, V., Doll, J.A., Cornwell, M., Arensman, R.M., Crawford, S.E., 2003. Wilms' tumor growth is suppressed by antiangiogenic pigment epithelium–derived factor in a xenograft model. J. Pediatr. Surg. 38, 336–342.

Aguirre Ghiso, J.A.A., Kovalski, K., Ossowski, L., 1999. Tumor dormancy induced by downregulation of urokinase receptor in human carcinoma involves integrin and MAPK signaling. J. Cell Biol. 147, 89–104.

Andreasen, P.A., Kjøller, L., Christensen, L., Duffy, M.J., 1997. The urokinase-type plasminogen activator system in cancer metastasis: a review. Int. J. Cancer 72, 1–22.

Antalis, T.M., Buzza, M.S., Hodge, K.M., Hooper, J.D., Netzel-Arnett, S., 2010. The cutting edge: membrane-anchored serine protease activities in the pericellular microenvironment. Biochem. J. 428, 325–346.

Ateeq, B., Tomlins, S.A., Laxman, B., Asangani, I.A., Cao, Q., Cao, X., Varambally, S., 2011. Therapeutic targeting of SPINK1-positive prostate cancer. Sci. Transl. Med. 3, 72ra17.

Bajou, K., Noël, A., Gerard, R.D., Masson, V., Brunner, N., Holst-Hansen, C., Foidart, J.M., 1998. Absence of host plasminogen activator inhibitor 1 prevents cancer invasion and vascularization. Nat. Med. 4, 923–928.

Bajou, K., Peng, H., Laug, W.E., Maillard, C., Noel, A., Foidart, J.M., DeClerck, Y.A., 2008. Plasminogen activator inhibitor-1 protects endothelial cells from FasL-mediated apoptosis. Cancer Cell 14, 324–334.

Baldi, A., De Luca, A., Morini, M., Battista, T., Felsani, A., Baldi, F., Natali, P.G., 2002. The HtrA1 serine protease is down-regulated during human melanoma progression and represses growth of metastatic melanoma cells. Oncogene 21, 6684.

Bass, R., Fernández, A.M.M., Ellis, V., 2002. Maspin inhibits cell migration in the absence of protease inhibitory activity. J. Biol. Chem. 277, 46845–46848.

Bastians, H., Topper, L.M., Gorbsky, G.L., Ruderman, J.V., 1999. Cell cycle–regulated proteolysis of mitotic target proteins. Mol. Biol. Cell 10, 3927–3941.

Belkacemi, L., Zhang, S.X., 2016. Anti-tumor effects of pigment epithelium-derived factor (PEDF): implication for cancer therapy. A mini-review. J. Exp. Clin. Cancer Res. 35, 4.

Bhatt, A.S., Erdjument-Bromage, H., Tempst, P., Craik, C.S., Moasser, M.M., 2005. Adhesion signaling by a novel mitotic substrate of src kinases. Oncogene 24, 5333.

Biliran, H., Sheng, S., 2001. Pleiotrophic inhibition of pericellular urokinase-type plasminogen activator system by endogenous tumor suppressive maspin. Cancer Res. 61, 8676–8682.

Blasi, F., 1997. uPA, uPAR, PAI-I: key intersection of proteolytic, adhesive and chemotactic highways? Immunol. Today 18, 415–417.

Borgoño, C.A., Diamandis, E.P., 2004. The emerging roles of human tissue kallikreins in cancer. Nat. Rev. Cancer 4, 876.

Borgono, C.A., Michael, I.P., Diamandis, E.P., 2004. Human tissue kallikreins: physiologic roles and applications in cancer. Mol. Cancer Res. 2, 257–280.

Borissenko, L., Groll, M., 2007. Diversity of proteasomal missions: fine tuning of the immune response. Biol. Chem. 388, 947–955.

Bowden, M.A., Di Nezza-Cossens, L.A., Jobling, T., Salamonsen, L.A., Nie, G., 2006. Serine proteases HTRA1 and HTRA3 are down-regulated with increasing grades of human endometrial cancer. Gynecol. Oncol. 103, 253–260.

Boy, R.G., Knapp, E.M., Eisenhut, M., Haberkorn, U., Mier, W., 2008. Enzymes/transporters. In: Molecular Imaging II. Springer, pp. 131–143.

Bugge, T.H., List, K., Szabo, R., 2007. Matriptase-dependent cell surface proteolysis in epithelial development and pathogenesis. Front. Biosci. 12, 5060–5070.

Cai, Z., Li, Y.F., Liu, F.Y., Feng, Y.L., Hou, J.H., Zhao, M.Q., 2007. The expression and clinical significance of uPA and PAI-1 in epithelial OC. Chin. J. Cancer 26, 312–317.

Canfield, A.E., Hadfield, K.D., Rock, C.F., Wylie, E.C., Wilkinson, F.L., 2007. HtrA1: a novel regulator of physiological and pathological matrix mineralization? Biochem. Soc. Trans. 35, 669–671.

Castro-Guillén, J.L., Garcia-Gasca, T., Blanco-Labra, A., 2010. Protease inhibitors as anticancer agents. In: Vazquez, V.C.M., Navarro, S. (Eds.), New Approaches in the Treatment of Cancer. Nova Science Publishers, pp. 91–124. ISBN: 978-1-61728-304-8 (Chapter V).

Chen, L.M., Skinner, M.L., Kauffman, S.W., Chao, J., Chao, L., Thaler, C.D., Chai, K.X., 2001. Prostasin is a glycosylphosphatidyl inositol-anchored active serine protease. J. Biol. Chem. 276, 21434–21442.

Chen, V.W., Ruiz, B., Killeen, J.L., Coté, T.R., Wu, X.C., Correa, C.N., Howe, H.L., 2003a. Pathology and classification of ovarian tumors. Cancer 97, 2631–2642.

Chen, Z., Fan, Z., McNEAL, J.E., Nolley, R., Caldwell, M.C., Mahadevappa, M., Stamey, T.A., 2003b. Hepsin and maspin are inversely expressed in laser capture microdissectioned prostate cancer. J. Urol. 169, 1316–1319.

Chen, E.I., Florens, L., Axelrod, F.T., Monosov, E., Barbas III, C.F., Yates III, J.R., Smith, J.W., 2005. Maspin alters the carcinoma proteome. FASEB J. 19, 1123–1124.

Cheng, M.F., Tzao, C., Tsai, W.C., Lee, W.H., Chen, A., Chiang, H., Jin, J.S., 2006. Expression of EMMPRIN and matriptase in esophageal squamous cell carcinoma: correlation with clinicopathological parameters. Dis. Esophagus 19, 482–486.

Cheung, L.W., Au, S.C., Cheung, A.N., Ngan, H.Y., Tombran-Tink, J., Auersperg, N., Wong, A.S., 2006. Pigment epithelium-derived factor is estrogen sensitive and inhibits the growth of human OC and ovarian surface epithelial cells. Endocrinology 147, 4179–4191.

Chien, J., Staub, J., Hu, S.I., Erickson-Johnson, M.R., Couch, F.J., Smith, D.I., Shridhar, V., 2004. A candidate tumor suppressor HtrA1 is downregulated in OC. Oncogene 23, 1636.

Chien, J., Aletti, G., Baldi, A., Catalano, V., Muretto, P., Keeney, G.L., Lee, Y.K., 2006. Serine protease HtrA1 modulates chemotherapy-induced cytotoxicity. J. Clin. Invest. 116, 1994–2004.

Chim, S.S., Tong, Y.K., Chiu, R.W., Lau, T.K., Leung, T.N., Chan, L.Y., Lo, Y.D., 2005. Detection of the placental epigenetic signature of the maspin gene in maternal plasma. Proc. Natl. Acad. Sci. 102, 14753–14758.

Choi, K.Y., Swierczewska, M., Lee, S., Chen, X., 2012. Protease-activated drug development. Theranostics 2, 156.

Clausen, T., Southan, C., Ehrmann, M., 2002. The HtrA family of proteases: implications for protein composition and cell fate. Mol. Cell 10, 443–455.

Collen, D., Lijnen, H.R., 1991. Basic and clinical aspects of fibrinolysis and thrombolysis. Blood 78, 3114–3124.

Colman, R.W., 2006. Regulation of angiogenesis by the kallikrein-kinin system. Curr. Pharm. Des. 12, 2599–2607.

Costa, F.P., Batista Junior, E.L., Zelmanowicz, A., Svedman, C., Devenz, G., Alves, S., Garicochea, B., 2009. Prostasin, a potential tumor marker in OC: a pilot study. Clinics 64, 641–644.

Crawford, S.E., Stellmach, V., Ranalli, M., Huang, X., Huang, L., Volpert, O., Bouck, N., 2001. Pigment epithelium-derived factor (PEDF) in neuroblastoma: a multifunctional mediator of Schwann cell antitumor activity. J. Cell Sci. 114, 4421–4428.

Dass, K., Ahmad, A., Azmi, A.S., Sarkar, S.H., Sarkar, F.H., 2008. Evolving role of uPA/uPAR system in human cancers. Cancer Treat. Rev. 34, 122–136.

Dawson, D.W., Volpert, O.V., Gillis, P., Crawford, S.E., Xu, H.J., Benedict, W., Bouck, N.P., 1999. Pigment epithelium-derived factor: a potent inhibitor of angiogenesis. Science 285, 245–248.

Declerck, P.J., Gils, A., 2013, June. Three decades of research on plasminogen activator inhibitor-1: a multifaceted serpin. Semin. Thromb. Hemost. 39 (04), 356–364. Thieme Medical Publishers.

Desriviéres, S., Lu, H., Peyri, N., Soria, C., Legrand, Y., Ménashi, S., 1993. Activation of the 92 kDa type IV collagenase by tissue kallikrein. J. Cell. Physiol. 157, 587–593.

Diamandis, E.P., Yousef, G.M., 2002. Human tissue kallikreins: a family of new cancer biomarkers. Clin. Chem. 48, 1198–1205.

Duffy, M.J., 2002. Urokinase plasminogen activator and its inhibitor, PAI-1, as prognostic markers in breast cancer: from pilot to level 1 evidence studies. Clin. Chem. 48, 1194–1197.

Egeblad, M., Werb, Z., 2002. New functions for the matrix metalloproteinases in cancer progression. Nat. Rev. Cancer 2, 161.

El Wahed, M.M.A., 2005. Expression and subcellular localization of maspin in human ovarian epithelial neoplasms: correlation with clinicopathologic features. J. Egypt Natl. Canc. Inst. 17, 173–183.

Emanueli, C., Madeddu, P., 2001. Targeting kinin receptors for the treatment of tissue ischaemia. Trends Pharmacol. Sci. 22, 478–484.

Esposito, V., Campioni, M., De Luca, A., Spugnini, E.P., Baldi, F., Cassandro, R., Baldi, A., 2006. Analysis of HtrA1 serine protease expression in human lung cancer. Anticancer Res. 26, 3455–3459.

Fesik, S.W., 2005. Promoting apoptosis as a strategy for cancer drug discovery. Nat. Rev. Cancer 5, 876.

Fisher, J.L., Mackie, P.S., Howard, M.L., Zhou, H., Choong, P.F.M., 2001. The expression of the urokinase plasminogen activator system in metastatic murine osteosarcoma: an in vivo mouse model. Clin. Cancer Res. 7, 1654–1660.

Frenette, G., Tremblay, R.R., Lazure, C., Dube, J.Y., 1997. Prostatic kallikrein hK2, but not prostate-specific antigen (hK3), activates single-chain urokinase-type plasminogen activator. Int. J. Cancer 71, 897–899.

Gaber, A., Johansson, M., Stenman, U.H., Hotakainen, K., Pontén, F., Glimelius, B., Birgisson, H., 2009. High expression of tumour-associated trypsin inhibitor correlates with liver metastasis and poor prognosis in colorectal cancer. Br. J. Cancer 100, 1540.

Giusti, B., Serratì, S., Margheri, F., Papucci, L., Rossi, L., Poggi, F., Kahaleh, B., 2005. The anti-angiogenic tissue kallikrein pattern of endothelial cells in systemic sclerosis. Arthritis Rheum. 52, 3618–3628.

Gocheva, V., Joyce, J.A., 2007. Cysteine cathepsins and the cutting edge of cancer invasion. Cell Cycle 6, 60–64.

Gondi, C.S., Kandhukuri, N., Dinh, D.H., Gujrati, M., Rao, J.S., 2007. Down-regulation of uPAR and uPA activates caspase-mediated apoptosis and inhibits the PI3K/AKT pathway. Int. J. Oncol. 31, 19–27.

Gray, C.W., Ward, R.V., Karran, E., Turconi, S., Rowles, A., Viglienghi, D., Savopoulos, J., 2000. Characterization of human HtrA2, a novel serine protease involved in the mammalian cellular stress response. Eur. J. Biochem. 267, 5699–5710.

Guan, M., Jiang, H., Xu, C., Xu, R., Chen, Z., Lu, Y., 2007. Adenovirus-mediated PEDF expression inhibits prostate cancer cell growth and results in augmented expression of PAI-2. Cancer Biol. Ther. 6, 419–425.

Han, Q., Leng, J., Bian, D., Mahanivong, C., Carpenter, K.A., Pan, Z.K., Huang, S., 2002. Rac1-MKK3-p38-MAPKAPK2 pathway promotes urokinase plasminogen activator mRNA stability in invasive breast cancer cells. J. Biol. Chem. 277, 48379–48385.

Hasui, Y., Marutsuka, K., Suzumiya, J., Kitada, S., Osada, Y., Sumiyoshi, A., 1992. The content of urokinase-type plasminogen activator antigen as a prognostic factor in urinary bladder cancer. Int. J. Cancer 50, 871–873.

He, X., Khurana, A., Maguire, J.L., Chien, J., Shridhar, V., 2012. HtrA1 sensitizes OC cells to cisplatin-induced cytotoxicity by targeting XIAP for degradation. Int. J. Cancer 130, 1029–1035.

He, X., Cheng, R., Benyajati, S., Ma, J.X., 2015. PEDF and its roles in physiological and pathological conditions: implication in diabetic and hypoxia-induced angiogenic diseases. Clin. Sci. 128, 805–823.

Hildenbrand, R., Gandhari, M., Stroebel, P., Marx, A., Allgayer, H., Arens, N., 2008. The urokinase-system—role of cell proliferation and apoptosis. Histol. Histopathol. 23, 227–236.

Hirai, K., Yokoyama, M., Asano, G., Tanaka, S., 1999. Expression of cathepsin B and cystatin C in human colorectal cancer. Hum. Pathol. 30, 680–686.

Hirota, M., Ohmuraya, M., Baba, H., 2006. Genetic background of pancreatitis. Postgrad. Med. J. 82, 775–778.

Hooper, J.D., Nicol, D.L., Dickinson, J.L., Eyre, H.J., Scarman, A.L., Normyle, J.F., Antalis, T.M., 1999. Testisin, a new human serine proteinase expressed by premeiotic testicular germ cells and lost in testicular germ cell tumors. Cancer Res. 59, 3199–3205.

Hooper, J.D., Clements, J.A., Quigley, J.P., Antalis, T.M., 2001. Type II transmembrane serine proteases insights into an emerging class of cell surface proteolytic enzymes. J. Biol. Chem. 276, 857–860.

Hu, S.I., Carozza, M., Klein, M., Nantermet, P., Luk, D., Crowl, R.M., 1998. Human HtrA, an evolutionarily conserved serine protease identified as a differentially expressed gene product in osteoarthritic cartilage. J. Biol. Chem. 273, 34406–34412.

Inagaki, A., Nishizawa, H., Ota, S., Suzuki, M., Inuzuka, H., Miyamura, H., Udagawa, Y., 2012. Upregulation of HtrA4 in the placentas of patients with severe pre-eclampsia. Placenta 33, 919–926.

Jedeszko, C., Sloane, B.F., 2004. Cysteine cathepsins in human cancer. Biol. Chem. 385, 1017–1027.

Ji, M., Li, S., Xie, Y., Zhao, Z., Chang, W., Li, Y., Wang, Z., 2017. Expression and prognostic value of matriptase in ovarian serous adenocarcinoma. Oncol. Lett. 13, 1741–1744.

Jin, J.S., Hsieh, D.S., Loh, S.H., Chen, A., Yao, C.W., Yen, C.Y., 2006. Increasing expression of serine protease matriptase in ovarian tumors: tissue microarray analysis of immunostaining score with clinicopathological parameters. Mod. Pathol. 19, 447.

Johnston, E.K., Francis, M.K., Knepper, J.E., 2015. Recombinant pigment epithelium-derived factor PEDF binds vascular endothelial growth factor receptors 1 and 2. In Vitro Cell. Dev. Biol. Anim. 51, 730–738.

Joossens, J., Van der Veken, P., Surpetanu, G., LAmbeit, A.-M., El-Sayed, I., Ali, O.M., Augustyns, K., Haemers, A., 2006. Diphenyl phosphonate inhibitors for the urokinase-type plasminogen activator: optimization of the P4 position. J. Med. Chem. 49, 5785–5793.

Joyce, J.A., Hanahan, D., 2004. Multiple roles for cysteine cathepsins in cancer. Cell Cycle 3, 1516–1519.

Kang, J.Y., Dolled-Filhart, M., Ocal, I.T., Singh, B., Lin, C.Y., Dickson, R.B., Camp, R.L., 2003. Tissue microarray analysis of hepatocyte growth factor/Met pathway components reveals a role for Met, matriptase, and hepatocyte growth factor activator inhibitor 1 in the progression of node-negative breast cancer. Cancer Res. 63, 1101–1105.

Kazal, L.A., Spicer, D.S., Brahinsky, R.A., 1948. Isolation of a Crystalline Trypsin Inhibitor-Anticoagulant Protein from Pancreas1a. J. Am. Chem. Soc. 70, 3034–3040.

Kazama, Y., Hamamoto, T., Foster, D.C., Kisiel, W., 1995. Hepsin, a putative membrane-associated serine protease, activates human factor VII and initiates a pathway of blood coagulation on the cell surface leading to thrombin formation. J. Biol. Chem. 270, 66–72.

Kim, J., Yu, W., Kovalski, K., Ossowski, L., 1998. Requirement for specific proteases in cancer cell intravasation as revealed by a novel semiquantitative PCR-based assay. Cell 94, 353–362.

Kirchhofer, D., Peek, M., Lipari, M.T., Billeci, K., Fan, B., Moran, P., 2005. Hepsin activates pro-hepatocyte growth factor and is inhibited by hepatocyte growth factor activator inhibitor-1B (HAI-1B) and HAI-2. FEBS Lett. 579, 1945–1950.

Klasa-Mazurkiewicz, D., Narkiewicz, J., Milczek, T., Lipińska, B., Emerich, J., 2009. Maspin overexpression correlates with positive response to primary chemotherapy in OC patients. Gynecol. Oncol. 113, 91–98.

Kobayashi, H., Suzuki, M., Kanayama, N., Terao, T., 2004. A soybean Kunitz trypsin inhibitor suppresses ovarian cancer cell invasion by blocking urokinase upregulation. Clin. Exp. Metastasis 21, 159–166.

Kotliarov, Y., Steed, M.E., Christopher, N., Walling, J., Su, Q., Center, A., Fine, H.A., 2006. High-resolution global genomic survey of 178 gliomas reveals novel regions of copy number alteration and allelic imbalances. Cancer Res. 66, 9428–9436.

Kuwata, K., Hirota, M., Shimizu, H., Nakae, M., Nishihara, S., Takimoto, A., Ogawa, M., 2002. Functional analysis of recombinant pancreatic secretory trypsin inhibitor protein with amino-acid substitution. J. Gastroenterol. 37, 928–934.

Lee, M., Fridman, R., Mobashery, S., 2004. Extracellular proteases as targets for treatment of cancer metastases. Chem. Soc. Rev. 33, 401–409.

Lee, M.S., Kiyomiya, K.I., Benaud, C., Dickson, R.B., Lin, C.Y., 2005. Simultaneous activation and hepatocyte growth factor activator inhibitor 1-mediated inhibition of matriptase induced at activation foci in human mammary epithelial cells. Am. J. Physiol. Cell Physiol. 288, C932–C941.

Li, Z., Shi, H.Y., Zhang, M., 2005. Targeted expression of maspin in tumor vasculatures induces endothelial cell apoptosis. Oncogene 24, 2008.

Lin, Y.C., Brown, K., Siebenlist, U., 1995. Activation of NF-kappa B requires proteolysis of the inhibitor I kappa B-alpha: signal-induced phosphorylation of I kappa B-alpha alone does not release active NF-kappa B. Proc. Natl. Acad. Sci. U. S. A. 92, 552–556.

Lin, C.Y., Wang, J.K., Torri, J., Dou, L., Sang, Q.A., Dickson, R.B., 1997. Characterization of a novel, membrane-bound, 80-kDa matrix-degrading protease from human breast cancer cells monoclonal antibody production, isolation, and localization. J. Biol. Chem. 272, 9147–9152.

Linington, R.G., Edwards, D.J., Shuman, C.F., McPhail, K.L., Matainaho, T., Gerwick, W.H., 2008. Symploxacine A, a potent cytotoxin and chymotrypsin inhibitor from the marine Cyanobacterium *Symploca* sp. J. Nat. Prod. 71, 22–27.

Lipinska, B., Zylicz, M., Georgopoulos, C., 1990. The HtrA (DegP) protein, essential for *Escherichia coli* survival at high temperatures, is an endopeptidase. J. Bacteriol. 172, 1791–1797.

List, K., 2009. Matriptase: a culprit in cancer? Future Oncol. 5, 97–104.

López-Otín, C., Matrisian, L.M., 2007. Emerging roles of proteases in tumour suppression. Nat. Rev. Cancer 7, 800.

Lu, P., Takai, K., Weaver, V.M., Werb, Z., 2011. Extracellular matrix degradation and remodeling in development and disease. Cold Spring Harb. Perspect. Biol. 3, a005058.

Magee, J.A., Araki, T., Patil, S., Ehrig, T., True, L., Humphrey, P.A., Milbrandt, J., 2001. Expression profiling reveals hepsin overexpression in prostate cancer. Cancer Res. 61, 5692–5696.

Mason, S.D., Joyce, J.A., 2011. Proteolytic networks in cancer. Trends Cell Biol. 21, 228–237.

Matarrese, P., Ascione, B., Ciarlo, L., Vona, R., Leonetti, C., Scarsella, M., Malorni, W., 2010. Cathepsin B inhibition interferes with metastatic potential of human melanoma: an in vitro and in vivo study. Mol. Cancer 9, 207.

McGowen, R., Biliran, H., Sager, R., Sheng, S., 2000. The surface of prostate carcinoma DU145 cells mediates the inhibition of urokinase-type plasminogen activator by maspin. Cancer Res. 60, 4771–4778.

McKeehan, W.L., Sakagami, Y., Hoshi, H., McKeehan, K.A., 1986. Two apparent human endothelial cell growth factors from human hepatoma cells are tumor-associated proteinase inhibitors. J. Biol. Chem. 261, 5378–5383.

McQueney, M.S., Amegadzie, B.Y., D'Alessio, K., Hanning, C.R., McLaughlin, M.M., McNulty, D., Jones, C.S., 1997. Autocatalytic activation of human cathepsin K. J. Biol. Chem. 272, 13955–13960.

Menashi, S., Fridman, R., Desrivieres, S., Lu, H., Legrand, Y., Soria, C., 1994. Regulation of 92-kDa gelatinase B activity in the extracellular matrix by tissue Kallikrein. Ann. N. Y. Acad. Sci. 732, 466–468.

Mercatali, L., Valenti, V., Calistri, D., Calpona, S., Rosti, G., Folli, S., Flamini, E., 2006. RT-PCR determination of maspin and mammaglobin B in peripheral blood of healthy donors and breast cancer patients. Ann. Oncol. 17, 424–428.

Milkiewicz, M., Ispanovic, E., Doyle, J.L., Haas, T.L., 2006. Regulators of angiogenesis and strategies for their therapeutic manipulation. Int. J. Biochem. Cell Biol. 38, 333–357.

Mishur, R.J., Zheng, C., Gilbert, T.M., Bose, R.N., 2008. Synthesis, X-ray crystallographic, and NMR characterizations of platinum (II) and platinum (IV) pyrophosphato complexes. Inorg. Chem. 47, 7972–7982.

Mohamed, M.M., Sloane, B.F., 2006. Cysteine cathepsins: multifunctional enzymes in cancer. Nat. Rev. Cancer 6, 764.

Mok, S.C., Chao, J., Skates, S., Wong, K.K., Yiu, G.K., Muto, M.G., Cramer, D.W., 2001. Prostasin, a potential serum marker for OC: identification through microarray technology. J. Natl. Cancer Inst. 93, 1458–1464.

Moran, P., Li, W., Fan, B., Vij, R., Eigenbrot, C., Kirchhofer, D., 2006. Pro-urokinase-type plasminogen activator is a substrate for hepsin. J. Biol. Chem. 281, 30439–30446.

Narkiewicz, J., Lapinska-Szumczyk, S., Zurawa-Janicka, D., Skorko-Glonek, J., Emerich, J., Lipinska, B., 2009. Expression of human HtrA1, HtrA2, HtrA3 and TGF-β1 genes in primary endometrial cancer. Oncol. Rep. 21, 1529–1537.

Nekarda, H., Siewert, J., Schmitt, M., Ulm, K., 1994. Tumour-associated proteolytic factors uPA and PAI-1 and survival in totally resected gastric cancer. Lancet 343, 117.

Nie, G., Li, Y., Hale, K., Okada, H., Manuelpillai, U., Wallace, E.M., Salamonsen, L.A., 2006. Serine peptidase HTRA3 is closely associated with human placental development and is elevated in pregnancy serum. Biol. Reprod. 74, 366–374.

Nishioka, N., Matsuoka, T., Yashiro, M., Hirakawa, K., Olden, K., Roberts, J.D., 2012. Plasminogen activator inhibitor 1 RNAi suppresses gastric cancer metastasis in vivo. Cancer Sci. 103, 228–232.

Oberst, M., Anders, J., Xie, B., Singh, B., Ossandon, M., Johnson, M., Lin, C.Y., 2001. Matriptase and HAI-1 are expressed by normal and malignant epithelial cells in vitro and in vivo. Am. J. Pathol. 158, 1301–1311.

Oberst, M.D., Johnson, M.D., Dickson, R.B., Lin, C.Y., Singh, B., Stewart, M., Sellar, G.C., 2002. Expression of the serine protease matriptase and its inhibitor HAI-1 in epithelial OC: correlation with clinical outcome and tumor clinicopathological parameters. Clin. Cancer Res. 8, 1101–1107.

Oberst, M.D., Williams, C.A., Dickson, R.B., Johnson, M.D., Lin, C.Y., 2003. The activation of matriptase requires its noncatalytic domains, serine protease domain, and its cognate inhibitor. J. Biol. Chem. 278, 26773–26779.

Oka, T., Ishida, T., Nishino, T., Sugimachi, K., 1991. Immunohistochemical evidence of urokinase-type plasminogen activator in primary and metastatic tumors of pulmonary adenocarcinoma. Cancer Res. 51, 3522–3525.

Oka, C., Tsujimoto, R., Kajikawa, M., Koshiba-Takeuchi, K., Ina, J., Yano, M., Matsumoto, M., 2004. HtrA1 serine protease inhibits signaling mediated by Tgfβ family proteins. Development 131, 1041–1053.

Ozaki, N., Ohmuraya, M., Hirota, M., Ida, S., Wang, J., Takamori, H., Yamamura, K.I., 2009. Serine protease inhibitor Kazal type 1 promotes proliferation of pancreatic cancer cells through the epidermal growth factor receptor. Mol. Cancer Res. 1541–7786.

Pemberton, P.A., Tipton, A.R., Pavloff, N., Smith, J., Erickson, J.R., Mouchabeck, Z.M., Kiefer, M.C., 1997. Maspin is an intracellular serpin that partitions into secretory vesicles and is present at the cell surface. J. Histochem. Cytochem. 45, 1697–1706.

Poddar, N.K., Maurya, S.K., Saxena, V., 2017. Role of serine proteases and inhibitors in cancer. In: Proteases in Physiology and Pathology. Springer, Singapore, pp. 257–287.

Preissner, K.T., Kanse, S.M., May, A.E., 2000. Urokinase receptor: a molecular organizer in cellular communication. Curr. Opin. Cell Biol. 12, 621–628.

Puente, X.S., Sanchez, L.M., Gutierrez-Fernandez, A., Velasco, G., Lopez-Otin, C., 2005. A genomic view of the complexity of mammalian proteolytic systems. Biochem. Soc. Trans. 33, 331–334.

Qin, L., Zhang, M., 2010. Maspin regulates endothelial cell adhesion and migration through an integrin signaling pathway. J. Biol. Chem. 285, 32360–32369.

Rakashanda, S., Rana, F., Rafiq, S., Masood, A., Amin, S., 2012. Role of proteases in cancer: a review role of proteases in cancer: a review. Biotechnol. Mol. Biol. Rev. 7, 90–101.

Ramsay, A.J., Reid, J.C., Velasco, G., Quigley, J.P., Hooper, J.D., 2008. The type II transmembrane serine protease matriptase-2–identification, structural features, enzymology, expression pattern and potential roles. Front. Biosci. 13, 569–579.

Ramsay, A.J., Hooper, J.D., Folgueras, A.R., Velasco, G., López-Otín, C., 2009a. Matriptase-2 (TMPRSS6): a proteolytic regulator of iron homeostasis. Haematologica 94, 840–849.

Ramsay, A.J., Quesada, V., Sanchez, M., Garabaya, C., Sardà, M.P., Baiget, M., López-Otín, C., 2009b. Matriptase-2 mutations in iron-refractory iron deficiency anemia patients provide new insights into protease activation mechanisms. Hum. Mol. Genet. 18, 3673–3683.

Rawlings, N.D., Barrett, A.J., Bateman, A., 2010. MEROPS: the peptidase database. Nucleic Acids Res. 38, D227–D233.

Rawlings, N.D., Barrett, A.J., Bateman, A., 2014. Using the MEROPS database for proteolytic enzymes and their inhibitors and substrates. Curr. Protoc. Bioinformatics 48, 1–25.

Reid, B.M., Permuth, J.B., Sellers, T.A., 2017. Epidemiology of OC: a review. Cancer Biol. Med. 14, 9.

Ribeiro, J.R., Gaudet, H.M., Khan, M., Schorl, C., James, N.E., Oliver, M.T., Yano, N., 2018. Human epididymis protein 4 promotes events associated with metastatic OC via regulation of the extracelluar matrix. Front. Oncol. 7, 332.

Richter, C., Tanaka, T., 1998. Mechanism of activation of the gastric aspartic proteinases: pepsinogen, progastricsin and prochymosin. Biochem. J. 335, 481–490.

Saleem, M., Adhami, V.M., Zhong, W., Longley, B.J., Lin, C.Y., Dickson, R.B., Mukhtar, H., 2006. A novel biomarker for staging human prostate adenocarcinoma: overexpression of matriptase with concomitant loss of its inhibitor, hepatocyte growth factor activator inhibitor-1. Cancer Epidemiol. Biomarkers Prev. 15, 217–227.

Sanders, A.J., Webb, S.L., Parr, C., Mason, M.D., Jiang, W.G., 2010. The type II transmembrane serine protease, matriptase-2: possible links to cancer? Anticancer Agents Med. Chem. 10, 64–69.

Saunders, W.B., Bayless, K.J., Davis, G.E., 2005. MMP-1 activation by serine proteases and MMP-10 induces human capillary tubular network collapse and regression in 3D collagen matrices. J. Cell Sci. 118, 2325–2340.

Schmitt, M., Magdolen, V., Yang, F., Kiechle, M., Bayani, J., Yousef, G.M., Dorn, J., 2013. Emerging clinical importance of the cancer biomarkers kallikrein-related peptidases (KLK) in female and male reproductive organ malignancies. Radiol. Oncol. 47, 319–329.

Schwartz, A.L., Ciechanover, A., 1999. The ubiquitin-proteasome pathway and pathogenesis of human diseases. Annu. Rev. Med. 50, 57–74.

Seruga, B., Ocana, A., Tannock, I.F., 2011. Drug resistance in metastatic castration-resistant prostate cancer. Nat. Rev. Clin. Oncol. 8, 12.

Sheng, S., Pemberton, P.A., Sager, R., 1994. Production, purification, and characterization of recombinant maspin proteins. J. Biol. Chem. 269, 30988–30993.

Sheng, S., Truong, B., Fredrickson, D., Wu, R., Pardee, A.B., Sager, R., 1998. Tissue-type plasminogen activator is a target of the tumor suppressor gene maspin. PNAS 95, 499–504.

Shi, Y.E., Torri, J., Yieh, L., Wellstein, A., Lippman, M.E., Dickson, R.B., 1993. Identification and characterization of a novel matrix-degrading protease from hormone-dependent human breast cancer cells. Cancer Res. 53, 1409–1415.

Shi, H.Y., Zhang, W., Liang, R., Kittrell, F., Templeton, N.S., Medina, D., Zhang, M., 2003. Modeling human breast cancer metastasis in mice: maspin as a paradigm. Histol. Histopathol. 18, 201–206.

Sidenius, N., Blasi, F., 2003. The urokinase plasminogen activator system in cancer: recent advances and implication for prognosis and therapy. Cancer Metastasis Rev. 22, 205–222.

Singh, H., Li, Y., Fuller, P.J., Harrison, C., Rao, J., Stephens, A.N., Nie, G., 2013. HtrA3 is downregulated in cancer cell lines and significantly reduced in primary serous and granulosa cell ovarian tumors. J. Cancer 4, 152.

Song, Z., Lin, Y., Zhang, X., Ye, X., Yang, G., Feng, C., Dong, C., 2016. Expression of FAP is correlated with clinical prognosis in OC patients. Int. J. Clin. Exp. Med. 9, 11379–11384.

Sood, A.K., Fletcher, M.S., Gruman, L.M., Coffin, J.E., Jabbari, S., Khalkhali-Ellis, Z., Hendrix, M.J., 2002. The paradoxical expression of maspin in ovarian carcinoma. Clin. Cancer Res. 8, 2924–2932.

Soon, W.W., Miller, L.D., Black, M.A., Dalmasso, C., Chan, X.B., Pang, B., Liu, E.T., 2011. Combined genomic and phenotype screening reveals secretory factor SPINK1 as an invasion and survival factor associated with patient prognosis in breast cancer. EMBO Mol. Med. 3, 451–464.

Spiess, C., Beil, A., Ehrmann, M., 1999. A temperature-dependent switch from chaperone to protease in a widely conserved heat shock protein. Cell 97, 339–347.

Steele, F.R., Chader, G.J., Johnson, L.V., Tombran-Tink, J., 1993. Pigment epithelium-derived factor: neurotrophic activity and identification as a member of the serine protease inhibitor gene family. Proc. Natl. Acad. Sci. U. S. A. 90, 1526–1530.

Stenman, U.H., 2011. SPINK1: a new therapeutic target in cancer? Clin. Chem. 57, 1474–1475.

Stenman, U.H., Huhtala, M.L., Koistinen, R., Seppälä, M., 1982. Immunochemical demonstration of an OC-associated urinary peptide. Int. J. Cancer 30, 53–57.

Suzuki, Y., Imai, Y., Nakayama, H., Takahashi, K., Takio, K., Takahashi, R., 2001. A serine protease, HtrA2, is released from the mitochondria and interacts with XIAP, inducing cell death. Mol. Cell 8, 613–621.

Suzuki, K., Yano, T., Sadzuka, Y., Sugiyama, T., Seki, T., Asano, R., 2005. Restoration of connexin 43 by Bowman-Birk protease inhibitor in M5067 bearing mice. Oncol. Rep. 13, 1247–1250.

Szabo, R., Bugge, T.H., 2008. Type II transmembrane serine proteases in development and disease. Int. J. Biochem. Cell Biol. 40, 1297–1316.

Szabo, R., Molinolo, A., List, K., Bugge, T.H., 2007. Matriptase inhibition by hepatocyte growth factor activator inhibitor-1 is essential for placental development. Oncogene 26, 1546.

Takayama, T.K., McMullen, B.A., Nelson, P.S., Matsumura, M., Fujikawa, K., 2001. Characterization of hK4 (prostase), a prostate-specific serine protease: activation of the precursor of prostate specific antigen (pro-PSA) and single-chain urokinase-type plasminogen activator and degradation of prostatic acid phosphatase. Biochemist 40, 15341–15348.

Tamir, A., Gangadharan, A., Balwani, S., Tanaka, T., Patel, U., Hassan, A., Yoon, S., 2016. The serine protease prostasin (PRSS8) is a potential biomarker for early detection of OC. J. Ovarian Res. 9, 20.

Tanimoto, H., Yan, Y., Clarke, J., Korourian, S., Shigemasa, K., Parmley, T.H., O'Brien, T.J., 1997. Hepsin, a cell surface serine protease identified in hepatoma cells, is overexpressed in OC. Cancer Res. 57, 2884–2887.

Tannock, I.F., Rotin, D., 1989. Acid pH in tumors and its potential for therapeutic exploitation. Cancer Res. 49, 4373–4384.

Tseng, I.C., Xu, H., Chou, F.P., Li, G., Vazzano, A.P., Kao, J.P., Lin, C.Y., 2010. Matriptase activation, an early cellular response to acidosis. J. Biol. Chem. 285, 3261–3270.

Tu, C., Ortega-Cava, C.F., Chen, G., Fernandes, N.D., Cavallo-Medved, D., Sloane, B.F., Band, H., 2008. Lysosomal cathepsin B participates in the podosome-mediated extracellular matrix degradation and invasion via secreted lysosomes in v-Src fibroblasts. Cancer Res. 68, 9147–9156.

Turk, B., Stoka, V., 2007. Protease signalling in cell death: caspases versus cysteine cathepsins. FEBS Lett. 581, 2761–2767.

Turk, B., Turk, D., Turk, V., 2012. Protease signaling: the cutting edge. EMBO J. 31, 1630–1643.

Vasiljeva, O., Turk, B., 2008. Dual contrasting roles of cysteine cathepsins in cancer progression: apoptosis versus tumour invasion. Biochimie 90, 380–386.

Velasco, G., Cal, S., Quesada, V., Sánchez, L.M., López-Otín, C., 2002. Matriptase-2, a membrane-bound mosaic serine proteinase predominantly expressed in human liver and showing degrading activity against extracellular matrix proteins. J. Biol. Chem. 277, 37637–37646.

Verbovšek, U., Van Noorden, C.J., Lah, T.T., 2015. Complexity of cancer protease biology: cathepsin K expression and function in cancer progression. Semin. Cancer Biol. 35, 71–84. Academic Press.

Verghese, G.M., Gutknecht, M.F., Caughey, G.H., 2006. Prostasin regulates epithelial monolayer function: cell-specific Gpld1-mediated secretion and functional role for GPI anchor. Am. J. Physiol. Cell Physiol. 291, C1258–C1270.

Verhagen, A.M., Silke, J., Ekert, P.G., Pakusch, M., Kaufmann, H., Connolly, L.M., Moritz, R.L., 2002. HtrA2 promotes cell death through its serine protease activity and its ability to antagonize inhibitor of apoptosis proteins. J. Biol. Chem. 277, 445–454.

Wang, M.C., Yang, Y.M., Li, X.H., Dong, F., Li, Y., 2004. Maspin expression and its clinicopathological significance in tumorigenesis and progression of gastric cancer. World J. Gastroenterol. 10, 634.

Wang, L., Diao, Y.C., Jiao, J.W., Wang, C., Yu, J., Li, B., Dai, S.Z., 2016. HtrA2/Omi protease in epithelial ovarian carcinoma: clinical significance and antineoplastic efficacy of its overexpression on subcutaneous transplanted tumor in nude mice model. Int. J. Clin. Exp. Pathol. 9, 3161–3169.

Webb, S.L., Sanders, A.J., Mason, M.D., Jiang, W.G., 2011. Type II transmembrane serine protease (TTSP) deregulation in cancer. Front. Biosci. 16, 539–552.

Webb, S.L., Sanders, A.J., Mason, M.D., Jiang, W.G., 2012. The influence of matriptase-2 on prostate cancer in vitro: a possible role for β-catenin. Oncol. Rep. 28, 1491–1497.

Xu, H., Xu, Z., Tseng, I.C., Chou, F.P., Chen, Y.W., Wang, J.K., Lin, C.Y., 2011. Mechanisms for the control of matriptase activity in the absence of sufficient HAI-1. Am. J. Physiol. Cell Physiol. 302, C453–C462.

Yang, Y., Hong, H., Zhang, Y., Cai, W., 2009. Molecular imaging of proteases in cancer. Cancer Growth Metastasis 2, CGM-S2814.

Zhang, M., Maass, N., Magit, D., Sager, R., 1997. Transactivation through Ets and Ap1 transcription sites determines the expression of the tumor-suppressing gene maspin. Cell Growth Differ. 8, 179–186.

Zhang, M., Volpert, O., Shi, Y.H., Bouck, N., 2000. Maspin is an angiogenesis inhibitor. Nat. Med. 6, 196.

Zhang, B., Cai, F.F., Zhong, X.Y., 2011. An overview of biomarkers for the OC diagnosis. Eur. J. Obstet. Gynecol. Reprod. Biol. 158, 119–123.

Zhu, M., Gokhale, V.M., Szabo, L., Munoz, R.M., Baek, H., Bashyam, S., Hurley, L.H., Von Hoff, D.D., Han, H., 2007. Identification of novel inhibitor of urokinase-type plasminogen activator. Mol. Cancer Ther. 6, 1348–1356.

Zou, Z., Anisowicz, A., Hendrix, M.J., Thor, A., Neveu, M., Sheng, S., Sager, R., 1994. Maspin, a serpin with tumor-suppressing activity in human mammary epithelial cells. Science 263, 526–529.

Zucker, S., Cao, J., Chen, W.T., 2000. Critical appraisal of the use of matrix metalloproteinase inhibitors in cancer treatment. Oncogene 19, 6642.

Zumbrunn, J., Trueb, B., 1996. Primary structure of a putative serine protease specific for IGF-binding proteins. FEBS Lett. 398, 187–192.

Zurawa-Janicka, D., Jarzab, M., Polit, A., Skorko-Glonek, J., Lesner, A., Gitlin, A., Lipinska, B., 2013. Temperature-induced changes of HtrA2 (Omi) protease activity and structure. Cell Stress Chaperones 18, 35–51.

Further reading

Eatemadi, A., Aiyelabegan, H.T., Negahdari, B., Mazlomi, M.A., Daraee, H., Daraee, N., Sadroddiny, E., 2017. Role of protease and protease inhibitors in cancer pathogenesis and treatment. Biomed. Pharmacother. 86, 221–231.

Latha, K., Zhang, W., Cella, N., Shi, H.Y., Zhang, M., 2005. Maspin mediates increased tumor cell apoptosis upon induction of the mitochondrial permeability transition. Mol. Cell. Biol. 25, 1737–1748.

Paschos, K.A., Canovas, D., Bird, N.C., 2009. The role of cell adhesion molecules in the progression of colorectal cancer and the development of liver metastasis. Cell. Signal. 21, 665–674.

Chapter 8

Serine proteases leading to prostate cancer: Structures, functions, and development of anticancer drugs

B.S. Harish, Kiran Babu Uppuluri

Bioprospecting Laboratory, Department of Biotechnology, School of Chemical and Biotechnology, SASTRA Deemed University, Thanjavur, India

8.1 Introduction

The prostate is a small gland with the size of a walnut and is placed in front of the rectum between the bladder and penis. The prostate gland secretes seminal fluid to nourish and protect sperm. The seminal fluid also helps the sperm to travel and survive. One of the most common forms of visceral malignancy in men is Prostate cancer (PCa). Prostate cancer usually starts in the peripheral region of the prostate near the rectum. That is the reason for conducting the digital rectal exam (DRE) for examining the prostate. The risk of prostate cancer increases after the age of 40. Incidences were high in people with more consumption of saturated fat, low dietary selenium, vitamins E and D, and exposure to radiation. The genetic cause is less than 5% in all prostate cancer cases (Dall'Era et al., 2008; Mazhar and Waxman, 2002). The majority of the PCa deaths are due to the development of metastatic diseases primarily in the bone. PCa can induce an osteoblastic reaction within the bone, which is rarely found in other bone-metastatic cancer (Ganguly et al., 2014).

Localized PCa is treated either by surgery to remove or by chemotherapy to destroy the cancerous lesions. There is no effective therapy for advanced PCa with hormone-refractory or metastatic phenotypes (Cheng et al., 2013). The cancer growth in the early stages of prostate cancer is androgen-dependent and treated by androgen deprivation therapy (ADT). ADT is recommended for the patient with metastatic disease after the surgical removal of the primary tumor. In the later stages, androgen deprivation is ineffective as cancer growth becomes androgen-independent (Ganguly et al., 2014; McCulloch et al., 2000).

Cancer-Leading Proteases. https://doi.org/10.1016/B978-0-12-818168-3.00008-5

The death from prostate cancer is mainly because of invasion and metastasis. Malignancy is progressed by the degradation of the basal membrane (BM) and extracellular matrix (ECM) followed by invasion. Matrix-degrading serine proteases and metalloproteases are involved in the dissolution of BM (Webber et al., 1995). About 95% of all prostate cancers are adenocarcinomas (that arises in the cells of glands). Approximately 4% are transitional cell carcinomas that are spread from the transitional epithelium of the urethra or ducts. Tumors from other organs can also spread into the prostate (Mazhar and Waxman, 2002)

8.2 Proteases and PCa progression

The key genes involved in the cancer formation are the C-oncogenes and tumor suppressor genes. Recent studies revealed that specific ECM-degrading proteases also participate in the genesis of animal cancers (Duffy, 2004). ECM degradation, including basement membrane and interstitial stroma, is required for tumor migration through anatomic barriers and invasion to distant tissues. The stromal compartment or tumor microenvironment is heterogeneous consisting of fibroblasts, endothelial cells, and immune cells. It also has several growth factors and cytokines. The cancer cells interact with the stromal compartment and lead to invasion, angiogenesis, and metastatic progression of cancer cells to distal sites. In prostate gland with PCa lesions, the smooth muscle cells of the stromal compartment are differentiated into myofibroblasts with overexpression of vimentin and matrix remodeling enzymes such as collagen-I and tenascin. The interaction of the PCa cells with the remodeled matrix is the first critical step in the cancer progression (Ganguly et al., 2014).

The progression of prostate adenocarcinoma is due to the degradation of the basement membrane present over the prostatic ducts and invasion of PCa cells into the stromal compartment. Invasive growth of cancer cells is a complex biological process, including cell proliferation, cell-cell interaction, and migration across the basal membrane and colonization to distant sites. Proteolysis of the basement membrane and stromal ECM is one of the first steps in invasion and metastatic dissemination (Ganguly et al., 2014; Saleem et al., 2006; Uhland, 2006). Invasive growth is normally found during tissue regeneration, maintenance, and pathological processes, such as tumor progression (Uhland, 2006). Proteases play vital roles in cancer progression by participating in ECM degradation, cell growth, adhesion, and migration. Hence any aberrantly expressed proteases may be a suitable candidate as cancer biomarker (Dudani et al., 2018; Wu et al., 2010). For its action, proteases are required to penetrate into and out of the vasculature and lymphatics (Ganguly et al., 2014). The elevated enzymatic activity of membrane-associated and pericellular proteases on the surface of cancer cells and in the transformed stroma is the feature of aggressive metastatic prostate cancer (LeBeau et al., 2015). The elevated peritumoral proteolytic activity is the result of protease overexpression, mislocalization, and/or reduced expression of endogenous protease inhibitors (LeBeau and Denmeade, 2015).

Even though several proteases participate in the process of invasion and metastasis, most of the studies were devoted to matrix metalloproteinases (MMPs). MMPs such as gelatinases, interstitial collagenases, stromelysin, matrilysin, and membrane-type metalloproteinases participate in the degradation of collagen and fibronectin which are the main constituents of stromal ECM (Friedrich et al., 2002; Ganguly et al., 2014). In addition to MMPs, serine proteases such as urokinase-type plasminogen activator (uPA), elastase, plasmin, and cathepsin G are also implicated to extracellular matrix degradation and cell-substratum adhesion in tumor cells (Klezovitch et al., 2004). Type II transmembrane serine proteases such as matriptase and hepsin participate in the breakdown of basement membrane in prostate cancer (Friedrich et al., 2002; Ganguly et al., 2014). Three members of serine protease family, prostate-specific antigen (KLK3), human kallikrein 2 (KLK2), and kallikrein 4 (KLK4), and the transmembrane metalloprotease, prostate-specific membrane antigen (PSMA) have been considered as PCa biomarkers (LeBeau and Denmeade, 2015).

In this chapter, serine proteases identified in prostate cancer progression are grouped into four different groups, plasminogen activation system, human kallikreins, type II transmembrane serine protease, and other serine proteases.

8.2.1 Plasminogen activation system

The components of the plasminogen activation (PA) system contribute to a wide range of physiological and pathological processes. The significance of the PA system and its elements is established in most of the tumors, and their expression not only reveals its role but also carries a prognostic value. They are, in turn, modulated by several other proteases, cytokines, and growth factors which are upregulated during cancer progression (Kwaan and McMahon, 2009). Proteolytic activity of plasmin and other proteases contributes to the breakdown of the extracellular matrix, which is critical in cancer invasion and metastasis (Danø et al., 2005). Plasmin is activated by plasminogen activation system. The PA system consists of several serine proteases, its activators, inhibitors, and receptors. The main components of PA system are urokinase-type plasminogen activator (uPA), its inactive precursor (pro-uPA), cell surface uPA receptor (uPAR), plasminogen activator inhibitors (PAIs), tissue-type plasminogen activator (tPA), and α_2-antiplasmin. The involvement of the PA system is established for all types of cancer, and its function in the metastasis makes PA system a potential therapeutic target. Moreover, uPA may serve as an active molecular marker for predicting poor prognosis of PCa (Sheng, 2001). The role of serine proteases in cancer progression is depicted in Fig. 8.1.

Bone metastasis is the most common complication leading to mortality in prostate cancer patients. Once reaching the bone, the PCa cells interact with the resident cells, and an elevated proteolytic activity was observed that could result in the degradation of bone matrix and activation of growth factors leading to cancer cell proliferation. The level of uPA is related to prostatic malignancy and

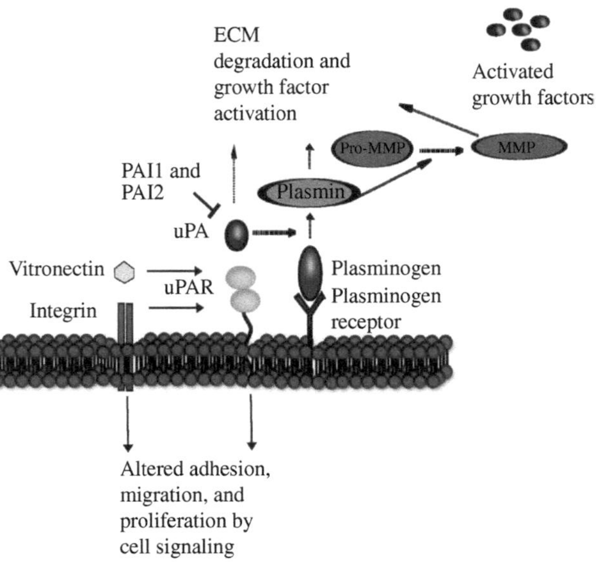

FIG. 8.1 Plasminogen activation system in the progression of cancer. Binding of pro-uPA to its specific receptor, uPAR, activates uPA and catalyzes the proteolytic conversion of plasminogen into plasmin. Plasmin further catalyzes the conversion of pro-uPA into uPA by feedback type activation, and this, in turn, accelerates plasminogen activation. PAI-1 inhibits this sequential series of events by binding to the uPA-uPAR complex. Plasmin can degrade several components of the extracellular matrix and activates some MMPs and growth factors, thereby contributing to tumor cell invasion and metastasis. uPAR can bind to vitronectin and modulate cell adhesion by regulating integrin signaling.

PCa invasion (Dong et al., 2008). The higher than normal levels of circulating uPA and uPAR in serum are considered to be associated with the tumor invasion and osteoblastic metastases (Shariat et al., 2007). uPA expression is a negative prognostic parameter, predicting invasive phenotype in human prostate, colon, brain, breast, and lung tumors (Soff et al., 1995). uPA and uPAR levels are moderately increased in benign prostate hyperplasia (BPH) and significantly increased in PCa. The elevated levels of uPA and uPAR in serum are correlated with that of prostate-specific antigen (PSA) (Sheng, 2001).

The molecular mechanism for the upregulation of uPA and uPAR in PCa is complicated. This may be due to the accumulated genetic changes in the PCa cell such as gene amplification, or may due to the evolving epigenetic stimulations during PCa progression. The transcription of uPA is activated by numerous paracrine growth factors, including androgen, interleukins, thrombin, bombesin, lipopolysaccharide, IGF, EGF, and TGF-β (Sheng, 2001). The PCa-associated uPA can activate the latent form of TGF-β derived from osteoblasts. The activated TGF-β, in turn, stimulates the overexpression of both uPA and PAI-1, resulting in metastasis by increasing pericellular plasminogen activation and activation of MMP-9 (Sheng, 2001).

8.2.1.1 Structure of uPA

uPA is a protein of 411 residues long consisting of two α-helices and two antiparallel β-strands. A zymogen pro-uPA undergoes proteolytic cleavage at Lys158-Ile159 bond and gets activated to uPA after binding to its receptor, uPAR. Either plasmin catalyzes uPA activation through feedback type activation or by other proteases such as cathepsin B, cathepsin L, and human kallikrein type 2 (hK2) (Dass et al., 2008; Duffy, 2004). Other convertases, such as mast cell tryptase and matriptase, can also activate uPA (Uhland, 2006). The mature uPA is a heterodimeric protein of two chains linked by a disulfide bond between Cys 148 and Cys 279. It consists of N-terminal A chain that could attach to uPAR and the C-terminal catalytic B chain (Sheng, 2001). A chain contains a growth factor-like domain and a kringle domain, while B chains have both the catalytic and inhibitor binding sites (Duffy, 2004). uPA aids the activation of plasmin by converting plasminogen to plasmin through proteolysis of the arginine-valine bond (Binder and Mihaly, 2008).

uPAR is cysteine-rich glycoprotein attached to the plasma membrane by linking to the GPI (glycosylphosphatidylinositol) anchor using its carboxy terminal. The function of uPAR is to focus protease actions to the leading edge of invading cells. Moreover, it serves as a signal receptor for specific extracellular or transmembrane proteins. uPAR consists of three domains with relatively low sequence identity, D1, D2, and D3 (Duffy, 2004). Domain 1 is considered as critical for binding to uPA. Both precursor form and active uPA can bind to uPAR with high affinity (k_d, approximately 0.1–0.5 nM) (Duffy, 2004). The downregulation of uPAR was reported to inhibit cancer growth and reduced cancer invasion and metastasis. The upregulation of uPA and uPAR is a hallmark of clinically unfavorable conditions during cancer, and hence both are considered as biomarkers for cancer (Binder and Mihaly, 2008; Dass et al., 2008).

PAI-1 and PAI-2 belong to the serpin family of protease inhibitors with relatively low sequence similarity. PAI-1 is a single-chain glycoprotein with a molecular weight of 43 kDa and can react rapidly with uPA. It forms a stable complex with a stoichiometry of 1:1 and thus regulated cellular proliferation. It can also bind to an ECM protein, vitronectin, and thereby modulating cellular adhesion and migration. PAI-1 is a double-edged sword that can also inhibit apoptosis. The ability to inhibit apoptosis and modulation of cell adhesion appears to be independent of its uPA inhibitory ability. Inhibition of apoptosis may be either by binding to proteases such as caspases or by interfering with crucial signaling pathways such as P13K/Akt and Jak/STAT pathways (Balsara and Ploplis, 2008). PAI-2 is found in two forms, a 47 kDa intracellular nonglycosylated form, and a 60 kDa extracellular glycosylated form. The inhibitory activity of PAI-2 is slower than PAI-1 and believed to block apoptosis (Duffy, 2004).

8.2.1.2 Function of uPA

The plasminogen activation system has a significant role in tissue remodeling, invasion, and angiogenesis with distinct and overlapping functions.

Primarily, it modulates plasminogen activation, thereby regulating the extracellular proteolytic activity. Second, it governs the interaction between cell and ECM by functioning as an adhesion receptor for vitronectin and by modulating integrin function. Third, uPA/uPAR regulates cell migration by acting as a signal transduction molecule and by its intrinsic chemotactic activity. The components of the PA system are upregulated in cancer and thus believed to promote invasion and metastasis (Uhland, 2006).

The zymogen of uPA, pro-uPA, is activated by attaching with uPAR. The active uPA can convert plasminogen to plasmin. uPA can also activate plasminogen homologues such as hepatocyte growth factor/scatter factor (HGF/SF) and macrophage-stimulating protein (MSP) in a similar manner (Sheng, 2001). In vitro studies revealed that in the presence of free sulfhydryl donors (FSD), uPA converts plasminogen to another product angiostatin, which can inhibit tumor-induced angiogenesis (Sheng, 2001).

In malignancies, the PA system plays a significant role in the degradation of collagen, laminin, fibronectin, and other components of the extracellular matrix (ECM), either directly or by activating of other proteases (Rabbani et al., 1995). uPA has a restricted specificity toward the ECM components, and till date, it has identified only to digest fibronectin directly. Whereas, plasmin can degrade most of the noncollagenous proteins, including fibrin, laminin, fibronectin, and perlecan (a heparin sulfate proteoglycan) (Duffy, 2004). Plasmin activates a cascade of proteases, including metalloproteinases (such as MMP-3, MMP-9, MMP-12, and MMP-13) and progrowth factors (such as FGF2 and TGFβ) for the degradation of a wide spectrum of extracellular matrix components (Binder and Mihaly, 2008; Duffy, 2004). uPAR also participates in various signaling events required for the differentiation and migration of cells within the tumor environment (Shariat et al., 2007). uPAR directly interacts with the integrin receptors present in ECM proteins and proteins on adjacent cells.

The uPA can be specifically inhibited by several serine protease inhibitors, including plasminogen activator inhibitor type-1 (PAI-1), plasminogen activator inhibitor type-2 (PAI-2), and maspin. PAI-1 and PAI-2 inhibit uPA bound with its receptor more efficiently than free-uPA, whereas maspin could inhibit only cell surface-associated uPA. The serpins inhibit uPA by inserting their reactive center loop (RCL) into the active site of the protease and form a stable uPA-serpin complex (Sheng, 2001). The docking of RCL present in PAI-1 to the active site of uPA is shown in Fig. 8.2 as a representative example (Qureshi et al., 2016).

The progression of tumor cell can be reduced either by blocking the binding of uPA to its receptor or by inhibiting its proteolytic activity (Rabbani et al., 1995). Dong et al. (2008) showed an association between uPA expression and intraosseous tumor burden in PC3 cells (cell line established from bone metastasis of human prostate cancer). They reported a lower tumor burden and reduced trabecular bone degradation in uPA silenced PC3 cells (Dong et al., 2008). However, studies on different PCa cell lines showed that there is a variation on

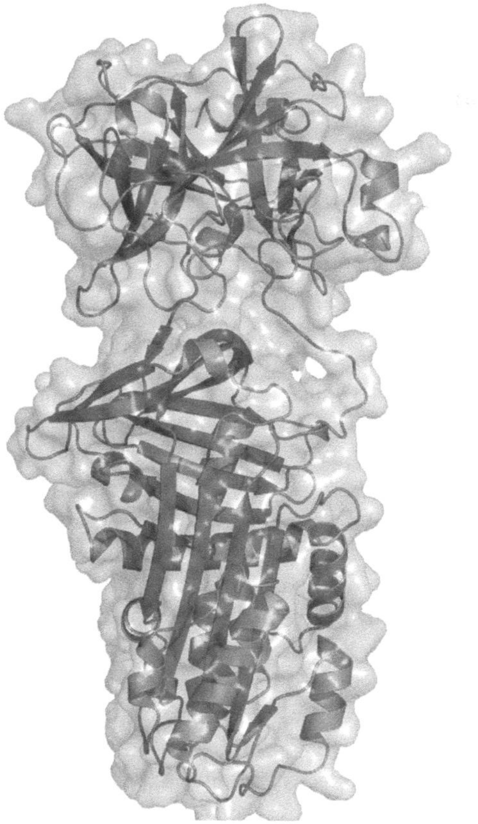

FIG. 8.2 Distinct encounter complexes of PAI-1 with plasminogen activators and vitronectin revealed by changes in the conformation and dynamics of the reactive center loop. *(Reprinted from Qureshi, T., Goswami, S., McClintock, C.S., Ramsey, M.T., Peterson, C.B., 2016. Distinct encounter complexes of PAI-1 with plasminogen activators and vitronectin revealed by changes in the conformation and dynamics of the reactive center loop. Protein Sci. 25, 499–510. Online Publication. US National Library of Medicine. Open Access Publication.)*

the levels of amplification of PCa. An amplified uPA gene was found in PC3 cells with high sensitivity to uPA inhibitors, whereas DU145 cells did not have amplified expression of uPA and showed less sensitivity to the inhibitors. The invasion property follows different mechanisms in these two cell lines. Hence it might not be a relevant treatment target in common form of the disease (Porkka and Visakorpi, 2004).

uPAR also can bind to vitronectin (VN) and induces cell adhesion by regulating integrin signaling. The integration activates the migratory signaling pathways through integrin-dependent regulation of Rho guanosine triphosphatase's activity involving p130-Cas adaptor molecule. uPAR-mediated VN adhesion can also activate mitogenic signaling pathway by initiating intracellular signaling through enhanced mitogen-activated protein kinase (MAPK) activity. The activation of these migratory and mitogenic signaling pathways could enhance tumor growth and metastasis dissemination in vivo (Pirazzoli et al., 2013).

8.2.2 Human kallikreins in prostate cancer

The members of the kallikrein family belong to the chymotrypsin family of serine proteases. Tissue kallikrein, KLK1, is the first member of the kallikrein family and is the most abundant protease present in the pancreas. The word kallikrein was derived from the Greek name "kallikreas" meaning pancreas. Kallikrein family of serine proteases was established with the identifications of other kallikreins, kallikrein 2 (hK2) and kallikrein 3 (hK3/prostate-specific antigen, PSA). Twelve more kallikrein genes were later identified to be located near to the previously identified KLK-encoding genes, of approximately 280 kb at chromosomal region 19q13.4 of the human genome (Hong, 2014).

Kallikreins are considered as a significant biomarker for a wide range of diseases in humans as they have a broad expression profile. One among the 15 kallikreins has been observed in all types of tissue samples other than nerves. Higher levels of kallikreins are detected in salivary gland and prostate. Steroids and other hormones control kallikrein expression. Kallikreins are often regarded as markers of hormone receptor activity such as androgen receptor activity. In the prostate, the appearance of human kallikreins, particularly KLK2 and KLK3, is regulated by androgens. The action of the androgen receptor is often measured by monitoring changes in the levels of prostate-specific kallikreins, KLK2 or KLK3. They are found to stimulate invasion and proliferation of prostate cancer (Lawrence et al., 2010). The role of kallikreins in PCa progression is depicted in Fig. 8.3.

8.2.2.1 Prostate-specific antigen (hK3/KLK3)

Prostate-specific antigen (PSA) belongs to the kallikrein-related family of serine proteases (LeBeau and Denmeade, 2015). PSA was first isolated and characterized by Wang et al. in 1979 and was reported to be found only in normal, benign hyperplastic, and malignant prostate tissue and absent in any other human tissue. PSA is a glycoprotein with a molecular weight of 33 kDa and carbohydrate content of approximately 7% (Lilja, 1993). Although the therapeutic application of PSA was suggested immediately after its discovery, it took several years of intensive studies for its utility in monitoring PCa. The determination of PSA level to aid the prognosis and management of patients with PCa was approved by the Food and Drug Administration (FDA) in 1986 (Rittenhouse et al., 1998). In seminal plasma, PSA is present as enzymatically active free form, whereas PSA is found as an inactivated form in the serum by binding with protease inhibitors (Stura et al., 2011). Serum PSA is predominantly found complexed with α-1-antichymotrypsin and α-2-macroglobulin (LeBeau and Denmeade, 2015; Stura et al., 2011). A minor fraction of total PSA is circulated as free PSA (fPSA),

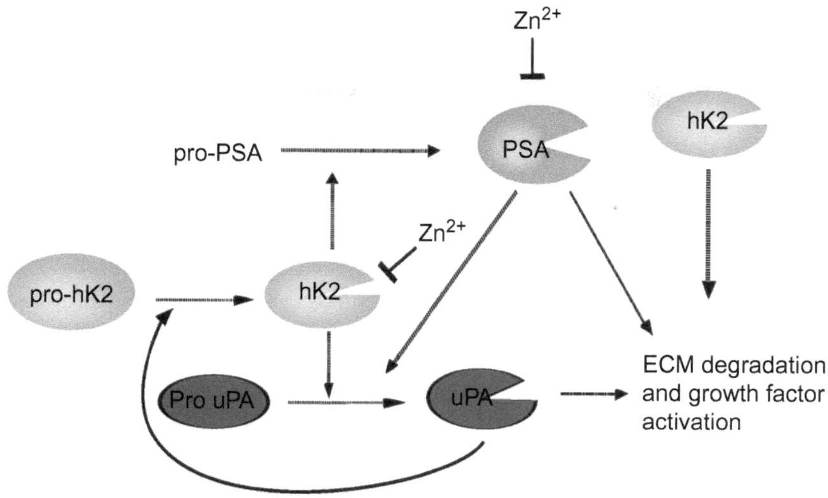

FIG. 8.3 Human kallikreins in the progression of prostate cancer. hK2 and hK3 (PSA) are the prostate-specific human kallikreins. It can act directly on ECM proteins and growth factors, and indirectly by activating urokinase.

which includes precursor isoforms of PSA (proPSA), benign PSA (BPSA), and mature inactive PSA (iPSA) (Gilgunn et al., 2013; Hong, 2014; Stura et al., 2011). Studies revealed that men with larger proportions of bound PSA are more probable to have PCa. Men with PCa have a lower percentage of fPSA (%fPSA) compared to BPH (Hong, 2014). For PCa diagnosis, the total PSA is first determined, and for those with a level of PSA >10 ng/mL, PCa is confirmed by coupling with digital rectal examination and biopsy. If the total PSA is in the gray zone of 4 and 10 ng/mL, then the measurement of %fPSA increase diagnostic accuracy (Stura et al., 2011). The commonly used %fPSA threshold is in the range of 20%–27%. The prostate cancer determined at %fPSA > 25% were of smaller volume and lower grade (Hong, 2014).

Moreover, the measurement of cancer-associated glycans of PSA can improve the specificity of PSA measurement in PCa as the tumor environment alters key elements of glycan biosynthesis apparatus (Gilgunn et al., 2013). Glycosylation of PSA has a significant effect on its activity against substrates as Asn69 residing near the substrate binding cleft is linked to the large glycan. During PCa development, there may be a change in the pattern of glycosylation, which leads to enzymatic dysfunction (Gilgunn et al., 2013).

Structure of PSA

The human PSA gene is located on chromosome 19 (Webber et al., 1995). The 244 amino acids PSA zymogen is secreted by prostate epithelium consisting of a leader peptide followed by a short activation peptide. The activation peptide is released by proteolytic cleavage at carboxy terminal of Arg (-1) by trypsin-like protease. The activation of zymogen happens before mixing of ejaculatory secretions from the male accessory sex glands. The mature PSA is a single-chain glycoprotein consisting of 237 amino acids showing restricted chymotrypsin-like activity. The polypeptide chain corresponds for a molecular mass of 26,079, and the backbone consists of a single carbohydrate unit constituting of 7%–12% attached at Asp 45 that increases the mass by another 2–3 kDa. The catalytic triad consists of His-41, Asp-96, and Ser-189 (Bélanger et al., 1995; Lilja, 1993) and hence placed in the serine protease family, which includes trypsin and chymotrypsin. The amino acid sequence showed that it is structurally comparable with hK1 and thus grouped in the kallikrein family of serine proteases (Rittenhouse et al., 1998). However, the protease activity of PSA is weak and have chymotrypsin-like activity, unlike other kallikreins with trypsin-like activity (Rittenhouse et al., 1998).

The mature inactive uncomplexed form of PSA is assumed to have kallikrein loop which blocks the access of substrate to S1 pocket. The inactive form can be activated by anti-free PSA monoclonal antibody 5D3D11 or anti-total PSA mAB 8G8F5 (Ménez et al., 2008). The crystallization of human-derived glycoproteins is complicated, and moreover, PSA is a protease. The presence of cleaved PSA molecules also makes the crystal studies difficult. Antibody fragments were used to overcome these problems, and two crystal studies are available.

The first crystal structure of PSA with its monoclonal antibody, 8G8F5, revealed that PSA formed a crystallographic dimer with the asymmetric molecule. His57, Asp102, and Ser195 constitute the catalytic triad. The kallikrein loop spans the stretch 95–101 with the insertion of 11-residues, 95A-95K. Unlike chymotrypsin, the access to the substrate-binding site in PSA can be blocked by the residues 95C-95I present in the kallikrein loop, which is believed to confer the enzyme better substrate specificity. A single N-oligosaccharide chain is linked to Asn61, which is near the entrance of the catalytic cleft and near to the kallikrein loop but far from the dimer interface (Ménez et al., 2008).

Stura et al. (2011) presented the crystal structure of the sandwiched complex of PSA with two monoclonal antibodies. The first one was complexed with 5D5A5, an anti-total-PSA antibody with higher affinity than 858F5. The second one was selective mAb 5D3D1, which had been developed as a capture antibody for sandwich immunoassays. The overall structure consisted of 10 individual polypeptide chains with four each of mAbs and two different subforms of PSA chains (P and Q). In overall, PSA P was better ordered than Q. There is a difference between the carbohydrates attached to the two different PSA subforms. In proximity to Thr125, present in P chain, the electron density was found too large to fit the water molecules, and likely represents O-linked glycosylation. These carbohydrates contribute to the epitope of 5D3D11 mAb (Stura et al., 2011).

Function of PSA

The primary function of PSA is the dissolution of the sperm-entrapping gel present in the freshly ejaculated sperm by proteolytically cleaving the gel-forming proteins semenogelin I and II and fibronectin. The proteolysis leads to the liquefaction of the ejaculate and release of progressively motile spermatozoa (Lilja, 1993). Zn^{2+}, which is found 100 times more abundant in semen than in serum, can strongly inhibit PSA activity. The inhibition of PSA by Zn^{2+} is relieved in the presence of semenogelins, which can strongly bind to zinc. Thus zinc plays a significant role in modulating the physiological activities of PSA (Ménez et al., 2008).

Measuring the serum levels of PSA is one of the significant methods in the screening of PCa. But PSA is susceptible to various noncancer comorbidities (Dudani et al., 2018). Normally PSA is secreted into seminal plasma by the prostate epithelium through prostate ducts and has minimal leakage into the bloodstream (Lawrence et al., 2010). But in PCa, PSA enters into the blood due to the loss of glandular architecture and degradation of basement membrane within the tumor (Lawrence et al., 2010).

PSA may facilitate PCa progression through the degradation of insulin-like growth factor binding protein 3 and 4 to increase the bioavailability of insulin-like growth factor (Ménez et al., 2008). Webber et al. (1995) demonstrated the degradation of extracellular glycoproteins fibronectin and laminin in vitro in LNCaP human prostate carcinoma cells leading to the invasion of PCa cells. Blocking of PSA activity in turn reduced the invasion. They proposed that PSA, along with uPA, produced by the prostate epithelium, participate in a cascade of proteolytic reactions during PCa invasion and metastasis (Webber et al., 1995). PSA can activate uPA by cleaving single chain pro-uPA and thus facilitates cancer cell invasion (Tang and Porter, 1997). PSA is a specific marker for prostate and not for cancer (Lawrence et al., 2010). Infection and benign prostatic hyperplasia lead to elevated levels of PSA (Dudani et al., 2018). PSA tests may be significant to younger men, where benign prostatic hyperplasia is uncommon (Lawrence et al., 2010). The common threshold for a biopsy is greater than 4 ng/mL with a positive predictive value of 30% in men aged above 50 years or more and negative predictive value of about 85% in men of median age 69 years at biopsy (Hayes and Barry, 2014). The discovery of the extracellular matrix-degrading ability of PSA makes it a target for the prevention and intervention of prostate cancer (Webber et al., 1995).

8.2.3 Kallikrein 2

Human glandular kallikrein 2 (hK2) is the last of the three human kallikreins produced by prostate epithelial cells. hK2 is prostate-specific and considered as one of the biological markers for PCa. hK2 is prostate-specific, PSA-like kallikrein generated by the epithelial cells of the prostate (Partin et al., 1999). PSA and hK2 constitute 10%–30% of the seminal plasma proteins by mass (Rittenhouse et al., 1998). The levels of hK2 in prostate, semen, and serum are only 2% of the PSA level (Hong, 2014). The production of recombinant hK2 showed that hK2 is secreted as inactive proform, and this zymogen is transient and is matured by autoactivation. Autoactivation is absent in hK1 and PSA (Rittenhouse et al., 1998).

The gene for hK2 is located 12 kb downstream of the PSA gene. The complete cDNA for hK2 was isolated in 1992, and the primary sequence of hK2 was found to be approximately 80% homologous to the PSA gene. Similar to that of PSA, the mRNA is detected in the prostatic epithelium and upregulated by androgen. The striking homology of hK2 with PSA along with the common location of both hK2 and PSA in prostate suggested a close resemblance between the biological function of the two proteases (Rittenhouse et al., 1998). Androgen response elements were identified in the hK2 promoter, and the enhancer fragment is located 12.3 kb upstream of the hK2 gene (Yu et al., 1999). Like PSA, hK2 is bounded to protease inhibitors in the serum and is present in both free and bound forms. Free-hK2 comprises of pro-hK2 and mature free-hK2; and their level increases in prostate cancer. An elevation in free hK2 level after radiation therapy can predict recurrence (Guerrico et al., 2017).

The levels of kallikrein 2 and kallikrein3 are differentially regulated suggesting hK2 as a suitable diagnostic and prognostic marker (Darson et al., 1997; Yu et al., 1999). There is a difference in the relative quantity of PSA and hK2 expression in benign hyperplasia and PCa cells. hK2 was found in every prostate cancer, and the level of hK2 protein expression increased from benign epithelium to high-grade prostatic intraepithelial neoplasia and adenocarcinoma. So it can give unique information in the diagnosis of PCa. PSA is usually highly expressed in well-differentiated tumors of benign tissue than in poorly differentiated prostate tumors, whereas hK2 is expressed more in poorly differentiated PCa cells. Hence hK2 is considered more tumor-associated than PSA (Rittenhouse et al., 1998).

PSA is a significant component of seminal plasma with a concentration range of 0.5–3.0 mg/mL and hK2 in the range of 2–12 μg/mL. The separation of prostate kallikreins is more difficult from prostate tissue and seminal plasma as one million times more PSA and 10,000-fold concentrations of hK2 is present than within the blood. Some anatomic barriers prevent the release of both these kallikreins from the normal healthy prostate into the blood. Physical trauma or prostate diseases such as BPH, prostatitis, and malignant transformation leads to the leakage of PSA and hK2. Hence the elevated serum levels of PSA and hK2 are sensitive indicators of prostate disease or trauma. In prostate tissue, both PSA and hK2 are uncomplexed with a significant portion of PSA in matured state and hK2 as pro-hK2 (Rittenhouse et al., 1998).

8.2.3.1 Structure of kallikrein 2

Kallikrein 2 has two six-stranded β-barrels similar to those in trypsin-like serine proteases and a short β strand formed by residues 20–21 adjacent to strand B present in C-terminal barrel adapted for kallikreins. Similar to all other kallikreins, hK2 has five disulfide bonds and typical cis-pro-219. It also contains the kallikrein loop which is a special surface loop containing 11 more residues than the corresponding 99-loop present in chymotrypsin. The 1.9 Å crystal structure of hK2-small molecule inhibitor complex revealed the role of kallikrein loop in the regulation of its activity. The 99-loop is responsible for the reversible inhibition by Zn^{2+} even in micromolar concentrations and irreversible inactivation by autocatalytic cleavage. The autolysis site was identified between the residues 95e and 95f in the 99-loop, the removal of which prevent both the autolysis of the mature enzyme and permanent inactivation (Skala et al., 2014). A slightly negative potential was found in the substrate binding site of hK2 predominantly in the S1 pocket. Two regions with positive surface potential are present. The first region is between the residues Trp-67 and Arg-82 while the second one is present between His-48 and the C-terminal residues (Arg-235, Lys-236, and Lys-239). These regions correspond to anion-binding exosite II of thrombin and may allow the binding of allosteric effectors like heparin which can hasten the association of hK2 and PCI by fourfolds. The 99-loop, 148-loop, and 220-loop can be in open or closed conformations, thereby allowing or preventing substrate access to the binding site. This property may aid the enzyme in the conformational selection of substrates (Skala et al., 2014).

8.2.3.2 Function of kallikrein 2

The physiological role of hK2 is liquefaction of sperm. The maximum hK2 activity was found immediately after ejaculation, and the activity reduces within 10 min by binding with PCI (protein C inhibitor). It complements PSA activity for sperm liquefaction (Skala et al., 2014). In contrast with the PSA, hK2 shows trypsin-like activity with selective cleavage at arginine residues. Moreover, hK2 is more effective than PSA with almost 20,000-fold higher activity (Rittenhouse et al., 1998). hK2 can also participate in the activation or maturation of PSA by cleaving 244 residues long proPSA to generate 237 residues long enzymatically active PSA (Rittenhouse et al., 1998; Yu et al., 1999). Seminal plasma-derived hK2 can also cleave semenogelin I and II and fibronectin at arginyl residues. However, the hK2 activity on semenogelin proteins is slower when compared with PSA (Rittenhouse et al., 1998). In prostate cancer, hK2 may promote growth and metastasis by interacting with the uPA system. hK2 can activate the zymogen form of uPA which in turn through a positive feedback loop can activate pro-hK2. hK2 can also form complex with plasminogen activator inhibitor-1, insulin growth factor-binding proteins 2-5, and PAR-2 (protease-activated receptor 2) (Skala et al., 2014).

Protein inhibitors of kallikreins include serpins (MEROPS class I4), kazal type inhibitors, and (I1) and α-macroglobulin (I39). Although serpins are the best-studied inhibitors of kallikrein, no serpin-KLK complex crystal structure is available, and hence, their physiological connection is unclear (Goettig et al., 2010). The complex formation between kallikreins and serpins is believed to be by the standard mechanism with the insertion of RCL into the active site of the protease as discussed elsewhere (Fig. 8.2). hK2 is inhibited by α_1-antichymotrypsin, α_2-antiplasmin, antithrombin III, protein C inhibitor, protease inhibitor 6, and plasminogen activator inhibitor I. Whereas, PSA is inhibited by α_1-antitrypsin, α_1-antichymotrypsin, antithrombin III, protein C inhibitor, and monocyte/neutrophil elastase inhibitor. α_1-Antichymotrypsin is widely used for immunoassays of prostate cancer as it forms complexes with PSA (Masurier et al., 2018).

8.2.4 Type II transmembrane serine protease (TTSP)

Type II transmembrane serine protease (TTSP) family consists of 20 members possessing similar structures but different functions and expression patterns (List, 2009). TTSP family serine proteases are membrane-bound proteases involved in various physiological and pathological processes such as digestion, tissue remodeling, blood coagulation, fertility, inflammatory responses, tumor cell invasion, and programmed cell death (Vest et al., 2010). Several types of cancer are associated with dysregulated expression of TTSPs. Recent studies have shown more evidence on the functional roles of TTSPs in cancer progression, and metastasis and hence can be considered as a promising target for cancer therapy. The development of sensitive and specific imaging agents and inhibitors of TTSPs may aid in the diagnosis, treatment, and evaluation of treatment efficacy (Murray et al., 2016). All TTSPs consists of a short N-terminal intracellular domain, a single pass hydrophobic transmembrane domain, and larger C-terminal extracellular region. The extracellular region is constituted by a variable stem region and the C-terminal serine protease domain (Tanabe and List, 2017). The domain organization of TTSPs is shown in Fig. 8.4.

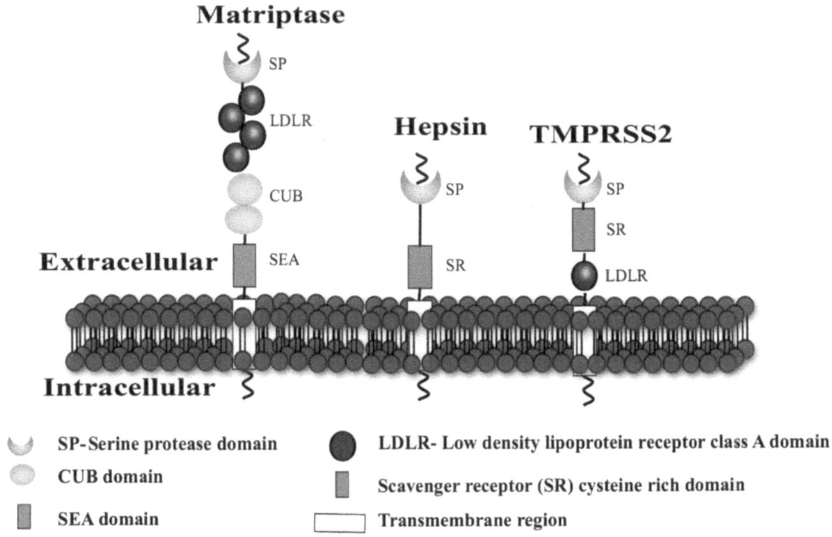

FIG. 8.4 Domain organization of matriptase, hepsin, and TMPRSS2 in the cell membrane.

In vertebrates, different TTSPs are distributed in four phylogenetically distinct subfamilies, namely matriptase subfamily, hepsin/TMPRSS (transmembrane protease serine subfamily), human air-way trypsin-like (HAT)/differentially expressed in squamous cell carcinoma (DESC) subfamily, and corin subfamily. TTSPs are synthesized as zymogens and require proteolytic cleavage for activation. TTSPs such as matriptase, hepsin, TMPRSS2, TMPRSS3, and TMPRSS4 are capable of auto-activation (Tanabe and List, 2017). Among them, TMPRSS2, matriptase1, matriptase2, and hepsin participate in the progression of prostate cancer (Gaweł-Bęben et al., 2018)

8.2.4.1 TMPRSS2

TMPRSS2 gene is another specific and significant marker for PCa, which is located in chromosome 21. TMPRSS2 is an androgen responsive gene encoding a Type II transmembrane serine protease (TTSP) (Vest et al., 2010). TMPRSS2 belongs to membrane-anchored serine protease (MASP) family and is predominantly expressed in the prostate (Ko et al., 2015).TMPRSS2 is also present in samples of colon, lung, kidney, and pancreas in smaller quantity. In comparison with BPH (Benign prostatic hyperplasia) cells, significant levels of TMPRSS2 genes were expressed in poorly differentiated and untreated prostate cancer cells (Vest et al., 2010). TMPRSS2 level is found to be correlated with PCa progression.

In normal prostate epithelia, TMPRSS2 is localized in the cell membrane. However, in prostate cancer, mislocalization of TMPRSS2 to the cytoplasm is observed. Higher levels of TMPRSS2 in primary and metastatic prostate tumors suggest its prooncogenic and prometastatic role in prostate cancer (Murray et al., 2016). In patients with prostate cancer, a chromosomal rearrangement is observed with 5′ untranslational region of TMPRSS2 merging to ETS (E26 transformation-specific) transcription factors such as ERG, ETV1, or ETV4. This fusion makes the expression of TMPRSS2 as androgen-inducible (Ko et al., 2015; Tanabe and List, 2017). ERG and ETV1 are found to be merged with TMPRSS2 in approximately 50%–79% PCa cases, and TMPRSS2-ETS fusion is associated with a poor prognosis in localized PCa (Tanabe and List, 2017). This recurrent gene fusion is believed as an early and perhaps causative genomic abnormality in PCa. This gene fusion also brings the expression of ETS transcription factor under the control of ARE-regulated TMPRSS2 promoter (Dehm and Tindall, 2007). No recombinant protein is formed for the fused gene as the coding sequence of TMPRSS2 is not engaged in the gene fusion. Moreover, with gene fusion, the promoter-less copy of TMPRSS2 is silenced, leading to the reduced expression of TMPRSS2 mRNA (Chen et al., 2010).

Androgenic ligands and the androgen receptor control the secretion of TMPRSS2. The knockdown of TMPRSS2 in TRAMP (transgenic adenocarcinoma of the mouse) significantly reduces metastasis with increased primary tumor size; suggesting that different factors regulate metastasis and primary tumor growth. TMPRSS2 is indicated to be critical in tumor metastatic behavior (Tanabe and List, 2017).

Structure of TMPRSS2

Despite its significant role in metastasis, the complete characterization of TMPRSS2 is not available and remains confusing. Even though the apparent molecular mass of TMPRSS2 is determined as approximately 54 kDa, many studies had reported around 70 and 32 kDa for the full-length protein and serine protease domain of TMPRSS2, respectively (Chen et al., 2010). TMPRSS2 gene is predicted to encode a protein of 492 amino acids consisting of five domains, a C-terminal serine protease domain of S1 family, a scavenger receptor cysteine-rich domain (a class A low-density lipoprotein), a transmembrane region, and an N-terminal cytoplasmic region (Lin et al., 1999) as shown in Fig. 8.4.

Function of TMPRSS2

The physiological function of TMPRSS2 and its substrates is yet to be determined. However, the study of the role of TMPRSS2 in prostate cancer was extensively started after the discovery of the oncogenic gene fusion of TMPRSS2 gene with ETS transcription factors, such as ERG (Murray et al., 2016). TMPRSS2 cleaves and activates other proteases involved in metastasis such as PAR-2, HGF, and matriptase (Tanabe and List, 2017). Moreover, TMPRSS2 acts as a cell receptor conducting external signaling and interacts with the extracellular matrix using its extracellular protein binding domains (Chen et al., 2010). TMPRSS2 promotes tumorigenicity and metastasis by aiding the degradation of ECM components such as nidogen-1 and laminin β-1(Fig. 8.5). The androgen-activated TMPRSS2 can also activate other pericellular proteases such as matriptase which initiate a proteolytic cascade to disrupt the network integrity of extracellular matrix and promote PCa cell invasion, tumor growth, and metastasis (Ko et al., 2015).

8.2.4.2 Matriptase (MT-SP1, TADG-15, epithin, ST14)

Matriptase is an epithelial-derived, trypsin-like, type II transmembrane serine protease which is expressed in all types of epithelium. Matriptase is involved in the epithelial development and maintenance of epithelial integrity. Matriptase is present in mast cells, peripheral blood monocytes, and B cells suggesting the role of matriptase in immune response (Zhao et al., 2013). Matriptase is highly expressed in both primary human tissues and in vitro cell lines of prostate, breast, ovarian, and colorectal epithelium. Matriptase is also expressed in lower levels in kidney, liver, lung, and spleen (Galkin et al., 2004).

The serine protease, matriptase, encoded by tumor-associated differentially, expressed gene-15 (TADG 15) was first isolated from human breast cancer cells (List, 2009; Saleem et al., 2006). Matriptase was initially isolated for its gelatinolytic activity and believed to be involved in the ECM degradation or tissue remodeling (Uhland, 2006). Takeuchi et al. cloned and characterized both MT-SP1 (membrane-type serine protease 1) from the human prostatic cancer cell line and its mouse homolog, epithin (Galkin et al., 2004). In human breast

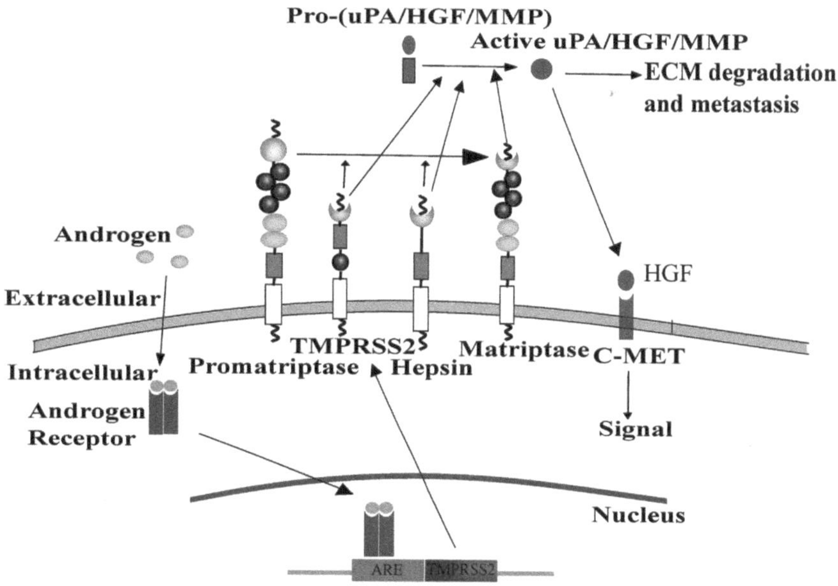

FIG. 8.5 Type II serine protease inhibitors in PCa progression. Androgen signals can activate expression of TTSPs such as TMPRSS2 and hepsin. TMPRSS2 and hepsin can activate matriptase. These membrane-bound serine proteases can activate uPA and MMPs. TTSPs activation can directly or indirectly degrade ECM degradation.

cancer cells, MT-SP1 primarily present as a free enzyme. Meanwhile, in human milk and other normal tissues, matriptase forms a complex with hepatocyte activator inhibitor 1 (HAI-1) (Friedrich et al., 2002).

Matriptase activation

Similar to other trypsin-like serine proteases, matriptase is also produced as an inactive zymogen. Matriptase is activated by proteolytic cleavage in a highly conserved activation site resulting in the conversion of the single-chain zymogen to the active form containing two-chains linked together by a disulfide bond. The activation can be either by other proteases or by autoactivation. The process of autoactivation is complex and incompletely understood (List, 2009). Several agents such as androgens, EGF, sphingosine 1-phosphate, and suramin stimulate the activation of matriptase in mammalian epithelial, breast, and prostate cancer cells (Cheng et al., 2013). In cancer cells, matriptase is expressed with a glycosylation pattern that gives the enzyme resistance to proteolytic activity at the cell surface. This suggests that posttranslational modifications can enhance matiptase activity (Galkin et al., 2004).

Wu et al. (2010) showed that ErbB-2 signaling through the phosphatidylinositol 3-kinase pathway could upregulate the activation of matriptase in C-81 LNCaP cells (Wu et al., 2010). ErbB-2 signaling induces PCa invasion by matriptase zymogen activation (Cheng et al., 2013). ErbB-2 signaling induces phenotypic changes such as cell motility, cell proliferation, and/or invasive ability associated with aggressive diseases. ErbB-2 activation can happen either by ligand-dependent or by ligand-independent manner. Ligand-dependent ErbB-2 activation involves heterodimerization of an ErbB-2 receptor to another ligand-activated ErbB receptor such as EGF receptor, ErbB-1, ErbB-3, and ErbB-4. In prostate cancer, ErbB ligand EGF is found to induce the formation of both ErbB-1/ErbB-1 homodimer and ErbB-1/ErbB-2 heterodimers. ErbB-2 has a functional tyrosine kinase domain, and the kinase activity has a significant role in EGF-induced matriptase activation and shedding. Ligand-independent ErbB-2 activation is due to the overexpression of ErbB-2, which leads to spontaneous homodimerization and autoactivation. Patients with clinically significant PCa shows elevated ErbB-2 levels. The overexpression of ErbB-2 can promote the growth of PCa cells through MAPK and/orphosphatidylinositol 3-kinase (P13K)/Akt pathway in the absence of androgens. The activation of matriptase increases both the protease activity at the cell surface and the invasive ability of the cells (Wu et al., 2010).

Structure of matriptase

The 855-residue matriptase has a multidomain structure (Fig. 8.4) with a putative N-terminal cytoplasmic region, a transmembrane region that attaches the enzyme to the cell surface, an SEA domain, two tandem repeats of complement proteases CUB (C1r/C1s-urchin embryonic growth factor-bone morphogenetic protein) domain, four tandem repeats of Class A low-density lipoprotein domain, and a C-terminal serine protease domain (Friedrich et al., 2002; Saleem et al., 2006). Matriptase is usually found in complex with HAI-1, a glycoprotein with 478 residues consisting of two Kunitz-type domains separated by an LDLR domain and a transmembrane segment. The crystal structure of MT-SP1 with benzamidine revealed that the catalytic domain folds into two adjacent six-stranded β-barrels strapped together by three trans-domain segments. The surface has several turn structures, a 3_{10}-helix and two α-helices. The catalytic triad is present along the junction of the barrels, and the catalytic site cleft runs perpendicular to the intersection. The active matriptase consists of two chains connected by disulfide linkage, Cys122 of B chain is linked to Cys1 of A chain. The B chain has three disulfide bridges between Cys42-Cys 58, Cys 168-Cys 182 and Cys 191-Cys 220. The surrounding surface loops flanking around the active site cleft, specifically 60-loop, are responsible for the narrow substrate specificity of MT-SP1. The catalytic triad is formed by Ser 195, His 57, and Asp 102 and the oxyanion hole is formed by the amino chain nitrogen of Gly 193 and Ser 295 (Friedrich et al., 2002).

Function of matriptase

Matriptase is a significant protease responsible for regulating a cascade of proteolytic activity by initiating the activation of several downstream enzymes as represented in Fig. 8.5 (Wu et al., 2010). Matriptase is found in various tissues of epithelial origin and cell lines in vitro (Saleem et al., 2006). Based on the substrate preference profiling with the help of a positional scanning synthetic combinatorial library and substrate phage display, three surface localized protein substrates such as protease-activated receptor 2 (PAR-2), the zymogen form of uPA (pro-uPA) and the inactive proform of the hepatocyte growth factor (pro-HGF/Scatter factor) were identified (Uhland, 2006).

Matriptase can also act on various other substrates involved in cell adhesion. It can also cleave fibronectin and laminin that mediates cell attachment and migration. Matriptase participates in the activation of PAR-2, a G-protein-coupled receptor that is involved in cell adhesion and early inflammatory processes (Uhland, 2006). Another substrate of matriptase that is involved in cell adhesion is angiomodulin (AGM), also known as insulin-like growth factor binding protein-related protein-1 (IGFB-rP1)/mac25/prostacyclin-stimulating factor (Uhland, 2006).

Matriptase has multiple functions such as the development of epidermis, hair follicles, and cellular immune system. It also participates in the activation of profilaggrin to filaggrin, a significant protein in keratin aggregation and terminal epidermal differentiation (Uhland, 2006). The proteolytic activation removes filaggrin monomer domains, and the N-terminal filaggrin S-100 regulatory protein (List, 2009). It can also activate profilaggrin indirectly by activating growth factors or remodeling the ECM (Uhland, 2006).

Matriptase is considered as an attractive therapeutical target in cancer treatment because of its role in extracellular matrix degradation, cell invasion, and growth factor activation (Galkin et al., 2004). Matriptase is overexpressed during tumor growth, invasion, and progression of breast, cervical, and ovarian cancer in humans (Saleem et al., 2006). Even though the importance of matriptase in PCa is found, little is known about its substrate or molecular actions. Matriptase is a potential activator of key molecules such as uPA and protease-activated receptor-2 that are involved in ECM degradation (Saleem et al., 2006). Another reported target of matriptase is Laminin-5 deposited in the basement membrane of the prostatic duct primarily by the basal epithelial cells (Ganguly et al., 2014).

The studies of Ustach et al. unveiled the signaling axis of matriptase/PDGF-D/β-PDGFR in PCa. Platelet-derived growth factors (PDGF) can induce cell migration, proliferation, and transformation. PDGF-A and PDGF-B are secreted as active growth factors and can immediately activate their respective receptors, α-PDGFR, and β-PDGFR, whereas PDGF-C and PDGF-D are secreted as latent homodimers consisting of an N-terminal CUB domain and a C-terminal growth factor domain (GFD). The CUB domain is removed to activate PDGF-C and PDGF-D. Matriptase activates PDGF-D by proteolytically removing CUB domain in a two-stage process. In the first stage, a hemidimer is formed followed by the second stage in which growth factor domain dimer (GFD-D) is generated. It can also deactivate PDGF-D by proteolysis within GFD and thus having a biphasic regulation (Ustach et al., 2010).

8.2.4.3 Hepsin

Hepsin is another serine protease which is overexpressed in PCa cells. Hepsin is also overexpressed in ovarian carcinomas and renal cell carcinomas (Magee et al., 2001). The hepsin upregulation is correlated with cancer progression. The hepsin mRNA levels were elevated in about 90% of prostate cancer examined in which most of the cases have more than 10-fold compared with those in noncancerous controls. Since hepsin is explicitly overexpressed in prostate cancer cells, it could be an ideal therapeutic target for treating PCa. The hepsin overexpression in the prostate epithelium leads to the degradation of the basement membrane, and the overexpression in prostate cancer cells promotes lymph node metastasis (Ganguly et al., 2014). Moreover, in vitro, anti-hepsin antibodies could inhibit the human PCa invasion (Wu and Parry, 2007).

Function of hepsin

Hepsin participates in ECM degradation either directly or indirectly (Fig. 8.5). It is proposed to activate pro-MMPs and other protease zymogens that are involved in matrix remodeling scenarios such as cancer metastasis and invasion (Wilkinson et al., 2017). Hepsin can activate HGF by cleaving pro-HGF, secreted by activated fibroblasts present in the stroma, which may in turn activate tyrosine kinase Met signaling pathway leading to scattering, migration, and invasion of the epithelial cell (Ganguly et al., 2014). Like matriptase, hepsin is also reported to target Laminin-5, a major constituent of the basement membrane present in the prostate which is lost during the development of prostate cancer (Ganguly et al., 2014).

Structure of hepsin

Hepsin is encoded by HPN gene, and the cDNA encodes a polypeptide of 417 amino acids (Kelly et al., 2008; Wu and Parry, 2007). Hepsin is a type II transmembrane serine protease with N-terminal cytoplasmic domain, a membrane-spanning domain, and a 373-residue extracellular domain. The crystal structure of hepsin showed that the extracellular region of hepsin forms an elongated structure with two distinct domains. The larger C-terminal 255-residue extracellular domain contains a serine protease region (Fig. 8.4). The remaining residues of the extracellular region showed no significant similarity to other known sequences and referred to as a noncatalytic chain. The crystal structure revealed that the region forms a scavenger receptor cysteine-rich (SRCR) domain. The sequence of the larger domains is homologous with the members of the chymotrypsin family of serine proteases (Wu and Parry, 2007). Hepsin is synthesized as a single chain, and during the activation process, the proteolytic cleavage between Arg162 and Ile 163 separates the serine protease domain from the rest of the protein. The two chains remain covalently bound through a disulfide bond between Cys277 of the serine protease domain and Cys153 of the noncatalytic region (Somoza et al., 2003). This disulfide bond attaches the protease domain on the cell surface. The association between the domains is further stabilized by an extensive network of hydrophobic interactions and salt bridges (Somoza et al., 2003).

The serine protease region of hepsin showed similar architecture to that of the chymotrypsin family consisting of two six-stranded β-barrels of approximately equal size joined together to form the active site and substrate binding site. The primary sequence alignment of this serine protease region showed the conservation of sequence with the related enzymes. The residues 163-404 of hepsin are homologous to enterokinase, matriptase, and chymotrypsin with a similarity of 44%, 42%, and 41%, respectively (Somoza et al., 2003).

The residues in the noncatalytic region 50–159 consist of three regions of regular secondary structure such as a 12-residue α-helix, a twisted five-stranded antiparallel β-sheet, and a second two-standard antiparallel β-sheet. The two β-sheets are located roughly right angles to each other with the helix located between the two. The noncatalytic region is held together by three intradomain disulfide bonds, between Cys190-Cys150; Cys 119-Cys138, and Cys77-Cys140. The residues present in the noncatalytic region from 50 to 151 forms a fairly compact structure with remaining eight residues extends away from the rest of the domain at the C terminus. This extended region plays a critical role in binding to the serine protease domain (Somoza et al., 2003).

TTSPs are mostly regulated by membrane-anchored Kunitz-type inhibitor and Hepatocyte activator inhibitor (HAI-1) (List, 2009). HAI-1 consists of two Kunitz domains, a low-density lipoprotein receptor class A, and a transmembrane region (List, 2009). The crystal structures of prototypic bovine pancreatic trypsin inhibitor and HAI-1 with matriptase were solved. Kunitz domain 1 is responsible for the inhibitory action of HAI-1. The substrate binding cleft and 60-loop region of matriptase binds to the Kunitz domain 1 of HAI-1. Similar to other Kunitz-type inhibitors, the side chain of reactive loop P1 residue (Arg-260) of the inhibitor is inserted deep into the S1 pocket of matriptase. Apart from HAI-1, α_1-antitrypsin and α_2-antiplasmin can also inhibit matriptase, whereas only a few protein inhibitors were identified to inhibit hepsin.

8.2.5 Other serine proteases

Some other serine proteases were also identified to affect the progression and treatment of prostate cancer. Among them, dipeptidyl peptidase IV, site-1 protease, and site-2protease were studied in prostate cancer.

Dipeptidyl peptidase IV (DPPIV/CD26) is a 110kDa glycoprotein that is present in the cell surface and belongs to the serine protease family. DPPIV is present on various tissues including T lymphocyte, endothelial cells, and epithelial cells. DPPIV controls the activities of mitogenic growth factors and neuropeptides. The protease activity inactivates and degrades these peptides. DPPIV is involved in various physiological functions such as cell differentiation, adhesion, immunomodulation, and apoptosis. DPPIV is usually expressed in normal epithelial cells and melanocytes. The lost activity of DPPIV in various cancers suggests its role in cancer progression. The reexpression of DPPIV in melanoma and lung cancers had shown there occurrence of exogenous growth factors (Havre et al., 2008; Sun et al., 2008; Wesley et al., 2005). In prostate cancer, it can degrade basic fibroblast growth factor (bFGF) (Wesley et al., 2005) or stromal derived factor (SDF-1/CXCL12) (Sun et al., 2008).

A membrane-bound serine protease, site-1 protease (S1P), along with S2P site-2 protease (S2P) is involved in cancer progression indirectly. S2P is a membrane-bound metalloprotease with a luminally disposed active site. S1P and S2P are involved in trafficking of SREBP-1 to the nucleus which is required for the de novo lipogenesis in cancer cells. The lipogenic phenotype is the major characteristic of cancer, which makes the cancer cells independent of systemic regulation. SREBP-1 is highly activated in cancer cells and plays a crucial role in connecting oncogenic signaling-regulated glucose and glutamine metabolism to *de novo* lipid synthesis. Genetic and pharmacological targeting of SREBP-1 can significantly inhibit tumor cell growth (Guan et al., 2011, 2015; Verhelst, 2017). But studies revealed that targeting S2P is more efficient than S1P in treating prostate cancer (Guan et al., 2012).

8.3. Targeting serine proteases for cancer therapy

Currently available FDA approved drugs for the treatment of prostate cancer fall in one among the following classes—antiandrogen (Abiraterone Acetate, Apalutamide, Bicalutamide, and Cabazitaxel), inhibitors of type II topoisomerase such as Mitoxantrone Hydrochloride, stimulators of the immune system such as Sipuleucel-T, and a radioactive therapeutic agent such as Radium 223 Dichloride. Till date protease inhibitors are only approved by FDA as antiretroviral drugs.

For designing drugs that target proteases, it is needed to understand the complexity of the physiological processes in which they are involved, the mechanism of action, and even their structure and biochemistry. Proteases participating in extracellular matrix degradation during cancer progression belong to multiple classes of proteases. The activation of a single protease may require consecutive proteolytic actions of several other proteases.

MMPs were the first protease targets considered for cancer therapy. Several hydroxamates and nonhydroxamates were developed as MMP inhibitors. Several of these inhibitors were tested in advanced clinical trials, but all failed because of several side effects without significant therapeutic benefit. Most of MMP inhibitors have a broad-spectrum activity that could inhibit proteases required for normal biological processes. Moreover, they were found ineffective against late-stage tumors. For all these reasons, further studies on MMP inhibitors were abandoned (Winer et al., 2018).

8.3.1 Protease-targeted drug discovery against prostate cancer

A protein target should have altered activity during the disease and often due to change in expression of the enzyme. Proteases are regulated either at the transcriptional level or by the action of inhibitors on the matured enzyme. Several inhibitors of serine proteases were earlier reported for anticancer activity. Among them, the Bowman-Birk inhibitor from soybean with chymotrypsin and trypsin inhibitory activity was reported to have a positive effect in treating oral cancer in phase II clinical trials. It is believed to work similarly to bortezomib (Velcade; Millennium) a proteasome inhibitor approved for cancer therapy (Turk, 2006).

HIV-1 protease inhibitors such as ritonavir, saquinavir, and indinavir were found to have antiproliferative activity on DU145 and PC-3 androgen-independent prostate cancer cells. Ritonavir increased the antiproliferative and proapoptotic effects of other anticancer drugs such as docetaxel in DU145 cells by inhibiting NFκB which is one of the reasons for drug resistance in cancer cells (Ikezoe et al., 2004). Another HIV-1 protease inhibitor nelfinavir inhibited growth and induced apoptosis in LNCaP, DU145, and PC-3 cells of prostate cancer. Nelfinavir was found to block AR signaling by downregulating nuclear levels of androgen receptor and PSA. Moreover, nelfinavir disrupted STAT3 and AKT signaling. It can also block interleukin-6-induced phosphorylation of STAT3 and inhibits STAT3 DNA binding activity in LNCaP and DU145 cells (Yang et al., 2005).

Some research is going on to produce neutralizing antibodies against protease targets in prostate cancer. A set of monoclonal antibodies that neutralize hepsin was generated and found to suppress the tumor invasion, although it failed to suppress the tumor growth. The study revealed that hepsin has a significant role in tumor invasion and not in tumor growth (Xuan et al., 2006).

A novel class of targeted anticancer agents called therapeutic oncolytic viruses (virotherapeutics) is also studied for treating prostate cancer (Liu et al., 2007). In 1997, Rodriguez et al. developed a replication-competent, cytolytic Ad5 adenovirus named as CN706 (renamed to CV706) which was used as a PSA-promoter-enhancer element to control E1A expression and thus to limit expression only in PSA-producing cells (Rodriguez et al., 1997). In 2001, CV706 (now known as CG7060) was found safe after phase I clinical trials. It has not shown irreversible grade 3 or any grade 4 toxicity (DeWeese et al., 2001). Another oncolytic virus studied against prostate cancer was CG7870 using rat probasin promoter to control E1A expression and PSA promoter-enhancer to control E1B expression. In phase I trial of intravenous administration of GG7870 flu-like symptoms were found as most common adverse events. Further clinical trials were halted even though there is no clinically significant adverse effects (Small et al., 2006).

Maspin, a serine protease inhibitor, was found to inhibit tumor invasion and metastasis by inhibiting cell surface-associated uPA in DU145 PCa cell line. In fact, maspin itself is a protein that in humans is encoded by SERPINB5 gene.

The inhibitory activity of this maspin was found to be almost equal to that of plasminogen activator inhibitor 1 and plasminogen activator inhibitor 2 with K_i of 20 nM (McGowen et al., 2000).

Unlike the serine proteases mentioned above with proliferation effect and serine protease inhibitor with antiproliferation effects, there are serine proteases like Dipeptidyl peptidase IV (DPPIV) with tumor suppression activity and serine protease inhibitor such as SLPI (secretory leukocyte peptidase inhibitor) which can aid proliferation and inhibit apoptosis. DPPIV is a membrane glycoprotein and found to regulate the mitogenic growth factors and neuropeptides by inactivation or degradation of these peptides. It regulates growth factors such as bFGF and ERK1/2, which may, in turn, promote uPA production (Wesley et al., 2005). SLPI is overexpressed in LNCaP cell lines, and it aids tumor proliferation by protecting the growth factor progranulin from elastase and by suppressing apoptosis which is independent of its antiprotease effect (Zheng et al., 2016).

8.4. Conclusions

Serine proteases, the most abundant proteases in nature, are involved in all physiological activities, including cancer progression. Targeting the pericellular and membrane-bound serine proteases involved in PCa progression is a significant therapeutical strategy. Among the serine proteases involved in cancer, PSA is specific to prostate cancer, and it is validated as a prominent diagnostic and prognostic biomarker. Another major serine protease, which is ubiquitously found in all types of cancer, is uPA. Other serine proteases such as kallikreins and membrane-associated serine proteases can activate a cascade of proteolytic activities directly or by activating other types of proteases such as MMPs and growth factors. The activated proteases and growth factors lead to extracellular matrix degradation and metastasis. Much research is going on to find specific regulators of these proteases involved in PCa progression. Even though there is no current FDA approved drugs available for treating prostate cancer, some antiretroviral FDA approved protease inhibitors such as saquinavir and nelfinavir are in clinical trials for treating prostate cancer.

Acknowledgments

B.S. Harish earnestly acknowledges SASTRA Deemed University for teaching assistantship. KBU (SB/FTP/ETA-212/2012) thank Department of Science and Technology, Government of India for the financial support.

References

Balsara, R.D., Ploplis, V.A., 2008. Plasminogen activator inhibitor-1: the double edged sword in apoptosis. Thromb. Haemost. 100, 1029–1036.

Bélanger, A., Van Halbeek, H., Graves, H.C., Grandbois, K., Stamey, T.A., Huang, L., et al., 1995. Molecular mass and carbohydrate structure of prostate specific antigen: studies for establishment of an international PSA standard. Prostate 27, 187–197.

Binder, B.R., Mihaly, J., 2008. The plasminogen activator inhibitor "paradox" in cancer. Immunol. Lett. 118, 116–124.

Chen, Y.-W., Lee, M.-S., Lucht, A., Chou, F.-P., Huang, W., Havighurst, T.C., et al., 2010. TM-PRSS2, a serine protease expressed in the prostate on the apical surface of luminal epithelial cells and released into semen in prostasomes, is misregulated in prostate cancer cells. Am. J. Pathol. 176, 2986–2996.

Cheng, T.-S., Chen, W.-C., Lin, Y.-Y., Tsai, C.-H., Liao, C.-I., Shyu, H.-Y., et al., 2013. Curcumin-targeting pericellular serine protease matriptase role in suppression of prostate cancer cell invasion, tumor growth and metastasis. Cancer Prev. Res. 6, 495–505.

Dall'Era, M.A., Cooperberg, M.R., Chan, J.M., Davies, B.J., Albertsen, P.C., Klotz, L.H., et al., 2008. Active surveillance for early-stage prostate cancer: review of the current literature. Cancer 112, 1650–1659.

Danø, K., Behrendt, N., Høyer-Hansen, G., Johnsen, M., Lund, L.R., Ploug, M., et al., 2005. Plasminogen activation and cancer. Thromb. Haemost. 93, 676–681.

Darson, M.F., Pacelli, A., Roche, P., Rittenhouse, H.G., Wolfert, R.L., Young, C.Y., et al., 1997. Human glandular kallikrein 2 (hK2) expression in prostatic intraepithelial neoplasia and adenocarcinoma: a novel prostate cancer marker. Urology 49, 857–862.

Dass, K., Ahmad, A., Azmi, A.S., Sarkar, S.H., Sarkar, F.H., 2008. Evolving role of uPA/uPAR system in human cancers. Cancer Treat. Rev. 34, 122–136.

Dehm, S.M., Tindall, D.J., 2007. Androgen receptor structural and functional elements: role and regulation in prostate cancer. Mol. Endocrinol. 21, 2855–2863.

DeWeese, T.L., van der Poel, H., Li, S., Mikhak, B., Drew, R., Goemann, M., et al., 2001. A phase I trial of CV706, a replication-competent, PSA selective oncolytic adenovirus, for the treatment of locally recurrent prostate cancer following radiation therapy. Cancer Res. 61, 7464–7472.

Dong, Z., Saliganan, A.D., Meng, H., Nabha, S.M., Sabbota, A.L., Sheng, S., et al., 2008. Prostate cancer cell-derived urokinase-type plasminogen activator contributes to intraosseous tumor growth and bone turnover. Neoplasia 10, 439–449.

Dudani, J.S., Ibrahim, M., Kirkpatrick, J., Warren, A.D., Bhatia, S.N., 2018. Classification of prostate cancer using a protease activity nanosensor library. Proc. Natl. Acad. Sci. U. S. A. 115, 8954–8959.

Duffy, M.J., 2004. The urokinase plasminogen activator system: role in malignancy. Curr. Pharm. Des. 10, 39–49.

Friedrich, R., Fuentes-Prior, P., Ong, E., Coombs, G., Hunter, M., Oehler, R., et al., 2002. Catalytic domain structures of MT-SP1/matriptase, a matrix-degrading transmembrane serine proteinase. J. Biol. Chem. 277, 2160–2168.

Galkin, A.V., Mullen, L., Fox, W.D., Brown, J., Duncan, D., Moreno, O., et al., 2004. CVS-3983, a selective matriptase inhibitor, suppresses the growth of androgen independent prostate tumor xenografts. Prostate 61, 228–235.

Ganguly, S.S., Li, X., Miranti, C.K., 2014. The host microenvironment influences prostate cancer invasion, systemic spread, bone colonization, and osteoblastic metastasis. Front. Oncol. 4, 364.

Gaweł-Bęben, K., Ali, N., Ellis, V., Velasco, G., Poghosyan, Z., Ager, A., et al., 2018. TMEFF2 shedding is regulated by oxidative stress and mediated by ADAMs and transmembrane serine proteases implicated in prostate cancer. Cell Biol. Int. 42, 273–280.

Gilgunn, S., Conroy, P.J., Saldova, R., Rudd, P.M., O'kennedy, R.J., 2013. Aberrant PSA glycosylation—a sweet predictor of prostate cancer. Nat. Rev. Urol. 10, 99.

Goettig, P., Magdolen, V., Brandstetter, H., 2010. Natural and synthetic inhibitors of kallikrein-related peptidases (KLKs). Biochimie 92, 1546–1567.

Guan, M., Fousek, K., Jiang, C., Guo, S., Synold, T., Xi, B., et al., 2011. Nelfinavir induces liposarcoma apoptosis through inhibition of regulated intramembrane proteolysis of SREBP-1 and ATF6. Clin. Cancer Res. 17, 1796–1806.

Guan, M., Fousek, K., Chow, W.A., 2012. Nelfinavir inhibits regulated intramembrane proteolysis of sterol regulatory element binding protein-1 and activating transcription factor 6 in castration-resistant prostate cancer. FEBS J. 279, 2399–2411.

Guan, M., Su, L., Yuan, Y.-C., Li, H., Chow, W.A., 2015. Nelfinavir and nelfinavir analogs block site-2 protease cleavage to inhibit castration-resistant prostate cancer. Sci. Rep. 5, 9698.

Guerrico, A.G., Hillman, D., Karnes, J., Davis, B., Gaston, S., Klee, G., 2017. Roles of kallikrein-2 biomarkers (free-hK2 and pro-hK2) for predicting prostate cancer progression-free survival. J. Circ. Biomark. 6, 1–8.

Havre, P.A., Abe, M., Urasaki, Y., Ohnuma, K., Morimoto, C., Dang, N.H., 2008. The role of CD26/dipeptidyl peptidase IV in cancer. Front. Biosci. 13, 1634–1645.

Hayes, J.H., Barry, M.J., 2014. Screening for prostate cancer with the prostate-specific antigen test: a review of current evidence. JAMA 311, 1143–1149.

Hong, S.K., 2014. Kallikreins as biomarkers for prostate cancer. Biomed. Res. Int. 2014, 1–10.

Ikezoe, T., Hisatake, Y., Takeuchi, T., Ohtsuki, Y., Yang, Y., Said, J.W., et al., 2004. HIV-1 protease inhibitor, ritonavir: a potent inhibitor of CYP3A4, enhanced the anticancer effects of docetaxel in androgen-independent prostate cancer cells in vitro and in vivo. Cancer Res. 64, 7426–7431.

Kelly, K.A., Setlur, S.R., Ross, R., Anbazhagan, R., Waterman, P., Rubin, M.A., et al., 2008. Detection of early prostate cancer using a hepsin-targeted imaging agent. Cancer Res. 68, 2286–2291.

Klezovitch, O., Chevillet, J., Mirosevich, J., Roberts, R.L., Matusik, R.J., Vasioukhin, V., 2004. Hepsin promotes prostate cancer progression and metastasis. Cancer Cell 6, 185–195.

Ko, C.-J., Huang, C.-C., Lin, H.-Y., Juan, C.-P., Lan, S.-W., Shyu, H.-Y., et al., 2015. Androgen-induced TMPRSS2 activates matriptase and promotes extracellular matrix degradation, prostate cancer cell invasion, tumor growth and metastasis. Cancer Res. 74, 2949–2960.

Kwaan, H.C., McMahon, B., 2009. The role of plasminogen-plasmin system in cancer. In: Coagulation in Cancer, Cancer Treatment and Research. vol. 148. Springer, pp. 43–66.

Lawrence, M.G., Lai, J., Clements, J.A., 2010. Kallikreins on steroids: structure, function, and hormonal regulation of prostate-specific antigen and the extended kallikrein locus. Endocr. Rev. 31, 407–446.

LeBeau, A.M., Denmeade, S.R., 2015. Protease-activated pore-forming peptides for the treatment and imaging of prostate cancer. Mol. Cancer Ther. 14, 659–668.

LeBeau, A.M., Sevillano, N., Markham, K., Winter, M.B., Murphy, S.T., Hostetter, D.R., et al., 2015. Imaging active urokinase plasminogen activator in prostate cancer. Cancer Res. 75, 1225–1235.

Lilja, H., 1993. Structure, function, and regulation of the enzyme activity of prostate-specific antigen. World J. Urol. 11, 188–191.

Lin, B., Ferguson, C., White, J.T., Wang, S., Vessella, R., True, L.D., et al., 1999. Prostate-localized and androgen-regulated expression of the membrane-bound serine protease TMPRSS2. Cancer Res. 59, 4180–4184.

List, K., 2009. Matriptase: a culprit in cancer? Future Oncol. 5, 97–104.

Liu, T.-C., Galanis, E., Kirn, D., 2007. Clinical trial results with oncolytic virotherapy: a century of promise, a decade of progress. Nat. Rev. Clin. Oncol. 4, 101–117.

Magee, J.A., Araki, T., Patil, S., Ehrig, T., True, L., Humphrey, P.A., et al., 2001. Expression profiling reveals hepsin overexpression in prostate cancer. Cancer Res. 61, 5692–5696.

Masurier, N., Arama, D.P., El Amri, C., Lisowski, V., 2018. Inhibitors of kallikrein-related peptidases: an overview. Med. Res. Rev. 38, 655–683.

Mazhar, D., Waxman, J., 2002. Prostate cancer. Postgrad. Med J. 78, 590–595.

McCulloch, D.R., Harvey, M., Herington, A.C., 2000. The expression of the ADAMs proteases in prostate cancer cell lines and their regulation by dihydrotestosterone. Mol. Cell. Endocrinol. 167, 11–21.

McGowen, R., Biliran, H., Sager, R., Sheng, S., 2000. The surface of prostate carcinoma DU145 cells mediates the inhibition of urokinase-type plasminogen activator by maspin. Cancer Res. 60, 4771–4778.

Ménez, R., Michel, S., Muller, B.H., Bossus, M., Ducancel, F., Jolivet-Reynaud, C., et al., 2008. Crystal structure of a ternary complex between human prostate-specific antigen, its substrate acyl intermediate and an activating antibody. J. Mol. Biol. 376, 1021–1033.

Murray, A.S., Varela, F.A., List, K., 2016. Type II transmembrane serine proteases as potential targets for cancer therapy. Biol. Chem. 397, 815–826.

Partin, A.W., Catalona, W.J., Finlay, J.A., Darte, C., Tindall, D.J., Young, C.Y.-F., et al., 1999. Use of human glandular kallikrein 2 for the detection of prostate cancer: preliminary analysis. Urology 54, 839–845.

Pirazzoli, V., Ferraris, G.M.S., Sidenius, N., 2013. Direct evidence of the importance of vitronectin and its interaction with the urokinase receptor in tumor growth. Blood 121, 2316–2323.

Porkka, K.P., Visakorpi, T., 2004. Molecular mechanisms of prostate cancer. Eur. Urol. 45, 683–691.

Qureshi, T., Goswami, S., McClintock, C.S., Ramsey, M.T., Peterson, C.B., 2016. Distinct encounter complexes of PAI-1 with plasminogen activators and vitronectin revealed by changes in the conformation and dynamics of the reactive center loop. Protein Sci. 25, 499–510.

Rabbani, S., Harakidas, P., Davidson, D.J., Henkin, J., Mazar, A.P., 1995. Prevention of prostate-cancer metastasis in vivo by a novel synthetic inhibitor of urokinase-type plasminogen activator (uPA). Int. J. Cancer 63, 840–845.

Rittenhouse, H.G., Finlay, J.A., Mikolajczyk, S.D., Partin, A.W., 1998. Human kallikrein 2 (hK2) and prostate-specific antigen (PSA): two closely related, but distinct, kallikreins in the prostate. Crit. Rev. Clin. Lab. Sci. 35, 275–368.

Rodriguez, R., Schuur, E.R., Lim, H.Y., Henderson, G.A., Simons, J.W., Henderson, D.R., 1997. Prostate attenuated replication competent adenovirus (ARCA) CN706: a selective cytotoxic for prostate-specific antigen-positive prostate cancer cells. Cancer Res. 57, 2559–2563.

Saleem, M., Adhami, V.M., Zhong, W., Longley, B.J., Lin, C.-Y., Dickson, R.B., et al., 2006. A novel biomarker for staging human prostate adenocarcinoma: overexpression of matriptase with concomitant loss of its inhibitor, hepatocyte growth factor activator inhibitor-1. Cancer Epidemiol. Biomarkers Prev. 15, 217–227.

Shariat, S.F., Roehrborn, C.G., McConnell, J.D., Park, S., Alam, N., Wheeler, T.M., et al., 2007. Association of the circulating levels of the urokinase system of plasminogen activation with the presence of prostate cancer and invasion, progression, and metastasis. J. Clin. Oncol. 25, 349–355.

Sheng, S., 2001. The urokinase-type plasminogen activator system in prostate cancer metastasis. Cancer Metastasis Rev. 20, 287–296.

Skala, W., Utzschneider, D.T., Magdolen, V., Debela, M., Guo, S., Craik, C.S., et al., 2014. Structure-function analyses of human kallikrein-related peptidase 2 establish the 99-loop as master regulator of activity. J. Biol. Chem. 289, 34267–34283.

Small, E.J., Carducci, M.A., Burke, J.M., Rodriguez, R., Fong, L., Van Ummersen, L., et al., 2006. A phase I trial of intravenous CG7870, a replication-selective, prostate-specific antigen–targeted oncolytic adenovirus, for the treatment of hormone-refractory, metastatic prostate cancer. Mol. Ther. 14, 107–117.

Soff, G.A., Sanderowitz, J., Gately, S., Verrusio, E., Weiss, I., Brem, S., et al., 1995. Expression of plasminogen activator inhibitor type 1 by human prostate carcinoma cells inhibits primary tumor growth, tumor-associated angiogenesis, and metastasis to lung and liver in an athymic mouse model. J. Clin. Invest. 96, 2593–2600.

Somoza, J.R., Ho, J.D., Luong, C., Ghate, M., Sprengeler, P.A., Mortara, K., et al., 2003. The structure of the extracellular region of human hepsin reveals a serine protease domain and a novel scavenger receptor cysteine-rich (SRCR) domain. Structure 11, 1123–1131.

Stura, E.A., Muller, B.H., Bossus, M., Michel, S., Jolivet-Reynaud, C., Ducancel, F., 2011. Crystal structure of human prostate-specific antigen in a sandwich antibody complex. J. Mol. Biol. 414, 530–544.

Sun, Y.-X., Pedersen, E.A., Shiozawa, Y., Havens, A.M., Jung, Y., Wang, J., et al., 2008. CD26/dipeptidyl peptidase IV regulates prostate cancer metastasis by degrading SDF-1/CXCL12. Clin. Exp. Metastasis 25, 765–776.

Tanabe, L.M., List, K., 2017. The role of type II transmembrane serine protease-mediated signaling in cancer. FEBS J. 284, 1421–1436.

Tang, D.G., Porter, A.T., 1997. Target to apoptosis: a hopeful weapon for prostate cancer. Prostate 32, 284–293.

Turk, B., 2006. Targeting proteases: successes, failures and future prospects. Nat. Rev. Drug Discov. 5, 785–799.

Uhland, K., 2006. Matriptase and its putative role in cancer. Cell. Mol. Life Sci. 63, 2968–2978.

Ustach, C.V., Huang, W., Conley-LaComb, M.K., Lin, C.-Y., Che, M., Abrams, J., et al., 2010. A novel signaling axis of matriptase/PDGF-D/β-PDGFR in human prostate cancer. Cancer Res. 70, 9631–9640.

Verhelst, S.H., 2017. Intramembrane proteases as drug targets. FEBS J. 284, 1489–1502.

Vest, D., Schalken, J.A., Muir, G., Dasgupta, P., 2010. Transmembrane protease serine 2 in prostate cancer. BJU Int. 105, 1490–1492.

Webber, M.M., Waghray, A., Bello, D., 1995. Prostate-specific antigen, a serine protease, facilitates human prostate cancer cell invasion. Clin. Cancer Res. 1, 1089–1094.

Wesley, U.V., McGroarty, M., Homoyouni, A., 2005. Dipeptidyl peptidase inhibits malignant phenotype of prostate cancer cells by blocking basic fibroblast growth factor signaling pathway. Cancer Res. 65, 1325–1334.

Wilkinson, D.J., Desilets, A., Lin, H., Charlton, S., Arques, M.C., Falconer, A., et al., 2017. The serine proteinase hepsin is an activator of pro-matrix metalloproteinases: molecular mechanisms and implications for extracellular matrix turnover. Sci. Rep. 7, 16693.

Winer, A., Adams, S., Mignatti, P., 2018. Matrix metalloproteinase inhibitors in cancer therapy: turning past failures into future successes. Mol. Cancer Ther. 17, 1147–1155.

Wu, Q., Parry, G., 2007. Hepsin and prostate cancer. Front. Biosci. 12, 5052–5059.

Wu, S.-R., Cheng, T.-S., Chen, W.-C., Shyu, H.-Y., Ko, C.-J., Huang, H.-P., et al., 2010. Matriptase is involved in ErbB-2-induced prostate cancer cell invasion. Am. J. Pathol. 177, 3145–3158.

Xuan, J.-A., Schneider, D., Toy, P., Lin, R., Newton, A., Zhu, Y., et al., 2006. Antibodies neutralizing hepsin protease activity do not impact cell growth but inhibit invasion of prostate and ovarian tumor cells in culture. Cancer Res. 66, 3611–3619.

Yang, Y., Ikezoe, T., Takeuchi, T., Adachi, Y., Ohtsuki, Y., Takeuchi, S., et al., 2005. HIV-1 protease inhibitor induces growth arrest and apoptosis of human prostate cancer LNCaP cells in vitro and in vivo in conjunction with blockade of androgen receptor STAT3 and AKT signaling. Cancer Sci. 96, 425–433.

Yu, D.-C., Sakamoto, G.T., Henderson, D.R., 1999. Identification of the transcriptional regulatory sequences of human kallikrein 2 and their use in the construction of calydon virus 764, an attenuated replication competent adenovirus for prostate cancer therapy. Cancer Res. 59, 1498–1504.

Zhao, B., Yuan, C., Li, R., Qu, D., Huang, M., Ngo, J.C.K., 2013. Crystal structures of matriptase in complex with its inhibitor hepatocyte growth factor activator inhibitor-1. J. Biol. Chem. 288, 11155–11164.

Zheng, D., Gui, B., Gray, K., Tinay, I., Rafiei, S., Huang, Q., et al., 2016. Secretory leukocyte protease inhibitor is a survival and proliferation factor for castration-resistant prostate cancer. Oncogene 35, 4807–4815.

Chapter 9

HCV NS3 serine protease as a drug target for the development of drugs against hepatocellular carcinoma (liver cancer)

Rishitha Gundala, Himani Balutia, R. Lavanya, Ravichandiran Velayutham, Kuldeep K. Roy
National Institute of Pharmaceutical Education and Research (NIPER), Kolkata, India

9.1 Introduction

Chronic HCV infection is the major cause of advanced liver fibrosis, cirrhosis, and hepatocellular carcinoma (HCC) and thus, HCV infection represents a major public health problem worldwide. In fact, HCV-induced HCC is a progressive disease affected by the duration and genotype of HCV infection (Bruno et al., 2007) and is the second leading cause of cancer-related death worldwide (Axley et al., 2018; Bosetti et al., 2014). According to the World Health Organization report, approximately 3% of the world population are infected with HCV, while 130–170 million people are persistently infected with HCV and they remain at high risk of developing HCC and other associated liver disorders in later stage of their life. The prevalence of HCV-related HCC varies over different geographic location and ethnicity. In the United States, Europe, Japan, and South America, the HCC is mainly caused by HCV infection; while on the other hand, in majority of Asia and Africa, it is mainly caused by HBV (Hepatitis B virus). In Japan, an estimated 85% of patients with HCC are infected with HCV (Sievert et al., 2011), while in contrast, around 50%–60% of patients with HCC are infected with HCV in the United States (Altekruse et al., 2014). Despite the advent of highly effective treatment option using direct-acting antiviral (DAA) agents, the morbidity and incidence of HCV-related HCC remain high. Therefore, for the successful prevention and control of HCV infection and HCV-induced HCC, there is an urgent need of novel and effective therapeutics.

There is a wide genetic diversity in HCV with six genotypes and several subtypes of different global distribution and prevalence (Abro et al., 2010). After an extensive effort, an oral cancer vaccine called Hepcortespenlisimut-L

Cancer-Leading Proteases. https://doi.org/10.1016/B978-0-12-818168-3.00009-7

(Hepko-V5) has received U.S. Food and Drug Administration (FDA) approval for HCC and is given an orphan drug designation (Pan et al., 2015). The objective of HCV therapy is to eradicate the infection, reduce the transmission rate from patients to other individuals, and decrease the risk of progressive development of HCC. Direct-acting antiviral agents are promising HCV treatment options with limitations of side effects and emerging cases of drug resistance (Kohli et al., 2014). Based on the mode of action, DAAs for HCV treatment can be classified into HCV NS3/4A serine protease inhibitors, NS3 NTPase/helicase inhibitors, NS5B polymerase inhibitors, NS5A inhibitors, and others. The HCV NS3/4A protease is a leading therapeutic target that has provided five FDA-approved drugs, e.g., telaprevir, boceprevir, simeprevir, paritaprevir, and grazoprevir, as NS3/4A protease inhibitors (PIs) for HCV treatment. In addition, a number of candidate molecules, such as asunaprevir, vaniprevir, danoprevir, sovaprevir, deldeprevir, GS-9256, and IDX320 are in different phases of clinical development. In addition, various DAAs including RNA-dependent RNA polymerase inhibitors and NS5A inhibitors are under clinical evaluation against HCV infection. Although the DAAs targeting NS3/4A protease inhibition has improved the treatment of HCV genotype-1, all protease inhibitors have shown lower potency against HCV genotype 3. In fact, certain HCV genotypes are linked with superior risk for development of HCC. Studies in a large cohort of patients from the USA Veterans Affairs medical system have revealed that in comparison to HCV genotype 1, the genotype 3 was linked with 80% higher risk of HCC (Kanwal et al., 2014). While less frequent in developed countries, HCV genotype 6 leads to a higher risk of HCC (Lai et al., 2017; Lee et al., 2017). This chapter covers the wide variety of HCV NS3/4A protease inhibitors that have been either FDA-approved or under clinical trials for HCV treatment, and have a great potential for the prevention of HCV-induced HCC.

9.2 HCV genomic organization and progression of HCV to HCC

HCV is a hepatotropic single-stranded RNA virus belonging to the *Hepacivirus* genus in the *Flaviviridae* family (Dubuisson and Cosset, 2014; Karayiannis, 2017; Kim and Chang, 2013). These viruses consist of 9.6 kb of a single-stranded RNA that encodes a polyprotein of 3000 amino acids length (Dubuisson and Cosset, 2014; Karayiannis, 2017; Kim and Chang, 2013). The sequential cleavage of HCV polyprotein leads to 10 different products: core protein (C), envelope glycoproteins E1 and E2, p7, nonstructural proteins NS2, NS3, NS4A, NS4B, NS5A, and NS5B. Fig. 9.1 describes distinct functions attributed to 10 protein products resulting from the HCV polyprotein cleavage. The progression of HCV infection into HCC is a slow and gradual process that may span over 20–40 years (Vescovo et al., 2016). HCV enters host, replicates in hepatocytes, and releases its protein component in cytosol that leads to a variety of cellular and immune mediated changes leading to HCC. The HCV-infected patients

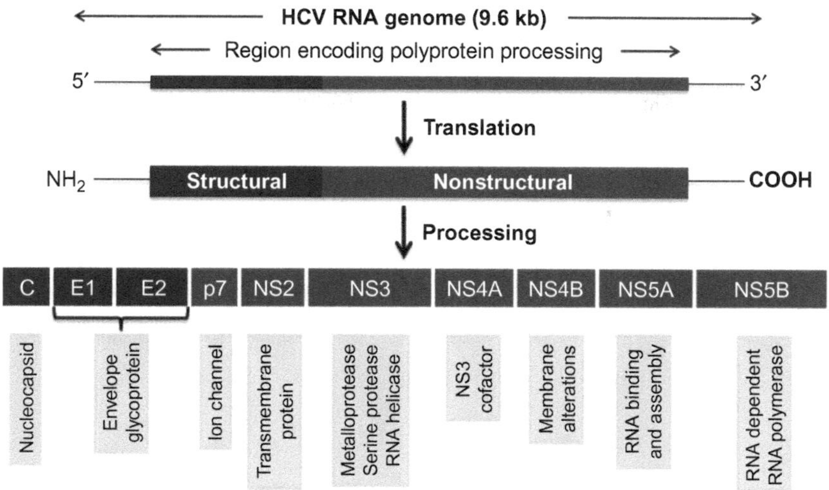

FIG. 9.1 Schematic representation of the HCV genome structure and various functions of the structural and nonstructural proteins of the polyprotein encoded by the HCV genome.

fail to clear the virus and thus, HCV resides in the host for an extended duration (more than 20 years) causing chronic HCV infection and a high risk for HCV-induced progressive liver diseases like cirrhosis and HCC. Although direct confirmation of oncogenic potential of HCV on hepatocytes (liver cells) is restricted to animal models, it is well established that HCV proteins, which have a major role in driving viral replication and HCV particle assembly, can influence directly on cell signaling pathways and metabolic mechanisms to induce or promote HCC. Both structural and nonstructural proteins produced after the cleavage of the HCV polyprotein interact with various host proteins to regulate malignancy of hepatocytes (Fig. 9.1). The direct role of HCV in the induction of HCC through interaction of its individual protein with various cellular pathways are illustrated in Table 9.1.

9.3 HCV NS3 protease: Structural perspective

The HCV NS3 protease is a 631 amino acids long bifunctional protein under the chymotrypsin family. The NS3 protease structure consists of two subdomains: N-terminal serine protease (180 amino acids) and C-terminal helicase (451 amino acids) domains [18], and each domain has a β-barrel, with the catalytic triad residues, namely His57, Asp81, and Ser139, located at the interdomain interface (Fig. 9.2) (Bartenschlager et al., 1993; Failla et al., 1995). Amino acids, His57 and Asp81, are part of the N-terminal β-barrel and Ser139 lie in the C-terminal β-barrel. Unlike other proteins in chymotrypsin family, the NS3 protease is small in size, structurally unstable independently, and involves the binding of zinc (Zn^{2+}) ion to maintain its structural integrity (Kim et al., 1996).

TABLE 9.1 Direct role of HCV in causing liver fibrosis, cirrhosis, and hepatocellular carcinoma.

HCV proteins	Reaction pathways[a]	End effects
Core	p53, p73, pRb, Ras, Wnt/β-catenin, Raf1/MAPK, TGF-β, PPAR-α, NFκB	Steatosis, oxidative stress, insulin resistance, proliferation, apoptosis
E1 and E2	PKR, ATF-2, TGF-β-TLR, MAPK/ERK	Proliferation, EMT, mitochondrial dysregulation
NS2	Cyclin D—CDK4, p53/p21	Proliferation, apoptosis
NS3	PKA-p38, p53/p21, NFκB, IRF3	Proliferation, apoptosis, innate response
NS4A and NS4B	Wnt/β-catenin	Proliferation
NS5A	JAK/STAT3, p53, BCL2, NFκB, VEGF, PI3K/akt/mTOR, Wnt/β-catenin, TGF-β-TLR	Lipid metabolism, oxidative stress, EMT, proliferation, apoptosis
NS5B	E2F1/Rb	Proliferation, genomic instability

[a] *MAPK, mitogen-activated protein kinase; TGF, transforming growth factor; PPAR-α, peroxisome proliferator-activated receptor alpha; NFκB, nuclear factor-κB; PKR, protein kinase; ERK, extracellular signal regulated protein kinase; CDK, cyclin-dependent kinase; PKA, protein kinase A; IRF, interferon-regulatory factor; VEGF, vascular endothelial growth factor; TNF-α, tumor necrosis factor-α; EMT, epithelial to mesenchymal trans-differentiation.*

The complex of NS3 protease and Zn has enzymatic activity, but requires an association with the NS4A protein, comprising 54 amino acids, or association with at least a peptide containing its central hydrophobic part of 14 amino acids, which adopts a β-strand conformation and contributes to the N-terminal β-barrel (Kim et al., 1996; Penin et al., 2004; Venkatakrishnan and Zlotnick, 2016).

9.3.1 HCV NS3 protease zinc-binding site

The structure of the NS3 protease is not stable due to its small size and hence it involves the binding of zinc ion (Zn^{2+}) to maintain its structural integrity. In fact, zinc ion is necessary for the structural integrity and stability of the properly folded protein, and its exclusion from the structure leads to the enzyme inactivation. X-ray structures of NS3 protease showed that there is a tetradentate zinc-binding site located in cleft between two β-barrels, where zinc is coordinated with the side chain of four amino acids, namely Cys97, Cys99, Cys145, and His149 (Fig. 9.2) (Kim et al., 1996). This zinc binding site is located at the opposite end of the catalytic triad. Mutagenesis and NMR experiments revealed the vital role of three cysteine residues in zinc coordination and enzyme activity,

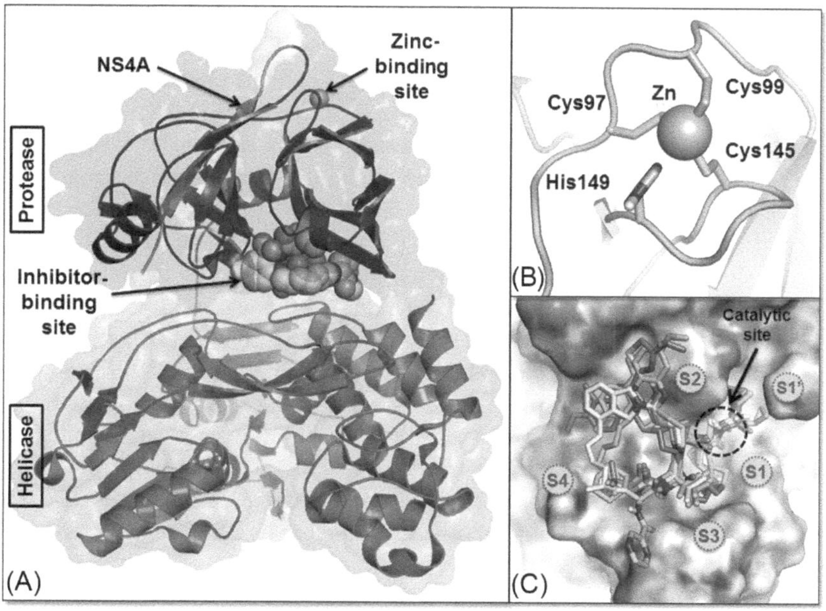

FIG. 9.2 Schematic depiction of: (A) the full-length HCV NS3/4A protease, (B) the zinc-binding site in NS3/4A coordinated with Cys97, Cys99, Cys145, and His149, and (C) the overlay of the selected inhibitors of NS3/4A protease into the substrate-binding pocket.

while indicating a subtle role of His149. In fact, NMR studies indicated that the side chain of His149 participates indirectly to zinc coordination through a bridging hydroxyl ion (Penin et al., 2004; Venkatakrishnan and Zlotnick, 2016).

9.3.2 HCV NS3 protease substrate binding site

Like other proteins of the chymotrypsin family, the HCV NS3 protease has some highly conserved characteristics, e.g., a catalytic triad, comprising amino acids namely His57, Asp81, and Ser139, located at the interdomain interface, and an oxyanion hole formed by the backbone of Gly137 and Ser139. The overlay of selected protease inhibitors into the binding site is shown in Fig. 9.2C. The small size of the NS3 protease results into a comparatively shallow and solvent-exposed substrate binding cleft/groove, a significant deviation from other proteins of the chymotrypsin family, where several loops interact with the substrate or inhibitor to form a well-defined substrate binding cleft (Barbato et al., 2000; Penin et al., 2004; Venkatakrishnan and Zlotnick, 2016). As a result, the selective recognition of the substrate with HCV NS3 protease relies on various weak interactions along an extended contact surface of the binding pocket, and hence, the design of selective and high-affinity small-molecule HCV NS3 protease inhibitors has been a very daunting task, which may be solved with the application of various cutting-edge computer-aided drug design techniques using various available X-ray crystal structures of HCV NS3/4A protease.

Many site-directed mutagenesis studies have demonstrated that the P1 residue is the primary determinant of substrate specificity, while the S1 pocket accounts for the preference for a cysteine residue in this position (Bartenschlager et al., 1995). Apparently, the P1′ residue might also play some role in governing the substrate (or inhibitor) binding into the S1′ pocket and hence specificity of the substrate (or inhibitor). The amino acids over the P2–P4 regions are not shown to account for specificity, mainly because of the fact that the substrate binding groove is shallow, wide, and solvent exposed (De Francesco et al., 1999). Analysis of X-ray structures revealed that the S1 pocket is primarily characterized by three hydrophobic residues, namely Leu135, Phe154, and Ala157 (Kim et al., 1996; Love et al., 1996). Phe154 is located at the bottom of the S1 pocket, in an orientation to exhibit favorable van der Waals interactions with the P1 side chain of the substrate. The small and hydrophobic nature of this S1 pocket is complementary to a relatively small and lipophilic side chain of a cysteine amino acid, and hence, the S1 pocket has preference to a cysteine residue in this position of a substrate. In addition, the sulfhydryl group of a cysteine residue is known to form a favorable electrostatic interaction with Phe154 (Failla et al., 1996; Koch and Bartenschlager, 1997). All types of HCV NS3 cleavage sites possess an acidic amino acid, usually Asp, at the P6 position. Based on the facts that substrates are stabilized in the NS3 binding pocket via interaction extended over several peptide bonds, it is suggested that the minimal length required for an efficient substrate of NS3 protease is 10 amino acids (Steinkuhler et al., 1996).

9.4 HCV NS3/4A interaction complex and mechanistic role of NS4A in the activation of HCV NS3 protease

The NS3 protease has a serine protease domain at N-terminus and a RNA helicase domain at C-terminus, where the former is essential for the enzymatic activity (De Francesco et al., 1999). NS3 interacts with NS4A cofactor to form a functional HCV NS3/4A complex, which is essential for the cleavage at NS3/4A and NS4B/5A sites of HCV polyprotein. Moreover, the NS3/4A complex also enhances cleavage at all other sites of HCV polyprotein. Such processing of HCV polyprotein results in the formation of various active forms of HCV proteins, which are vital for viral replication. Therefore, inhibiting the formation of the stable and functional NS3/4A complex in turn will stop the viral replication.

The HCV NS3/4A complex adopts a canonical chymotrypsin-like fold consisting of N-terminal and C-terminal β-barrel domains of NS3 protease (Lesk and Fordham, 1996). The C-terminal β-barrel domain of NS3 protease closely resembles the six-stranded β-barrel present in other chymotrypsin like serine proteases, while N-terminal β-barrel domain has two additional β-strands, one contributed by N-terminal of NS3 protease and the other by the NS4A peptide

(De Francesco et al., 1999). NS4A has 14 hydrophobic amino acids and the central portion (residues 21–32) binds in a hydrophobic channel between β-strands of the N-terminal β-barrel domain of NS3 protease (Zhu and Briggs, 2011) and contributes a β-strand that intercalates in a β-strands within the N-terminal β-barrel domain of NS3 protease (De Francesco et al., 1999). The binding of NS4A brings conformational changes that results in the stabilization and activation of HCV NS3 protease (De Francesco et al., 1999). In the absence of NS4A peptide as a cofactor, the N-terminal domain of NS3 protease adopts an open chain conformation, while stabilization aided by binding with NS4A peptide results in the formation of molecular clamp-like conformation which locks the NS4A cofactor onto the NS3 protease N-terminal β-barrel (De Francesco et al., 1999).

The interaction of NS4A with the NS3 protease involves an extensive array of 15 antiparallel main-chain H-bonds. In addition, NS4A forms one main-chain H-bond with helix and two main-chain H-bonds with β-strands in another place. Most of these 18 main-chain H-bonds are quite stable in the NS3/4A complex system. It is further suggested that these main-chain H-bonds stabilize the remotely located catalytic site. It may further enable the NS4A to allosterically dictate the conformation of the catalytic site. The catalytic site having catalytic triad, consisting of His57, Asp81, and Ser139 amino acids, is located deep at the interface between the N- and C-domains of NS3 protease. His57 and Asp81 are located within the N-terminal β-barrel domain (De Francesco et al., 1999). In the apo-form crystal structure of NS3 protease, the carboxylate side chain of Asp81 directs itself away from His57 and is engaged via H-bond formation with the side chain of Arg155. While, on the other hand, in the crystal structure of NS3/4A complex, the carboxylate side chain of Asp81 is shown to form a H-bond with imidazole side chain of His57, and the polarized form of the latter acts as general base catalyst and abstracts a proton from the hydroxyl side chain group of catalytic Ser139 amino acid. Therefore, it is inferred that particular rotameric state of Asp81 is induced upon binding of the NS4A peptide or cofactor (Love et al., 1998), which might be leading to the enhancement of the proteolytic activity by activating the NS3 protease (De Francesco et al., 1999). In fact, the NS3/4A complex itself cannot be targeted by small molecules/peptides because the NS4A cofactor is deeply embedded inside NS3 and the NS3/4A interaction occurs very rapidly during polyprotein folding and prior to processing/cleavage of the NS3/NS4A precursor, and it would thus be a very daunting task to intervene the formation of this complex (De Francesco et al., 1999).

9.5 HCV NS3/4A protease inhibitors and the molecular basis of binding with NS3/4A protease

Based on the modes of interaction with the HCV NS3/4A protease, various known inhibitors can be classified into reversible covalent (first generation) and noncovalent inhibitors (second generation). Table 9.2 summarizes key details of various NS3/4A protease inhibitors. Fig. 9.3 depicts chemical structures of selected NS3/4A protease inhibitors. Both generations of protease inhibitors are highly potent inhibitors of the HCV NS3/4A enzyme. Notably, the second generations of protease inhibitors have advantages over the first generations in terms of improved safety profile (Salam and Akimitsu, 2013). A diverse set of molecules from different open and macrocyclic classes have been explored and reported till-date, which are comprehensively reviewed in the literature

TABLE 9.2 Current HCV NS3-4A protease inhibitors approved as drugs or in clinical phases/pipeline.

Type	Name	HCV genotype	Company	Current status
Reversible covalent inhibitors	Boceprevir	1	Merck	Approved
	Telaprevir	1	Vertex	Approved
Noncovalent inhibitors	Paritaprevir (ABT-450)	1	Abbott	Approved
	Simeprevir (TMC-435)	1, 2, 5, 6	Janssen	Approved
	Faldaprevir (BI 201335)	1	Boehringer-Ingelheim	Phase-III, but discontinued
	Danoprevir (ITMN-191/R-7227)	1	Ascletis	Phase-II
	Vaniprevir (MK-7009)	1	Merck	Phase-II
	Grazoprevir (MK-5172)	1, 2	Merck	Approved
	Asunaprevir (BMS-650032)	1, 4	Bristol-Myers Squibb	Phase-III
	Sovaprevir (ACH-1625)	1	Achillion	Phase-II
	GS-9256	1	Gliead	Phase-II
	Deldeprevir (ACH-2684)	1, 3	Achillion	Phase-II
	Vedroprevir (GS-9451)	1a, 1b	Gliead	Phase-IIb
	Narlaprevir (SCH 900518)	1	Merck	Approved
	IDX320	1, 1b, 3a, and 4a	Idenix	Phase-II
	Voxilaprevir (GS-9857)	1–6	Gilead	Approved
	Glecaprevir (ABT-493)	1–6	Abbvie	Approved

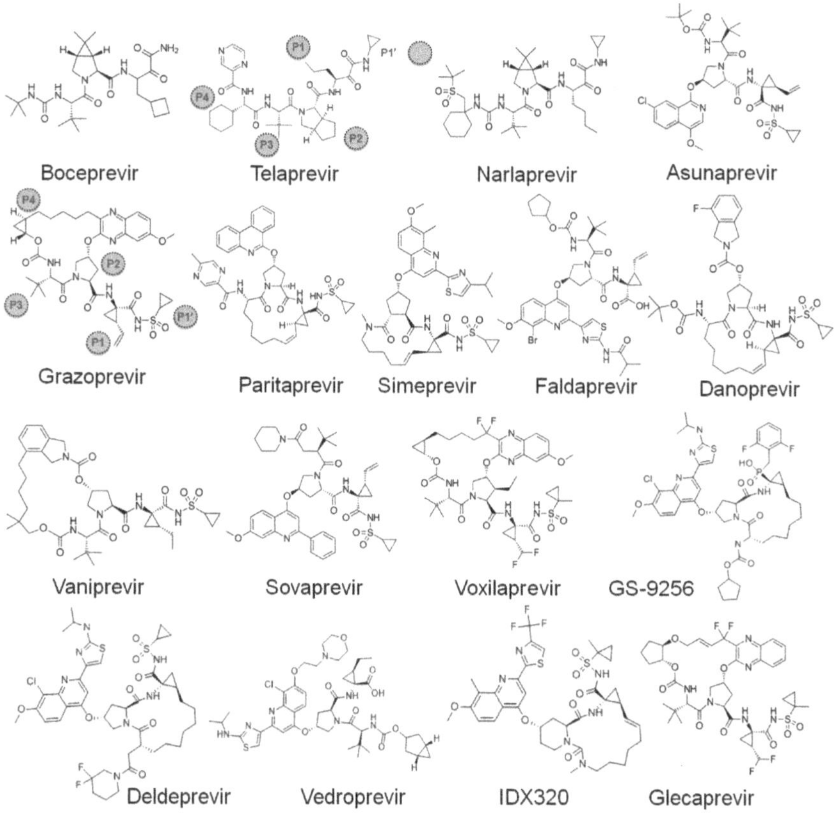

FIG. 9.3 Chemical structure of HCV NS3/4A protease inhibitors marketed as drug or under clinical investigation.

(McCauley and Rudd, 2016; Pillaiyar et al., 2016). In this chapter, an emphasis is given various candidate molecules that have reached to the market or discontinued due to the observed adverse effects during the clinical trial.

9.5.1 Reversible covalent inhibitors

Early attempt to discover peptide based inhibitors by incorporating fused proline cores led to the two linear α-ketoamide derivatives, boceprevir (Howe and Venkatraman, 2013; Prongay et al., 2007) and telaprevir (Kwong et al., 2011; Romano et al., 2012), as HCV NS3/4A protease inhibitors that received FDA approval. Subsequent investigation centered on ketoamide class led to narlaprevir (Fig. 9.3). These drugs form a covalent bond with the active site amino acid of the HCV NS3/4A protease in a reversible way, and are intended for the treatment of chronic HCV genotype 1 infection in combination with other antiviral drugs (Table 9.2).

9.5.2 Noncovalent inhibitors

These inhibitors are mostly linear and macrocyclic structures. Boehringer Ingelheim discovered a highly potent macrocycle, ciluprevir, as a noncovalent inhibitor of HCV NS3/4A protease. This compound displayed multilog drops in viral load during the Phase-I clinical trial; however, it was discontinued from further development due to the cardiovascular side effects. On the other hand, Bristol-Myers Squibb (BMS) reported a candidate molecule BMS-605339 with in vivo efficacy, but was later discontinued due to cardiac side effects. Researchers at BMS made further exploration in this candidate class that led to asunaprevir that gained approval in Japan for use in combination with pegylated interferon (PEG-IFN) and ribavirin (RBV) (Scola et al., 2014). BMS is conducting Phase III clinical trials on this compound for the treatment of hepatitis C (McCauley and Rudd, 2016; Pillaiyar et al., 2016).

Medivir AB and Janssen Pharmaceutica developed simeprevir (Cummings et al., 2010; Rosenquist et al., 2014) for the treatment of HCV genotype 1 and 4. It received approval for use in the United States in 2013. Boehringer-Ingelheim developed faldaprevir (Llinas-Brunet et al., 2010; White et al., 2010) that reached Phase-III clinical trial for the treatment of HCV. Further development of this investigational drug was, however, discontinued later due to observed cardiac toxicity. Danoprevir (Jiang et al., 2014), a macrocyclic inhibitor of HCV NS3/4A protease, is found effective against multiple HCV genotypes 1–6. Danoprevir was initially developed by Array BioPharma, which was then licensed to Merck for further development and commercialization. Vaniprevir (MK-7009) (McCauley et al., 2010) is a macrocyclic inhibitor of HCV NS3/4A protease developed by Merck & Co. It received approval in Japan in 2014 for the treatment of HCV. Grazoprevir (Romano et al., 2012; Williams et al., 2016) is a drug developed by Merck for the treatment of HCV. Abbott Laboratories developed paritaprevir (ABT-450) (Trifan et al., 2017) as an inhibitor of the NS3/4A protease for the treatment of HCV. Sovaprevir (ACH-1625) (De Clercq, 2014) is a nonmacrocyclic acylsulfonamide as a NS3/4A inhibitor undergoing clinical development by Achillion Pharmaceuticals, that is intended for the treatment of HCV. It has received the fast track status of FDA for clinical development. GS-9256 is a P1-P3 macrocyclic P1-phosphinic acid derivative and a candidate drug being developed by Gilead, which is currently in Phase II clinical development. Deldeprevir (ACH-2684) (De Clercq, 2014) is a P1–P3 macrocyclic acylsulfonamide derivative identified by Achillion Pharmaceuticals that acts as HCV NS3/4A protease inhibitor. Vedroprevir (GS-9451) (De Clercq, 2014) is another candidate drug being developed by Gilead. It has shown clinical efficacy in combination with sofosbuvir and ledipasvir in a pilot-scale proof-of-concept study and is under Phase IIb clinical development. Meanwhile, Gilead is conducting Phase-II clinical trial on GS-9256 for HCV infection (Sheng et al., 2012; Yang et al., 2017). Narlaprevir (SCH 900518) (Arasappan et al., 2010) is a FDA approved drug acting as NS3/4A protease inhibitor. It is used for the treatment of HCV genotype 1 infection in combination with other antiviral drugs. IDX-320 is a candidate drug being developed by Idenix for the treatment of HCV, which is currently undergoing Phase II clinical development (Parsy et al., 2015). Voxilaprevir (GS-9857) is a drug acting as HCV NS3/4A protease inhibitor, developed by Gilead for use in combination with sofosbuvir and velpatasvir for the treatment of HCV genotypes 1–6 (Soriano et al., 2017; Voaklander and Jacobson, 2017). It received approval of FDA in July 2017. Glecaprevir (ABT-493) (Flamm et al., 2019) was discovered and developed jointly by AbbVie and Enanta Pharmaceuticals. The medication of glecaprevir in combination with another HCV NS5A inhibitor pibrentasvi has been approved by the United States and Europe in 2017 for treatment of chronic HCV genotypes 1–6 (Table 9.2 and Fig. 9.3).

Investigation of various X-ray crystal structures of HCV NS3/4A protease complexed with approved drugs or clinical candidates, namely boceprevir (PDB-ID: 2OC8) (Prongay et al., 2007), telaprevir (PDB-ID: 3SV6) (Romano et al., 2012), simprevir (PDB-ID: 3KEE) (Cummings et al., 2010), grazoprevir (PDB-ID: 3SUD) (Romano et al., 2012), asunaprevir (PDB-ID: 4WF8) (Soumana et al., 2014), danoprevir (PDB-ID: 3M5L) (Romano et al., 2010), and vaniprevir (PDB-ID: 3SU3) (Romano et al., 2012), are studied and the corresponding three-dimensional and two-dimensional profiles revealed that the inhibitors share the same substrate-binding cavity and bind with binding site residues in a similar fashion. Comparative analysis of X-ray structures revealed that the transformation of open to macrocyclic structure did not affect the positioning of key functional groups in the protease inhibitors, thus forming the basis of the inhibitor potency and specificity. The detailed protein-ligand interaction profiles of the selected candidate drugs or approved drugs are depicted in Figs. 9.4–9.6. Reader should note that the amino acid numbering in Figs. 9.4–9.6 somewhere differs by 1000 positions, e.g., Phe154 or Phe1154, Leu135 or Leu1135, etc., as a result of the numbering assigned in various X-ray crystal structures, and hence it should not be a source of confusion to reader.

As demonstrated using site-directed mutagenesis studies, the P1 residue is the primary determinant of substrate specificity, while the S1 pocket has the preference for a cysteine residue or cysteine surrogate. Analysis of X-ray structures of HCV NS3/4A with bound inhibitors revealed that the S1 pocket is primarily characterized by three hydrophobic residues, namely Leu135 (or Leu1135), Phe154 (Phe1154), and Ala157 (or Ala1157) (Kim et al., 1996; Love et al., 1996). Phe154 is located at the bottom of the S1 pocket in an orientation to exhibit favorable van der Waals interactions with the P1 residue or cysteine surrogates. The small and hydrophobic nature of this S1 pocket is complementary to a relatively small and lipophilic side chain of a cysteine amino acid, and hence, the S1 pocket has preference to a cysteine surrogates as present in various high-affinity and selective inhibitors (Figs. 9.3–9.6). Apparently, the P1′ residue might also play some role in governing the substrate (or inhibitor) binding into the S1′ pocket formed by Gln41 (or Gln1041), His57 (or His1057), Lys136 (or

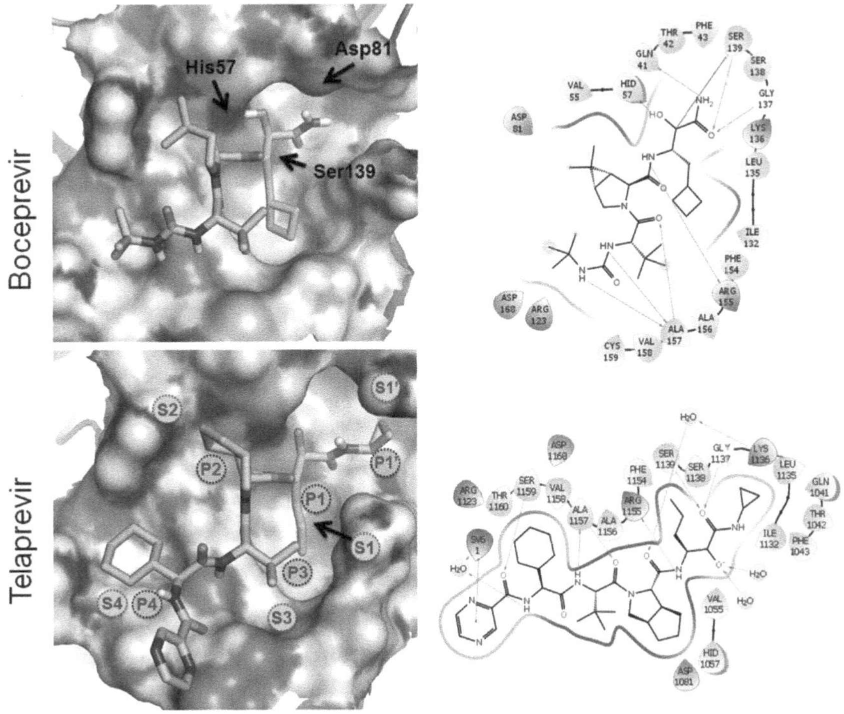

FIG. 9.4 A stereo view of interactions of inhibitors, boceprevir (PDB-ID: 2OC8) and telaprevir (PDB-ID: 3SV6), with the HCV NS3/4A protease. The protein surface view and the bioactive conformation (sticks) are shown on the left side, while 2D protein-ligand interaction is depicted on the right side.

Lys1136), Gly137 (or Gly1137), Ser138 (or Ser1138), and Ser139 (or Ser1139), hence specificity of the substrate or inhibitor. The amide or sulfonamide groups in the inhibitors are engaged in hydrogen bonding with surrounding amino acids, including Gly1137, Ser1139, Lys1136, and others (Figs. 9.4–9.6). The amino acids over the P2–P4 region are not shown to account for specificity, mainly because of the fact that the substrate binding groove is shallow, wide, and solvent exposed (De Francesco et al., 1999). Hence, the major variation among various NS3/4A protease inhibitors are in the P2–P4 regions, in particular the largest variation occurs at P2 region (Fig. 9.3). The P2 region occupies the S2 pocket lined by His1057, Asp1081, and Arg1155, where the aromatic rings in the P2 region of protease inhibitors like grazoprevir, asunaprevir, danoprevir, and vaniprevir and others stack parallel against the guanidinium and carboxylate groups of Arg1155 and Asp1081, respectively (Figs. 9.5 and 9.6). Such molecular interaction modifies the electrostatic network involving Arg1123, Asp1168, Arg1155, and Asp1081, and thus mutation of any of these vital amino acids disrupts the packing and stability of the bound inhibitor into the substrate-binding pocket, as demonstrated using molecular dynamics simulations.

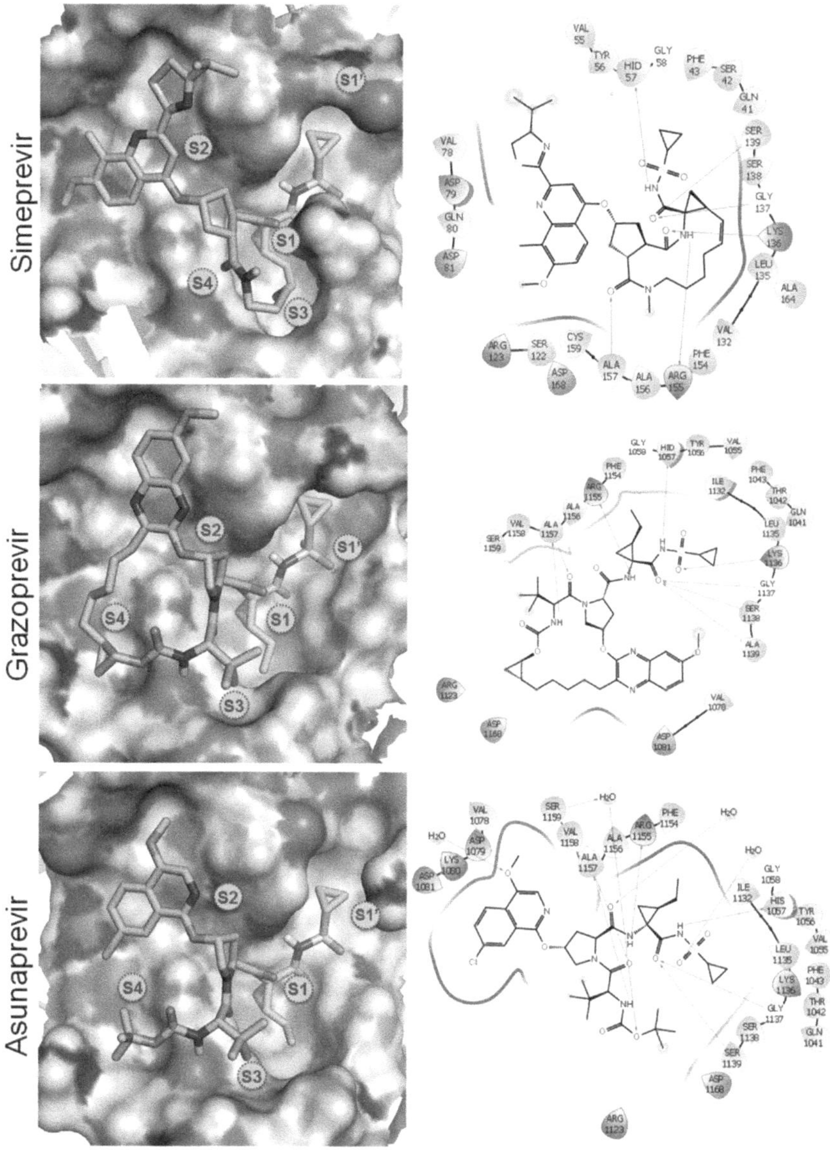

FIG. 9.5 A stereo view of interactions of inhibitors, simeprevir (PDB-ID: 3KEE), grazoprevir (PDB-ID: 3SUD), and asunaprevir (PDB-ID: 4WF8), with the HCV NS3/4A protease. The protein surface view and the bioactive conformation (sticks) are shown on the left side, while 2D protein-ligand interaction is depicted on the right side.

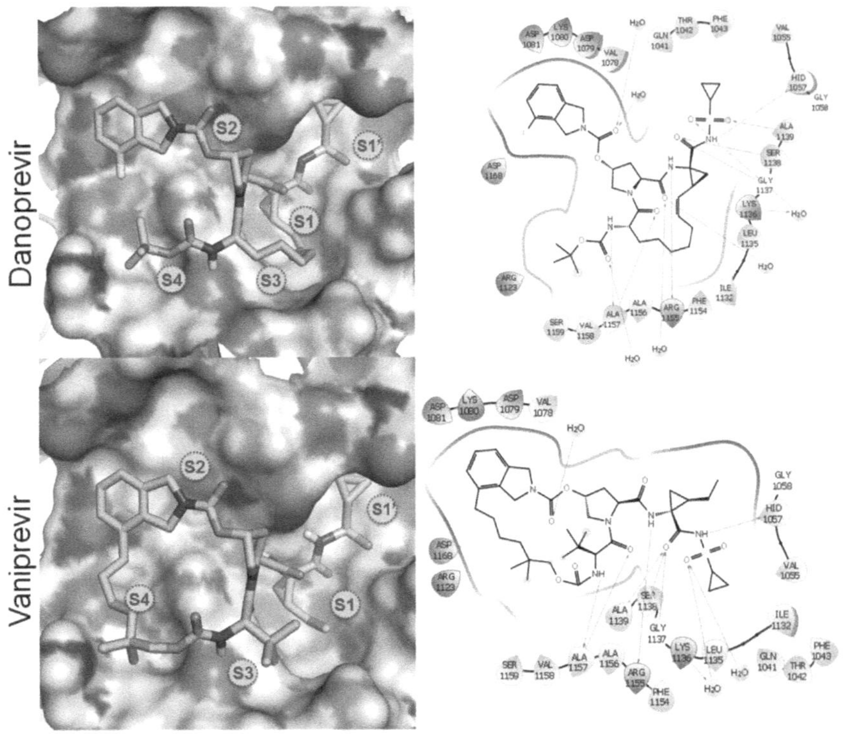

FIG. 9.6 A stereo view of interactions of inhibitors, danoprevir (PDB-ID: 3M5L) and vaniprevir (PDB-ID: 3SU3), with the HCV NS3/4A protease. The protein surface view and the bioactive conformation (sticks) are shown on the left side, while 2D protein-ligand interaction is depicted on the right side.

Because of this fact, mutations at Arg1155 or Asp1168 would lead to the drug resistance, as can be rationalized with the proposed drug resistance mutations Arg1155Lys and Asp1168Val. The short and bulky P3 residue fits into the small S3 pocket lined with Ala1157, Ile1132, and Ser1159 amino acids. The P1 and P3 residues (backbone atoms) of all inhibitors are hydrogen bonded with the carbonyl oxygens of Arg1155 and Ala1157, respectively. The P4 residue or the region connecting P1 and p3 regions in case of macrocyclic structures, reside in the shallow and extended S4 pocket, mainly lined by Asr1123, Asp1168, and Als1157 and exhibit a combination of hydrophobic and direct interactions (Figs. 9.4–9.6).

9.6 Emergence of drug resistance against HCV NS3/4A protease inhibitors

There are six genotypes and multiple subtypes of HCV with different distribution and prevalence worldwide. The long-term effectiveness of the DAAs as

HCV NS3/4A protease inhibitors is challenged by the emergence of resistant hepatitis C virus variants (Romano et al., 2012; Soumana et al., 2016). Through detailed assessment of 16 high-resolution cocrystal structures of HCV NS3/4A protease, Romano and coworkers have described the loss of inhibitor potency because of resistance mutations (Romano et al., 2012). As the mutations occur in the substrate binding regions, inhibitors are vulnerable to resistance as these mutations lead to disruption of drug binding with minimal effect on substrate proteolysis (Romano et al., 2010).

Substrate-binding-site mutations including Arg155 (or Arg1155), Ala156 (or Ala1156), and Asp168 (or Asp1168) have been found to confer resistance to almost all NS3/4A protease inhibitors in market or clinical development (Table 9.3). Notably, HCV NS3/4A protease amino acids around the substrate-binding or active site, including Arg155, Ala156, and Asp168 are highly conserved in all HCV genotypes except genotype 3 viruses (Soumana et al., 2014). HCV genotype 3 possesses mutated residues Gln168 and Thr123 instead of Asp168 and Arg123 as found in other HCV genotypes. The strong electrostatic interaction between aromatic region of the inhibitor and the S2 residues

TABLE 9.3 Drug resistance mutations near the substrate-binding pocket in HCV NS3/4A protease.

Residue	Mutation	Drug
Val36 or Val1036	Ala, Met, Leu, Gly	boceprevir, telaprevir
Gln41 or Gln1041	Arg	boceprevir, danoprevir
Phe43 or Phe1043	Ser, Cys, Val, Ile	boceprevir, telaprevir, danoprevir, simeprevir
Val55 or Val1055	Ala	boceprevir
Thr54 or Thr1054	Ala, Ser	boceprevir, telaprevir
Ser138 or Ser1138	Thr	danoprevir, simeprevir
Arg155 or Arg1155	K, T, I, M, G, L, S, Q	boceprevir, telaprevir, danoprevir, ciluprevir, simeprevir
Ala156 or Ala1156	Val, Thr, Ser, Ile, Gly	boceprevir, telaprevir, danoprevir, ciluprevir, simeprevir
Val158 or Val1158	Ile	boceprevir
Asp168 or Asp1168	Ala, Val, Glu, Gly, Asn, Thr, Tyr, His, Ile	danoprevir, ciluprevir, simeprevir
Val170 or Val1170	Ala	boceprevir, telaprevir
Met175 or Met1175	Leu	boceprevir

can modify the electrostatic network involving Arg1123, Asp1168, Arg1155, and Asp1081 (Romano et al., 2012) and thus, mutation(s) of any of these vital amino acids disrupt the packing and stability of the bound inhibitor into the substrate-binding pocket, as demonstrated using molecular dynamics simulations (Soumana et al., 2016). It may be emphasized that it is very important to have a detailed molecular level of understanding using the crystal structures of these HCV NS3/4A protease inhibitors that could facilitate the future drug design strategies for finding novel robust therapies against this rapidly evolving virus and the underlying diseases, e.g., HCV-induced HCC and several others.

9.7 Conclusions

Hepatocellular carcinoma, caused by the chronic HCV infection, is the second leading cause of cancer-related death worldwide. Despite of the advent of highly effective treatment option using direct-acting antivirals, the morbidity and incidence of HCV-related HCC remain high. The NS3 protease has a serine protease domain at N-terminus and a RNA helicase domain at C-terminus and has a zinc ion at the zinc binding site. NS3 interacts with NS4A cofactor, involving an extensive array of 15 antiparallel main-chain H-bonds to form a functional HCV NS3/4A complex, which is essential for the cleavage at NS3/4A and NS4B/5A sites of HCV polyprotein. Moreover, the NS3/4A complex also enhances cleavage at all other sites of HCV polyprotein, and thus regulates the formation of other protein products. Such processing of HCV polyprotein results in the formation of various active forms of HCV proteins, both structural and nonstructural, which are vital for viral replication and can influence directly on cell signaling pathways and metabolic mechanisms to promote HCC. Therefore, the HCV NS3/4A protease is a leading therapeutic target that has provided five FDA-approved drugs, e.g., telaprevir, boceprevir, simeprevir, paritaprevir, and grazoprevir, and several clinical candidates as NS3/4A protease inhibitors for HCV treatment, and for the prevention and control of HCV-induced HCC.

Based on the site-directed mutagenesis studies, the P1 residue is concluded to be the primary determinant of substrate specificity, while the S1 pocket has the preference for a cysteine residue or cysteine surrogate. The amino acids over the P2–P4 region are not shown to account for specificity, mainly because of the fact that the substrate binding groove is shallow, wide, and solvent exposed. Hence, the major variations among various NS3/4A protease inhibitors lie in the P2–P4 regions.

The six genotypes of HCV are linked to different level of risk for development of HCC and different potency against existing drugs as protease inhibitors. Meanwhile, there are emerging cases of viral resistance to all existing anti-HCV drugs mainly due to single-point mutations including Arg155, Ala156, and Asp168. The strong electrostatic interaction between aromatic region of the inhibitor (or drug) and the S2 residues can alter the electrostatic network involving Arg1123, Asp1168, Arg1155, and Asp1081 and thus, mutation of any of these vital amino acids disrupts the packing and stability of the bound inhibitor into the substrate-binding pocket. The HCV genome organization, HCV-to-HCC progression, structure, and function of NS3/4A protease, and wide variety of HCV NS3/4A protease inhibitors including protein-ligand interaction profiles, and emerging drug resistance cases, covered in detail in this chapter, may help the reader to understand this area and to target HCV NS3/4A protease considering the existing single-point mutation and with the judicious use of drug design techniques that may lead to novel robust therapies against this rapidly evolving virus and for the prevention of HCV-induced HCC and others.

Additional information

The X-ray structures of the various HCV NS3/4A with bound inhibitors were downloaded from the Protein Data Bank (www.rcsb.org) online. The ligands were sketched in ChemDraw [PerkinElmer Ltd.] or Maestro, while the raw coordinates of protein structures were prepared using the Protein Preparation Wizard implemented in the Schrodinger suite [Small-Molecule Drug Discovery Suite 2018-4, Schrödinger, LLC, New York, NY, 2018]. The graphics were created using Maestro tools and PyMol [PyMOL: The PyMOL Molecular Graphics System, Version 2.0 Schrödinger, LLC].

References

Abro, A.H., Al-Dabal, L., Younis, N.J., 2010. Distribution of hepatitis C virus genotypes in Dubai, United Arab Emirates. J. Pak. Med. Assoc. 60, 987–990.

Altekruse, S.F., Henley, S.J., Cucinelli, J.E., McGlynn, K.A., 2014. Changing hepatocellular carcinoma incidence and liver cancer mortality rates in the United States. Am. J. Gastroenterol. 109, 542–553.

Arasappan, A., Bennett, F., Bogen, S.L., Venkatraman, S., Blackman, M., Chen, K.X., Hendrata, S., Huang, Y., Huelgas, R.M., Nair, L., Padilla, A.I., Pan, W., Pike, R., Pinto, P., Ruan, S., Sannigrahi, M., Velazquez, F., Vibulbhan, B., Wu, W., Yang, W., Saksena, A.K., Girijavallabhan, V., Shih, N.Y., Kong, J., Meng, T., Jin, Y., Wong, J., McNamara, P., Prongay, A., Madison, V., Piwinski, J.J., Cheng, K.C., Morrison, R., Malcolm, B., Tong, X., Ralston, R., Njoroge, F.G., 2010. Discovery of narlaprevir (SCH 900518): a potent, second generation HCV NS3 serine protease inhibitor. ACS Med. Chem. Lett. 1, 64–69.

Axley, P., Ahmed, Z., Ravi, S., Singal, A.K., 2018. Hepatitis C virus and hepatocellular carcinoma: a narrative review. J. Clin. Transl. Hepatol. 6, 79–84.

Barbato, G., Cicero, D.O., Cordier, F., Narjes, F., Gerlach, B., Sambucini, S., Grzesiek, S., Matassa, V.G., De Francesco, R., Bazzo, R., 2000. Inhibitor binding induces active site stabilization of the HCV NS3 protein serine protease domain. EMBO J. 19, 1195–1206.

Bartenschlager, R., Ahlborn-Laake, L., Mous, J., Jacobsen, H., 1993. Nonstructural protein 3 of the hepatitis C virus encodes a serine-type proteinase required for cleavage at the NS3/4 and NS4/5 junctions. J. Virol. 67, 3835–3844.

Bartenschlager, R., Lohmann, V., Wilkinson, T., Koch, J.O., 1995. Complex formation between the NS3 serine-type proteinase of the hepatitis C virus and NS4A and its importance for polyprotein maturation. J. Virol. 69, 7519–7528.

Bosetti, C., Turati, F., La Vecchia, C., 2014. Hepatocellular carcinoma epidemiology. Best Pract. Res. Clin. Gastroenterol. 28, 753–770.

Bruno, S., Crosignani, A., Maisonneuve, P., Rossi, S., Silini, E., Mondelli, M.U., 2007. Hepatitis C virus genotype 1b as a major risk factor associated with hepatocellular carcinoma in patients with cirrhosis: a seventeen-year prospective cohort study. Hepatology 46, 1350–1356.

Cummings, M.D., Lindberg, J., Lin, T.I., de Kock, H., Lenz, O., Lilja, E., Fellander, S., Baraznenok, V., Nystrom, S., Nilsson, M., Vrang, L., Edlund, M., Rosenquist, A., Samuelsson, B., Raboisson, P., Simmen, K., 2010. Induced-fit binding of the macrocyclic noncovalent inhibitor TMC435 to its HCV NS3/NS4A protease target. Angew. Chem. Int. Ed. Engl. 49, 1652–1655.

De Clercq, E., 2014. Current race in the development of DAAs (direct-acting antivirals) against HCV. Biochem. Pharmacol. 89, 441–452.

De Francesco, R., Pessi, A., Steinkuhler, C., 1999. Mechanisms of hepatitis C virus NS3 proteinase inhibitors. J. Viral Hepat. 6 (Suppl. 1), 23–30.

Dubuisson, J., Cosset, F.L., 2014. Virology and cell biology of the hepatitis C virus life cycle: an update. J. Hepatol. 61, S3–S13.

Failla, C., Tomei, L., De Francesco, R., 1995. An amino-terminal domain of the hepatitis C virus NS3 protease is essential for interaction with NS4A. J. Virol. 69, 1769–1777.

Failla, C.M., Pizzi, E., De Francesco, R., Tramontano, A., 1996. Redesigning the substrate specificity of the hepatitis C virus NS3 protease. Fold. Des. 1, 35–42.

Flamm, S., Mutimer, D., Asatryan, A., Wang, S., Rockstroh, J., Horsmans, Y., Kwo, P.Y., Weiland, O., Villa, E., Heo, J., Gane, E., Ryder, S.D., Welzel, T.M., Ruane, P.J., Agarwal, K., Ng, T.I., Xue, Z., Lovell, S.S., Krishnan, P., Kopecky-Bromberg, S., Trinh, R., Mensa, F.J., Wyles, D.L., 2019. Glecaprevir/pibrentasvir in patients with chronic HCV genotype 3 infection: an integrated phase 2/3 analysis. J. Viral Hepat. 26, 337–349.

Howe, A.Y., Venkatraman, S., 2013. The discovery and development of boceprevir: a novel, first-generation inhibitor of the hepatitis C virus NS3/4A serine protease. J. Clin. Transl. Hepatol. 1, 22–32.

Jiang, Y., Andrews, S.W., Condroski, K.R., Buckman, B., Serebryany, V., Wenglowsky, S., Kennedy, A.L., Madduru, M.R., Wang, B., Lyon, M., Doherty, G.A., Woodard, B.T., Lemieux, C., Geck Do, M., Zhang, H., Ballard, J., Vigers, G., Brandhuber, B.J., Stengel, P., Josey, J.A., Beigelman, L., Blatt, L., Seiwert, S.D., 2014. Discovery of danoprevir (ITMN-191/R7227), a highly selective and potent inhibitor of hepatitis C virus (HCV) NS3/4A protease. J. Med. Chem. 57, 1753–1769.

Kanwal, F., Kramer, J.R., Ilyas, J., Duan, Z., El-Serag, H.B., 2014. HCV genotype 3 is associated with an increased risk of cirrhosis and hepatocellular cancer in a national sample of U.S. Veterans with HCV. Hepatology 60, 98–105.

Karayiannis, P., 2017. Hepatitis B virus: virology, molecular biology, life cycle and intrahepatic spread. Hepatol. Int. 11, 500–508.

Kim, C.W., Chang, K.M., 2013. Hepatitis C virus: virology and life cycle. Clin. Mol. Hepatol. 19, 17–25.

Kim, J.L., Morgenstern, K.A., Lin, C., Fox, T., Dwyer, M.D., Landro, J.A., Chambers, S.P., Markland, W., Lepre, C.A., O'Malley, E.T., Harbeson, S.L., Rice, C.M., Murcko, M.A., Caron, P.R., Thomson, J.A., 1996. Crystal structure of the hepatitis C virus NS3 protease domain complexed with a synthetic NS4A cofactor peptide. Cell 87, 343–355.

Koch, J.O., Bartenschlager, R., 1997. Determinants of substrate specificity in the NS3 serine proteinase of the hepatitis C virus. Virology 237, 78–88.

Kohli, A., Shaffer, A., Sherman, A., Kottilil, S., 2014. Treatment of hepatitis C: a systematic review. JAMA 312, 631–640.

Kwong, A.D., Kauffman, R.S., Hurter, P., Mueller, P., 2011. Discovery and development of telaprevir: an NS3-4A protease inhibitor for treating genotype 1 chronic hepatitis C virus. Nat. Biotechnol. 29, 993–1003.

Lai, T.S., Lee, M.H., Yang, H.I., You, S.L., Lu, S.N., Wang, L.Y., Yuan, Y., L'Italien, G., Chien, K.L., Chen, C.J., REVEAL-HCV Study Group, 2017. Hepatitis C viral load, genotype, and increased risk of developing end-stage renal disease: REVEAL-HCV study. Hepatology 66, 784–793.

Lee, M.H., Hsiao, T.I., Subramaniam, S.R., Le, A.K., Vu, V.D., Trinh, H.N., Zhang, J., Jin, M., Wong, V.W., Wong, G.L., Nguyen, M.H., 2017. HCV genotype 6 increased the risk for hepatocellular carcinoma among asian patients with liver cirrhosis. Am. J. Gastroenterol. 112, 1111–1119.

Lesk, A.M., Fordham, W.D., 1996. Conservation and variability in the structures of serine proteinases of the chymotrypsin family. J. Mol. Biol. 258, 501–537.

Llinas-Brunet, M., Bailey, M.D., Goudreau, N., Bhardwaj, P.K., Bordeleau, J., Bos, M., Bousquet, Y., Cordingley, M.G., Duan, J., Forgione, P., Garneau, M., Ghiro, E., Gorys, V., Goulet, S., Halmos, T., Kawai, S.H., Naud, J., Poupart, M.A., White, P.W., 2010. Discovery of a potent and selective noncovalent linear inhibitor of the hepatitis C virus NS3 protease (BI 201335). J. Med. Chem. 53, 6466–6476.

Love, R.A., Parge, H.E., Wickersham, J.A., Hostomsky, Z., Habuka, N., Moomaw, E.W., Adachi, T., Hostomska, Z., 1996. The crystal structure of hepatitis C virus NS3 proteinase reveals a trypsin-like fold and a structural zinc binding site. Cell 87, 331–342.

Love, R.A., Parge, H.E., Wickersham, J.A., Hostomsky, Z., Habuka, N., Moomaw, E.W., Adachi, T., Margosiak, S., Dagostino, E., Hostomska, Z., 1998. The conformation of hepatitis C virus NS3 proteinase with and without NS4A: a structural basis for the activation of the enzyme by its cofactor. Clin. Diagn. Virol. 10, 151–156.

McCauley, J.A., Rudd, M.T., 2016. Hepatitis C virus NS3/4a protease inhibitors. Curr. Opin. Pharmacol. 30, 84–92.

McCauley, J.A., McIntyre, C.J., Rudd, M.T., Nguyen, K.T., Romano, J.J., Butcher, J.W., Gilbert, K.F., Bush, K.J., Holloway, M.K., Swestock, J., Wan, B.L., Carroll, S.S., DiMuzio, J.M., Graham, D.J., Ludmerer, S.W., Mao, S.S., Stahlhut, M.W., Fandozzi, C.M., Trainor, N., Olsen, D.B., Vacca, J.P., Liverton, N.J., 2010. Discovery of vaniprevir (MK-7009), a macrocyclic hepatitis C virus NS3/4a protease inhibitor. J. Med. Chem. 53, 2443–2463.

Pan, Q.Z., Pan, K., Wang, Q.J., Weng, D.S., Zhao, J.J., Zheng, H.X., Zhang, X.F., Jiang, S.S., Lv, L., Tang, Y., Li, Y.Q., He, J., Liu, Q., Chen, C.L., Zhang, H.X., Xia, J.C., 2015. Annexin A3 as a potential target for immunotherapy of liver cancer stem-like cells. Stem Cells 33, 354–366.

Parsy, C.C., Alexandre, F.R., Bidau, V., Bonnaterre, F., Brandt, G., Caillet, C., Cappelle, S., Chaves, D., Convard, T., Derock, M., Gloux, D., Griffon, Y., Lallos, L.B., Leroy, F., Liuzzi, M., Loi, A.G., Moulat, L., Chiara, M., Rahali, H., Roques, V., Rosinovsky, E., Savin, S., Seifer, M., Standring, D., Surleraux, D., 2015. Discovery and structural diversity of the hepatitis C virus NS3/4A serine protease inhibitor series leading to clinical candidate IDX320. Bioorg. Med. Chem. Lett. 25, 5427–5436.

Penin, F., Dubuisson, J., Rey, F.A., Moradpour, D., Pawlotsky, J.M., 2004. Structural biology of hepatitis C virus. Hepatology 39, 5–19.

Pillaiyar, T., Namasivayam, V., Manickam, M., 2016. Macrocyclic hepatitis C virus NS3/4A protease inhibitors: an overview of medicinal chemistry. Curr. Med. Chem. 23, 3404–3447.

Prongay, A.J., Guo, Z., Yao, N., Pichardo, J., Fischmann, T., Strickland, C., Myers Jr., J., Weber, P.C., Beyer, B.M., Ingram, R., Hong, Z., Prosise, W.W., Ramanathan, L., Taremi, S.S., Yarosh-Tomaine, T., Zhang, R., Senior, M., Yang, R.S., Malcolm, B., Arasappan, A., Bennett, F., Bogen, S.L., Chen, K., Jao, E., Liu, Y.T., Lovey, R.G., Saksena, A.K., Venkatraman, S., Girijavallabhan, V., Njoroge, F.G., Madison, V., 2007. Discovery of the HCV NS3/4A protease inhibitor (1R,5S)-N-[3-amino-1-(cyclobutylmethyl)-2,3-dioxopropyl]-3- [2(S)-[[[(1,1-dimethylethyl) amino]carbonyl]amino]-3,3-dimethyl-1-oxobutyl]-6,6-dimethyl-3-azabicyclo[3.1.0]hexan-2(S)-carboxamide (Sch 503034) II. Key steps in structure-based optimization. J. Med. Chem. 50, 2310–2318.

Romano, K.P., Ali, A., Royer, W.E., Schiffer, C.A., 2010. Drug resistance against HCV NS3/4A inhibitors is defined by the balance of substrate recognition versus inhibitor binding. Proc. Natl. Acad. Sci. U. S. A. 107, 20986–20991.

Romano, K.P., Ali, A., Aydin, C., Soumana, D., Ozen, A., Deveau, L.M., Silver, C., Cao, H., Newton, A., Petropoulos, C.J., Huang, W., Schiffer, C.A., 2012. The molecular basis of drug resistance against hepatitis C virus NS3/4A protease inhibitors. PLoS Pathog. 8, e1002832.

Rosenquist, A., Samuelsson, B., Johansson, P.O., Cummings, M.D., Lenz, O., Raboisson, P., Simmen, K., Vendeville, S., de Kock, H., Nilsson, M., Horvath, A., Kalmeijer, R., de la Rosa, G., Beumont-Mauviel, M., 2014. Discovery and development of simeprevir (TMC435), a HCV NS3/4A protease inhibitor. J. Med. Chem. 57, 1673–1693.

Salam, K.A., Akimitsu, N., 2013. Hepatitis C virus NS3 inhibitors: current and future perspectives. Biomed. Res. Int. 2013, 467869.

Scola, P.M., Sun, L.Q., Wang, A.X., Chen, J., Sin, N., Venables, B.L., Sit, S.Y., Chen, Y., Cocuzza, A., Bilder, D.M., D'Andrea, S.V., Zheng, B., Hewawasam, P., Tu, Y., Friborg, J., Falk, P., Hernandez, D., Levine, S., Chen, C., Yu, F., Sheaffer, A.K., Zhai, G., Barry, D., Knipe, J.O., Han, Y.H., Schartman, R., Donoso, M., Mosure, K., Sinz, M.W., Zvyaga, T., Good, A.C., Rajamani, R., Kish, K., Tredup, J., Klei, H.E., Gao, Q., Mueller, L., Colonno, R.J., Grasela, D.M., Adams, S.P., Loy, J., Levesque, P.C., Sun, H., Shi, H., Sun, L., Warner, W., Li, D., Zhu, J., Meanwell, N.A., McPhee, F., 2014. The discovery of asunaprevir (BMS-650032), an orally efficacious NS3 protease inhibitor for the treatment of hepatitis C virus infection. J. Med. Chem. 57, 1730–1752.

Sheng, X.C., Casarez, A., Cai, R., Clarke, M.O., Chen, X., Cho, A., Delaney, W.E.t., Doerffler, E., Ji, M., Mertzman, M., Pakdaman, R., Pyun, H.J., Rowe, T., Wu, Q., Xu, J., Kim, C.U., 2012. Discovery of GS-9256: a novel phosphinic acid derived inhibitor of the hepatitis C virus NS3/4A protease with potent clinical activity. Bioorg. Med. Chem. Lett. 22, 1394–1396.

Sievert, W., Altraif, I., Razavi, H.A., Abdo, A., Ahmed, E.A., Alomair, A., Amarapurkar, D., Chen, C.H., Dou, X., El Khayat, H., Elshazly, M., Esmat, G., Guan, R., Han, K.H., Koike, K., Largen, A., McCaughan, G., Mogawer, S., Monis, A., Nawaz, A., Piratvisuth, T., Sanai, F.M., Sharara, A.I., Sibbel, S., Sood, A., Suh, D.J., Wallace, C., Young, K., Negro, F., 2011. A systematic review of hepatitis C virus epidemiology in Asia, Australia and Egypt. Liver Int. 31 (Suppl. 2), 61–80.

Soriano, V., Benitez-Gutierrez, L., Arias, A., Carrasco, I., Barreiro, P., Pena, J.M., de Mendoza, C., 2017. Evaluation of sofosbuvir, velpatasvir plus voxilaprevir as fixed-dose co-formulation for treating hepatitis C. Expert Opin. Drug Metab. Toxicol. 13, 1015–1022.

Soumana, D.I., Ali, A., Schiffer, C.A., 2014. Structural analysis of asunaprevir resistance in HCV NS3/4A protease. ACS Chem. Biol. 9, 2485–2490.

Soumana, D.I., Kurt Yilmaz, N., Ali, A., Prachanronarong, K.L., Schiffer, C.A., 2016. Molecular and dynamic mechanism underlying drug resistance in genotype 3 hepatitis C NS3/4A protease. J. Am. Chem. Soc. 138, 11850–11859.

Steinkuhler, C., Urbani, A., Tomei, L., Biasiol, G., Sardana, M., Bianchi, E., Pessi, A., De Francesco, R., 1996. Activity of purified hepatitis C virus protease NS3 on peptide substrates. J. Virol. 70, 6694–6700.

Trifan, A., Stanciu, C., Gheorghe, L., Iacob, S., Curescu, M., Cijevschi Prelipcean, C., Stefanescu, G., Girleanu, I., Chiriac, S., Mihai, C., Brisc, C., Goldis, A., Sporea, I., Miftode, E., Bataga, S., Rogoveanu, I., Preda, C., Caruntu, F.A., Singeap, A.M., 2017. Efficacy and safety of paritaprevir/ritonavir, ombitasvir, and dasabuvir with ribavirin for the treatment of HCV genotype 1b compensated cirrhosis in patients aged 70 years or older. Medicine (Baltimore) 96, e9271.

Venkatakrishnan, B., Zlotnick, A., 2016. The structural biology of hepatitis B virus: form and function. Annu. Rev. Virol. 3, 429–451.

Vescovo, T., Refolo, G., Vitagliano, G., Fimia, G.M., Piacentini, M., 2016. Molecular mechanisms of hepatitis C virus-induced hepatocellular carcinoma. Clin. Microbiol. Infect. 22, 853–861.

Voaklander, R., Jacobson, I.M., 2017. Sofosbuvir, velpatasvir and voxilaprevir combination for the treatment of hepatitis C. Expert Rev. Gastroenterol. Hepatol. 11, 789–795.

White, P.W., Llinas-Brunet, M., Amad, M., Bethell, R.C., Bolger, G., Cordingley, M.G., Duan, J., Garneau, M., Lagace, L., Thibeault, D., Kukolj, G., 2010. Preclinical characterization of BI 201335, a C-terminal carboxylic acid inhibitor of the hepatitis C virus NS3-NS4A protease. Antimicrob. Agents Chemother. 54, 4611–4618.

Williams, M.J., Kong, J., Chung, C.K., Brunskill, A., Campeau, L.C., McLaughlin, M., 2016. The discovery of quinoxaline-based metathesis catalysts from synthesis of grazoprevir (MK-5172). Org. Lett. 18, 1952–1955.

Yang, H., Yang, C., Wang, Y., Rhodes, G., Robinson, M., Cheng, G., Qi, X., Mo, H., Tian, Y., Pakdaman, R., Sheng, X.C., Kim, C.U., Delaney, W.E.t., 2017. Preclinical characterization of the novel HCV NS3 protease inhibitor GS-9256. Antivir. Ther. 22, 413–420.

Zhu, H., Briggs, J.M., 2011. Mechanistic role of NS4A and substrate in the activation of HCV NS3 protease. Proteins 79, 2428–2443.

Chapter 10

Collagenases and gelatinases and their inhibitors as anticancer agents

Nilanjan Adhikari, Sk. Abdul Amin, Tarun Jha
Natural Science Laboratory, Division of Medicinal and Pharmaceutical Chemistry, Department of Pharmaceutical Technology, Jadavpur University, Kolkata, India

10.1 Introduction

Collagen is one of the important structural proteins in various connective tissues present in the body (Tortora et al., 2007). It is a key component of the animal extracellular matrix. It is the most abundant protein in mammals (about 30% of the whole-body protein). Collagen is mostly found in fibrous tissues such as bones, tendons, ligaments, and skin (Tortora et al., 2007). Collagen tissues may be classified into three types based on the degree of mineralization: (a) rigid collagen (e.g., bone), (b) compliant collagen (e.g., tendon), (c) collagen having a gradient from rigid to compliant (e.g., cartilage). The name collagen comes from the Greek words κόλλα (kólla) and -γέν (-gen). Greek ward κόλλα means "glue" and the suffix -γέν represents "generation". Denatured collagen is gelatin.

Collagens are broken down by the enzymes collagenases. Collagenases cleave the peptide bonds present in collagen (Di Lullo et al., 2002). Collagenases help the destruction of extracellular structures and are considered as a virulence factor (Riley and Herman, 2005). They normally target the connective tissue in muscle and other body organs. The International Union of Biochemistry and Molecular Biology (IUBMB) recognized peptidases in two sets of subclasses such as endopeptidases and exopeptidases. The endopeptidases are mainly divided into six types (Fig. 10.1).

Out of these endopeptidases, metalloproteinases are one of the important peptidases. Matrix metalloproteinases (MMPs) belong to the zinc metallopeptidases family and are divided into several types (Amin et al., 2017). Till date, 28 different MMPs are identified, out of which 23 belong to humans, having unique characteristic features. Based on structures, cellular localization, and substrate specificity (Hu et al., 2007; Whittaker et al., 1999), these MMPs are categorized

Cancer-Leading Proteases. https://doi.org/10.1016/B978-0-12-818168-3.00010-3

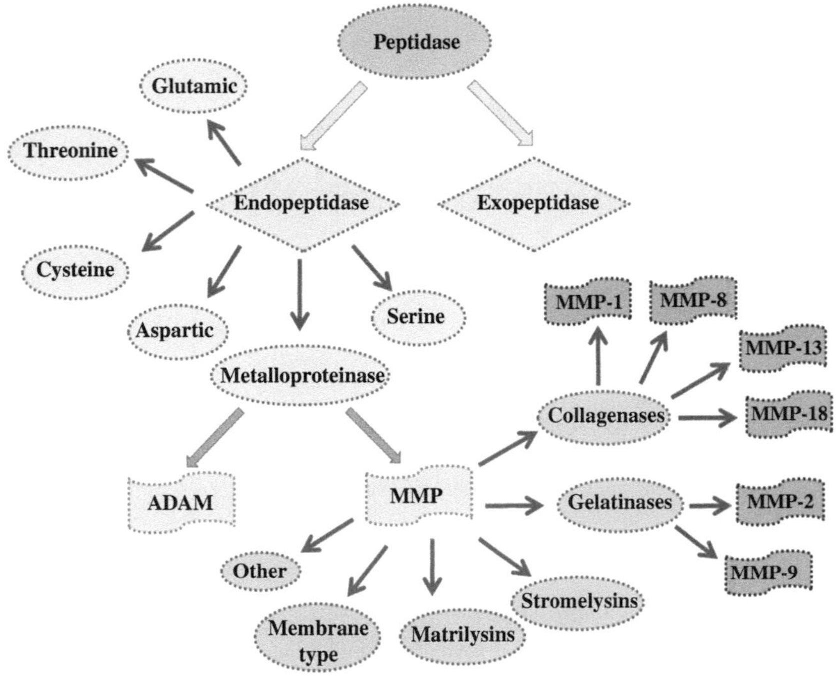

FIG. 10.1 A diagram showing different types of peptidases.

into several classes such as collagenases (MMP-1, -8, -13 and -18) (Nagase and Fushimi, 2008; Chung et al., 2004), matrilysins (MMP-7 and -26) (Benjamin and Khalil, 2012), gelatinases (MMP-2 and -9) (Patterson et al., 2001; Nagase et al., 2006; Adhikari et al., 2017a,b,c), stromelysins (MMP-3, -10, and -11) (Pei and Weiss, 1995), membrane-type MMPs (MMP-14, -15, -16, -17, -24, and -25) (Ohuchi et al., 1997; Holmbeck et al., 1999), enamelysin (MMP-20) (Ryu et al., 1999), epilysin (MMP-28) (Lohi et al., 2001; Benjamin and Khalil, 2012), and other MMPs (MMP-12, -20, and -27) (Benjamin and Khalil, 2012). Among these different MMPs, collagenases play important roles in cleaving or breakdown of fibrillar collagen types I-III into fragments. Four types of collagenases such as MMP-1 (collagenase 1), MMP-8 (collagenase 2), MMP-13 (collagenase 3), and MMP-18 (collagenase 4 found in Xenopus) are found. The other three can be obtained from human beings (Fig. 10.1). The hemopexin domain cleaves the native fibrillar collagen. The catalytic domains cleave the noncollagen substrate (Nagase and Fushimi, 2008; Chung et al., 2004).

On the other hand, the two MMPs that are closely associated with the metastatic ability are MMP-2 and -9, known together as gelatinases (gelatinase A and gelatinase B) (Adhikari et al., 2016, 2017a,b,c, 2018a,b; Jha et al., 2018). They are secreted as zymogen and finally cleaved into the active form. It is confirmed from different experiments that MMP-2 has a crucial role in a variety of cancers. MMP-2 is also found to play important role in neovascularization as confirmed by different angiogenesis models such as retinal angiogenesis, aortic ring assay, and choroidal neovascularization models (Gupta and Patil, 2012). Additional studies suggested that expression of MMP-2 is highly associated with metastasis of tumors in a variety of tumors and malignant type of cancers (Liu et al., 2006; Kast and Halatsch, 2012). MMP-2 has the ability to trigger intravasation of tumors and subsequently promote neoangiogenesis to form leaky blood vessels. Therefore, MMP-2 may be considered as an important predictor of poor prognosis in cancers. MMP-9 is also considered as another important culprit that may lead to cancer (Groblewska et al., 2012). Numerous studies suggested MMP-9 as very crucial for the advanced stage of cancer (Lakka et al., 2002; Fabre et al., 2013; Overall and Kleifeld, 2006). Though MMPs, in general, have been recognized as important targets to develop drugs against various diseases, very few have been fruitfully exploited for the development of anticancer drugs as in general MMP inhibitors possess broad spectrum of MMP inhibition that lead to inflammation and musculoskeletal pain. In this respect, however, collagenases and gelatinases have provided great hope. This chapter therefore describes their specific biological functions and roles as drug targets for the development of anticancer drugs.

10.2 Structures of MMPs

In general all MMPs belong to the metzincin group of proteases. The members of the metzincin group contain catalytic Zn^{2+} ion as well as the conserved methionine residue at the catalytic site. MMPs are secreted as pro-enzymes, activation of which results in a loss of N-terminal pro-peptide sequence comprising 80 amino acid residues. The pro-domain consists of a "cysteine switch" PRCGXPD consensus sequence. MMPs have a fairly similar catalytic domain comprised of a highly conserved HExxHxxGxxH catalytic zinc binding motif. The catalytic Zn^{2+} ion is located in a bigger and relatively shallow cleft that facilitates binding of substrates and inhibitors. In addition, MMPs contain some hydrophobic pockets including S1, S2, S1′ pockets. The hydrophobic S1′ pocket is important as the substrate binding site. The specificity of this pocket is pivotal for the selectivity of inhibitors. Based on the depth and size of the S1′ pocket, human MMPs are classified as (i) shallow (MMP-1 and -7), (ii) intermediate (MMP-2, -8, -9, -12, and -14), and (iii) deep (MMP-3, -10, and -13) MMPs.

10.2.1 Structures of collagenases

Collagenases are nothing but MMP-1, -8, and -13, which may be referred to as collagenase-1, collagenase-2, and collagenase-3. These collagenases consist of a canonical multidomain MMP structure. They include N-terminal signal peptide, propeptide, catalytic domain, and proline-rich hinge region as well

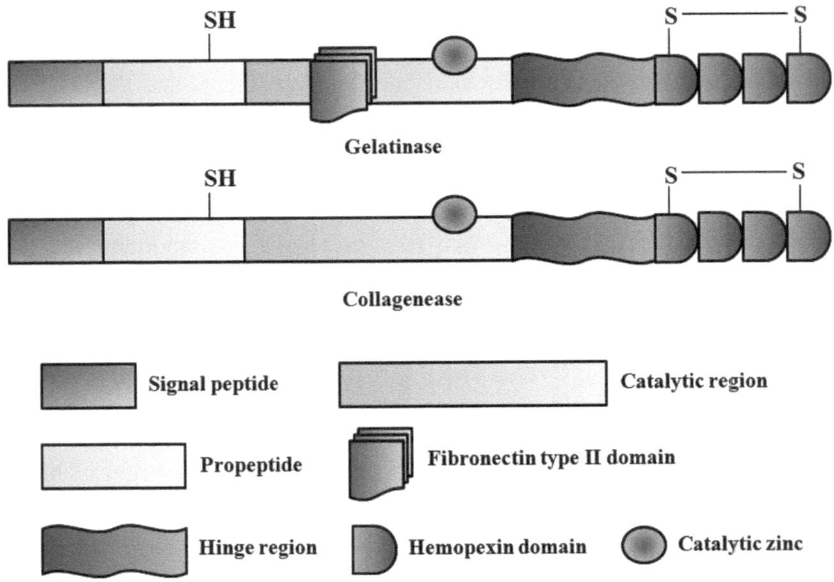

FIG. 10.2 The domain structures of collagenase and gelatinase.

as hemopexin domain. The domain structure of collagenase is responsible for cleaving collagens and closely related gelatinase which breaks down gelatins (denatured collagens) as shown in Fig. 10.2.

As far as the multidomain structures of collagenases are concerned, the N-terminal signal peptide shows pivotal role to direct the newly produced pre-procollagenase to secret (Ala-Aho and Kähäri, 2005). The propeptide consists of a conserved cysteine residue that is known as cysteine switch. Propeptide also produces a covalent linkage with the catalytic Zn^{2+} ion at the active site. This domain consists of a highly conserved zinc binding sequence known as HEXXHXXGXXH. This region is crucial for the proteolytic ability of MMPs. Interestingly, collagenases contain a hemopexin domain that has a sequential similarity to a heme-binding protein hemopexin. This hemopexin domain is highly conserved among different MMPs. It is linked to the catalytic region through proline-rich hinge region. Two cysteine residues are found to form a disulfide bridge that folds the domain into a four-bladed propeller structure. The hemopexin domain is important not only for the substrate specificity but also for proteolytic activity. It also helps in the binding of tissue inhibitors of metalloproteinases (TIMPs). Unlike gelatinases (MMP-2 and -9), collagenases do not have an additional fibronectin-II like inserts (Fig. 10.2). Crystal structures of the different human collagenases (collagenases 1, 2, 3) are shown in Fig. 10.3 and a brief description of them is given below.

Collagenase-1 (MMP-1) is the first member of MMP family which was purified from the tail of a tadpole. The first human MMP-1 was obtained from adult skin fibroblasts. Expression of human MMP-1 is found in numerous

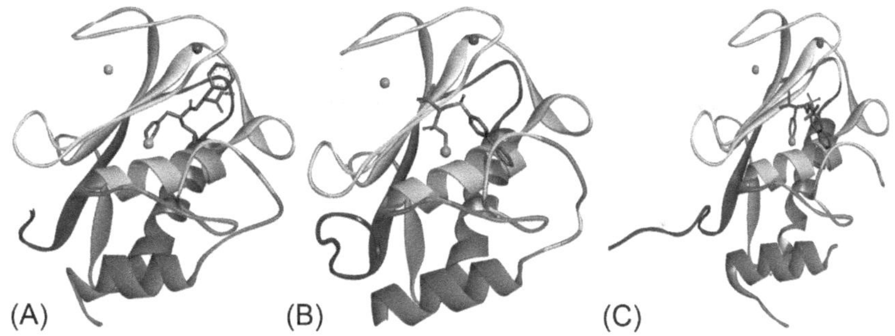

FIG. 10.3 Crystal structure of the collagenases including MMP-1 (A), MMP-8 (B), and MMP-13 (C).

physiological processes from wound healing to embryonic development. It is involved in various pathological processes from chronic cutaneous ulcers to malignant tumors. The X-ray crystal structure of MMP-1 highlighted that its S1′ pocket is shallow. For MMP-1, the amino acid residue Arg214 closes the S1′ pocket and, therefore, the specific conformation of the Ω-loop is not pivotal for designing MMP-1 inhibitors. This amino acid residue Arg214 may constitute a steric hindrance to the ligands, preventing the interactions of ligands with residues of the Ω-loop. A 2D interaction plot of MMP-1 (PDB: 1HFC) and MMP-1 inhibitor is depicted in Fig. 10.4.

Collagenase-2 (MMP-8) is biosynthesized by the neutrophils during their maturation in bone marrow and thus, collagenase-2 is also called neutrophil collagenase. It is found to be stored in intracellular granules and subsequently released in response to extracellular stimuli. A number of X-ray crystal structures of the complex catalytic domain of MMP-8 have been reported so far. The S1′ pocket of MMP-8 is relatively larger in size than that of MMP-2 and so is the case of its Ω-loop. This offers certain inhibitors to achieve selectivity toward MMP-8 over MMP-2 as the bulky groups of these inhibitors can occupy the S1′ pocket. However, the size of the S1′ pocket of MMP-8 is comparatively smaller than that of MMP-13. Interestingly, MMP-8 and MMP-13 inhibitors with bulky P1′ group provide them selectivity over MMP-2. The 2D interaction of a representative MMP-8 inhibitor, bis-phosphonate (ML115), with MMP-8 is depicted in Fig. 10.5.

Collagenase-3 (MMP-13) was originally cloned from the human breast cancer tissue (Freije et al., 1994). MMP-13 shows a restricted pattern of expression but has a broad range of substrate specificity. A number of X-ray crystal structures of the human MMP-13 and MMP-1 with bound inhibitors provide a primary knowledge of the selectivity pattern of inhibitors. The intrinsic flexibility of the S1′ pocket of human collagenases is different. In comparison to that of other collagenases, the S1′ pocket of MMP-13 is long and deep (Fig. 10.3). The Ω-loop of MMP-13 is composed of 13 residues. The "bottom" of its S1′ pocket is completely solvent exposed and is able to accommodate the large P1′ group. The hydroxamate-based inhibitors interact with the catalytic zinc ion and

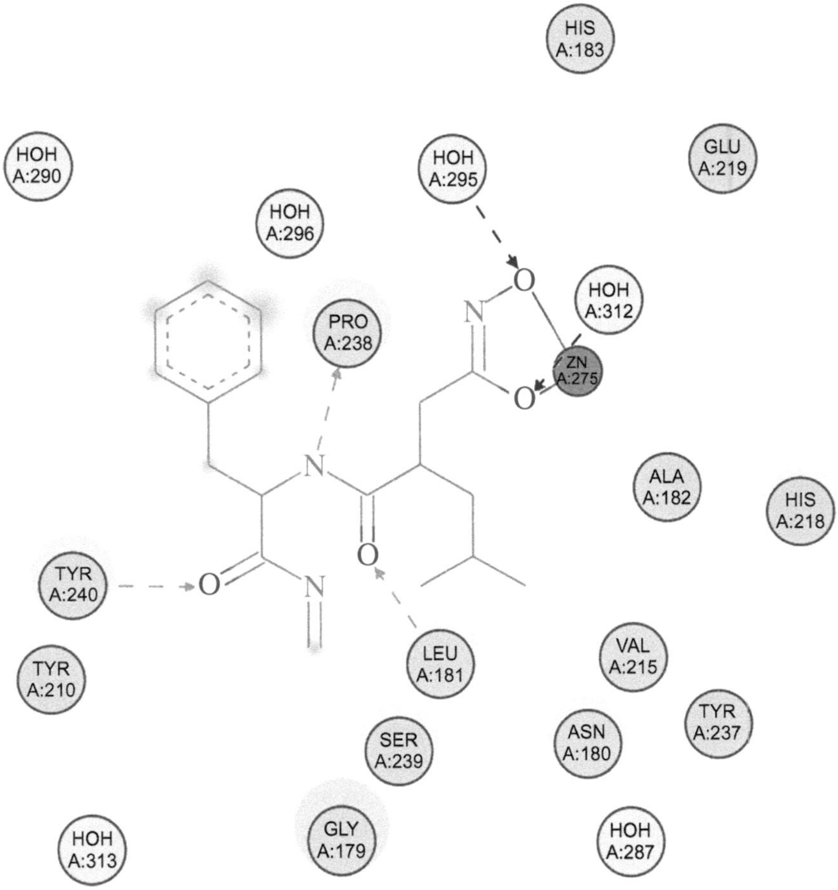

FIG. 10.4 2D interaction plot of MMP-1 (PDB: 1HFC) and one of its inhibitors.

their sulfonamide moieties interact with the backbone of the protein as shown in Fig. 10.6. Fig. 10.6 also shows that enhancing the rigidity of inhibitors is conducive to MMP-13 inhibition that offers to adapt the aromatic substituent. Therefore, the differences in relative size and shape between the S1′ pockets of human collagenases are critical and determinant factors for the selectivity of inhibitors.

10.2.2 Structures of gelatinases

Gelatinases are nothing but MMP-2 and MMP-9 and called as gelatinase-A and gelatinase-B, respectively. Crystal structures of human gelatinases are as shown in Fig. 10.7. Gelatinase-A is one of the important targets for cancer. Seven X-ray structures of gelatinase-A are found in the PDB. Its Ω-loop is shorter than that of collagenase-2 and collagenase-3. This attribute helps to achieve selectivity of certain

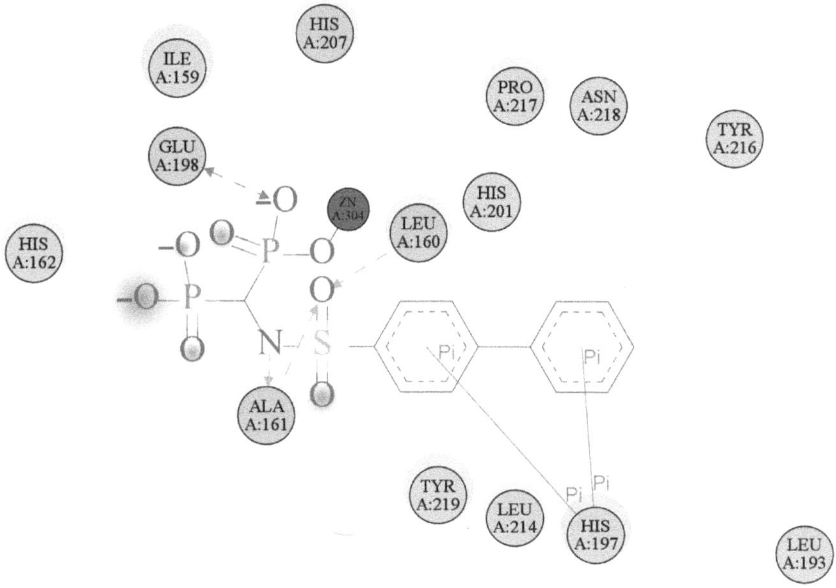

FIG. 10.5 2D interaction plot of MMP-8 (PDB: 4QKZ) and one of its inhibitors.

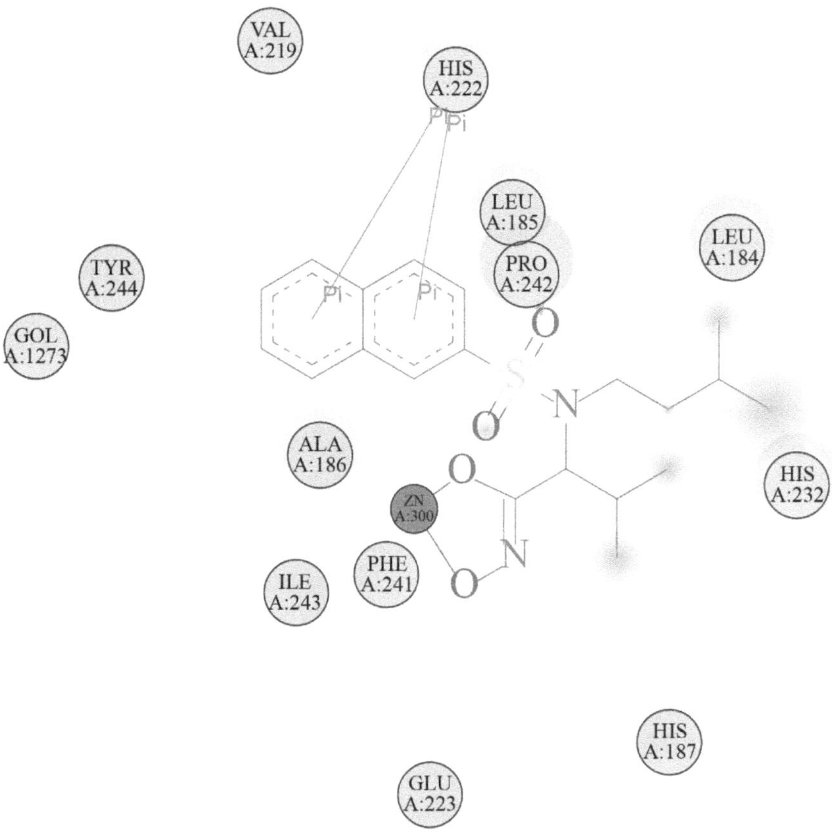

FIG. 10.6 2D interaction plot of MMP-13 (PDB: 3ZXH) and one of its inhibitors.

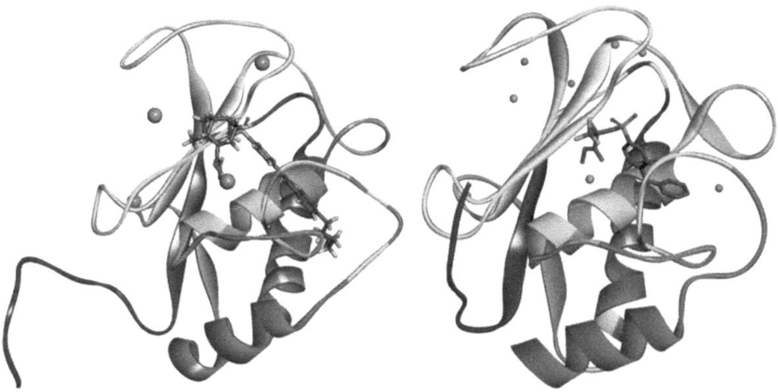

FIG. 10.7 Crystal structure of the gelatinases including MMP-2 (A) and MMP-9 (B).

inhibitors by occupying the S1′ pocket as exhibited in Fig. 10.8. Therefore, the design of gelatinase-A inhibitors with less bulky groups in the S1′ pocket should give them selectivity over collagenase-2 and collagenase-3. The different binding pattern can be attributed to the difference in length of the Ω-loop between gelatinase-B and collegenase-2, providing a possible explanation for the selectivity observed for their inhibitors.

Twenty five X-ray crystal structures of gelatinase-B were deposited in the PDB. The Ω-loop in it is special in the sense that it presents two consecutive proline residues (Pro254 and Pro255) (Fig. 10.9). Because of the conformational rigidity of proline and the low spatial variability of the Ω-loop residues, it can be inferred that the presence of these two proline residues significantly reduces the flexibility of the Ω-loop of this gelatinase. The rigidity of the Ω-loop and small size of S1′ pocket allows an easier entry of the inhibitors in it.

10.3 Roles of collagenases and gelatinases in human diseases

10.3.1 Collagenases

Collagenases are associated with a variety of disease conditions. Their overexpression is related with malignant tumors. Collagenase-3 (MMP-13) is highly overexpressed in osteoarthritis and rheumatoid arthritis (Li et al., 2017; Withrow et al., 2016; Wan et al., 2018), and liver fibrosis (Louka and Ramzy, 2016). A high level of it is associated with the retinal detachment and proliferative vitreoretinopathy (Kim et al., 2014). Nevertheless, it plays a major role in neuroprotection and repair after cerebral ischemia (Ma et al., 2016). Collegenase-3 is overexpressed in cancer also. On the other hand, collagenase-2 (MMP-8) is found to be associated with the inflammatory responses related to obesity and insulin resistance (Lauhio et al., 2016) as well as to be linked with other

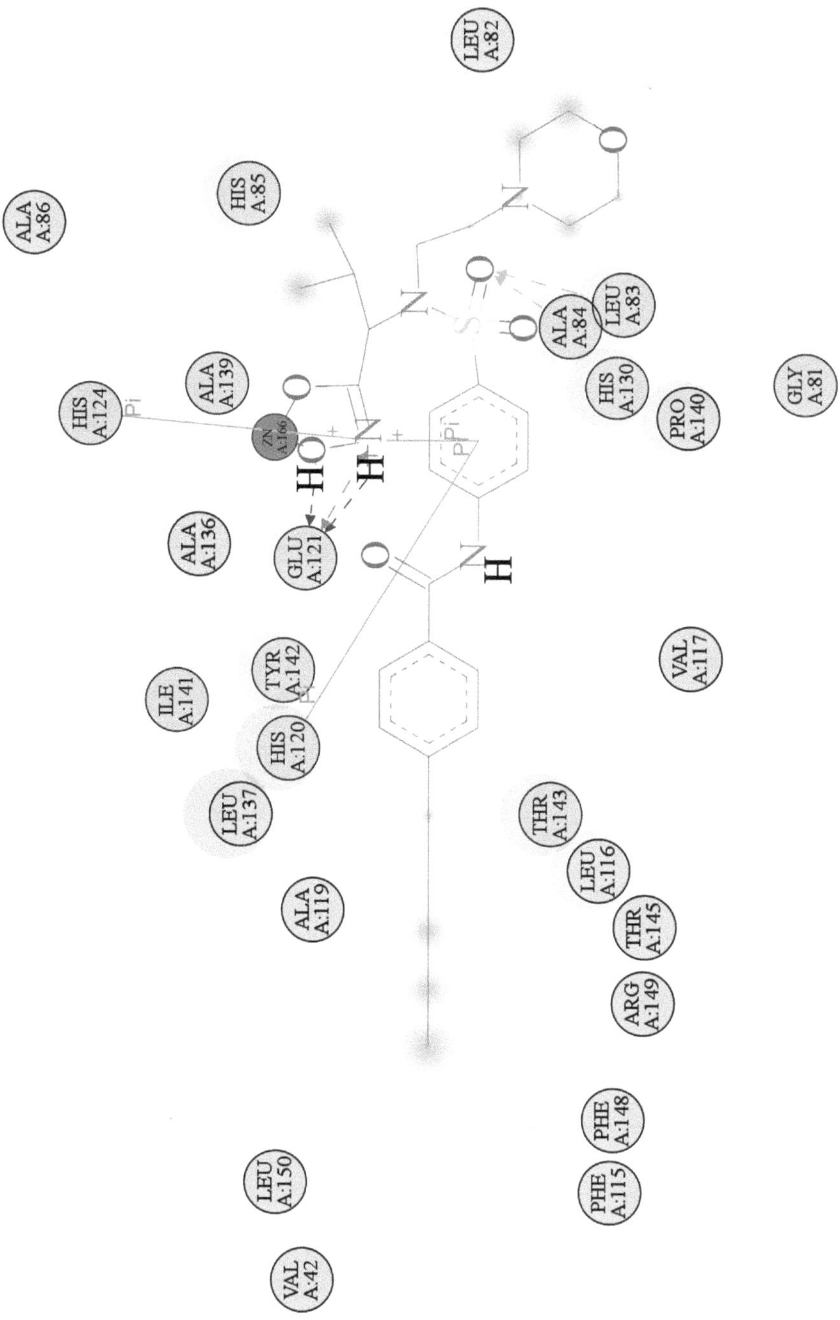

FIG. 10.8 2D interaction plot of MMP-2 (PDB: 1H0V) and one of its inhibitors.

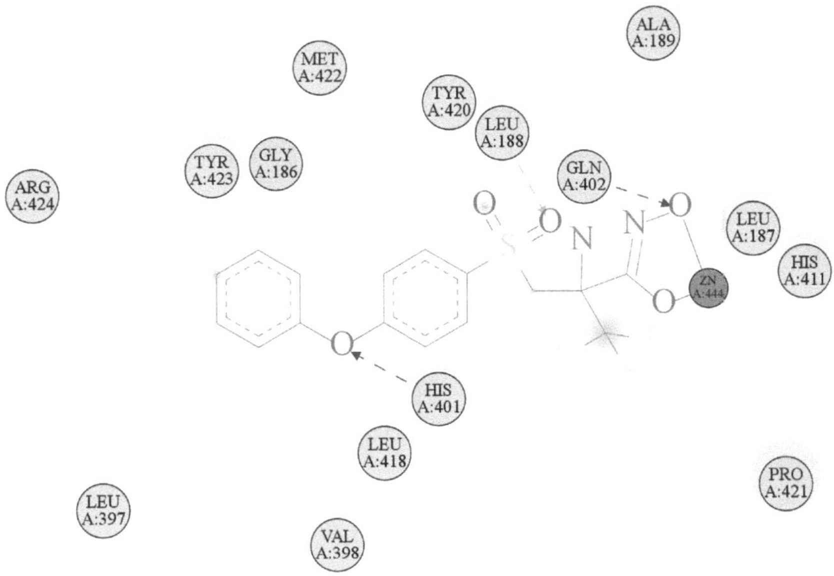

FIG. 10.9 2D interaction plot of MMP-9 (PDB: 2OW1) and one of its inhibitors.

disease conditions such as ischemic stroke (Palm et al., 2018), chronic tonsillitis (Ilmarinen et al., 2017), and periodontitis (Mauramo et al., 2018). In addition, collagenase-2 is found to be overexpressed in ovarian cancer. Likewise, collagenase-1 (MMP-1) has also been observed to be overexpressed in cancer. Moreover, high level of collagenase-1 is reported to be associated with coronary artery diseases (Kondapalli et al., 2016). Below are some important roles of collagenases in various cancers.

10.3.1.1 Collagenases in cancers

MMPs are important enzymes that degrade the extracellular matrix (ECM) and are crucial for the invasiveness of malignant cells (Ala-Aho and Kähäri, 2005). The correlation between collagenase overexpression and malignant tumors points their roles in cancer cell invasion (Ala-Aho and Kähäri, 2005; Overall and López-Otín, 2002; Egeblad and Werb, 2002; Vihinen and Kähäri, 2002). Apart from their physical situations and conditions, collagenases have been found to be overexpressed in numerous tumor cells or malignant type of cancers as shown in Fig. 10.10 (Ala-Aho and Kähäri, 2005).

Collagenase-1 (MMP-1) is the first discovered collagenase. This collagenase has been observed to be overexpressed in several cancers, e.g., breast cancer (Nakopoulou et al., 1999), ovarian cancer (Murray et al., 1998a,b), melanoma (Nikkola et al., 2002; Airola et al., 1999; Ala-Aho and Kähäri, 2005; Murray et al., 1996; Ito et al., 1999), pancreatic cancer (Nikkola-Paakkarinen et al., 2005), gastric cancer (Murray et al., 1998a,b), esophageal

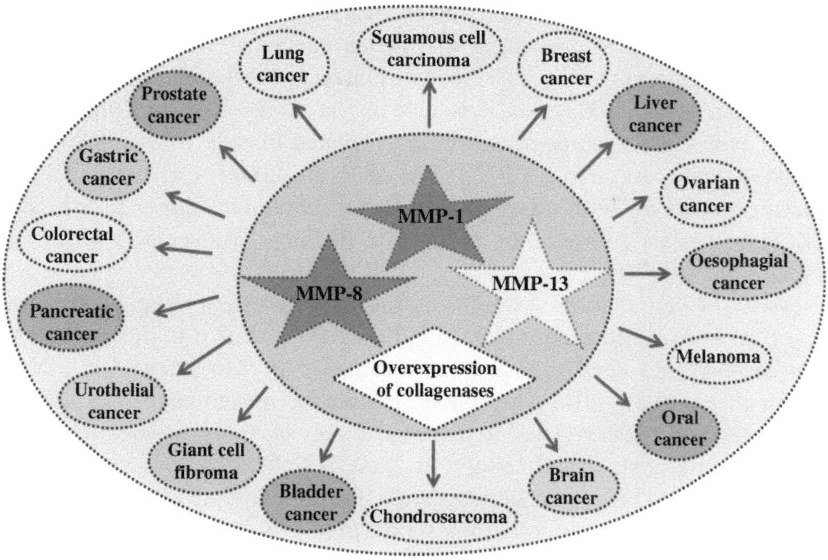

FIG. 10.10 Collagenase overexpression in different cancers.

cancer (Murray et al., 1998a,b), and colorectal cancer (Ghilardi et al., 2001), while collagenase-2 (MMP-8) has been found to be overexpressed only in ovarian cancers (Stadlmann et al., 2003). However, collagenase-3 (MMP-3) also has been observed to be overexpressed in many cancers such as breast cancer (Freije et al., 1994), head and neck squamous cell carcinoma (Johansson et al., 1997), chondrosarcoma (Mengshol et al., 2001), melanoma (Airola et al., 1999; Nikkola et al., 2002), esophageal cancer (Etoh et al., 2000), and urothelial cancer (Boström et al., 2000).

Collegenase-1 obtained from fibroblasts modulates the signaling cascade related to protease activated receptor type-1 (PAR-1), promoting the invasion and migration of breast cancer cells (Boire et al., 2005). The pro-angiogenic effect of MMP-1 is noticed in different types of cancers including melanoma (Blackburn et al., 2007), prostate (Pulukuri and Rao, 2008), breast (Eck et al., 2009), and brain tumors (Pullen et al., 2012). Collegenase-1 triggers the mitogen-activated protein kinases (MAPKs) signaling through mediating PAR-1 and modulates genetic expression to promote angiogenesis (Blackburn and Brinckerhoff, 2008). Collegenase-1 and collegenase-8 together are involved in the pathogenesis of giant cell fibroma (GCF) (Kotepui et al., 2016). During cancer cell proliferation, collagenase, along with other MMPs (such as MMP-2, -3, -7, -9, -11 and -19), is found to cleave the IGF-binding proteins (Nakamura et al., 2005; Loechel et al., 2000; Gialeli et al., 2011). As far as the tumor angiogenesis is concerned, collagenases as well as gelatinases have their profound effect on them (Rundhaug, 2003). Collagenases are found to degrade collagen and subsequently release vascular endothelial growth factor (VEGF) and basic fibroblast growth factor (bFGF) to promote angiogenic effects (Gialeli et al., 2011).

Collegenase-2 plays crucial role in ovarian cancer progression. Its expression is related to the stages of ovarian cancer along with tumor size and its higher expression is also modulated by inflammatory cytokines (Stadlmann et al., 2003). As it is one of the most effective collagenases for the type I collagen degradation, it is related closely to the invasion in squamous cell carcinomas (SCC) (Balbín et al., 2003). Collagenase-1 and gelatinase-1 along with other growth factors modulate tumor progression and angiogenesis followed by metastasis in lungs (Alaseem et al., 2019; Gupta et al., 2007).

As ECM degradation seems to be the major process of metastasis and tumor invasion, collagenase-2 is found to play crucial role during expression of head and neck squamous cell carcinomas (Moilanen et al., 2002; Dejonckheere et al., 2011). Moreover, in case of ovarian cancer, expression of collegenase-2 is correlated to different stages of tumor progression along with poor prognosis (Stadlmann et al., 2003). Nevertheless, variation in its genes is found to be correlated with the risk for bladder cancer (Kader et al., 2006) and its overexpression along with TIMP-1 is found to be highly correlated with the poor prognosis of colorectal cancer (Böckelman et al., 2018). However, its overexpression is found to be modulated by interleukin-1 beta (IL-1β). The proinflammatory cytokines promote the invasion and progression in ovarian cancer (Stadlmann et al., 2003), while collagenase-2 is found to induce the expression of the key regulators of tumor growth, i.e., interleukin-6 (IL-6) and interleukin -8 (IL-8) in breast cancer cells (Thirkettle et al., 2013).

In tongue cancer, however, collagenase-2 has a positive role (Korpi et al., 2008). It is interesting to note that the deficiency of collagenase-2 may produce tongue and skin cancers as evidenced in wild-type mice (Balbín et al., 2003; Korpi et al., 2008), while its expression may be involved in the decrease of breast tumor as well as metastasis in lungs (Soria-Valles et al., 2014). The serum collagenase-2, TIMP-1, and their ratio may be potential prognostic biomarkers in gastric cancer (Laitinen et al., 2018).

It is interesting to note that no such expression of collegenase-3 has been noticed during premalignant tumors of human skin (Airola et al., 1997). However, its expression in the head and neck SCC correlates with the metastasis and invasive properties of tumors and thus, indicates its capability for being an indicator in SCC (Johansson et al., 1997; Cazorla et al., 1998). Its expression is considered to be a marker of the transformation of squamous cell. As it is not found to be expressed in most adult human tissues, its inhibition may be a safe and effective strategy for targeted anticancer therapy where it is expressed (Ala-Aho and Kähäri, 2005). The tumor necrosis factor-α (TNF-α) stimulates its overexpression by regulating the ataxia-telangiectasia mutated (ATM) regulation, favoring the metastasis in lungs (Yan et al., 2016). Collagenase is highly expressed in cancers related to breast along with metastasis in lymph nodes (Kotepui et al., 2016).

10.3.2 Gelatinases

Gelatinases have been found to play major roles in cancer. Among the two gelatinases, gelatinase-A (MMP-2) has been identified as the most crucial target for anticancer therapy, while the gelatinase-B (MMP-9) has been recognized as an antitarget in advance stage of cancer (Fabre et al., 2013, 2014; Overall and Kleifeld, 2006; Serra et al., 2012; Zapico et al., 2015). Apart from cancer, gelatinases have been found to be involved in vasculo-Behçet's disease complicated with aneurysm formation (Pay et al., 2007). Activity of both the gelatinases has been found in corneal and ocular surface disorders as evidenced by gelatin zymography (Singh et al., 2012). Both have clinical significance in chronic obstructive pulmonary disorders (Cataldo et al., 2000), chronic liver diseases (Kuyvenhoven et al., 2003), neurocysticercosis (Verma et al., 2011), chronic arthritis (Giannelli et al., 2005), and atherosclerosis (Kuzuya et al., 2006). The various roles of gelatinases are highlighted in details in our earlier communications (Adhikari et al., 2017a,b,c; Amin et al., 2017).

10.3.2.1 Gelatinases in cancer

So far cancer is concerned, enhanced level of both gelatinases is found to be localized at the site of colon tumor invasion (Emmert-Buck et al., 1994) and their overexpression is found in a variety of cancers including lung, liver, breast, ovary, and colon cancers (Egeblad and Werb, 2002). Their expression is highly correlated with the metastatic events and invasive features of such type of cancers. Therefore, the chance for survival is highly reduced. Nevertheless, the expression of gelatinase is completely dependent on the stages of cancer. Gelatinases are involved in different stages of tumor progression including primary tumor growth, angiogenesis, migration, and invasion of tumor cells in secondary organs along with the progression of the tumor at the metastatic site (Bjorklund and Koivunen, 2005). Gelatinases are involved in the angiogenic events during cancer progression (Schnaper et al., 1993; Seftor et al., 2001) involving multiple pathways. A number of animal studies indicated that both of them are involved in the cancer metastasis (Bjorklund and Koivunen, 2005).

It was found (Decock et al., 2005) that plasma gelatinase-A level is markedly enhanced for patients bearing Her2/neu overexpressing tumors. It suggested that Her2/neu has a direct relation in the signaling pathways of activation of gelatinase-A in breast cancer. Gelatinase-A is related to the cancer progression in human as evidenced by different experiments with gelatinase-A knockout mice. Gelatinase-A also plays crucial roles in angiogenesis and neovascularization (Cathcart et al., 2015a,b; Kessenbrock et al., 2011). Furthermore, its overexpression has been implicated in the progression of different types of malignancies (Chien et al., 2013; Herszényi et al., 2012; Liu et al., 2006). Numerous in vitro and in vivo animal studies (Adhikari et al., 2017a) have shown that gelatinase-A overexpression leads to tumor progression, angiogenesis, and metastasis, resulting in U87MG glioblastoma (Nuti et al., 2011), HT1080 fibrosarcoma (Fabre et al., 2013; Rossello et al., 2004), B16F10 melanoma (Chollet et al., 2002), chemoinvasion model in human umbilical endothelial cell (HUVEC) cells (Nuti et al., 2015; Rossello et al., 2005), human ovarian carcinoma (Zhang et al., 2014), A-549 lung carcinoma (Halder et al., 2015), and human dermal fibroblasts (Park and Kim, 2012). However, the proliferation and invasive features of acute myeloid leukemia (AML) and acute lymphoblastic leukemia (ALL) have been controlled by gelatinase overexpression (Klein et al., 2004). A variety of leukemic cells (such as U-937, K-562, NB4, and SH-1) also disclosed that gelatinase-A helps to migrate the leukemia as evidenced by several matrigel-based invasion studies (Amin et al., 2017).

Like gelatinase-A, gelatinase-B in serum is found to play a crucial role in gastric cancer progression as detected by SDS-PAGE and SDS-PAGE zymography assays (Dragutinović et al., 2006). Chiranjeevi et al. (2014) showed the importance of gelatinase-B gene polymorphism in breast cancer patients along with identification of risk of developing breast cancer. Niu et al. (1998) reported that the $\alpha_v\beta_6$ integrin is expressed in colon cancers which in turn triggers gelatinase-B secretion and subsequently involves the protein-kinase-C pathway activation. Further study by Agrez et al. (1999) showed that $\alpha_v\beta_6$-mediated secretion of gelatinase-B has a crucial role in colon cancer progression. For breast and colon cancers, its overexpression is associated with decreased survival rate and metastasis (Bjorklund and Koivunen, 2005; Zeng et al., 1996; Pacheco et al., 1998; Takeha et al., 1997; Scorilas et al., 2001). Again, for melanoma, increased gelatinase-B expression is found in earlier stages but the decreased expression is found in later stages (van den Oord et al., 1997). It is found that gelatinase-B has a direct correlation with poor prognosis in breast tumors (van't Veer et al., 2002). Nevertheless, in gelatinase-B deficient mice, intravenous injection of melanoma or lung cancer cells exhibited a decrease in metastatic colonies (Itoh et al., 1999), suggesting the importance of gelatinase-B in metastasis. Gelatinase-B is also found to be induced by VEGF during lung metastasis and subsequently its deficiency is found to reduce the metastasis (Hiratsuka et al., 2002). This member of MMP family has been observed to play a crucial role in several cancers associated with inflammation (Bjorklund and Koivunen, 2005). Of the gelatinases, the gelatinase-B in particular has been found to be related with negative regulation of immune response to cancer by cleaving IL-2α as well as through shedding of ICAM-1 and TGF-β activation (Bjorklund and Koivunen, 2005; Yu and Stamenkovic, 2000; Fiore et al., 2002; Sheu et al., 2001).

10.4 Inhibitors of collagenases and gelatinases as anticancer agents

It is clearly evidenced from the above-mentioned instances that both collagenases and gelatinases have important roles and functions in the various types of cancer progression. Therefore, their inhibitors may be effective remedies to combat various types of cancers. As these enzymes are Zn^{2+}-dependent metalloenzymes, compounds possessing various zinc binding groups (ZBGs) may be investigated to find potent inhibitors for them acting as effective anticancer agents. For the affinity of most MMP inhibitors, however, two molecular features are required. One is chelating moiety that can interact with the zinc ion and the other is a hydrophobic extension capable to interact with S1′ pocket of the enzyme and thus, achieve selectivity. Thus, most of the MMP inhibitors were hydroxamate-based, i.e., they contained a hydroxamate (–CONHOH) group. These inhibitors displayed an excellent anticancer activity in tumor cells, but since they were broad-spectrum inhibitors and could inhibit many subtypes of MMPs leading to many side effects, the clinical performance of these drugs against cancer was disappointing. Thus, some molecular modifications are needed in the structures of these inhibitors which can be achieved by including a substituted aryl moiety and a sulfonamide group along with a hydroxamate zinc-binding group. The MMP inhibitors designed based on these structural features are known as new-generation hydroxamate-based MMP inhibitors.

The synthetic inhibitors that were designed based on the above features included peptidomimetics, nonpeptidomimetics inhibitors, and tetracycline derivatives as reported by some authors and listed in Table 10.1 (Mannello et al., 2005; Li et al., 2013). As this table shows, these inhibitors were not selective to any specific MMP, but majority of them were selective to collagenases (MMP-1, -8, and -13) and gelatinases (MMP-2 and -9). However, using antisense strategies and small interfering RNA (siRNA) technology some selectivity can be achieved (Mannello, 2006; Jiang et al., 2003, 2005). Table 10.1 also lists some natural compounds, like neovastat and genistein. Structures of all those compounds listed in Table 10.1 are given in Fig. 10.11. When the structures of MMP inhibitors were adjusted to impart selectivity and abolish toxicity, they could achieve clinical impact in cancer therapy (Fisher and Mobashery, 2006), e.g., a pyrimidine-based inhibitor (**13**, Fig. 10.12) was found to be very selective and potent MMP-13 (collagenase-3) inhibitor that could be a good candidate for future development to treat diseases related to MMP-13 (Fisher and Mobashery, 2006). The compound has a specificity loop within the S1′ pocket and its 3-methyl-4-fluoro group is proximal enough to the zinc to change the water entity. It possesses good oral bioavailability. Similarly, a carbamoyl phosphonate inhibitor (**14**, Fig. 10.12) was developed that affected MMP-2 and -9 (gelatinase-A and gelatinase-B) sparing other MMPs and showed inhibitory activity on cell invasion and tumor colonization. Inhibitors with carbamoyl phosphonate zinc binding groups are water-soluble at physiological pH (Jacobsen et al., 2010). Doxycycline (**15**, Fig 10.12), a tetracycline derivative, is an MMP inhibitor approved for cancer therapy (Lee et al., 2009; Cathcart et al., 2015a,b). This drug reduces laminin degradation by inhibiting gelatinase-B activity (Lee et al., 2009).

TABLE 10.1 Important MMP inhibitors.

MMPIs[a]	Other names	Company	Activity
Peptidomimetics			
Batimastat	BB-94	British Biotech	MMP-1-3, -7, -9
Marimastat	BB-2516	British Biotech	Nonselective
Nonpeptidomimetics			
Tanomastat	BAY 12-9566	Bayer	MMP-2-3, -9
Prinomastat	AG3340	Agouron	MMP-2-3, -7, -9, -13
Rebimastat	BMS-275291	Bristol-Myers Squibb	Gelatinases
MMI-270	CGS27023A	Novartis	MMP-1-3
Tetracyclines			
Minocycline	Minocin	Lederle	MMP-1-3
Metastat	COL-3	State University of New York	MMP-1-2, -8-9, -13
Mechanism-based			
SB-3CT	IN 1250	Wayne State University	Gelatinases
Off-Target			
Zoledronic acid	Zoledronate	Ciba-Geigy	Gelatinases
Letrozole	CGS20267	Novartis	Gelatinases
Natural			
Neovastat	AE-941	AEterna	MMP-1-2, -7, -9, -13
Genistein	Genisteol	Roche	Gelatinases, MMP-14-16

[a] *Structures of these inhibitors can be found in Fig. 10.11.*

Activities of MMPs are regulated at various levels by endogenous inhibitors, where the tissue inhibitors of metalloproteinases (TIMPs) are of prime importance that specifically inhibit MMPs and assist in maintaining the balance between extracellular matrix destruction and formation. However, they have hardly been exploited for pharmacological applications due to their short half-lives in vivo.

Some natural compounds, such as neostat and genistein listed in Table 10.1, were also found to inhibit selectively collagenases and gelatinases and tested for anticancer effects. Neostat, which is an extract of shark cartilage, went through

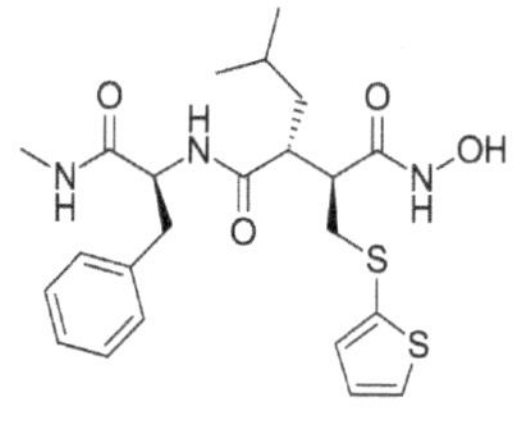

1, Batimastat

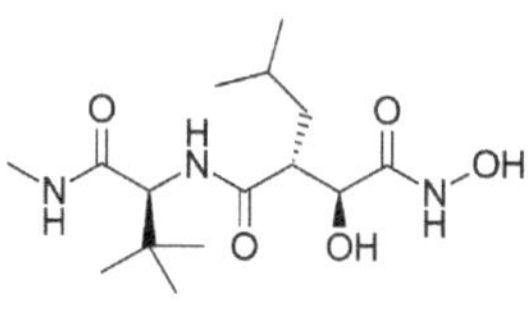

2, Marimastat

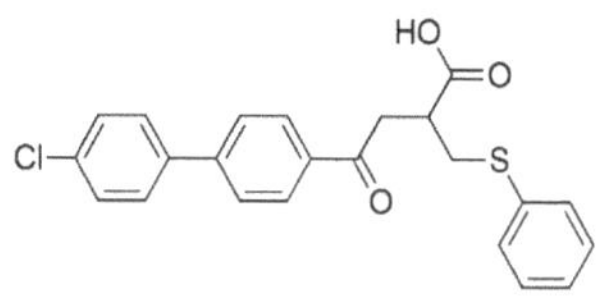

3, Tanomastat

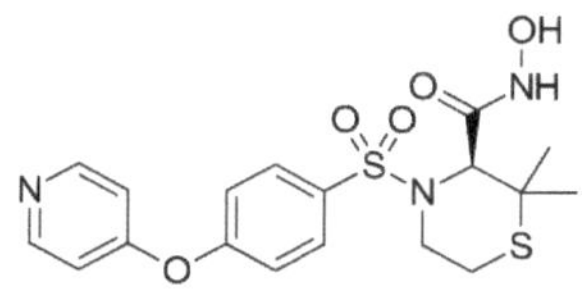

4, Prinomastat

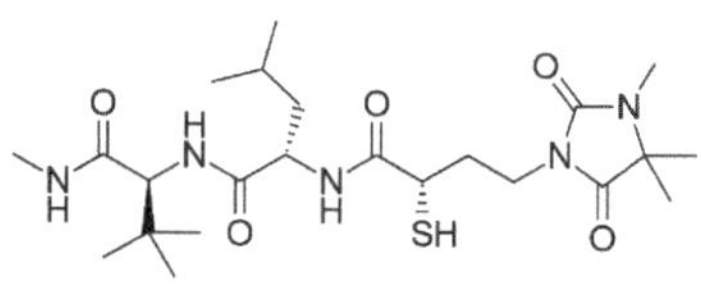

5, Rebimastat

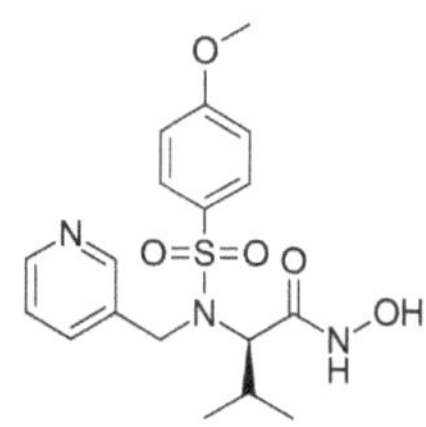

6, MMI-270

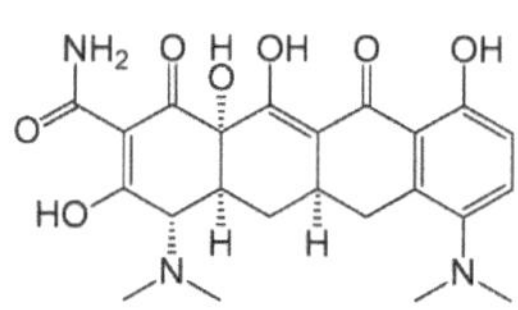

7, Minocycline

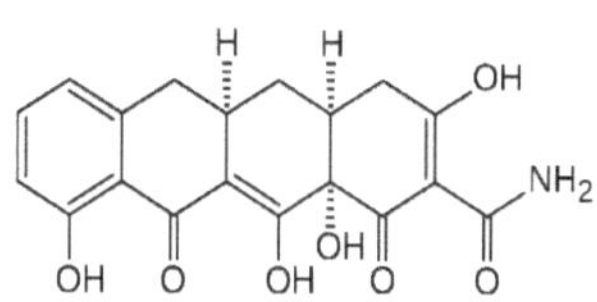

8, Metastat

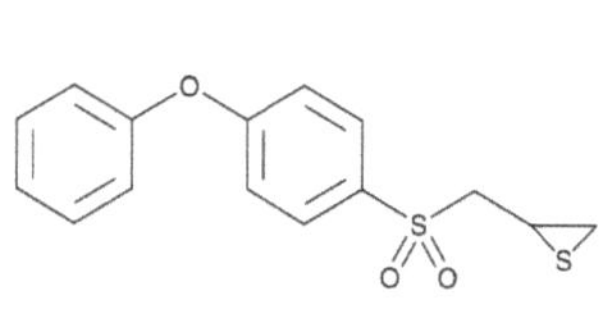

9, SB-3CT

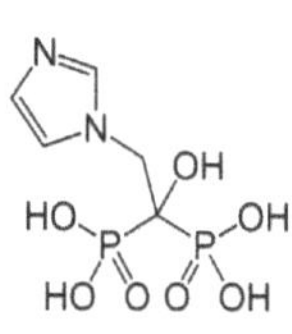

10, Zoledronic acid

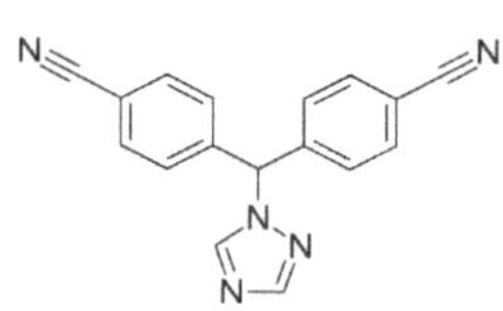

11, Letrozole

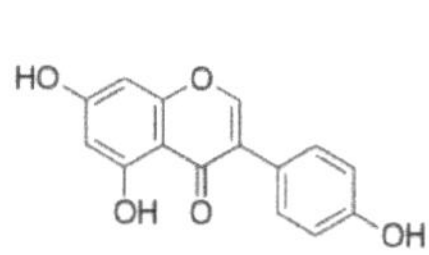

12, Genistein

FIG. 10.11 Structures of potential matrix metalloproteinase inhibitors listed in Table 10.1 and a few more.

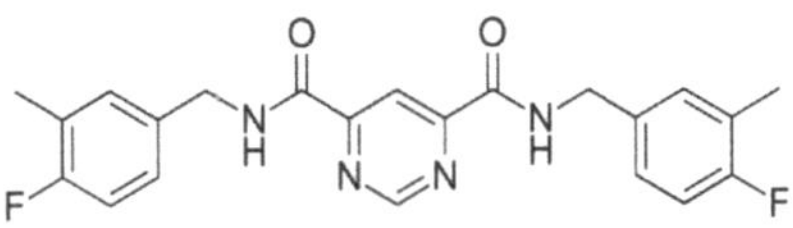

13, Compound 544678-85-5

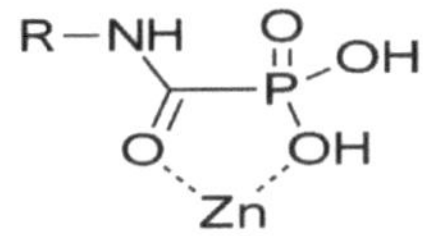

14, A carbamoyl phosphonate

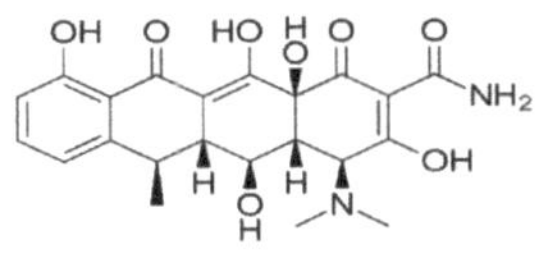

15, Doxycycline

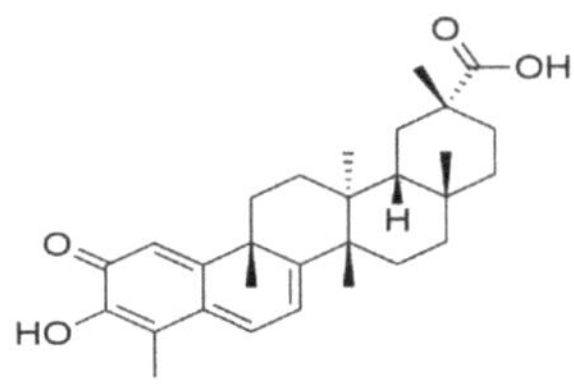

16, Celastrol

FIG. 10.12 MMP inhibitors showing selectivity for collagenase-3 (**13**) and gelatinases (**14–16**).

phase III trials for patients with advanced breast cancer, colorectal cancer, kidney cancer, and stage III nonsmall cell lung cancer, but found to have no significant effects. Genistein, a soy isoflavonoid, was found to be a potent inhibitor of gelatinases and thus, to have some effect on tumor growth and invasion (Huang et al., 2005; Kousidou et al., 2005). Several studies, in fact, indicated that it could lead to a lower risk of cancer development and cancer-related death, particularly due to breast and prostate cancers (Gu et al., 2005; Holzbeierlein et al., 2005). Celastrol (**16**, Fig 10.12), a quinone methide triterpene, from *Tripterygium wilfordii* dose-dependently suppressed TNF-α-induced gelatinase-B gene expression in MDA-MB-231 cells (Mi et al., 2014). However, if natural compounds had been so successful in blocking the MMPs, there was nothing to be worried about management of cancers. But, in in vitro testing paradigms, there are no immune systems, and only a few variables are considered. But in vivo systems are extremely complex and the efficacy of the phytochemicals in preventing the activation of MMPs cannot be claimed.

For selective inhibition of gelatinases, Table 10.1 mentions some off-target compounds, such as zoledronic acid and letrozole. Off-target MMP inhibitors (MMPIs) refer to compounds that show beneficial effects on MMPs but they are not their intended primary targets. Zoledronic acid is a third-generation bisphosphonate to be used as a standard treatment for preventing skeletal complications associated with bone metastases, but it was also found to be associated with downregulation of MMP-2 and -9 expressions (Li et al., 2012). Similarly, letrozole is a reversible nonsteroidal inhibitor of the P450 aromatase and is widely used in hormone therapy for breast cancer patients, but it was also found to suppress the release of gelatinases (MMP-2 and -9) by breast cancer cells in a dose-dependent manner (Mitropoulou et al., 2003; Thürlimann et al., 2005).

Another selective inhibitor of gelatinases is SB-3CT (Table 10.1), which is known as novel mechanism-based inhibitor. It is a potent, selective, slow binding, and the first competitive mechanism-based inhibitor of human gelatinases, whose inhibitory mechanism involves in its fundamental step an enzyme-catalyzed ring opening of thiirane, resulting in a stable zinc-thiolate species (Gu et al., 2005). In mouse model studies, SB-3CT (Table 10.1) has been found to suppress liver metastasis and increase animal survival (Krüger et al., 2005).

Another selective inhibitor of gelatinases has been rebimastat (Table 10.1), but when it went through phase III trial in combination with some other drugs (paclitaxel and carboplatin) for patients with advanced nonsmall cell lung cancer, the result was disappointing due to increased toxicity with no improvements in survival.

The remaining MMP inhibitors of Table 10.1, i.e., batimastat, marimastat, tanomastat, prinomastat, MMI-270, minocycline, metastat, that were not too selective to collagenases or gelatinases but inhibited other MMPs too, also went through several trial phases for anticancer chemotherapy, but none of them showed any super efficacy in terms of patients survival when compared with standard chemotherapy or placebo (Sparano et al., 2004; Shepherd et al., 2002; Bramhall et al., 2002), rather each one had some side effects. However, the clinical trials of these MMPIs have suggested that MMPIs have great promise to develop effective anticancer drugs, provided we could improve the methodology to avoid or minimize the adverse events. Despite promising results in mice, MMPIs did not help cancer patients live longer and some patients developed serious side effects. As more specific MMPIs are now available, new trials should be investigated to test their antimetastatic properties in early-stage tumors, and endpoints should focus on parameters other than decreasing metastatic tumor burden.

In fact, in the failure of clinical trials so far specificity of MMPIs has been a challenging issue (Winer et al., 2018). Now since it has surfaced that some MMPs have antitumor effects in some types of cancers, efforts are being made to the design of MMPIs that are highly selective and possibly inhibit only deleterious functions of specific, tumor-associated MMPs. A turning point in this effort is that the activity of an MMP can be inhibited specifically by targeting its molecular structure outside of the catalytic domain, so-called exosite (Levin et al., 2017). An exosite is a secondary binding site in the structure of the enzyme remote from the active site, similar to allosteric site but differing in the fact that, in order for an enzyme to be active, the exosite typically must be occupied. Unlike the catalytic domains, different exosites are present in different MMPs and it is believed that if they are targeted by synthetic, low-molecular-weight compounds or antibodies, selective inhibition of even a specific function of a single MMP can be achieved. This approach has led to the generation of highly selective monoclonal antibodies (mAbs), AB0041 and AB0046, to MMP-9. These mAbs and a humanized version of AB0041, GS-5745, have shown efficacy in a mouse xenograft model of colorectal carcinoma (Levin et al., 2017).

One of the first anti-MMP-9 antibodies reported was a murine monoclonal antibody (mAb), REGA-3G12 (Paemen et al., 1995). A selective and potent MMP-2/9 inhibitory antibody developed by Sela-Passwell et al. (2012)

was SDS3. It was generated by immunizing mice with a small synthetic, inorganic metal ligand molecule, tris-imidazole zinc complex (zinc-tripod) which was specifically designed to mimic structural and chemical motifs of the relatively ex-posed catalytic zinc-protein machinery in the active form of MMPs. Structural and biochemical analysis indicated that SDS3 has hybrid like interaction with MMP-2/9.

Selective MMP inhibition can also be achieved by the use of "endogenous" or "intrinsic" MMP inhibitors. However, selective and specific MMPIs could also be developed using sophisticated biochemical techniques such as protein engineering and directed evolution to improve the inhibitory activity of antibodies and TIMPs. Protein engineering has been used to generate TIMP variants that specifically inhibit MMP-14. Since the failure of the last trials in the past, further trials of MMPIs have been on hold. However, specific inhibitors are currently being developed and the mAbs discussed above are perhaps the most promising of the new MMPIs.

In fact, a culture shift is needed to reveal the true effects of MMPIs. Now there are multiple techniques that allow the gene expression in few, or even single cells that can be identified by laser capture microscopy (Winer et al., 2018).

In fact, MMP inhibition in vivo is extremely challenging and straight forward techniques to design inhibitors, such as substrate-based peptidomimetic, are not compatible with this family due to high structural homology, substrate promiscuity, and cross-reactivity. This raises the need for novel approaches to be applied to increase inhibitors' selectivity and specificity. Thus, new-age design of MMP inhibitors is focused mainly on specificity and selectivity between the MMPs and the closely related ADAM family. For this, protein engineering (PE) methodologies, such as computational design and directed evolution (DE), have been found quite encouraging.

10.5 Conclusions

Though a little is known about the relation between the collagenases and gelatinases expression and cancer progression, it is clearly observed that collagenases and gelatinases have implication in tumorogenesis, angiogenesis, and apoptotic mechanisms in numerous cancers as these collagenases are directly interlinked to other zinc-dependent MMPs related to cancer. Therefore, it is possible that expression of different MMPs in cancerous condition may influence each other. In this context, it may be inferred that collagenases and gelatinases, apart from the direct relation, may have an indirect role in tumor progression. Therefore, collagenase and gelatinase inhibitors may be targeted for effective management of anticancer therapy and related diseases. However, in vivo inhibition of MMPs is not an easy task and the usual methods to design inhibitors for them are not compatible for this class of enzymes due to high structural homology, substrate promiscuity, and cross-reactivity. Thus, attention has been focused to apply new approaches that can provide specificity and selectivity between the MMPs. Now new age design of MMPIs has been directed to protein engineering (PE) methodologies, such as computational design and directed evolution (DE). A turning point in this effort is that the activity of an MMP can be inhibited specifically by targeting its molecular structure outside of the catalytic domain, so-called exosite, a secondary binding site in the structure of the enzyme remote from the active site. It is believed that if exosites are targeted by synthetic, low-molecular-weight compounds or antibodies, selective inhibition of even a specific function of a single MMP can be achieved. This approach has led to the generation of highly selective monoclonal antibodies (mAbs) that have shown efficacy in a mouse xenograft model of colorectal carcinoma.

Acknowledgments

Nilanjan Adhikari and Sk. Abdul Amin gratefully acknowledge the grant of Research Assistant (RA) Fellowship (RAF) and Senior Research Fellowship (SRF), respectively, by Council of Scientific and Industrial Research (CSIR), New Delhi, India and Tarun Jha thanks UGC, New Delhi, for the financial support from UPE Phase II and RUSA 2.0 programs as implemented by Jadavpur University, Kolkata, India. Also all the authors gratefully acknowledge the research facilities provided by the Department of Pharmaceutical Technology, Jadavpur University, Kolkata, India as well as help rendered by S.P. Gupta, Editor of this volume, who wrote the "inhibitors" portion of this chapter.

References

Adhikari, N., Halder, A.K., Mallick, S., Saha, A., Saha, K.D., Jha, T., 2016. Robust design of some selective matrix metalloproteinase-2 inhibitors over matrix metalloproteinase-9 through in silico/fragment-based lead identification and de novo lead modification: syntheses and biological assays. Bioorg. Med. Chem. 24, 4291–4309.

Adhikari, N., Amin, S.A., Saha, A., Jha, T., 2017a. Understanding chemico-biological interactions of glutamate MMP-2 inhibitors through rigorous alignment-dependent 3D-QSAR analyses. ChemistrySelect 2, 7888–7898.

Adhikari, N., Mukherjee, A., Saha, A., Jha, T., 2017b. Arylsulfonamides and selectivity of matrix metalloproteinase-2: an overview. Eur. J. Med. Chem. 129, 72–109.

Adhikari, N., Baidya, S., Saha, A., Jha, T., 2017c. Advances in studies on enzyme inhibitors as drugs. Volume 2: miscellaneous drugs. In: Gupta, S.P. (Ed.), Design and Development of Matrix Metalloproteinase Inhibitors Containing Zinc-Binding Groups, Without Zinc-Binding Groups, and Mechanism-Based. Nova Science Publishers, New York, USA, pp. 135–208.

Adhikari, N., Amin, S.A., Saha, A., Jha, T., 2018a. Exploring in-house glutamate inhibitors of matrix metalloproteinase-2 through validated robust chemico-biological quantitative approaches. Struct. Chem. 29, 285–295.

Adhikari, N., Amin, S.A., Saha, A., Jha, T., 2018b. Structural exploration for the refinement of anticancer matrix metalloproteinase-2 inhibitor designing approaches through robust validated multi-QSARs. J. Mol. Struct. 1156, 501–515.

Agrez, M., Gu, X., Turton, J., Meldrum, C., Niu, J., Antalis, T., Howard, E.W., 1999. The alpha v beta 6 integrin induces gelatinase B secretion in colon cancer cells. Int. J. Cancer 81, 90–97.

Airola, K., Johansson, N., Kariniemi, A.L., Kähäri, V.M., Saarialho-Kere, U., 1997. Human collagenase-3 is expressed in malignant squamous epithelium of the skin. J. Invest. Dermatol. 109, 225–231.

Airola, K., Karonen, T., Vaalamo, M., Lehti, K., Lohi, J., Kariniemi, A.L., Keski-Oja, J., Saarialho-Kere, U.K., 1999. Expression of collagenases-1 and -3 and their inhibitors TIMP-1 and -3 correlates with the level of invasion in malignant melanomas. Br. J. Cancer 80, 733–743.

Ala-Aho, R., Kähäri, V.M., 2005. Collagenases in cancer. Biochimie 87, 273–286.

Alaseem, A., Alhazzani, K., Dondapati, P., Alobid, S., Bishayee, A., Rathinavelu, A., 2019. Matrix metalloproteinases: a challenging paradigm of cancer management. Semin. Cancer Biol. 56, 100–115.

Amin, S.A., Adhikari, N., Jha, T., 2017. Is dual inhibition of metalloenzymes HDAC-8 and MMP-2 a potential pharmacological target to combat hematological malignancies? Pharmacol. Res. 122, 8–19.

Balbín, M., Fueyo, A., Tester, A.M., Pendás, A.M., Pitiot, A.S., Astudillo, A., Overall, C.M., Shapiro, S.D., López-Otín, C., 2003. Loss of collagenase-2 confers increased skin tumor susceptibility to male mice. Nat. Genet. 35, 252–257.

Benjamin, M.M., Khalil, R.A., 2012. Matrix metalloproteinase inhibitors as investigative tools in the pathogenesis and management of vascular disease. In: Gupta, S.P. (Ed.), Matrix Metalloproteinase Inhibitors. Springer, Basel, pp. 209–279 (Chapter 7).

Bjorklund, M., Koivunen, E., 2005. Gelatinase-mediated migration and invasion of cancer cells. Biochim. Biophys. Acta 1755, 37–69.

Blackburn, J.S., Brinckerhoff, C.E., 2008. Matrix metalloproteinase-1 and thrombin differentially activate gene expression in endothelial cells via PAR-1 and promote angiogenesis. Am. J. Pathol. 173, 1736–1746.

Blackburn, J.S., Rhodes, C.H., Coon, C.I., Brinckerhoff, C.E., 2007. RNA interference inhibition of matrix metalloproteinase-1 prevents melanoma metastasis by reducing tumor collagenase activity and angiogenesis. Cancer Res. 67, 10849–10858.

Böckelman, C., Beilmann-Lehtonen, I., Kaprio, T., Koskensalo, S., Tervahartiala, T., Mustonen, H., Stenman, U.H., Sorsa, T., Haglund, C., 2018. Serum MMP-8 and TIMP-1 predict prognosis in colorectal cancer. BMC Cancer 18, 679.

Boire, A., Covic, L., Agarwal, A., Jacques, S., Sherifi, S., Kuliopulos, A., 2005. PAR1 is a matrix metalloprotease-1 receptor that promotes invasion and tumorigenesis of breast cancer cells. Cell 120, 303–313.

Boström, P.J., Ravanti, L., Reunanen, N., Aaltonen, V., Söderström, K.O., Kähäri, V.M., Laato, M., 2000. Expression of collagenase-3 (matrix metalloproteinase-13) in transitional cell carcinoma of the urinary bladder. Int. J. Cancer 88, 417–423.

Bramhall, S.R., Schulz, J., Nemunaitis, J., Brown, P.D., Baillet, M., Buckels, J.A., 2002. A double-blind placebo-controlled, randomized study comparing gemcitabine and marimastat with gemcitabine and placebo as first line therapy in patients with advanced pancreatic cancer. Br. J. Cancer 87, 161–167.

Cataldo, D., Munaut, C., Noël, A., Frankenne, F., Bartsch, P., Foidart, J.M., Louis, R., 2000. MMP-2- and MMP-9-linked gelatinolytic activity in the sputum from patients with asthma and chronic obstructive pulmonary disease. Int. Arch. Allergy Immunol. 123, 259–267.

Cathcart, J., Pulkoshi-Gross, A., Cao, J., 2015a. Targeting matrix metalloprpteinases in cancer: bringing new life to old ideas. Genes Dis. 2, 26–34.

Cathcart, J., Pulkoski-Gross, A., Cao, J., 2015b. Targeting matrix metalloproteinases in cancer: bringing new life to old ideas. Genes Dis. 2, 26–34.

Cazorla, M., Hernandez, L., Nadal, A., Balbín, M., López, J.M., Vizoso, F., Fernandez, P.L., Iwata, K., Cardesa, A., López-Otín, C., Campo, E., 1998. Collagenase-3 expression is associated with advanced local invasion in human squamous cell carcinomas of the larynx. J. Pathol. 186, 144–150.

Chien, M.H., Lin, C.W., Cheng, C.W., Wen, Y.C., Yang, S.F., 2013. Matrix metalloproteinase-2 as a target for head and neck cancer therapy. Expert Opin. Ther. Targets 17, 203–216.

Chiranjeevi, P., Spurthi, K.M., Rani, N.S., Kumar, G.R., Aiyengar, T.M., Saraswati, M., Srilatha, G., Kumar, G.K., Sinha, S., Kumari, C.S., Reddy, B.N., Vishnupriya, S., Rani, H.S., 2014. Gelatinase B (-1562C/T) polymorphism in tumor progression and invasion of breast cancer. Tumour Biol. 35, 1351–1356.

Chollet, A.M., Le Diguarher, T., Kucharczyk, N., Loynel, A., Bertrand, M., Tucker, G., Guilbaud, N., Burbridge, M., Pastoureau, P., Fradin, A., Sabatini, M., Fauchère, J.L., Casara, P., 2002. Solid-phase synthesis of alpha-substituted 3-bisarylthio N-hydroxy propionamides as specific MMP inhibitors. Bioorg. Med. Chem. Lett. 10, 531–544.

Chung, L., Dinakarpandian, D., Yoshida, N., Lauer-Fields, J.L., Fields, G.B., Visse, R., Nagase, H., 2004. Collagenase unwinds triple-helical collagen prior to peptide bond hydrolysis. EMBO J. 23, 3020–3030.

Decock, J., Hendrickx, W., Wildiers, H., Christiaens, M.R., Neven, P., Drijkoningen, M., Paridaens, R., 2005. Plasma gelatinase levels in patients with primary breast cancer in relation to axillary lymph node status, Her2/neu expression, and other clinicopathological variables. Clin. Exp. Metastasis 22, 495–502.

Dejonckheere, E., Vandenbroucke, R.E., Libert, C., 2011. Matrix metalloproteinase 8 has a central role in inflammatory disorders and cancer progression. Cytokine Growth Factor Rev. 22, 73–81.

Di Lullo, G.A., Sweeney, S.M., Korkko, J., Ala-Kokko, L., San Antonio, J.D., 2002. Mapping the ligand-binding sites and disease-associated mutations on the most abundant protein in the human, type i collagen. J. Biol. Chem. 277, 4223–4231.

Dragutinović, V.V., Radovanović, N.S., Izrael-Živković, L.T., Vrvić, M.M., 2006. Detection of gelatinase B activity in serum of gastric cancer patients. World J. Gastroenterol. 12, 105–109.

Eck, S.M., Hoopes, P.J., Petrella, B.L., Coon, C.I., Brinckerhoff, C.E., 2009. Matrix metalloproteinase-1 promotes breast cancer angiogenesis and osteolysis in a novel in vivo model. Breast Cancer Res. Treat. 116, 79–90.

Egeblad, M., Werb, Z., 2002. New functions for the matrix metalloproteinases in cancer progression. Nat. Rev. Cancer 2, 161–174.

Emmert-Buck, M.R., Roth, M.J., Zhuang, Z., Campo, E., Rozhin, J., Sloane, B.F., Liotta, L.A., Stetler-Stevenson, W.G., 1994. Increased gelatinase A (MMP-2) and cathepsin B activity in invasive tumor regions of human colon cancer samples. Am. J. Pathol. 145, 1285–1290.

Etoh, T., Inoue, H., Yoshikawa, Y., Barnard, G.F., Kitano, S., Mori, M., 2000. Increased expression of collagenase-3 (MMP-13) and MT1-MMP in oesophageal cancer is related to cancer aggressiveness. Gut 47, 50–56.

Fabre, B., Filipiak, K., Zapico, J.M., Diaz, N., Carbajo, R.J., Schott, A.K., Martinez-Alcazar, M.P., Suarez, D., Pineda-Lucena, A., Ramos, A., de Pascual-Teresa, B., 2013. Progress towards water-soluble triazole-based selective MMP-2 inhibitors. Org. Biomol. Chem. 11, 6623–6641.

Fabre, B., Filipiak, K., Diaz, N., Zapico, J.M., Suarez, D., Ramos, A., de Pascual-Teresa, B., 2014. An integrated computational and experimental approach to gaining selectivity for MMP-2 within the gelatinase subfamily. ChemBioChem 15, 399–412.

Fiore, E., Fusco, C., Romero, P., Stamenkovic, I., 2002. Matrix metalloproteinase-9 (MMP-9/gelatinase B) proteolytically cleaves ICAM-1 and participates in tumor cell resistance to natural killer cell-mediated cytotoxicity. Oncogene 21, 5213–5223.

Fisher, J.F., Mobashery, S., 2006. Recent advances in MMP inhibitor design. Cancer Metastasis Rev. 25, 115–136.

Freije, J.M., Diéz-Itza, I., Balbín, M., Sánchez, L.M., Blasco, R., Tolivia, J., López-Otín, C., 1994. Molecular cloning and expression of collagenase-3, a novel human matrix metalloproteinase produced by breast carcinomas. J. Biol. Chem. 269, 16766–16773.

Ghilardi, G., Biondi, M.L., Mangoni, J., Leviti, S., DeMonti, M., Guagnellini, E., Scorza, R., 2001. Matrix metalloproteinase-1 promoter polymorphism 1G/2G is correlated with colorectal cancer invasiveness. Clin. Cancer Res. 7, 2344–2346.

Gialeli, C., Theocharis, A.D., Karamanos, N.K., 2011. Roles of matrix metalloproteinases in cancer progression and their pharmacological targeting. FEBS J. 278, 16–27.

Giannelli, G., Iannone, F., Marinosci, F., Covelli, M., Lapadula, G., Antonaci, S., 2005. Infliximab therapy does not modify MMP-2 and MMP-9 serum concentrations in chronic arthritis. Clin. Exp. Rheumatol. 23, 867–872.

Groblewska, M., Siewko, M., Mroczko, B., Szmitkowski, M., 2012. The role of matrix metalloproteinases (MMPs) and their inhibitors (TIMPs) in the development of esophageal cancer. Folia Histochem. Cytobiol. 50, 12–19.

Gu, Z., Cui, J., Brown, S., et al., 2005. A highly specific inhibitor of matrix metalloproteinase-9 rescues laminin from proteolysis and neurons from apoptosis in transient focal cerebral ischemia. J. Neurosci. 25, 6401–6408.

Gupta, S.P., Patil, V.M., 2012. Specificity of binding and structure-activity relationships. In: Gupta, S.P. (Ed.), Matrix Metalloproteanases, first ed. Springer, Basel, pp. 35–56.

Gupta, G.P., Nguyen, D.X., Chiang, A.C., Bos, P.D., Kim, J.Y., Nadal, C., Gomis, R.R., Manova-Todorova, K., Massagué, J., 2007. Mediators of vascular remodelling co-opted for sequential steps in lung metastasis. Nature 446, 765–770.

Halder, A.K., Mallick, S., Shikha, D., Saha, A., Saha, K.D., Jha, T., 2015. Design of dual MMP-2/HDAC-8 inhibitors by pharmacophore mapping, molecular docking, synthesis and biological activity. RSC Adv. 5, 72373–72386.

Herszényi, L., Hritz, I., Lakatos, G., Varga, M.Z., Tulassay, Z., 2012. The behaviour of matrix metalloproteinases and their inhibitors in colorectal cancer. Int. J. Mol. Sci. 13, 13240–13263.

Hiratsuka, S., Nakamura, K., Iwai, S., Murakami, M., Itoh, T., Kijima, H., Shipley, J.M., Senior, R.M., Shibuya, M., 2002. MMP9 induction by vascular endothelial growth factor receptor-1 is involved in lung specific metastasis. Cancer Cell 2, 289–300.

Holmbeck, K., Bianco, P., Caterina, J., Yamada, S., Kromer, M., Kuznetsov, S.A., Mankani, M., Robey, P.G., Poole, A.R., Pidoux, I., Ward, J.M., Birkedal-Hansen, H., 1999. MT1-MMP-deficient mice develop dwarfism, osteopenia, arthritis, and connective tissue disease due to inadequate collagen turnover. Cell 99, 81–92.

Holzbeierlein, J.M., McIntosh, J., Thrasher, J.B., 2005. The role of soy phytoestrogens in prostate cancer. Curr. Opin. Urol. 15, 17–22.

Hu, J., Van den Steen, P.E., Sang, Q.X., Opdenakker, G., 2007. Matrix metalloproteinase inhibitors as therapy for inflammatory and vascular diseases. Nat. Rev. Drug Discov. 6, 480–498.

Huang, X., Chen, S., Xu, L., et al., 2005. Genistein inhibits p38 map kinase activation, matrix metalloproteinase type 2, and cell invasion in human prostate epithelial cells. Cancer Res. 65, 3470–3478.

Ilmarinen, T., Lont, T., Hagström, J., Tervahartiala, T., Sorsa, T., Haglund, C., Munck-Wickland, E., Ramqvist, T., Dalianis, T., Aaltonen, L.M., 2017. Systemic matrix metalloproteinase-8 response in chronic tonsillitis. Infect. Dis. (Lond.) 49, 302–307.

Ito, T., Ito, M., Shiozawa, J., Naito, S., Kanematsu, T., Sekine, I., 1999. Expression of the MMP-1 in human pancreatic carcinoma: relationship with prognostic factor. Mod. Pathol. 12, 669–674.

Itoh, T., Tanioka, M., Matsuda, H., Nishimoto, H., Yoshioka, T., Suzuki, R., Uehira, M., 1999. Experimental metastasis is suppressed in MMP-9-deficient mice. Clin. Exp. Metastasis 17, 177–181.

Jacobsen, J.A., Major Jourden, J.L., Miller, M.T., Cohen, S.M., 2010. To bind zinc or not to bind zinc: an examination of innovative approaches to improved metalloproteinase inhibition. Biochim. Biophys. Acta 1803, 72–94.

Jha, T., Adhikari, N., Saha, A., Amin, S.A., 2018. Multiple molecular modeling studies on some derivatives and analogues of glutamic acid as matrix metalloproteinase-2 inhibitors. SAR QSAR Environ. Res. 29, 43–68.

Jiang, X., Dutton, C.M., Qi, W., et al., 2003. Inhibition of MMP-1 expression by antisense RNA decreases invasiveness of human chondrosarcoma. J. Orthop. Res. 21, 1063–1070.

Jiang, X., Dutton, C.M., Qi, W.N., Block, J.A., Garamszegi, N., Scully, S.P., 2005. siRNA mediated inhibition of MMP-1 reduces invasive potential of a human chondrosarcoma cell line. J. Cell. Physiol. 202, 723–730.

Johansson, N., Airola, K., Grénman, R., Kariniemi, A.L., Saarialho-Kere, U., Kähäri, V.-M., 1997. Expression of collagenase-3 (matrix metalloproteinase-13) in squamos cell carcinomas of the head and neck. Am. J. Pathol. 151, 499–508.

Kader, A.K., Shao, L., Dinney, C.P., Schabath, M.B., Wang, Y., Liu, J., Gu, J., Grossman, H.B., Wu, X., 2006. Matrix metalloproteinase polymorphisms and bladder cancer risk. Cancer Res. 66, 11644–11648.

Kast, R.E., Halatsch, M.E., 2012. Matrix metalloproteinase-2 and -9 in glioblastoma: a trio of old drugs-captopril, disulfiram and nelfinavirare inhibitors with potential as adjunctive treatments in glioblastoma. Arch. Med. Res. 43, 243–247.

Kessenbrock, K., Plaks, V., Werb, Z., 2011. Matrix metalloproteinases: regulators of the tumor microenviroment. Cell 141, 52–67.

Kim, B., Abdel-Rahman, M.H., Wang, T., Pouly, S., Mahmoud, A.M., Cebulla, C.M., 2014. Retinal MMP-12, MMP-13, TIMP-1, and TIMP-2 expression in murine experimental retinal detachment. Invest. Ophthalmol. Vis. Sci. 55, 2031–3040.

Klein, G., Vellenga, E., Fraaije, M.W., Kamps, W.A., de Bont, E.S., 2004. The possible role of matrix metalloproteinase (MMP)-2 and MMP-9 in cancer, e.g. acute leukemia. Crit. Rev. Oncol. Hematol. 50, 87–100.

Kondapalli, M.S., Galimudi, R.K., Gundapaneni, K.K., Padala, C., Cingeetham, A., Gantala, S., Ali, A., Shyamala, N., Sahu, S.K., Nallari, P., Hanumanth, S.R., 2016. MMP 1 circulating levels and promoter polymorphism in risk prediction of coronary artery disease in asymptomatic first degree relatives. Gene 595, 115–120.

Korpi, J.T., Kervinen, V., Mäklin, H., Väänänen, A., Lahtinen, M., Läärä, E., Ristimäki, A., Thomas, G., Ylipalosaari, M., Aström, P., Lopez-Otin, C., Sorsa, T., Kantola, S., Pirilä, E., Salo, T., 2008. Collagenase-2 (matrix metalloproteinase-8) plays a protective role in tongue cancer. Br. J. Cancer 98, 766–775.

Kotepui, M., Punsawad, C., Chupeerach, C., Songsri, A., Charoenkijkajorn, L., Petmitr, S., 2016. Differential expression of matrix metalloproteinase-13 in association with invasion of breast cancer. Contemp. Oncol. (Pozn) 20, 225–228.

Kousidou, O.C., Mitropoulou, T.N., Roussidis, A.E., Kletsas, D., Theocharis, A.D., Karamanos, N.K., 2005. Genistein suppresses the invasive potential of human breast cancer cells through transcriptional regulation of metalloproteinases and their tissue inhibitors. Int. J. Oncol. 26, 1101–1109.

Krüger, A., Arlt, M.J., Gerg, M., et al., 2005. Antimetastatic activity of a novel mechanism-based gelatinase inhibitor. Cancer Res. 65, 3523–3526.

Kuyvenhoven, J.P., van Hoek, B., Blom, E., van Duijn, W., Hanemaaijer, R., Verheijen, J.H., Lamers, C.B., Verspaget, H.W., 2003. Assessment of the clinical significance of serum matrix metalloproteinases MMP-2 and MMP-9 in patients with various chronic liver diseases and hepatocellular carcinoma. Thromb. Haemost. 89, 718–725.

Kuzuya, M., Nakamura, K., Sasaki, T., Cheng, X.W., Itohara, S., Iguchi, A., 2006. Effect of MMP-2 deficiency on atherosclerotic lesion formation in apoE-deficient mice. Arterioscler. Thromb. Vasc. Biol. 26, 1120–1125.

Laitinen, A., Hagström, J., Mustonen, H., Kokkola, A., Tervahartiala, T., Sorsa, T., Böckelman, C., Haglund, C., 2018. Serum MMP-8 and TIMP-1 as prognostic biomarkers in gastric cancer. Tumor Biol. 40, 1–10. https://doi.org/10.1177/1010428318799266.

Lakka, S.S., Rajan, M., Gondi, C., Yanamandra, N., Chandrasekar, N., Jasti, S.L., Adachi, Y., Siddique, K., 2002. Adenovirus-mediated expression of antisense MMP-9 in glioma cells inhibits tumour growth and invasion. Oncogene 21, 8011–8019.

Lauhio, A., Färkkilä, E., Pietiläinen, K.H., Åström, P., Winkelmann, A., Tervahartiala, T., Pirilä, E., Rissanen, A., Kaprio, J., Sorsa, T.A., Salo, T., 2016. Association of MMP-8 with obesity, smoking and insulin resistance. Eur. J. Clin. Investig. 46, 757–765.

Lee, H., Park, J.W., Kim, S.P., Lo, E.H., Lee, S.R., 2009. Doxycycline inhibits matrix metalloproteinase-9 and laminin degradation after transient global cerebral ischemia. Neurobiol. Dis. 34, 189–198.

Levin, M., Udi, Y., Solomonov, I., Sagi, I., 2017. Next generation matrix metalloproteinase inhibitors—novel strategies bring new prospects. Biophys. Acta Mol. Cell Res. 1864, 1927–1939.

Li, X.Y., Lin, Y.C., Huang, W.L., et al., 2012. Zoledronic acid inhibits proliferation and impairs migration and invasion through downregulating VEGF and MMPs expression in human nasopharyngeal carcinoma cells. Med. Oncol. 29, 714–720.

Li, W., Saji, S., Fumiaki Sato, F., Noda, M., Toi, M., 2013. Potential clinical applications of matrix metalloproteinase inhibitors and their future prospects. Int. J. Biol. Markers 28, 117–130.

Li, H., Wang, D., Yuan, Y., Min, J., 2017. New insights on the MMP-13 regulatory network in the pathogenesis of early osteoarthritis. Arthritis Res. Ther. 19, 248. https://doi.org/10.1186/s13075-017-1454-2.

Liu, S.C., Yang, S.F., Yeh, K.T., Chiou, H.L., Lee, C.Y., Chou, M.C., Hsieh, Y.S., 2006. Relationships between the level of matrix metalloproteinase-2 and tumour size of breast cancer. Clin. Chim. Acta 371, 92–96.

Loechel, F., Fox, J.W., Murphy, G., Albrechtsen, R., Wewer, U.M., 2000. ADAM 12-S cleaves IGFBP-3 and IGFBP-5 and is inhibited by TIMP-3. Biochem. Biophys. Res. Commun. 278, 511–515.

Lohi, J., Wilson, C.L., Roby, J.D., Parks, W.C., 2001. Epilysin, a novel human matrix metalloproteinase (MMP-28) expressed in testis and keratinocytes and in response to injury. J. Biol. Chem. 276, 10134–10144.

Louka, M.L., Ramzy, M.M., 2016. Involvement of fibroblast-specific protein 1 (S100A4) and matrix metalloproteinase-13 (MMP-13) in CCl4-induced reversible liver fibrosis. Gene 579, 29–33.

Ma, F., Martínez-San Segundo, P., Barceló, V., Morancho, A., Gabriel-Salazar, M., Giralt, D., Montaner, J., Rosell, A., 2016. Matrix metalloproteinase-13 participates in neuroprotection and neurorepair after cerebral ischemia in mice. Neurobiol. Dis. 91, 236–246.

Mannello, F., 2006. Natural bio-drugs as matrix metalloproteinase inhibitors: new perspectives on the horizon? Recent Pat. Anticancer Drug Discov. 1, 91–103.

Mannello, F., Tonti, G., Papa, S., 2005. Matrix metalloproteinase inhibitors as anticancer therapeutics. Curr. Cancer Drug Targets 5, 285–298.

Mauramo, M., Ramseier, A.M., Mauramo, E., Buser, A., Tervahartiala, T., Sorsa, T., Waltimo, T., 2018. Associations of oral fluid MMP-8 with periodontitis in Swiss adult subjects. Oral Dis. 24, 449–455.

Mengshol, J.A., Vincenti, M.P., Brinckerhoff, C.E., 2001. IL-1 induces collagenase-3 (MMP-13) promoter activity in stably transfected chondrocytic cells: requirement for Runx-2 and activation by p38 MAPK and JNK pathways. Nucleic Acids Res. 29, 4361–4372.

Mi, C., Shi, H., Ma, J., Han, L.Z., Lee, J.J., Jin, X., 2014. Celastrol induces the apoptosis of breast cancer cells and inhibits their invasion via downregulation of MMP-9. Oncol. Rep. 32, 2527–2532.

Mitropoulou, T.N., Tzanakakis, G.N., Kletsas, D., Kalofonos, H.P., Karamanos, N.K., 2003. Letrozole as a potent inhibitor of cell proliferation and expression of metalloproteinases (MMP-2 and MMP-9) by human epithelial breast cancer cells. Int. J. Cancer 104, 155–160.

Moilanen, M., Pirila, E., Grenman, R., Sorsa, T., Salo, T., 2002. Expression and regulation of collagenase-2 (MMP-8) in head and neck squamous cell carcinomas. J. Pathol. 197, 72–81.

Murray, G.I., Duncan, M.E., O'Neil, P., Melvin, W.T., Fothergill, J.E., 1996. Matrix metalloproteinase-1 is associated with poor prognosis in colorectal cancer. Nat. Med. 2, 461–462.

Murray, G.I., Duncan, M.E., Arbuckle, E., Melvin, W.T., Fothergill, J.E., 1998a. Matrix metalloproteinases and their inhibitors in gastric cancer. Gut 43, 791–797.

Murray, G.I., Duncan, M.E., O'Neil, P., McKay, J.A., Melvin, W.T., Fothergill, J.E., 1998b. Matrix metalloproteinase-1 is associated with poor prognosis in oesophageal cancer. J. Pathol. 185, 256–261.

Nagase, H., Fushimi, K., 2008. Elucidating the function of non-catalytic domains of collagenases and aggrecanases. Connect. Tissue Res. 49, 169–174.

Nagase, H., Visse, R., Murphy, G., 2006. Structure and function of matrix metalloproteinases and TIMPs. Cardiovasc. Res. 69, 562–573.

Nakamura, M., Miyamoto, S., Maeda, H., Ishii, G., Hasebe, T., Chiba, T., Asaka, M., Ochiai, A., 2005. Matrix metalloproteinase-7 degrades all insulin-like growth factor binding proteins and facilitates insulinlike growth factor bioavailability. Biochem. Biophys. Res. Commun. 333, 1011–1016.

Nakopoulou, L., Giannopoulou, I., Gakiopoulou, H., Liapis, H., Tzonou, A., Davaris, P.S., 1999. Matrix metalloproteinase-1 and -3 in breast cancer: correlation with progesterone receptors and other clinicopathologic features. Hum. Pathol. 30, 436–442.

Nikkola, J., Vihinen, P., Vlaykova, T., Hahka-Kemppinen, M., Kähäri, V.M., Pyrhönen, S., 2002. High expression levels of collagenase-1 (MMP-1) and stromelysin-1 (MMP-3) correlate with shorter diseasefree survival in human metastatic melanoma. Int. J. Cancer 97, 432–438.

Nikkola-Paakkarinen, J., Vihinen, P., Vuoristo, M., Kellokumpu-Lehtinen, P., Kähäri, V.M., Pyrhönen, S., 2005. Prognostic value of serum gelatinase-B (MMP-9) and collagenase-1 (MMP-1) and collagenase-3 (MMP-13) in human metastatic melanoma. Clin. Cancer Res. 11, 5158–5166.

Niu, J., Gu, X., Turton, J., Meldrum, C., Howard, E.W., Agrez, M., 1998. Integrin-mediated signaling of gelatinase B secretion in colon cancer cells. Biochem. Biophys. Res. Commun. 249, 287–291.

Nuti, E., Casalini, F., Santamaria, S., Gabelloni, P., Bendinelli, S., Da Pozzo, E., Costa, B., Marinelli, L., La Pietra, V., Novellino, E., Margarida Bernardo, M., Fridman, R., Da Settimo, F., Martini, C., Rossello, A., 2011. Synthesis and biological evaluation in U87MG glioma cells of (ethynylthiophene)sulfonamido-based hydroxamates as matrix metalloproteinase inhibitors. Eur. J. Med. Chem. 46, 2617–2629.

Nuti, E., Cantelmo, A.R., Gallo, C., Bruno, A., Bassani, B., Camodeca, C., Tuccinardi, T., Vera, L., Orlandini, E., Nencetti, S., Stura, E.A., Martinelli, A., Dive, V., Albini, A., Rossello, A., 2015. N-O-isopropyl sulfonamido-based hydroxamates as matrix metalloproteinase inhibitors: hit selection and in vivo antiangiogenic activity. J. Med. Chem. 58, 7224–7240.

Ohuchi, E., Imai, K., Fujii, Y., Sato, H., Seiki, M., Okada, Y., 1997. Membrane type 1 matrix metalloproteinase digests interstitial collagens and other extracellular matrix macromolecules. J. Biol. Chem. 272, 2446–2451.

Overall, C.M., Kleifeld, O., 2006. Validating matrix metalloproteinases as drug targets and anti-targets for cancer therapy. Nat. Rev. 6, 227–239.
Overall, C.M., López-Otín, C., 2002. Strategies for MMP inhibition in cancer: innovations for the post-trial era. Nat. Rev. Cancer 2, 657–672.
Pacheco, M.M., Mourao, M., Mantovani, E.B., Nishimoto, I.N., Brentani, M.M., 1998. Expression of gelatinases A and B, stromelysin-3 and matrilysin genes in breast carcinomas: clinico-pathological correlations. Clin. Exp. Metastasis 16, 577–585.
Paemen, L., Martens, E., Masure, S., Opdenakker, G., 1995. Monoclonal antibodies specific for natural human neutrophil gelatinase B used for affinity purification, quantitation by two-site ELISA and inhibition of enzymatic activity. Eur. J. Biochem. 234, 759–765.
Palm, F., Pussinen, P.J., Safer, A., Tervahartiala, T., Sorsa, T., Urbanek, C., Becher, H., Grau, A.J., 2018. Serum matrix metalloproteinase-8, tissue inhibitor of metalloproteinase and myeloperoxidase in ischemic stroke. Atherosclerosis 271, 9–14.
Park, I.H., Kim, M.M., 2012. Spermidine inhibits MMP-2 via modulation of histone acetyltransferase and histone deacetylase in HDFs. Int. J. Biol. Macromol. 51, 1003–1007.
Patterson, M.L., Atkinson, S.J., Knauper, V., Murphy, G., 2001. Specific collagenolysis by gelatinase A, MMP-2, is determined by the hemopexin domain and not the fibronectin-like domain. FEBS Lett. 503, 158–162.
Pay, S., Abbasov, T., Erdem, H., Musabak, U., Simsek, I., Pekel, A., Akdogan, A., Sengul, A., Dinc, A., 2007. Serum MMP-2 and MMP-9 in patients with Behçet's disease: do their higher levels correlate to vasculo-Behçet's disease associated with aneurysm formation? Clin. Exp. Rheumatol. 25, S70–S75.
Pei, D., Weiss, S.J., 1995. Furin-dependent intracellular activation of the human stromelysin-3 zymogen. Nature 375, 244–247.
Pullen, N.A., Anand, M., Cooper, P.S., Fillmore, H.L., 2012. Matrix metalloproteinase-1 expression enhances tumorigenicity as well as tumor-related angiogenesis and is inversely associated with TIMP-4 expression in a model of glioblastoma. J. Neuro-Oncol. 106, 461–471.
Pulukuri, S.M., Rao, J.S., 2008. Matrix metalloproteinase-1 promotes prostate tumor growth and metastasis. Int. J. Oncol. 32, 757–765.
Riley, K.N., Herman, I.M., 2005. Collagenase promotes the cellular responses to injury and wound healing in vivo. J. Burns. Wounds 4, e8.
Rossello, A., Nuti, E., Orlandini, E., Carelli, P., Rapposelli, S., Macchia, M., Minutolo, F., Carbonaro, L., Albini, A., Benelli, R., Cercignani, G., Murphy, G., Balsamo, A., 2004. New N-arylsulfonyl-N-alkoxyaminoacetohydroxamic acids as selective inhibitors of gelatinase A (MMP-2). Bioorg. Med. Chem. Lett. 12, 2441–2450.
Rossello, A., Nuti, E., Carelli, P., Orlandini, E., Macchia, M., Nencetti, S., Zandomeneghi, M., Balzano, F., Uccello Barretta, G., Albini, A., Benelli, R., Cercignani, G., Murphy, G., Balsamo, A., 2005. N-i-propoxy-N-biphenylsulfonylaminobutylhydroxamic acids as potent and selective inhibitors of MMP-2 and MT1-MMP. Bioorg. Med. Chem. Lett. 15, 1321–1326.
Rundhaug, E.J., 2003. Matrix metalloproteinases, angiogenesis, and cancer. Clin. Cancer Res. 9, 551–554.
Ryu, O.H., Fincham, A.G., Hu, C.C., Zhang, C., Qian, Q., Bartlett, J.D., Simmer, J.P., 1999. Characterization of recombinant pig enamelysin activity and cleavage of recombinant pig and mouse amelogenins. J. Dent. Res. 78, 743–750.
Schnaper, H.W., Grant, D.S., Stetler-Stevenson, W.G., Fridman, R., D'Orazi, G., Murphy, A.N., Bird, R.E., Hoythya, M., Fuerst, T.R., French, D.L., Quigley, J.P., Kleinman, H.K., 1993. Type IV collagenase(s) and TIMPs modulate endothelial cell morphogenesis in vitro. J. Cell. Physiol. 156, 235–246.

Scorilas, A., Karameris, A., Arnogiannaki, N., Ardavanis, A., Bassilopoulos, P., Trangas, T., Talieri, M., 2001. Overexpression of matrixmetalloproteinase-9 in human breast cancer: a potential favourable indicator in node-negative patients. Br. J. Cancer 84, 1488–1496.

Seftor, R.E., Seftor, E.A., Koshikawa, N., Meltzer, P.S., Gardner, L.M., Bilban, M., Stetler-Stevenson, W.G., Quaranta, V., Hendrix, M.J., 2001. Cooperative interactions of laminin 5 gamma2 chain, matrix metalloproteinase-2, and membrane type-1-matrix/metalloproteinase are required for mimicry of embryonic vasculogenesis by aggressive melanoma. Cancer Res. 61, 6322–6327.

Sela-Passwell, N., Kikkeri, R., Dym, O., Rozenberg, H., Raanan Margalit, R., Rina Arad-Yellin, R., et al., 2012. Antibodies targeting the catalytic zinc complex of activated matrix metalloproteinases show therapeutic potential. Nat. Med. 18, 143–147.

Serra, P., Bruczko, M., Zapico, J.M., Puckpwska, A., Garcia, M.A., Martin-Santamaria, S., Ramos, A., de Pascual-Teresa, B., 2012. MMP-2 selectivity in hydroxamate-type inhibitors. Curr. Med. Chem. 19, 1036.

Shepherd, F.A., Giaccone, G., Seymour, L., et al., 2002. Prospective, randomized, double-blind, placebo-controlled trial of marimastat after response to first-line chemotherapy in patients with small-cell lung cancer: a trial of the National Cancer Institute of Canada-Clinical Trials Group and the European Organization for Research and Treatment of Cancer. J. Clin. Oncol. 20, 4434–4439.

Sheu, B.C., Hsu, S.M., Ho, H.N., Lien, H.C., Huang, S.C., Lin, R.H., 2001. A novel role of metalloproteinase in cancer-mediated immunosuppression. Cancer Res. 61, 237–242.

Singh, A., Maurya, O.P.S., Jagannadhan, M.V., Patel, A., 2012. Matrix metalloproteinases (MMP-2 and MMP-9) activity in corneal ulcer and ocular surface disorders determined by gelatin zymography. J. Ocul. Biol. Dis. Inform. 5, 31–35.

Soria-Valles, C., Gutiérrez-Fernández, A., Guiu, M., Mari, B., Fueyo, A., Gomis, R.R., López-Otín, C., 2014. The anti-metastatic activity of collagenase-2 in breast cancer cells is mediated by a signaling pathway involving decorin and miR-21. Oncogene 33, 3054–3063.

Sparano, J.A., Bernardo, P., Stephenson, P., et al., 2004. Randomized phase III trial of marimastat versus placebo in patients with metastatic breast cancer who have responding or stable disease after first-line chemotherapy: Eastern Cooperative Oncology Group trial E2196. J. Clin. Oncol. 22, 4683–4690.

Stadlmann, S., Pollheimer, J., Moser, P.L., Raggi, A., Amberger, A., Margreiter, R., Offner, F.A., Mikuz, G., Dirnhofer, S., Moch, H., 2003. Cytokine-regulated expression of collagenase-2 (MMP-8) is involved in the progression of ovarian cancer. Eur. J. Cancer 39, 2499–2505.

Takeha, S., Fujiyama, Y., Bamba, T., Sorsa, T., Nagura, H., Ohtani, H., 1997. Stromal expression of MMP-9 and urokinase receptor is inversely associated with liver metastasis and with infiltrating growth in human colorectal cancer: a novel approach from immune/inflammatory aspect. Jpn. J. Cancer Res. 88, 72–81.

Thirkettle, S., Decock, J., Arnold, H., Pennington, C.J., Jaworski, D.M., Edwards, D.R., 2013. Matrix metalloproteinase 8 (collagenase 2) induces the expression of interleukins 6 and 8 in breast cancer cells. J. Biol. Chem. 288, 16282–16294.

Thürlimann, B., Keshaviah, A., Coates, A.S., et al., 2005. A comparison of letrozole and tamoxifen in postmenopausal women with early breast cancer. N. Engl. J. Med. 353, 2747–2757.

Tortora, G.J., Funke, B.R., Case, C.L., 2007. Microbiology: An Introduction. Pearson Benjamin Cummings, ISBN: 0-321-39603-0.

van den Oord, J.J., Paemen, L., Opdenakker, G., de Wolf-Peeters, C., 1997. Expression of gelatinase B and the extracellular matrix metalloproteinase inducer EMMPRIN in benign and malignant pigment cell lesions of the skin. Am. J. Pathol. 151, 665–670.

van't Veer, L.J., Dai, H., van de Vijver, M.J., He, Y.D., Hart, A.A., Mao, M., Peterse, H.L., van der Kooy, K., Marton, M.J., Witteveen, A.T., Schreiber, G.J., Kerkhoven, R.M., Roberts, C., Linsley, P.S., Bernards, R., Friend, S.H., 2002. Gene expression profiling predicts clinical outcome of breast cancer. Nature 415, 530–536.

Verma, A., Prasad, K.N., Nyati, K.K., Singh, S.K., Singh, A.K., Paliwal, V.K., Gupta, R.K., 2011. Association of MMP-2 and MMP-9 with clinical outcome of neurocysticercosis. Parasitology 138, 1423–1428.

Vihinen, P., Kähäri, V.M., 2002. Matrix metalloproteinases in cancer: prognostic markers and therapeutic targets. Int. J. Cancer 99, 157–166.

Wan, Y., Li, W., Liao, Z., Yan, M., Chen, X., Tang, Z., 2018. Selective MMP-13 inhibitors: promising agents for the therapy of Osteoarthritis. Curr. Med. Chem. https://doi.org/10.2174/0929867326666181217153118. (in press).

Whittaker, M., Floyd, C.D., Brown, P., Gearing, A.J., 1999. Design and therapeutic application of matrix metalloproteinase inhibitors. Chem. Rev. 99, 2735–2776.

Winer, A., Adams, S., Mignatti, P., 2018. Matrix metalloproteinase inhibitors in cancer therapy: turning past failures into future successes. Mol. Cancer Ther. 17, 1147–1155.

Withrow, J., Murphy, C., Liu, Y., Hunter, M., Fulzele, S., Hamrick, M.W., 2016. Extracellular vesicles in the pathogenesis of rheumatoid arthritis and osteoarthritis. Arthritis Res. Ther. 18, 286.

Yan, H.Q., Zhang, D., Shi, Y.Y., You, X., Shi, L., Li, Q., Gao, F.G., 2016. Ataxia-telangiectasia mutated activation mediates tumor necrosis factor-alpha induced MMP-13 up-regulation and metastasis in lung cancer cells. Oncotarget 7, 62070–62083.

Yu, Q., Stamenkovic, I., 2000. Cell surface-localized matrix metalloproteinase-9 proteolytically activates TGF-beta and promotes tumor invasion and angiogenesis. Genes Dev. 14, 163–176.

Zapico, J.M., Puckowska, A., Filipiak, K., Coderch, C., de Pascual-Teresa, B., Ramos, A., 2015. Design and synthesis of potent hydroxamate inhibitors with increased selectivity within the gelatinase family. Org. Biomol. Chem. 13, 142–156.

Zeng, Z.S., Huang, Y., Cohen, A.M., Guillem, J.G., 1996. Prediction of colorectal cancer relapse and survival via tissue RNA levels of matrix metalloproteinase-9. J. Clin. Oncol. 14, 3133–3140.

Zhang, J., Li, X., Jiang, Y., Feng, J., Li, X., Zhang, Y., Xu, W., 2014. Design, synthesis and preliminary evaluation of α-sulfonyl γ-(glycinyl-amino)proline peptidomimetics as matrix metalloproteinase inhibitors. Bioorg. Med. Chem. 22, 3055–3064.

Chapter 11

c-Met as a potential therapeutic target in triple negative breast cancer

Sapana Sameer Chaudhary[a], Sameer Choudhary[a], Sakshi Rawat[a], Gouri Ahir[a], Anwar L. Bilgrami[b], Ghulam Md Ashraf[c,d]

[a]*RASA Life science Informatics, Pune, India,* [b]*Deanship of Scientific Research, King Abdulaziz University, Jeddah, Saudi Arabia,* [c]*King Fahd Medical Research Center, King Abdulaziz University, Jeddah, Saudi Arabia,* [d]*Department of Medical Laboratory Technology, Faculty of Applied Medical Sciences, King Abdulaziz University, Jeddah, Saudi Arabia*

Abbreviations

ER	estrogen receptor
HER2	human epidermal growth factor receptor 2
HGF	hepatocyte growth factor
HGFR	hepatocyte growth factor receptor
PR	progesterone receptor
SF	scatter factor
TNBC	triple negative breast cancer

11.1 Introduction

C-Met was identified as a proto-oncogene by Cooper et al. (1984). It was first isolated from human osteosarcoma cell lines which was treated with an anticarcinogen known as *N*-methyl-*N*-nitro-so-guanidine, found as a fusion oncogene (Cooper et al., 1984). C-Met transfers signals from extracellular matrix to cytoplasm through binding with its single-ligand hepatocyte growth factor/scatter factor (HGF/SF) (Bottaro et al., 1991; Sonnenberg et al., 1993; Birchmeier et al., 2003). Some cells like mesenchymal cells of fibroblast and smooth muscle cells secrete HGF (Sonnenberg et al., 1993; Stoker et al., 1987; Ma et al., 2003). c-Met is majorly expressed in epithelial cells of liver, gastrointestinal tract, thyroid, kidney, stomach lining, brain, bone marrow, muscle, and the small and the large intestine besides been found in the basal keratinocytes of esophagus and skin during embryogenesis and adulthood (Prat et al., 1991). Ligand

Cancer-Leading Proteases. https://doi.org/10.1016/B978-0-12-818168-3.00011-5

binding on surface induces auto-phosphorylation of c-Met in its intracellular trans-membrane domain that provides c-terminal docking site for downstream signaling (Ponzetto et al., 1994). Activated c-Met interacts with GAB1, GRB2, PI3KR, SRC, and STAT3 and leads to activation of several signaling cascades including RAS-ERK, MAPK, PI3K-AKT, STAT, and IκBα-NF-κB (Birchmeier et al., 2003; Weidner et al., 1996; Boccaccio et al., 1998; Trusolino et al., 2010). c-Met signaling by HGF/SF helps in transiting information between epithelial and stromal compartments required for many physiological processes including proliferation, scattering, morphogenesis and cell survivality (Birchmeier et al., 2003; Thiery, 2003; Christensen et al., 2005; Forte et al., 2006). C-Met signaling plays an important role in wound healing, organ regeneration, and tissue remodeling. Angiogenesis occurs in kidney during embryogenesis, gastrulation, development and migration of muscle, and neural precursors (Trusolino et al., 2010; Boccaccio and Comoglio, 2006; Neuss et al., 2004; Borowiak et al., 2004; Andermarcher et al., 1996). Researchers have found that c-Met in oncogenic transformation and wide spread spectrum of tumor malignancies. It plays a key role in metastasis and poop prognosis of cancer, suggesting that inhibition of c-Met signaling may help in abrogating cancer growth and enhancing therapeutic efficacy. c-Met signaling promotes breast cancer, of aggressive phenotype. In all breast cancers c-Met is overexpressed in 20%–30% of the cases and around 52% in triple negative breast cancer.

11.2 c-MET structure and functions

The c-MET gene, or c-MET proto-oncogene is a receptor tyrosine kinase that was named by Human Genome Nomenclature Committee (HGNC). It is located in chromosome 7-band 7q21-q31 and is >120-kilo base pairs in length as depicted in Fig. 11.1. It consists of 21 exons which are separated by 20 introns (Duh et al., 1997). The gene is also known as hepatocyte growth factor receptor (HGFR), AUTS9, RCCP2, c-Met, or DFNB97 (NCBI: Gene Database). c-MET gene encodes for a protein belonging to family of the receptor tyrosine kinase as well as the proto-oncogene c-MET product, which is proteolytically processed to synthesize α and β subunits that form mature receptor via disulfide bonds formation. The β subunit will further proceed resulting in the formation of M10 peptide which plays an important role in the reduction of lung fibrosis. Binding of hepatocyte growth factor, which acts as its ligand, can induce dimerization

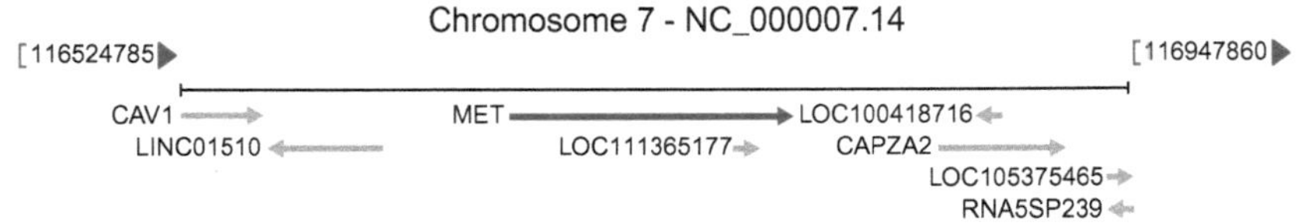

FIG. 11.1 Genomic Location of cMET: c-MET gene on chromosome location 7.

activation of the receptor. This makes the bio-molecule play a vital role in embryogenesis, cellular invasion, and migration along with cellular survival. Genetic mutations in this gene can lead to overexpression and amplification of c-MET gene leading to association with different types of human cancers, like cancer in various head and neck regions, hepatocellular carcinoma, and papillary renal cell carcinoma to be named among the many. The translated product of this gene is c-MET tyrosine kinase or c-MET receptor which is 1390 bp long (1390 Amino Acids) (Entrez: Gene). A precursor at furin site, which is located between 307 and 308 residues, is cleaved into extracellular α chain which is linked by disulfide bond to extended transmembrane β chain, demonstrating catalytic activity.

c-Met has four important functional domains as shown in Fig. 11.2.

Sema domain: The first 500 residues at N-terminal forms Sema domain. The word Sema refers to actually Semaphorin-like. The similar Sema domain is also present in the Semaphorins and Plexins family. It consists of whole α chain and first 212 residues of β chain. This domain plays important role in extracellular ligand (Hepatocyte growth factor/scatter factor) binding (Trusolino et al., 2010).

PSI domain: It is named so as it is found in Plexins, Semaphorins, and Integrins. It contains approximately 50 residues and includes four conserved disulfide bonds. It is connected with trans-membrane helix via four immuneglobulins like domains (IPT). It functions as linking molecule which is responsible for orientation of the extracellular fragment of c-MET for proper ligand binding.

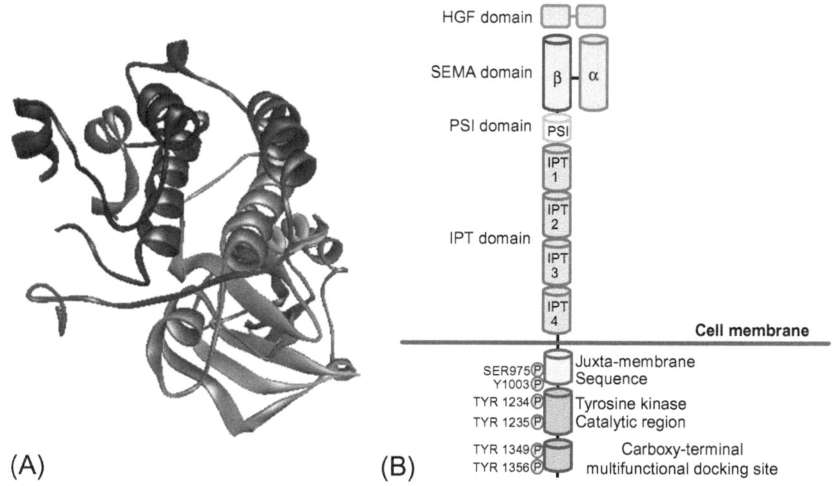

FIG. 11.2 Met structure as visualized via protein visualizing tool, Discovery Studio visualizer (Dassault Systèmes BIOVIA, Discovery Studio Visualizer, Discovery Studio v 16.1.0.15350, San Diego: Dassault Systèmes, 2016). (B) Diagram showing important functional domains of c-MET.

IPT domain: It is named because it is found in immunoglobulin-like, plexins, and transcription factors. It covers 400 residues and forms 4 IPT domains to connect PSI domain to transmembrane helix.

Transmembrane domain: It is intracellular segment of c-Met. It contains single α-helix like other tyrosine kinases (Trusolino et al., 2010; Cecchi et al., 2011). It is composed of three important regions:

- *Juxta-membrane region (JM)*: This region covers two protein phosphorylation sites: S985, which downregulated kinase activity (Gandino et al., 1994) and Y1003, which recruits c-Cbl, mono-ubiquitination of c-MET and interacts with endophilin, targeting c-Met for internalization and degradation (Peschard et al., 2001). It contains a PEST sequence which serves as site for ubiquitination (Cecchi et al., 2011).
- *Tyrosine kinase catalytic region*: Kinase activity is positively modulated by trans-phosphorylation of Tyr 1234 and Tyr 1235 residues following the HGF binding with c-Met.
- *Carboxy-terminal multifunctional docking site*: It phosphorylates two docking tyrosine residues: Tyr1349 and Tyr1356. It recruits several intracellular adapters and transducers that transmit signals downstream. Transformation and Metastasis require intact docking sites (Ponzetto et al., 1994; Trusolino et al., 2010; Cecchi et al., 2011).

11.3 c-Met signaling

c-Met is a protein that mediates extracellular signals across the cell membrane into cytoplasm. Hepatocyte growth factor (HGF)/scatter factor (SF) is the single ligand which activates c-Met tyrosine kinase signaling cascades (Nakamura, 1991). As known, mesenchymal cells secrete HGF, present in its inactive form bounded with heparin proteoglycans in extracellular matrix. The signaling starts when extracellular serine protease produced by liver cleaves inactive HGF into active α-β heterodimer linked with di-sulfide bond which binds with c-Met and triggers its tyrosine kinase activity (Boccaccio and Comoglio, 2006). This triggers trans-phosphorylation and dimerization of two tyrosine residues in tyrosine catalytic region (Tyr1234 and Tyr1235) in trans-membrane domain. Subsequently, this results in phosphorylation of two more tyrosine (Tyr1349 and Tyr1356) residues having multitasking docking site in carboxy-terminal tail of c-Met. The c-Met-HGF signaling mediates connection between mesenchymal and epithelial cells (Sonnenberg et al., 1993). It is essential for normal processes like stimulation of angiogenesis, morphogenesis, cellular behavior which describes its property of invasive growth, proliferation, survival (resistant to apoptotic signals), increased cell motility, cell dissociation (scattering), epithelial tubulogenesis, and infiltration of tissues (Nakamura, 1991). This process recruits intracellular adaptors, transducers, cytoskeleton connectors, and structure homologous coreceptors.

11.3.1 c-Met and adaptor protein

The tyrosine residues on C-terminal docking site of c-Met, Tyr1349, and Tyr1356 bind on phosphorylation with substrates such as Gab1 and Grb2, PI3K (phosphatidylinositol 3-kinase), phospholipase Cγ1, CRK (v-crk sarcoma virus CT10 oncogene homolog), STAT3 transcription factor activator and signal transducer, and Src-homology-2 domain, containing protein tyrosine phosphatase-2 Shp-2 (Ponzetto et al., 1994; Weidner et al., 1996; Fixman et al., 1996; Zhang et al., 2002). It can also recruit indirectly through c-Met binding the GRB2, which provides extra binding sites for molecules like P13K, SHC, SHP2, PLCγ1, CRK, and p120 RAS-GTPase-activating protein (p120-GAP) (Weidner et al., 1996; Lock et al., 2000; Schaeper et al., 2000; Fixman et al., 1996; Pelicci et al., 1995; Sakkab et al., 2000; Maulik et al., 2002; Gual et al., 2000; Montagner et al., 2005). The Gab1 multiadaptor is a scaffolding adaptor that recruits through a direct medium of unique 13 Amino acid c-Met-binding sites on Gab1. It acts downstream of receptor tyrosine kinase and upstream of Ras and Raf (important component of MAPK signal pathway which is activated on c-Met activation) (Cunnick et al., 2002). In tumors, c-Met activation also phosphorylates β4-subunit cytoplasmic domain (3 tyrosine residues) which recruits SHC, P13K, and SHP2. The α6β4 integrin and Gab1 thus behave as a platform for recruitment of additional transducers that unite with those which directly bind to c-MET and thus allow signal amplification at a contiguous level and lead to downstream transducers activation (Trusolino et al., 2001; Bertotti et al., 2005, 2006).

11.3.2 c-Met-CD44 links cytoskeleton

The CD44 is a trans-membrane cell adhesion molecule which acts as a linker molecule of extracellular and intracellular cytoskeleton (Ponta et al., 2003). CD44 family members have different extracellular domain, forming variable isoforms (Ponta et al., 2003; Prochazka et al., 2014). The v6 sequence of CD44 participates inc- Met-signaling by two-fold mechanism, like activating the extracellular domain and organizing ternary complexes between c-MET, HGF, and CD44. The CD44v6 molecule consists of an intracellular domain and handles the sub-membranous network which includes cytoplasmic region of F-actin, Grb2, and c-Met, ERM (radixin, moesin, and ezrin) proteins that connect actin microfilament to CD44 and Guanine nucleotide exchange factor SOS (son of sevenless). This allows activation of RAS by SOS (Orian-Rousseau et al., 2002, 2007). c-Met-induced signaling from the endosomes depends upon its collaboration with CD44v6 and ERM proteins of cytoskeleton upon hepatocyte growth factor initiation (Hasenauer et al., 2013). It is found that CD44v6 and c-Met proteins are upregulated in many cancers (Matzke-Ogi et al., 2016; Todaro et al., 2014).

The CD44v10 isoform partitions c-Met into insoluble, caveolin-enriched micro-domain together with T-lymphoma invasion and metastasis-inducing protein 1, cortactin (actin cytoskeleton regulator), and dynamin 2 (vesicular regulator)

(Singleton et al., 2007). CD44 increases aggressiveness in tumors through formation of vasculogenic structures (Paulis et al., 2015).

11.3.3 HGF-independent c-Met-activation

The extracellular domain of Met shares structural homology with broad ligand and receptor pair family, semaphorins and plexins (Giordano et al., 2002). c-Met and class B plexins share highly homologous semidomain that form seven bladed β-propeller which support interaction between c-Met and some Class B plexins (Conrotto et al., 2004). The c-Met is activated in HGF-independent manner by semaphorins on oligomerization with plexins, stimulating c-Met downstream effectors and executing Met-dependent biological responses (Conrotto et al., 2005; Wickramasinghe and Kong-Beltran, 2005). Soong and Scott (2013) found that plexin B1 and semaphorin 4D play an important role in c-Met signaling by blocking SHP2 (downstream adaptor protein of Met).

11.3.4 c-Met-receptor endocytosis

The Juxta-membrane region of c-Met contains two additional protein phosphorylation sites at S985 and Y1003 and acts as negative regulator (Gandino et al., 1994; Petrelli et al., 2002). This is absent in Tpr-c-Met onco-protein. The phosphorylation of Y1003 recruits the Cbl, an E3 ubiquitin ligase, that results in mono-ubiquitination of c-Met (Peschard and Park, 2007; Jeffers et al., 1997; Peschard et al., 2001). Cbl interaction with c-Met can also be aided through Grb2. This mechanism thus leads to termination of c-Met signaling (Birchmeier et al., 2003; Maroun and Rowlands, 2014). Rolle et al. (2017) demonstrated that altered c-CBL expression is related to c-MET overexpression in head and neck squamous cell carcinoma, which may influence tumorigenesis. The study by Tan et al. (2017) on CBL mutant and wild-type cells in nonsmall-cell lung cancer has shown that CBL mutant type cells have higher c-Met expression and lower c-Met ubiquitination than CBL wild-type cells.

11.4 c-Met and biological signaling pathways

The c-Met kinase is a type of receptor tyrosine kinase expressed mostly in epithelial and endothelial cells. The natural ligand of c-Met is hepatocyte growth factor (HGF), also known as a scatter factor. It plays a vital role in organogenesis, normal development, and homeostasis. Auto-phosphorylation and dimerization of Tyr1234 and Tyr1235 are caused by activation of c-Met by the scatter factor. Phosphorylation of c-Met further results in triggering activation of various downstream signaling pathways, like c-Src, Ras, or MAPK and PI3K/Akt pathways as shown in Fig. 11.3. These things lead to induction of various invasive programs such as migration, invasion, cell survival, and cell proliferation, which play an essential role in various physiological events like liver regeneration, morphogenesis, and wound healing. Variant HGF/c-Met signaling in multiple tumor oncogenic

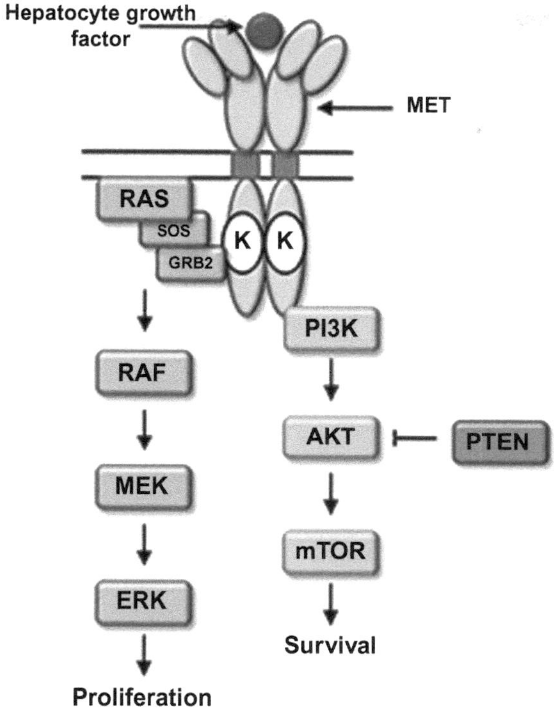

FIG. 11.3 Signaling pathways are regulated by scatter factor (HGF) binding to MET and resulting and in activation of various pathways.

processes, such as cell survival, mitogenesis, angiogenesis along with invasive cell growth during metastatic process, can be caused due to gene mutations, aberrant gene amplifications, autocrine loop activations, etc. (Gherardi et al., 2012; Birchmeier et al., 2003; Boccaccio and Comoglio, 2006; Ma et al., 2008). cMet and scatter factor have drawn lot of attention as cancer therapeutic targets due to overexpression leading to corelation between various cellular processes, like poor cell prognosis, invasive growth of cells, or metastatic progression in a number of human cancers in different regions like lung, breast, etc. (Cui, 2014). c-Met have a unique receptor-associated signaling model of scaffolding adaptor and surface signal transducers which elicit signaling cascade, biochemical events, and chain of signaling pathways. c-Met controls many essential signal transduction pathways which transform information from cell membrane to nucleus, via downstream transducers, finally affecting the cellular responses (Fig. 11.4). The biological pathways controlled by c-Met are as discussed below.

11.4.1 MAPK (mitogen-activated protein kinase) cascade

MAPK cascade is involved in various cellular functions like cell migration, proliferation, and differentiation. Hence it is a highly conserved module.

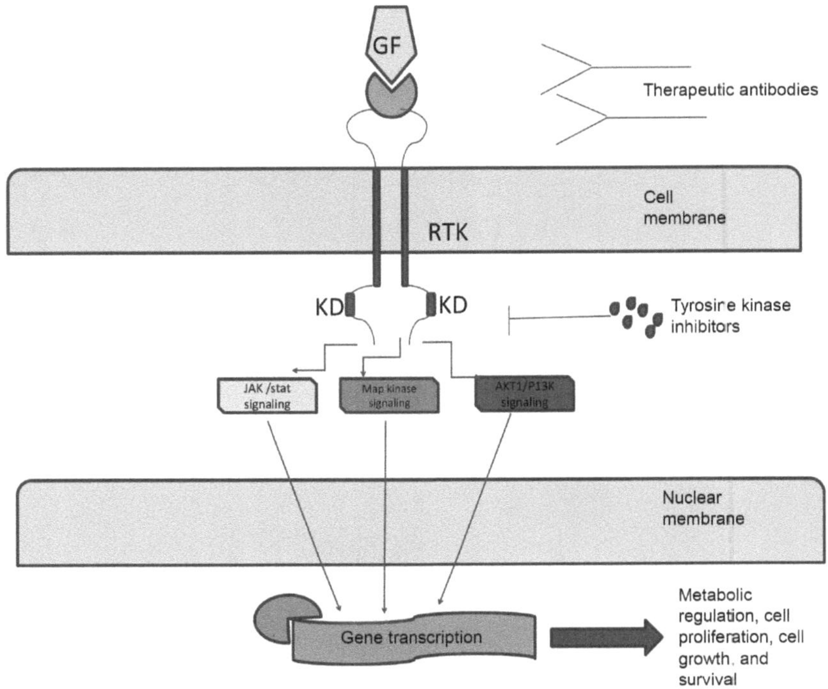

FIG. 11.4 Positive regulation of MET for different cellular processes like metabolic regulation, cell proliferation, cell growth, and survival.

Particularly in mammals, there are four distinctive regulation groups of MAPK, mainly, Jun amino-terminal kinases (JNK1/2/3), ERK5, p38 proteins (p38alpha/beta/gamma/delta), and extracellular signal-related kinases (ERK)-1/2 which are activated by specific MAPKKs, like MKK4/7 (JNKK1/2) for the JNKs, MEK5 for ERK5, MKK3/6 for the p38, and MEK1/2 for ERK1/2. However, these extracellular signal-related kinases can also be activated MAPKKs, leading to increased diversity and complexity in MAPK signaling. Presumptions depict that each MAPKKK can lead to distinct stimuli which is conferred to the responsiveness. For example, MAPKKK c-Raf is responsible for activation of ERK1/2 due to associated growth factors, but pro-inflammatory stimuli can signal other MAPKKKs to activate ERK1/2 in response. c-Met binding with SHC and Grb2 stimulates the activity of RAS (rat sarcoma viral oncogene homology) through c-Met-Grb2 forming complex as well as guanine nucleotide exchange factor SOS (son of seven less), c-Met-Grb2-SOS complex (Lock et al., 2000; Graziani et al., 1993). This leads to indirect activation of RAF kinase (v-raf murine sarcoma viral oncogene homology) that phosphorylates and activates MEK (MEK1 and MEK2) and MAPK effector kinase. It subsequently activates

MAPK (It is serine/tyrosine/threonine kinase), ERK1, and ERK2, which translocate to nucleus and affect cell functioning. It alters translation of mRNA and activates several transcription factors (which controls regulation of large number of genes) leading to the regulation of cell proliferation, cell motility, and cell cycle progression (Schaeper et al., 2000; Fixman et al., 1996; Paumelle et al., 2002). ERK2 is the main downstream signal transducer of activated c-Met signaling in cell motility (Gusenbauer et al., 2015).

Another pathway that leads to RAS-ERK activation through tyrosine phosphatase SHP2, which dephosphorylates p120-RAS-GAP binding site on GAB1, subsequently recruits p120-RAS-GAP which usually deactivates RAS and promotes activation of RAS, extending the duration of MAPK phosphorylation (Montagner et al., 2005; Maroun et al., 2000). c-Met also controls the activation of JNK (Jun N-terminal kinase) and p38 MAPK, stimulated by Rac (a small GTPase) and activated by PAS-PI3K mediated pathway. MEK kinase phosphorylation of MEK 4 and MEK 7 leads to activation of JNK 1, JNK 2, and JNK3. Phosphorylation of MEK 3 and MEK 7 leads to activation of p38α, p38β, p38γ, and p38δ. JNK and p38 control cellular responses, like cell proliferation, differentiation, transformation, and apoptosis (Rodrigues et al., 1997; Recio and Merlino, 2002; Coltella et al., 2006). The hepatocyte growth factor (HGF) receptor-induced p38 MAPK and P13K-Akt signaling pathways upregulate COX2 and MMP-9 expression, leading to cell invasion (Kuang et al., 2017).

11.4.2 PI3K-Akt pathway

This is another major c-Met-dependent biological signaling pathway. Met is able to activate PI3K directly or indirectly via GAB1-RAS (Ponzetto et al., 1994; Rosário and Birchmeier, 2003). Different types of toxic insults and cellular stimuli result in activation of phosphatidylinositol 3′-kinase (PI3K)-Akt signaling pathway. It is involved in the regulation of fundamental cell functions, like cell survival, growth, and proliferation along with transcription and translation. PI3K activation results in the formation of phosphatidylinositol-3,4,5-triphosphate (PtdIns-3,4,5-P3) which recruits PH Domain (pleckstrin homology domain) of AKT (Ser/Thr kinase) resulting in translocation of AKT to plasma membrane, where it suppresses apoptosis through inactivation of BCL-2 pro-apoptotic protein BAD antagonist of cell death, and activation of MDM2 (E3 ubiquitin-protein ligase MDM2) which stimulates p53 (tumor suppressor) degradation. AKT also inactivates GSK3β (glycogen synthase kinase 3β), which antagonizes Myc and cyclin D1, activating mTOR (mechanistic target of rapamycin), a serine/threonine protein kinase which regulates different cellular processes, like protein synthesis, cell motility, cell proliferation, and cell growth (Fan et al., 2000; Xiao et al., 2001; Derksen et al., 2003; Tulasne and Foveau, 2008; Zhou et al., 2014). c-Met-dependent PI3K-Akt-mTOR signaling pathway is related to epithelial-mesenchymal transition (EMT) and angiogenesis (Jiao et al.,

2016). The cross talk between MAPK and P13K-Akt signaling pathways has been implicated in cancer initiation, progression, and metastasis (Ciuffreda et al., 2014). The binding of growth factors to their receptor tyrosine kinase (RTK) or G protein-coupled receptor (GPCR) stimulates class Ia and Ib PI3K isoforms, respectively. Phosphatidylinositol-3,4,5-triphosphate (PIP3), which acts as a secondary messenger and helps in the activation of Akt produced at the cell membrane, is catalyzed by PI3K. Activation of Akt leads to controlling cellular functions, due to phosphorylation of substrates, which are involved in cell cycle, apoptosis, metabolism, and protein synthesis.

11.4.3 NF-κB pathway

NF-κB belongs to transcription factor family and is present in inactivated state in cytoplasm with IκBα, a family of inhibitor proteins (Oeckinghaus and Ghosh, 2009). The phosphorylation in IκBα protein is mediated by c-Met-activated PI3K-Akt pathway, which results in ubiquitination, dissociation of IκBα from NF-κB, and degradation of IκBα. This leads to translocation of activated NF-κB to nucleus and binds with DNA sequence known as RE (response elements). This complex recruits other proteins and stimulates transcription of various genes, including mitogenic and antiapoptotic regulators, resulting in change of cell function (Oeckinghaus and Ghosh, 2009; Fan et al., 2005). The PI3K-Akt-mTOR pathway also controls NF-κB activation and induces cell progression (Dan et al., 2008). HGF-induced NF-κB signal transduction pathway upregulates MMP2 expression in chondrosarcoma cells (malignant tumor) (Tsou et al., 2013). The interleukin-17 (IL-17) family is a subset of cytokines which consists of IL-17A-F that plays a vital role in both acute and chronic inflammatory responses. T-helper 17 (TH17) cell subset consists of a hallmark cytokine, known as IL-17A, and plays an important role in autoimmune disease promoting inflammatory pathology and also protecting the host against extracellular pathogens, whereas IL-17F is mainly involved in defense mechanisms of mucosal host. IL-17E (IL-25) acts as an amplifier of Th2 immune responses. IL-17C has biological functions similar to those of IL-17A. However, functions of IL-17B and IL-17D still remain largely elusive, wherein the IL-17 family signals via their correspondent receptors and activates downstream pathways that include NF-κB, C/EBPs, and MAPKs to induce the expression of cytokines, antimicrobial peptides, and chemokines. The receptor proximal adaptor Act1 (also known as an NF-κB activator 1) is considered as the master mediator in IL-17A signaling.

11.4.4 PTK2 pathway

c-Met regulates cellular migration through PTK2 or FAK (protein tyrosine kinase 2, also known as focal adhesion kinase). FAK is activated through phosphorylation of SRC family kinase, which is directly associated with c-Met (Ponzetto et al., 1994). This c-Met-SRC-FAK interaction results in cell migration and anchorage-independent growth (Hui et al., 2009). The SRC activation can also serve as positive feed-back mechanism for c-Met activation (Hui et al., 2009; Organ et al., 2011). c-Met-FAK cascade upregulates LCN2 (Lipocalin 2), a tumor-associated protein, regulated by T3/TR thyroid hormone, controls cell growth, development, and differentiation (Chung et al., 2015). For inflammation and immune surveillance, migration of leukocyte from blood into tissues is vital. During this process of migration, leukocytes bind to endothelial cell adhesion molecules (CAM) leading to migration across the vascular endothelium. Leukocyte, in adhesion to CAMs on the endothelial cells, when moves forward leads to retraction of its tail and edge protrusion. During this process, αL/β2 integrin is activated via Vav1. RhoA protein eventually activates the kinase p160ROCK resulting into phosphorylation of MLC, subsequently causing retraction of the actin cytoskeleton. Moreover, endothelial cell signaling is activated by leukocytes that stimulate endothelial cell retraction during localized dissociation of the endothelial cell junctions. An endothelial cell PKC and calcium flux is activated by ICAM-1-mediated signaling, which is essential for leukocyte migration that is ICAM-1 dependent. The "endothelial passage" is opened because of VCAM-1 through which extravasation of leukocytes occurs. Considering this, ligation of VCAM-1 induces activation of NADPH oxidase activation and eventually in a Rac-mediated manner produces reactive oxygen species (ROS), resulting in subsequent activation of matrix metalloproteinases (MMPs) and loss of VE-cadherin-mediated adhesion.

11.4.5 STAT pathway

STAT (signal transducers and activators of transcription) pathway also known as Janus kinase pathway (JAK) is a type of pleiotropic cascade used for multitude signal transduction for development process and homeostasis in animals, from humans to flies. In mammals, for a wide array of cytokines and other growth factors the principal signaling mechanism is done by JAK/STAT pathway. When cytokines bind to their cognate receptor, a member of JAK family of tyrosine kinases, it leads to STATs activation. Once activated, these molecules perform dimerization and translocation to the nucleus modulating target genes expression. Along with activating STATs, JAKs are also involved in mediating recruitment of other bio-molecules like PI3 kinase, and MAP kinases, which are processed in downstream signaling via PI3 kinase and the Ras-Raf-MAP kinase pathways, resulting in the activated transcription factors leading to gene expression. The c-Met-dependent tyrosine-phosphorylation of STAT3 on docking site of Met results in direct association of STAT3, stimulating STAT3 phosphorylation, which causes STAT to dissociate from receptor and homo-dimerization through SH2 domain that leads to its translocation to nucleus, where they control transcription factor to regulate gene expression of various genes responsible for cell proliferation or differentiation. This pathway results in tubulogenesis and invasion of cell (Boccaccio et al., 1998; Zhang et al., 2002; Syed et al., 2011). HGF/c-Met signaling-induced PI3K/Akt, MAPK, and STAT3 downstream pathways are involved in controlling HIF-1α (hypoxia inducible factor) transcriptional activity which regulates VEGF (vascular endothelial cell growth factor) expression (Matsumura et al., 2013). Mesenchymal stromal cells secret HGF that binds with c-MET downstream pathway and phosphorylates STAT3 that induces expansion of MDSCs (myeloid-derived suppressor cells) (Yen et al., 2013). High glucose levels can also induce c-Met downstream signaling of STAT3, Akt, and ERK independent of their ligand HGF/SF, via integrin α5β1 (Mesarosova et al., 2017).

11.4.6 Wnt/β-catenin pathway

The activated c-Met phosphorylates at Tyr1234 and Tyr1235, leading to phosphorylation of β-catenin (present in inner surface of cell membrane) at Tyr654 and Tyr670 resulting in its dissociation from cell membrane and accumulation in nucleus, where it acts as TCF/LEF transcription cofactor and activates the expression of many genes, including c-myc and cyclin D1 (cell proliferation), surviving (antiapoptosis), matrix-metalloproteinase (invasion), and VEGF (angiogenesis) (Monga et al., 2002; Nelson and Nusse, 2004; Apte et al., 2006; Kimelman and Xu, 2006; Huang et al., 2012). Inhibition of β-catenin mutant generates pro-oncogenic microenvironment which induces recurrence of tumor on treating primary tumor (Liang et al., 2017). According to the pathological research, progressive myocyte loss and fibro-fatty replacement, with a predilection for the right ventricle, are the causes of an inherited heart muscular disease, known as arrhythmogenic right ventricular cardiomyopathy (ARVC), which may lead to sudden death, heart failure, and arrhythmia. Genetic mutations in various components of the cardiac desmosome play an important role in pathogenesis of ARVC. Defective proteins cause disruption of desmosomal function which might lead to death of myocytes under mechanical stress. Also, inflammation accompanies myocardial injury. Fibrofatty replacement repair occurs due to regeneration limit of cardiac myocytes. As depicted by several studies, desmosome dysfunction leads to delocalization and nuclear translocation of plakoglobin, resulting in competition between plakoglobin and beta-catenin which may lead to the inhibition of Wnt/beta-catenin signaling and thus cause a shift from a myocyte fate towards an adipocyte fate of cells. Electromechanical coupling is crucially executed in the presence of ryanodine receptor which controls the release of calcium from the sarcoplasmic reticulum into the cytosol. Therefore, if there are any defects observed in this receptor it could result in an imbalance of calcium homeostasis triggering cell death.

11.5 c-Met in cancer

Until now, we have studied that c-Met signaling is a crucial and highly regulated process. The disregulation of c-Met-HGF/SF signaling and ectopic overexpression of c-Met and HGF/SF are responsible for tumorigenesis or cancer progression. The in vitro and in vivo experiments suggest that c-Met oncogenesis and metastasis are due to the following three main mechanisms.

(i) Ligand-dependent autocrine or paracrine mechanism
(ii) Specific genetic lesions occurrence includes translocation, gene amplification, and activation of mutations
(iii) Transcriptional upregulation of c-Met protein in absence of gene amplification (Danilkovitch-Miagkova and Zbar, 2001).

Park et al. (1986) were the first to identify c-Met as a fused oncogene, mutant form containing a chromosomal rearrangement, which fuses tyrosine kinase domain to upstream trans-locating promoter region (TPR), leading to dimerization and activation of encoded gene. Further studies by Soman et al. (1991) showed that TPR-c-MET translocation in humans can be found in gastric cancer precursor lesions and proximate mucosa in a normal state, suggesting that the occurrence of genetic lesion can make us prone to gastric carcinomas.

c-Met-activation in cancer is through aberrant autocrine or paracrine mechanism. The autocrine activation of HGF/SF c-Met ligand is produced by aberrant tumor cells consequent Met activation (Birchmeier et al., 2003; Zhang and Vande Woude, 2003). The HGF autocrine expression correlates with c-Met levels and shows high sensitivity to Met inhibition in vivo. The HGF level may also serve as biomarker in autocrine-induced tumors (Xie et al., 2012). In paracrine ligand production, HGF/SF ligand of c-Met is produced by stromal cells and basal myo-epithelial cells, thus controlling Met activation. Thus it is a ligand-independent activation of Met tyrosine kinase (Matsumoto and Nakamura, 2006). Other oncogenes, like RAS, also induce c-Met overexpression through transcriptional upregulation (Xie et al., 2001). HGF/c-MET autocrine and paracrine signaling pathways play important role in development and metastasis of tumor (Miller et al., 2006). The c-Met-gene amplification leads to overexpression of proteins, and increased kinase activity is seen in many primary human tumors, suggesting that Met gene amplification, acquired before or during tumor progression, leads to tumor metastasis (Kawakami et al., 2013; Kwak et al., 2015; Sequist et al., 2011). c-Met gene amplification is found to be one of the important mechanisms responsible for resistance to EGFR tyrosine kinase inhibitors (An et al., 2014). c-Met gene amplification and protein overexpression are significant in recurrent/metastatic gastric cancer patients after chemotherapy (Janbabai et al., 2015). Recent studies show correlation of c-MET gene amplification with a poor prognosis and survival in gastric carcinomas (Fuse et al., 2016; Kawakami et al., 2014). The c-Met gene amplification is an "oncogenic driver" (Li et al., 2015). The positive correlation between c-MET gene amplification and protein overexpression suggests that it is a therapeutic biomarker for prognosis of patients who can be benefited with MET inhibitors in advanced nasopharyngeal carcinoma. Met protein overexpression was found to be independent type of prognostic factors for overall survival and disease-free survival and Met gene amplification were found to be associated independently with poorer overall survival and disease-free survival (Kwak et al., 2015). c-Met gene amplification and overexpression are found in grade IV and not in grade II and III gliomas, and thus are partially linked with aggressiveness in gliomas (Catenacci et al., 2017). c-Met gene amplification by FISH (fluorescence in situ hybridization) and Met protein overexpression by SRM (mass spectrometry-based selected reaction monitoring) were observed to be independent prognostic biomarkers of survival in gastroesophageal adenocarcinoma (Xu et al., 2012).

The downregulation of RPTP-β (receptor-type protein tyrosine phosphatase β) levels, with or without c-Met protein overexpression, promotes Met activation in head and neck squamous cell carcinoma (Zhang et al., 2015). Micro-RNA (miRNA) is known as a cluster of small nonencoding RNA (snRNA) molecules ranging from 21 to 23 nucleotides in length, which via posttranscription controls gene suppression either through target mRNAs degradation or by inhibiting translation of proteins. Considering high-throughput profiling and studies, dis-regulation of mi-RNAs is widely observed to be involved in different stages of cancer. The upregulation (overexpression) of specific miRNAs can cause tumor suppressor gene repression, and contrastingly the downregulation of specific miRNAs can lead to onco-gene expression, resulting in induction of subsequent malignant effects on cell proliferation, differentiation, and apoptosis leading to tumor growth and progress. The miRNA signatures and hallmarks of cancer studies are observed to differ significantly. This regulation of genes can lead to differential expression of 26 genes which are directly and indirectly associated with cMET and eventually are affecting different regions of body.

MicroRNA (miR-206) is negative regulator of transcription factor PAX3 (paired box gene 3) which upregulates c-Met downstream signaling in gastric cancer metastasis (Kitajima et al., 2008). Hypoxia, lack of oxygen at center of tumor, activates c-Met promoter through transcription factor HIF1α (hypoxia inducible factor 1α), which is regulated by intracellular oxygen concentration. HIF1α transactivates hepatocyte growth factor activator (HGFA) is a serine protease that accelerates processing of HGF in fibroblast and activates it (hepatocyte growth factor) leading to the activation of c-MET signaling (Peinado et al., 2012). The tumor-derived exosomes support tumorigenesis and metastasis. The high level of c-Met and exosomes were expressed in melanoma cells. The bone marrow-derived exosomes increased Met activation and vascular permeability, which promote tumor migration and reprogram it to pro-angiogenic phenotype and aided angiogenesis, invasion, and metastasis (Schmidt et al., 1999).

There are evidences which prove that c-Met can lead cancer in humans by activating mutations in Met-kinase domain in both sporadic and inherited forms of human renal papillary cancer (Forbes et al., 2008). Mutations have also been found on HGF binding region of SEMA domain and c-Cbl binding site of Juxta-membrane domain (Petrini, 2015). The somatic mutations at c-Met tyrosine kinase domain were described at Tyr1248 and Tyr1253 in head and neck squamous cell carcinomas, at Gly113Val in gliomas, and at Ala1209Gly in mucinous ovarian carcinomas. In childhood, mutations are described in both tyrosine kinase domains at Thr1191lle and carboxyl-terminal, and at Lys1262Arg and Met1268lle in hepatocellular carcinomas (Navis et al., 2015). Another mutation is found in extracellular IPT domain of c-Met in high grade gliomas. The encoded protein lacks a part of IPT1 encoded exon 7 and IPT2 encoded exon 8 that form a single pseudo-IPT domain named as MET (Δ7–8). This variant MET (Δ7–8) is present in cytosol in constantly active form, but significance of this mutation is unknown (Saffroy et al., 2017). c-Met tyrosine kinase gene exon 14 skipping (METex14) alteration is an oncogenic driver in NSCLC and pulmonary sarcomatoid carcinomas (Ou et al., 2017). The METex14-positive NSCLC induces resistance to crizotinib with preexisting MET Y1230C mutation observed with noninvasive plasma-based ct-DNA assay (Cortot et al., 2017). Several case reports described that patients with MET exon 14 skipping (METex14) variant show positive response to MET-targeting tyrosine kinase inhibitors, suggesting it to be a new biomarker for treating cancer (Tuck et al., 1996).

11.5.1 c-Met in breast cancer

Multiple studies have recorded c-MET over-expression in invasive breast cancer (Jin et al., 1997; Edakuni et al., 2001; Ho-Yen et al., 2014, 2015; Gaule et al., 2014; Sierra and Tsao, 2011). In breast cancer like other cancers, HGF is present in stromal cells, adipocytes, fibroblasts, and endothelial cells. MET activation is via HGF induced paracrine signaling (Jin et al., 1997; Cao et al., 2013). Aberrant c-Met signaling stimulates cell proliferation, invasion, and angiogenesis. Many mechanisms cause this deregulation of c-Met pathway including, gene mutation, gene amplification, protein overexpression, and increase in paracrine induced autocrine signaling (Minuti and Landi, 2015; Yan et al., 2015). c-Met overexpression is associated with aggressiveness of breast cancer and studies have found that Met is prognostic in breast cancer (Mueller et al., 2012). Fig. 11.5 describes very well the overexpression of c-Met resulting in breast cancer.

11.5.2 c-Met in triple negative breast cancer (TNBC)

Triple-negative breast cancer (TNBC) is a kind of breast cancer that does not have any of the receptors commonly found in breast cancer. In recent studies it is found that c-Met is overexpressed in around 52% of TNBC (Triple negative breast cancer), and disease-free survival and overall survival is worse in TNBC with high c-Met expression (Knight et al., 2013). The study suggests that

FIG. 11.5 A diagram showing micro-RNA depicted involvement in overexpression of c-MET resulting in breast cancer.

c-Met pathway should be aimed for TNBC targeted therapy (Zhang et al., 2014). Another study shows that due to diversity in cancer it is implausible that anti-Met drug therapy will work for all TNBC patients (Sierra and Tsao, 2011). MET interacts with other oncogenic tyrosine kinases including epidermal growth-factor receptor (EGFR) and HER-3 and these interactions may be the reason of EGFR resistance. This suggests that targeting both MET and EGFR may prove as effective therapeutic strategy (Sohn et al., 2014; Linklater et al., 2016). A synergistic study found that c-Met expression and P53 loss result in development of claudin-low TNBC (Inanc et al., 2014). The c-Met over-expression and CK5/6 (breast cancer diagnostic marker) expressions with PTEN loss on disease prognosis may increase the risk of recurrence in TNBC patients leading to death (Yi et al., 2015).

BRCA1-associated breast cancer in Chinese women shows aggressive disease phenotype. BRACA1 mutation tumors are likely to be negative for ER, PR, and HER-2. The recurrent mutations may exist in Chinese women with inherent breast cancer (Smyth et al., 2014). A study in TNBC subtype, mesenchymal stem-like (MSL), shows that EGFR and c-MET were targeted together by downregulating ribosomal protein S6 (RPS6), which resulted in reduced proliferation of these cells (Zagouri et al., 2013). Another study found that c-Met inhibition has caused upregulation of Jag1-mediated Notch activation. This suggested that dual targeting of c-Met and Notch is necessary for TNBC patients showing lower Lfng and high Jag1 expression with Met over expression and Notch hyper-activation (Chae et al., 2016). A multivariate analysis was performed on coexpression of c-MET and EGFR along with phosphorylation, which proved that neither c-MET nor EGFR expression or its activation gives independent prognostic factor for survival (Chae et al., 2016).

11.6 Inhibitors of c-Met protein

Due to aberrations and mutations in the c-Met kinase protein with its adverse involvement in multiple types of cancer, it has emerged as an attractive target protein in drug designing. Researchers are involved in developing various types of antitumor agents using Met as target. Met has been found to be significant target because of its close relationship with multiple human cancers development. A series of novel c-Met kinase inhibitors can be identified with multiple workflows including X-ray crystallography, virtual screening, structural optimization, and biological evaluation.

Grouping of the c-Met kinase inhibitors is done due to inhibitor's binding mode in the binding sites. They can be of two types: ATP-competitive small molecule inhibitors and ATP-noncompetitive small molecule inhibitors. ATP-competitive small molecule inhibitors are also classified as Type I inhibitors and Type II inhibitors. c-Met inhibitors which follow a U-shaped binding mode in the ATP binding site are termed as Type I inhibitors. Fig. 11.6 depicts the topographical features of c-Met ATP binding site. Type II inhibitors are usually not as selective as those of Type I. Type II cMet inhibitors are multitargeted and possess a property of passing through the gateway channel of the cellular compartments and occupy a region of deep hydrophobic origin in the back pocket of cMET protein. On the other hand, Type I inhibitors exhibit good cellular selectivity profiles along with a limited number of hits for off-target. They compete with ATP for binding in the ATP binding site, mimicking the interactions between ATP and the binding site like the hydrogen bond interactions with the amino acids (residues) in the hinge region (Pro1158, Tyr1159, and Met1160). These two types of cMet competitive inhibitors are comparatively well studied than noncompetitive cMet inhibitors. Various cMet inhibitors belonging to Type I, II, and other types that are in various phases of clinical trials are given in Fig. 11.7. Among these, Crizotinib/PF-02341066 of Type I and Cabozantinib/XL-184 of Type II have been approved for the treatment of nonsmall cell lung carcinoma (Cui, 2014). Crizotinib more specifically inhibits hepatocyte growth factor receptor (HGFR, c-MET), anaplastic lymphoma kinase (ALK), and macrophage-stimulating protein receptor, also known as Recepteur d'Origine Nantais (RON) kinase. RON kinase is related

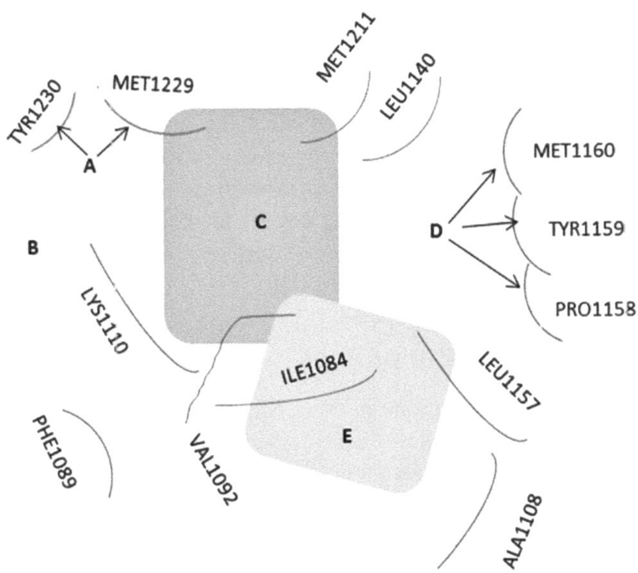

FIG. 11.6 The topographical features of the Met ATP binding site. A, tyrosine in the active loop; B, hydrophobic subpocket; C, central hydrophobic region; D, hinge region; and E, hydrophobic subpocket.

to c-Met receptor tyrosine kinase. Crizotinib also has an activity of inhibiting ALK tyrosine kinase resulting in decreased proliferation of cells carrying the genetic mutation and tumor survivability.

On the other hand, cabozantinib is considered as a nonspecific inhibitor of c-MET tyrosine kinase and was also approved as an inhibitory molecule in 2012. For thyroid cancer of metastatic medullary stage, cabozantinib is marketed as Cometriq which includes several warnings in a black box of marketing product for fistulas, gastrointestinal perforations, and hemorrhage. Also, cabozantinib was approved by the name cabometyx in April 2016 for treatment of patients suffering from advanced renal cell carcinoma. Apart from RTKs (receptor tyrosine kinases) and c-MET, cabozantinib is also a potent inhibitor of RET, KIT, AXL, FLT3, and VEGFR2 (Joly, 2006; Sennino et al., 2009). Along with the antitumor and antiangiogenic activity, it was also observed that cabozantinib treatment resulted in decreased metastasis and rate in tumor invasions (in vitro) as compared to agents targeting VEGF signaling, inhibiting phosphorylation without MET inhibition or the vehicle control (Sennino et al., 2009). Studies have suggested that cabozantinib is a promising inhibitor of metastasis in cancer and tumor angiogenesis with dysregulation of VEGFR and MET signaling (Yakes et al., 2011).

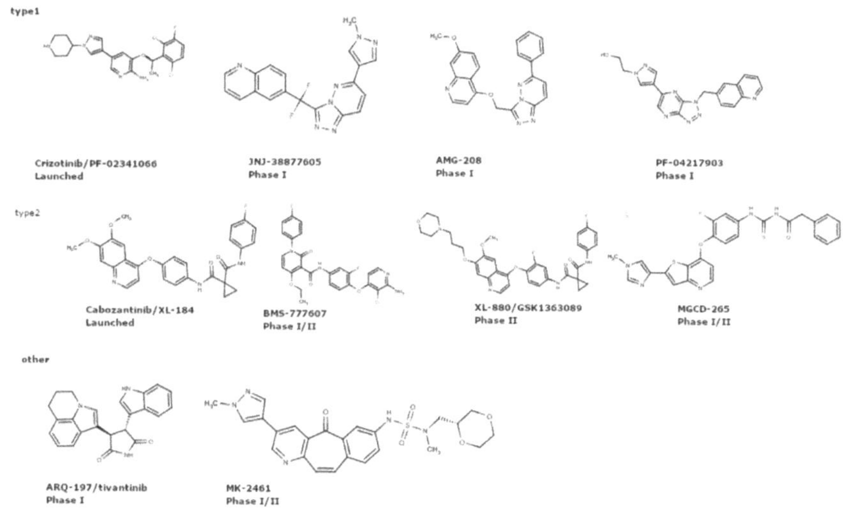

FIG. 11.7 c-MET inhibitors.

However, in addition to crizotinib and cabozantinib, many more compounds of those passing through various phases of clinical trials as mentioned in Fig. 11.7 may come out to be great importance. Additionally, Table 11.1 lists several other compounds that have been well studied for their cMet inhibition activity.

11.7 Conclusions

We have known c-Met/HGF signaling, and in vitro and in vivo evidences convince that this is an important pathway in mammary development and also for cancer progression. Several clinical investigations have suggested that expression of c-Met in breast cancer can develop the prognostic significance. There are many studies explaining the anti-c-Met drugs to act as a novel form of targeted therapy for triple negative breast cancer but it is yet to be investigated. We found that it is very crucial to select a certain group of patients for targeted therapy. This can only be achieved through standardized prognostic models for predicting biomarkers and increasing efficacy of anti-Met drug agents. The cross-talk of MET with other signaling pathways or tyrosine kinases seems to explain the failure of c-Met target therapies. So, it is important to determine the combination of anti-met agents with other targeted therapies. Anti-Met drugs have potential role in treating many cancers including triple negative breast cancer, but to maximize the efficacy proper selection and study are required.

TABLE 11.1 cMET inhibitors.

No.	Inhibitor	Activity on c-MET	References
1	Crizotinib	Crizotinib (PF-02341066) is a potent inhibitor of cMet and ALK with IC_{50} of 11 and 24 nM in cell-based assays, respectively.	Manchado et al. (2016)
2	Cabozantinib	Cabozantinib (XL184, BMS-907351) is a potent VEGFR2 inhibitor with IC_{50} of 0.035 nM and also inhibits c-Met, Ret, Kit, Flt-1/3/4, Tie2, and AXL with IC_{50} of 1.3 nM, 4 nM, 4.6 nM, 12 nM/11.3 nM/6 nM, 14.3 nM, and 7 nM in cell-free assays, respectively.	Subbiah et al. (2018)
3	Foretinib (GSK1363089)	Foretinib (GSK1363089) is an ATP-competitive inhibitor of HGFR and VEGFR, mostly for Met and KDR with IC50 of 0.4 nM and 0.9 nM in cell-free assays. Less potent against Ron, Flt-1/3/4, Kit, PDGFRα/β, and Tie-2, and little activity to FGFR1 and EGFR. Phase 2	Song et al. (2015)
4	PHA-665752	PHA-665752 is a potent, selective and ATP-competitive c-Met inhibitor with IC50 of 9 nM in cell-free assays, >50-fold selectivity for c-Met than RTKs or STKs.	Papadakis et al. (2015)
5	SU11274	SU11274 is a selective Met inhibitor with IC50 of 10 nM in cell-free assays, no effects on PGDFRβ, EGFR, or Tie2.	Gibot et al. (2016)
6	Pulsatilla saponin D	Pulsatilla saponin D, isolated from the root of Pulsatilla koreana, targets c-Met and exerts antiangiogenic and antitumor activities.	https://www.selleckchem.com/c-Met.html
7	Savolitinib (AZD6094, HMPL-504)	Savolitinib (volitinib, AZD6094, HMPL-504) is a novel, potent, and selective MET inhibitor currently in clinical development in various indications, including PRCC. The IC50 values of this compound for c-Met and p-Met are 5 and 3 nM, respectively. It shows exquisite selectivity for c-Met over 274 kinase.	https://www.selleckchem.com/c-Met.html
8	SGX-523	SGX-523 is a selective Met inhibitor with IC50 of 4 nM, no activity to BRAFV599E, c-Raf, Abl, and p38α. Phase 1.	Brauer et al. (2016)
9	BMS-777607	BMS-777607 is a Met-related inhibitor for cMet, Axl, Ron and Tyro3 with IC50 of 3.9, 1.1, 1.8, and 4.3 nM in cell-free assays, 40-fold more selective for Met-related targets versus Lck, VEGFR-2, and TrkA/B, and >500-fold greater selectivity versus all other receptor and nonreceptor kinases. Phase 1/2.	Werfel et al. (2018)

10	Tivantinib (ARQ 197)	Tivantinib (ARQ 197) is the first non-ATP-competitive c-Met inhibitor with K_i of 0.355 μM in a cell-free assay, little activity to Ron, and no inhibition to EGFR, InsR, PDGFRα or FGFR1/4. Phase 3.	Yang et al. (2013)
11	JNJ-38877605	JNJ-38877605 is an ATP-competitive inhibitor of c-Met with IC50 of 4 nM, 600-fold selective for c-Met than 200 other tyrosine and serine-threonine kinases. Phase 1.	Rebouissou et al. (2017)
12	PF-04217903	PF-04217903 is a selective ATP-competitive c-Met inhibitor with IC50 of 4.8 nM in A549 cell line, susceptible to oncogenic mutations (no activity to Y1230C mutant). Phase 1.	Lock et al. (2016)
13	MGCD-265 analog	MGCD-265 is a potent, multitarget and ATP-competitive inhibitor of c-Met and VEGFR1/2/3 with IC50 of 1 nM, 3 nM/3 nM/4 nM, respectively; also inhibits Ron and Tie2. Phase 1/2.	Bao et al. (2013)
14	Capmatinib (INCB28060)	Capmatinib (INCB28060) is a novel, ATP-competitive inhibitor of c-MET with IC50 of 0.13 nM in a cell-free assay, inactive against RONβ, as well as EGFR and HER-3. Phase 1.	Ai et al. (2018)
15	BMS-754807	BMS-754807 is a potent and reversible inhibitor of IGF-1R/InsR with IC50 of 1.8 nM/1.7 nM in cell-free assays, less potent to Met, Aurora A/B, TrkA/B and Ron, and shows little activity to Flt3, Lck, MK2, PKA, PKC, etc. Phase 2.	Matheny Jr. et al. (2015)
16	BMS-794833	BMS-794833 is a potent ATP competitive inhibitor of Met/VEGFR2 with IC50 of 1.7 nM/15 nM, also inhibits Ron, Axl and Flt3 with IC50 of <3 nM; a prodrug of BMS-817378. Phase 1.	https://www.selleckchem.com/c-Met.html
17	AMG-208	AMG 458 is a potent c-Met inhibitor with K_i of 1.2 nM, ~350-fold selectivity for c-Met than VEGFR2 in cells.	https://www.selleckchem.com/c-Met.html
18	NVP-BVU972	NVP-BVU972 is a selective and potent Met inhibitor with IC50 of 14 nM.	https://www.selleckchem.com/c-Met.html
19	Tepotinib (EMD 1214063)	Tepotinib (EMD 1214063) is a potent and selective c-Met inhibitor with IC50 of 4 nM, >200-fold selective for c-Met than IRAK4, TrkA, Axl, IRAK1, and Mer. Phase 1.	Yi et al. (2018)

Continued

TABLE 11.1 cMET inhibitors—cont'd

No.	Inhibitor	Activity on c-MET	References
20	AMG 337	AMG 337 is an oral, small molecule, ATP-competitive, highly selective inhibitor of the MET receptor with an IC50 of 1 nM.	https://www.selleckchem.com/c-Met.html
21	Merestinib (LY2801653)	LY2801653 is a type-II ATP competitive, slow-off inhibitor of MET tyrosine kinase with a dissociation constant (Ki) of 2 nM, a pharmacodynamic residence time (Koff) of 0.00132 min(−1) and t1/2 of 525 min.	https://www.selleckchem.com/c-Met.html
22	S49076	S49076 is a novel, potent inhibitor of MET, AXL/MER, and FGFR1/2/3 with IC50 values below 20 nmol/L.	https://www.selleckchem.com/c-Met.html
23	Norcantharidin	Norcantharidin is a synthetic anticancer compound which is a dual inhibitor for c-Met and EGFR in human colon cancers.	https://www.selleckchem.com/c-Met.html
24	NPS-1034	NPS-1034 is a dual Met/Axl inhibitor with IC50 of 48 and 10.3 nM, respectively.	https://www.selleckchem.com/c-Met.html

Content courtesy: https://www.selleckchem.com/c-Met.html

References

Ai, J., Chen, Y., Peng, X., Ji, Y., Xi, Y., Shen, Y., et al., 2018. Preclinical evaluation of SCC244 (glumetinib), a novel, potent, and highly selective inhibitor of c-Met in MET-dependent cancer models. Mol. Cancer Ther. 17 (4), 751–762.

An, X., Wang, F., Shao, Q., Wang, F.H., Wang, Z.Q., Wang, Z.Q., et al., 2014. MET amplification is not rare and predicts unfavorable clinical outcomes in patients with recurrent/metastatic gastric cancer after chemotherapy. Cancer 120, 675–682.

Andermarcher, E., Surani, M.A., Gherardi, E., 1996. Co-expression of the HGF/SF and c-met genes during early mouse embryogenesis precedes reciprocal expression in adjacent tissues during organogenesis. Dev. Genet. 18, 254–266.

Apte, U., Zeng, G., Muller, P., Tan, X., Micsenvi, A., Cieply, B., et al., 2006. Activation of Wnt/beta-catenin pathway during hepatocyte growth factor-induced hepatomegaly in mice. Hepatology 44, 992–1002.

Bao, N.R., Lu, M., Bin, F.W., Chang, Z.Y., Meng, J., Zhou, L.W., et al., 2013. Systematic screen with kinases inhibitors reveals kinases play distinct roles in growth of osteoprogenitor cells. Int. J. Clin. Exp. Pathol. 6 (10), 2082–2091.

Bertotti, A., Comoglio, P.M., Trusolino, L., 2005. Beta4 integrin is a transforming molecule that unleashes Met tyrosine kinase tumorigenesis. Cancer Res. 65 (23), 10674–10679.

Bertotti, A., Comoglio, P.M., Trusolino, L., 2006. Beta4 integrin activates a Shp2-Src signaling pathway that sustains HGF-induced anchorage-independent growth. J. Cell Biol. 175 (6), 993–1003.

Birchmeier, C., Birchmeier, W., Gherardi, E., Vande Woude, G.F., 2003. Met, metastasis, motility and more. Nat. Rev. Mol. Cell Biol. 4, 915–925.

Boccaccio, C., Comoglio, P.M., 2006. Invasive growth: a Met driven genetic program for cancer and stem cells. Nat. Rev. Cancer 6, 637–645.

Boccaccio, C., Andò, M., Tamagnone, L., Bardelli, A., Michieli, P., Battistini, C., 1998. Induction of epithelial tubules by growth factor HGF depends on the STAT pathway. Nature 391, 285–288.

Borowiak, M., Garratt, A.N., Wüstefeld, T., Strehle, M., Trautwein, C., Bircheier, C., 2004. Met provides essential signals for liver regeneration. Proc. Natl. Acad. Sci. U. S. A. 101, 10608–10613.

Bottaro, D.P., Rubin, J.S., Faletto, D.L., Chan, A.M., Kmiecik, T.E., Vande Woude, G.F., et al., 1991. Identification of the hepatocyte growth factor receptor as the c-met proto-oncogene product. Science 251, 802–804.

Brauer, R., Ge, L., Schlesinger, S.Y., Birkland, T.P., Huang, Y., Parimon, T., et al., 2016. Syndecan-1 attenuates lung injury during influenza infection by potentiating c-Met signaling to suppress epithelial apoptosis. Am. J. Respir. Crit. Care Med. 194 (3), 333–344.

Cao, W., Wang, X., Gao, Y., Yang, H., Li, J.C., 2013. BRCA1 germ-line mutations and tumor characteristics in eastern Chinese women with familial breast cancer. Anat. Rec. (Hoboken) 296 (2), 273–278.

Catenacci, D.V., Ang, A., Liao, W.L., Shen, J., O'Day, E., Loberg, R.D., et al., 2017. MET tyrosine kinase receptor expression and amplification as prognostic biomarkers of survival in gastroesophageal adenocarcinoma. Cancer 123 (6), 1061–1070.

Cecchi, F., Rabe, D.C., Bottaro, D.P., 2011. The hepatocyte growth factor receptor: structure, function and pharmacological targeting in cancer. Curr. Signal Transduct Ther. 6 (2), 146–151.

Chae, Y.K., Gagliato Dde, M., Pai, S.G., Carneiro, B., Mohindra, N., Giles, F.J., et al., 2016. The association between EGFR and cMET expression and phosphorylation and its prognostic implication in patients with breast cancer. PLoS One 11 (4), e0152585.

Christensen, J.G., Burrows, J., Salgia, R., 2005. c-Met as a target for human cancer and characterization of inhibitors for therapeutic intervention. Cancer Lett. 225, 1–26.

Chung, I.H., Chen, C.Y., Lin, Y.H., Chi, H.C., Huang, Y.H., Tai, P.J., et al., 2015. Thyroid hormone-mediated regulation of lipocalin 2 through the Met/FAK pathway in liver cancer. Oncotarget 6 (17), 15050–15064.

Ciuffreda, L., Incani, U.C., Steelman, L.S., Abrams, S.L., Falcone, I., Curatolo, A.D., et al., 2014. Signaling intermediates (MAPK and PI3K) as therapeutic targets in NSCLC. Curr. Pharm. Des. 20 (24), 3944–3957.

Coltella, N., Rasola, A., Nano, E., Bardella, C., Fassetta, M., Filigheddu, N., et al., 2006. p38 MAPK turns hepatocyte growth factor to a death signal that commits ovarian cancer cells to chemotherapy-induced apoptosis. Int. J. Cancer 118 (12), 2981–2990.

Conrotto, P., Corso, S., Gamberini, S., Comoglio, P.M., Giordano, S., 2004. Interplay between scatter factor receptors and B plexins controls invasive growth. Oncogene 23 (30), 5131–5137.

Conrotto, P., Valdembri, D., Corso, S., Serini, G., Tamagnone, L., Comoglio, P.M., et al., 2005. Sema4D induces angiogenesis through Met recruitment by Plexin B1. Blood 105 (11), 4321–4329.

Cooper, C.S., Park, M., Blair, D.G., Tainsky, M.A., Huebner, K., Croce, C.M., et al., 1984. Molecular cloning of a new transforming gene from a chemically transformed human cell line. Nature 311, 29–33.

Cortot, A.B., Kherrouche, Z., Descarpentries, C., Wislez, M., Baldacci, S., Furlan, A., et al., 2017. Exon 14 deleted MET receptor as a new biomarker and target in cancers. J Natl Cancer. Inst. 109 (5).

Cui, J.J., 2014. Targeting receptor tyrosine kinase MET in cancer: small molecule inhibitors and clinical progress. J. Med. Chem. 57, 4427e4453.

Cunnick, J.M., Meng, S., Ren, Y., Desponts, C., Wang, H.G., Djeu, J.Y., et al., 2002. Regulation of the mitogen activated protein kinase signaling pathway by SHP2. J. Biol. Chem. 277, 9498–9504.

Dan, H.C., Cooper, M.J., Cogswell, P.C., Duncan, J.A., Ting, J.P., Baldwin, A.S., 2008. Akt-dependent regulation of NF-{kappa}B is controlled by mTOR and Raptor in association with IKK. Genes Dev. 22, 1490–1500.

Danilkovitch-Miagkova, A., Zbar, B., 2001. Dysregulation of Met receptor tyrosine kinase activity in invasive tumors. J. Clin. Invest. 109 (7), 863–867.

Derksen, P.W., de Gorter, D.J., Meijer, H.P., Bende, R.J., van Dijk, M., Lokhorst, H.M., et al., 2003. The hepatocyte growth factor/Met pathway controls proliferation and apoptosis in multiple myeloma. Leukemia 17, 764–774.

Duh, F.M., Scherer, S.W., Tsui, L.C., Lerman, M.I., Zbar, B., Schmidt, L., 1997. Gene structure of the human MET proto-oncogene. Oncogene 15, 1583–1586.

Edakuni, G., Sasatomi, E., Satoh, T., Tokunaga, O., 2001. Miyazaki, K., Expression of the hepatocyte growth factor/c-Met pathway is increased at the cancer front in breast carcinoma. Pathol. Int. 51 (3), 172–178.

Fan, S., Ma, Y.X., Wang, J.A., Yuan, R.Q., Meng, Q., Cao, Y., et al., 2000. The cytokine hepatocyte growth factor/scatter factor inhibits apoptosis and enhances DNA repair by a common mechanism involving signaling through phosphatidyl inositol 3′ kinase. Oncogene 19, 2212–2223.

Fan, S., Gao, M., Meng, Q., Laterra, J.J., Symons, M.H., Coniglio, S., 2005. Role of NF-kappaB signaling in hepatocyte growth factor/scatter factor-mediated cell protection. Oncogene 24 (10), 1749–1766.

Fixman, E.D., Fournier, T.M., Kamikura, D.M., Naujokas, M.A., Park, M., 1996. Pathways downstream of Shc and Grb2 are required for cell transformation by the tpr-Met oncoprotein. J. Biol. Chem. 271 (22), 13116–13122.

Forbes, S.A., Bhamra, G., Bamford, S., Dawson, E., Kok, C., Clements, J., et al., 2008. The catalogue of somatic mutations in cancer (COSMIC). In: Curr Protoc Hum Genet. Chapter 10, Unit 10.11.

Forte, G., Minieri, M., Cossa, P., Antenucci, D., Sala, M., Gnocchi, V., et al., 2006. Hepatocyte growth factor effects on mesenchymal stem cells: proliferation, migration, and differentiation. Stem Cells 24, 23–33.

Fuse, N., Kuboki, Y., Kuwata, T., Nishina, T., Kadowaki, S., Shinozaki, E., et al., 2016. Prognostic impact of HER2, EGFR, and c-MET status on overall survival of advanced gastric cancer patients. Gastric Cancer 19 (1), 183–191.

Gandino, L., Longati, P., Medico, E., Prat, M., Comoglio, P.M., 1994. Phosphorylation of serine 985 negatively regulates the hepatocyte growth factor receptor kinase. J. Biol. Chem. 269 (3), 1815–1820.

Gaule, P.B., Crown, J., O'Donovan, N., Duffy, M.J., et al., 2014. cMET in triple-negative breast cancer: is it a therapeutic target for this subset of breast cancer patients? Expert Opin. Ther. Targets 18 (9), 999–1009.

Gherardi, E., Birchmeier, W., Birchmeier, C., Vande Woude, G., 2012. Targeting MET in cancer: rationale and progress. Nat. Rev. Cancer 12, 89e103.

Gibot, L., Galbraith, T., Kloos, B., Das, S., Lacroix, D.A., Auger, F.A., 2016. Cell-based approach for 3D reconstruction of lymphatic capillaries in vitro reveals distinct functions of HGF and VEGF-C in lymphangiogenesis. Biomaterials 78, 129–139.

Giordano, S., Corso, S., Conrotto, P., Artigiani, S., Gilestro, G., Barberis, D., et al., 2002. The semaphorin 4D receptor controls invasive growth by coupling with Met. Nat. Cell Biol. 4 (9), 720–724.

Graziani, A., Gramaglia, D., dalla Zonca, P., Comoglio, P.M., 1993. Hepatocyte growth factor/scatter factor stimulates the Ras-guanine nucleotide exchanger. J. Biol. Chem. 268 (13), 9165–9168.

Gual, P., Giordano, S., Williams, T.A., Rocchi, S., Van Obberghen, E., Comoglio, P.M., 2000. Sustained recruitment of phospholipase C-gamma to Gab1 is required for HGF-induced branching tubulogenesis. Oncogene 19 (12), 1509–1518.

Gusenbauer, S., Zanucco, E., Knyazev, P., Ullrich, A., 2015. Erk2 but not Erk1 regulates crosstalk between Met and EGFR in squamous cell carcinoma cell lines. Mol. Cancer 14, 54.

Hasenauer, S., Malinger, D., Koschut, D., Pace, G., Matzke, A., von Au, A., et al., 2013. Internalization of Met requires the co-receptor CD44v6 and its link to ERM proteins. PLoS One 8 (4), e62357.

Ho-Yen, C.M., Green, A.R., Rakha, E.A., Brentnall, A.R., Ellis, I.O., Kermorgant, S., et al., 2014. C-Met in invasive breast cancer: is there a relationship with the basal-like subtype? Cancer 120 (2), 163–171.

Ho-Yen, C.M., Jones, J.L., Kermorgant, S., 2015. The clinical and functional significance of c-Met in breast cancer. Breast Cancer Res. 17, 52.

Huang, F.I., Chen, Y.L., Chang, C.N., Yuan, R.H., Jeng, Y.M., 2012. Hepatocyte growth factor activates Wnt pathway by transcriptional activation of LEF1 to facilitate tumor invasion. Carcinogenesis 33 (6), 1142–1148.

Hui, A.Y., Meens, J.A., Schick, C., Organ, S.L., Qiao, H., Tremblay, E.A., et al., 2009. Src and FAK mediate cell-matrix adhesion-dependent activation of Met during transformation of breast epithelial cells. J. Cell. Biochem. 107 (6), 1168–1181.

Inanc, M., Ozkan, M., Karaca, H., Berk, V., Bozkurt, O., Duran, A.O., et al., 2014. Cytokeratin 5/6, c-Met expressions, and PTEN loss prognostic indicators in triple-negative breast cancer. Med. Oncol. 31 (1), 801.

Janbabai, G., Oladi, Z., Farazmandfar, T., Taghvaei, T., Naghshvar, F., 2015. The prognostic impact of EGFR, ErbB2 and MET gene amplification in human gastric carcinomas as measured by quantitative Real-Time PCR. J. Cancer Res. Clin. Oncol. 141 (11), 1945–1952.

Jeffers, M., Taylor, G.A., Weidner, K.M., Omura, S., Vande Woude, G.F., 1997. Degradation of the Met tyrosine kinase receptor by the ubiquitin-proteasome pathway. Mol. Cell. Biol. 17 (2), 799–808.

Jiao, D., Wang, J., Lu, W., Tang, X., Chen, J., Mou, H., et al., 2016. Curcumin inhibited HGF-induced EMT and angiogenesis through regulating c-Met dependent PI3K/Akt/mTOR signaling pathways in lung cancer. Mol. Ther. Oncol. 3, 16018.

Jin, L., Fuchs, A., Schnitt, S.J., Yao, Y., Joseph, A., Lamszus, K., et al., 1997. Expression of scatter factor and c-met receptor in benign and malignant breast tissue. Cancer 79 (4), 749–760.

Joly, A., 2006. Simultaneous blockade of VEGF and HGF receptors results in potent anti-angiogenic and anti-tumor effects. Eur. J. Cancer Suppl. 4, 35. KEGG Pathway Database.

Kawakami, H., Okamoto, I., Arao, T., Okamoto, W., Matsumoto, K., Taniguchi, H., et al., 2013. MET amplification as a potential therapeutic target in gastric cancer. Oncotarget 4 (1), 9–17.

Kawakami, H., Okamoto, I., Okamoto, W., Tanizaki, J., Nakagawa, K., Nishio, K., 2014. Targeting MET amplification as a new oncogenic driver. Cancers (Basel) 6 (3), 1540–1552.

Kimelman, D., Xu, W., 2006. beta-catenin destruction complex: insights and questions from a structural perspective. Oncogene 25 (57), 7482–7491.

Kitajima, Y., Ide, T., Ohtsuka, T., Miyazaki, K., 2008. Induction of hepatocyte growth factor activator gene expression under hypoxia activates the hepatocyte growth factor/c-Met system via hypoxia inducible factor-1 in pancreatic cancer. Cancer Sci. 99 (7), 1341–1347.

Knight, J.F., Lesurf, R., Zhao, H., Pinnaduwage, D., Davis, R.R., Saleh, S.M., et al., 2013. Met synergizes with p53 loss to induce mammary tumors that possess features of claudin-low breast cancer. Proc. Natl. Acad. Sci. U. S. A. 110 (14), E1301–E1310.

Kuang, W., Deng, Q., Deng, C., Li, W., Shu, S., Zhou, M., 2017. Hepatocyte growth factor induces breast cancer cell invasion via the PI3K/Akt and p38 MAPK signaling pathways to up-regulate the expression of COX2. Am. J. Transl. Res. 9 (8), 3816–3826.

Kwak, Y., Kim, S.-I., Park, C.-K., Paek, S.H., Lee, S.-T., Park, S.-H., 2015. C-MET over-expression and amplification in gliomas. Int. J. Clin. Exp. Pathol. 8 (11), 14932–14938.

Li, Y., Li, W., He, Q., Xu, Y., Ren, X., Tang, X., et al., 2015. Prognostic value of MET protein over-expression and gene amplification in locoregionally advanced nasopharyngeal carcinoma. Oncotarget 6 (15), 13309–13319.

Liang, Y., Feng, Y., Zong, M., Wei, X.F., Lee, J., Feng, Y., et al., 2017. β-Catenin deficiency in hepatocytes aggravates hepatocarcinogenesis driven by oncogenic β-catenin and MET. Hepatology 67 (5), 1807–1822.

Linklater, E.S., Tovar, E.A., Essenburg, C.J., Turner, L., Madaj, Z., Winn, M., et al., 2016. Targeting MET and EGFR crosstalk signaling in triple-negative breast cancers. Oncotarget 7 (43), 69903–69915.

Lock, L.S., Royal, I., Naujokas, M.A., Park, M., 2000. Identification of an atypical Grb2 carboxyl-terminal SH3 domain binding site in Gab docking proteins reveals Grb2-dependent and -independent recruitment of Gab1 to receptor tyrosine kinases. J. Biol. Chem. 275 (40), 31536–31545.

Lock, R., Ingraham, R., Maertens, O., Miller, A.L., Weledji, N., Legius, E., et al., 2016. Cotargeting MNK and MEK kinases induces the regression of NF1-mutant cancers. J. Clin. Invest. 126 (6), 2181–2190.

Ma, P.C., Maulik, G., Christensen, J., Salgia, R., 2003. c-Met: structure, functions and potential for therapeutic inhibition. Cancer Metastasis Rev. 22, 309–325.

Ma, P.C., Tretiakova, M.S., MacKinnon, A.C., Ramnath, N., Johnson, C., Dietrich, S., et al., 2008. Expression and mutational analysis of MET in human solid cancers. Genes Chromosom. Cancer 47, 1025–1037.

Manchado, E., Weissmueller, S., Morris 4th., J.P., Chen, C.C., Wullenkord, R., Lujambio, A., et al., 2016. A combinatorial strategy for treating KRAS-mutant lung cancer. Nature 534 (7609), 647–651.

Maroun, C.R., Rowlands, T., 2014. The Met receptor tyrosine kinase: a key player in oncogenesis and drug resistance. Pharmacol. Ther. 142 (3), 316–338.

Maroun, C.R., Naujokas, M.A., Holgado-Madruga, M., Wong, A.J., Park, M., 2000. The tyrosine phosphatase SHP-2 is required for sustained activation of extracellular signal-regulated kinase and epithelial morphogenesis downstream from the met receptor tyrosine kinase. Mol. Cell. Biol. 20 (22), 8513–8525.

Matheny Jr., R.W., Riddle-Kottke, M.A., Leandry, L.A., Lynch, C.M., Abdalla, M.N., Geddis, A.V., et al., 2015. Role of phosphoinositide 3-OH kinase p110β in skeletal myogenesis. Mol. Cell. Biol. 35 (7), 1182–1196.

Matsumoto, K., Nakamura, T., 2006. Hepatocyte growth factor and the Met system as a mediator of tumor-stromal interactions. Int. J. Cancer 119 (3), 477–483.

Matsumura, A., Kubota, T., Taiyoh, H., Fujiwara, H., Okamoto, K., Ichikawa, D., et al., 2013. HGF regulates VEGF expression via the c-Met receptor downstream pathways, PI3K/Akt, MAPK and STAT3, in CT26 murine cells. Int. J. Oncol. 42 (2), 535–542.

Matzke-Ogi, A., Jannasch, K., Shatirishvili, M., Fuchs, B., Chiblak, S., et al., 2016. Inhibition of tumor growth and metastasis in pancreatic cancer models by interference with CD44v6 signaling. Gastroenterology 150 (2), 513–525.

Maulik, G., Madhiwala, P., Brooks, S., Ma, P.C., Kijima, T., Tibaldi, E.V., et al., 2002. Activated c-Met signals through PI3K with dramatic effects on cytoskeletal functions in small cell lung cancer. J. Cell. Mol. Med. 6 (4), 539–553.

Mesarosova, L., Ochodnicky, P., Leemans, J.C., Florquin, S., Krenek, P., Klimas, J., 2017. High glucose induces HGF-independent activation of Met receptor in human renal tubular epithelium. J. Recept. Signal Transduct. Res. 37 (6), 535–542.

Miller, C.T., Lin, L., Casper, A.M., Lim, J., Thomas, D.G., Orringer, M.B., et al., 2006. Genomic amplification of MET with boundaries within fragile site FRA7G and upregulation of MET pathways in esophageal adenocarcinoma. Oncogene 25 (3), 409–418.

Minuti, G., Landi, L., 2015. MET deregulation in breast cancer. Ann. Transl. Med. 3 (13), 181.

Monga, S.P., Mars, W.M., Pediaditakis, P., Bell, A., Mulé, K., Bowen, W.C., et al., 2002. Hepatocyte growth factor induces Wnt-independent nuclear translocation of beta-catenin after Met-beta-catenin dissociation in hepatocytes. Cancer Res. 62 (7), 2064–2071.

Montagner, A., Yart, A., Dance, M., Perret, B., Salles, J.P., Raynal, P., 2005. A novel role for Gab1 and SHP2 in epidermal growth factor-induced Ras activation. J. Biol. Chem. 280 (7), 5350–5360.

Mueller, K.L., Madden, J.M., Zoratti, G.L., Kuperwasser, C., List, K., Boerner, J.L., 2012. Fibroblast-secreted hepatocyte growth factor mediates epidermal growth factor receptor tyrosine kinase inhibitor resistance in triple-negative breast cancers through paracrine activation of Met. Breast Cancer Res. 14 (4), R104.

Nakamura, T., 1991. Structure and function of hepatocyte growth factor. Prog. Growth Factor Res. 3 (1), 67–85.

Navis, A.C., van Lith, S.A., van Duijnhoven, S.M., de Pooter, M., Yetkin-Arik, B., Wesseling, P., 2015. Identification of a novel MET mutation in high-grade glioma resulting in an auto-active intracellular protein. Acta Neuropathol. 130 (1), 131–144.

Nelson, W.J., Nusse, R., 2004. Convergence of Wnt, beta-catenin, and cadherin pathways. Science 303 (5663), 1483–1487.

Neuss, S., Becher, E., Wöltje, M., Tietze, L., Jahnen-Dechent, W., 2004. Functional expression of HGF and HGF receptor/c-met in adult human mesenchymal stem cells suggests a role in cell mobilization, tissue repair, and wound healing. Stem Cells 22, 405–414.

Oeckinghaus, A., Ghosh, S., 2009. The NF-κB Family of Transcription Factors and Its Regulation. Cold Spring Harb. Perspect. Biol. 1 (4), a000034.

Organ, S.L., Tong, J., Taylor, P., St-Germain, J.R., Navab, R., Moran, M.F., et al., 2011. Quantitative phospho-proteomic profiling of hepatocyte growth factor (HGF)-MET signaling in colorectal cancer. J. Proteome Res. 10 (7), 3200–3211.

Orian-Rousseau, V., Chen, L., Sleeman, J.P., Herrlich, P., Ponta, H., 2002. CD44 is required for two consecutive steps in HGF/c-Met signaling. Genes Dev. 16 (23), 3074–3086.

Orian-Rousseau, V., Morrison, H., Matzke, A., Kastilan, T., Pace, G., Herrlich, P., et al., 2007. Hepatocyte growth factor-induced Ras activation requires ERM proteins linked to both CD44v6 and F-actin. Mol. Biol. Cell 18 (1), 76–83.

Ou, S.I., Young, L., Schrock, A.B., Johnson, A., Klempner, S.J., Zhu, V.W., et al., 2017. Emergence of preexisting MET Y1230C Mutation as a resistance mechanism to crizotinib in NSCLC with MET Exon 14 skipping. J. Thorac. Oncol. 12 (1), 137–140.

Papadakis, A.I., Sun, C., Knijnenburg, T.A., Xue, Y., Grernrum, W., Hölzel, M., et al., 2015. SMARCE1 suppresses EGFR expression and controls responses to MET and ALK inhibitors in lung cancer. Cell Res. 25 (4), 445–458.

Park, M., Dean, M., Cooper, C.S., Schmidt, M., O'Brien, S.J., Blair, D.G., et al., 1986. Mechanism of met oncogene activation. Cell 45 (6), 895–904.

Paulis, Y.W., Huijbers, E.J., van der Schaft, D.W., Soetekouw, P.M., Pauwels, P., Tjan-Heijnen, V.C., et al., 2015. CD44 enhance tumor aggressiveness by promoting tumor cell plasticity. Oncotarget 6 (23), 19634–19646.

Paumelle, R., Tulasne, D., Kherrouche, Z., Plaza, S., Leroy, C., Reveneau, S., et al., 2002. Hepatocyte growth factor/scatter factor activates the ETS1 transcription factor by a RAS-RAF-MEK-ERK signaling pathway. Oncogene 21 (15), 2309–2319.

Peinado, H., Alečković, M., Lavotshkin, S., Matei, I., Costa-Silva, B., Moreno-Bueno, G., et al., 2012. Melanoma exosomes educate bone marrow progenitor cells toward a pro-metastatic phenotype through MET. Nat. Med. 18 (6), 883–891.

Pelicci, G., Giordano, S., Zhen, Z., Salcini, A.E., Lanfrancone, L., Bardelli, A., et al., 1995. The motogenic and mitogenic responses to HGF are amplified by the Shc adaptor protein. Oncogene 10 (8), 1631–1638.

Peschard, P., Park, M., 2007. From Tpr-Met to Met, tumorigenesis and tubes. Oncogene 26 (9), 1276–1285.

Peschard, P., Fournier, T.M., Lamorte, L., Naujokas, M.A., Band, H., Langdon, W.Y., et al., 2001. Mutation of the c-Cbl TKB domain binding site on the Met receptor tyrosine kinase converts it into a transforming protein. Mol. Cell 8 (5), 995–1004.

Petrelli, A., Gilestro, G.F., Lanzardo, S., Comoglio, P.M., Migone, N., Giordano, S., 2002. The endophilin-CIN85-Cbl complex mediates ligand-dependent downregulation of c-Met. Nature 416 (6877), 187–190.

Petrini, I., 2015. Biology of MET: a double life between normal tissue repair and tumor progression. Ann. Transl. Med. 3 (6), 82.

Ponta, H., Sherman, L., Herrlich, P.A., 2003. CD44: from adhesion molecules to signaling regulators. Nat. Rev. Mol. Cell Biol. 4 (1), 33–45.

Ponzetto, C., Bardelli, A., Zhen, Z., Maina, F., Dalla Zonca, P., Giordano, S., et al., 1994. A multifunctional docking site mediates signaling and transformation by the hepatocyte growth factor/scatter factor receptor family. Cell 77, 261–271.

Prat, M., Narsimhan, R.P., Crepaldi, T., Nicotra, M.R., Natali, P.G., Comoglio, P.M., 1991. The receptor encoded by the human c-MET oncogene is expressed in hepatocytes, epithelial cells and solid tumors. Int. J. Cancer 49, 323–328.

Prochazka, L., Tesarik, R., Turanek, J., 2014. Regulation of alternative splicing of CD44 in cancer. Cell. Signal. 26 (10), 2234–2239.

Rebouissou, S., La Bella, T., Rekik, S., Imbeaud, S., Calatayud, A.L., Rohr-Udilova, N., et al., 2017. Proliferation markers Are associated with MET expression in hepatocellular carcinoma and predict tivantinib sensitivity in vitro. Clin. Cancer Res. 23 (15), 4364–4375.

Recio, J.A., Merlino, G., 2002. Hepatocyte growth factor/scatter factor activates proliferation in melanoma cells through p38 MAPK, ATF-2 and cyclin D1. Oncogene 21 (7), 1000–1008.

Rodrigues, G.A., Park, M., Schlessinger, J., 1997. Activation of the JNK pathway is essential for transformation by the Met oncogene. EMBO J. 16 (10), 2634–2645.

Rolle, C.E., Tan, Y.C., Seiwert, T.Y., Vora, S., Kanteti, R., Hasina, R., et al., 2017. Expression and mutational analysis of c-CBL and its relationship to the MET receptor in head and neck squamous cell carcinoma. Oncotarget 8 (12), 18726–18734.

Rosário, M., Birchmeier, W., 2003. How to make tubes: signaling by the Met receptor tyrosine kinase. Trends Cell Biol. 13 (6), 328–335.

Saffroy, R., Fallet, V., Girard, N., Mazieres, J., Sibilot, D.M., Lantuejoul, S., et al., 2017. MET exon 14 mutations as targets in routine molecular analysis of primary sarcomatoid carcinoma of the lung. Oncotarget 8 (26), 42428–42437.

Sakkab, D., Lewitzky, M., Posern, G., Schaeper, U., Sachs, M., Birchmeier, W., et al., 2000. Signaling of hepatocyte growth factor/scatter factor (HGF) to the small GTPase Rap1 via the large docking protein Gab1 and the adapter protein CRKL. J. Biol. Chem. 275 (15), 10772–10778.

Schaeper, U., Gehring, N.H., Fuchs, K.P., Sachs, M., Kempkes, B., Birchmeier, W., 2000. Coupling of Gab1 to c-Met, Grb2, and Shp2 mediates biological responses. J. Cell Biol. 149 (7), 1419–1432.

Schmidt, L., Junker, K., Nakaigawa, N., Kinjerski, T., Weirich, G., Miller, M., et al., 1999. Novel mutations of the MET proto-oncogene in papillary renal carcinomas. Oncogene 18 (14), 2343–2350.

Sennino, B., Naylor, R.M., Tabruyn, S.P., You, W.-K., Aftab, D.T., McDonald, D.M., 2009. Reduction of tumor invasiveness and metastasis and prolongation of survival of RIP-Tag2 mice after inhibition of VEGFR plus c-Met by XL184. Mol. Cancer Ther. 8, A13.

Sequist, L.V., Waltman, B.A., Dias-Santagata, D., Digumarthy, S., Turke, A.B., Fidias, P., et al., 2011. Genotypic and histological evolution of lung cancers acquiring resistance to EGFR inhibitors. Sci. Transl. Med. 3 (75), 75ra26.

Sierra, J.R., Tsao, M.S., 2011. c-MET as a potential therapeutic target and biomarker in cancer. Ther. Adv. Med. Oncol. 3 (1 Suppl), S21–S35.

Singleton, P.A., Salgia, R., Moreno-Vinasco, L., Moitra, J., Sammani, S., Mirzapoiazova, T., et al., 2007. CD44 regulates hepatocyte growth factor-mediated vascular integrity. Role of c-Met, Tiam1/Rac1, dynamin 2, and cortactin. J. Biol. Chem. 282 (42), 30643–30657.

Smyth, E.C., Sclafani, F., Cunningham, D., 2014. Emerging molecular targets in oncology: clinical potential of MET/hepatocyte growth-factor inhibitors. OncoTargets Ther. 7, 1001–1014.

Sohn, J., Liu, S., Parinyanitikul, N., Lee, J., Hortobagyi, G.N., Mills, G.B., et al., 2014. cMET activation and EGFR-directed therapy resistance in triple-negative breast cancer. J. Cancer 5 (9), 745–753.

Soman, N.R., Correa, P., Ruiz, B.A., Wogan, G.N., 1991. The TPR-MET oncogenic rearrangement is present and expressed in human gastric carcinoma and precursor lesions. Proc. Natl. Acad. Sci. U. S. A. 88 (11), 4892–4896.

Song, A., Kim, T.M., Kim, D.W., Kim, S., Keam, B., Lee, S.H., Heo, D.S., 2015. Molecular changes associated with acquired resistance to crizotinib in ROS1-rearranged non-small cell lung cancer. Clin. Cancer Res. 21 (10), 2379–2387.

Sonnenberg, E., Meyer, D., Weidner, K.M., Birchmeier, C., 1993. Scatter factor/hepatocyte growth factor and its receptor, the c-met tyrosine kinase, can mediate a signal exchange between mesenchyme and epithelia during mouse development. J. Cell Biol. 123, 223–235.

Soong, J., Scott, G., 2013. Plexin B1 inhibits MET through direct association and regulates Shp2 expression in melanocytes. J. Cell Sci. 126 (Pt 2), 688–695.

Stoker, M., Gherardi, E., Perryman, M., Gray, J., 1987. Scatter factor is a fibroblast-derived modulator of epithelial cell mobility. Nature 327, 239–242.

Subbiah, V., Gainor, J.F., Rahal, R., Brubaker, J.D., Kim, J.L., Maynard, M., et al., 2018. Precision targeted therapy with BLU-667 for RET-driven cancers. Cancer Discov. 8 (7), 836–849.

Syed, Z.A., Yin, W., Hughes, K., Gill, J.N., Shi, R., Clifford, J.L., 2011. HGF/c-met/Stat3 signaling during skin tumor cell invasion: indications for a positive feedback loop. BMC Cancer 11, 180.

Tan, Y.C., Mirzapoiazova, T., Won, B.M., Zhu, L., Srivastava, M.K., Vokes, E.E., et al., 2017. Differential responsiveness of MET inhibition in non-small-cell lung cancer with altered CBL. Sci. Rep. 7 (1), 9192.

Thiery, J.P., 2003. Epithelial-mesenchymal transitions in development and pathologies. Curr. Opin. Cell Biol. 15, 740–746.

Todaro, M., Gaggianesi, M., Catalano, V., Benfante, A., Iovino, F., Biffoni, M., et al., 2014. CD44v6 is a marker of constitutive and reprogrammed cancer stem cells driving colon cancer metastasis. Cell Stem Cell 14 (3), 342–356.

Trusolino, L., Bertotti, A., Comoglio, P.M., 2001. A signaling adapter functions for alpha6beta4 integrin in the control of HGF-dependent invasive growth. Cell 107 (5), 643–654.

Trusolino, L., Bertotti, A., Comoglio, P.M., 2010. Met signaling: principles and functions in development, organ regeneration and cancer. Nat. Rev. Mol. Cell Biol. 11, 834–848.

Tsou, H.K., Chen, H.T., Hung, Y.H., Chang, C.H., Li, T.M., Fong, Y.C., et al., 2013. HGF and c-Met interaction promotes migration in human chondrosarcoma cells. PLoS One 8 (1), e53974.

Tuck, A.B., Park, M., Sterns, E.E., Boag, A., Elliott, B.E., 1996. Coexpression of hepatocyte growth factor and receptor (Met) in human breast carcinoma. Am. J. Pathol. 148 (1), 225–232.

Tulasne, D., Foveau, B., 2008. The shadow of death on the MET tyrosine kinase receptor. Cell Death Differ. 15 (3), 427–434.

Weidner, K.M., Di Cesare, S., Sachs, M., Brinkmann, V., Behrens, J., Birchmeier, W., 1996. Interaction between Gab1 and the c-Met receptor tyrosine kinase is responsible for epithelial morphogenesis. Nature 384, 173–176.

Werfel, T.A., Elion, D.L., Rahman, B., Hicks, D.J., Sanchez, V., Gonzales-Ericsson, P.I., et al., 2018. Treatment-induced tumor cell apoptosis and secondary necrosis drive tumor progression in the residual tumor microenvironment through MerTK and IDO1. Cancer Res. 79 (1), 171–182.

Wickramasinghe, D., Kong-Beltran, M., 2005. Met activation and receptor dimerization in cancer: a role for the Sema domain. Cell Cycle 4 (5), 683–685.

Xiao, G.H., Jeffers, M., Bellacosa, A., Mitsuuchi, Y., Vande Woude, G.F., Testa, J.R., 2001. Anti-apoptotic signaling by hepatocyte growth factor/Met via the phosphatidylinositol 3-kinase/Akt and mitogen-activated protein kinase pathways. Proc. Natl. Acad. Sci. U. S. A. 98, 247–252.

Xie, Q., Liu, K.D., Hu, M.Y., Zhou, K., 2001. SF/HGF-c-Met autocrine and paracrine promote metastasis of hepatocellular carcinoma. World J. Gastroenterol. 7 (6), 816–820.

Xie, Q., Bradley, R., Kang, L., Koeman, J., Ascierto, M.L., Worschech, A., et al., 2012. Hepatocyte growth factor (HGF) autocrine activation predicts sensitivity to MET inhibition in glioblastoma. Proc. Natl. Acad. Sci. U. S. A. 109 (2), 570–575.

Xu, Y., Zhou, J., Carey, T.E., McHugh, J.B., Voorhees, J.J., Fisher, G.J., 2012. Receptor-type protein tyrosine phosphatase β regulates met phosphorylation and function in head and neck squamous cell carcinoma. Neoplasia 14 (11), 1015–1022.

Yakes, F.M., Chen, J., Tan, J., Yamaguchi, K., Shi, Y., Yu, P., et al., 2011. Cabozantinib (XL184), a novel MET and VEGFR2 inhibitor, simultaneously suppresses metastasis, angiogenesis, and tumor growth. Mol. Cancer Ther. 10 (12), 2298–2308.

Yan, S., Jiao, X., Zou, H., Li, K., 2015. Prognostic significance of c-Met in breast cancer: a meta-analysis of 6010 cases. Diagn. Pathol. 10, 62.

Yang, Q., Feng, F., Zhang, F., Wang, C., Lu, Y., Gao, X., et al., 2013. LINE-1 ORF-1p functions as a novel HGF/ETS-1 signaling pathway co-activator and promotes the growth of MDA-MB-231 cell. Cell. Signal. 25 (12), 2652–2660.

Yen, B.L., Yen, M.L., Hsu, P.J., Liu, K.J., Wang, C.J., Bai, C.H., et al., 2013. Multipotent human mesenchymal stromal cells mediate expansion of myeloid-derived suppressor cells via hepatocyte growth factor/c-met and STAT3. Stem Cell Rep. 1 (2), 139–151.

Yi, Y.W., You, K., Bae, E.J., Kwak, S.J., Seong, Y.S., Bae, I., 2015. Dual inhibition of EGFR and MET induces synthetic lethality in triple-negative breast cancer cells through downregulation of ribosomal protein S6. Int. J. Oncol. 47 (1), 122–132.

Yi, Y., Zeng, S., Wang, Z., Wu, M., Ma, Y., Ye, X., et al., 2018. Cancer-associated fibroblasts promote epithelial-mesenchymal transition and EGFR-TKI resistance of non-small cell lung cancers via HGF/IGF-1/ANXA2 signaling. Biochim. Biophys. Acta Mol. Basis Dis. 1864 (3), 793–803.

Zagouri, F., Bago-Horvath, Z., Rössler, F., Brandstetter, A., Bartsch, R., Papadimitriou, C.A., et al., 2013. High MET expression is an adverse prognostic factor in patients with triple-negative breast cancer. Br. J. Cancer 108 (5), 1100–1105.

Zhang, Y.W., Vande Woude, G.F., 2003. HGF/SF-met signaling in the control of branching morphogenesis and invasion. J. Cell. Biochem. 88 (2), 408–417.

Zhang, Y.W., Wang, L.M., Jove, R., Vande Woude, G.F., 2002. Requirement of STAT3 signaling for HGF/SF-Met mediated tumorigenesis. Oncogene 21 (2), 217–226.

Zhang, S., Chung, W.C., Miele, L., Xu, K., 2014. Targeting Met and Notch in the Lfng-deficient, Met-amplified triple-negative breast cancer. Cancer Biol. Ther. 15 (5), 633–642.

Zhang, L., Xia, L., Zhao, L., Chen, Z., Shang, X., Xin, J., et al., 2015. Activation of PAX3-MET pathways due to miR-206 loss promotes gastric cancer metastasis. Carcinogenesis 36 (3), 390–399.

Zhou, S., Liu, L., Li, H., Eilers, G., Kuang, Y., Shi, S., Yan, Z., et al., 2014. Multipoint targeting of the PI3K/mTOR pathway in mesothelioma. Br. J. Cancer 110 (10), 2479–2488.

Further reading

Al Moustafa, A.-E., 2013. Epithelial-mesenchymal transition and its regulators are major targets of triple-negative breast cancer. Cell Adhes. Migr. 7, 424–425.

Appleman, L.J., 2011. Met signaling pathway: a rational target for cancer therapy. J. Clin. Oncol. 29 (36), 4837–4838.

Di Renzo, M.F., Narsimhan, R.P., Olivero, M., Bretti, S., Giordano, S., Medico, E., 1991. Expression of the Met/HGF receptor in normal and neoplastic human tissues. Oncogene 6, 1997e2003.

Emsley, P., Lohkamp, B., Scott, W.G., Cowtan, K., 2010. Features and development of coot. Acta Crystallogr. D Biol. Crystallogr. 66 (4), 486–501.

Angeloni, D., Nickerson, M.L., Schmidt, L., Entrez Gene, n.d. Entrez Gene:MET met proto-oncogene (hepatocyte growth factor receptor) (http://atlasgeneticsoncology.org/Genes/GC_MET.html).

Gandino, L., Longati, P., Medico, E., Prat, M., Comoglio, P.M., 1999. Met-induced JNK activation is mediated by the adapter protein Crk and correlates with the Gab1-Crk signaling complex formation. Oncogene 18 (54), 7775–7786.

https://www.selleckchem.com/c-Met.html.

Tai, W., Lu, T., Yuan, H., Wang, F., Liu, H., Lu, S., et al., 2012. Pharmacophore modeling and virtual screening studies to identify new c-Met inhibitors. J. Mol. Model. 18, 3087–3100.

Timm, A., Kolesar, J.M., 2013. Crizotinib for the treatment of non-small-cell lung cancer. Am. J. Health Syst. Pharm. 70 (11), 943–947.

Yuan, H., Zhuang, J., Hu, S., Li, H., Xu, J., Hu, Y., et al., 2014. Molecular modeling of exquisitely selective c-Met inhibitors through 3DQSAR and molecular dynamics simulations. J. Chem. Inf. Model. 54 (9), 2544–2554.

Chapter 12

Rhomboid proteases leading to cancer: Structures, functions, and inhibition

Saroj Verma, Rajiv Kumar Tonk
Department of Pharmaceutical Chemistry, Delhi Pharmaceutical Sciences and Research University, New Delhi, India

12.1 Introduction

Cancer is a serious threat to health and treated as second leading cause of death globally. World health organization (WHO) reported 18.1 million new cancer cases and 9.6 million cancer related deaths in 2018 (WHO report, 2018). The available therapeutic options to address cancer are inadequate. Cancer treatment is a serious challenge due to uncertain prognosis, toxicity to other tissues/organs, emergence of drug resistance, and lack of selective drugs. There is an urgent need to explore new and promising biological targets for anticancer drug development (Chari, 2008; Mansoori et al., 2017). Several target-based studies are reported for cancer treatment (Olgen, 2018; Magalhaes et al., 2018; Perez-Herrero and Fernandez-Medarde, 2015). Among these, proteases have crucial role in cell growth and proliferation (Eatemadi et al., 2017; Yang et al., 2015). In view of this, they have been recognized as important therapeutic targets for cancer treatment. In cancer, uncontrolled cell growth and progression is attributed to failed regulation of apoptotic pathways which are responsible for cell homeostasis and signaling. Proteases are digestive enzymes. They cleave peptide bonds (basically hydrolysis process) of different substrate proteins (Zhou et al., 1999; Wallis et al., 2003). Therefore, these enzymes are held in hydrolase family (IUBMB, 2010). The proteolysis mechanism of protein is irreversible process. This helps in the regulation of cellular growth (Cooper, 2000). On the basis of mechanism of peptide bond cleavage, the proteases are divided into different classes (Eatemadi et al., 2017).

Rhomboids are most conserved family of intramembrane cleaving proteases. They are implicated in the progression of cancer cells. Rhomboid proteases were first discovered from a genetic screen in *Drosophila melanogaster*

Cancer-Leading Proteases. https://doi.org/10.1016/B978-0-12-818168-3.00012-7

as epidermal growth factor receptor (EGFR) regulator (Urban et al., 2001). As rhomboids are intramembrane proteins, they involved in proteolysis of cell surface proteins and secretory pathway (Urban et al., 2001). Dysfunction of EGFR signaling pathway is mainly responsible for the overexpression of rhomboid proteases in cancer cells (Wee and Wang, 2017; Harden, 2017). The active site of intramembrane proteases is positioned in the lipid bilayer of cell membranes. They cleave the peptide bond of transmembrane proteins within their transmembrane helices (Ha, 2009). In human beings, rhomboids are located in different parts of the cell and participate in various biological process associated with cell progression. In spite of extensive research, the rhomboid proteases' structure and function as well as biological course in triggering the cancer are not well understood (Dusterhoft et al., 2017).

The chapter reviews biological function and structure of rhomboid proteases to advance the understanding of the topic in the exploration of potential anticancer drugs. Earlier reviews on rhomboid proteases addressed some aspects of their role in diseases and scope as therapeutic targets (Dusterhoft et al., 2017; Bergbold and Lemberg, 2013). This chapter advances the discussion on the rhomboids in cancer therapy in terms of conceptual overview and by including recent reports on the subject. Here, we try to present information of primary, secondary, and tertiary structures of different rhomboids along with biological pathway/function involved in the cancer cell growth. Furthermore, experimental and theoretical studies for the development of inhibitors against rhomboid proteases are described. In the discussion, we used different bioinformatics databases and tools to illustrate the scope of the earlier reported data (Lemberg and Freeman, 2007; Kinch and Grishin, 2013). Attempts are also made to throw some light on the design and development of anticancer drug against rhomboids.

12.2 Rhomboid proteases

The human genome consists of different types of rhomboids that are phylogenetically classified as true active rhomboids, inactive rhomboids, and inactive rhomboid homologs (Table 12.1). The first class includes secretase/rhomboid-related proteins-1,2,3,4 (RHBL-1, 2, 3, 4) and presenilins-associated rhomboid-like protein (PARL). The second class includes rhomboids identified as degradation in endoplasmic reticulum protein 1 (Derlin-1) and iRhoms (also known as pseudoprotease since they lack essential catalytic residues in transmembrane domain). The third class is rhomboid-like homologous proteins. They lack catalytic residues and do not belong to either derlins or iRhoms (Lemberg and Freeman, 2007). Considering the importance of conserved transmembrane domain helices of rhomboids in the proteolytic cleaving of the substrate proteins, several groups (Dusterhoft et al., 2017; Ha et al., 2013; Urban and Dickey, 2011) have discussed their membrane topology with the help of available crystal structure of the core catalytic domain of the *Escherichia coli* (*E. coli*) rhomboid protease GlpG (Wang et al., 2006). They described conserved catalytic domain (Ser-His catalytic dyad)

TABLE 12.1 Detail of human/mammalian rhomboid proteases.

Gene	Protein	Chromosome location	UniProt ID	Amino acids	M. W. (D)	Location	Protein structure	Substrate/ interacting proteins	Function	Role in cancer
RHBDL1	RHBL-1	16	O75783	438	48,314	Golgi	–	–	–	–
RHBDL2	RHBL-2	1	Q9NX52	303	34,021	Endoplasmic reticulum	–	EphirineB2/B3, EGFR, EGF	Intramembrane cleavage of ephrin B2/B3	Tumor metastasis, tumor angiogenesis
RHBDL3	RHBL-3	17	P58872	404	45,245	Endosomes, golgi	–	–	–	–
RHBDD1	RHBL-4	2	Q8TEB9	315	35,823	Endoplasmic reticulam	5EPP	EGFR, proTGFα,TSAP6, proTGF,BIK1	EGFR activation, TGFα cleavage	Colorectal cancer metastasis, tumor markers
PARL	PARL	3	Q9H300	379	42,190	Mitochondrion	–	PINK1, OM1	Mitophagy, apoptosis	–
DERL1	Derlin-1	8	Q9BUN8	251	28,801	Endoplasmic reticulam, endosomes	5GLF	DERL2, DERL3, Sel1L-SYVN1/ HRD1, VIMP, Herp, VCP/p97	Translocation, degradation, ERAD	Breast, lung, colon cancers, squamous cell carcinoma of the head and neck
RHBDF1	iRhom-1	16	Q96CC6	855	97,401	Endoplasmic reticulam	–	EGF, TGFα	Degradation, ERAD	Esophageal cancer
RHBDF2	iRhom-2	17	Q6PJF5	856	96,686	Endoplasmic reticulam	–	EGF, TGFα	Cell signaling	Esophageal cancer

of rhomboids to typically have six/seven transmembrane helices (TMHs), which cleave substrates in or near the amino-terminus of the transmembrane domain. The number of TMHs in prokaryotes is often six, and in eukaryotes it is seven. These are divided into 1+6 TMH (mitochondria: N-terminal additional TMH) and 6+1 TMH (endoplasmic reticulum and Golgi body: C-terminal additional TMH) topology. Sequence alignment results from CLUSTALW have also indicated conservation of residues in human rhomboids (Larkin et al., 2007).

12.2.1 Rhomboid-related proteins/secretases (RHBL-1, 2, 3, 4)

The human rhomboid-related proteins are homologous to *Drosophila* rhomboid protein. Members of this family are found in both prokaryotes and eukaryotes and are thought to function as intramembrane serine proteases. There are four types of rhomboid-related proteins (RHBL-1 to RHBL-4). They are positioned all over the secretory pathway in mammals. Among these, the role of RHBL-2 and RHBL-4 is well studied. Correlation between the structural similarities between sequences of rhomboids can be used to explain the role of unexplored ones at primary level. With this view here we calculated the sequence similarities between the rhomboids with the help of CLUSTALW alignment tool (Larkin et al., 2007). The result indicated different similarity levels between each pair (rhomboid pair, alignment score: RHBL-1-RHBL-3, 51.73; RHBL-1-RHBL-2, 32.34; RHBL-2-RHBL-3, 31.35; RHBL-3-RHBL-4, 12.69; RHBL-1-RHBL-4, 12.06; and RHBL-2-RHBL-4, 10.89). The results infer that RHBL1 and RHBL3 possess highest similarity and both are very similar to RHBL2 (Fig. 12.1).

12.2.1.1 Rhomboid-related protein-2 (RHBL-2)

Human RHBL-2 is encoded by gene RHBDL2 and is localized in the plasma membrane. It is mostly detected in skin, airways, digestive system, and colon tissues (Adrain et al., 2011; Johnson et al., 2017). In human genome, RHBL-2 (Uniprot ID: Q9NX52) is located in chromosome position 1 (1p35.1) and consists of 303 amino acids. Its theoretical molecular mass is about 34,021 D (UniProt Consortium, 2011). The sequence includes 54.13% hydrophobic, 25.08% neutral, 11.22% basic, and 9.57% acidic amino acids (Peptide 2.0). The transmembrane proteins which possess hydrophobic surfaces are highly flexible and are expressed relatively low in comparison to proteins having hydrophilic surfaces (Vinothkumar and Henderson, 2010). The protein sequence from TMHMM Server v.2.0 showed (Krogh et al., 2001) six highly probable transmembrane domains (TMDs) at different position of the sequence such as TMH-1: $_{73}$VFIISISLAELAVFIYYAVW$_{92}$, TMH-2: $_{159}$VGLVYLAGVIAGSLASSIF$_{177}$, TMH-3:$_{182}$YLVGASGGVYA LMGGYFMNVLVN$_{204}$, TMH-4: $_{211}$AFGIFRLLIIILIIVLDMGFALY$_{233}$, TMH-5: 243SPVSFAAHIAGGFAGMSIGYTVF$_{265}$, TMH-6: $_{278}$FWIAIAAYLACVLFAVFFNIFLS$_{300}$ and one weaker TMH in between one and three TMH at N terminal domain (Fig. 12.2) (Ha et al., 2013; Dusterhoft et al., 2017).

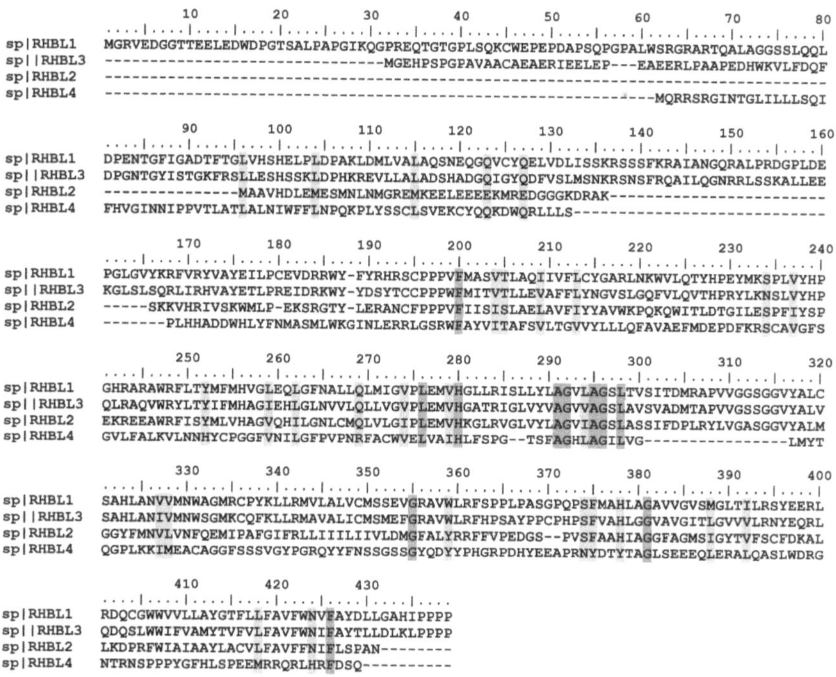

FIG. 12.1 ClustalW multiple alignments represent variation/similarity in sequences of *Human* RHBL-1, 2, 3, and 4. The similarity variations in residues in align sequences are marked with pink—gray in print version (identical) and cyan—light gray in print version (similar) colors.

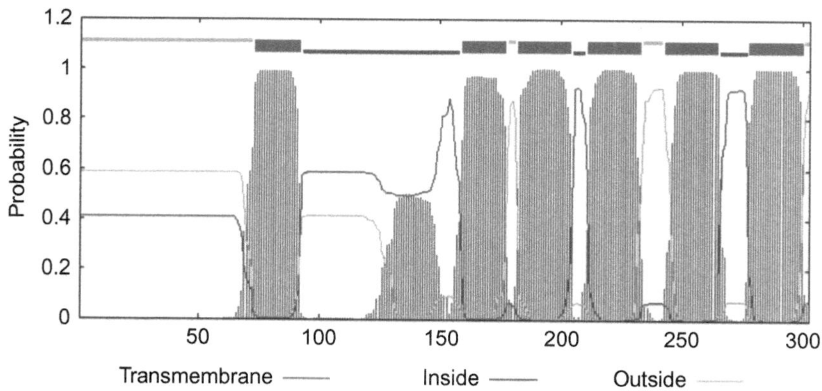

FIG. 12.2 The graphical representation generated by TMHMM Server v. 2.0 showing amino acids contribution in formation of transmembrane helices at different position of *Human* RHBL-2 sequence. Red region (gray in print version) represents transmembrane helices; blue (dark gray in print version) and pink (light gray in print version) colors respectively represent inside and outside helices.

Eph receptors and their ephrin substrates represent the largest subfamily of receptor tyrosine kinases (RTKs) and are an important part of the cell signaling pathways involved in cell growth (Arvanitis and Davy, 2008). In Eph receptors, B-type ephrins (EFNB2, EFNB3) are potential substrates of RHBDL2. They are cleaved within the TMD (Pascall and Brown, 2004). Ephrin overexpression has been seen in several human cancers such as gastrointestinal cancer, colorectal cancer, pancreatic cancer, and malignant glioma (Herath and Boyd, 2010; Nakada et al., 2011). Among ephrins, EFNB3 is lightly coexpress on the cell surface of RHBDL2 and cleaved by proteases. The results demonstrated that RHBDL2-mediated proteolytic enzymatic activity is regulated by intercellular interactions between EFNB3 and eph receptors (Pascall and Brown, 2004). Studies suggested that RHBDL2 also cleaves EFNB2 but to a lesser extent (Cheng et al., 2011). RHBDL2 catalyzed cleavage mechanism of EFNB2 and EFNB3 shows similarly in remodeling of cell-cell adhesion which remains to be addressed. String interaction network pathway also showed that RHBL-2 has strong connection with EFNB2 and EFNB3 B-type ephrins (Fig. 12.3).

Drosophila rhomboids catalyze the release of EGFR substrates. However, in mammals the mechanism initially seems to be catalyzed by ADAM-family metalloproteases. Work has been done in this direction to explore the role of mammalian rhomboids in the release of EGFR substrate. The study has demonstrated

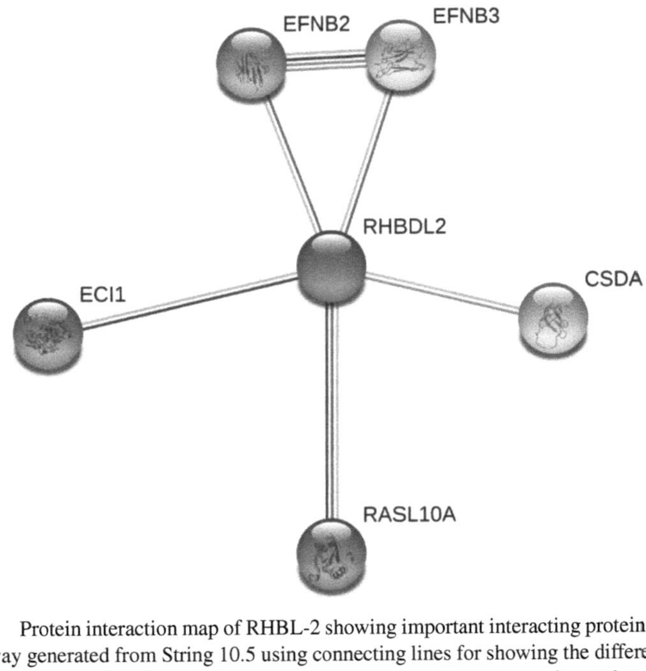

FIG. 12.3 Protein interaction map of RHBL-2 showing important interacting proteins in pathway. The pathway generated from String 10.5 using connecting lines for showing the different evidences (fusion evidence, neighborhood evidence, co-occurrence evidence, experimental evidence, text-mining evidence, database evidence, the co-expression evidence) of connectivity between proteins.

that mammalian rhomboid RHBDL2 is involved in the secretion of EGF substrate instead of ADAM-family metalloproteases. This has provided first evidence indicating the association of mammalian rhomboids in EGFR signaling (Adrain et al., 2011). The EGFR (also called as ErbB-1 and HER1 in humans) is a receptor of tyrosine kinase (RTK) family that is usually upregulated in various cancers such as breast, lung, pancreas, colon, glioblastoma, head, and neck (Wee and Wang, 2017; Sasaki, 2013; Masuda 2012). Several factors are responsible for the upregulation of EGFR, including mutations and extracellular domain truncation. These EGFR structure anomalies overactivate downstream pro-oncogenic mitogen-activated protein kinase/extracellular signal-regulated kinase (RAS-RAF-MEK-ERK/MAPK) signaling pathways. They then sensitize many cellular reactions that are favorable for cancer cell growth, including chronic initiation and progression of the cell cycle. EGFR has several substrates that are involved in signaling mechanism. However, rhomboids specifically bind with EGF and TGFα (transforming growth factor alpha) substrates. They are homologous (35%–40% homology) to each other and bind with the same affinity to EGFR (Wee and Wang, 2017).

RHBDL2 is able to cleave and activate proEGF in several tumor cell lines. No other RHBDL is known to show similar mechanism. The TMD of proEGF does not have Spitz type helix breaking amino acids, revealing that RHBDL2 can recruit its substrate by different mechanisms. As other rhomboid proteases, RHBDL2 cleaves proEGF outside the TMD. In the absence of helix breaking amino acids in the TMD, the sequence specificity of proEGF provides special control in cleaving mechanism (Cheng et al., 2014). The RHBDL2 knockdown or the cleaving site mutation has not shown any effect on ADAM (a disintegrin and metalloproteinase) protease-dependent EGF shedding process. This has indicated that rhomboid and metalloprotease-dependent pathways work parallelly rather than in sequence (Adrain et al., 2011).

Ras-like protein family members 10A (RAS10A), cold shock domain (CSD), and enoyl-CoA delta isomerase 1 (ECI1) are other proteins which also showed connectivity with RHBL-2 in string 10.5 predicted pathway (Fig. 12.3) (Szklarczyk et al., 2017). Overexpression of RAS gene has been indicated in cancer cells (Fernandez-Medarde and Santos, 2011).

12.2.1.2 Rhomboid-related protein-4/rhomboid domain containing protein-1 (RHBL-4)

Human RHBL-4 is encoded by gene RHBDD1 and is localized in endoplasmic reticulum (ER), involved in protein folding and transportation. It is abundantly expressed in testis, brain, and adrenal muscle tissues (Ren et al., 2013). In human genome, RHBL-4 (Uniprot ID: Q8TEB9) is located in chromosome positions 2 (2q36.3) and consists of 315 amino acids with molecular mass of about 35,823 D (UniProt Consortium, 2011). The sequence includes 44.44% hydrophobic, 35.87% neutral, 12.06% basic, and 7.62% acidic amino acids (Peptide 2.0). The topology and function of RHBL-4 is highly different from other three rhomboids (RHBL-1, 2, 3) of mammalian secretory pathway (Kinch and Grishin, 2013; Ha et al., 2013; Dusterhoft et al., 2017). It plays important role in the digestion of different substrates such as p97, EGFR, TGFα, tumor suppressor activated pathway-6 (TSAP6), and the pro-apoptotic protein (BCL-2/3 or Bik).

Human cells possess ER quality control/pre-emptive quality control (ER pQC) system to regulate ER associated stress that selectively refold or degrade misfolded proteins via retro-translocation/dislocation or ER-associated degradation (ERAD) pathway. Conversely, deregulation in the ERAD pathway causes accumulation of misfolded proteins in the ER that can contribute to different human diseases, including cancer (Kim et al., 2015). RHBL-4 is an ER an intramembrane protease and it is upregulated upon ER stress. RHBL-4 cuts transmembrane proteins (e.g., spanning and polytopic membrane protein) within unstable TMD helices (pre-T-cell receptor α, pTα), leading to their rapid degradation through the ERAD pathway. Molecular binding between RHBL-4 and AAA+-ATPase p97/VCP suggested that proteolytic processing and translocation into the cytosol are linked functionally (Fleig et al., 2012; Greenblatt et al., 2012). Recently, the first X-ray complex structure (PDB: 5EPP) of VCP-binding motif (VBM) with p97 N-terminal domain (p97N) at 1.88 Å resolution has been reported (Fig. 12.4). AAA+-ATPase involved in several cellular processes due to the large number of cofactors that interact with this protein such as p97/VCP-binding motif (VBM), p97/VCP-interacting motif (VIM), SHP motif (also known as binding site 1 (BS1), ubiquitin regulatory X (UBX), ubiquitin-binding domain, and UBX-like element. The crystallization study identified new binding conformation of RHBL-4-VBM motif to p97N that involves combination of two types of p97-cofactor specificities observed in the UBX and VIM

MQRRSRGINTGLILLLSQIFHVGINNIP
PVTLATLALNIWFFLNPQKPLYSSCLS
VEKCYQQKDWQRLLLSPLHHADDWH
LYFNMASMLWKGINLERRLGSRWFA
YVITAFSVLTGVVYLLLQFAVAEFMD
EPDFKRSCAVGFSGVLFALKVLNNHY
CPGGFVNILGFPVPNRFACWVELVAIH
LFSPGTSFAGHLAGILVGLMYTQGPLK
KIMEACAGGFSSSVGYPGRQYYFNSS
GSSGYQDYYPHGRPDHYEEAPRNYDT
YTAGLSEEEQLERALQASLWDRGNTR
NSPPPYGFHLSPEEMRRQRLHRFDSQ

(A)

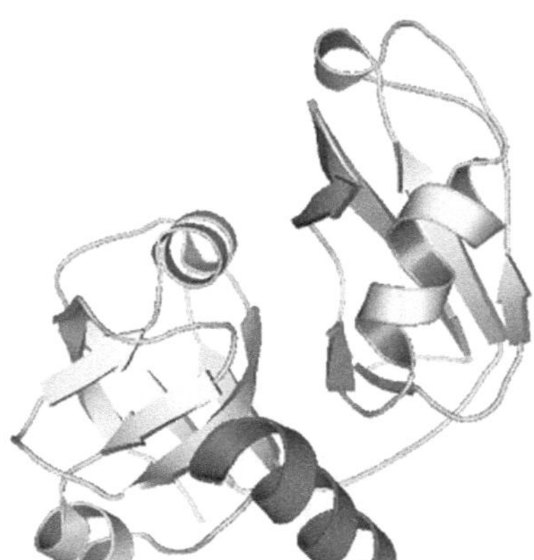

(B)

FIG. 12.4 (A) Primary structure/sequence of RHBL-4 (UniProt ID: Q8TEB9), amino acids represents in red color (underlined sequence in print version) showing VBM motif; (B) 3D structure of RHBDL4 VBM motif (red—dark gray in print version) complexed with p97N-a (yellow—light gray in print version).

interactions. The mutational and biochemical analysis described the specific interaction between VBM and p97N. It explained the importance of conservation of VBM in other VBM-containing proteins. The finding also revealed that RHBL-4, ubiquitins, and p97 help in retrotranslocation of polyubiquitinated substrate (Lim et al., 2016a). Phylogenetic relationship between RHBL-4 and derlin suggested that substrates involved in the intramembrane proteolysis and the ERAD pathway of protein translocation shared similar mechanisms (Fleig et al., 2012; Wunderle et al., 2016). The AAA ATPase p97 is one of the most important targets which help in regulation of protein homeostasis. It is targeted for the treatment of cancer through disruption of protein homeostasis. The CB-5083 is a potent, selective, and orally bioavailable inhibitor of p97. Its inhibitory effect is mediated by the disruption of protein homeostasis (Zhou et al., 2015; Anderson et al., 2015; Le Moigne et al., 2017).

Recently, the role of RHBL-4 rhomboid has also been reported in EGFR signaling pathway. RHBL-4 specifically binds with proTGFα (transforming growth factor α precursor) and facilitates the ADAM-independent cleavage and secretion of proTGFα. After that, released TGFα participates in the activation of the MAPK/ERK signaling pathway (Fig. 12.5) (Song et al., 2015). The positive correlation between expression of RHBL-4 and MAPK/ERK signaling pathway has also been confirmed in a murine model of colitis-associated colorectal cancer. These investigations suggested growth promoting role of RHBL-4 in colorectal cancer may prime the development of biomarkers and thereby anticancer treatment (Song et al., 2015; Wunderle et al., 2016).

Tumor suppressor-activated pathway-6 (TSAP6), a multipass transmembrane protein, is another potential substrate of RHBL-4. TSAP6 belongs to

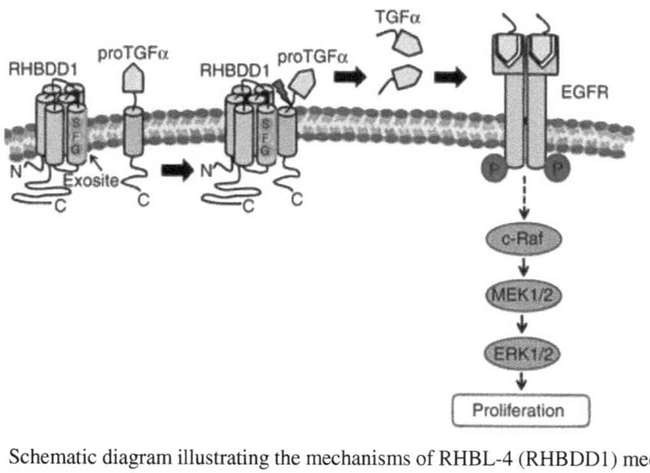

FIG. 12.5 Schematic diagram illustrating the mechanisms of RHBL-4 (RHBDD1) mediated cancer cell proliferation. *(Reprinted from Song, W., Liu, W., Zhao, H., Li, S., Guan, X., Ying, J., Zhang, Y., Miao, F., Zhang, M., Ren, X., Li, X., Wu, F., Zhao, Y., Tian, Y., Wu, W., Fu, J., Liang, J., Wu, W., Liu, C., Yu, J., Zong, S., Miao, S., Zhang, X., Wang, L., 2015. Rhomboid domain containing 1 promotes colorectal cancer growth through activation of the EGFR signaling pathway. Nat. Commun. 6, 8022. Open Access publication.)*

the six-transmembrane epithelial antigen of the prostate (STEAP) family. It is highly involved in the regulation of nonclassical exosomal secretions. Several studies have identified the role and importance of exosomes in different cellular processes and cancer progression. RHBL-4 helps in the proteolysis of TSAP6 in quantitative manner. The cleaving mechanism is not restricted to its glycosylation form and it occurred at different places of TSAP6. The mutagenesis and mass spectrometry data indicated that proteolytic cleavage of TSAP6 occurred at C-terminal of TMD. Exosome secretion was observed in inactivated RHBL-4 cell lines (HCT116 and RKO) of colon cancer and it is confirmed by the detection of exosomal components (Tsg101, Tf-R, FasL, and Trail). This finding demonstrated that the RHBDL4 and TSAP6 (knock in/knock down of substrate) are interdependent in the regulation of exosomal trafficking (Wan et al., 2012).

Mutation study at G142 and S144 of RHBDL4 indicated that both residues play important role in catalytic activity in cleaving the BIK (Bcl-2-interacting killer) at TMD. The finding suggested that RHBDL4 regulates the BIK-mediated apoptosis (Wang et al., 2008a). RHBL-4 inhibits cell apoptosis by upregulating the activator protein 1 (AP-1) activity and its downstream target B-cell lymphoma 3-encoded protein (Bcl-3; pro-apoptotic protein) (Ren et al., 2013). AP-1 is a transcription factor that regulates the protein expression and controls number of cellular processes such as differentiation, proliferation, and apoptosis. String interaction network pathway indicated additional connection of RHBL-4 with PARL and cystinosin (CTNS) proteins (Fig. 12.6) (Szklarczyk et al., 2017). However, experimental evidence is not reported.

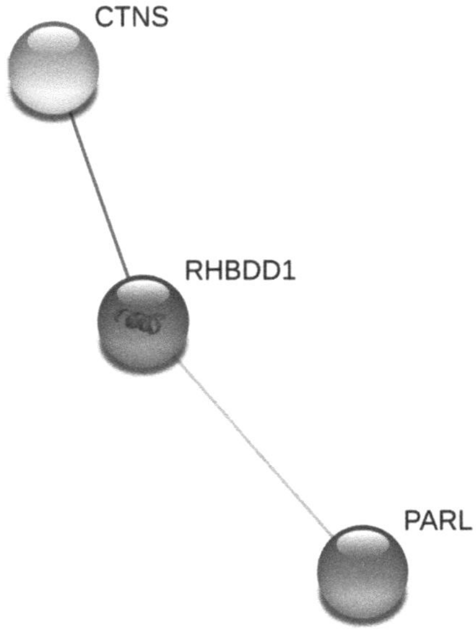

FIG. 12.6 Protein interaction map of RHBL-4/RHBDD1 showing interaction with PARL and CTNS proteins in pathway. Map generated by String 10.5.

12.2.1.3 Rhomboid-related protein-1 (RHBL-1)

Human RHBL-1 is encoded by gene RHBDL1 localized in the Golgi body. The HomoloGene (NCBI database) indicated that RHBDL1 is highly conserved in chimpanzee, dog, cow, mouse, rat, chicken, and zebrafish. Several species are orthologs to human gene RHBDL1. The BioGPS and transcriptome database analysis indicated that RHBDL1 is highly expressed in heart, brain, skeletal muscle, kidney tissues, and neurons (Cahoy et al., 2008; Wu et al., 2016a). Human RHBDL1 was identified by sequence similarity with *Drosophila* rhomboid-1 (Pascall and Brown, 1998). In human genome, RHBL-1 (Uniprot ID: O75783) is located in chromosome positions 16 (16p13.3). It consists of 438 amino acids with theoretical molecular mass of about 48,314 D. The sequence includes 49.77% hydrophobic, 31.28% neutral, 10.96% basic, and 7.99% acidic amino acids (Peptide 2). It possesses seven transmembrane helices (TMHs). The human RHBL-1 sequence (Uniprot ID: O75783) from TMHMM Server v. 2.0 (Krogh et al., 2001) also predicted seven transmembrane helices namely TMH-1: $_{194}$CPPPVFMASVTLAQIIVFLCYGA$_{216}$, TMH-2: $_{245}$AWRFLTYMFMHVGLEQLGFNALL$_{267}$, TMH-3: $_{280}$GLLRI SLLYLAGVLAGSLTVSIT$_{302}$, TMH-4: $_{306}$APVVGGSGGVYALCSAHLA NVVM$_{328}$, TMH-5: $_{240}$LRMVLALVCMSSEVGRAVWL$_{359}$, $_{374}$FMAHLAG AVVGVSMGLTIL$_{392}$ and $_{404}$GWWVVLLAYGTFLLFAVFWNVFA$_{426}$ at the N terminal domain (Fig. 12.7) (Ha et al., 2013; Dusterhoft et al., 2017).

The RHBDL1 promotes the cleavage of the TGFα-like growth factor Spitz (glycine-alanine motif), which helps in the activation of *Drosophila* EGF substrate. RHBDL1 is highly conserved across the species and studies indicated that human RHBDL1 promotes Spitz cleavage by a similar mechanism. Therefore,

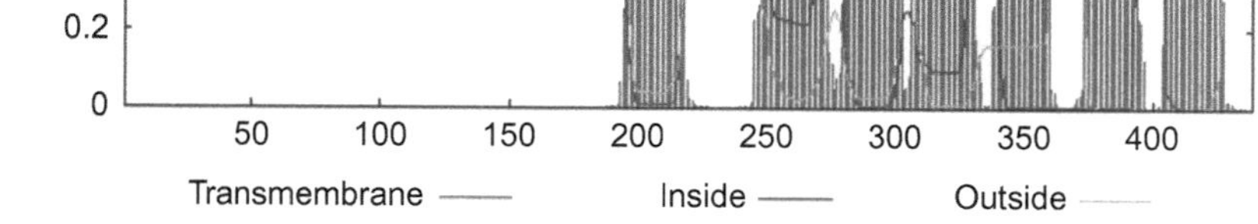

FIG. 12.7 The graphical representation generated by TMHMM Server v. 2.0 showing amino acids contribution in formation of transmembrane helices at different position of *Human* RHBL-1 sequence. Red region (gray in print version) represents transmembrane helices; blue (dark gray in print version) and pink (light gray in print version) regions represent inside and outside helices, respectively.

the EGFR cell proliferation signaling mechanism may be widespread process (Urban et al., 2001). These biological alterations in EGFR proteins are associated with high probability to respond against anti-EGFR agents. Although EGFR proteins and their substrates form a complex, the type and the duration of the intracellular signals derived from the protein activation alter the binding interactions between the proteins and substrates. ErbB (EGF) family proteins form homo- and hetero-dimmers (Roskoski Jr., 2014). In each case, dimer represents different affinity toward substrates as well as different signaling properties. The available evidence indicates that cooperation of multiple ErbB proteins and consensus substrates is necessary to induce cell transformation. The growth and the survival of cancer cells appear to be sustained by protein-protein/protein-substrate interactions involved in the pathway of the ErbB family. The pathway is considered to be important in cancer therapy. Its response to anti-EGFR agents depends on the total level of expression of ErbB proteins and substrates in tumor cells (Flynn et al., 2009). These investigations suggested that the RHBL-1 is possibly associated with EGFR signaling pathway responsible for cancer progression. String interaction network pathway showed that RHBL-1 also has connections with other genes such as Disks large homolog 3 (DLG3), membrane-associated guanylate kinase (MAGI3), urotensin-2 receptor (UTS2R), and PARL (Fig. 12.8) (Szklarczyk et al., 2017). They are indirectly related to cancer genesis.

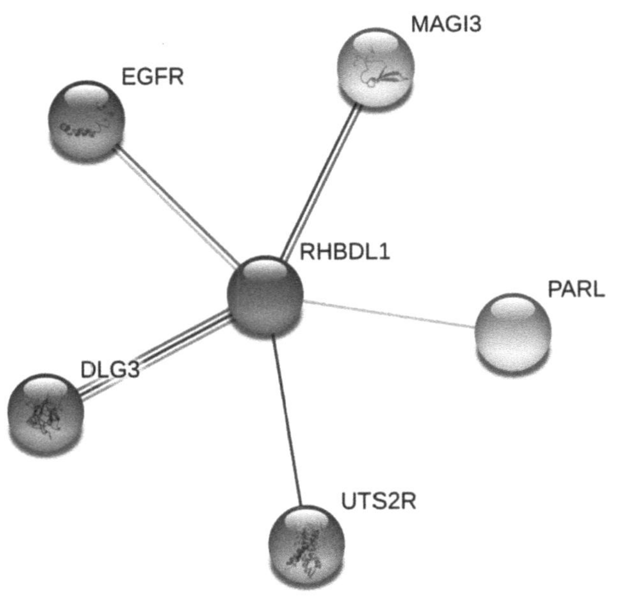

FIG. 12.8 Protein interaction map of RHBL-1/RHBDL1 showing important interacting proteins in pathway.

12.2.1.4 Rhomboid-related protein-3/ventrhoid transmembrane protein (RHBL-3)

Human RHBL-3 is encoded by gene RHBDL3 and is localized in the Golgi apparatus. This protein is mostly found in the brain, adrenal gland, and muscle tissues (Kumar et al., 2013). In human genome, RHBL-3 (Uniprot ID: P58872) is located in chromosome position 17 (17q11.2). It is made of 404 amino acids and has theoretical molecular mass of about 45,245 D. The sequence includes 50.99% hydrophobic, 28.96% neutral, 11.88% basic and 8.17% acidic amino acids (Peptide 2.0). The protein consists of six probable TMDs namely TMH-1: $_{217}$YIFMHAGIEHLGLNVVLQLLVGV$_{239}$, TMH-2: $_{246}$GATRIGLVYV-AGVVAGSLAVSVA$_{268}$, TMH-3: $_{274}$VVGSSGGVYALVSAHLANIVMNW$_{296}$, TMH-4: $_{303}$FKLLRMAVALICMSMEFGRAVWL$_{325}$, TMH-5: $_{340}$FVAHLGGVAVGITLGVVVL$_{358}$,$_{370}$LWWIFVAMYTVFVLFAVFWNIFA$_{392}$ and one weaker TMH at near the C terminal domain of protein sequence (Fig. 12.9) (Krogh et al., 2001; Ha et al., 2013; Dusterhoft et al., 2017).

The pancreatic gene expression profiling in embryonic mice demonstrated that RHBDL3 plays important role in pancreas development. Recently in a microarray experiment, autopsy of the human brain indicated a strong correlation between *RHBDL3* gene expression and chronological aging (Kumar et al., 2013). The mechanism involved in the aging process is still unclear. At the same time the activity of RHBDL3 in aging cells and its substrates are to be identified. String interaction network pathway indicated that RHBL-3 has link with obscurin (OBSCN), striated muscle enriched protein kinase (SPEG) and myocin-Va, Vb, Vc (MYO5A, B, C) proteins (Fig. 12.10). Obscurin, kinase and myocin are sarcomeric cytoskeleton proteins. Sarcomeres are highly ordered organization of striated muscles, essential for the fast and directional expansion

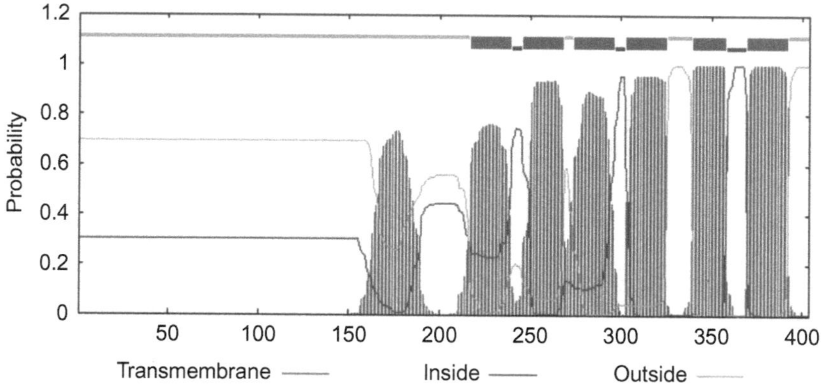

FIG. 12.9 The graphical representation generated by TMHMM Server v. 2.0 showing amino acids contribution in formation of transmembrane helices at different position of *Human* RHBL-3 sequence. Red region (gray in print version) represents transmembrane helices; blue (dark gray in print version) and pink (light gray in print version) regions represent inside and outside helices, respectively.

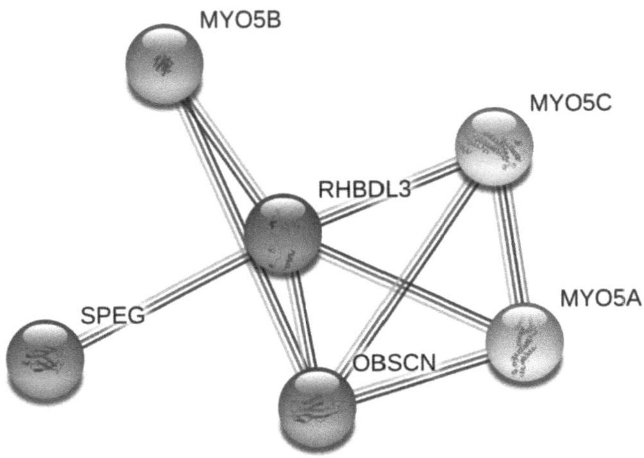

FIG. 12.10 Protein interaction map of RHBL-3/RHBDL3 showing important interacting proteins in pathway. Map generated by String 10.5.

of force and motion in skeletal muscle contraction. This group of proteins is crucial for the ordered sequence arrangement of actin and myosin into sarcomeres, via coordination of mechanical, architectural and signaling regulation (Gautel and Djinovic-Carugo, 2016). The overexpression of obscurin and myocin are observed in cancer cells (Rajendran and Deng, 2017; Wang et al., 2016).

12.2.2 Presenilins-associated rhomboid-like protein (PARL)

In human genome, PARL (Uniprot ID: Q9H300) is located in chromosome position 3 (3q27.1). It has 379 amino acids and calculated molecular mass of about 42,190 D (UniProt Consortium, 2011). The sequence is made up of 47.49% hydrophobic, 34.04% neutral, 12.66% basic, and 5.8% acidic amino acids (Peptide 2.0). The human PARL sequence (Uniprot ID: Q9H300.2) from TMHMM Server v.2.0 also showed a higher probability for six helices namely TMH-1: $_{102}$LFFTVGFTGCAFGSAAIWQ$_{121}$, TMH-2: $_{168}$TVTGIIAANVLVFCLWRVPS$_{187}$, TMH-3: $_{208}$PMLLSTFSHFSLFHMAANMYVLW$_{230}$, TMH-4: $_{245}$FMAVYLSAGVISNFVSYV$_{262}$, TMH-5: $_{296}$LAIIFLPMFTFTAGNALKAIIAM$_{318}$ and TMH-6: $_{333}$AAHLGGALFGIWYVTYGHELIW$_{354}$ (Fig. 12.11). One weaker TMH was also observed in the sequence, located in between TMH-4 and -5 (Fig. 12.11) (Ha et al., 2013; Dusterhoft et al., 2017; Krogh et al., 2001). The N-terminal domain of the protein is exposed to the mitochondrial matrix and is associated with the cleaving mechanism of mitochondrial membrane, termed as α and β cleavage. Jeyaraju et al. have observed that α cleavage helps in the import of PARL into the mitochondria and β cleavage led to the mitochondrial fragmentation (Jeyaraju et al., 2006).

The PARL protein, an intramembrane serine protease, is localized in the inner mitochondrial membrane. This is also known as mitochondrial intramembrane cleaving protease (Sik et al., 2004). The structure of mitochondria is very dynamic

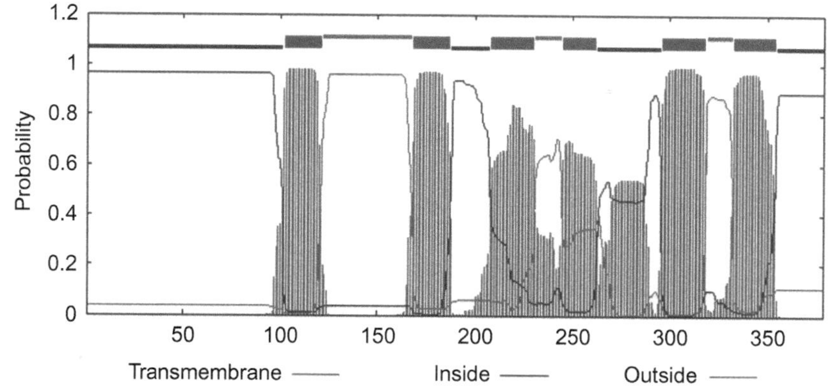

FIG. 12.11 The graphical representation generated by TMHMM Server v. 2.0 showing amino acids contribution in formation of transmembrane helices at different position of *Human* PARL sequence. Red region (gray in print version) represents transmembrane helices; blue (dark gray in print version) and pink (light gray in print version) regions represent inside and outside helices, respectively.

in nature and undergoes continuous changes. This is regulated by different enzymes of its organelles (Gottlieb and Bernstein, 2016). The remodeling process of mitochondria go through the following morphological changes namely (a) fusion: the mechanism that generates fewer, larger, and elongated mitochondria; (b) fission: the mechanism that generates several, smaller and circular mitochondria; (c) autophagy or mitophagy: the selective degradation of damaged mitochondria; (d) biogenesis: the process that increases their individual mitochondrial number and/or mass by increased expression of both mitochondrial and nuclear transcripts; (e) apoptosis: the process that is responsible for programmed cell death (Gottlieb and Bernstein, 2016). Experimental studies revealed that mitochondrial fission, fusion, mitophagy, biogenesis and apoptosis, and enzymes involved therein are interdependent and alteration in one activity has indirect influence on others.

Mitochondria organelles possess several conserved proteins. PARL is one among them and helps in the regulation of morphological changes and remodeling mechanism of mitochondria. Mitochondrial rhomboid PARL regulates apoptosis through molecular interactions with GTPase optic atrophy 1 (OPA1) and the B-cell CLL/lymphoma 2/oncogene B-cell leukemia 2 (Bcl-2) family-related HCLS1-associated protein X1 (HAX1) (Fig. 12.12). The study on mouse embryonic fibroblasts (MEFs) demonstrated that OPA1 acts as cristae remodeling controller by forming oligomers that participate in cristae junction formation and maintenance to regulate cytochrome *c* release during apoptosis. This crucial process is related to OPA1 oligomerization and was linked with cleavage of OPA1 by PARL protein. It is also identified that oligomerization of OPA1 protein regulates apoptosis by retaining the tightness of mitochondrial cristae junctions (Frezza, et al., 2006). OPA1 regulates the fusion process in the mitochondrial membrane after proteolysis of PARL (Song et al., 2007). Proteolysis plays a key role in mitochondrial remodeling and apoptosis. Proteolysis is a

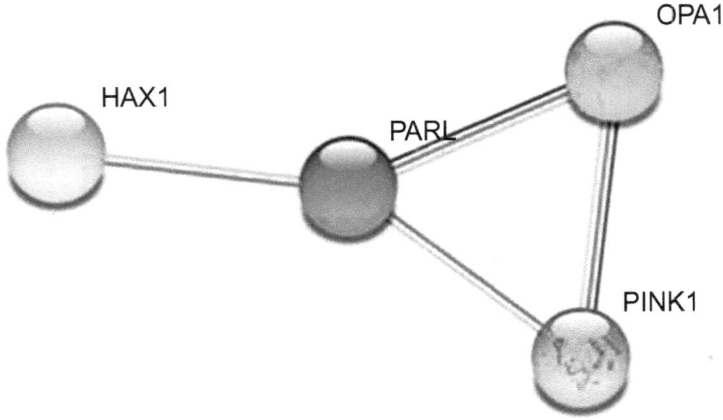

FIG. 12.12 Protein interaction map of PARL with OPA1, PINK1, HAX1. Map generated by String 10.5.

regulatory biological action that regulates several cellular processes ranging from transcription control to intracellular/extracellular signaling through irreversible modification in the protein's structure. In proteolysis, PARL releases small peptides (P-β), which may get transferred to the nucleus (Sik et al., 2004). The changes in mitochondrial structure may provide a selective advantage to the cells allowing them to survive and grow under stress created by carcinogenesis.

Phosphatase and tensin homolog (PTEN)-induced kinase 1 (PINK1), also known as mitochondrial serine/threonine-protein kinase, is another important protein in metabolic pathways which interacts with PARL and recognizes the damaged mitochondria to specifically target it for degradation. Normally mitochondria maintain a membrane potential. This helps in importing PINK1 into the inner membrane where the damaged mitochondrion is cleaved by PARL and cleared from the outer membrane (Fig. 12.12). The study of human cells showed that PARL cleaves the 66-kD isoform of PINK1 to a 55-kD isoform upon removal of the leader sequence of mitochondria. Both isoforms are localized in the inner and outer membranes of mitochondria (Meissner et al., 2011). Other findings also suggested that PARL cleaves PINK1 in between Ala-103 and Phe-104 amino acid to generate ΔN-PINK1 (Deas et al., 2011). They revealed that decrease in the ability to cleave PINK1 and the subsequent aggregation of protein length result in mitochondrial functional disorders, including disruption of the mitochondrial dynamic network and reduction in mitochondrial mass. Recently, various research groups identified that PINK1 regulates several cellular processes which are having significance in cancer cell biology, namely mitochondrial homeostasis, cell survival, stress resistance, and cell cycle (O'Flanagan and O'Neill, 2014). The mutational changes in PINK1 alter its biological function and are responsible for the pathogenesis of Parkinson's disease (Meissner et al., 2011). PARL interacting proteins are also predicted in the string interconnection map.

As the mitochondria's structure is very dynamic in nature, its deregulation may be responsible for the cancer cell growth and tumorigenesis (Srinivasan et al., 2017). Generally in cancer cells, apoptosis, autophagy, and mitochondrial biogenesis machinery are seen to be uncontrolled in comparison to normal cells. Several studies indicated that oncogenes and tumor suppressors work as a biological response modulator of mitochondrial morphology and dynamics (Srinivasan et al., 2017; Han et al., 2018). Exploration of targets responsible for mitochondrial structural/biological changes and designing of compounds to suppress the cell growth is a challenging task.

12.2.3 Derlin-1

In human genome derlin-1 (Uniprot ID: Q9BUN8) located in chromosome position 8 (location: 8q24.13) contains 251 amino acids and has calculated molecular mass of about 28,801 D (UniProt Consortium, 2011). The sequence contains 53.78% hydrophobic, 33.07% neutral, 8.37% basic, and 4.78% acidic amino acids. Derlins considered as conserved family proteins in ERAD pathway (Schekman 2004). In *Homo sapiens* three conserved transmembrane domains, namely derlin-1, derlin-2, and derlin-3 are present. Derlin-1, derlin-2, and derlin-3 form homo/hetero-oligomers (Lilley and Ploegh, 2005; Ye et al., 2004) and play important role in the channels which translocate ERAD substrates (Schekman 2004). Among these, the derlin-1 mainly participates in ERAD pathway. Derlin-1 possesses five TMHs. The human derlin-1 sequence (Uniprot ID: Q9BUN8.1) from TMHMM Server v. 2.0 (Krogh, et al., 2001) predicted five highly probable transmembrane helices namely TMH-1: $_{20}$AATVAVPLVGKLGLISPAYLFLW$_{42}$, TMH-2: $_{57}$TATFYFPVGP-GTGFLYLVNLYFL$_{79}$, TMH-3: $_{99}$LFMLLF NWICIVITGLAM$_{116}$, TMH-4: $_{120}$LLMIPLIMS-VLYVWAQLN$_{137}$, TMH-5: $_{157}$WVILGFNYIIGGSVINELIGNLV$_{179}$ and one weaker TMH in protein sequence (Fig. 12.13) (Ha et al., 2013; Dusterhoft et al., 2017).

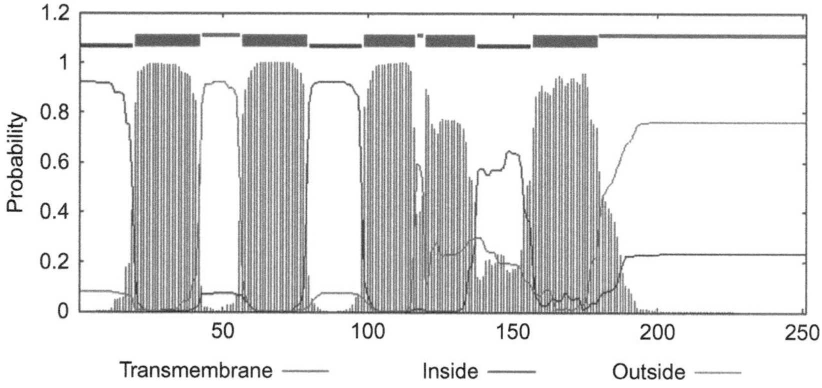

FIG. 12.13 The graphical representation generated by TMHMM Server v. 2.0 showing amino acids contribution in formation of transmembrane helices at different position of *Human* derlin-1 sequence. Red region (gray in print version) represent transmembrane helices, blue (dark gray in print version) and pink (light gray in print version) regions inside and pink (light gray in print version) represent inside and outside helices, respectively.

Derlin-1 is known as degradation in endoplasmic reticulum (ER) protein and is encoded by gene DERL1. Derlin family proteins are the part of ERAD pathway and participate in the ER-associated degradation mechanism and retro-translocation/dislocation of proteins from the ER lumen to the cytosol for proteasomal degradation (Ye et al., 2004). Mammalian derlins namely derlin-1, derlin-2, and derlin-3 form homo/hetero-oligomers (Lilley and Ploegh, 2005; Oda et al., 2006; Ye et al., 2004) and interact with different proteins involve in ERAD pathway such as E3 ubiquitin-protein ligase synoviolin (SYVN1/HRD1), Protein sel-1 homolog 1 (Suppressor of lin-12-like protein 1/SEL1L), Transitional endoplasmic reticulum ATPase (TER ATPase/Valosin-containing protein/VCP/15S Mg(2+)-ATPase p97 subunit/CDC48), E3 ubiquitin-protein ligase AMFR (Autocrine motility factor receptor/AMFR/RING finger protein 45/RING-type E3 ubiquitin transferase AMFR/gp78), Selenoprotein S (SelS/VCP-interacting membrane protein/VIMP), Large proline-rich protein BAG6 (HLA-B-associated transcript 3/Protein Scythe/BCL2-associated athanogene 6) and Homocysteine-responsive endoplasmic reticulum-resident ubiquitin-like domain member 1 protein (Methyl methanesulfonate inducible fragment protein 1/Herp) (Fig. 12.14) (Preston and Brodsky, 2017).

The Sel1L-SYVN1/HRD1 protein complex is the most conserved complex in ERAD pathway and is associated with other proteins including derlin, VIMP, Herp, and VCP/p97 (Schulz et al., 2017). Here VIMP is the smallest protein (189 amino acids) and acts as a linker between derlin-1 and VCP/p97. It works as unfolding motor supporting ubiquitination and responsible for final degradation of proteins. Herp is an ubiquitin like membrane protein induced by ER stress. It helps HRD1 to bind to derlin1. The AMFR/gp78 protein regulates downstream with the Sel1L-SYVN1/HRD1 to increase the solubility of retrotranslocated protein substrates for proteasomal degradation of misfolded proteins. Derlins are important proteins in the ERAD pathway that can reroute specific ER proteins from the translocon to the proteasome through interactions with the signal recognition particle (SRP). Furthermore, the cytosolic chaperone VCP/p97 and Bag6 participate in the degradation of ER pQC substrates. These

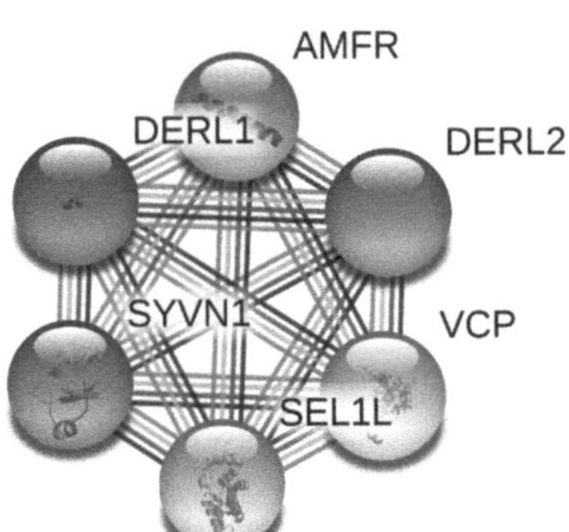

FIG. 12.14 Protein interaction map of Derlin-1/DERL1 showing important interacting proteins in ERAD pathway. Map generated by String 10.5.

results indicated that derlins facilitated substrate specific rerouting and VCP/p97-Bag6 facilitated proteasomal degradation for maintenance of ER homeostasis without the need for translocation. Derlin-1 (yeast protein homolog to mammalian derlins) is promising retrotranslocon protein in comparison to other derlins. In rhomboid family, derlins were confirmed as inactive members of intramembrane proteases and play a key role in retrotranslocation by conserved functional domains in place of the catalytic domain (Greenblatt et al., 2011). The X-ray crystal (5GLF, resolution: 2.25Å) of derlin-1 SHP (C-terminal binding segment 1(BS1) motif, a short antiparallel β-strand showed strong binding interaction with the β-sheet of p97N-a site) revealed the importance of derlin-1 in retrotranslocation of polyubiquitinated substrates in the ER-associated degradation pathway (Fig. 12.15) (Lim et al., 2016b).

Several studies have strongly indicated that derlin-1 plays a key role in cancer progression. Documented reports indicate that the overexpression of derlin-1 in human is responsible for breast, lung, colon cancers, and squamous cell carcinoma of the head and neck (Tan et al., 2015; Wu et al., 2016b). Derlin-1-directed antibodies selectively targeted and inhibited colon tumor cell growth in isogenic mice (Ran et al., 2008). Derlin-1 overexpression was observed in 66.7% of the breast carcinoma tissues, whereas it was rarely expressed in normal mammary glands. Its expression is related to tumor grade and axillary lymph node metastasis. ERAD pathway-induced stress is responsible for derlin-1 overexpression. Derlin-1 is also overexpressed in nonsmall cell lung cancer (NSCLC) and causes invasion through EGFR and extracellular signal regulated kinase (ERK) signaling pathway mediated upregulation of matrix metalloproteinase (MMP)-2 and MMP-9 (Wang et al., 2008b). Overexpression of derlin-1 also observed in bladder cancer and it is resembled with a high tumor grade and metastasis (Wu et al., 2016b). These findings strongly indicated that derlin-1 is a new oncogene and potential drug target for cancer therapy. However, the mechanism of derlin-1 and

MSDIGDWFRSIPAITRYWFA
ATVAVPLVGKLGLISPAYLF
LWPEAFLYRFQIWRPITATF
YFPVGPGTGFLYLVNLYFL
YQYSTRLETGAFDGRPADY
LFMLLFNWICIVITGLAMD
MQLLMIPLIMSVLYVWAQL
NRDMIVSFWFGTRFKACYL
PWVILGFNYIIGGSVINELIG
NLVGHLYFFLMFRYPMDLG
GRNFLSTPQFLYRWLPSRRG
GVSGFGVPPASMRRAADQN
GGGGRHNWGQGFRLGDQ
(A)

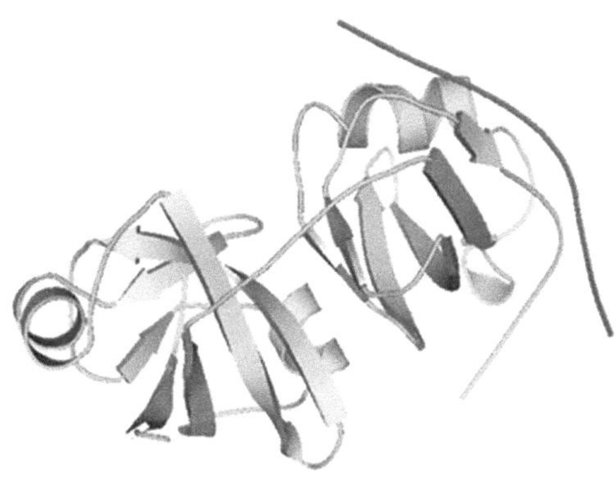
(B)

FIG. 12.15 (A) Primary structure/sequence of derlin-1 (UniProt ID: Q9BUN), amino acids represents in red color (underlined sequence in print version) showing SHP motif; (B) 3D structure of derlin-1 SHP motif (red—dark gray in print version) complexed with p97N-a (yellow—light gray in print version).

cancer cell growth is not very clear. It gives scope to researcher to explore new potential molecules and their mechanism of action against cancer cell growth.

12.2.4 iRhoms

iRhoms are inactive homolog rhomboids also called as nonprotease rhomboids. They are lacking catalytic residues important for proteolytic activity. In human genome iRhom-1 (Uniprot ID: Q96CC6) and iRhom-2 (Uniprot ID: Q6PJF5) are located in chromosome positions 16 and 17, and contain 855 and 856 amino acids with calculated molecular mass of about 97,401 D and 96,686 D, respectively (UniProt Consortium, 2011). The sequences of iRhom-1 and iRhom-2 share 58% identity and represent same profiling for hydrophobic (43.39% and 43.22%) residues (Fig. 12.16) (BLAST, Peptide 2.0). They possess seven TMHs. TMHMM tool also predicted 6 highly probable and one weaker TMH in sequences of iRhom-1 and iRhom-2. Also most of these TMHs are localized at N-terminal site of sequences (Fig. 12.17) (Krogh et al., 2001; Ha et al., 2013; Dusterhoft et al., 2017).

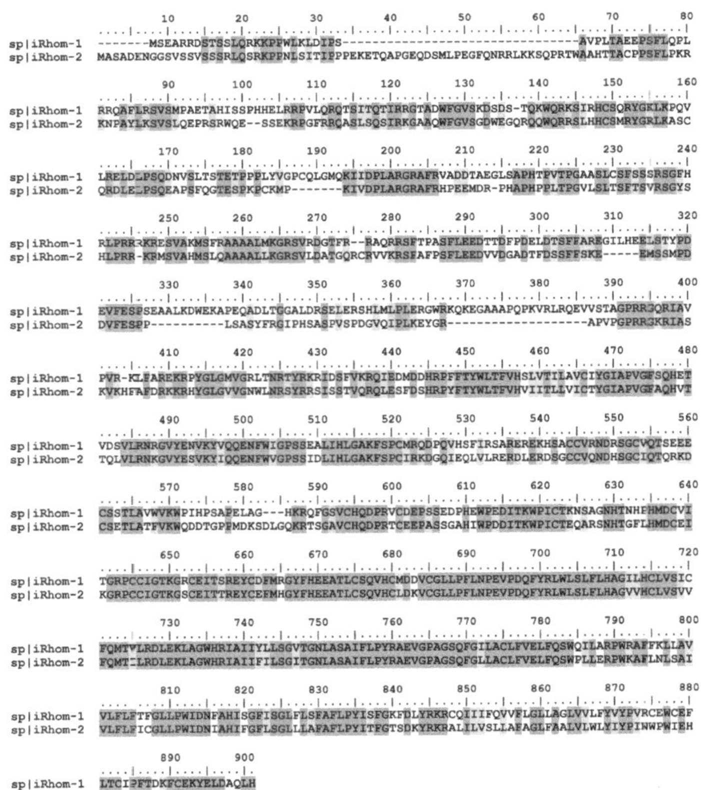

FIG. 12.16 ClustalW alignment represents variation/similarity between *Human* iRhom-1 and iRhom-2. The similarity variations in residues in aligned sequences marked with pink—gray in print version (identical) and cyan—light gray in print version (similar) colors.

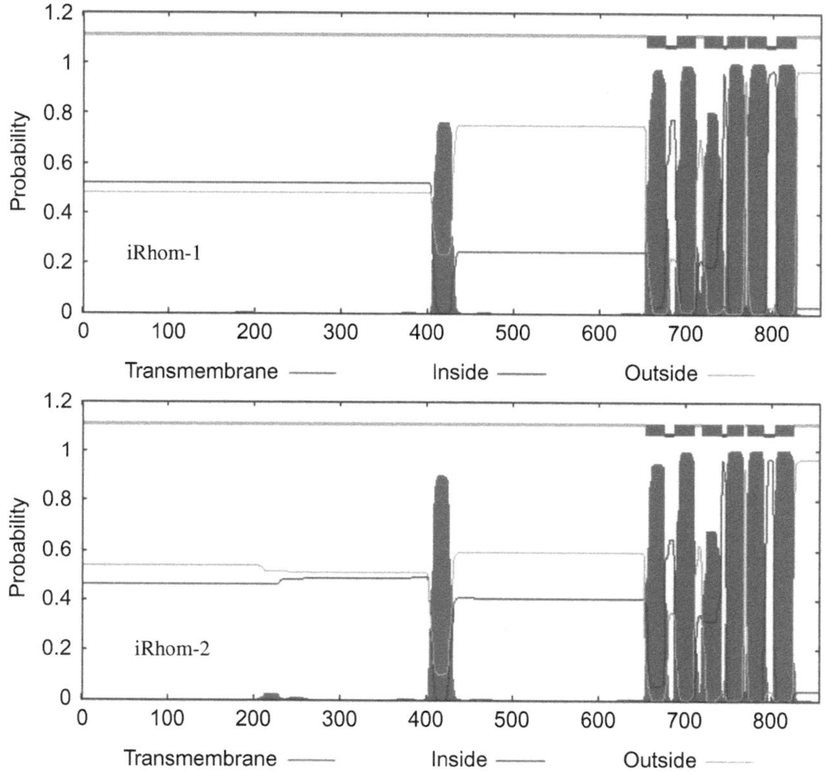

FIG. 12.17 The graphical representation generated by TMHMM Server v. 2.0 showing amino acids contribution in formation of transmembrane helices at different position of *Human* iRhom-1 and iRhom-2 sequences. Red region (gray in print version) represents transmembrane helices; blue (dark gray in print version) and pink (light gray in print version) regions represent inside and outside helices, respectively.

The role of iRhoms was initially identified in *Drosophila*. Human iRhoms are essential for regulation of ADAM metallopeptidase domain 17 (ADAM17)/tumor necrosis factor-α-converting enzyme (TACE) that help in the maturation and trafficking of tumor necrosis factor-alpha (TNF-α) from ER to plasma membrane. The study also suggested that ADAM17 activates EGFR by releasing pro-EGFR substrates. iRhoms-regulated activation/downregulation of EGFR signaling pathways is responsible for various human diseases, including breast, esophageal, and ovarian cancer (Wojnarowicz et al., 2012; Lee et al., 2016).

12.3 Inhibitors of rhomboid proteases

Rhomboid proteases mediate an array of essential physiological functions such as cell signaling, mitochondrial remodeling, cell membrane/protein metabolism, and wound healing in various organisms. Considering the importance of rhomboid proteases in biological functions, diverse chemical scaffolds have been explored (Fig. 12.18). The dichloroisocoumarins (DCIs) were the first identified intramembrane serine proteases or rhomboid protease inhibitors that contain highly reactive electrophilic groups. These compounds also showed great affinity toward other serine proteases (Fig. 12.18) (Harper et al., 1985). The discovery was supported by the sensitivity of serine protease inhibitors DCI and tosyl phenylalanine chloromethyl ketone (TPCK) to *Drosophila* rhomboid-1 dependent Spitz cleavage assay (Urban et al., 2001). Recently, some benzoxazin-4-ones were developed as inhibitors of rhomboid proteases, which showed activity in the micromolar range. The compounds were prepared from anthranilic acid derivatives in a one-step synthesis. Preparation of these analogs is very economic and easy in comparison to other available rhomboid protease inhibitors (Yang et al., 2015). This provides lots of scope to explore rhomboid protease inhibitors in order to optimize their activity profile (Fig. 12.18).

The first cocrystal of isocoumarin and *E. coli* GlpG rhomboid protease indicated the importance of oxyanion hole, and the S1- and S2′-binding subsites in inhibition/catalytic mechanism of inhibitor/substrate. These are key structural characteristics of serine proteases (Vinothkumar et al., 2010). The catalytic domain of GlpG consists of six membrane spanning segments (S1–S6)

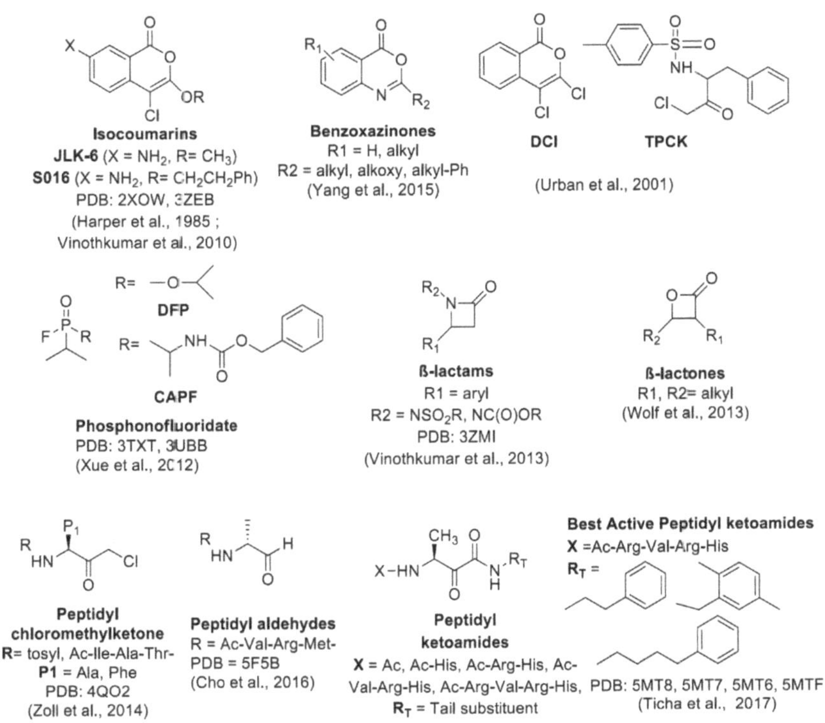

FIG. 12.18 The different chemical scaffolds reported as inhibitors of rhomboid proteases.

(Koonin et al., 2003). The oxyanion hole/pocket of rhomboid protease is formed by the side chains of conserved amino acid residues His150 and Asp154 and the main chain amide of Ser201. In the binding pocket, isocoumarin covalently binds with catalytic dyad of serine and histidine. The nucleophilic reaction between the serine and carbonyl group of isocoumarin facilitates ring opening of isocoumarin and formation of acyl enzyme. Consequently, nucleophilic reaction with histidine gives doubly covalent-bonded alkylated acyl enzyme (Vinothkumar et al., 2010). The phosphonofluoridate (DFP, CAPF) chemical scaffold covalently bonded with serine leads to changes in many transmembrane helices to get accommodated in binding site (Xue et al., 2012). High-throughput screening of 60,000 molecules library with a fluorogenic FRET (fluorescence/Foerster resonance energy transfer) substrate and AarA (rhomboid serine protease) indicated monocyclic β-lactams as new rhomboid protease inhibitors. The carbonyl oxygen of lactams ring covalently binds with catalytic serine and faces away from the oxyanion hole of GlpG and shows very low potency in in vitro and in vivo studies (Vinothkumar et al., 2013). Considering the importance of reactive electrophiles, a small library of molecules consisting isocoumarins, phosphonates, phosphoramidates, β-sultams, β-lactones, epoxides, and thiiranes were screened with ABP fluorescence polarization assay. This produced β-lactones as a new class of moderate inhibitor of GlpG. They are similar to monocyclic β-lactams. They also shared covalent irreversible bonding with the serine of GlpG (Wolf et al., 2013).

In order to modify the activity of TPCK, researchers have considered several peptidyl chloromethyl ketones (CMKs) derived from the natural rhomboid substrate TatA of bacterium providencia stuartii with a longer peptide chain which binds with GlpG in substrate like manner. However, these compounds were not found to be very potent. The cocrystal structure revealed that S1 and S4 subsites are important for protease activity. The molecular dynamics simulation experiment supported the substrate's binding to the active site of GlpG. These compounds formed hemi-ketal by alkylation on reaction with serine and histidine of GlpG active site. The study also revealed that homologous rhomboid-like proteins may contain similar substrate- or client-protein-binding function (Zoll et al., 2014). The peptidyl aldehydes are noncompetitive and reversible mechanism-based inhibitors that help in kinetic analysis and structurally mimic the transition state. At catalytic site the tetrahedral intermediate of peptidyl aldehydes showed covalent interaction with serine 201. The His150 and Asn154 are other important residues involved in the side chain interactions (Cho et al., 2016). The inhibitors with electrophilic head groups and long peptide chains are suggested to bind to the active site of GlpG. Here the active site can accommodate about 6 residues and display distinct sequence preferences at several positions (Zoll et al., 2014; Cho et al., 2016). However, all these discovered chemical scaffolds did not culminate in clinically viable inhibitors due to lack of selectivity and potency in biological screening. However, they have been put to use in validation of therapeutic potential of rhomboids, and as templates for drug design and development (Strisovsky, 2016). Recently, in a breakthrough discovery, peptidyl ketoamides have been shown as potential inhibitors of rhomboid proteases in the nanomolar range, which surpassed the other rhomboid inhibitors by up to three orders of magnitude. The discovered ketoamides showed selectivity for rhomboids, without affecting most of the human serine hydrolases. The cocrystal study showed that peptidyl ketoamide moieties of the inhibitors interaction with His150, Asn154, and Ser201 of rhomboid protease oxyanion pocket and form tetrahedral intermediate like substrate. Among these interactions, ketoamide is covalently bonded by its proximal carbon to the side chain oxygen of the catalytic Ser201 (Fig. 12.19). The kinetic analysis revealed their slow-binding, noncompetitive, and reversible behavior (Ticha et al., 2017). Most of the rhomboid inhibitors including peptidyl ketoamides showed stereo-chemical changes during the course of reaction progression (Fig. 12.19) (Strisovsky, 2016; Ticha et al., 2017).

The conformational flexibility/variation between native (PDB: 2XOV) and acyl enzyme (PDB: 2XOW) crystal structures of rhomboid proteases has been observed, which confirms the importance of structural flexibility in proteolysis mechanism but the nature of flexibility is not clearly understood (Wang et al., 2006; Vinothkumar et al., 2010; Vosyka et al., 2013). The backbone conformational variation has been observed between the inhibitors (PDB: 2XOW, 3ZEB, 5MTF, 4QO2, 5F5B, 3UBB, 3ZMI) bound and native (2XOV) crystal structures of GlpG (Pymol viewer). Among all, the maximum variation was observed in peptidyl chloromethylketone (RMSD: 0.788) and peptidyl ketoamides (RMSD: 0.704) bound crystal structure and minimum variation in lactam (RMSD: 0.232) bound crystal structures (Fig. 12.20). These results indicated that the binding

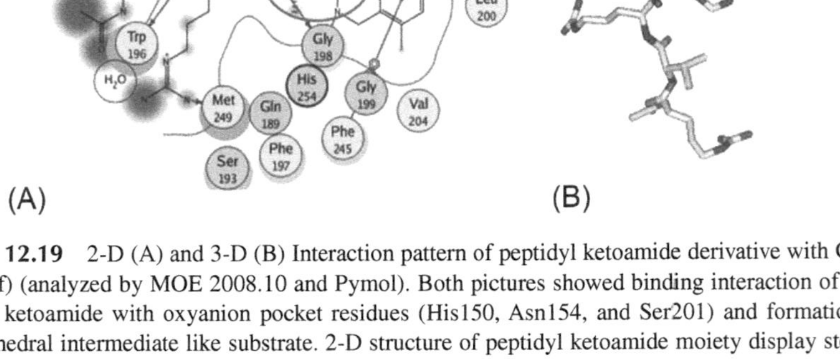

FIG. 12.19 2-D (A) and 3-D (B) Interaction pattern of peptidyl ketoamide derivative with GlpG (5mtf) (analyzed by MOE 2008.10 and Pymol). Both pictures showed binding interaction of peptidyl ketoamide with oxyanion pocket residues (His150, Asn154, and Ser201) and formation of tetrahedral intermediate like substrate. 2-D structure of peptidyl ketoamide moiety display stereochemical changes during reaction mechanism.

FIG. 12.20 Align structure (RMSD: 0.564, calculated from Pymol) of native (PDB: 2XOV, red—dark gray in print version) and mechanism-based isocoumarin (PDB: 2XOW, green—light gray in print version) bound rhomboid proteases. Isocoumarin binding (PDB: 2XOV) showing reasonable conformational variation in binding site.

pocket of rhomboid proteases is flexible in nature and can be modulated by size and structural flexibility of inhibitors.

12.4 Conclusions

In proteolytic rhomboids, the sequences of RHBDL1, RHBDL2, and RHBDL3 are reasonably homologous to each other and share similar TMDs in comparison to others. This finding gives an indication that RHBDL1, RHBDL2, and RHBDL3 possibly share same mechanism in EGF signaling pathway. While RHBDL4 is dissimilar from other rhomboids (RHBDL1, RHBDL2, and RHBDL3), it shows association with TGF-β signaling pathway, and regulation of apoptosis via BIK, AP-1, and exosome secretion. PARL is another important proteolytic rhomboid and its correlation with cancer is not yet understood. However, the connecting proteins in its pathway, such as PINK1 showed link with cancer cells. In cell cycle, ERAD is an important pathway where RHBDL4 and derlin-1 (pseudoprotease) work together to regulate the translocation and deregulation mechanism to control the homeostasis of cells. iRhom 1 and 2 (pseudo proteases) are highly similar in structure and work as key upstream regulators of ADAM17-dependent EGFR signaling. Cell colocalization of rhomboids also indicated similarities in biological processes. These mechanisms uncovered that the rhomboids can act as attractive targets to treat ERAD- and EGFR-dependent diseases such as cancer. Multiple biological assays and crystallography studies have been done to explore inhibitors of rhomboid proteases. Most of the inhibitors investigated are covalent binder and have electrophilic warhead. Among membrane spanning segments (S1–S6) of rhomboids, S1, S2, S4, and S5 subsites, are important for catalytic activity. The binding pocket is very flexible in nature and can accommodate variety of inhibitors. With the accumulating knowledge of rhomboids, its structure, cellular mechanisms, inhibitors, and biological events in the spread of cancer open a window to design new potential inhibitors against metastatic disease. Although lots of challenges still exist to be addressed, it is anticipated that continuous efforts may uncover structural and mechanistic aspects of rhomboids that may be useful to discover new anticancer agents. Thus the chapter provided recent updates along with critical analysis and comparison of rhomboids. This may give new direction for the exploration of inhibitors of rhomboid proteases useful against cancer.

Acknowledgment

The authors thank Prof. Ramesh K. Goyal, Vice Chancellor, Delhi Pharmaceutical Sciences and Research University for the encouragement and support. This chapter is dedicated to Dr. Y.S. Prabhakar Medicinal & Process Chemistry Division, CSIR-CDRI, Lucknow, on his 60th birthday as a mark of respect for his commitment to scientific quest. Correspondence: Saroj Verma (ss2016@gmail.com).

References

Adrain, C., Strisovsky, K., Zettl, M., Hu, L., Lemberg, M.K., Freeman, M., 2011. Mammalian EGF receptor activation by the rhomboid protease RHBDL2. EMBO Rep. 12, 421–427.

Anderson, D.J., Le Moigne, R., Djakovic, S., Kumar, B., Rice, J., Wong, S., Wang, J., Yao, B., Valle, E., Kiss von Soly, S., Madriaga, A., Soriano, F., Menon, M.K., Wu, Z.Y., Kampmann, M., Chen, Y., Weissman, J.S., Aftab, B.T., Yakes, F.M., Shawver, L., Zhou, H.J., Wustrow, D., Rolfe, M., 2015. Targeting the AAA ATPase p97 as an approach to treat cancer through disruption of protein homeostasis. Cancer Cell 28, 653–665.

Arvanitis, D., Davy, A., 2008. Eph/ephrin signaling: networks. Genes Dev. 22, 416–429.

Bergbold, N., Lemberg, M.K., 2013. Emerging role of rhomboid family proteins in mammalian biology and disease. Biochim. Biophys. Acta 1828, 2840–2848.

Cahoy, J.D., Emery, B., Kaushal, A., Foo, L.C., Zamanian, J.L., Christopherson, K.S., Xing, Y., Lubischer, J.L., Krieg, P.A., Krupenko, S.A., Thompson, W.J., Barres, B.A., 2008. A transcriptome database for astrocytes, neurons, and oligodendrocytes: a new resource for understanding brain development and function. J. Neurosci. 28, 264–678.

Chari, R.V., 2008. Targeted cancer therapy: conferring specificity to cytotoxic drugs. Acc. Chem. Res. 41, 98–107.

Cheng, T.L., Wu, Y.T., Lin, H.Y., Hsu, F.C., Liu, S.K., Chang, B.I., Chen, W.S., Lai, C.H., Shi, G.Y., Wu, H.L., 2011. Functions of rhomboid family protease RHBDL2 and thrombomodulin in wound healing. J. Invest. Dermatol. 131, 2486–2494.

Cheng, T.L., Lai, C.H., Jiang, S.J., Hung, J.H., Liu, S.K., Chang, B.I., Shi, G.Y., Wu, H.L., 2014. RHBDL2 is a critical membrane protease for anoikis resistance in human malignant epithelial cells. Sci. World J. 2014, 902987.

Cho, S., Dickey, S., Urban, S., 2016. Crystal structures and inhibition kinetics reveal a two-stage catalytic mechanism with drug design implications for rhomboid proteolysis. Mol. Cell 61, 329–340.

Cooper, G.M., 2000. The Cell: A Molecular Approach, second ed. Sinauer Associates, Sunderland, MA.

Deas, E., Plun-Favreau, H., Gandhi, S., Desmond, H., Kjaer, S., Loh, S.H., Renton, A.E., Harvey, R.J., Whitworth, A.J., Martins, L.M., Abramov, A.Y., Wood, N.W., 2011. PINK1 cleavage at position A103 by the mitochondrial protease PARL. Hum. Mol. Genet. 20, 867–879.

Dusterhoft, S., Kunzel, U., Freeman, M., 2017. Rhomboid proteases in human disease: mechanisms and future prospects. Biochim. Biophys. Acta, Mol. Cell Res. 1864, 2200–2209.

Eatemadi, A., Aiyelabegan, H.T., Negahdari, B., Mazlomi, M.A., Daraee, H., Daraee, N., Eatemadi, R., Sadroddiny, E., 2017. Role of protease and protease inhibitors in cancer pathogenesis and treatment. Biomed. Pharmacother. 86, 221–231.

Fernandez-Medarde, A., Santos, E., 2011. Ras in cancer and developmental diseases. Genes Cancer 2, 344–358.

Fleig, L., Bergbold, N., Sahasrabudhe, P., Geiger, B., Kaltak, L., Lemberg, M.K., 2012. Ubiquitin-dependent intramembrane rhomboid protease promotes ERAD of membrane proteins. Mol. Cell 47, 558–569.

Flynn, J.F., Wong, C., Wu, J.M., 2009. Anti-EGFR therapy: mechanism and advances in clinical efficacy in breast Cancer. J. Oncol. 2009, 1–16.

Frezza, C., Cipolat, S., Martins de Brito, O., Micaroni, M., Beznoussenko, G.V., Rudka, T., Bartoli, D., Polishuck, R.S., Danial, N.N., De Strooper, B., Scorrano, L., 2006. OPA1 controls apoptotic cristae remodeling independently from mitochondrial fusion. Cell 126, 177–189.

Gautel, M., Djinovic-Carugo, K., 2016. The sarcomeric cytoskeleton: from molecules to motion. J. Exp. Biol. 2016 (219), 135–145.

Gottlieb, R.A., Bernstein, D., 2016. Mitochondrial remodeling: rearranging, recycling, and reprogramming. Cell Calcium 60, 88–101.

Greenblatt, E.J., Olzmann, J.A., Kopito, R.R., 2011. Derlin-1 is a rhomboid pseudoprotease required for the dislocation of mutant α-1 antitrypsin from the endoplasmic reticulum. Nat. Struct. Mol. Biol. 18, 1147–1152.

Greenblatt, E.J., Olzmann, J.A., Kopito, R.R., 2012. Making the cut: intramembrane cleavage by a rhomboid protease promotes ERAD. Nat. Struct. Mol. Biol. 19, 979–981.

Ha, Y., 2009. Structure and mechanism of intramembrane protease. Semin. Cell Dev. Biol. 20, 240–250.

Ha, Y., Akiyama, Y., Xue, Y., 2013. Structure and mechanism of rhomboid protease. J. Biol. Chem. 288, 15430–15436.

Han, Y., Cho, U., Kim, S., Park, I.S., Cho, J.H., Dhanasekaran, D.N., Song, Y.S., 2018. Tumour microenvironment on mitochondrial dynamics and chemoresistance in cancer. Free Radic. Res, 1–17.

Harden, N., 2017. New insights from *Drosophila* into the regulation of EGFR signaling. In: Wang, Z. (Ed.), ErbB Receptor Signaling. Methods in Molecular Biology. vol. 1652. Humana Press, New York, NY.

Harper, J.W., Hemmi, K., Powers, J.C., 1985. Reaction of serine proteases with substituted isocoumarins: discovery of 3,4-dichloroisocoumarin, a new general mechanism based serine protease inhibitor. Biochemistry 24, 1831–1841.

Herath, N.I., Boyd, A.W., 2010. The role of Eph receptors and ephrin ligands in colorectal cancer. Int. J. Cancer 126, 2003–2011.

IUBMB, 2010. Hydrolases Enzymes, Generated from the ExplorEnz Database, September 2010, IUBMB. Enzyme Nomenclature: Recommendations of the Nomenclature Committee of the International Union of Biochemistry and Molecular Biology. Academic Press, San Diego, CA. Accessible at: http://www.enzyme-database.org/downloads/ec3.pdf. (accessed 30.11.18).

Jeyaraju, D.V., Xu, L., Letellier, M.C., Bandaru, S., Zunino, R., Berg, E.A., McBride, H.M., Pellegrini, L., 2006. Phosphorylation and cleavage of presenilin-associated rhomboid-like protein (PARL) promotes changes in mitochondrial morphology. Proc. Natl. Acad. Sci. U. S. A. 103, 18562–18567.

Johnson, N., Brezinova, J., Stephens, E., Burbridge, E., Freeman, M., Adrain, C., Strisovsky, K., 2017. Quantitative proteomics screen identifies a substrate repertoire of rhomboid protease RHBDL2 in human cells and implicates it in epithelial homeostasis. Sci. Rep. 7, 7283.

Kim, H., Bhattacharya, A., Qi, L., 2015. Endoplasmic reticulum quality control in cancer: friend or foe. Semin. Cancer Biol. 33, 25–33.

Kinch, L.N., Grishin, N.V., 2013. Bioinformatics perspective on rhomboid intramembrane protease evolution and function. Biochim. Biophys. Acta 1828, 2937–2943.

Koonin, E.V., Makarova, K.S., Rogozin, I.B., Davidovic, L., Letellier, M.C., Pellegrini, L., 2003. The rhomboids: a nearly ubiquitous family of intramembrane serine proteases that probably evolved by multiple ancient horizontal gene transfers. Genome Biol. 4, R19.

Krogh, A., Larsson, B., von Heijne, G., Sonnhammer, E.L., 2001. Predicting transmembrane protein topology with a hidden Markov model: application to complete genomes. J. Mol. Biol. 305, 567–580.

Kumar, A., Gibbs, J.R., Beilina, A., Dillman, A., Kumaran, R., Trabzuni, D., Ryten, M., Walker, R., Smith, C., Traynor, B.J., Hardy, J., Singleton, A.B., Cookson, M.R., 2013. Age-associated changes in gene expression in human brain and isolated neurons. Neurobiol. Aging 34, 1199–1209.

Larkin, M.A., Blackshields, G., Brown, N.P., Chenna, R., McGettigan, P.A., McWilliam, H., Valentin, F., Wallace, I.M., Wilm, A., Lopez, R., Thompson, J.D., Gibson, T.J., Higgins, D.G., 2007. Clustal W and clustal X version 2.0. Bioinformatics 23, 2947–2948.

Lee, M.Y., Nam, K.H., Choi, K.C., 2016. iRhoms; its functions and essential roles. Biomol. Ther. (Seoul) 24, 109–114.

Lemberg, M.K., Freeman, M., 2007. Functional and evolutionary implications of enhanced genomic analysis of rhomboid intramembrane proteases. Genome Res. 17, 1634–1646.

Le Moigne, R., Aftab, B.T., Djakovic, S., Dhimolea, E., Valle, E., Murnane, M., King, E.M., Soriano, F., Menon, M.K., Wu, Z.Y., Wong, S.T., Lee, G.J., Yao, B., Wiita, A.P., Lam, C., Rice, J., Wang, J., Chesi, M., Bergsagel, P.L., Kraus, M., Driessen, C., Kiss von Soly, S.,Yakes, F.M., Wustrow, D., Shawver, L., Zhou, H.J., Martin, T.G. 3rd, Wolf, J.L., Mitsiades, C.S., Anderson, D.J., Rolfe, M., 2017. The p97 inhibitor CB-5083 is a unique disrupter of protein homeostasis in models of multiple myeloma. Mol. Cancer Ther 16, 2375–2386.

Lilley, B.N., Ploegh, H.L., 2005. Multiprotein complexes that link dislocation, ubiquitination, and extraction of misfolded proteins from the endoplasmic reticulum membrane. Proc. Natl. Acad. Sci. U. S. A. 102, 14296–14301.

Lim, J.J., Lee, Y., Ly, T.T., Kang, J.Y., Lee, J.G., An, J.Y., Youn, H.S., Park, K.R., Kim, T.G., Yang, J.K., Jun, Y., Eom, S.H., 2016a. Structural insights into the interaction of p97 N-terminus domain and VBM in rhomboid protease, RHBDL4. Biochem. J. 473, 2863–2880.

Lim, J.J., Lee, Y., Yoon, S.Y., Ly, T.T., Kang, J.Y., Youn, H.S., An, J.Y., Lee, J.G., Park, K.R., Kim, T.G., Yang, J.K., Jun, Y., Eom, S.H., 2016b. Structural insights into the interaction of human p97 N-terminal domain and SHP motif in Derlin-1 rhomboid pseudoprotease. FEBS Lett. 590, 4402–4413.

Magalhaes, L.G., Ferreira, L.L.G., Andricopulo, A.D., 2018. Recent advances and perspectives in cancer drug design. An. Acad. Bras. Cienc. 90, 1233–1250.

Mansoori, B., Mohammadi, A., Davudian, S., Shirjang, S., Baradaran, B., 2017. The different mechanisms of Cancer drug resistance: a brief review. Adv. Pharm. Bull. 7, 339–348.

Masuda, H., Zhang, D., Bartholomeusz, C., Doihara, H., Hortobagyi, G.N., Ueno, N.T., 2012. Role of epidermal growth factor receptor in breast cancer. Breast Cancer Res. Treat. 136, 331–345.

Meissner, C., Lorenz, H., Weihofen, A., Selkoe, D.J., Lemberg, M.K., 2011. The mitochondrial intramembrane protease PARL cleaves human Pink1 to regulate Pink1 trafficking. J. Neurochem. 117, 856–867.

Nakada, M., Kita, D., Watanabe, T., Hayashi, Y., Teng, L., Pyko, I.V., Hamada, J., 2011. Aberrant signaling pathways in glioma. Cancers (Basel) 3, 3242–3278.

O'Flanagan, C.H., O'Neill, C., 2014. PINK1 signalling in cancer biology. Biochim. Biophys. Acta 1846, 590–608.

Oda, Y., Okada, T., Yoshida, H., Kaufman, R.J., Nagata, K., Mori, K., 2006. Derlin-2 and Derlin-3 are regulated by the mammalian unfolded protein response and are required for ER-associated degradation. J. Cell Biol. 172, 383–393.

Olgen, S., 2018. Overview on anticancer drug design and development. Curr. Med. Chem. 25, 1704–1719.

Pascall, J.C., Brown, K.D., 1998. Characterization of a mammalian cDNA encoding a protein with high sequence similarity to the Drosophila regulatory protein rhomboid. FEBS Lett. 429, 337–340.

Pascall, J.C., Brown, K.D., 2004. Intramembrane cleavage of ephrinB3 by the human rhomboid family protease, RHBDL2. Biochem. Biophys. Res. Commun. 317, 244–252.

Peptide 2.0 (Peptide Hydrophobicity/Hydrophilicity Analysis). Available from: https://www.peptide2.com/N_peptide_hydrophobicity_hydrophilicity.php Accessed 30 November 2018.

Perez-Herrero, E., Fernandez-Medarde, A., 2015. Advanced targeted therapies in cancer: drug nanocarriers, the future of chemotherapy. Eur. J. Pharm. Biopharm. 93, 52–79.

Preston, G.M., Brodsky, J.L., 2017. The evolving role of ubiquitin modification in endoplasmic reticulum-associated degradation. Biochem. J. 474, 445–469.

Rajendran, B.K., Deng, C.X., 2017. A comprehensive genomic meta-analysis identifies confirmatory role of OBSCN gene in breast tumorigenesis. Oncotarget 8, 102263–102276.

Ran, Y., Hu, H., Hu, D., Zhou, Z., Sun, Y., Yu, L., Sun, L., Pan, J., Liu, J., Liu, T., Yang, Z., 2008. Derlin-1 is overexpressed on the tumor cell surface and enables antibody-mediated tumor targeting therapy. Clin. Cancer Res. 14, 6538–6545.

Ren, X., Song, W., Liu, W., Guan, X., Miao, F., Miao, S., Wang, L., 2013. Rhomboid domain containing 1 inhibits cell apoptosis by upregulating AP-1 activity and its downstream target Bcl-3. FEBS Lett. 587, 1793–1798.

Roskoski Jr., R., 2014. The ErbB/HER family of protein-tyrosine kinases and cancer. Pharmacol. Res. 79, 34–74.

Sasaki, T., Hiroki, K., Yamashita, Y., 2013. The role of epidermal growth factor receptor in cancer metastasis and microenvironment. Biomed. Res. Int. 2013, 546318.

Schekman, R., 2004. Cell biology: a channel for protein waste. Nature 429, 817–818.

Schulz, J., Avci, D., Queisser, M.A., Gutschmidt, A., Dreher, L.S., Fenech, E.J., Volkmar, N., Hayashi, Y., Hoppe, T., Christianson, J.C., 2017. Conserved cytoplasmic domains promote

Hrd1 ubiquitin ligase complex formation for ER-associated degradation (ERAD). J. Cell Sci. 130, 3322–3335.

Sik, A., Passer, B.J., Koonin, E.V., Pellegrini, L., 2004. Self-regulated cleavage of the mitochondrial intramembrane-cleaving protease PARL yields Pbeta, a nuclear-targeted peptide. J. Biol. Chem. 279, 15323–15329.

Song, Z., Chen, H., Fiket, M., Alexander, C., Chan, D.C., 2007. OPA1 processing controls mitochondrial fusion and is regulated by mRNA splicing, membrane potential, and Yme1L. Cell Biol. 178, 749–755.

Song, W., Liu, W., Zhao, H., Li, S., Guan, X., Ying, J., Zhang, Y., Miao, F., Zhang, M., Ren, X., Li, X., Wu, F., Zhao, Y., Tian, Y., Wu, W., Fu, J., Liang, J., Wu, W., Liu, C., Yu, J., Zong, S., Miao, S., Zhang, X., Wang, L., 2015. Rhomboid domain containing 1 promotes colorectal cancer growth through activation of the EGFR signalling pathway. Nat. Commun. 6, 8022.

Srinivasan, S., Guha, M., Kashina, A., Avadhani, N.G., 2017. Mitochondrial dysfunction and mitochondrial dynamics—the cancer connection. Biochim. Biophys. Acta Bioenerg. 1858, 602–614.

Strisovsky, K., 2016. Why cells need intramembrane proteases—a mechanistic perspective. FEBS J. 283, 837–845.

Szklarczyk, D., Morris, J.H., Cook, H., Kuhn, M., Wyder, S., Simonovic, M., Santos, A., Doncheva, N.T., Roth, A., Bork, P., Jensen, L.J., von Mering, C., 2017. The STRING database in 2017: quality-controlled protein-protein association networks, made broadly accessible. Nucleic Acids Res. 45, D362–D368.

Tan, X., He, X., Jiang, Z., Wang, X., Ma, L., Liu, L., Wang, X., Fan, Z., Su, D., 2015. Derlin-1 is overexpressed in human colon cancer and promotes cancer cell proliferation. Mol. Cell. Biochem. 408, 205–213.

Ticha, A., Stanchev, S., Vinothkumar, K.R., Mikles, D.C., Pachl, P., Began, J., Skerle, J., Svehlova, K., Nguyen, M.T.N., Verhelst, S.H.L., Johnson, D.C., Bachovchin, D.A., Lepsík, M., Majer, P., Strisovsky, K., 2017. General and modular strategy for designing potent, selective, and pharmacologically compliant inhibitors of rhomboid proteases. Cell Chem. Biol. 24, 1523–1536. e4.

UniProt Consortium, 2011. Ongoing and future developments at the universal protein resource. Nucleic Acids Res. 39, D214–D219.

Urban, S., Dickey, S.W., 2011. The rhomboid protease family: a decade of progress on function and mechanism. Genome Biol. 12, 231.

Urban, S., Lee, J.R., Freeman, M., 2001. *Drosophila* rhomboid-1 defines a family of putative intramembrane serine proteases. Cell 107, 173–182.

Vinothkumar, K.R., Henderson, R., 2010. Structures of membrane proteins. Q. Rev. Biophys. 43, 65–158.

Vinothkumar, K.R., Strisovsky, K., Andreeva, A., Christova, Y., Verhelst, S., Freeman, M., 2010. The structural basis for catalysis and substrate specificity of a rhomboid protease. EMBO J. 29, 3797–3809.

Vinothkumar, K.R., Pierrat, O.A., Large, J.M., Freeman, M., 2013. Structure of rhomboid protease in complex with β-lactam inhibitors defines the S2' cavity. Structure 21, 1051–1058.

Vosyka, O., Vinothkumar, K.R., Wolf, E.V., Brouwer, A.J., Liskamp, R.M., Verhelst, S.H., 2013. Activity-based probes for rhomboid proteases discovered in a mass spectrometry-based assay. Proc. Natl. Acad. Sci. U. S. A. 110, 2472–2477.

Wallis, D.D., Putnam, E.A., Cretoiu, J.S., Carmical, S.G., Cao, S.N., Thomas, G., Milewicz, D.M., 2003. Profibrillin-1 maturation by human dermal fibroblasts: proteolytic processing and molecular chaperones. J. Cell. Biochem. 90, 641–652.

Wan, C., Fu, J., Wang, Y., Miao, S., Song, W., Wang, L., 2012. Exosome-related multi-pass transmembrane protein TSAP6 is a target of rhomboid protease RHBDD1-induced proteolysis. PLoS One 7, e37452.

Wang, Y., Zhang, Y., Ha, Y., 2006. Crystal structure of a rhomboid family intramembrane protease. Nature 44, 179–180.

Wang, Y., Guan, X., Fok, K.L., Li, S., Zhang, X., Miao, S., Zong, S., Koide, S.S., Chan, H.C., Wang, L.A., 2008a. Novel member of the rhomboid family, RHBDD1, regulates BIK-mediated apoptosis. Cell. Mol. Life Sci. 65, 3822–3829.

Wang, J., Hua, H., Ran, Y., Zhang, H., Liu, W., Yang, Z., Jiang, Y., 2008b. Derlin-1 is overexpressed in human breast carcinoma and protects cancer cells from endoplasmic reticulum stress-induced apoptosis. Breast Cancer Res. 10, R7.

Wang, Z., Ying, M., Wu, Q., Wang, R., Li, Y., 2016. Overexpression of myosin VI regulates gastric cancer cell progression. Gene 593, 100–109.

Wee, P., Wang, Z., 2017. Epidermal growth factor receptor cell proliferation signaling pathways. Cancers (Basel) 9. pii: E52.

WHO Cancer report, 2018. Latest global cancer data: Cancer burden rises to 18.1 million new cases and 9.6 million cancer deaths in 2018. Available from: https://www.who.int/cancer/PRGlobocanFinal.pdf. (accessed 30.11.18).

Wojnarowicz, P.M., Provencher, D.M., Mes-Masson, A.M., Tonin, P.N., 2012. Chromosome 17q25 genes, RHBDF2 and CYGB, in ovarian cancer. Int. J. Oncol. 40, 1865–1880.

Wolf, E.V., Zeißler, A., Vosyka, O., Zeiler, E., Sieber, S., Verhelst, S.H., 2013. A new class of rhomboid protease inhibitors discovered by activity-based fluorescence polarization. PLoS One 8, e72307.

Wu, C., Jin, X., Tsueng, G., Afrasiabi, C., Su, A.I., 2016a. BioGPS: building your own mash-up of gene annotations and expression profiles. Nucleic Acids Res. 44, D313–D316.

Wu, Z., Wang, C., Zhang, Z., Liu, W., Xu, H., Wang, H., Wang, Y., Zhang, W., Wang, S.L., 2016b. High expression of derlin-1 is associated with the malignancy of bladder cancer in a Chinese han population. PLoS One 11, e0168351.

Wunderle, L., Knopf, J.D., Kuhnle, N., Morle, A., Hehn, B., Adrain, C., Strisovsky, K., Freeman, M., Lemberg, M.K., 2016. Rhomboid intramembrane protease RHBDL4 triggers ER-export and non-canonical secretion of membrane-anchored TGFα. Sci. Rep. 6, 27342.

Xue, Y., Chowdhury, S., Liu, X., Akiyama, Y., Ellman, J., Ha, Y., 2012. Conformational change in rhomboid protease GlpG induced by inhibitor binding to its S′ subsites. Biochemistry 51, 3723–3731.

Yang, P., Li, Z.Y., Li, H.Q., 2015. Potential roles of protease inhibitors in cancer progression. Asian Pac. J. Cancer Prev. 16, 8047–8052.

Ye, Y., Shibata, Y., Yun, C., Ron, D., Rapoport, T.A., 2004. A membrane protein complex mediates retro-translocation from the ER lumen into the cytosol. Nature 429, 841–847.

Zhou, A., Webb, G., Zhu, X., Steiner, D.F., 1999. Proteolytic processing in the secretory pathway. J. Biol. Chem. 274, 20745–20748.

Zhou, H.J., Wang, J., Yao, B., Wong, S., Djakovic, S., Kumar, B., Rice, J., Valle, E., Soriano, F., Menon, M.K., Madriaga, A., Kiss von Soly, S., Kumar, A., Parlati, F., Yakes, F.M., Shawver, L., Le Moigne, R., Anderson, D.J., Rolfe, M., Wustrow, D., 2015. Discovery of a first-in-class, potent, selective, and orally bioavailable inhibitor of the p97 AAA ATPase (CB-5083). J. Med. Chem. 58, 9480–9497.

Zoll, S., Stanchev, S., Began, J., Skerle, J., Lepsik, M., Peclinovska, L., Majer, P., Strisovsky, K., 2014. Substrate binding and specificity of rhomboid intramembrane protease revealed by substrate-peptide complex structures. EMBO J. 33, 2408–2421.

Chapter 13

KRAS: Structure, function, and development of anticancer drugs

Dolly A. Parasrampuria, Alex Yu, Nahor Haddish-Berhane
Janssen Research & Development, LLC, Spring House, PA, United States

13.1 Introduction

The *RAS* oncogenes are the focus of intense research since they are mutated in a wide range of cancers and make these malignancies particularly intractable to current therapies. As of the writing of this chapter, there are no approved therapies that directly target *RAS*, despite almost 40 years of intensive research to understand the gene and its mutations, function, structure, and impact on cellular transformation from normal to a malignant cell.

In the 1960s, research using murine leukemia viruses set the stage for the later discovery of the oncogenic potential of the *RAS* genes, as retroviruses from infected animals were found to cause cancer in inoculated new-born rodents. The earliest reports were from Jennifer Harvey, who reported the development of cancer in new-born rodents inoculated with leukemic cells containing a murine sarcoma virus from rats (Harvey, 1964). This was followed by a series of publications by Kirsten et al. that showed the transformative potential of leukemic cells when injected into newborn or young rodents (Kirsten and Mayer, 1967; Kirsten and Platz, 1964). These were postulated to be caused by retroviruses carrying the *RAS* oncogene.

The Harvey murine sarcoma virus (Ha-MSV) was first cloned in 1979 (Hager et al., 1979), followed by cloning of the Kirsten murine sarcoma virus (Ki-MSV) (Tsuchida and Uesugi, 1981). In 1982, Chang and others first identified that the retroviruses, Ha-MuSV and Ki-MuSV, contained *v-RAS* genes and postulated the existence of at least two homologous human genes, leading to the cloning of two *C-HA-RAS* genes and two *C-KI-RAS* genes (Chang et al., 1982). This was followed by the characterization and molecular cloning of the *NRAS* gene, located on chromosome 1 (Cox and Der, 2010). The N prefix signifies its neuroblastoma cell line origins. The gene products of *C-HA-RAS* and

Cancer-Leading Proteases. https://doi.org/10.1016/B978-0-12-818168-3.00013-9

NRAS appear to be essential for cellular growth; and disruptions in these genes result in uncontrolled tumor growth. In 1984, Santos et al. (1984) discovered that a single point mutation from guanine to cytosine at the amino acid position 12 was responsible for the conversion of the wild-type *KRAS* oncogene to a malignant form. These findings have since driven the study of RAS structure, biochemistry, and biology (Karnoub and Weinberg, 2008).

The *KRAS* isoform is found to be mutated in 84% of all *RAS*-mutant cancers making it a high value target for drug therapy (Waters and Der, 2018). Point mutations in *KRAS* are most common at codons 12 and 13 with point mutations occurring less frequently in codons 18, 61, 117, and 146 (Bamford et al., 2004). The type of *KRAS* mutations appears to determine the biochemical activity and transforming capacity. Experiments with murine NIH/3T3 indicate that codon 12 mutations induce higher level of resistance to apoptosis and predisposition to anchorage-independent growth over codon 13 (Guerrero et al., 2000). In the clinical setting, colorectal cancer (CRC) patients with codon 13 mutations reportedly respond better to anti-EGFR therapy (cetuximab) compared to patients with codon 12 mutations (De Roock et al., 2010; Tural et al., 2013). This aligns with findings that codon 13 mutations are associated with increased EGFR expression (Stolze et al., 2015). *KRAS-G12D*, *G12V*, *G13D*, and *K117N* mediate EGF-independent proliferation, whereas anchorage-independent growth is primarily induced by *K117N* and *Q61H* mutant *KRAS* (Stolze et al., 2015).

The *KRAS* gene is located on the short arm of chromosome 12 at position 12.1 (12p12.1) (Cox et al., 2014). It encodes KRAS4A and KRAS4B, which result from alternative splicing of the *KRAS* gene, with a 25 amino acid difference between the two isoforms. Protein interaction preference between the two isoform can vary, for example, v-ATPase a2 and eIF2Bδ interact only with KRAS4B (Zhang et al., 2018), whereas KRAS4A binds RAF-1 (Rapidly accelerated fibrosarcoma) more strongly and is more effective in promoting ERK (Extracellular signal-Regulated protein Kinase) phosphorylation and anchorage-independent growth than *KRAS4B* (Zhang et al., 2018).

There are numerous research and review articles that focus on each individual aspect of the structure, signaling and function of the KRAS and other *RAS* genes. In this chapter, while we briefly review the Ras family, the key focus is on the role of KRAS in oncogenesis where a clinically effective treatment remains elusive despite extensive research.

13.2 RAS superfamily: Highly conserved structure and function

RAS proteins are regarded as part of the superfamily of Ras-related small GTPases that contribute to many aspects of fundamental cellular processes (Wennerberg et al., 2005).

The Ras superfamily of genes consists of over 150 genes that roughly constitute five major families, which are functionally and structurally similar (Fig. 13.1).

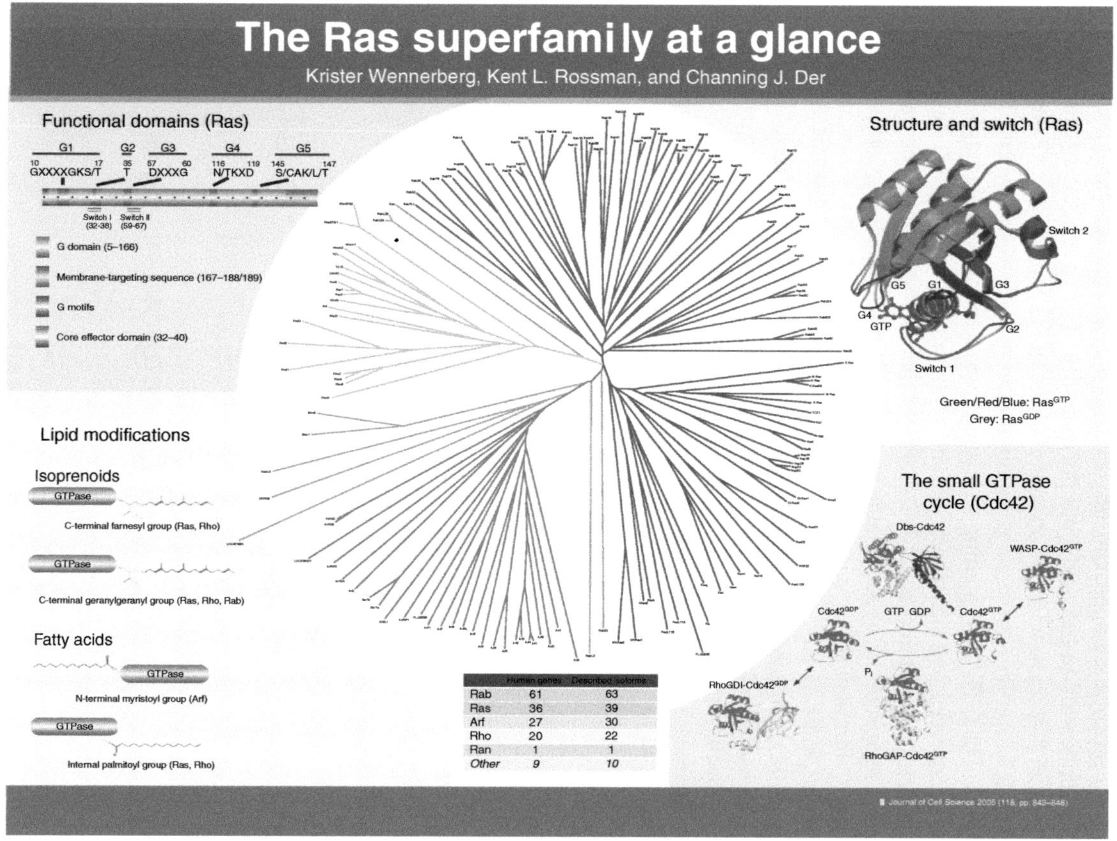

FIG. 13.1 The Ras superfamily: structural, functional, lipid modifications and the GTPase cycle. *(Reproduced with permission from Wennerberg, K., Rossman, K.L., Der, C.J., 2005. The Ras superfamily at a glance. J. Cell Sci. 118, 843–846.)*

These families include: Ras, Ran, Rab, Rho, and Arf/Sar (Rojas et al., 2012). They share high sequence homology (>50%) and common features.

13.2.1 Structure

The RAS proteins are approximately 21 kDa in molecular mass and consist of equal numbers of amino acids and polypeptides. The structure consists of α-helices and β-strands, with two structural domains (G and C) (Fig. 13.2).

The RAS protein structure is highly conserved (~90%) between different isoforms. The GTP/GDP binding sites and the effector protein binding sites are highly conserved and occur near the amino terminal consisting of the 1–166 amino acids. The amino acids 167–188/189 that are adjacent to the carboxyl terminal represent the hypervariable region, with <20% homology. The hypervariable C-terminal region ends in a highly conserved CAAX (C for cysteine, A for any aliphatic moiety, X for an uncharged amino acid) motif that serves as the recognition sequence for farnesyltransferase (Hancock et al., 1990).

RAS itself is a 21-kDa monomeric G-protein that is localized to the cytosolic side of the plasma membrane. Occasionally, it may also be located on other cellular organelle membranes such as the Golgi bodies or endosomal membranes. It is tethered to membranes by lipid moieties attached to the carboxyl terminal. Following cytoplasmic synthesis, RAS isoforms undergo posttranslational

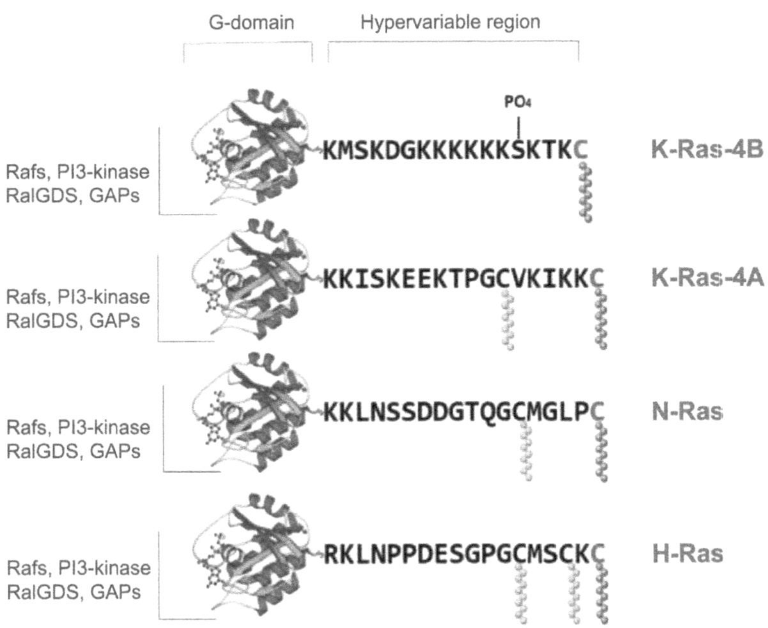

FIG. 13.2 Schematic representation of the Ras isoforms. *(Reproduced with permission from Stephen, A.G., Esposito, D., Bagni, R.K., McCormick, F., 2014. Dragging Ras back in the ring. Cancer Cell 25, 272–281. Copyright 2014 Elsevier.)*

modifications whereby the cysteine in the C-terminal CAAX motif is prenylated by farnesyltransferases. This is followed by removal of the AAX portion by RAS-converting enzyme 1. Then the exposed carboxyl group is methylated by the isoprenylcysteine carboxyl methyltransferase (ICMT). KRAS then uses the farnesylated cysteine and the hexa-lysine polybasic domain for membrane tethering (Sogabe et al., 2017). H-RAS and N-RAS undergo palmitoylation at cysteine 184 and 181, respectively (Sogabe et al., 2017).

Posttranslational modifications, necessary for biochemical function of RAS proteins, are the required steps for membrane binding and triggering differentiation and transformation. RAS proteins differ in the posttranslational modifications after prenylation. Prenylation is the insertion of farnesyl isoprenoid at the C-terminal of CAAX motif facilitated by farnesyl protein transferase (FPT). While H-RAS and NRAS undergo further lipidation by palmitoylation, KRAS proteins possess a polybasic domain that can be reversibly phosphorylated. Palmitoylation of HRAS and NRAS improves the association of these proteins to plasma membranes and triggers differentiation and translation. Affinity to FPT is another difference present in the RAS proteins posttranslational processing. When treated with FPT inhibitors, it has been shown that KRAS and NRAS can be alternatively geranylgeranylated in vitro and KRAS undergoes both geranylgeranylated and farnesylated in vivo (Lerner et al., 1997; Rowell et al., 1997; Sogabe et al., 2017; Whyte et al., 1997). Consequently, the inhibition of oncogenic KRAS can be achieved by inhibiting both enzymes, farnesyl- and geranylgeranyl transferases (Sun et al., 1998). With HRAS, farnesylation is not a necessary step for palmitoylation and hence can support differentiation and transformation in addition to membrane binding (Booden et al., 1999).

13.2.2 Function

RAS is also a proto-oncogene, involved in cellular signaling that controls proliferation, differentiation, and apoptosis. The key feature of these members is that they are small guanosine triposphatases (GTPases), and act as binary (ON/OFF) switches. These proteins are all regulated in the same manner by two sets of regulatory proteins: the guanosine nucleotide exchange factors (GEFs) and GTPase-activating proteins (GAPs). The GEFs promote the formation of GTP-bound active (ON) form, whereas the GAPs favor the formation of the GDP-bound inactive (OFF) form. Unlike the RAS proteins, the GEFs and GAPs are large, multiple-domain proteins, with molecular weights of 150–300 kDa. They control the RAS protein cycling between the ON and OFF positions through interactions with a host of other proteins, lipids, and regulatory molecules, but require proximal positioning through translocation of the effector proteins to the cell surface (Simanshu et al., 2017). This initiates the signaling downstream cascade.

Conformationally, the ON and OFF forms differ only in the high affinity effector binding switch regions: switch 1 (residues 30–38) and switch 2 (residues 59–67).

Following binding to GDP or GTP, the conformational changes are detected by the effector and regulatory proteins that then trigger the signaling processes by activating a specific set of downstream events (Wennerberg et al., 2005). Despite their small structure, the RAS proteins are able to modulate a wide array of signaling and cellular processes due to a combinatorial set of interactions with different effector proteins, posttranslational modifications that determine their cellular location and polymerization, as well as interactions with regulator proteins (Fig. 13.1). This allows for a very large and complex set of downstream cell-signaling events, and the ability to control a wide set of cellular functions involving cell growth, proliferation, and apoptosis.

As small GTPases, RAS proteins activate in response to various extracellular stimuli ultimately regulating numerous signaling cascades in many cellular processes (Rajalingam et al., 2007). Intrinsically, these GTPases have high affinity for binding to GDP and GTP, but the GTP hydrolysis capability is low. Under normal conditions, RAS can switch in a binary way from the inactive (GDP-bound) form to active (GTP-bound) form and revert to the inactive form. The off-rate of GDP is slow ($T_{1/2}=6\,\text{min}$; koff$=2\times10^{-3}$/s at 20°C) (Simanshu et al., 2017).

RAS binds to GTP and GDP with high affinity; dissociation constants are in the picomolar range. The common oncogenic mutations at positions 12, 13, and 61 occur near the nucleotide binding site. It is hypothesized that the nucleotide exchange rates may determine signaling behaviors; however, for mutants other than G13D, the nucleotide exchange kinetics are similar for wild-type and mutant RAS. The GDP exchange rate for G13D is 14 times faster than wild type, and GTP exchange rate is nine times faster for mutants (Hunter et al., 2015).

The wild-type RAS is complex and has been reported to function both as a tumor suppressor and as a tumor promoter. The functionality seems to be dependent on the interaction with mutant KRAS as well as mutant NRAS or HRAS, where sometimes it acts paradoxically. The activity of wild-type RAS is further determined by the loss of negative RAS regulators or by the amplification or overexpression of positive regulatory elements such as GEFs, which activate the tumorigenic function of wild-type KRAS (Zhou et al., 2016).

During mitogenic stimulation, rapid and transient GDP/GTP cycling occurs (within minutes or less), which is several orders of magnitude faster than the intrinsic GTPase and GDP/GTP exchange activities (in the order of 1 h or more) possessed by RAS proteins (Bos et al., 2007). To achieve the rapid cycling rate, the GTpase activating proteins (GAPs) and guanine exchange factors (GEFs) play a pivotal role. The binding of GAPs to RAS-GTP complex facilitates fast hydrolysis by creating an active site for GTP hydrolysis. GEFs on the other hand act as positive regulators promoting guanine nucleotide exchange. GAPs and GEFs are multidomain proteins in turn regulated by extracellular and localized signals that control cellular events. These proteins act as potential therapeutic targets.

With defects, the RAS protein becomes primarily locked into the active form. As RAS proteins control signaling pathways that include proliferation and differentiation, these defects lead to malignant cell transformation. Three *RAS* genes are the most common oncogenes in human cancer: Kirsten rat sarcoma 2 viral homolog (*KRAS*), *NRAS*, and Harvey rat sarcoma (*HRAS*).

13.2.3 Signaling

The RAS signaling pathway is complex (Fig. 13.3). The structural conformation of KRAS, and therefore its biological activity, is governed by its nucleotide binding state. The GDP-bound KRAS is the inactive state and GTP-bound KRAS is the active state. The ratio of KRAS•GDP to KRAS•GTP is controlled by the relative rates of exchange and hydrolysis and the oncogenic activity of mutant KRAS results from an increase in the rate of intrinsic nucleotide dissociation and/or a decrease in the rate of intrinsic or GAP-induced hydrolysis (Haigis, 2017). In cancer, the cyclic process is disrupted and KRAS stays in the GTP-bound active state. This disrupts the cellular signaling pathways establishing homeostasis. Instead, cell division and proliferation continue unchecked.

Members of the Ras sub family are GTPase and participate in many signal transduction pathways. RAS proteins are posttranslationally modified by a process called prenylation. This modification, besides facilitating membrane targeting, also has important consequence for protein-protein interaction. Prenylation-dependent interactions of RAS proteins with protein acceptors in cytoplasmic membranes and guanine nucleotide exchange factors are well documented (Ahearn et al., 2018; Chen et al., 2000; Okada et al., 1996). This modification appears to be essential for activation but not for transformation, due to alternative plasma membrane targeting (Hart and Donoghue, 1997).

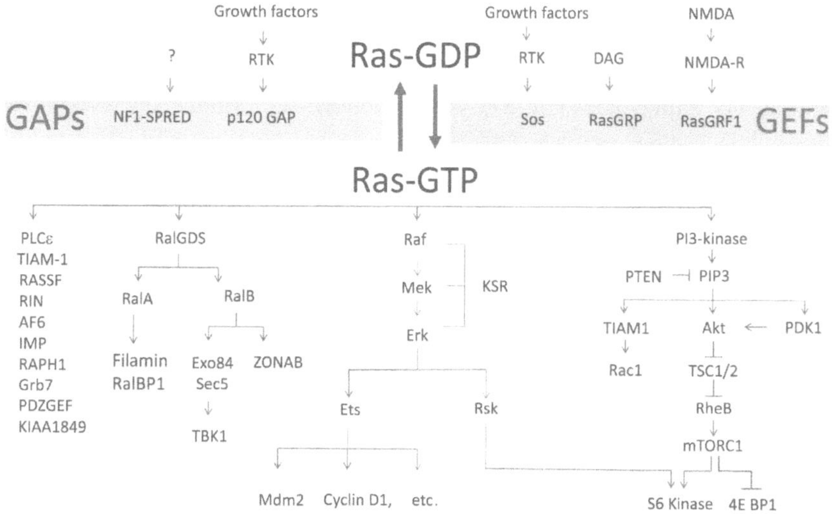

FIG. 13.3 Simplified view of the Ras pathway. *(Reproduced with permission from Stephen, A.G., Esposito, D., Bagni, R.K., McCormick, F., 2014. Dragging Ras back in the ring. Cancer Cell 25, 272–281. Copyright 2014 Elsevier.)*

Upon activation by kinases such as tyrosine kinase, the inactive GDP-bound RAS acquires a phosphate and is converted to active GTP-bound conformationally different form that is available to interact with effector proteins through RAS binding domain (RBD). The active form binds to effector proteins at the RAS binding domain. These in turn activate one or many downstream signaling pathways. The three major pathways include the Raf/MAPK (Rapidly Accelerated Fibrosarcoma/Mitogen Activated Protein Kinase) pathway, the tissue-dependent activation of the phosphatidylinositol 3-kinase (PI3K) pathway, and the less fully characterized Ral guanine nucleotide dissociation stimulator (RalGDS) pathway (Fig. 13.3) (Ferrer et al., 2018).

13.2.4 KRAS activation and role of effectors

RAS proteins affect numerous phenotypes despite a highly conserved structure. This is thought to occur through interactions of RAS proteins with a diverse set of effector proteins, resulting in a large set of combinations that affect a wide range of cellular functions from unmitigated cell proliferation, genomic instability, changes in metabolism and motility, to loss of contact inhibition. The built-in redundancies and compensatory activation, as well as differential effects depending on cell cycle state, pose challenges to robust investigation and targeting of these RAS-effector interactions.

Following GTP binding, RAS proteins undergo a conformational change to allow binding of the active state to effector proteins (Nakhaeizadeh et al., 2016). These interactions are mediated through the RBD. Five distinct regions (R1–R5) have been identified, with R1 playing a key role in effector interactions. The R1 domain, located in the middle of the KRAS protein adopts an antiparallel β-sheet configuration to facilitate intermolecular main-chain-main-chain interactions involving hydrogen bonds between the N-H group and the carbonyl oxygen. The amino acids Glu-37, Asp-38, and Ser-39 form the key recognition sites in R1. The RAS-effector protein interactions are potentially stabilized by the side chains on either side of the complexes via long range interactions, electrostatic steering, and/or allosteric modulation. The K_d values for RAS-RAF/MAPK interactions range from 0.048 to 0.142 μM.

Cellular lineage, secondary mutations, and energy states appear to dictate which KRAS-effector interactions will be preferred among many possible choices (Yuan et al., 2018). Yuan et al. have shown that most mutant cancers stratify into KRAS-addicted cancers, and non-KRAS-addicted cancers (RSK). The KRAS-addicted cancers bind to a few effectors and try to maximize the activation of the RAF-MAPK pathway, thereby maintaining the epithelial phenotype and driving glycolysis. The RSK subtype modulates signaling through activation of the mTOR pathway, maintains the mesenchymal phenotype, and drives flux through oxidative phosphorylation. The RAL subtype is dependent on RAL and PI3K signaling.

Various mutations appear to show preference for specific effector interactions. For example, G12C-mutated KRAS preferentially binds to RalGDS, while

G12D-mutated KRAS binds to PI3K over RalGDS. Similarly, in nonsmall cell lung cancer (NSCLC) cell lines, G12D-mutant KRAS activates PI3K and MEK signaling while G12C- or G12V-mutated KRAS activates Ral and AKT signaling (Roberts and Stinchcombe, 2013).

The heterogeneity of effector interactions suggests that not all *KRAS* mutations have similar effects in all tissues (Yuan et al., 2018). In pancreatic cancer, *KRAS* mutations appear to be the initiators as well as drivers of disease progression. In lung adenocarcinoma, *KRAS* mutations function as initiators, but additional mutations in tumor suppressor genes may result in oncogene addiction switch in response to microenvironments. In colon cancer, while KRAS mutations are prevalent and coexist with other mutations, they do not appear to be involved in tumor initiation; the initiating event appears to be beta catenin signaling.

13.2.5 Oligomers

RAS proteins may occur as monomers, dimers (about 56%), or oligomers (about 44%), forming nanoclusters with or without being bound to guanosine di- or tri-phosphate. These nanoclusters have been observed using electron microscopy and other visualization techniques and are thought to play a key role in signaling through RAS proteins. Nussinov et al. (2019) have hypothesized that mutant Ras clusters form at the membrane, and these nanoclusters are essential for dimerization of the kinase domains and subsequent signaling mediated by the Raf-MEK1/2-ERK1/2 oncogenic MAPK pathways leading to cell proliferation. The presence of wild-type KRAS dilutes the nanoclusters thereby attenuating the signaling by the oncogenic mutant KRAS. The PI3Kα/Akt pathway is not dependent on RAS nanoclustering; instead it is activated by the calcium-dependent calmodulin (Nussinov et al., 2015). In adenocarcinomas, which have a calcium-rich environment and abundant KRAS4B, Ca^{2+}-bound calmodulin forms a complex with KRAS4B, fully activating PI3Kα, which is not achieved by mutant KRAS4B alone. The calmodulin/KRAS4B/PI3K complex then initiates phosphorylation and activates Akt initiating signaling leading to mTORC1-dependent cell proliferation and migration. Calmodulin has the opposite effect on the MEK-ERK signaling pathway. Thus, it appears that calmodulin selectively activates the PI3Kα/Akt pathway, which plays a key role in cell growth and cell proliferation.

13.3 Role in disease and mutations

13.3.1 Role in disease

RAS genes are ubiquitously expressed in all tissues and mutations are associated with resistance to therapy, poor prognosis, and mortality. Despite being one of the first oncogenes to be discovered, there are no approved therapies that directly target the *KRAS* oncogene. Mutations in *RAS* genes are implicated in more than 30 types of cancers in humans. In general, *KRAS* is the most frequently mutated gene in cancer, followed by *NRAS* and then *HRAS* (NIH, 2019). The rate of *RAS* gene mutations in human cancers are in pancreas (*KRAS*—95%), colorectal (*KRAS*—45%), lung (*KRAS*—45%), acute myeloid leukemia (*NRAS*—15%), melanoma (*NRAS*—15%), and bladder (*HRAS*—10%) (NCI, 2016). *KRAS* mutations alone can be seen in the top three causes of death in the United States (lung, colorectal, and pancreatic cancer) (Waters and Der, 2018).

It is unclear whether *RAS*-transformed cells are dependent on the RAS pathway and/or require cooperating oncogenes and/or loss of tumor suppressors. Studies using temperature-sensitive *RAS* mutants or neutralizing antibody injections demonstrated a dependence on the continued presence of RAS (Stephen et al., 2014). The efficacy of tyrosine kinase inhibitors further supported the dependence on cooperating oncogenes (McCormick, 2015). The lack of efficacy seen with farnesyl transferase inhibitors (FTI) that were meant to inhibit the RAS membrane association highlighted the importance of alternative lipid modification pathways that were available to RAS thereby rendering the FTIs useless (Cox et al., 2015). A wide range of cell lines derived from tumors expressing oncogenic *KRAS* have been found to be dependent on KRAS for survival in both 2D and 3D cultures or in vivo (Singh et al., 2009; Zhang et al., 2006). While these studies have supported the concept that *Ras*-transformed cells that are dependent on the RAS pathway to varying degrees, the elusiveness of a drug therapy might suggest an incomplete understanding of a complex mechanism through which RAS proteins contribute to oncogenesis.

In addition to cancer, RAS has been implicated in a group of inherited disorders, collectively referred to as RASopathies. These are the most common genetic defects and affect >1 in 1000 individuals, representing one of the most prevalent groups of malformation syndromes (Tidyman and Rauen, 2016). The RASopathies include Noonan syndrome (NS) affecting 1 in 1000–2000 newborns, Costello syndrome (CS), Cardiofaciocutaneous (CFC) syndrome, and Neurofibromatosis type 1 (NF1) (Rauen, 2013). They originate due to mutations in the genes or regulators encoding the RAS/MAPK pathway that is responsible for essential cellular functions from growth and development to differentiation and eventual senescence. These mutations have profound and detrimental effects on the embryonic and later developmental stages imparting characteristic overlapping multiorgan phenotypic defects impacting cardiac, neurologic, musculoskeletal, cutaneous, ocular, and gastrointestinal functions as well as growth and developmental delays and distinct facial features. Although distinct from cancer mutations, which tend to be somatic, therapies targeting cancers might also be beneficial to patients with RASopathies.

13.3.2 Mutations

RAS mutations occur at high frequency in all human cancers, occurring in about 30% of all human cancers. Cancers harboring *RAS* mutations have been shown to be intractable to standard chemotherapeutic agents, and the overall survival outcomes of patients with *KRAS* mutations are poor compared to those with wild-type *KRAS*. Oncogenic mutations alter the RAS structure preventing the business end of RAS-GTP complex from triggering GTP hydrolysis. This results in accumulation of RAS-GTP complex, which leads to the persistent ON state of RAS. Overwhelming majority of available data, from biochemical to cellular to clinical/epidemiological, pertain to *KRAS* compared to *NRAS* or *HRAS* (Haigis, 2017) due to its unique role and considerably higher mutation frequency in human cancer compared to *HRAS* and *NRAS*. Additionally, the *KRAS* gene encodes two distinct splice variant proteins (*KRAS4A* and *KRAS4B*). Potential differences between specific mutations influence the activated oncoproteins (Simanshu et al., 2017; Cox and Der, 2010). In 98% of cases, *KRAS* mutations represent single nucleotide substitutions at glycine-12 (G12), glycine-13 (G13), or glutamine-61 (Q61), resulting in missense mutations that preferentially trap the KRAS protein in the GTP-bound active conformation resulting in mitogenic activation of cells (Waters and Der, 2018).

The oncogenic activity of KRAS mutants is not solely determined by the core biochemical properties, namely hydrolysis and exchange. Besides the nucleotide binding state, which is affected by mutations, the oncogenic activity is also a function of interaction with downstream effectors. The affinity to downstream effectors (e.g., RAF) differs between mutants as well as the wild-type (Hunter et al., 2015). To link the biochemical activity and subtype frequency in human tumors, a useful correlation termed as the in vitro biochemical activation score that accounts for GTPase activity and effector binding in cancers has been proposed (Haigis, 2017). The biochemical activation score predicts the frequency of subtype frequency in primary human tumors.

Haigis provides an alternative conceptualization to the molecular switch representation of KRAS protein function that accounts for the relationships between oncogenic activity, biochemical properties, and interaction with downstream effectors (Haigis, 2017). He postulates that given the population of wild-type *KRAS* and the different mutations at the population level, there is no strict ON or OFF state. Instead, he compares the phenomenon to a dimmer switch, the infinite quantitative levels of functional activation in the dial arise from the graded level of GTPase binding states and various effector affinities of KRAS mutational subtypes. This implies that human cancers with different mutational subtypes may have different KRAS activation states. Also, what may not be known is the accumulation effect of "weak" subtypes on KRAS activation states. Whether biochemical profiling and identification of different mutational subtypes will lead to rational selection of therapies against KRAS-driven tumors remains to be seen.

The most common KRAS-activating mutations cluster around the nucleotide binding pocket at codons 12, 13, 61, 117, and 146 (Hobbs et al., 2016). G12 and G13 are located on the P-loop, which is necessary to stabilize the nucleotide in the active site, but they give rise to different effects on the biochemistry of

KRAS. Q61 is located at the N-terminus of switch II. These activating mutations alter the action of the on-off switch either by reducing GTP hydrolysis or by increasing the rate of GTP loading. The hallmark of most codon 12 mutants is that both intrinsic and GAP-induced hydrolyses are affected while the rate of nucleotide exchange remains unchanged. On the other hand, codon 13 mutants affect hydrolysis and also increase intrinsic exchange by approximately 10-fold (Hunter et al., 2015; Smith et al., 2013). Activating mutation at codon 61 participates in the conformational changes at the N-terminus of switch II during the interconversion between structural states. Among all *KRAS* alleles, Q61 mutants have the lowest hydrolysis rates and it is hypothesized that Q61 helps to coordinate and stabilize the transition state of the hydrolysis reaction (Donovan et al., 2002; Hunter et al., 2015). In comparison to other mutants, *KRAS* G13D shows rapid nucleotide exchange kinetics (Hunter et al., 2015).

RAS mutations appear to be organ specific. About 94.1% of pancreatic cancers harbor KRAS mutations; this percentage increases to almost 100% in pancreatic ductal adenocarcinomas (Waters and Der, 2018), with high rates of KRAS mutations also found in adenocarcinomas of lung and CRCs. Squamous cell carcinomas appear to have a lower rate of KRAS mutations (Table 13.1). NRAS mutations are found in cutaneous melanomas and acute myelogenous leukemia, with HRAS mutations predominating in bladder and head and neck squamous cell carcinomas.

In cancers, a single point mutation in KRAS disrupts the signaling pathway resulting in a loss of GTPase activity. The mutations at G13 and Q61 positions trap the protein in the active, GTP-bound state thereby making it oncogenic. Among the point mutations, codon 12 mutations are most common comprising 89% followed by G13 mutations in 9% while the remaining 1% are Q61 (Prior et al., 2012). The likelihood of different point mutation changes at the codon 12 location is dependent on cancer type (Zehir et al., 2017). Of the G12 mutations the most frequently mutated site is the G12D (36%) followed by G12V (23%) and G12C (14%) (Tsuchida et al., 2016). In the Catalogue of Somatic Mutations in Cancer (COSMIC), the highest frequency KRAS mutations are located at the G12, G13, and Q61 amino acids, with the largest number of mutations occurring in the large intestine and lungs (Table 13.1) (Sanger Institute, 2019). When KRAS is mutated (at G12, G13, or Q61 positions), the rate of conversion of the GTP-bound (ON) state to the inactive GDP-bound state is disrupted, thereby trapping the RAS proteins in signaling states.

KRAS mutations appear to confer resistance to many therapies. For example, NSCLC patients with KRAS mutations treated with EGFR-specific tyrosine-kinase inhibitor drugs, gefitinib and erlotinib, had shorter time to progression and survival, whereas patients with wild-type KRAS had significantly better outcomes (Eberhard et al., 2005). Similarly, metastatic colorectal patients with mutated KRAS had significantly shorter overall survival when treated with cetuximab in combination with folic acid, fluorouracil, and irinotecan (Jean and Shah, 2008), and chronic myeloid leukemia (CML) patients with mutated

TABLE 13.1 The most common mutations and tissue distribution.

Rank (based on number of samples)	CDS mutation (nucleotide sequence position)	Mutation (amino acid)	Total number of unique mutated samples	Top 5 tissue distribution by mutation				
				Rank #1	Rank #2	Rank #3	Rank #4	Rank #5
1	35G>A	G12D	15,078	Large intestine (57%)	Pancreas (21%)	Lung (9%)	Biliary tract (3%)	Ovary (2%)
2	35G>T	G12V	10,321	Large intestine (54%)	Pancreas (21%)	Lung (15%)	Ovary (3%)	Biliary tract (2%)
3	38G>A	G13D	5601	Large intestine (82%)	Hematopoietic and lymphoid (4%)	Lung (4%)	Pancreas (2%)	Endometrium (1%)
4	34G>T	G12C	5116	Lung (50%)	Large intestine (39%)	Pancreas (4%)	Endometrium (1%)	Biliary tract (1%)
5	35G>C	G12A	2398	Large intestine (60%)	Lung (23%)	Pancreas (4%)	Endometrium (3%)	Hematopoietic and lymphoid (2%)
10	183A>C	Q61H	277	Large intestine (35%)	Pancreas (24%)	Hematopoietic and lymphoid (16%)	Lung (9%)	Biliary tract (4%)

Notes: Percentages are based on total number of unique mutated samples for a particular type of mutation.
Data from COSMIC database, (Accessed 3 February 2019).

RAS were shown to be resistant to the standard of care drug, imatinib mesylate (Agarwal et al., 2008). Thus, patients with KRAS are often excluded from treatment with many of the novel cancer therapies that have proven very effective in a wide range of cancers.

Somatic mutations have been identified in pancreatic, lung, and CRCs, whereas germline mutations have been discovered in diseases and disorders such as cardiofaciocutaneous syndrome, and related disorders including the Noonan syndrome and Costello syndrome (NIH, 2019).

13.3.2.1 Pancreatic cancer

The incidence of death caused by pancreatic cancer has been increasing. In the United States, in 2016, it was the third leading cause of death with a 5-year survival rate of only 8% (Siegel et al., 2016). By 2020, it is expected to become the second leading cause of cancer-related deaths (Rahib et al., 2014). Hence, there is urgency in developing cures for this highly lethal form of cancer. Pancreatic cancer has a high rate of *KRAS* mutations that in combination with mutations in *TP53*, *SMAD4*, and *CDKN2A* result in rapid progression, metastases, and a high rate of mortality.

G12D is most frequently mutated in pancreatic cancer (41%), followed by G12V (34%), and G12R (16%) (Waters and Der, 2018). The Q61H mutation occurs at a frequency of 3.9%, and the rest of the mutations account for 5% of pancreatic cancers. In pancreatic ductal adenocarcinoma (PDAC), the G12D subtype was identified as an independent prognostic marker in primary tumors and with chemotherapy-pretreated patients. This subtype is associated with lower probability of survival compared to the patients with G12V and more so with G12R mutation. G12D is the most common point mutation (Bournet et al., 2016).

The highly lethal pancreatic cancer has a high rate of KRAS mutations of approximately 74% in Caucasians and 64% in Asians (Tao et al., 2016), with almost 80% of KRAS mutations at codon 12. Patients with KRAS mutations are associated with poor overall survival irrespective of ethnicity. The wild-type KRAS appears to function as a tumor suppressor in PDAC, with loss of WT resulting in metastases (Qiu et al., 2011).

In pancreatic ductal adenocarcinoma (PDAC), which is the most common type of pancreatic cancer, the *KRAS* mutations are considered to be the initiating genetic event that transform normal pancreatic tissue to PDAC in a stepwise process over a 12-year period (Iacobuzio-Donahue et al., 2012), and are considered necessary to maintain the growth and metastases. During this period, normal pancreatic duct epithelium transforms into noninvasive pancreatic intraepithelial neoplasm (PanINs), where KRAS mutations are found at higher than 90% frequency (Kanda et al., 2012). The tumor initiation is followed by a loss of tumor suppressor function, facilitating the progression to unchecked cell growth and tumorigenesis. The G12D mutation is implicated in the formation of PanIN and onset of PDAC (Waters and Der, 2018).

13.3.2.2 Lung cancer

Lung cancer patients with *KRAS* mutations are likely to have worse survival outcomes. *KRAS* mutations are most prevalent in lung cancer patients, with higher prevalence in smokers (34%) than nonsmokers (6%) (Dogan et al., 2012). *KRAS* G12C mutation is the most prevalent mutation in lung adenocarcinomas, with a 39% prevalence of G12C, and 18% prevalence of both G12D and G12V mutations (El Osta et al., 2017). The G12C mutation is present at a much higher frequency in women, with a G→T transversion, whereas never smokers are more likely to have a *KRAS* G→A mutation. For instance, in nonsmall cell lung cancer (NSCLC), the G12C and G12V are the most frequent *KRAS* mutations associated with smoking-induced mutation.

In NSCLC, overall *KRAS* mutations are associated with shorter survival. Mutant *KRAS* G12C and mutant *KRAS* G12V compared with other mutant *KRAS* or *KRAS* wild-type are associated with a statistically significant decrease in progression-free survival and median progression-free survival (Ihle et al., 2012). Despite limited prognostic impact, it appears that resected stage I NSCLC patients with frequent G12V and G12C mutations do better than those with rarer codon 12 mutation (Izar et al., 2014). In late stage lung cancers, G12V late stage lung cancer patients have better response to platinum-based chemotherapy than do cancers expressing other KRAS subtypes (Cserepes et al., 2014). This G12V-selective sensitivity to cisplatin was validated in isogenic cells lines ectopically expressing different codon 12 alleles, indicating that it is an intrinsic property of G12V-mutant lung cancers (Garassino et al., 2011). In stage III–IV NSCLC, while KRAS mutation status per se is neither prognostic nor predictive, subtype-specific analysis to identify clinically relevant subgroups of patients is recommended, which ultimately may influence treatment decisions (Cserepes et al., 2014).

13.3.2.3 Colorectal cancer

In CRC, KRAS mutation rate is approximately 35%–40%, with majority of mutations at codon 12 (Tan and Du, 2012). The mortality rate for smokers is much higher for both genders than nonsmokers for overall CRC, with the risk of rectal and proximal colon cancer being higher in smoker males with CRC (Parajuli et al., 2014). However, for CRC patients with KRAS mutations, nonsmokers and smokers generally have similar outcomes, but differential effects are observed by anatomical site (Samadder et al., 2012).

In CRC, the overall KRAS mutation is predictive of inferior response, similar to NSCLC. Multiple investigators have explored the relationship of the different subtypes and treatment outcomes in multiple CRC populations (Andreyev et al., 2001; Jones et al., 2017; Margonis et al., 2015) (Imamura et al., 2012). These independent studies looking into large number of patients arrived at the conclusion that codon 12 is associated with worse survival. Among the codon 12 subtypes G12V is common to all the different populations such as postresection of colorectal liver metastases (Margonis et al., 2015), *BRAF*-wild-type CRC (Imamura et al., 2012), and other different CRC populations (Andreyev et al., 2001; Jones et al., 2017).

The importance of subtype variation in KRAS-implicated tumors appears to have clinical importance considering all the epidemiological and genetic or genomic variation data. These genomic and genetic data should however be employed as one aspect in the search for prognostic or predictive factors. Partly, the limitation comes from inherent variabilities in the studies these associations are derived from such as the confounding factors of cohort size, variations, and limitations in the experimental methods and the diversity of the biology of the disease itself. Interethnic variations in KRAS mutations have been reported (Table 13.2).

As noted earlier (Section 13.2.4), there are interactions between the functions of these mutational subtypes and downstream effector proteins. For instance, in PIK3CA-mutated CRC, the likelihood of KRAS mutant development is higher (Rosty et al., 2013) indicating the influence and/or dependence of one event over the other. However, in NSCLC, PIK3A and KRAS mutations rarely coexist, and PIK3A mutation is an independent factor for poor prognosis and treatment outcome (Wang et al., 2014).

13.3.2.4 Mutations in RASopathies

Of all the HRAS mutations that cause CS, mutations that occur at position 12 or 13 are the most prevalent with >80% of CS individuals having a p.G12S substitution, the second most common being p.G12A (Gibbs et al., 1984; Gremer et al., 2011; McGrath et al., 1984). These mutations ultimately result in increased effector activity including MAPK activity via the disruption of guanine nucleotide binding causing a reduction in intrinsic and GTPase-activating protein (GAP)-induced GTPase activity.

TABLE 13.2 Ethnic variation in key KRAS mutation-driven cancers.

Type of cancer	Ethnic variation	References
Pancreatic ductal adenocarcinoma	74% in Caucasians 64% in Asians	Tao et al. (2016)
Lung adenocarcinoma	Western 26.1% Asian 11.2%	Dearden et al. (2013)
Lung squamous cell carcinoma	Western 6.4% Asian 1.8%	
Colon cancer	Whites (86%) Nonwhites (14%)	Gonsalves et al. (2014) Sinicrope et al. (2015)

Germline KRAS mutations at amino acid positions K5, V14, Q22, P34, I36, T58, G60, V152, D153, and F156 cause remarkably broad phenotypic spectrum and comprise NS, CFC, and, more rarely, a phenotype consistent with CS (Gremer et al., 2011; Niihori et al., 2006; Schubbert et al., 2007). These mutations cause increased MAPK signaling through reduced intrinsic GTPase activity of Ras conferring decreased Ras inactivation compared to the wild type. Moreover, despite some germ-line mutants having normal GTPase activity cause GTPase activation independent of GEF binding (Schubbert et al., 2007).

NRAS mutations have been found to cause clinical phenotype of NS in some individuals, which occur at or near the switch II region of NRAS. It is believed that these mutations interfere with GTPase function that cause enhanced phosphorylation of downstream MAPK effectors (Tidyman and Rauen, 2016).

13.4 KRAS targeted drug development

Eventually, the objective of the exploration into RAS structure and function and the different mutations is to design treatment strategies for the multifaceted RAS-driven human tumors. Despite more than three decades of research, there has yet to be an effective RAS inhibitor to reach the patient (Waters and Der, 2018). Membrane association of RAS proteins through which these proteins exert downstream signaling has long been recognized as a required precondition for their biological activity (Jackson et al., 1990; Willumsen et al., 1984). Inhibition of the enzymatic process of lipid modification by a farnesyl isoprenoid which is a necessary step in this association was the first effort to develop anti-RAS drugs (reviewed by Berndt et al. (2011) and Tamanoi and Der (2013)). However, farnesyltransferase inhibitors showed disappointing results as anticancer drugs in the clinic which led to the misguided conception that blocking RAS membrane association was a flawed approach for cancer treatment (Cox et al., 2015). While this failure was wrongly attributed to RAS being a poor target, tumor regression has been demonstrated after ablation of KRAS from established tumors in mice (Collins et al., 2012). This suggests that KRAS may be a target that is at par with other oncogenes.

The two necessary conditions for targeting the Ras oncogene are: (i) the dependence of cancers on the expression of the oncogene and (ii) availability and accessibility of suitable pockets for small molecule drug binding. For KRAS specifically, one of the challenges with identifying compounds that bind directly to KRAS and block subsequent functions is that there are very few binding pockets that would be suitable for high affinity binding. The GDP/GTP binding pocket is not regarded as feasible due to the high affinity and specificity of the RAS-GTP binding, while the off rate is slow for the bound nucleotide. In addition, given the high cellular concentrations of GTP and GDP, a competitive inhibitor is difficult to develop. Furthermore, in normal cells, HRAS, KRAS, and NRAS may have overlapping effects so targeting KRAS alone may not be sufficient (McCormick, 2015). However, due to the key role that RAS plays, a drug that blocks all RAS isoforms (HRAS, NRAS, KRAS4A, and KRAS 4B) would likely be extremely toxic. Therefore, it is not clear whether a drug that targets KRAS needs to be specific for a mutant allele or whether targeting both mutant and wild-type KRAS is necessary. On the other hand, targeting specifically for the mutant allele is a logically sound approach. Due to the high mutation rate of KRAS in cancers, targeting KRAS mutations is a very active area of drug development. Current strategies broadly fall into the following six strategies (Papke and Der, 2017) (Ferrer et al., 2018):

(1) Direct targeting: Molecules that directly bind RAS disrupt its interaction with guanine nucleotide exchange factors or with effectors such as the RAF serine-threonine kinases.
(2) Targeting membrane-KRAS interactions: Proteins modulating RAS spatial organization and association with the plasma membrane (e.g., farnesyltransferase and PDEδ)
(3) Targeting RAS-effector signaling (e.g., RAF and PI3K)
(4) Synthetic lethal interactors of mutant RAS
(5) RAS-regulated metabolic processes in cancer cells
(6) Immunotherapy

13.4.1 Direct targeting of RAS

Direct targeting of KRAS has been challenging as KRAS is a small molecule with limited opportunities for conformational disruption. The two switch regions offer binding interfaces, where KRAS inhibitors could bind and potentially disrupt the downstream signaling, if mutant KRAS can be trapped in the GDP-bound inactive state. However, this approach is challenging as KRAS preferentially binds to GDP and GTP with extremely high (picomolar) affinity, and due to the high abundance (millimolar) of both GDP and GTP within the cell. Hunter et al. (2014) have postulated that targeting the guanine nucleotide (GN) in the switch regions represents the most promising approach for direct inhibition of KRAS as it would trap the protein conformationally in the inactive state. One of the more promising strategies appears to be to conformationally constrain the mutant KRAS in the inactive position by targeting the cysteine located at the G12. The approach employed by Ostrem et al. (2013) selectively targets the mutant KRAS 12C and has shown activity in cell lines. Another compound focuses on the KRAS guanine-nucleotide binding site as a selective, direct acting covalent inhibitor with in vitro assays confirming it renders the KRAS mutant inactive (Lim et al., 2014). Allele-specific KRAS inhibitors have been developed that trap the GDP-bound KRAS, making it unavailable for nucleotide cycling, and over time reducing the intracellular concentration of the active KRAS-GTP-bound form (Lito et al., 2016). Combining the small molecule with another drug (EGFR inhibitor such as erlotinib) that targets downstream signaling proteins or effectors may result in synergistic effects.

Similarly, inhibiting both KRAS and GEF stimulation may also provoke a synergistic response.

In 2012, several groups found molecules that were capable of interacting with KRAS4B but had poor affinity in vitro (Maurer et al., 2012; Shima et al., 2013; Sun et al., 2012). While these did not lead to clinical candidates, the successes demonstrated the potential for a direct inhibitor. For this strategy to be successful, the RAS-selective small molecules must bind with high affinity, target a face of KRAS4B that is essential for oncogenic function, and have the pharmacologic properties needed for clinical development (Papke and Der, 2017).

13.4.2 Targeting membrane-KRAS interactions

RAS proteins require membrane association to achieve biological activity making it a logical target for anti-RAS therapeutics. Farnesol modification was found to be essential for KRAS4B transformation (Jackson et al., 1990). As RAS isoforms are initially inactive proteins, a logical approach was to interfere with the membrane association and trafficking of RAS (Cox et al., 2015). This led to the natural pursuit of farnesyltransferase inhibitors (FTIs) being developed as potential drugs. Two inhibitors (lonafarnib and tipifarnib) were tested in cancers in KRAS mutations but showed no efficacy. This could be due to KRAS4B and NRAS isoforms being retained by the membrane despite FTIs, as the isoforms are modified by geranylgeranyl isoprenoid (Karnoub and Weinberg, 2008).

With this in mind, studies have now furthered the selectivity in regard to RAS isoform. Fendiline, an L-type calcium channel blocker, was found to inhibit KRAS plasma membrane localization and blocks KRAS signal transmission (van der Hoeven et al., 2013). Fendiline did not inhibit KRAS posttranslational processing but significantly reduced nanoclustering of KRAS and redistributed KRAS from the plasma membrane to the endoplasmic reticulum (ER), Golgi apparatus, endosomes, and cytosol (van der Hoeven et al., 2013). Fendiline was determined to block the proliferation of pancreatic, colon, lung, and endometrial cancer cell lines expressing oncogenic mutant KRAS.

A recently identified target is the prenyl-binding protein phosphodiesterase δ (PDEδ) that can be used to affect the spatial organization of KRAS as KRAS signaling is dependent on the level of enrichment on the plasma membrane (Schmick et al., 2014). PDEδ facilitates the transit of RAS proteins to the Golgi or recycling endosomes and then to the plasma membrane. Deltarasin has been identified as a compound that can inhibit KRAS-PDEδ interactions leading to impairment of cell growth and KRAS activity (Leung et al., 2018). This should overcome the concerns encountered with FTIs; however PDEδ's role in regulating other farnesylated proteins may result in unintended effects (Papke and Der, 2017).

13.4.3 Synthetic lethal interactions

Synthetic lethality occurs when the simultaneous perturbation of two genes or a gene and small molecule leads to cellular death (Nijman, 2011). This was realized by the interaction between BRCA defects and PARP inhibition. In the context of RAS, synthetic lethal interactions would depend on gene functions that are essential in mutant but not in wild-type Ras (Fig. 13.4).

One major approach is to use isogenic cell lines along with cancer cell lines with differing KRAS mutation status. This can be accomplished by deleting or adding the mutant KRAS allele from HCT116 colon cancer cells and immortalized cells, respectively (Hahn et al., 1999; Shirasawa et al., 1993). An alternative approach is to use a panel of cell lines with varying mutant KRAS and to seek genes which selectively kill mutant but not wild-type KRAS allele.

Several synthetic lethal interactors of mutant RAS have been identified such as STK33 and TBK1 (Papke and Der, 2017). Despite the search for synthetic lethal interactions spanning more than 10 years, there has yet to be any basis for optimism that this method will lead to a promising therapeutic approach in the clinic (Downward, 2015). To a certain extent, a portion of the difficulty experienced can be attributed to challenges in screening. This can range from the need to use a large number of cell lines to overcome noise from individual mutations (Boehm and Hahn, 2011) to siRNA-based screening technologies having problems with off-target effects (Jackson and Linsley, 2010).

While it is possible that a specific combination of tissue type and mutational background would render RAS-mutant tumors to be susceptible to synthetic lethal interactions, there is currently no universal RAS synthetic lethal target that is as effective as targeting RAS proteins directly (Downward, 2015).

13.4.4 Inhibiting RAS-regulated metabolic processes in cancer cells

Like other cancers, oncogenic RAS also exhibits the need for increased nutrient requirements. To date, studies have found oncogene KRAS to play a central role in controlling tumor metabolism including stimulation of glucose uptake, differential channeling of glucose intermediates, reprogrammed glutamine metabolism, and increased autophagy as well as micropinocytosis (Bryant et al., 2014).

RAS wild type	+	Gene X	→	Viable
RAS wild type	+	~~Gene X~~	→	Viable
RAS mutant	+	Gene X	→	Viable
RAS mutant	+	~~Gene X~~	→	Lethal

FIG. 13.4 Scheme demonstrating the basis of synthetic lethality with RAS mutation exploited in RAS synthetic lethal screens. *(Reproduced from Downward, J., 2015. RAS synthetic lethal screens revisited: still seeking the elusive prize? Clin. Cancer Res. 21, 1802–1809.)*

KRAS has been found to promote glucose intake by upregulation of the glucose transporter GLUT1. The result is an increase in glycolytic activity and increased pyruvate to lactate production (Gaglio et al., 2011) This leads to KRAS cell lines surviving in low glucose environments (Yun et al., 2009). Additionally, RAS also regulates enzymes that router glucose intermediates into nonoxidative pentose phosphate and hexosamine biosynthetic pathways (Papke and Der, 2017). For KRAS, this regulation is conducted through the RAF-MEK-ERK pathways and as such, ERK-MAPK pathway inhibitors may block the mutant KRAS.

Oncogenic Ras cells also can be noted for the increased dependence on glutamine which is required for the maintenance of mitochondrial membrane potential/integrity and for support of the NADPH production needed for redox control as well as macromolecular synthesis (Wise and Thompson, 2010). In terms of impact of treatment, inhibition of glutamine metabolism has been demonstrated to sensitize PDAC cells to radiotherapy (Li et al., 2015). The altered glutamine metabolism in oncogenic KRAS also makes it more dependent on transaminases leading to redox balance (Son et al., 2013). As such, therapy targeting KRAS-regulated metabolism may potentiate the effect of reactive oxygen species treatments such as chemotherapy or radiation (Choi and Park, 2018).

Autophagy is another method by which cancer cells can obtain the requisite macromolecules for cell proliferation by degrading unneeded or dysfunctional intracellular components. An assessment of samples from 71 different clinical studies with PDAC patients found that those that exhibited activated autophagy and a high LC3 protein expression (a key component of autophagy) had a poorer patient outcome (Fujii et al., 2008). However, the role of autophagy in cancer is complex, and with pancreatic cancers having a distinct dependence on autophagy, targeting this mechanism may be a viable therapeutic alternative. For this specific case, chloroquine, which is a relatively nonspecific inhibitor of autophagy, was found to impair PDAC growth in mice (Yang et al., 2011). With over 90% of pancreatic carcinomas containing mutations of the KRAS gene, inhibiting the autophagy process may prove to be an attractive target.

In macropinocytosis, the cell uses the plasma membrane to acquire nutrient-containing fluids. Similar to autophagy, KRAS-mutant PDAC cell lines and mouse models have found increased macropinocytotic activity (Maurer et al., 2012). Unlike autophagy, however, there are no clear pharmacologic inhibitors that selectively block micropinocytosis. 5-(*N*-ethyl-*N*-isopropyl) amiloride was found to inhibit this process and impact PDAC tumor formation in vivo (Papke and Der, 2017). While the increase in micropinocytosis activity can be associated with mutant RAS, the mechanism is still poorly understood.

13.4.5 Immunotherapy

The infusion of autologous T cells is emerging as a new approach to providing powerful therapy for cancer and chronic infections. This treatment method of transferring lymphocytes to mediate an effector function has named Adoptive cell transfer (ACT) (Billingham et al., 1954). A tumor-infiltrating lymphocyte

(TIL) is a type of immune cell that attacks the tumor after moving from blood. To treat cancer, TILs are removed from a patient's tumor and processed in vitro to better kill the cancer cells. This approach has been used via the infusion of CD8+ cells targeting mutant KRAS-mediated effective antitumor immunotherapy against a cancer that expressed mutant KRAS G12D and HLA-C*08:02 (Tran et al., 2016). In this single patient study, the final outcome after resection of a single progressing lesion (with other six indicated regression) was a clinically disease-free patient.

While there are now multiple clinical studies regarding ACT methods such as TIL and Chimeric Antigen Receptor T-cell (CAR-T), no therapies have been approved by regulatory agencies. However, the direct efficacious nature may prove promising in finding means to treat KRAS tumors which have otherwise been impossible thus far.

13.4.6 Recent advances in direct targeting of KRAS G12C

Several small molecules have been discovered, which target the KRAS G12C mutant protein by covalently binding and trapping it in the OFF state (Janes et al., 2018). In vitro and animal studies have shown promising results. Despite weak affinity, these small molecules slide into the shallow switch II binding pocket and are able to access the Cys12 and form a covalent bond, thereby trapping the mutant protein in the GDP-bound inactive form (Hansen et al., 2018). Amino amide substituted quinazoline KRAS G12C selective inhibitors have been discovered that also access the switch II pocket and covalently bind to Cys12 bonds (Fig. 13.5). For these molecules, the electrophilic acrylamide is important to imparting selectivity to the mutant KRAS. The key features of these molecules include spatial approach of electrophilic acrylamide to allow binding to Cys12, steric displacement of Met72 in the switch II binding pocket, hydrogen-bonding with Asp69 stabilizing the KRAS-inhibitor complex, and His95 interacting with amide substituents (Zeng et al., 2017). It remains to be seen if this approach will result in therapeutically active drugs.

13.5 Challenges in developing therapies to target KRAS

RAS genes are ubiquitously expressed in all tissues. With more than 30% of all human cancers are driven by mutations of the *RAS* genes, it is no surprise that there is intensive research to find drugs that can target the *RAS* gene, gene product, or signaling mechanisms controlled by *RAS* (NCI, 2016). The discovery of germline RAS mutations in a class of development syndromes (RASopathies) expand the possible scope beyond cancer (Tidyman and Rauen, 2009). Despite intense research over three decades, no molecules have been shown to be effective in treating KRAS-driven cancers. The ubiquity of the protein, the high affinity with which it binds to the GDP and GTP, the small size, presence of both wild-type and mutant KRAS, heterogeneity due to the presence of multiple

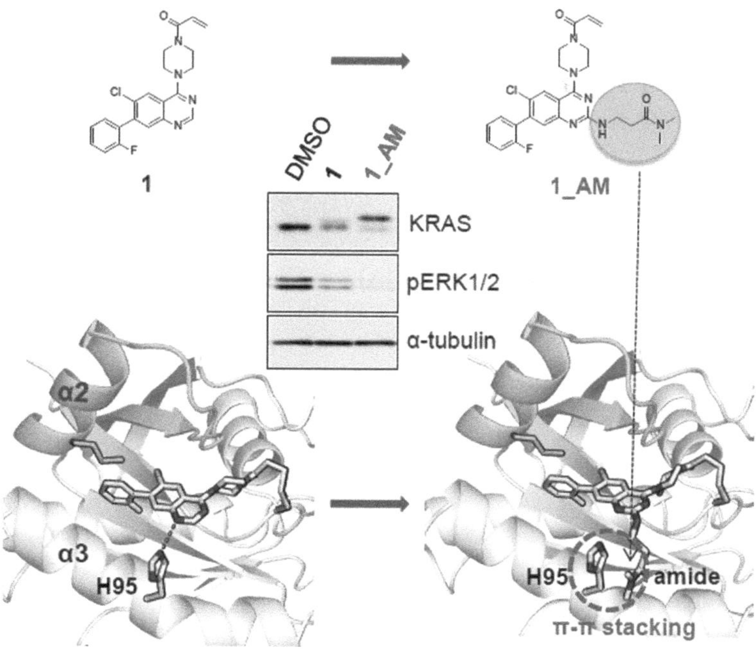

FIG. 13.5 Amino amide substituted quinazoline scaffold enhances binding to KRAS G12C. *(Reproduced with permission from Zeng, M., Lu, J., Li, L., Feru, F., Quan, C., Gero, T.W., et al., 2017. Potent and selective covalent quinazoline inhibitors of KRAS G12C. Cell Chem. Biol. 24, 1005–1016.e1003. Copyright 2017 Elsevier.)*

mutations, redundant and alternative pathways, and spontaneous mutations represent some of the challenges in targeting KRAS.

Significant advances have been made to understand the RAS gene structure, function, and its role in oncogenesis. However, there are numerous unknown and unanswered questions that are pivotal in developing targeted therapies. Mutant cells do not spontaneously result in oncogenesis; a second signal/trigger is needed. This raises the basic question of the dependence of cancers to the oncogene in that inhibition of KRAS may not be sufficient in arresting cancers. KRAS plays an integral role in cell signaling. Multiple mutations have been identified and these mutations are somatic. So, it is challenging to develop a common therapy for multiple mutations, will one drug work for all mutants? It appears that a diverse set of spontaneous mutations have been observed in KRAS and the potential biological difference between many KRAS activating mutations is not well appreciated. These unanswered questions pose challenges in developing drugs with optimal pharmacokinetic and pharmacodynamic properties to achieve sufficient exposure, the level of inhibition required for efficacy and at the same time have manageable safety profiles (what dose?).

The microenvironment appears to play an important role in tumorigenesis. Rescue mechanisms in cells are able to overcome inhibition of one pathway, and copresence of mutated and wild-type KRAS, and their interactions are not fully understood. Conceptually, targeting farnesyl transferases that catalyze the attachment of a C15 farnesyl isoprenoid lipid to the cysteine in the CAAX motif, thereby playing an integral role in RAS trafficking and consequent membrane association, represented a rational approach in targeting mutant KRAS by intercepting it prior to membrane association. However, the Phase 3 clinical failures of lonafarnib and tipifarnib farnesyl transferase inhibitors (Cox and Der, 1997; Cox et al., 2015) highlighted the lack of understanding of potential alternative prenylation pathway when the primary farnesyl transferase pathway was inhibited (James et al., 1995; Rowell et al., 1997; Whyte et al., 1997).

Besides playing a role in early tumorigenesis, RAS is critical for tumor maintenance. In this regard, efforts in the development of covalent small molecules that directly and selectively target G12C mutant for NSCLC have recently been underway rendering the G12C as a potentially druggable target. A series of Switch II pocket G12C KRAS inhibitors are able to covalently react with the GDP-bound state of KRAS, trapping it in the inactive confirmation. It has been shown that these compounds, besides effectively preventing the GTP loading of KRAS G12C, suppress MAPK phosphorylation and growth of G12C driven cancer cells in vitro and in vivo. Notwithstanding the promising results of direct targeting for patients with KRAS G12C-driven cancers, the clinical therapeutic potential is yet to be explored. Potency in cell lines and mouse models may not translate into humans for various reasons: KRAS is ubiquitous and targeting somatic cell mutations in various cancers, it is unknown how many mutant KRAS need to be inhibited for termination of tumor growth. It appears that near-complete KRAS engagement under constant exposure may be needed to achieve tumor growth inhibition in vivo (Janes et al., 2018). This may result in high drug doses that will pose significant challenges in optimizing the safety profile of such drugs as well as developing suitable formulation.

13.6 Conclusions

Several hypotheses have been advanced, but no fixed paradigm is established. Many mutations occur in RAS genes, but each mutation does not consistently lead to cancer. A variety of other factors may be necessary. The sweet spot hypothesis advanced by Li et al. (2018) challenges in developing covalent binding compounds that are thought to be reactive. In this regard, the recent advances in covalent inhibitors may result in new investigational drugs that will soon enter the clinic and may provide proof of concept, yet the eventual success to develop the drugs with benefits for patients remains to be seen. Although there has been extensive research in trying to understand the structure, function, and mutational status of KRAS, no drugs have been proven to be effective and it is unclear which approach will be most effective.

References

Agarwal, A., Eide, C.A., Harlow, A., Corbin, A.S., Mauro, M.J., Druker, B.J., et al., 2008. An activating KRAS mutation in imatinib-resistant chronic myeloid leukemia. Leukemia 22, 2269–2272.

Ahearn, I., Zhou, M., Philips, M.R., 2018. Posttranslational modifications of RAS proteins. Cold Spring Harb. Perspect. Med. 8. a031484.

Andreyev, H.J., Norman, A.R., Cunningham, D., Oates, J., Dix, B.R., Iacopetta, B.J., et al., 2001. Kirsten ras mutations in patients with colorectal cancer: the 'RASCAL II' study. Br. J. Cancer 85, 692–696.

Bamford, S., Dawson, E., Forbes, S., Clements, J., Pettett, R., Dogan, A., et al., 2004. The COSMIC (Catalogue of Somatic Mutations in Cancer) database and website. Br. J. Cancer 91, 355–358.

Berndt, N., Hamilton, A.D., Sebti, S.M., 2011. Targeting protein prenylation for cancer therapy. Nat. Rev. Cancer 11, 775–791.

Billingham, R.E., Brent, L., Medawar, P.B., 1954. Quantitative studies on tissue transplantation immunity. II. The origin, strength and duration of actively and adoptively acquired immunity. Proc. R. Soc. Lond. B Biol. Sci. 143, 58–80.

Boehm, J.S., Hahn, W.C., 2011. Towards systematic functional characterization of cancer genomes. Nat. Rev. Genet. 12, 487–498.

Booden, M.A., Baker, T.L., Solski, P.A., Der, C.J., Punke, S.G., Buss, J.E., 1999. A non-farnesylated Ha-Ras protein can be palmitoylated and trigger potent differentiation and transformation. J. Biol. Chem. 274, 1423–1431.

Bos, J.L., Rehmann, H., Wittinghofer, A., 2007. GEFs and GAPs: critical elements in the control of small G proteins. Cell 129, 865–877. https://doi.org/10.1016/j.cell.2007.05.018.

Bournet, B., Muscari, F., Buscail, C., Assenat, E., Barthet, M., Hammel, P., et al., 2016. KRAS G12D mutation subtype is a prognostic factor for advanced pancreatic adenocarcinoma. Clin. Transl. Gastroenterol. 7. e157.

Bryant, K.L., Mancias, J.D., Kimmelman, A.C., Der, C.J., 2014. KRAS: feeding pancreatic cancer proliferation. Trends Biochem. Sci. 39, 91–100.

Chang, E.H., Gonda, M.A., Ellis, R.W., Scolnick, E.M., Lowy, D.R., 1982. Human genome contains four genes homologous to transforming genes of Harvey and Kirsten murine sarcoma viruses. Proc. Natl. Acad. Sci. U. S. A. 79, 4848–4852.

Chen, R.A., Michaeli, T., Van Aelst, L., Ballester, R., 2000. A role for the noncatalytic N terminus in the function of Cdc25, a Saccharomyces cerevisiae Ras-guanine nucleotide exchange factor. Genetics 154, 1473–1484.

Choi, Y.-K., Park, K.-G., 2018. Targeting glutamine metabolism for cancer treatment. Biomol. Ther. 26, 19–28.

Collins, M.A., Brisset, J.C., Zhang, Y., Bednar, F., Pierre, J., Heist, K.A., et al., 2012. Metastatic pancreatic cancer is dependent on oncogenic Kras in mice. PLoS ONE 7. e49707.

Cox, A.D., Der, C.J., 1997. Farnesyltransferase inhibitors and cancer treatment: targeting simply Ras? Biochim. Biophys. Acta 1333, F51–F71.

Cox, A.D., Der, C.J., 2010. Ras history: the saga continues. Small GTPases 1, 2–27.

Cox, A.D., Fesik, S.W., Kimmelman, A.C., Luo, J., Der, C.J., 2014. Drugging the undruggable RAS: mission possible? Nat. Rev. Drug Discov. 13, 828–851.

Cox, A.D., Der, C.J., Philips, M.R., 2015. Targeting RAS membrane association: back to the future for anti-RAS drug discovery? Clin. Cancer Res. 21, 1819–1827.

Cserepes, M., Ostoros, G., Lohinai, Z., Raso, E., Barbai, T., Timar, J., et al., 2014. Subtype-specific KRAS mutations in advanced lung adenocarcinoma: a retrospective study of patients treated with platinum-based chemotherapy. Eur. J. Cancer 50, 1819–1828.

Dearden, S., Stevens, J., Wu, Y.L., Blowers, D., 2013. Mutation incidence and coincidence in non small-cell lung cancer: meta-analyses by ethnicity and histology (mutMap). Ann. Oncol. 24, 2371–2376. https://doi.org/10.1093/annonc/mdt205.

De Roock, W., Jonker, D.J., Di Nicolantonio, F., Sartore-Bianchi, A., Tu, D., Siena, S., et al., 2010. Association of KRAS p.G13D mutation with outcome in patients with chemotherapy-refractory metastatic colorectal cancer treated with cetuximab. JAMA 304, 1812–1820.

Dogan, S., Shen, R., Ang, D.C., Johnson, M.L., D'Angelo, S.P., Paik, P.K., et al., 2012. Molecular epidemiology of EGFR and KRAS mutations in 3,026 lung adenocarcinomas: higher susceptibility of women to smoking-related KRAS-mutant cancers. Clin. Cancer Res. 18, 6169–6177.

Donovan, S., Shannon, K.M., Bollag, G., 2002. GTPase activating proteins: critical regulators of intracellular signaling. Biochim. Biophys. Acta 1602, 23–45.

Downward, J., 2015. RAS synthetic lethal screens revisited: still seeking the elusive prize? Clin. Cancer Res. 21, 1802–1809.

Eberhard, D.A., Johnson, B.E., Amler, L.C., Goddard, A.D., Heldens, S.L., Herbst, R.S., et al., 2005. Mutations in the epidermal growth factor receptor and in KRAS are predictive and prognostic indicators in patients with non-small-cell lung cancer treated with chemotherapy alone and in combination with erlotinib. J. Clin. Oncol. 23, 5900–5909.

El Osta, B.E., Behera, M., Kim, S., Berry, L.D., Sica, G., Pillai, R.N., et al., 2017. Characteristics and outcomes of patients (pts) with metastatic KRAS mutant lung adenocarcinomas: Lung Cancer Mutation Consortium (LCMC) database. J. Clin. Oncol. 35, 9021.

Ferrer, I., Zugazagoitia, J., Herbertz, S., John, W., Paz-Ares, L., Schmid-Bindert, G., 2018. KRAS-mutant non-small cell lung cancer: from biology to therapy. Lung Cancer 124, 53–64.

Fujii, S., Mitsunaga, S., Yamazaki, M., Hasebe, T., Ishii, G., Kojima, M., et al., 2008. Autophagy is activated in pancreatic cancer cells and correlates with poor patient outcome. Cancer Sci. 99, 1813–1819.

Gaglio, D., Metallo, C.M., Gameiro, P.A., Hiller, K., Danna, L.S., Balestrieri, C., et al., 2011. Oncogenic K-Ras decouples glucose and glutamine metabolism to support cancer cell growth. Mol. Syst. Biol. 7, 523.

Garassino, M.C., Marabese, M., Rusconi, P., Rulli, E., Martelli, O., Farina, G., et al., 2011. Different types of K-Ras mutations could affect drug sensitivity and tumour behaviour in non-small-cell lung cancer. Ann. Oncol. 22, 235–237.

Gibbs, J.B., Sigal, I.S., Poe, M., Scolnick, E.M., 1984. Intrinsic GTPase activity distinguishes normal and oncogenic ras p21 molecules. Proc. Natl. Acad. Sci. U. S. A. 81, 5704–5708.

Gonsalves, W.I., Mahoney, M.R., Sargent, D.J., Nelson, G.D., Alberts, S.R., Sinicrope, F.A., Goldberg, R.M., Limburg, P.J., Thibodeau, S.N., Grothey, A., Hubbard, J.M., Chan, E., Nair, S., Berenberg, J.L., McWilliams, R.R., 2014. Patient and tumor characteristics and BRAF and KRAS mutations in colon cancer, NCCTG/Alliance N0147. J. Natl. Cancer Inst. 106. https://doi.org/10.1093/jnci/dju106.

Gremer, L., Merbitz-Zahradnik, T., Dvorsky, R., Cirstea, I.C., Kratz, C.P., Zenker, M., et al., 2011. Germline KRAS mutations cause aberrant biochemical and physical properties leading to developmental disorders. Hum. Mutat. 32, 33–43.

Guerrero, S., Casanova, I., Farre, L., Mazo, A., Capella, G., Mangues, R., 2000. K-ras codon 12 mutation induces higher level of resistance to apoptosis and predisposition to anchorage-independent growth than codon 13 mutation or proto-oncogene overexpression. Cancer Res. 60, 6750–6756.

Hager, G.L., Chang, E.H., Chan, H.W., Garon, C.F., Israel, M.A., Martin, M.A., et al., 1979. Molecular cloning of the Harvey sarcoma virus closed circular DNA intermediates: initial structural and biological characterization. J. Virol. 31, 795–809.

Hahn, W.C., Counter, C.M., Lundberg, A.S., Beijersbergen, R.L., Brooks, M.W., Weinberg, R.A., 1999. Creation of human tumour cells with defined genetic elements. Nature 400, 464–468.

Haigis, K.M., 2017. KRAS alleles: the devil is in the detail. Trends Cancer 3, 686–697.

Hancock, J.F., Paterson, H., Marshall, C.J., 1990. A polybasic domain or palmitoylation is required in addition to the CAAX motif to localize p21ras to the plasma membrane. Cell 63, 133–139.

Hansen, R., Peters, U., Babbar, A., Chen, Y., Feng, J., Janes, M.R., et al., 2018. The reactivity-driven biochemical mechanism of covalent KRASG12C inhibitors. Nat. Struct. Mol. Biol. 25, 454–462.

Hart, K.C., Donoghue, D.J., 1997. Derivatives of activated H-ras lacking C-terminal lipid modifications retain transforming ability if targeted to the correct subcellular location. Oncogene 14, 945.

Harvey, J.J., 1964. An unidentified virus which causes the rapid production of tumours in mice. Nature 204, 1104–1105.

Hobbs, G.A., Der, C.J., Rossman, K.L., 2016. RAS isoforms and mutations in cancer at a glance. J. Cell Sci. 129, 1287–1292.

Hunter, J.C., Gurbani, D., Ficarro, S.B., Carrasco, M.A., Lim, S.M., Choi, H.G., et al., 2014. In situ selectivity profiling and crystal structure of SML-8-73-1, an active site inhibitor of oncogenic K-Ras G12C. Proc. Natl. Acad. Sci. U. S. A. 111, 8895–8900.

Hunter, J.C., Manandhar, A., Carrasco, M.A., Gurbani, D., Gondi, S., Westover, K.D., 2015. Biochemical and structural analysis of common cancer-associated KRAS mutations. Mol. Cancer Res. 13, 1325.

Iacobuzio-Donahue, C.A., Velculescu, V.E., Wolfgang, C.L., Hruban, R.H., 2012. Genetic basis of pancreas cancer development and progression: insights from whole-exome and whole-genome sequencing. Clin. Cancer Res. 18, 4257–4265.

Ihle, N.T., Byers, L.A., Kim, E.S., Saintigny, P., Lee, J.J., Blumenschein, G.R., Tsao, A., Liu, S., Larsen, J.E., Wang, J., Diao, L., Coombes, K.R., Chen, L., Zhang, S., Abdelmelek, M.F., Tang, X., Papadimitrakopoulou, V., Minna, J.D., Lippman, S.M., Hong, W.K., Herbst, R.S., Wistuba, I.I., Heymach, J.V., Powis, G., 2012. Effect of KRAS oncogene substitutions on protein behavior: implications for signaling and clinical outcome. J. Natl. Cancer Inst. 104, 228–239. https://doi.org/10.1093/jnci/djr523.

Imamura, Y., Morikawa, T., Liao, X., Lochhead, P., Kuchiba, A., Yamauchi, M., et al., 2012. Specific mutations in KRAS codons 12 and 13, and patient prognosis in 1075 BRAF wild-type colorectal cancers. Clin. Cancer Res. 18, 4753–4763.

Izar, B., Zhou, H., Heist, R.S., Azzoli, C.G., Muzikansky, A., Scribner, E.E.F., et al., 2014. The prognostic impact of KRAS, its codon and amino acid specific mutations, on survival in resected stage I lung adenocarcinoma. J. Thorac. Oncol. 9, 1363–1369.

Jackson, A.L., Linsley, P.S., 2010. Recognizing and avoiding siRNA off-target effects for target identification and therapeutic application. Nat. Rev. Drug Discov. 9, 57–67.

Jackson, J.H., Cochrane, C.G., Bourne, J.R., Solski, P.A., Buss, J.E., Der, C.J., 1990. Farnesol modification of Kirsten-ras exon 4B protein is essential for transformation. Proc. Natl. Acad. Sci. 87, 3042–3046.

James, G.L., Goldstein, J.L., Brown, M.S., 1995. Polylysine and CVIM sequences of K-RasB dictate specificity of prenylation and confer resistance to benzodiazepine peptidomimetic in vitro. J. Biol. Chem. 270, 6221–6226.

Janes, M.R., Zhang, J., Li, L.S., Hansen, R., Peters, U., Guo, X., et al., 2018. Targeting KRAS mutant cancers with a covalent G12C-specific inhibitor. Cell 172, 578–589. e517.

Jean, G.W., Shah, S.R., 2008. Epidermal growth factor receptor monoclonal antibodies for the treatment of metastatic colorectal cancer. Pharmacotherapy 28, 742–754.

Jones, R.P., Sutton, P.A., Evans, J.P., Clifford, R., McAvoy, A., Lewis, J., et al., 2017. Specific mutations in KRAS codon 12 are associated with worse overall survival in patients with advanced and recurrent colorectal cancer. Br. J. Cancer 116, 923–929.

Kanda, M., Matthaei, H., Wu, J., Hong, S.M., Yu, J., Borges, M., et al., 2012. Presence of somatic mutations in most early-stage pancreatic intraepithelial neoplasia. Gastroenterology 142, 730–733. e739.

Karnoub, A.E., Weinberg, R.A., 2008. Ras oncogenes: split personalities. Nat. Rev. Mol. Cell Biol. 9, 517–531.

Kirsten, W.H., Mayer, L.A., 1967. Morphologic responses to a murine erythroblastosis virus. J. Natl. Cancer Inst. 39, 311–335.

Kirsten, W.H., Platz, C.E., 1964. Early and late leukemias in rats after transplantation of leukemic cells from AKR mice. Cancer Res. 24, 1056–1062.

Lerner, E.C., Zhang, T.-T., Knowles, D.B., Qian, Y., Hamilton, A.D., Sebti, S.M., 1997. Inhibition of the prenylation of K-Ras, but not H- or N-Ras, is highly resistant to CAAX peptidomimetics and requires both a farnesyltransferase and a geranylgeranyltransferase I inhibitor in human tumor cell lines. Oncogene 15, 1283.

Leung, E.L.H., Luo, L.X., Liu, Z.Q., Wong, V.K.W., Lu, L.L., Xie, Y., et al., 2018. Inhibition of KRAS-dependent lung cancer cell growth by deltarasin: blockage of autophagy increases its cytotoxicity. Cell Death Dis. 9, 216.

Li, D., Fu, Z., Chen, R., Zhao, X., Zhou, Y., Zeng, B., et al., 2015. Inhibition of glutamine metabolism counteracts pancreatic cancer stem cell features and sensitizes cells to radiotherapy. Oncotarget 6, 31151–31163.

Li, S., Balmain, A., Counter, C.M., 2018. A model for RAS mutation patterns in cancers: finding the sweet spot. Nat. Rev. Cancer 18, 767–777.

Lim, S.M., Westover, K.D., Ficarro, S.B., Harrison, R.A., Choi, H.G., Pacold, M.E., et al., 2014. Therapeutic targeting of oncogenic K-Ras by a covalent catalytic site inhibitor. Angew. Chem. Int. Ed. Eng. 53, 199–204.

Lito, P., Solomon, M., Li, L.-S., Hansen, R., Rosen, N., 2016. Allele-specific inhibitors inactivate mutant KRAS G12C by a trapping mechanism. Science (New York, N.Y.) 351, 604–608.

Margonis, G.A., Kim, Y., Spolverato, G., Ejaz, A., Gupta, R., Cosgrove, D., et al., 2015. Association between specific mutations in KRAS codon 12 and colorectal liver metastasis. JAMA Surg. 150, 722–729.

Maurer, T., Garrenton, L.S., Oh, A., Pitts, K., Anderson, D.J., Skelton, N.J., et al., 2012. Small-molecule ligands bind to a distinct pocket in Ras and inhibit SOS-mediated nucleotide exchange activity. Proc. Natl. Acad. Sci. 109, 5299–5304.

McCormick, F., 2015. KRAS as a therapeutic target. Clin. Cancer Res. 21, 1797–1801.

McGrath, J.P., Capon, D.J., Goeddel, D.V., Levinson, A.D., 1984. Comparative biochemical properties of normal and activated human ras p21 protein. Nature 310, 644–649.

Nakhaeizadeh, H., Amin, E., Nakhaei-Rad, S., Dvorsky, R., Ahmadian, M.R., 2016. The RAS-effector interface: isoform-specific differences in the effector binding regions. PLoS ONE 11. e0167145.

NCI, 2016. Learn About the RAS Initiative. https://www.cancer.gov/research/key-initiatives/ras/about. (Accessed 23 January 2019).

NIH, 2019. KRAS Gene. https://ghr.nlm.nih.gov/gene/KRAS#conditions. (Accessed 25 January 2019).

Niihori, T., Aoki, Y., Narumi, Y., Neri, G., Cavé, H., Verloes, A., et al., 2006. Germline KRAS and BRAF mutations in cardio-facio-cutaneous syndrome. Nat. Genet. 38, 294.

Nijman, S.M.B., 2011. Synthetic lethality: general principles, utility and detection using genetic screens in human cells. FEBS Lett. 585, 1–6.

Nussinov, R., Muratcioglu, S., Tsai, C.J., Jang, H., Gursoy, A., Keskin, O., 2015. The key role of calmodulin in KRAS-driven adenocarcinomas. Mol. Cancer Res. 13, 1265–1273.

Nussinov, R., Tsai, C.J., Jang, H., 2019. Is Nanoclustering essential for all oncogenic KRas pathways? Can it explain why wild-type KRas can inhibit its oncogenic variant? Semin. Cancer Biol. 54, 114–120.

Okada, T., Masuda, T., Shinkai, M., Kariya, K.-i., Kataoka, T., 1996. Post-translational modification of H-Ras is required for activation of, but not for association with, B-Raf. J. Biol. Chem. 271, 4671–4678.

Ostrem, J.M., Peters, U., Sos, M.L., Wells, J.A., Shokat, K.M., 2013. K-Ras(G12C) inhibitors allosterically control GTP affinity and effector interactions. Nature 503, 548–551.

Papke, B., Der, C.J., 2017. Drugging RAS: know the enemy. Science (New York, N.Y.) 355, 1158–1163.

Parajuli, R., Bjerkaas, E., Tverdal, A., Le Marchand, L., Weiderpass, E., Gram, I.T., 2014. Cigarette smoking and colorectal cancer mortality among 602,242 Norwegian males and females. Clin. Epidemiol. 6, 137–145. https://doi.org/10.2147/clep.s58722.

Prior, I.A., Lewis, P.D., Mattos, C., 2012. A comprehensive survey of Ras mutations in cancer. Cancer Res. 72, 2457–2467.

Qiu, W., Sahin, F., Iacobuzio-Donahue, C.A., Garcia-Carracedo, D., Wang, W.M., Kuo, C.Y., et al., 2011. Disruption of p16 and activation of Kras in pancreas increase ductal adenocarcinoma formation and metastasis in vivo. Oncotarget 2, 862–873.

Rahib, L., Smith, B.D., Aizenberg, R., Rosenzweig, A.B., Fleshman, J.M., Matrisian, L.M., 2014. Projecting cancer incidence and deaths to 2030: the unexpected burden of thyroid, liver, and pancreas cancers in the United States. Cancer Res. 74, 2913–2921.

Rajalingam, K., Schreck, R., Rapp, U.R., Albert, Š., 2007. Ras oncogenes and their downstream targets. Biochim. Biophys. Acta 1773, 1177–1195.

Rauen, K.A., 2013. The RASopathies. Annu. Rev. Genomics Hum. Genet. 14, 355–369.

Roberts, P.J., Stinchcombe, T.E., 2013. KRAS mutation: should we test for it, and does it matter? J. Clin. Oncol. 31, 1112–1121.

Rojas, A.M., Fuentes, G., Rausell, A., Valencia, A., 2012. The Ras protein superfamily: evolutionary tree and role of conserved amino acids. J. Cell Biol. 196, 189–201.

Rosty, C., Young, J.P., Walsh, M.D., Clendenning, M., Sanderson, K., Walters, R.J., et al., 2013. PIK3CA activating mutation in colorectal carcinoma: associations with molecular features and survival. PLoS ONE 8, e65479.

Rowell, C.A., Kowalczyk, J.J., Lewis, M.D., Garcia, A.M., 1997. Direct demonstration of geranylgeranylation and farnesylation of Ki-Ras in vivo. J. Biol. Chem. 272, 14093–14097.

Samadder, N.J., Vierkant, R.A., Tillmans, L.S., Wang, A.H., Lynch, C.F., Anderson, K.E., et al., 2012. Cigarette smoking and colorectal cancer risk by KRAS mutation status among older women. Am. J. Gastroenterol. 107, 782–789.

Sanger Institute, 2019. Catalogue Of Somatic Mutations in Cancer: Gene KRAS. https://cancer.sanger.ac.uk/cosmic/gene/analysis?ln=KRAS#variants. (Accessed 3 February 2019).

Santos, E., Martin-Zanca, D., Reddy, E.P., Pierotti, M.A., Della Porta, G., Barbacid, M., 1984. Malignant activation of a K-ras oncogene in lung carcinoma but not in normal tissue of the same patient. Science (New York, N.Y.) 223, 661–664.

Schmick, M., Vartak, N., Papke, B., Kovacevic, M., Truxius, D.C., Rossmannek, L., et al., 2014. KRas localizes to the plasma membrane by spatial cycles of solubilization, trapping and vesicular transport. Cell 157, 459–471.

Schubbert, S., Bollag, G., Lyubynska, N., Nguyen, H., Kratz, C.P., Zenker, M., et al., 2007. Biochemical and functional characterization of germ line KRAS mutations. Mol. Cell. Biol. 27, 7765–7770.

Shima, F., Yoshikawa, Y., Ye, M., Araki, M., Matsumoto, S., Liao, J., et al., 2013. *In silico* discovery of small-molecule Ras inhibitors that display antitumor activity by blocking the Ras–effector interaction. Proc. Natl. Acad. Sci. 110, 8182–8187.

Shirasawa, S., Furuse, M., Yokoyama, N., Sasazuki, T., 1993. Altered growth of human colon cancer cell lines disrupted at activated Ki-ras. Science (New York, N.Y.) 260, 85–88.

Siegel, R.L., Miller, K.D., Jemal, A., 2016. Cancer statistics, 2016. CA Cancer J. Clin. 66, 7–30.

Simanshu, D.K., Nissley, D.V., McCormick, F., 2017. RAS proteins and their regulators in human disease. Cell 170, 17–33.

Singh, A., Greninger, P., Rhodes, D., Koopman, L., Violette, S., Bardeesy, N., et al., 2009. A gene expression signature associated with "K-Ras addiction" reveals regulators of EMT and tumor cell survival. Cancer Cell 15, 489–500.

Sinicrope, F.A., Shi, Q., Smyrk, T.C., Thibodeau, S.N., Dienstmann, R., Guinney, J., Bot, B.M., Tejpar, S., Delorenzi, M., Goldberg, R.M., Mahoney, M., Sargent, D.J., Alberts, S.R., 2015. Molecular markers identify subtypes of stage III colon cancer associated with patient outcomes. Gastroenterology 148, 88–99. https://doi.org/10.1053/j.gastro.2014.09.041.

Smith, M.J., Neel, B.G., Ikura, M., 2013. NMR-based functional profiling of RASopathies and oncogenic RAS mutations. Proc. Natl. Acad. Sci. U. S. A. 110, 4574–4579.

Sogabe, S., Kamada, Y., Miwa, M., Niida, A., Sameshima, T., Kamaura, M., et al., 2017. Crystal structure of a human K-Ras G12D mutant in complex with GDP and the cyclic inhibitory peptide KRpep-2d. ACS Med. Chem. Lett. 8, 732–736.

Son, J., Lyssiotis, C.A., Ying, H., Wang, X., Hua, S., Ligorio, M., et al., 2013. Glutamine supports pancreatic cancer growth through a KRAS-regulated metabolic pathway. Nature 496, 101–105.

Stephen, A.G., Esposito, D., Bagni, R.K., McCormick, F., 2014. Dragging Ras back in the ring. Cancer Cell 25, 272–281.

Stolze, B., Reinhart, S., Bulllinger, L., Fröhling, S., Scholl, C., 2015. Comparative analysis of KRAS codon 12, 13, 18, 61, and 117 mutations using human MCF10A isogenic cell lines. Sci. Rep. 5, 8535.

Sun, J., Qian, Y., Hamilton, A.D., Sebti, S.M., 1998. Both farnesyltransferase and geranylgeranyltransferase I inhibitors are required for inhibition of oncogenic K-Ras prenylation but each alone is sufficient to suppress human tumor growth in nude mouse xenografts. Oncogene 16, 1467.

Sun, Q., Burke, J.P., Phan, J., Burns, M.C., Olejniczak, E.T., Waterson, A.G., et al., 2012. Discovery of small molecules that bind to K-Ras and inhibit Sos-mediated activation. Angew. Chem. Int. Ed. Eng. 51, 6140–6143.

Tamanoi, F., Der, C.J., 2013. Inhibitors of the Ras superfamily of small G-proteins. Preface. Enzyme 34 (Pt. B), ix.

Tan, C., Du, X., 2012. KRAS mutation testing in metastatic colorectal cancer. World J. Gastroenterol. 18, 5171–5180.

Tao, L.Y., Zhang, L.F., Xiu, D.R., Yuan, C.H., Ma, Z.L., Jiang, B., 2016. Prognostic significance of K-ras mutations in pancreatic cancer: a meta-analysis. World J. Surg. Oncol. 14, 146.

Tidyman, W.E., Rauen, K.A., 2009. The RASopathies: developmental syndromes of Ras/MAPK pathway dysregulation. Curr. Opin. Genet. Dev. 19, 230–236.

Tidyman, W.E., Rauen, K.A., 2016. Pathogenetics of the RASopathies. Hum. Mol. Genet. 25, R123–R132.

Tran, E., Robbins, P.F., Lu, Y.-C., Prickett, T.D., Gartner, J.J., Jia, L., et al., 2016. T-cell transfer therapy targeting mutant KRAS in cancer. N. Engl. J. Med. 375, 2255–2262.

Tsuchida, N., Uesugi, S., 1981. Structure and functions of the Kirsten murine sarcoma virus genome: molecular cloning of biologically active Kirsten murine sarcoma virus DNA. J. Virol. 38, 720–727.

Tsuchida, N., Murugan, A.K., Grieco, M., 2016. Kirsten Ras* oncogene: significance of its discovery in human cancer research. Oncotarget 7, 46717–46733.

Tural, D., Selcukbiricik, F., Erdamar, S., Ozkurt, C.U., Yanmaz, T., Mandel, N.M., et al., 2013. Association KRAS G13D tumor mutated outcome in patients with chemotherapy refractory metastatic colorectal cancer treated with cetuximab. Hepato-Gastroenterology 60, 1035–1040.

van der Hoeven, D., Cho, K.-j., Ma, X., Chigurupati, S., Parton, R.G., Hancock, J.F., 2013. Fendiline inhibits K-Ras plasma membrane localization and blocks K-Ras signal transmission. Mol. Cell. Biol. 33, 237–251.

Wang, L., Hu, H., Pan, Y., Wang, R., Li, Y., Shen, L., et al., 2014. PIK3CA mutations frequently coexist with EGFR/KRAS mutations in non-small cell lung cancer and suggest poor prognosis in EGFR/KRAS wild type subgroup. PLoS ONE 9 e88291.

Waters, A.M., Der, C.J., 2018. KRAS: the critical driver and therapeutic target for pancreatic cancer. Cold Spring Harb. Perspect. Med. 8 a031435.

Wennerberg, K., Rossman, K.L., Der, C.J., 2005. The Ras superfamily at a glance. J. Cell Sci. 118, 843–846.

Whyte, D.B., Kirschmeier, P., Hockenberry, T.N., Nunez-Oliva, I., James, L., Catino, J.J., et al., 1997. K- and N-Ras are geranylgeranylated in cells treated with farnesyl protein transferase inhibitors. J. Biol. Chem. 272, 14459–14464.

Willumsen, B.M., Christensen, A., Hubbert, N.L., Papageorge, A.G., Lowy, D.R., 1984. The p21 ras C-terminus is required for transformation and membrane association. Nature 310, 583–586.

Wise, D.R., Thompson, C.B., 2010. Glutamine addiction: a new therapeutic target in cancer. Trends Biochem. Sci. 35, 427–433.

Yang, S., Wang, X., Contino, G., Liesa, M., Sahin, E., Ying, H., et al., 2011. Pancreatic cancers require autophagy for tumor growth. Genes Dev. 25, 717–729.

Yuan, T.L., Amzallag, A., Bagni, R., Yi, M., Afghani, S., Burgan, W., et al., 2018. Differential effector engagement by oncogenic KRAS. Cell Rep. 22, 1889–1902.

Yun, J., Rago, C., Cheong, I., Pagliarini, R., Angenendt, P., Rajagopalan, H., et al., 2009. Glucose deprivation contributes to the development of KRAS pathway mutations in tumor cells. Science (New York, N.Y.) 325, 1555–1559.

Zehir, A., Benayed, R., Shah, R.H., Syed, A., Middha, S., 2017. Mutational landscape of metastatic cancer revealed from prospective clinical sequencing of 10,000 patients. Nat. Med. 23, 703–713.

Zeng, M., Lu, J., Li, L., Feru, F., Quan, C., Gero, T.W., et al., 2017. Potent and selective covalent quinazoline inhibitors of KRAS G12C. Cell Chem. Biol. 24, 1005–1016. e1003.

Zhang, Z., Jiang, G., Yang, F., Wang, J., 2006. Knockdown of mutant K-ras expression by adenovirus-mediated siRNA inhibits the in vitro and in vivo growth of lung cancer cells. Cancer Biol. Ther. 5, 1481–1486.

Zhang, X., Cao, J., Miller, S.P., Jing, H., Lin, H., 2018. Comparative nucleotide-dependent interactome analysis reveals shared and differential properties of KRas4a and KRas4b. ACS Cent. Sci. 4, 71–80.

Zhou, B., Der, C.J., Cox, A.D., 2016. The role of wild type RAS isoforms in cancer. Semin. Cell Dev. Biol. 58, 60–69.

Chapter 14

Tumor-suppressive proteases revisited: Role in inhibiting tumor progression and metastasis

Devendra Shukla[a], Tanima Mandal[a], Priyanka Saha[a], Deepak Kumar[b], Sanjay Kumar[c], Amit Kumar Srivastava[a]
[a]*Cancer Biology & Inflammatory Disorder Division, Council of Scientific and Industrial Research-Indian Institute of Chemical Biology, Kolkata, India,* [b]*Organic & Medicinal Chemistry, Council of Scientific and Industrial Research-Indian Institute of Chemical Biology, Kolkata, India,* [c]*Division of Biology, Indian Institute of Science Education & Research Tirupati, Tirupati, India*

14.1 Introduction

Proteolysis is one of the significant biochemical reactions performed by a group of proteolytic enzymes. Proteolytic activity has been ascribed to a family of enzymes called proteases. These enzymes are present in many parts of human body and are involved in a series of significant biological processes and linked with various pathological conditions, including a variety of human cancers (Yang et al., 2009). A considerable body of research suggests that there are two types of proteases, i.e., extracellular and intracellular, which can function as signaling molecules in various cellular and physiological processes that lead to cancer progression. These proteases regulate various different processes including cell division, proliferation, self-renewal, migration, adhesion, angiogenesis, differentiation, senescence, autophagy, apoptosis, and activation of the immune system (López-Otín and Matrisian, 2007).

Proteases catalyze irreversible hydrolysis of peptide bonds (CO-NH) via attacking the carbonyl moiety involved in the peptide bond formation in the protein. Proteases have been categorized into various families on the basis of structural similarities in the primary structure, and groups that are homologous and assembled as clans. A clan consists of proteases that follow same catalytic mechanism based on the active site amino acids, i.e., cysteine, aspartic, metallo, serine, threonine, and glutamic acid. However, there are also proteolytic enzymes where active site amino acids are not known or mixed in addition to the

Cancer-Leading Proteases. https://doi.org/10.1016/B978-0-12-818168-3.00014-0

asparagine peptide lyases (Rawlings et al., 2011). Recently, the whole genome sequence of human and certain organisms has simplified the identification and characterization of the entire family of proteases, which has been termed as degradome (Lopez-Otin and Overall, 2002). The human degradome contains >569 proteolytic enzymes and homologs grouped into five catalytic classes: 196 matrix metalloproteinases (MMPs), 176 serine, 150 cysteine, 21 aspartate, and 28 threonine proteases. However, only a few proteases have been known to take part in tumor progression and metastasis (Puente et al., 2003). In the last few years, a large body of research has been performed using both in vitro and in vivo model systems, which offers substantial proof for the existence of tumor-suppressive extra- and intracellular proteases (Overall and Kleifeld, 2006; Balbín et al., 2003; McCawley et al., 2004). These two groups of proteases are described below.

14.2 Extracellular proteases with tumor-suppressive activity

Extracellular proteases may mutually affect extracellular matrix degradation, tumor initiation, and progression via regulating proteolytic signaling cascades, with individual proteolytic enzymes having separate functions in cancer development and angiogenesis (Koblinski et al., 2000). A range of families of extracellular proteases might act to reduce tumor progression. The increasing list of extracellular proteases with tumor-suppressive activity includes matrix metalloproteinases, neprilysin, cysteine cathepsins, kallikreins, prostasin serine protease, testisin, dipeptidyl peptidase 4, and ADAMTSs (A disintegrin and metalloprotease domains with thrombospondin motifs) Among all extracellular proteolytic enzymes, MMPs are most studied proteases. However, recent findings suggest that proteases belonging to other classes might also display anticancerous properties (Mohamed and Sloane, 2006; Borgono and Diamandis, 2004).

14.2.1 Matrix metalloproteinases

In human, MMP family includes 23 endopeptidases which have been reported to play a pivotal role in cancer progression. They are categorized into five subclasses on the basis of their domain structure and specificity to bind with substrate: gelatinases, stromelysins, collagenases, membrane-type MMPs, and matrilysins. These MMPs play central role in various cellular, physiological, and pathological processes including cancer progression. A huge portion of research has shown the antitumor properties of multiple members of the MMP family and these MMPs may inhibit the cancer progression at different stages of cancer progression (Fig. 14.1). For instance, MMP-8, also termed as collagenase-2 or neutrophil collagenase mainly produced by neutrophils, was the primary metalloproteinase recognized to be a probable pharmacological target for cancer treatment. MMP-8 can inhibit growth and progression of breast, skin, and melanoma cancer cells in various in vitro and in vivo model systems (Balbín et al., 2003; Agarwal et al., 2003; Palavalli et al., 2009). Mutation of MMP-8 increased the incidence of skin cancer in male group of mice (Balbín et al., 2003). This study elucidated that loss of MMP-8 results in increased susceptibility of mouse skin for tumor growth after treatment with a carcinogen. In another study, conducted by Agarwal et al. (2003), anticancerous properties of MMP-8 have been revealed against tongue squamous carcinoma. Taken together, these findings reflect that MMP-8 is an essential tumor-protective protease which can significantly modulate cancer-related molecular signaling. MMP-9, also known as gelatinase-B, though has been linked with cancer development, in some cases, has been reported to play an anticancerous role (Egeblad and Werb, 2002). For example, loss of MMP-9 abundantly increases the incidence of skin tumor in mice model. Despite eliciting a proinflammatory response, MMP-9 plays a tumor-suppressive role in colitis-associated cancer via regulating Notch and $p21^{WAF1/Cip1}$ signaling activation (Garg et al., 2010). Additionally, Walter et al. (2017) have shown the protective role of MMP-9 in colitis-linked cancer by modulating MMP-9-Notch1-ARF-p53 axis.

MMP-12 or macrophage metalloelastase is mostly secreted by macrophages but is also detected in osteoclasts and hypertrophic chondrocytes, and its expression has been correlated with retarded tumor growth rates in various animal models (Gorrin-Rivas et al., 2000a, b). As mentioned below, a series of findings have established the tumor suppressive role of MMP-12 but its cancer promoting/pro-inflammatory functions have also been reported (Hofmann et al., 2005; Kerkelä et al., 2000). This inconsistency may be partially attributed to the use of varying cancer models and different cellular sources of MMP-12

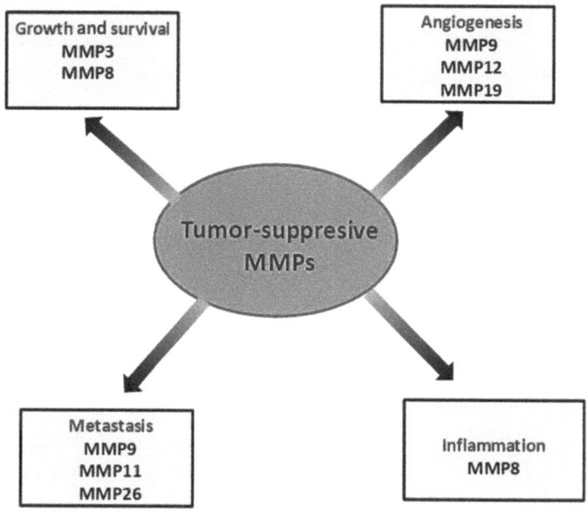

FIG. 14.1 Tumor-suppressive role of MMPs at different stages of cancer development.

production (Kerkelä et al., 2002). MMP-12 reduces the lung adenocarcinoma development both in experimental and spontaneous metastasis models (Houghton et al., 2006). In the same way, enhanced MMP-12 expression in liver carcinomas was observed to be linked with reduced tumor vascularity and improved overall survival (Gorrin-Rivas et al., 1998; Shi et al., 2006). Moreover, in vivo orthotopic colon cancer Balb/c mouse models have shown strong evidences of antitumorigenic and antiangiogenic properties for MMP-12 (Shi et al., 2006; Xu et al., 2008). Elevated expression of MMP-12 remarkably reduces the tumor xenograft growth and vascularization of colon cancer cells (Shi et al., 2008) and increases overall survival significantly. In addition, injection of cancer cells with enforced MMP-12 expression in orthotopic nu/nu (CD-1) BR mice model system resulted in significant reduction of tumor volume as compared to control (Xu et al., 2008). Human MMP-11, also termed as stromelysin-3, belongs to stromelysin subgroup and was first reported in the stromal cells of breast cancer (Basset et al., 1990). Loss of MMP-11 results in higher rate of metastasis and cell proliferation in mammary cancer models (Andarawewa et al., 2003). A good number of evidences suggest that MMP-11 is involved in regulation of cancer-specific signaling cascades or complex tumor microenvironment, reflecting a more crucial role in cancer progression than its proteolysis action.

MMP-3, belonging to stromelysin subfamily of MMPs, was first mentioned as a robust pro-tumorigenic protease (Blavier et al., 2006; Pedersen et al., 2005). However, recent finding exhibited its tumor-suppressive role in in vivo squamous cell carcinoma model (Suojanen et al., 2009). MMP-3-deficient mice showed a significant suppression in the number of tumor associated neutrophils and infiltrating macrophages, suggesting its tumor-suppressive role during cancer development (McCawley et al., 2004). Additionally, in vivo animal models with enhanced expression of MMP-3 in their mammary glands were observed to develop a smaller number of carcinogen-induced tumors as compared to control group, further reflecting the anticancerous property of this class of MMPs (Witty et al., 2005). Overexpression of MMP-3-induced apoptosis of cancer cells might help to defend its anticancerous properties (Witty et al., 2005).

MMP-26, also termed as matrilysin-2 or endometas, is the newly discovered member of the MMP family which could play a specific role in human cells and organs (Uria and Lopez-Otin, 2000). Enhanced expression of MMP-26 was observed during the early stages of several types of malignancies and was linked with overall improved survival. In the high-grade carcinomas, MMP-26 levels were shown to be reduced (Savinov et al., 2006). The anticancer potential of this protease may, because of its ability to modulate estrogen receptor β-gene expression, regulate estrogen signaling in various hormone-dependent diseases, such as endometrial and breast carcinomas (Savinov et al., 2006). However, more research is needed to fully understand the function of MMP-26 in cancer progression and metastasis, particularly in estrogen-related malignancies. Like other MMPs, MMP-19 also plays dual role in cancer, i.e., protumorigenic/proinflammatory and antitumorigenic role. It has been observed that MMP-19 null mice are more vulnerable to carcinogen-induced skin cancer as compared to wild type, suggesting that MMP-19 may promote tumor growth and progression (Pendás et al., 2004). However, its antitumor properties in early stages of malignancies have been reported, indicating the dual function of MMP-19 in the regulation of cancer signaling (Jost et al., 2006). In the last few years, extensive research has been made related to functional role of MMPs which enhanced our knowledge about MMPs and presented better clarification about the complexity of their roles in various physiological and pathological conditions. A large number of studies using various model systems reveal that MMPs have contradictory roles in tumor progression. Although some MMPs, specifically those that are discussed here, appear more consistently to have tumor-suppressive potential, most of the MMPs, such as MMP-1 and MMP-14, mainly enhance cancer development. However, further research will strengthen our knowledge about the underlying mechanisms of cancer promoting and/or preventing actions of MMPs.

14.2.2 Neprilysin

Neprilysin, also known as neutral endopeptidase, is an approximately 90–110-KDa cell surface peptidase that catalytically breaks peptide bonds (OC-NH) on the N-terminal side of hydrophobic amino acids and degrades neuropeptide substrate compounds and acts as a tumor suppressor due to its proteolysis activity and interactions with other proteins (Goodman et al., 2006). The presence of neprilysin has been detected in various organs including prostate, endometrium, adrenal glands, kidney, intestine, and lung (Dai et al., 2001). Reduced expression or loss of neprilysin has been observed in various types of human malignancies, including nonsmall cell lung carcinoma, small cell lung carcinoma, bladder cancer, renal cancer, endometrial cancer, gastrointestinal cancer, and prostate cancer (Papandreou et al., 1998; Osman et al., 2004). Decreased expression of neprilysin results in the buildup of higher neuropeptide amount that promote cancer development (Nanus, 2003). It has been reported that neprilysin suppresses angiogenesis via proteomic degradation of fibroblast growth factor-2 (FGF2) and activates the expression of tumor suppressor gene PTEN (phosphatase and tensin homolog) via protein-protein interaction (Goodman et al., 2006; Sumitomo et al., 2004). Stephen et al. (2016) have shown that neprilysin acts as a critical modulator of breast cancer invasion and metastasis, thus illuminating its utility as a prospective biomarker for breast cancer progression. Moreover, in prostate cancer, necrolysis protein is expressed in androgen-sensitive cell lines, e.g., LNCaP, but not in androgen-independent prostate cancer cells (Papandreou et al., 1998; Shen et al., 2000). Moreover, Dai et al. (2001) have reported that neprilysin can stall prostate cell proliferation and tumor growth, and thus could be a potential therapy for androgen-independent prostate cancer.

14.2.3 Cysteine cathepsins

It has been reported that cysteine cathepsins play multiple roles in disease progression including cancer. Recently, cysteine cathepsin proteases have attained much attention because of their essential function in various cellular and physiological processes including cell growth and proliferation, apoptosis, tumor initiation, progression, angiogenesis, and invasion (Joyce and Hanahan, 2004). In humans, this family of proteases contains 11 members (cathepsins B, C, H, F, K, L, O, S, V, W, X/Z) (Turk et al., 2002). Cysteine cathepsins are mainly localized in lysosomal compartments of normal cells, and their primary role is protein degradation and processing in the acidic environment of lysosomes (Turk et al., 2002). In the last few years, other important functions of cysteine cathepsins have been identified in normal cells. For instance, these proteases regulate protein processing in intracellular compartments such as secretory granules and nucleus (Goulet et al., 2004) and found to play precise roles in cellular and various other physiological processes, such as bone regeneration, regulation of MHC class I and II molecules activity, and epidermal homeostasis (Yasothornsrikul et al., 2003). Cysteine cathepsins play a crucial role in carcinogenesis as they are highly expressed in various malignant tumors. Cathepsins are secreted into the extracellular matrix and have multiple roles during tumor progression. Many cathepsins have been reported to promote angiogenesis but cathepsin L may show a contrasting role in the formation of blood vessels via producing endostatin, an endogenous angiogenesis inhibitor, and thus can cleave collagen XVIII in vitro (Felbor et al., 2000). Moreover, depletion of cathepsin L in a Human papillomavirus-16 (HPV16)-induced skin cancer mouse model leads to early and enhanced tumor growth as compared to vehicle control mice (Reinheckel et al., 2005). These studies represent the strong tumor-suppressive role of cysteine cathepsins, although further research is required to evaluate its protective roles in other types of cancer.

14.2.4 Kallikreins

Kallikreins (hKs) comprise a family of 15 homologous trypsin- or chymotrypsin-like serine proteinases, the expression of which is often altered in hormonally associated human malignancies (Borgono and Diamandis, 2004). Emerging experimental data suggest that kallikrein gene/protein expression and proteolytic activity are altered in various kinds of malignancies, especially aggressive tumors, and often associated with patient survival. Data of numerous experiments also suggest that kallikreins may be primarily involved in neoplastic transformation. Kallikreins might display multiple and often opposite effects on the tumor niche (Borgono and Diamandis, 2004). Accumulating evidences suggest that 12 kallikreins genes are upregulated in ovarian cancer (Obiezu et al., 2001; Adib et al., 2004). Contrary to this, many kallikrein genes have been found to be typically downregulated in breast (Yu et al., 1996, 1998; Welsh et al., 2003), prostate (Petraki et al., 2003), and testicular (Luo et al., 2003) tumors. In addition to steroid hormone-dependent malignancies, kallikreins are dysregulated in cancers like nonsmall cell lung carcinoma (Bhattacharjee et al., 2001), pancreatic carcinoma (Iacobuzio-Donahue et al., 2003; Yousef et al., 2004), and head and neck squamous cell carcinoma (Chung et al., 2004). Whether hKs employ tumor-promoting or suppressive behavior depends on the type of tissue and tumor niche. However, detecting increased expression of hKs in some carcinoma, a promising outcome, suggested their importance as anticancer proteases. Tumor-suppressive role of both hK3 and hK10 has been studied. Moreover, hK3 can suppress the growth and proliferation of the estrogen-receptor (ER)+breast cancer cells (MCF-7) via inducing the transformation of the potent estrogen estradiol to the less potent estrone (Lai et al., 1996). It has been reported that hK3 can activate transforming growth factor-β (TGFβ) which may suppress cell growth and induce programmed cell death in many normal and malignant cells (Derynck et al., 2001), thus further reflecting a tumor-suppressive role of hK3. Furthermore, downregulation of hK3 in many types of cancers, such as prostate, breast, testicular cancer, and acute lymphoblastic leukemia (ALL), suggests its cancer protective roles (Liu et al., 1996; Goyal et al., 1998; Dhar et al., 2001; Roman-Gomez et al., 2004; Yousef et al., 2000). Overexpression of KLK10 into the breast cancer cells reduced its cell growth and proliferation, colony formation ability, and xenograft formation. Thus, KLK10 can reduce the tumor progression in various in vitro and in vivo model systems. Many studies have shown that hK3, 6, and 13 are associated with angiogenesis reduction via the release of angiostatin-like fragments directly from plasminogen (Sotiropoulou et al., 2003; Heidtmann et al., 1999; Fortier et al., 1999). These findings may help to clarify why few kallikreins act as a prognostic marker for cancer detection. Overall, in conclusion, hK proteases have potent anticancer effects and might open a new research direction in the development of cancer chemotherapy. Thus, another crucial objective for the future will involve further clarifying the clinical implication of kallikreins as predictive biomarkers for cancer, alone or in combination with other genes/proteins in a multiparametric model. Therefore, the postgenomic period displays a new challenge for research in this subclass of the human proteolytic enzymes.

14.2.5 Prostasin serine protease

Prostasin, also termed as prostate-abundant serine protease, was first identified in seminal human fluid (Yu et al., 1995). Recently, lower expression of prostasin has been noticed in metastatic prostate cancer and its enforced expression in aggressive prostate carcinoma cell lines reduces invasion and progression of cancer cells (Chen et al., 2001). These enzymes are trypsin-like serine peptidase, mainly found in epithelial cells with high level in the seminal fluid and normal prostate gland and low expression in other organs/tissues (Yu et al., 1995). The expression of prostasin serine protease has been shown to alter various malignancies including ovary, prostate, breast, and gastric cancers (Mok et al., 2001; Chen and Chai, 2002; Sakashita et al., 2008; Lu et al., 2004). In the last few years, it has been claimed that the expression of prostasin could be used as potential biomarker, alone or in combination with CA125, for early detection of ovarian cancer (Costa et al., 2009). It has been suggested that prostasin suppresses cancer cell growth, proliferation, and invasion in breast and prostate cancers (López-Otín and Matrisian, 2007). Prostasin is also known as channel-activating protease 1, which is known to play a pivotal role in the regulation of sodium channel of epithelial cells; thus it is important for cardiovascular diseases (Rickert et al., 2008; Planes et al., 2010; Li et al., 2011). Thus, it is implicated in a broad spectrum of cellular, metabolic, and pathophysiological conditions. In summary, these findings suggest that prostasin is a potential pharmacological target molecule for treatment/reduction of gynecological malignancies like breast and ovarian, including chemo-resistant tumors. The signaling pathway and molecular mechanism findings suggest that prostasin may regulate tumor cell survival and/or drug resistance by modulating various signaling networks. Further, research in this regard will highlight the possible function of prostasin as a prognostic marker for malignancies or a therapeutic agent for therapy of persistent and metastatic tumors.

14.2.6 Testisin

Testisin is a serine protease linked with glycosyl-phosphatidylinositol (GPI) moiety which is anchored to the cell membrane by transmembrane domains or a GPI anchor (Martin et al., 2015). Localization of GPI-linked serine proteases on cell surface, their restricted mosaic expression, and partial physiological functions of a few members of this family of proteolytic enzymes indicate that they may be potential cell membrane-bound targets for anticancer therapies (Martin et al., 2015). The membrane-bound testisin protease (*PRSS21*) is made of 17-amino acid, carboxyl-terminal hydrophobic segment that is posttranscriptionally altered by a GPI bond which then localizes the protease to the cell surface (Scarman et al., 2001; Inoue et al., 1999; Hooper et al., 1999; Honda et al., 2002). Testisin has unusual tissue-specific distribution. Higher expression of testisin has been found in primary and secondary spermatocytes, where it plays an important role in maintaining male fertility (Kawano et al., 2010; Yamashita et al., 2008; Netzel-Arnett et al., 2009). However, altered expression of testisin has been noticed in various types of tumors (Mirandola et al., 2011). It is highly expressed in human high-grade cervical and ovarian cancers, while being undetectable in low-grade cervical or ovarian primary human tumor tissue. The study performed by Shigemasa et al. (2007) has shown that testisin was present in approximately 80%–90% of stage II or III diseases (Shigemasa et al., 2007). Similarly, Bignotti et al. (2007) also reported that testisin is expressed in primary and high-grade human ovarian cancers. Enforced expression of testisin in ovarian cancer cell lines results in enhanced growth of cancer as evident from colony formation assay and increased xenograft tumor growth in immunocompromised mice (Tang et al., 2005). In cervical cancer, overexpression of testisin significantly increases the invasion of cancer cells (Yeom et al., 2010). On the other hand, significant downregulation using transient siRNA has been reported where the reduction in cell growth, proliferation, migration, and invasion reduced cellular resistance to the chemotherapeutic drug (Tang et al., 2005; Yeom et al., 2010). The altered gene expression of testisin exhibited by metastatic ovarian and cervical tumors, as compared to its normally limited expression level in testicular cells, collectively with the relationship of testisin mRNA/protein expression to carcinogenesis processes, reflects that testisin is a promising pharmacological target for designing new anticancer remedial strategies. Moreover, enforced expression of testisin in testicular cancer cells suppresses the tumorigenicity of these cells and is downregulated in testicular tumors by DNA hypermethylation (Manton et al., 2005). Genetic engineering or chemical modifications of tumor-promoting proteases is a potential strategy for the generation of anticancer therapies (Choi et al., 2012; Weidle et al., 2014a, b). Targeting of proteases could be achieved using various approaches (Turk, 2006). Use of prodrug-like protease compounds that specifically target highly expressed proteolytic enzymes is a highly effective strategy to enhance specificity and efficacy with the reduction of off-target effects (Weidle et al., 2014a, b). Martin et al. (2015) have shown that testisin's proteolysis activities can be blocked on cancer cells using engineered PrAg-PCIS. It was proposed that the cell surface-bound proteolytic enzymes comprise active targets for chemically modified anthrax toxins. Moreover, these reports reflect that other concepts of prodrug-mediated targeting strategies, e.g., use of other protease-activated toxins (Lebeau et al., 2009; Williams et al., 2007; Potrich et al., 2005) or ACPPs (activatable cell penetrating peptides) (Hussain et al., 2014; Nguyen et al., 2015, 2010), could be considered to target the proteolytic enzyme activities of tumor cell expressed surface-bound proteolytic enzymes for treatment or early detection purposes.

14.2.7 Dipeptidyl peptidase 4

Dipeptidyl peptidase 4 (DPP-4), a cell surface-bound serine proteolytic enzyme, was first identified to reduce the cancerous characteristics of melanocytic cells (Wesley et al., 1999) and further found to be linked with antitumor roles in various human malignancies (Kajiyama et al., 2003; Wesley et al., 2005). DPP-4 inhibitors are well-known antidiabetic drugs and are used for the management of Type II diabetes. DPP-4 is a serine protease enzyme which reduces the activity of incretin hormone, which belongs to the class of hypoglycemic gut hormones. Given that two main types of incretin hormones are present in human, the first one is known as glucose-dependent insulinotropic peptide-GIP and the second is glucagon-like peptide-1 (GLP-1). DPP-4 inhibitors suppress the degradation of GIP and GLP-1 (McIntosh et al., 2005; Behme et al., 2003; Dupre et al., 1995).

Like other proteases, dual roles of DPP-4 inhibitors have also been reported. Reports related to this have clearly stated that DPP-4 promotes cancer cell's growth and proliferation but some studies have shown that they have anticancer property. A study by Amritha et al. (2015) has demonstrated that DPP-4 inhibitors have strong anticancer activity against colon cancer cells. It has been reported that enforced DPP-4 expression increases E-cadherin level and tissue inhibitors of MMPs, resulting in the reduction of the metastatic potential of ovarian cancer (Kajiyama et al., 2003). DPP-4 may also modulate cell-cell interaction properties and revoke the cancerous phenotype of prostate cancer cells (Wesley et al., 2005).

14.2.8 ADAMTSs

ADAMTSs are extracellular proteolytic enzymes which have been reported to exhibit dual role, tumor-promoting and suppressive properties. Until now, 19 ADAMTs proteases have been identified and characterized in humans. These proteases can be secreted by stromal and tumor cells and might contribute to modulation of the tumor niche via various molecular mechanisms. Therefore, ADAMTSs can either cleave or directly interact with several components of extracellular matrix or other regulatory entities and thus modulate cell division, adhesion, differentiation, proliferation, migration, and angiogenesis (Cal and López-Otín, 2015). ADAMTS-1 was reported to be an antiangiogenesis protease due to its ability to inhibit endothelial cell division and proliferation (Lee et al., 2006a, b, c, 2010). The carboxyl-terminus of the enzyme containing the TS1 motifs is thought to be the reason for this inhibitory effect. This inhibitory effect occurs by sequestration of two polypeptide chains of 165 amino acids of vascular endothelial growth factor (VEGF) (Vazquez et al., 1999; Kuno et al., 2004). Apart from ADAMTS-1, strong antiangiogenic effects of other ADAMTSs, e.g., ADAMTS-2 (Dubail et al., 2010), ADAMTS-4 (Hsu et al., 2012), ADAMTS-5 (Kumar et al., 2012), ADAMTS-8 or METH-2 (Dunn et al., 2006), ADAMTS-9 (Lo et al., 2010; Koo et al., 2010), and ADAMTS-12 (El Hour et al., 2010) have been studied using various cell culture and animal models. Different ADAMTSs may display their anticancerous potential through distinct molecular mechanisms. For instance, ADAMTS-6 inhibits tumor progression by inhibiting Erk phosphorylation, an essential signaling molecule that usually enhances cancer cells proliferation (Xie et al., 2016). Moreover, it has been reported that ADAMTS-1 can inhibit tumor xenograft growth in human fibrosarcoma, prostate cancer, and Chinese hamster ovary CHO-K1 cells (Obika et al., 2012). A recent study done by Ham et al. showed that ADAMTS-1 inhibits proliferation, invasion, and migration of breast tumor cells through modulating PPARδ (Ham et al., 2017). ADAMTS-9 exerts its tumor-suppressive role by inhibiting AKT/mTOR pathway (Du et al., 2013). ADAMTS-1 expression is significantly repressed in several cancers including breast, colon, and lung adenocarcinoma through the promotion of hypermethylation of cancer-specific genes (Porter et al., 2004). Likewise, enhanced expression of ADAMTS-15 may inhibit breast cancer via decreasing interaction between tumor cells and tumor microenvironment (Wagstaff et al., 2010). On the contrary, knockdown of various proteases like ADAMTS-1, ADAMTS-8, ADAMTS-9, and ADAMTS-15 enhances the tumor formation ability of cancer cells (Viloria et al., 2009; Du et al., 2013; Gigi and Richter-Levin, 2014). Similarly, ADAMTS-8 is observed to be significantly downregulated in various kinds of fatalities, which is often linked with hypermethylation of cancer-specific genes (Porter et al., 2004). These studies suggest that loss of ADAMTs metalloproteinases may lead to enhanced cancer progression and metastasis. Thus, ADAMTSs may regulate multiple cancer-related molecular signaling networks (Sulzmaier and Ramos, 2013). Still, further research would be required to observe if ADAMTs genes/ proteins mutations are common in various types of malignancies and also to determine the functional consequences of these mutations in tumor progression.

14.3 Intracellular proteases

The intracellular enzyme levels are described by the ratio of the rate of biosynthesis and the rate of degradation. So far, several intracellular proteolytic enzymes with strong tumor-suppressive potential have been identified. The growing list of intracellular proteases with tumor-suppressive potential includes caspases, deubiquitylases (DUBs), and autophagins.

14.3.1 Caspases

Deregulation of programmed cell death has been connected with the pathogenesis of various diseases including cancer (Cotter, 2009; Krammer et al., 2007). Apoptosis has two major pathways, i.e., death receptor pathway and mitochondrial-mediated pathway and in both pathways caspases play an important role (Wickman et al., 2012) (Fig. 14.2). The first report showing the strong proof in this regard came from research on neuroblastoma in which the caspase-8 gene was mutated or downregulated through epigenetics alteration DNA methylation (Teitz et al., 2000). Moreover, apart from apoptotic roles, a piece of mounting evidence showed their role in another physiological process. Caspase-8 is required for formation of blood vessel during early embryogenesis, survival, and proliferation of hematopoietic progenitors, and for mitogen- or antigen-activated T- and B-cell growth and proliferation (Su et al., 2005; Beisner et al., 2005). A large body of research has shown that loss of mutation in Caspase-8 in various malignancies, e.g., colon, head and neck, gastric and lung carcinomas, as well as several pediatric tumors (Mandruzzato et al., 1997; Soung et al., 2005; Harada et al., 2002). Their involvement in programmed cell death highlights their tumor-suppressive properties. Loss of caspase-8 expression has been often found to be associated with amplification of the Myc oncogene (Harada et al., 2002). Promoter methylation-independent suppression of caspase-8 gene expression has also been reported in primary human glioma tumor tissue (Ashley et al., 2005). Furthermore, caspase-8 mutations have also been observed at low level in gastric and colorectal malignancies (Soung et al., 2005; Kim et al., 2003). Reduced level of caspase-8 might have several effects on tumorigenesis process. Certainly, caspase-8 was reported to be involved in the reduction of cancerous phenotype and neoplastic transformation, independent of its function in apoptosis induced by death receptor pathway (Krelin et al., 2008). Indeed, caspase-8 deficiency might prompt cells to attain further oncogenic transformations, or permit spontaneous tumor-promoting mutations to accumulate easily. It is still unclear how caspase-8 deficiency promotes neoplastic transformation; thus, further research is needed to reveal the underlying mechanisms. Caspase-1 is proinflammatory caspase, which plays an important role in prostate and bladder cancer suppression via interaction with p63. In another study done by Ho et al. (2009) it has been revealed that deficiency of caspase-2 expression results in an enhanced ability of cells to attain malignant and aggressive phenotype, representing that caspase-2 is a potent anticancer protein. Moreover, caspase-2 expression is suppressed in mantle cell lymphoma and childhood ALL (Holleman et al., 2005; Hofmann et al., 2001). Similarly, other members of caspase family, such as caspase-3, caspase-4, caspase-5, caspase-6, and caspase-7, have been found to be

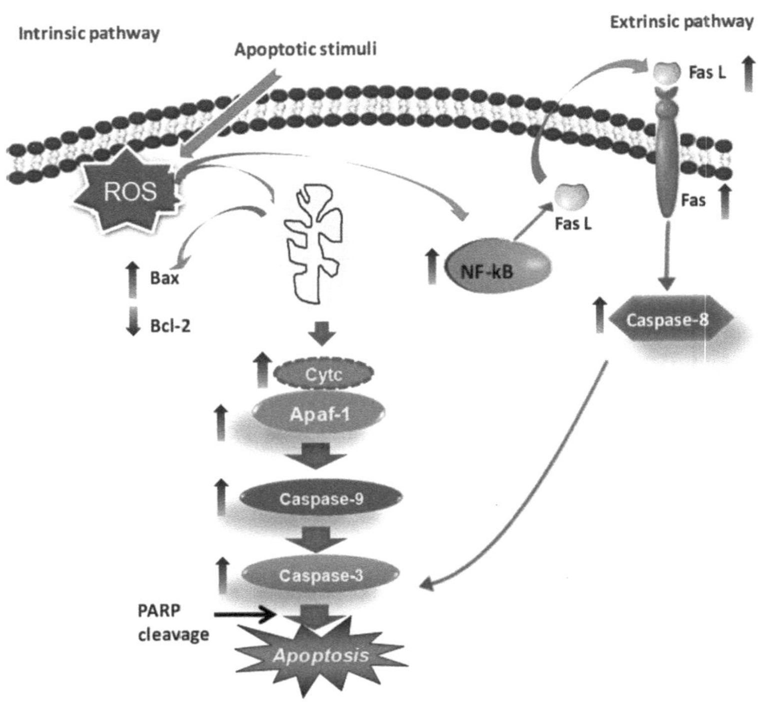

FIG. 14.2 Schematic diagram showing extrinsic and intrinsic pathways of apoptosis.

irregularly deleted or mutated in various malignancies (Soung et al., 2003, 2004; Offman et al., 2005; Lee et al., 2006a, b, c). In a study performed on breast tumor tissue obtained from patients undergoing breast cancer treatment, it was noticed that around 70%–80% of the tumor samples lacked caspase-3 gene expression (Devarajan et al., 2002). Additionally, it has been observed that in 1%–3% colon and lung cancers caspase-3 gene is mutated (Soung et al., 2004). Till date, the function of caspase-3 in tumor initiation, progression, and tumor response for treatment of chemotherapeutic drugs is unknown. Caspase-6 is an effective caspase that activates downstream caspases (caspase-3 and caspase-7) in apoptosome-mediated apoptosis (Inoue et al., 2009). Only a few reports have shown the association of caspase-6 with cancer, but reduced expression of caspase-3 has been shown in about 50% of gastric tumor samples (Yoo et al., 2004). Caspase-3 shares many functional resemblances with caspase-7; both caspases are effector caspases and are substrates for initiator caspases in mitochondrial or death receptor apoptotic pathways. The extent of participation of caspase-8 mutations in the progression of various human malignancies has been studied by next-generation sequencing techniques. Caspase-7 mutations were detected 1 out of 50 esophageal tissue, 2 out of 98 colon cancer samples, and 1 out of 33 head and neck carcinoma tissues (Song et al., 2003). Likewise, fibroblasts deficient in both caspase-3 and -7 were vastly resistant to apoptosis (Larsson and Henriksson, 2010). However, these studies suggest that the loss of caspases may promote tumor development. Whatsoever, it is still unknown whether these mutations are real driver mutations that accumulate during the course of cancer development.

14.3.2 Deubiquitylases

Deubiquitination is a posttranslational reversible modification in which ubiquitin moiety can be detached from target proteins by a group of proteases known as DUBs (Murtaza et al., 2015). Recent studies showed crucial roles of DUBs in the development of several diseases such as neurodegeneration, cardiovascular, respiratory, and cancer (Turk, 2006). Deubiquitinating enzymes (DUBs) are proteolytic enzymes that remove ubiquitin or ubiquitin-like moiety from target proteins. In humans, approximately 100 DUBs have been discovered that function to destabilize and cleave ubiquitin moiety. The dynamic interconversion between deubiquitylation and ubiquitylation sets the measure for functional roles and protein turnover. Interestingly, depending on the type of malignancies, DUBs can act as either tumor promoting or suppressive. For instances, enhanced expression of USP9X may stabilize MCL-1, a pro-apoptotic protein belonging to BCL-2 family of proteins, thus leading to the onset of multiple myeloma lymphoma (Schwickart et al., 2010). On the other hand, in a genetic screening for anticancer genes of pancreatic cancer performed in in vivo model, USP9X was reported to be frequently mutated gene in around >50% of primary human tumor samples (Pérez-Mancera et al., 2012), suggesting its potent antitumor activity. Moreover, in a study, Xu et al. (2014) have shown that USP9X reduces breast cancer development by enhancing the stability of LATS2 (large tumor suppressor kinase 2) protein in the Hippo pathway. A similar study performed by Toloczko et al. (2017) has shown that USP9X inhibits tumor growth via core components and LATS kinase of the Hippo pathway.

The p53 is a well-known tumor suppressor and its stability is of utmost importance to maintain the antitumor activity. USP-7, or HAUSP (herpesvirus-associated ubiquitin-specific protease), has been reported to increase the stability of p53 via deubiquitylating it, even in the presence of high Mdm2 protein expression. USP-7 belongs to ubiquitin-specific processing protease (UBP) group of DUBs. It has been found that both amino and carboxyl-terminal of HAUSP interact with p53. Additionally, HAUSP has also been found to stop proteomic lysis of Mdm2 in a p53-independent manner (Li et al., 2004). These exciting findings reflect a feedback loop modulation of p53 by Mdm2 and USP-7. Moreover, it has been noticed that HAUSP deubiquitylates tumor suppressor protein PTEN and partially regulates its tumor-suppressive activity (Song et al., 2008). USP10 (Ubiquitin-specific protease 10) is another member of DUB family that stabilizes the cellular level of p53 protein. It directly interacts with other proteins to sustain cellular level of p53 in normal as well as disease condition (Jochemsen and Shiloh, 2010). However, USP10 only interacts with p53 and stabilizes it and does not interact with Mdm2, which indicates that USP10 is just a p53-specific deubiquitylate. Therefore, it is a potential pharmacological target for the development of new cancer therapeutics. After the onset of DNA damage, USP10 migrates to the nuclear compartment from cytosol, and deubiquitinate p53, and eventually regulates p53-dependent DNA damage signaling pathway (Zhang et al., 2016). Moreover, USP10 modulates autophagy via mediating deubiquitination of coiled-coil myosin-like BCL2-interacting protein (BECN1) (Liu et al., 2011). Clinically, the involvement of USP10 in various types of cancers has been elucidated, for instance, Sun et al. (2018) have reported that USP10 reduces lung tumor growth and metastasis by increasing tumor suppresser gene PTEN level. USP22 (ubiquitin-specific peptidase 22) belongs to DUBs family and has been categorized as a tumor-promoting protease, i.e., a promising biomarker for predicting the prospect of treatment failure and tumor relapse in cancer patients (Glinsky, 2006; Verdecia et al., 2003). A large body of research suggests the oncogenic potential of USP22 and its expression is significantly enhanced in high grade carcinoma of several tissues such as those present in skeletal muscle myocardial muscle and lung adenocarcinoma (Lee et al., 2006a, b, c). Also, it can be used as a biomarker for predicting the tumor relapse and its resistance to chemotherapeutic drugs (Glinsky et al., 2005). It has been found that USP22 positively regulates the tumor growth and its knockdown induces cell cycle arrest (Zhang et al., 2008). The p53 is known as "the guardian of the genome" as it plays a central role in inducing various cellular and physiological responses. Altered regulation of p53 is a main driving power for cancer initiation and progression. Thus, an accurate understanding of ubiquitin molecular signaling networks that control p53 regulation will open a new avenue for pharmacological target identification in cancer.

14.3.3 Autophagins

Autophagins are cysteine proteolytic enzymes that belong to a group of four structurally similar enzymes involved in degradation of proteins linked with autophagy function (Marino et al., 2003). Autophagy is a self tuned regulated mechanism of the cell for the removal of dysfunctional and unwanted components. Precisely, it is an enzymatic mediated catabolic degradation process in which cellular bodies are engulfed to maintain cellular homeostasis (Levine and Klionsky, 2004; Mizushima, 2007). Recently, several studies have shown the importance of autophagy in cancer progression. A series of studies have proved that autophagy is a tumor-suppressive mechanism. For instance, inactivation of autophagy gene beclin1 (*BECN1*, also known as *ATG6*) was found in various cancers including ovarian, prostate, and breast cancers. In addition, autophagy-defective Becnl-heterozygous (Qu et al., 2003) and autophagin 3 (also known as Atg4C)-mutant (Marino et al., 2007) animal models are more susceptible to tumor formation. These findings suggest that autophagin 3 has tumor-suppressive potential and thus opens the prospect of assessing similar antitumor roles in the residual members of this class of cysteine proteases.

14.4 Conclusion and future prospective

Proteolytic enzymes are involved in each step starting from cancer initiation to metastasis but sometimes exhibit complex roles. Redundancy in protease function and altered expression of proteases in different tissue and tumor microenvironment underline the importance of validating proteolytic enzymes levels in the various human malignancies. Moreover, it will be imperative to know differences between protease expression level and cleavage-level changes caused by altered protease activity. In addition, it is important to understand the patient-to-patient variation in protease expression level for a type and site of the cancer. The recent identification of repeatedly mutated proteolytic enzymes in several types of human malignancies highlights the increasing list of proteases with protective roles against cancer initiation and progression. In this chapter >30 proteases with the ability to repress tumor growth or modulate some aspects of cancer have been described. However, the molecular mechanisms through which these proteolytic enzymes exert their tumor-promoting or suppressive properties at the cellular and molecular levels are not well known and represent a major challenge to be addressed in the near future. Interestingly, several proteolytic enzymes might have dual functions either to promote or suppress cancer development on the basis of cell types or tissue in which they are expressed. This presents an additional challenge in the explanation of this inventory of anticancer suppressive proteolytic enzymes. Given that few proteolytic enzymes can exert tumor promoting activity and show opposite function in different types of malignancies or steps of tumor development, a necessary step for personalized cancer treatment is now the identification and characterization of the most suitable tumor-suppressive protease for clinical implications in each case. These proteases are logical targets for initial efforts to produce novel synthetic mimics to target chemotherapy and tumor relapse. In spite of extensive research on the tumor-suppressive proteases in last few years, more functional and mechanistic studies are required to completely reveal how these proteolytic enzymes could control tumor niche to induce tumor volume regression. There are many challenges in near future for translating this knowledge for clinical utility in cancer patients but, hopefully, we attempted to give portrayal of the tumor-suppressive proteases which will help in the building of a conceptual foreground to classify the tumor promoting and suppressing proteolytic enzymes and, eventually, to identify real friends and enemy proteolytic enzymes in the war against cancer.

References

Adib, T.R., Henderson, S., Perrett, C., Hewitt, D., Bourmpoulia, D., Ledermann, J., et al., 2004. Predicting biomarkers for ovarian cancer using gene-expression microarrays. Br. J. Cancer 90, 686–692.

Agarwal, D., Goodison, S., Nicholson, B., Tarin, D., Urquidi, V., 2003. Expression of matrix metalloproteinase 8 (MMP-8) and tyrosinase-related protein-1 (TYRP1) correlates with the absence of metastasis in an isogenic human breast cancer model. Differentiation 71, 114–125.

Amritha, C.A., Kumaravelu, P., Chellathai, D.D., 2015. Evaluation of anticancer effects of DPP-4 inhibitors in colon cancer- an *in vitro* study. J. Clin. Diag. Res. 9, 14–16.

Andarawewa, K.L., Boulay, A., Masson, R., Mathelin, C., Stoll, I., Tomasetto, C., et al., 2003. Dual stromelysin-3 function during natural mouse mammary tumor virus-ras tumor progression. Cancer Res. 63, 5844–5849.

Ashley, D.M., Riffkin, C.D., Muscat, A.M., Knight, M.J., Kaye, A.H., Novak, U., et al., 2005. Caspase 8 is absent or low in many *ex vivo* gliomas. Cancer 104, 1487–1496.

Balbín, M., Fueyo, A., Tester, A.M., Pendás, A.M., Pitiot, A.S., Astudillo, A., et al., 2003. Loss of collagenase-2 confers increased skin tumor susceptibility to male mice. Nat. Genet. 35, 252–257.

Basset, P., Bellocq, J.P., Wolf, C., Stoll, I., Hutin, P., Limacher, J.M., et al., 1990. A novel metalloproteinase gene specifically expressed in stromal cells of breast carcinomas. Nature 348, 699–704.

Behme, M.T., John, D., McDonald, T.J., 2003. Glucagon-like peptide 1 improved glycaemic control in type 1 diabetes. BMC Endocr. Disord. 3, 1–9.

Beisner, D.R., Ch'en, I.L., Kolla, R.V., Hoffmann, A., Hedrick, S.M., 2005. Cutting edge: innate immunity conferred by B cells is regulated by caspase-8. J. Immunol. 175, 3469–3473.

Bhattacharjee, A., Richards, W.G., Staunton, J., Li, C., Monti, S., Vasa, P., et al., 2001. Classification of human lung carcinomas by mRNA expression profiling reveals distinct adenocarcinoma subclasses. Proc. Natl. Acad. Sci. 98, 13790–13795.

Bignotti, E., Tassi, R.A., Calza, S., Ravaggi, A., Bandiera, E., Rossi, E., et al., 2007. Gene expression profile of ovarian serous papillary carcinomas: identification of metastasis-associated genes. Am. J. Obstet. Gynecol. 196. 245. e1-11.

Blavier, L., Lazaryev, A., Dorey, F., Shackleford, G.M., DeClerck, Y.A., 2006. Matrix metalloproteinases play an active role in Wnt1-induced mammary tumorigenesis. Cancer Res. 66, 2691–2699.

Borgono, C.A., Diamandis, E.P., 2004. The emerging roles of human tissue kallikreins in cancer. Nat. Rev. Cancer 4, 876–890.

Cal, S., López-Otín, C., 2015. ADAMTS proteases and cancer. Matrix Biol. 44-46, 38–45.

Chen, L.M., Chai, K.X., 2002. Prostasin serine protease inhibits breast cancer invasiveness and is transcriptionally regulated by promoter DNA methylation. Int. J. Cancer 97, 323–329.

Chen, L.M., Hodge, G.B., Guarda, L.A., Welch, J.L., Greenberg, N.M., Chai, K.X., 2001. Down-regulation of prostasin serine protease, a potential invasion suppressor in prostate cancer. Prostate 48, 93–103.

Choi, K.Y., Swierczewska, M., Lee, S., Chen, X., 2012. Protease-activated drug development. Theranostics 2, 156–178.

Chung, C.H., Parker, J.S., Karaca, G., Wu, J., Funkhouser, W.K., Moore, D., et al., 2004. Molecular classification of head and neck squamous cell carcinomas using patterns of gene. Cancer Cell 5, 489–500.

Costa, F.P., Batista, E.L., Zelmanowicz, A., Svedman, C., Devenz, G., Alves, S., et al., 2009. Prostasin, a potential tumor marker in ovarian cancer-a pilot study. Clinics 64, 641–644.

Cotter, T.G., 2009. Apoptosis and cancer: the genesis of a research field. Nat. Rev. Cancer 9, 501–507.

Dai, J., Shen, R., Sumitomo, M., Goldberg, J.S., Geng, Y., Navarro, D., et al., 2001. Tumor-suppressive effects of neutral endopeptidase in androgen-independent prostate cancer cells. Clin. Cancer Res. 7, 1370–1377.

Derynck, R., Akhurst, R.J., Balmain, A., 2001. TGF-βsignaling in tumor suppression and cancer progression. Nat. Genet. 29, 117–129.

Devarajan, E., Sahin, A.A., Chen, J.S., Krishnamurthy, R.R., Aggarwal, N., Brun, A.M., et al., 2002. Down-regulation of caspase 3 in breast cancer: a possible mechanism for chemoresistance. Oncogene 21, 8843–8851.

Dhar, S., Bhargava, R., Yunes, M., Li, B., Goyal, J., Naber, S.P., et al., 2001. Analysis of normal epithelial cell specific-1 (NES1)/Kallikrein 10 mRNA expression by in situ hybridization, a novel marker for breast cancer. Clin. Cancer Res. 7, 3393–3398.

Du, W., Wang, S., Zhou, Q., Li, X., Chu, J., Chang, Z., et al., 2013. ADAMTS9 is a functional tumor suppressor through inhibiting AKT/mTOR pathway and associated with poor survival in gastric cancer. Oncogene 32, 3319–3328.

Dubail, J., Kesteloot, F., Deroanne, C., Motte, P., Lambert, V., Rakic, J.M., et al., 2010. ADAMTS-2 functions as anti-angiogenic and anti-tumoral molecule independently of its catalytic activity. Cell. Mol. Life Sci. 67, 4213–4232.

Dunn, J.R., Reed, J.E., du Plessis, D.G., Shaw, E.J., Reeves, P., Gee, A.L., et al., 2006. Expression of ADAMTS-8, a secreted protease with antiangiogenic properties, is downregulated in brain tumours. Br. J. Cancer 94, 1186–1193.

Dupre, J., Behme, M.T., Hramiak, I.M., McFarlane, P., Williamson, M.P., Zabel, P., 1995. Glucagon like peptide I reduces postprandial glycaemic excursions in IDDM. Diabetes 44, 626–630.

Egeblad, M., Werb, Z., 2002. New functions for the matrix metalloproteinases in cancer progression. Nat. Rev. Cancer 2, 161–174.

El Hour, M., Moncada-Pazos, A., Blacher, S., Masset, A., Cal, S., Berndt, S., et al., 2010. Higher sensitivity of Adamts12-deficient mice to tumor growth and angiogenesis. Oncogene 29, 3025–3032.

Felbor, U., Dreier, L., Bryant, R.A., Ploegh, H.L., Olsen, B.R., Mothes, W., 2000. Secreted cathepsin L generates endostatin from collagen XVIII. EMBO J. 19, 1187–1194.

Fortier, A.H., Nelson, B.J., Grella, D.K., Holaday, J.W., 1999. Antiangiogenic activity of prostate-specific antigen. J. Natl. Cancer Inst. 91, 1635–1640.
Garg, P., Sarma, D., Jeppsson, S., Patel, N.R., Gewirtz, A.T., Merlin, D., et al., 2010. MMP-9 functions as a tumor suppressor in colitis-associated cancer. Cancer Res. 70, 792–801.
Gigi, E., Richter-Levin, G., 2014. The hidden price of repeated traumatic exposure. Stress 17, 343–351.
Glinsky, G.V., Berezovska, O., Glinskii, A.B., 2005. Microarray analysis identifies a death-from cancer signature predicting therapy failure in patients with multiple types of cancer. J. Clin. Invest. 115, 1503–1521.
Glinsky, G.V., 2006. Genomic models of metastatic cancer: functional analysis of death-from-cancer signature genes reveals aneuploid, anoikis-resistant, metastasis-enabling phenotype with altered cell cycle control and activated Polycomb Group (PcG) protein chromatin silencing pathway. Cell Cycle 5, 1208–1216.
Goodman, O.B., Febbraio, M., Simantov, R., Zheng, R., Shen, R., Silverstein, R.L., et al., 2006. Neprilysin inhibits angiogenesis via proteolysis of fibroblast growth Factor-2. J. Biol. Chem. 281, 33597–33605.
Gorrin-Rivas, M.J., Arii, S., Furutani, M., Harada, T., Mizumoto, M., Nishiyama, H., et al., 1998. Expression of human macrophage metalloelastase gene in hepatocellular carcinoma: correlation with angiostatin generation and its clinical significance. Hepatology 28, 986–993.
Gorrin-Rivas, M.J., Arii, S., Furutani, M., Mizumoto, M., Mori, A., Hanaki, K., et al., 2000a. Mouse macrophage metalloelastase gene transfer into a murine melanoma suppresses primary tumor growth by halting angiogenesis. Clin. Cancer Res. 6, 1647–1654.
Gorrin-Rivas, M.J., Arii, S., Mori, A., Takeda, Y., Mizumoto, M., Furutani, M., et al., 2000b. Implications of human macrophage metalloelastase and vascular endothelial growth factor gene expression in angiogenesis of hepatocellular carcinoma. Ann. Surg. 231, 67–73.
Goulet, B., Baruch, A., Moon, N.S., Poirier, M., Sansregret, L.L., Erickson, A., et al., 2004. A cathepsin L isoform that is devoid of a signal peptide localizes to the nucleus in S phase and processes the CDP/Cux transcription factor. Mol. Cell 14, 207–219.
Goyal, J., Smith, K.M., Cowan, J.M., Wazer, D.E., Lee, S.W., Band, V., 1998. The role for NES1 serine protease as a novel tumor suppressor. Cancer Res. 58, 4782–4786.
Ham, S.A., Yoo, T., Lee, W.J., Hwang, J.S., Hur, J., Paek, K.S., et al., 2017. ADAMTS1-mediated targeting of TSP-1 by PPARδ suppresses migration and invasion of breast cancer cells. Oncotarget 8, 94091–94103.
Harada, K., Toyooka, S., Shivapurkar, N., Maitra, A., Reddy, J.L., Matta, H., et al., 2002. Deregulation of caspase 8 and 10 expression in pediatric tumors and cell lines. Cancer Res. 62, 5897–5901.
Heidtmann, H.H., Nettelbeck, D.M., Mingels, A., Jager, R., Welker, H.G., Kontermann, R.E., 1999. Generation of angiostatin-like fragments from plasminogen by prostate-specific antigen. Br. J. Cancer 81, 1269–1273.
Ho, L., Taylor, R., Dorstyn, L., Cakouros, D., Bouillet, P., Kumar, S., 2009. A tumor suppressor function for caspase-2. Proc. Natl. Acad. Sci. 106, 5336–5341.
Hofmann, H.S., Hansen, G., Richter, G., Taege, C., Simm, A., Silber, R.E., et al., 2005. Matrix metalloproteinase-12 expression correlates with local recurrence and metastatic disease in non-small cell lung cancer patients. Clin. Cancer Res. 11, 1086–1092.
Hofmann, W.K., de Vos, S., Tsukasaki, K., Wachsman, W., Pinkus, G.S., Said, J.W., et al., 2001. Altered apoptosis pathways in mantle cell lymphoma detected by oligonucleotide microarray. Blood 98, 787–794.
Holleman, A., den Boer, M.L., Kazemier, K.M., Beverloo, H.B., von Bergh, A.R., Janka-Schaub, G.E., et al., 2005. Decreased PARP and procaspase-2 protein levels are associated with cellular drug resistance in childhood acute lymphoblastic leukemia. Blood 106, 1817–1823.

Honda, A., Yamagata, K., Sugiura, S., Watanabe, K., Baba, T.A., 2002. Mouse serine protease TESP5 is selectively included into lipid rafts of sperm membrane presumably as a glycosylphosphatidylinositol-anchored protein. J. Biol. Chem. 277, 16976–16984.

Hooper, J.D., Nicol, D.L., Dickinson, J.L., Eyre, H.J., Scarman, A.L., Normyle, J.F., et al., 1999. Testisin, a new human serine proteinase expressed by premeiotic testicular germ cells and lost in testicular germ cell tumors. Cancer Res. 59, 3199–3205.

Houghton, A.M., Grisolano, J.L., Baumann, M.L., Kobayashi, D.K., Hautamaki, R.D., Nehring, L.C., et al., 2006. Macrophage elastase (matrix metalloproteinase-12) suppresses growth of lung metastases. Cancer Res. 66, 6149–6155.

Hsu, Y.P., Staton, C.A., Cross, N., Buttle, D.J., 2012. Anti-angiogenic properties of ADAMTS-4 in vitro. Int. J. Exp. Pathol. 93, 70–77.

Hussain, T., Savariar, E.N., Diaz-Perez, J.A., Messer, K., Pu, M., Tsien, R.Y., et al., 2014. Surgical molecular navigation with a ratio metric activatable cell penetrating peptide improves intraoperative identification and resection of small salivary gland cancers. Head Neck 38, 715–723.

Iacobuzio-Donahue, C.A., Ashfaq, R., Maitra, A., Adsay, N.V., Shen-Ong, G.L., Berg, K., et al., 2003. Highly expressed genes in pancreatic ductal adenocarcinomas: a comprehensive characterization and comparison of the transcription profiles obtained from three major technologies. Cancer Res. 63, 8614–8622.

Inoue, M., Isobe, M., Itoyama, T., Kido, H., 1999. Structural analysis of esp-1 gene (PRSS 21). Biochem. Biophys. Res. Commun. 266, 564–568.

Inoue, S., Browne, G., Melino, G., Cohen, G.M., 2009. Ordering of caspases in cells undergoing apoptosis by the intrinsic pathway. Cell Death Differ. 16, 1053–1061.

Jochemsen, A.G., Shiloh, Y., 2010. USP10: friend and foe. Cell 140, 308–310.

Jost, M., Folgueras, A.R., Frérart, F., Pendas, A.M., Blacher, S., Houard, X., et al., 2006. Earlier onset of tumoral angiogenesis in matrix metalloproteinase-19-deficient mice. Cancer Res. 66, 5234–5241.

Joyce, J.A., Hanahan, D., 2004. Multiple roles for cysteine cathepsins in cancer. Cell Cycle 3, 1516–1519.

Kajiyama, H., Kikkawa, F., Khin, E., Shibata, K., Ino, K., Mizutani, S., 2003. Dipeptidyl peptidase IV overexpression induces up-regulation of E-cadherin and tissue inhibitors of matrix metalloproteinases, resulting in decreased invasive potential in ovarian carcinoma cells. Cancer Res. 63, 2278–2283.

Kawano, N., Kang, W., Yamashita, M., Koga, Y., Yamazaki, T., Hata, T., et al., 2010. T. Mice lacking two sperm serine proteases, ACR, and PRSS21, are subfertile, but the mutant sperm are infertile *in vitro*. Biol. Reprod. 83, 359–369.

Kerkelä, E., Ala-Aho, R., Jeskanen, L., Rechardt, O., Grénman, R., Shapiro, S.D., et al., 2000. Expression of human macrophage metalloelastase (MMP-12) by tumor cells in skin cancer. J. Invest. Dermatol. 114, 1113–1119.

Kerkelä, E., Ala-aho, R., Klemi, P., Grénman, S., Shapiro, S.D., Kähäri, V.M., et al., 2002. Metalloelastase (MMP-12) expression by tumour cells in squamous cell carcinoma of the vulva correlates with invasiveness, while that by macrophages predicts better outcome. J. Pathol. 198, 258–269.

Kim, H.S., Lee, J.W., Soung, Y.H., Ki, C.J., Jeong, S.W., Nam, S.W., et al., 2003. Inactivating mutations of caspase-8 gene in colorectal carcinomas. Gastroenterology 125, 708–715.

Koblinski, J.E., Ahram, M., Sloane, B.F., 2000. Unraveling the role of proteases in cancer. Clin. Chim. Acta 291, 113–135.

Koo, B.H., Coe, D.M., Dixon, L.J., Somerville, R.P., Nelson, C.M., Wang, L.W., et al., 2010. ADAMTS9 is a cell-autonomously acting anti-angiogenic metalloprotease expressed by microvascular endothelial cells. Am. J. Pathol. 176, 1494–1504.

Krammer, P.H., Arnold, R., Lavrik, I.N., 2007. Life and death in peripheral T cells. Nat. Rev. Immunol. 7, 532–542.

Krelin, Y., Zhang, L., Kang, T.B., Appel, E., Kovalenko, A., Wallach, D., 2008. Caspase-8 deficiency facilitates cellular transformation *in vitro*. Cell Death Differ. 15, 1350–1355.

Kumar, S., Sharghi-Namini, S., Rao, N., Ge, R., 2012. ADAMTS5 functions as an anti-angiogenic and anti-tumorigenic protein independent of its proteoglycanase activity. Am. J. Pathol. 181, 1056–1068.

Kuno, K., Bannai, K., Hakozaki, M., Matsushima, K., Hirose, K., 2004. The carboxyl-terminal half region of ADAMTS-1 suppresses both tumorigenicity and experimental tumor metastatic potential. Biochem. Biophys. Res. Commun. 319, 1327–1333.

Lai, L.C., Erbas, H., Lennard, T.W., Peaston, R.T., 1996. Prostate-specific antigen in breast cyst fluid: possible role of prostate-specific antigen in hormone-dependent breast cancer. Int. J. Cancer 66, 743–746.

Larsson, L.G., Henriksson, M.A., 2010. The Yin and Yang functions of the Myc oncoprotein in cancer development and as targets for therapy. Exp. Cell Res. 316, 1429–1437.

Lebeau, A.M., Brennen, W.N., Aggarwal, S., Denmeade, S.R., 2009. Targeting the cancer stroma with a fibroblast activation protein-activated promelittinprotoxin. Mol. Cancer Ther. 8, 1378–1386.

Lee, H.J., Kim, M.S., Shin, J.M., Park, T.J., Chung, H.M., Baek, K.H., 2006a. The expression patterns of deubiquitinating enzymes, USP22 and Usp22. Gene Expr. Patterns 6, 277–284.

Lee, J.W., Kim, M.R., Soung, Y.H., Nam, S.W., Kim, S.H., Lee, J.Y., et al., 2006b. Mutational analysis of the CASP6 gene in colorectal and gastric carcinomas. APMIS 114, 646–650.

Lee, N.V., Sato, M., Annis, D.S., Loo, J.A., Wu, L., Mosher, D.F., et al., 2006c. ADAMTS1 mediates the release of antiangiogenic polypeptides from TSP1 and 2. EMBO J. 25, 5270–5283.

Lee, Y.J., Koch, M., Karl, D., Torres-Collado, A.X., Fernando, N.T., Rothrock, C., et al., 2010. Variable inhibition of thrombospondin 1 against liver and lung metastases through differential activation of metalloproteinase ADAMTS1. Cancer Res. 70, 948–956.

Levine, B., Klionsky, D.J., 2004. Development by self-digestion: molecular mechanisms and biological functions of autophagy. Dev. Cell. 6, 463–477.

Li, M., Brooks, C.L., Kon, N., Gu, W., 2004. A dynamic role of HAUSP in the p53-Mdm2 pathway. Mol. Cell 13, 879–886.

Li, N.F., Zhang, J.H., Chang, J.H., Yang, J., Wang, H.M., Zhou, L.H., 2011. Association of genetic variations of the prostasin gene with essential hypertension in the Xinjiang Kazakh population. Chin. Med. J. 124, 2107–2112.

Liu, X.L., Wazer, D.E., Watanabe, K., Band, V., 1996. Identification of a novel serine protease-like gene, the expression of which is down-regulated during breast cancer progression. Cancer Res. 56, 3371–3379.

Liu, J., Xia, H., Kim, M., Xu, L., Li, Y., Zhang, L., et al., 2011. Beclin1 controls the levels of p53 by regulating the deubiquitination activity of USP10 and USP13. Cell 147, 223–234.

Lo, P.H., Lung, H.L., Cheung, A.K., Apte, S.S., Chan, K.W., Kwong, F.M., et al., 2010. Extracellular protease ADAMTS9 suppresses esophageal and nasopharyngeal carcinoma tumor formation by inhibiting angiogenesis. Cancer Res. 70, 5567–5576.

López-Otín, C., Matrisian, L.M., 2007. Emerging roles of proteases in tumour suppression. Nat. Rev. Cancer 7, 800–808.

Lopez-Otin, C., Overall, C.M., 2002. Protease degradomics: a new challenge for proteomics. Nat. Rev. Mol. Cell Biol. 3, 509–519.

Lu, K.H., Patterson, A.P., Wang, L., Marquez, R.T., Atkinson, E.N., Baggerly, K.A., et al., 2004. Selection of potential markers for epithelial ovarian cancer with gene expression arrays and recursive descent partition analysis. Clin. Cancer Res. 10, 3291–3300.

Luo, L.Y., Rajpert-De Meyts, E.R., Jung, K., Diamandis, E.P., 2003. Expression of the normal epithelial cell-specific 1 (NES1; KLK10) candidate tumour suppressor gene in normal and malignant testicular tissue. Br. J. Cancer 85, 220–224.

Mandruzzato, S., Brasseur, F., Andry, G., Boon, T., Bruggen, V.D., 1997. CASP-8 mutation recognized by cytolytic T lymphocytes on a human head and neck carcinoma. J. Exp. Med. 186, 785–793.

Manton, K.J., Douglas, M.L., Netzel-Arnett, S., Fitzpatrick, D.R., Nicol, D.L., Boyd, A.W., et al., 2005. Hypermethylation of the 5′ CpG island of the gene encoding the serine protease testisin promotes its loss in testicular tumorigenesis. Br. J. Cancer 92, 760–769.

Marino, G., Salvador-Montoliu, N., Fueyo, A., Knecht, E., Mizushima, N., López-Otín, C., 2007. Tissue-specific autophagy alterations and increased tumorigenesis in mice deficient in Atg4C/autophagin-3. J. Biol. Chem. 282, 18573–18583.

Marino, G., Uría, J.A., Puente, X.S., Quesada, V., Bordallo, J., López-Otín, C., 2003. Human autophagins, a family of cysteine proteinases potentially implicated in cell degradation by autophagy. J. Biol. Chem. 278, 3671–3678.

Martin, E.W., Buzza, M., Driesbaugh, K.H., Liu, S., Fortenberry, Y.M., Leppla, S.H., et al., 2015. Targeting the membrane-anchored serine protease testisin with a novel engineered anthrax toxin prodrug to kill tumor cells and reduce tumor burden. Oncotarget 6, 33534–33553.

McCawley, L.J., Crawford, H.C., King Jr., L.E., Mudgett, J., Matrisian, L.M., 2004. A protective role for matrix metalloproteinase-3 in squamous cell carcinoma. Cancer Res. 64, 6965–6972.

McIntosh, C., Demuth, H., Pospisilik, J., Pederson, R., 2005. Dipeptidyl peptidase IV inhibitors: How do they work as new antidiabetic agents? Regul. Pept. 128, 159–165.

Mirandola, L., Cannon, J., Cobos, E., Bernardini, G., Jenkins, M.R., Kast, W.M., 2011. Chiriva-Internati M. Cancer testis antigens: novel biomarkers and targetable proteins for ovarian cancer. Int. Rev. Immunol. 30, 127–137.

Mizushima, N., 2007. Autophagy: process and function. Genes Dev. 21, 2861–2873.

Mohamed, M.M., Sloane, B.F., 2006. Cysteine cathepsins: multifunctional enzymes in cancer. Nat. Rev. Cancer 6, 764–775.

Mok, S.C., Chao, J., Skates, S., Wong, K., Yiu, G.K., Muto, M.G., et al., 2001. Prostasin, a potential serum marker for ovarian cancer: identification through microarray technology. J. Natl. Cancer Inst. 93, 1458–1464.

Murtaza, M., Jolly, L.A., Gecz, J., Wood, S.A., 2015. La FAM fatale: USP9X in development and disease. Cell. Mol. Life Sci. 72, 2075–2089.

Nanus, D.M., 2003. Of peptides and peptidases: the role of cell surface peptidases in cancer. Clin. Cancer Res. 9, 6307–6309.

Netzel-Arnett, S., Bugge, T.H., Hess, R.A., Carnes, K., Stringer, B.W., Scarman, A.L., et al., 2009. The glycosylphosphatidylinositol-anchored serine protease PRSS21 (testisin) imparts murine epididymal sperm cell maturation and fertilizing ability. Biol. Reprod. 81, 921–932.

Nguyen, L.T., Yang, X.Z., Du, X., Wang, J.W., Zhang, R., Zhao, J., et al., 2015. Enhancing tumor-specific intracellular delivering efficiency of cell-penetrating peptide by fusion with a peptide targeting to EGFR. Amino Acids 47, 997–1006.

Nguyen, Q.T., Olson, E.S., Aguilera, T.A., Jiang, T., Scadeng, M., Ellies, L.G., et al., 2010. Surgery with molecular fluorescence imaging using activatable cell-penetrating peptides decreases residual cancer and improves survival. Proc. Natl. Acad. Sci. 107, 4317–4322.

Obiezu, C.V., Scorilas, A., Katsaros, D., Massobrio, M., Yousef, G.M., Fracchioli, S., et al., 2001. Higher human kallikrein gene 4 (klk4) expression indicates poor prognosis of ovarian cancer patients. Clin. Cancer Res. 7, 2380–2386.

Obika, M., Ogawa, H., Takahashi, K., Li, J., Hatipoglu, O.F., Cilek, M.Z., et al., 2012. Tumor growth inhibitory effect of ADAMTS1 is accompanied by the inhibition of tumor angiogenesis. Cancer Sci. 103, 1889–1897.

Offman, J., Gascoigne, K., Bristow, F., Macpherson, P., Bignami, M., Casorelli, I., et al., 2005. Repeated sequences in CASPASE-5 and FANCD2 but not NF1 are targets for mutation in microsatellite-unstable acute leukemia/myelodysplastic syndrome. Mol. Cancer Res. 3, 251–260.

Osman, I., Yee, H., Taneja, S.S., Levinson, B., Zeleniuch-Jacquotte, A., Chang, C., et al., 2004. Neutral endopeptidase protein expression and prognosis in localized prostate cancer. Clin. Cancer Res. 10, 4096–4100.

Overall, C.M., Kleifeld, O., 2006. Validating matrix metalloproteinases as drug targets and anti-targets for cancer therapy. Nat. Rev. Cancer 6, 227–239.

Palavalli, L.H., Prickett, T.D., Wunderlich, J.R., Wei, X., Burrell, A.S., Porter-Gill, P., et al., 2009. Analysis of the matrix metalloproteinase family reveals that MMP 8 is often mutated in melanoma. Nat. Genet. 41, 518–520.

Papandreou, C.N., Usmani, B., Geng, Y., Bogenrieder, T., Freeman, R., Wilk, S., et al., 1998. Neutral endopeptidase 24.11 loss in metastatic human prostate cancer contributes to androgen-independent progression. Nat. Med. 4, 50–57.

Pérez-Mancera, P.A., Rust, A.G., Van der Weyden, L., Kristiansen, G., Li, A., Sarver, A.L., et al., 2012. The deubiquitinase USP9X suppresses pancreatic ductal adenocarcinoma. Nature 486, 266–270.

Pedersen, T.X., Pennington, C.J., Almholt, K., Christensen, I.J., Nielsen, B.S., Edwards, D.R., et al., 2005. Extracellular protease mRNAs are predominantly expressed in the stromal areas of microdissected mouse breast carcinomas. Carcinogenesis 26, 1233–1240.

Pendás, A.M., Folgueras, A.R., Llano, E., Caterina, J., Frerard, F., Rodríguez, F., et al., 2004. Diet-induced obesity and reduced skin cancer susceptibility in matrix metalloproteinase 19-deficient mice. Mol. Cell. Biol. 24, 5304–5313.

Petraki, C.D., Gregorakis, A.K., Papanastasiou, P.A., Karavana, V.N., Luo, L.Y., Diamandis, E.P., 2003. Immunohistochemical localization of human kallikreins 6, 10 and 13 in benign and malignant prostatic tissues. Prostate Cancer Prostatic Dis. 6, 223–227.

Planes, C., Randrianarison, N.H., Charles, R.P., Frateschi, S., Cluzeaud, F., Vuagniaux, G., et al., 2010. ENaC-mediated alveolar fluid clearance and lung fluid balance depend on the channel-activating protease 1. EMBO Mol. Med. 2, 26–37.

Porter, S., Scott, S.D., Sassoon, E.M., Williams, M.R., Jones, J.L., Girling, A.C., et al., 2004. Dysregulated expression of adamalysin-thrombospondin genes in human breast carcinoma. Clin. Cancer Res. 10, 2429–2440.

Potrich, C., Tomazzolli, R., Dalla, S.M., Anderluh, G., Malovrh, P., Macek, P., et al., 2005. Cytotoxic activity of a tumor protease-activated pore-forming toxin. Bioconjug. Chem. 16, 369–376.

Puente, X.S., Sanchez, L.M., Overall, C.M., Lopez-Otin, C., 2003. Human and mouse proteases: a comparative genomic approach. Nat. Rev. Genet. 4, 544–558.

Qu, X., Yu, J., Bhagat, G., Furuya, N., Hibshoosh, H., Troxel, A., et al., 2003. Promotion of tumorigenesis by heterozygous disruption of the *beclin 1* autophagy gene. J. Clin. Invest. 112, 1809–1820.

Rawlings, N.D., Barrett, A.J., Bateman, A., 2011. Asparagine peptide lyases: a seventh catalytic type of proteolytic enzymes. J. Biol. Chem. 286, 38321–38328.

Reinheckel, T., Hagemann, S., Dollwet-Mack, S., Martinez, E., Lohmüller, T., Zlatkovic, G., et al., 2005. The lysosomal cysteine protease cathepsin L regulates keratinocyte proliferation by control of growth factor recycling. J. Cell Sci. 118, 3387–3395.

Rickert, K.W., Kelley, P., Byrne, N.J., Diehl, R.E., Hall, D.L., Montalvo, A.M., et al., 2008. Structure of human prostasin, a target for the regulation of hypertension. J. Biol. Chem. 283, 34864–34872.

Roman-Gomez, J., Jimenez-Velasco, A., Agirre, X., Castillejo, J.A., Barrios, M., Andreu, E.J., et al., 2004. The normal epithelial cell-specific 1 (NES1) gene, a candidate tumor suppressor gene on chromosome 19q13.3-4, is downregulated by hypermethylation in acute lymphoblastic leukemia. Leukemia 18, 362–365.

Sakashita, K., Mimori, K., Tanaka, F., Tahara, K., Inoue, H., Sawada, T., et al., 2008. Clinical significance of low expression of Prostasin mRNA in human gastric cancer. J. Surg. Oncol. 98, 559–564.

Savinov, A.Y., Remacle, A.G., Golubkov, V.S., Krajewska, M., Kennedy, S., Duffy, M.J., et al., 2006. Matrix metalloproteinase 26 proteolysis of the NH2-terminal domain of the estrogen receptor β correlates with the survival of breast cancer patients. Cancer Res. 66, 2716–2724.

Scarman, A.L., Hooper, J.D., Boucaut, K.J., Sit, M.L., Webb, G.C., Normyle, J.F., et al., 2001. Organization and chromosomal localization of the murine testisin gene encoding a serine protease temporally expressed during spermatogenesis. Eur. J. Biochem. 268, 1250–1258.

Schwickart, M., Huang, X., Lill, J.R., Liu, J., Ferrando, R., French, D.M., et al., 2010. Deubiquitinase USP9X stabilizes MCL1 and promotes tumour cell survival. Nature 463, 103–107.

Shen, R., Sumitomo, M., Dai, J., Hardy, D.O., Navarro, D., Usmani, B., et al., 2000. Identification and characterization of two androgen response regions in the human neutral endopeptidase gene. Mol. Cell. Endocrinol. 170, 131–142.

Shi, H., Xu, J.M., Hu, N.Z., Wang, X.L., Mei, Q., Song, Y., 2006. Transfection of mouse macrophage metalloelastase gene into murine CT-26 colon cancer cells suppresses orthotopic tumor growth, angiogenesis and vascular endothelial growth factor expression. Cancer Lett. 233, 139–150.

Shi, Y., Desponts, C., Do, J.T., Hahm, H.S., Schöler, H.R., Ding, S., 2008. Induction of pluripotent stem cells from mouse embryonic fibroblasts by Oct4 and Klf4 with small-molecule compounds. Cell Stem Cell 3, 568–574.

Shigemasa, K., Underwood, L.J., Beard, J., Tanimoto, H., Ohama, K., Parmley, T.H., et al., 2007. Overexpression of testisin, a serine protease expressed by testicular germ cells, in epithelial ovarian tumor cells. J. Soc. Gynecol. Investig. 7, 358–362.

Song, H., Wong, K.K., Chon, K.K., 2003. Modelling and forecasting the demand for Hong Kong tourism. Int. J. Hosp. Manag. 22, 435–451.

Song, M.S., Salmena, L., Carracedo, A., Egia, A., Lo-Coco, F., Teruya-Feldstein, J., et al., 2008. The deubiquitinylation and localization of PTEN are regulated by a HAUSP-PML network. Nature 455, 813–817.

Sotiropoulou, G., Rogakos, V., Tsetsenis, T., Pampalakis, G., Zafiropoulos, N., Simillides, G., et al., 2003. Emerging interest in the kallikrein gene family for understanding and diagnosing cancer. Oncol. Res. 13, 381–391.

Soung, Y.H., Lee, J.W., Kim, S.Y., Park, W.S., Nam, S.W., Lee, J.Y., et al., 2004. Somatic mutations of CASP3 gene in human cancers. Hum. Genet. 115, 112–115.

Soung, Y.H., Lee, J.W., Kim, H.S., Park, W.S., Kim, S.Y., Lee, J.H., et al., 2003. Inactivating mutations of CASPASE-7 gene in human cancers. Oncogene 22, 8048–8052.

Soung, Y.H., Lee, J.W., Kim, S.Y., Jang, J., Park, Y.G., Park, W.S., et al., 2005. CASPASE-8 gene is inactivated by somatic mutations in gastric carcinomas. Cancer Res. 65, 815–821.

Stephen, H.M., Khoury, R.J., Majmudar, P.R., Blaylock, T., Hawkins, K., Salama, M.S., et al., 2016. Epigenetic suppression of neprilysin regulates breast cancer invasion. Oncogene 5, e207.

Su, H., Bidere, N., Zheng, L., Cubre, A., Sakai, K., Dale, J., et al., 2005. Requirement for caspase-8 in NF-kappaB activation by antigen receptor. Science 307, 1465–1468.

Sulzmaier, F.J., Ramos, J.W., 2013. RSK isoforms in cancer cell invasion and metastasis. Cancer Res. 73, 6099–6105.

Sumitomo, M., Iwase, A., Zheng, R., Navarro, D., Kaminetzky, D., Shen, R., et al., 2004. Synergy in tumor suppression by direct interaction of neutral endopeptidase with PTEN. Cancer Cell 5, 67–78.

Sun, J., Li, T., Zhao, Y., Huang, L., Sun, H., Wu, H., et al., 2018. USP10 inhibits lung cancer cell growth and invasion by upregulating PTEN. Mol. Cell. Biochem. 441, 1–7.

Suojanen, J., Salo, T., Koivunen, E., Sorsa, T., Pirilä, E., 2009. A novel and selective membrane type-1 matrix metalloproteinase (MT1-MMP) inhibitor reduces cancer cell motility and tumor growth. Cancer Biol. Ther. 8, 2362–2370.

Tang, T., Kmet, M., Corral, L., Vartanian, S., Tobler, A., Papkoff, J., 2005. Testisin, a glycosyl-phosphatidylinositol-linked serine protease, promotes malignant transformation *in vitro* and *in vivo*. Cancer Res. 65, 868–878.

Teitz, T., Wei, T., Valentine, M.B., Vanin, E.F., Grenet, J., Valentine, V.A., et al., 2000. Caspase 8 is deleted or silenced preferentially in childhood neuroblastomas with amplification of MYCN. Nat. Med. 6, 529–535.

Toloczko, A., Guo, F., Yuen, H.F., Wen, Q., Wood, S.A., Ong, Y.S., et al., 2017. Deubiquitinating enzyme USP9X suppresses tumor growth via LATS kinase and core components of the hippo pathway. Cancer Res. 77, 4921–4933.

Turk, B., 2006. Targeting proteases: successes, failures and prospects. Nat. Rev. Drug Discov. 5, 785–799.

Turk, V., Turk, B., Guncar, G., Turk, D., Kos, J., 2002. Lysosomal cathepsins: structure, role in antigen processing and presentation, and cancer. Adv. Enzym. Regul. 42, 285–303.

Uria, J.A., Lopez-Otin, C., 2000. Matrilysin-2, a new matrix metalloproteinase expressed in human tumors and showing the minimal domain organization required for secretion, latency, and activity. Cancer Res. 60, 4745–4751.

Vazquez, F., Hastings, G., Ortega, M.A., Lane, T.F., Oikemus, S., Lombardo, M., et al., 1999. METH-1, a human ortholog of ADAMTS1, and METH-2 are members of a new family of proteins with angio-inhibitory activity. J. Biol. Chem. 274, 23349–23357.

Verdecia, M.A., Joazeiro, C.A., Wells, N.J., Ferrer, J.L., Bowman, M.E., Hunter, T., et al., 2003. Conformational flexibility underlies ubiquitin ligation mediated by the WWP1 HECT domain E3 ligase. Mol. Cell 11, 249–259.

Viloria, C.G., Obaya, A.J., Moncada-Pazos, A., Llamazares, M., Astudillo, A., Capella, G., et al., 2009. Genetic inactivation of ADAMTS15 metalloprotease in human colorectal cancer. Cancer Res. 69, 4926–4934.

Wagstaff, L., Kelwick, R., Decock, J., Arnold, H., Pennington, C., Jaworski, D., et al., 2010. ADAMTS15 metalloproteinase inhibits breast cancer cell migration. Breast Cancer Res. 12, P15.

Walter, L., Pujada, A., Bhatnagar, N., Białkowska, A.B., Yang, V.W., Laroui, H., et al., 2017. Epithelial derived-matrix metalloproteinase (MMP9) exhibits a novel defensive role of tumor suppressor in colitis associated cancer by activating MMP9-Notch1-ARF-p53 axis. Oncotarget 8, 364–378.

Weidle, U.H., Tiefenthaler, G., Georges, G., 2014a. Proteases as activators for cytotoxic prodrugs in antitumor therapy. Cancer Genom. Proteom. 11, 67–79.

Weidle, U.H., Tiefenthaler, G., Schiller, C., Weiss, E.H., Georges, G., Brinkmann, U., 2014b. Prospects of bacterial and plant protein-based immunotoxins for treatment of cancer. Cancer Genom. Proteom. 11, 25–38.

Welsh, J.B., Sapinoso, L.M., Kern, S.G., Brown, D.A., Liu, T., Bauskin, A.R., et al., 2003. Large-scale delineation of secreted protein biomarkers overexpressed in cancer tissue and serum. Proc. Natl. Acad. Sci. 100, 3410–3415.

Wesley, U.V., Albino, A.P., Tiwari, S., Houghton, A.N., 1999. A role for dipeptidyl peptidase IV in suppressing the malignant phenotype of melanocytic cells. J. Exp. Med. 190, 311–322.

Wesley, U.V., McGroarty, M., Homoyouni, A., 2005. Dipeptidyl peptidase inhibits malignant phenotype of prostate cancer cells by blocking basic fibroblast growth factor signaling pathway. Cancer Res. 65, 1325–1334.

Wickman, G., Julian, L., Olson, M.F., 2012. How apoptotic cells aid in the removal of their own cold dead bodies. Cell Death Differ. 19, 735–742.

Williams, S.A., Merchant, R.F., Garrett-Mayer, E., Isaacs, J.T., Buckley, J.T., Denmeade, S.R., 2007. A prostate-specific antigen-activated channel-forming toxin as therapy for prostatic disease. J. Natl. Cancer Inst. 99, 376–385.

Witty, J.P., Lempka, T., Coffey Jr., R.J., Matrisian, L.M., 2005. Decreased tumor formation in 7,12-dimethylbenzanthracene-treated stromelysin-1 transgenic mice is associated with alterations in mammary epithelial cell apoptosis. Cancer Res. 55, 1401–1406.

Xie, Y., Gou, Q., Xie, K., Wang, Z., Wang, Y., Zheng, H., 2016. ADAMTS6 suppresses tumor progression via the ERK signaling pathway and serves as a prognostic marker in human breast cancer. Oncotarget 7, 61273–61283.

Xu, Z., Shi, H., Li, Q., Mei, Q., Bao, J., Shen, Y., et al., 2008. Mouse macrophage metalloelastase generates angiostatin from plasminogen and suppresses tumor angiogenesis in murine colon cancer. Oncol. Rep. 20, 81–88.

Xu, X., Tang, X., Lu, M., Tang, Q., Zhang, H., Zhu, H., et al., 2014. Overexpression of MAGE-A9 predicts unfavorable outcome in breast cancer. Exp. Mol. Pathol. 97, 579–584.

Yamashita, M., Honda, A., Ogura, A., Kashiwabara, S., Fukami, K., Baba, T., 2008. Reduced fertility of mouse epididymal sperm lacking Prss21/Tesp5 is rescued by sperm exposure to uterine microenvironment. Genes Cells 13, 1001–1013.

Yang, Y., Hong, H., Zhang, Y., Cai, W., 2009. Molecular imaging of proteases in cancer. Cancer Growth Metastasis 2, 13–27.

Yasothornsrikul, S., Greenbaum, D., Medzihradszky, K.F., Toneff, T., Bundey, R., Miller, R., et al., 2003. Cathepsin L in secretory vesicles functions as a prohormone-processing enzyme for production of the enkephalin peptide neurotransmitter. Proc. Natl. Acad. Sci. 100, 9590–9595.

Yeom, S.Y., Jang, H.L., Lee, S.J., Kim, E., Son, H.J., Kim, B.G., et al., 2010. Interaction of testisin with maspin and its impact on invasion and cell death resistance of cervical cancer cells. FEBS Lett. 584, 1469–1475.

Yoo, N.J., Lee, J.W., Kim, Y.J., Soung, Y.H., Kim, S.Y., Nam, S.W., et al., 2004. Loss of caspase-2, -6 and -7 expression in gastric cancers. APMIS 112, 330–335.

Yousef, G.M., Magklara, A., Diamandis, E.P., 2000. KLK12 is a novel serine protease and a new member of the human kallikrein gene family-differential expression in breast cancer. Genomics 69, 331–341.

Yousef, G.M., Borgoño, C.A., Popalis, C., Yacoub, G.M., Polymeris, M.E., Soosaipillai, A., et al., 2004. In-silico analysis of kallikrein gene expression in pancreatic and colon cancers. Anticancer Res. 24, 43–51.

Yu, H., Diamandis, E.P., Levesque, M., Giai, M., Roagna, R., Ponzone, R., et al., 1996. Prostate specific antigen in breast cancer, benign breast disease and normal breast tissue. Breast Cancer Res. Treat. 40, 171–178.

Yu, H., Levesque, M.A., Clark, G.M., Diamandis, E.P., 1998. Prognostic value of prostate-specific antigen for women with breast cancer: a large United States cohort study. Clin. Cancer Res. 4, 1489–1497.

Yu, J.X., Chao, L., Chao, J., 1995. Molecular cloning, tissue-specific expression and cellular localization of human prostasin mRNA. J. Biol. Chem. 270, 13483–13489.

Zhang, M., Wang, A., Xia, T., He, P., 2008. Effects of fluoride on DNA damage, S-phase cell-cycle arrest and the expression of NF-κB in primary cultured rat hippocampal neurons. Toxicol. Lett. 179 (1), 1–5.

Zhang, H., Liu, T., Zhang, Z., Payne, S.H., Zhang, B., McDermott, J.E., Zhou, J.Y., et al., 2016. Integrated proteogenomic characterization of human high-grade serous ovarian cancer. Cell 166, 755–765.

Further reading

Choi, G.C., Li, J., Wang, Y., Li, L., Zhong, L., Ma, B., et al., 2014. The metalloprotease ADAMTS8 displays antitumor properties through antagonizing EGFR-MEK-ERK signaling and is silenced in carcinomas by CpG methylation. Mol. Cancer Res. 12, 228–238.

Chu, Z., Xinyan, J., Haitao, Z., Qi, Z., Xiaolei, C., Mei, T., et al., 2018. Deubiquitylase USP9X suppresses tumorigenesis by stabilizing large tumor suppressor kinase 2 (LATS2) in the Hippo pathway. J. Biol. Chem. 293, 1178–1191.

Kuno, K., Kanada, N., Nakashima, E., Fujiki, F., Ichimura, F., Matsushima, K., 1997. Molecular cloning of a gene encoding a new type of metalloproteinase-disintegrin family protein with thrombospondin motifs as an inflammation associated gene. J. Biol. Chem. 272, 556–562.

Levine, B., 2007. Cell biology: autophagy and cancer. Nature 446, 745–747.

Li, M., Chen, D., Shiloh, A., Luo, J., Nikolaev, A.Y., Qin, J., et al., 2002. Deubiquitination of p53 by HAUSP is an important pathway for p53 stabilization. Nature 416, 648–653.

Sharghi-Namini, S., Fan, H., Sulochana, K.N., Potturi, P., Xiang, W., Chong, Y.S., et al., 2008. The first but not the second thrombospondin type 1 repeat of ADAMTS5 functions as an angiogenesis inhibitor. Biochem. Biophys. Res. Commun. 371, 215–219.

Suga, A., Hikasa, H., Taira, M., 2006. Xenopus ADAMTS1 negatively modulates FGF signaling independent of its metalloprotease activity. Dev. Biol. 295, 26–39.

Teitz, T., Lahti, J.M., Kidd, V.J., 2001. Aggressive childhood neuroblastomas do not express caspase-8: an important component of programmed cell death. J. Mol. Med. 79, 428–436.

Wagstaff, L., Kelwick, R., Decock, J., Edwards, D.R., 2011. The roles of ADAMTS metalloproteinases in tumorigenesis and metastasis. Front. Biosci. 16, 1861–1872.

Yousef, G.M., Magklara, A., Chang, A., Jung, K., Katsaros, D., Diamandis, E.P., 2001. Cloning of a new member of the human kallikrein gene family, KLK14, which is down-regulated in different malignancies. Cancer Res. 61, 3425–3431.

Chapter 15

Vitamin D as therapeutic agent acting against cancers caused by proteases

Ebtesam Abdullah Al-Suhaimi[a], Khulood Mohammed Al-Khater[b], Meneerah Abdurhman Aljafary[a], Vijaya Ravinayagam[c], Adeeb Shehzad[d], Hanan A. Al-Dossary[e], Reem A. Assuhaimi[e], Mohamad Tarhini[f], Abdelhamid Elaissari[f]

[a]*Department of Biology, College of Science, Imam Abdulrahman Bin Faisal University, Dammam, Saudi Arabia,* [b]*Department of Anatomy, College of Medicine, Imam Abdulrahman Bin Faisal University, Dammam, Saudi Arabia,* [c]*Nanomedicine Research Department, Institute for Research and Medical Consultations (IRMC), Deanship of Scientific Research, Imam Abdulrahman Bin Faisal University, Dammam, Saudi Arabia,* [d]*Department of Clinical Pharmacy, Institute for Research and Medical Consultations (IRMC), Imam Abdulrahman Bin Faisal University, Dammam, Saudi Arabia,* [e]*Institute for Research and Medical Consultations (IRMC), Imam Abdulrahman Bin Faisal University, Dammam, Saudi Arabia,* [f]*Univ Lyon, University Claude Bernard Lyon-1, CNRS, LAGEP-UMR 5007, Lyon, France*

15.1 Introduction

Vitamin D has been known as the sunshine vitamin, as it is produced with the exposure to sun, although unlike other vitamins the nutritional sources of vitamin D are few. Vitamin D is a hormone family, specifically belonging to the steroid family. As a prohormone, vitamin D is converted into active form in the presence of sun in the skin. This active hormone accumulates in many cells and tissues, where it mediates a wide range of actions. The deeper understanding of vitamin D and its interactions with different cells, tissues, and organs will enable the future pharmaceutical applications of vitamin D in the prevention and treatment of many disorders in the future.

There are two types of vitamin D, natural and synthetic. Natural vitamin D is obtained by dietary intake; animal origin (cholecalciferol) gives rise to vitamin D3, while vegetable origin (ergocalciferol) gives rise to vitamin D2. Other natural analogs of vitamin D are vitamin D1 (ergocalciferol: lumisterol), vitamin D4 (22-dihydroergocalciferol), and vitamin D5 (sitocalciferol). There are many synthetic vitamin D analogs such as 22-oxacalcitriol (OCT) and falecalcitriol

Cancer-Leading Proteases. https://doi.org/10.1016/B978-0-12-818168-3.00015-2

with a wider effect than vitamin D3. Dihydrotachysterol (DHT), another synthetic analog, does not need further hydroxylation in the kidney as it is activated directly in the liver. Calcipotriol and paricalcitol are vitamin D3-derived molecules (Caccamo et al., 2018).

Synthetic vitamin D is produced in the skin. A derivative of cholesterol (7-dehydrocholesterol) is produced in large quantities in the skin. When the skin is exposed to sunlight, the ultraviolet (UVB) radiation is absorbed by 7-dehydrocholesterol located in both the dermal and epidermal cells, transforming 7-dehydrocholesterol to a nonfunctional previtamin D3 (cholecalciferol). Cholecalciferol is then metabolized in the liver by the enzyme 25-hydroxylase encoded by the CYP2R1 gene and converted to 25-hydroxyvitamin D3, which is transported through the blood to the kidney, where it is transformed by the enzyme, 1-α-hydroxylase, synthesized by the CYP27B1 gene, to the functional form of vitamin D (1α,25-dihydroxyvitamin D3). Vitamin D can be measured in the body by assessment of 25-hydroxyvitamin D3 level in the blood (Fig. 15.1) (DeLuca, 2004; Holick, 2004a). Calcitriol, derived from Vitamin D2 or Vitamin D3, is known to be the active form of Vitamin D which mediates calcium metabolism and osteoblasts (Shrihari, 2018).

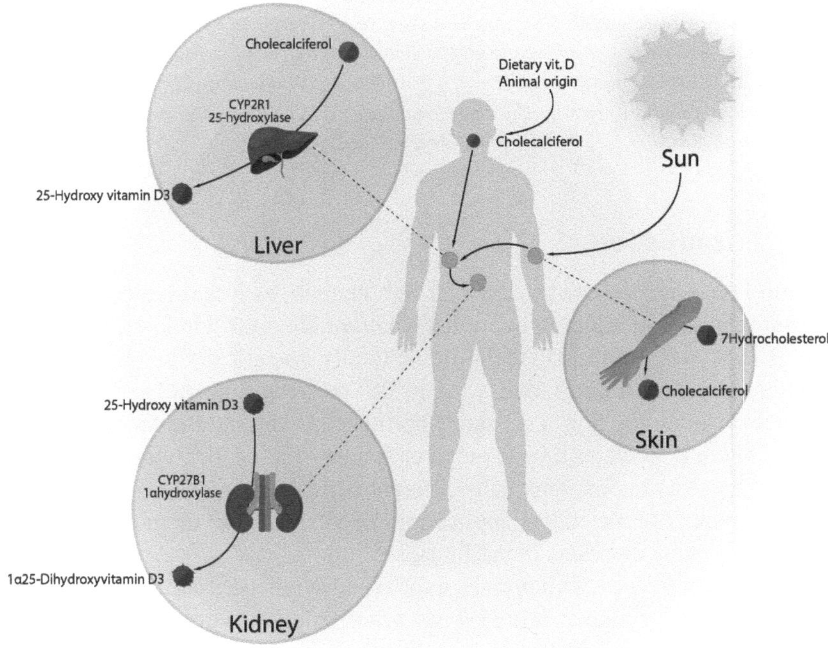

FIG. 15.1 Vitamin D synthesis begins in the skin where 7-hydrocholesterol is transformed into cholecalciferol. In the liver CYP2R1 gene synthesizes 25-hydroxylase, which transforms cholecalciferol into 25-hydroxyvitamin D3. CYP27B1 gene in the kidney synthesizes 25-hydroxy vitamin D3 into the active form 1α25-dihydroxyvitamin D3.

Vitamin D is found in oily fish, such as salmon, sardines, and mackerel. In addition to fish, cod liver oil and shitake mushrooms are also considered as a dietary source of Vitamin D. Some foods such as milk, yogurt, bread, orange juice, and some breakfast cereals are fortified with vitamin D. The most common source of vitamin D is the exposure to sun, by which it can be stored in fat cells and utilized during less exposure to sun (Holick and Chen, 2008).

15.2 Functions of vitamin D

Vitamin D and its analogs are natural molecules that bind to a nuclear vitamin D receptor (VDR). This receptor is widely distributed in many types of cells, tissues, and organs (Caccamo et al., 2018) and thus its essential functions range from cells to organs as described below.

15.2.1 Nuclear functions

The most active form of vitamin D "1α,25-dihydroxyvitamin D3 (1α, 25 $(OH)_2D3$)" is effective when it binds to the VDR. The VDR consists of three main regions where a C-terminal domain binds to 1α,25- dihydroxyvitamin D3 followed by a nonbinding region and ending with a DNA-binding N-terminal dual zinc finger domain. The changes in receptor caused by VDR during Vitamin D binding allow it to interact with the retinoid X receptor (RXR), which is in turn enabled to bind with vitamin D response elements (VDREs) in the DNA, facilitating gene transcription (Keane et al., 2018). Likewise nuclear steroids, Vitamin D has genomic and nongenomic functions. The genomic functions occur via the VDR on the nucleus of the cells, where transcription takes place, effecting gene regulation while the nongenomic function occurs via the VDR located outside of the nucleus, effecting and modulating the physiology of many cell types (Cui et al., 2017; Keane et al., 2018). Many tissues, immune apparatus, and epithelia types have been found to express 1-α-hydroxylase and synthesize vitamin D locally. Vitamin D allows the cell to respond to pathological and physiological signals by acting as a key to unlock the cell's DNA and allow the stimulated cell to transcribe the needed response (Fig. 15.2).

Targeted therapeutics based on hormones treatment using antiestrogen tamoxifen and antihuman epidermal growth factor receptor 2 therapies (Anti-HER2) was effective against breast cancer. However, therapeutic effect over triple-negative breast cancer remains negative against hormonal receptors (estrogen and anti-HER2) and remained a challenge for decades. Interestingly, hormonal receptors involving expression of vitamin D receptor (VDR) and androgen receptor (AR) can be targeted for treatment. Thakkar et al. have provided the benchmark scale for androgen expression. In addition, the role of vitamin D3 has been shown in inhibition of cell viability through VDR-dependent pathway. Combination of both receptor ligands has been found to be effective in reducing the cell viability and differentiation of cancer stem cells (Thakkar et al., 2016).

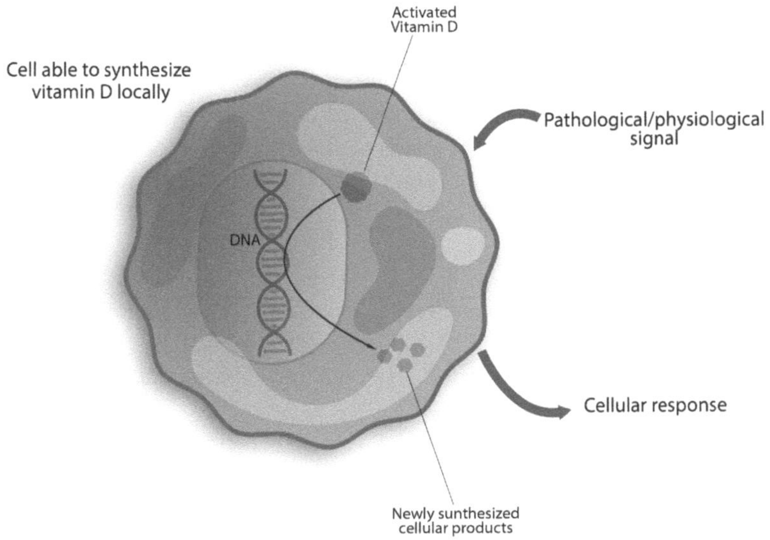

FIG. 15.2 Many types of cells have the ability to synthesize vitamin D locally. These cells react to physiological or pathological signals, vitamin D then allows the cell to respond through unlocking the cell's DNA, transcribing the needed response.

15.2.2 Vitamin D and the gastrointestinal tract

The classic function of vitamin D is to facilitate the absorption of calcium in the intestine, where calcium is actively transported across the intestinal mucosa. This occurs by the genomic effect of vitamin D aiding in the synthesis of calbindin (a calcium transport protein) which transports calcium from the brush border of the mucosal cells across to the basolateral side. Vitamin D has been found to protect the intestinal epithelial barrier from infection and inflammation, in addition to affecting gut immunity and gut microbiome. Vitamin D has been used for treatment in animals and in humans and has been found to protect the intestinal epithelia through regulating tight junction proteins and inhibiting cellular apoptosis. Vitamin D affects both innate and adaptive gut's immunity, as it is used to treat some inflammatory bowel diseases (IBD) through regulating inflammatory and inhibitory cytokines. Vitamin D was found to increase serum cathelicidin levels, an antimicrobial peptide stored in lysosomes of macrophages as an innate immune defense against bacterial infections which cause Crohn's disease (a type of IBD) causing inflammation involving different areas of the digestive tract, causing pain and severe diarrhea. Additionally, vitamin D also increases the expression of programed death receptor-1 in Crohn's disease. It has been suggested that vitamin D supplementations can be beneficial to Crohn's disease patients, as vitamin D deficiency contributes to Crohn's disease pathogenesis. Vitamin D is also effective on gut microbiome, as it increases bacterial richness in the upper gastrointestinal tract and decreases the abundance of Gammaproteo bacteria. It has been found that the active form of vitamin D induces differentiation and inhibits proliferation in colon cancer cells (Ferrer-Mayorga et al., 2019).

15.2.3 Vitamin D and liver

The function of the liver in the synthesis of vitamin D has been explained earlier. Any problem in the liver will cause deficiency in vitamin D, for example it has been found that the hepatitis C virus (HCV) may cause a decrease in 25(OH)D levels, which might be due to the changes in the lipids metabolism in the liver. The severity of the liver disease correlates with vitamin D deficiency (Keane et al., 2018).

15.2.4 Effect of vitamin D on the bone

One of the most essential roles of vitamin D is to maintain skeletal mineralization through maintaining the serum concentrations of calcium and phosphorus within normal ranges in order to normalize cellular functions. Vitamin D deficiency impacts all ages and it is seen to be the cause of metabolic bone diseases in elderly people, causing osteomalacia in addition to possibly aggravating osteoporosis. Rickets is an extreme case of vitamin D deficiency, affecting the bones of growing children and infants. There are two kinds of rickets, vitamin D-dependent rickets type I (VDDR I) which is thought to be caused by the deficiency of 1α-hydroxylase produced in the kidney, and vitamin D-dependent rickets type II (VDDR II) which is caused by vitamin D receptor (VDR) defects in response to VDR gene mutations (Takeda et al., 1997).

15.2.5 Effect of vitamin D on the kidney

Vitamin D is converted into its active form by an enzyme 1α-hydroxylase present within the kidney. Chronic kidney disease (CKD) decreases production of vitamin D in early stages of the disease, causing vitamin D deficiency. As one of the possible treatments, oral active vitamin D has been found to aid in the survival of patients on hemodialysis. In addition to the active form of vitamin D, vitamin D analogs have also been shown to exhibit therapeutic effects in many kidney disease models (González et al., 2004).

15.2.6 Effect of vitamin D on the brain

Vitamin D (1α, $25(OH)_2D3$) has been proven to modulate many brain functions, from brain development to neurotransmission, in addition to neuroprotection and immunomodulation. Although the exact mechanism underlying vitamin D functions still needs more clarification, as signaling of vitamin D occurs through the vitamin D receptors (VDR) found in neurons and glial cells (Cui et al., 2017). Vitamin D deficiency was seen to affect the brain in many conditions such as developmental disorders, autistic spectrum disorders, and schizophrenia, and disorders not related to development of the brain, such as depression and Alzheimer's disease. This effect of vitamin D on the brain indicates potential for the treatment of other neuroimmune diseases. Besides, vitamin D has been found to induce glioma cell death, giving rise to a new aspect in the management of brain tumors.

15.2.7 Vitamin D and immunity

Vitamin D affects both innate and adaptive immune responses. Enzymes metabolizing vitamin D and its receptors have been found in activated T and B lymphocytes in addition to their presence in monocytes. Both animal and human studies on the supplementations of vitamin D have shown its beneficial effects on autoimmune functions. Using animal models prone to the most common autoimmune diseases including type 1 diabetes, rheumatoid arthritis, and multiple sclerosis, it was found that if they receive vitamin D early in their life, these diseases can be successfully prevented (Holick, 2004b).

15.2.8 Vitamin D and hypertension

Vitamin D metabolizing enzymes and receptors were found in all heart cells and tissues. Renin-Angiotensin system (RAS) was found to be downregulated by vitamin D. RAS is responsible for the regulation of blood pressure, volume, and electrolyte homeostasis, and its abnormal activation causes the increase of blood pressure and cardiovascular death. Vitamin D may be a new method of controlling blood pressure (Pilz et al., 2009).

15.2.9 Effect of vitamin D on obesity

Obesity and insulin resistance are two disorders affected greatly by intra cellular calcium (Ca^{2+}), as it plays a key role in their metabolism. It was found that vitamin D regulates lipolysis and lipogenesis through modulating the adipocyte Ca^{2+} signaling. In addition, vitamin D plays an important role in adipose tissue energy homeostasis. Obesity was not linked to alter the production of vitamin D3 from skin, but can alter the release behavior of vitamin D3 into blood circulation. Thus, obesity does not affect the capacity of the skin to produce vitamin D3, but might alter the release of vitamin D3 from the skin into the circulation. It is possible that the subcutaneous fat, which is known to store vitamin D3, sequesters more of the cutaneous synthesized vitamin D3 in the obese than in the nonobese subjects because there may be more fat available for this process. On the other hand, obesity is linked to vitamin D deficiency and it is thought that the reason behind it is the increased amount of subcutaneous adipose tissue that stores vitamin D. This can be treated by oral vitamin D depending on the severity of the obesity (Wortsman et al., 2000).

15.2.10 Effect of vitamin D on reproduction

During pregnancy, a sufficient concentration of vitamin D is needed for both the fetal and mother health. Vitamin D deficiency affects maternal fertility and can cause gestational diabetes and an increased rate of caesarean sections. Vitamin D deficiency may affect the infant by causing skeletal problems, impaired growth, and low birth weight. Furthermore, it has been found that some autoimmune diseases have been linked to low vitamin D level during pregnancy and infancy. However, the optimal concentration of vitamin D in pregnancy is still unknown (Mulligan et al., 2010).

15.3 Vitamin D in cancer management and therapy

Cancer is a complex and multifactorial disease that is characterized by dysregulation of multiple signaling pathways with aberrant gene expression. Vitamin D is a secosteroid, which mediates a wide range of beneficial therapeutic effects by interaction with complex pathways including enzymes, precursors, receptors, and active metabolites. This interaction of vitamin D with several other molecular pathways makes it an ideal candidate for the treatment and prevention of various diseases including various cancers. The classical role of vitamin D is calcium and bone homeostasis but can mediate biological effects in immunity, inflammation, arthritis, and osteosarcomas (Holick, 2004a,b). Epidemiologic studies have shown lower prevalence and mortality rates of various cancers including colorectal cancer (Schwartz and Hulka, 1990), prostate cancer (Schwartz and Hanchette, 2006), and breast cancer (Garland et al., 2006) in regions that are more exposed to solar ultraviolet B radiations. It has been reported that vitamin D metabolite 1,25$(OH)_2$D3 downregulates oncogenic expression involved in protein degradation by modulating protease inhibitors, proteases, and components of Ubiquitin-Proteasome System at transcriptional and translational levels in various cancers (Hussain et al., 2009). There is compelling evidence that vitamin D operates like a transcription factor, which influences the central mechanisms of carcinogenesis: growth, cell differentiation, and apoptosis (Deeb et al., 2007).

Sterol regulatory element-binding proteins (SREBPs) are a type of proteins involved in lipid metabolism. Regulation of SREBP occurs through homeostatic processes involving negative feedback loop. In this process, binding with escort protein termed as SREBP cleaving activating protein (SCAP) tends to regulate the activation process. A list of molecules has been screened and shown that 25-hydroxyvitamin D (25OHD) acts as inhibitor for SREBP and tends to induce posttranslational modifications through proteolytic process and degrading escort protein through ubiquitin mediation leading to SREBP suppression independently of vitamin D receptor. Such target can be therapeutically utilized to control transcription factors (SREBP-SCAP) targeting cancer and other metabolic disorders (Asano et al., 2017).

The traditional pathway involved in the synthesis of vitamin D includes 25- and 1-alpha hydroxylation of Vit D2 and D3 in liver and kidneys, respectively. Previtamins, Vit D3 (from the skin) and Vit D2 and Vit D3 (from the diet), are first hydroxylated in the liver to biologically inert 25(OH)D (calcidiol) by metabolizing enzyme CYP2R1. Second hydroxylation occurs in the kidneys where it is converted into an active form 1,25$(OH)_2$D3 (calcitriol) by CYP27B1 and CYP24 (Holick, 2004a,b). Vitamin D metabolites are then transported to tissues having vitamin D receptors (VDRs) via specific bound proteins, vitamin D binding proteins (DBP).VDRs are not only present in the bone, intestine, and kidney, but are also expressed in the prostate, colon, lung, pancreas, breast, monocytes, and activated T and B lymphocytes where calcitriol can be synthesized and degraded.

The first insight regarding the anticancer effect of calcitriol against M-1 leukemic cells was reported in 1981. Treatment with 1,25$(OH)_2$D3 was found to suppress M-1 leukemic cells by causing M-1 cell differentiation (Miyaura et al., 1981). Similar response of VDR was also noted in human HL-60 leukemic cells (Tanaka et al., 1982). Apart from this, calcitriol inhibited cellular growth and induced differentiation in cultured colon, breast, prostate, lung, and skin cancer cell lines (DeLuca, 2004; Holick, 2004a). VDR-dependent inhibition of prostate, melanoma, lung, colon, and breast cancer cell lines with vitamin D has been reported (Skowronski et al., 1993). Calcitriol and its analogs induce cell cycle arrest in G0/G1 phase of cell cycle of proliferating cancer cells (Chiang and Chen, 2009) especially in prostate cancer cells (Krishnan et al., 2003). They upregulate the expression of p21 and p27 and cyclin-dependent kinase (CDK) inhibitors (Campbell et al., 1997) and downregulate cyclin-dependent kinase 2 activity, causing the hypophosphorylation of the retinoblastoma protein (pRb) in a p53-dependent manner (Stewart and Weigel, 2004). The aforementioned studies reveal that vitamin D regulates cell proliferation and differentiation and inhibits the tumor growth and development of in vitro and in vivo cancer models (Krishnan et al., 2003; González-Sancho et al., 2006).

15.4 Anticancer mechanism of vitamin D

Tumor promotion is a complex process that transforms normal cells into genetically mutated cells. A number of data provide evidence that vitamin D plays a crucial role in preventing malignant transformation of cells through downregulation of inflammatory cytokines and activation of antioxidant (Feldman et al., 2014). As shown in Fig. 15.3 it has various targets through which it can affect the cancer progression. Various mechanisms for the anticancer effect of vitamin D can be described as follows:

15.4.1 Antiinflammatory effect of vitamin D

Chronic inflammation is associated with the development and progression of various cancers including liver, colon, prostate, and stomach cells

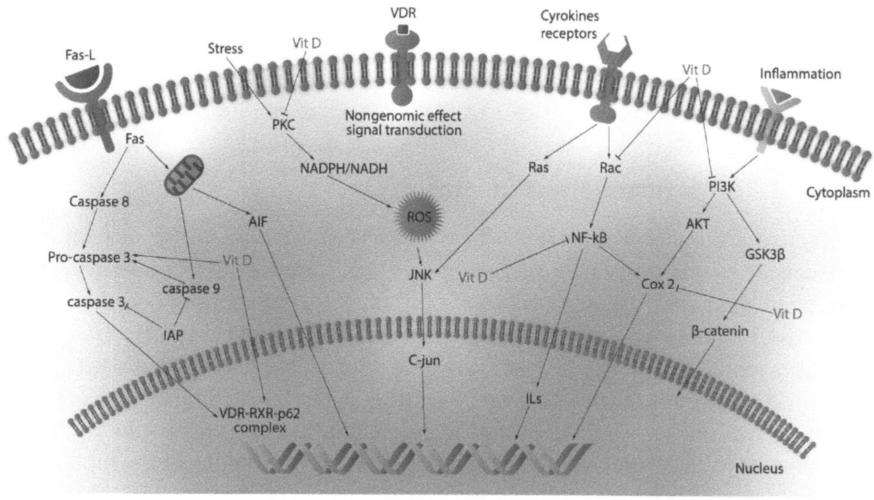

FIG. 15.3 Vitamin D molecular targets in cancer.

(Haverkamp et al., 2008). Inflammation is a slow process producing reactive oxygen species (ROS) and cytokines at inflammation site causing tumorigenesis and malignant transformation. Studies have shown that vitamin D can suppress the inflammatory mediator prostaglandin by inhibiting the expression of prostanoid receptors and cyclooxygenase-2 (COX-2) (Krishnan and Feldman, 2010). In prostate cancer cells, vitamin D was found to reduce the expression of prostanoid receptors EP2 and FP and inhibit COX-2 by increasing the expression level of 15-hydroxyprostaglandin-dehydrogenase (15-PGDH), an enzyme which degrades PGE2 (Krishnan and Feldman, 2010). In breast cancer cells, Vitamin D decreased COX-2 expression at transcriptional level and PGE2 production (Yuan et al., 2012). There is compelling evidence that VDR expression is inversely related to COX-2 expression in ovarian cancer tissues and malignant breast cell lines (Cordes et al., 2012). Furthermore, vitamin D inhibited MAPK-mediated activation of inflammatory responses. It was also found to inhibit proinflammatory cytokines, such as IL-6, and phosphorylation of p38 MAPK by activating MAPK phosphatases-5 (MAPK-5) in normal prostate epithelial cells and prostate cancer cells (Nonn et al., 2006). In human monocytes and murine macrophages derived from bone marrow, vitamin D suppressed Lipopolysaccharides (LPS)-induced IL-6 and tumor necrosis factor (TNF)-α through the activation of MKP-1 (Zhang et al., 2012). Vitamin D has also the ability to block NFκB and NFκB-associated downstream signaling pathway. Vitamin D was also observed to inhibit the phosphorylation of AKT and NFκB-mediated COX-2 expression through upregulation of thioesterase superfamily member 4 (THEM4) (Chen et al., 2013). In fibroblasts, Vitamin D regulates the interaction of VDR with IκBα kinase (IKK), consequently blocking NFκB (p65) nuclear translocation from cytoplasm (Bessler and Djaldetti, 2012). Additionally, vitamin D can modulate the tumor microenvironment between immune and cancer cells to repress inflammatory cytokines production. Vitamin D treatment can decrease the production of proinflammatory cytokines TNF-α, IL-6, and IL-10 in peripheral blood mononuclear cells (PBMCs) and colon cancer cell lines.

15.4.2 Antioxidant effect of vitamin D

Reactive oxygen species (ROS) has a very critical role in the development of cancer by causing DNA mutation, cell proliferation, and cell death. ROS-induced oxidative stress provokes proinflammatory responses and favors the process of tumorigenesis. Accumulating data have suggested that vitamin D can prevent DNA damage by activation of antioxidant defense system (Kállay et al., 2002). It has been shown that oxidative stress-induced DNA damage proportion was high in VDR-knockout mice. In addition, rats treated with vitamin D have been observed with decreased levels of malondialdehyde, which is the end product of lipid peroxidation, responsible for DNA damage (Fedirko et al., 2010). Studies have shown that daily intake of vitamin D can reduce the oxidative stress-induced DNA damage in human (Peehl et al., 2004). Vitamin D protects from ROS induced-DNA damage by activating various enzymes involved in the regulation of ROS generation. Vitamin D reduced production of ROS by activation of antioxidant enzymes such as superoxide dismutase 1 (SOD1) and 2 (SOD2) in epithelial and androgen-sensitive prostate cancer cells (Manna et al., 2017). In prostate and breast cancer cells, calcitriol reduced the antioxidant thioredoxin by inducing the expression of thioredoxin reductase 1 (TXNRD1). Moreover, NF-E2-related factor-2 (NRF2) has been shown to be regulated by vitamin D to modulate activation of antioxidant enzymes by increasing nuclear translocation and decreasing KEAP1-mediated degradation (Nakai et al., 2014).

15.4.3 Vitamin D effect on lymphangioleiomyomatosis (LAM)

LAM is a disease associated with blockage of bronchial tubes in lungs due to smooth muscle growth. Vitamin D binding protein was linked with abnormal condition and survival rate. Miller et al. (2018) have shown the presence of lower level of vitamin D in lungs affected with LAM. Vitamin D binding protein tends to improve the damage of lungs and increase the survival rate with LAM (Miller et al., 2018).

15.4.4 Vitamin D repair DNA damage

Vitamin D has the ability to regulate DNA damage repair processes (Kállay et al., 2002). Studies have shown that Vitamin D increases the expression of genes involved in repair of DNA damage including p53, proliferating cell nuclear antigen (*PCNA*) and BRCA1 in breast cancer cells (Ting et al., 2012). It has been reported that vitamin D can activate ATM and RAD50, consequently accelerating the damage process in prostate epithelial cells (Jiang et al., 2003) and increasing GADD45α in squamous cell carcinoma and ovarian cancer cells (Akhter et al., 1997). Summing up, vitamin D can enhance DNA damage repair process and thus prevent genetic mutations that promote tumor development.

15.4.5 Vitamin D regulate cell proliferation and differentiation

There is compelling evidence that Vitamin D can modulate differentiation and proliferation of normal and malignant cells (Slominski et al., 2017). Novel vitamin D metabolites 20(OH)D_2, 20(OH)D_3, 1,20$(OH)_2D_3$, and 20,23$(OH)_2D_3$ have been shown to inhibit proliferation and induce differentiation of cancer cells through VDR (Slominski et al., 2005). Vitamin D has been found to decrease cells viability by regulating cell cycle, growth factors, and signaling pathways of cancer cells. It enhances the expression of insulin-like growth factor (IGF)-binding protein 3 and the cyclin-dependent kinase (CDK) inhibitors p21 and p27, and suppresses CDK2 expression, leading to attenuation of IGF-1- and IGF-2 involved in cell proliferation and tumor development (Larriba et al., 2013). Furthermore, vitamin D was found to repress the configuration of TCF4-b-catenin complexes by increasing the expression of Wnt antagonist, Dickkopf-1 (DKK-1), to block Wnt/β-catenin signaling pathway (Pendás-Franco et al., 2008). Vitamin D also activated transcription factors FoxO3/4 which trigger transcription of genes that decreases cells viability and arrest cell cycle in neuroblastoma cells (Chen et al., 2002). It was also observed to inhibit cell growth by reducing expression level of telomerase reverse transcriptase (TERT) (Díaz et al., 2000) and induce the expression level of TGFβ and its receptors (Yang et al., 2001)

15.4.6 Vitamin D induces cancer cell death

Vitamin D induces apoptosis or program cell death by downregulating Bcl-2 and Bcl-XL (antiapoptotic proteins) and upregulating Bax, Bak, and Bad (pro-apoptotic proteins) in cancer cell lines (Pálmer et al., 2003). Vitamin D has the ability to upregulate proapoptotic proteins such as caspases, G0-G1 switch 2 (GOS2), death-associated protein (DAP-3), and Fas-associated death domain (FADD) in cancer cell lines (Swami et al., 2003). Vitamin D can also block AKT-mediated antiapoptotic signaling pathway by increasing the expression of phosphatase and phosphatase and tensin homolog (PTEN) (Sergeev, 2012). Further, vitamin D has been found to induce apoptotic process events by causing Ca^{2+}/calpain-dependent caspase-12 and Ca^{2+}-dependent μ-calpain activation of apoptotic effectors (Wilson et al., 2011). Autophagy is a catabolic process, which plays crucial role in necrosis and apoptosis-independent cell death. Vitamin D sensitizes breast cancer cells to radiotherapy by enhancing cytotoxicity of radiation (Sharma et al., 2014). Vitamin D can also induce autophagic cell death through upregulation of autophagy-related gene *beclin 1* (Tavera-Mendoza et al., 2006) and CDK inhibitors (Lisse et al., 2011). Besides, vitamin D can also induce the expression of DNA damage-inducible transcript 4 (*DDIT4*), ultimately inhibiting survival proteins, which suppresses autophagy (Lisse et al., 2011).

15.4.7 Vitamin D and protease inhibition

Vitamin D interacts with VDR (Vitamin D Receptor) through genomic and non-genomic mechanisms (Ordóñez-Morán et al., 2008). VDR forms heterodimers with retinoid X Receptor (RXR), which then interacts with vitamin D response elements (VDREs) in target genes (Carlberg and Seuter, 2009) that code for proteases or protease inhibitors. Calcitriol regulates the expression of cystatin D which inhibits several cysteine proteases of cathepsin family in colon cancer cells (Alvarez-Díaz et al., 2009).

Matrix metalloproteases (MMPs) are zinc-dependent proteases that degrade the components of the extracellular membrane and basement membrane. MMPs are regulated by tissue inhibitors of metalloproteases (TIMPs). MMPs and TIMPs are disrupted in cancer allowing the migration and invasion of cancer cells. Several studies have demonstrated the regulation of MMPs and TIMPs by calcitriol. Malignant cells in prostate and breast cancer decrease the expression of MMP-9 and increase TIMP-1 levels when treated with calcitriol, ultimately inhibiting invasion process (Koli and Keski-Oja, 2000). In squamous cell carcinoma, EB1089 (an analog for calcitriol) also inhibits MMP-13 and regulates the RNA expression of MMP-1 and MMP-3.

Three major groups of proteases, cathepsins (CPs), MMPs, and plasminogen activators (PAs), were examined for the changes in their activities and expressions when treated with calcitriol human prostate cancer cell lines. Calcitriol was observed to decrease the level of MMP-9 and CPs and increase the activity of tissue inhibitors of metalloproteinase-1 (TIMP-1) and cathepsin inhibitors. Furthermore, calcitriol increased the binding of AP-1 complexes to TIMP-1 promoter which enhanced the activity of TIMP-1, thus resulting in inhibition of MMPs activity and tumor progression. These findings strongly support the idea that Vitamin D-based therapies might be the future for managing advanced prostate cancer especially in patients who have established higher level of CPs and MMP-9 activities (Bao et al., 2006).

Uterine fibroids (UFs) are the benign tumors caused by excessive deposition of extracellular matrix (ECM)-associated proteins. To determine the relationship between vitamin D and UFs, the expression levels of VDR protein in human uterine fibroids were compared with the levels of normal myometrium. Western blot analysis showed that more than 60% of UFs analyzed expressed low levels of VDR. Calcitriol induced VDR in a concentration-dependent manner and reduced the level of ECM-associated proteins: collagen type 1, fibronectin, and PAI-1 expression in human uterine fibroid cell line (HuLM). It was also found that calcitriol reduced the expressions of proteoglycans such as versican, fibromodulin, and biglycan in HuLM cells. Altogether, seeing the results collectively, it is safe to suggest that treatment with vitamin D can potentially reduce the abnormal expression of ECM-associated proteins in the HuLM cells and might be an efficient, safe, and nonsurgical treatment option for human uterine fibroid treatment (Brakta et al., 2015).

Vitamin D also regulates the expression of urokinase (uPA) and tissue plasminogen (tPA) activators and their inhibitors (PAIs). These serine proteases convert inactive plasminogen into plasmin which degrades ECM and basement membrane proteins and activates pro-MMPs. In breast cancer cells, calcitriol decreases the expression of uPA and tPA and increases that of PAI (Koli and Keski-Oja, 2000). This finding was observed in breast cancer cells but not in prostate cancer cells (Koli and Keski-Oja, 2000). Quantitative RT-PCR studies on SW480-ADH colon cancer cell lines showed 2.3-fold increase in the expression of PAI-1 by calcitriol. Still, more work is required on colon cancer to evaluate the possible involvement of Vitamin D having its antitumor effects as an inhibitor via these pathways.

Vitamin D also regulates the expression of protease M, a member of serine protease family. It is also known as neurosin/zyme/kallikrein-6 (KLK-6), a target gene of calcitriol in squamous carcinoma and colon cancer cell lines identified through transcriptomic studies by using oligonucleotide micro-arrays (Pálmer et al., 2003). Protease M is from KLK family which is commonly regulated by steroid hormones in a number of cancer cell lines (Obiezu and Diamandis, 2005). The induction of protease M was confirmed by immunofluorescence and northern blotting when treated with calcitriol (Pálmer et al., 2003). In the same way as protease M, normal epithelial cell-specific 1 (NES1), another member of the KLK family (KLK-10), was found to be induced by calcitriol in SW480-ADH human colon cancer cells. The results were confirmed by using northern blot (Pálmer et al., 2003). Laboratory data also revealed that calcitriol induced KLK-7 RNA expression by 9.5-fold in these cells. Since there are no reported functional studies, the implicit role of these serine proteases due to the action of vitamin D is still not very known. In contradiction, recent studies have indicated that protease M is a poor marker for the diagnosis of colon and ovarian cancer, whereas NES1 can either be favorable or unfavorable for the diagnosis of the cancer, depending on the type (Paliouras et al., 2007). Up till now without any clear knowledge of the functions of these proteases, they are still considered to contribute to the anticancer action of vitamin D.

15.5 Role of vitamin D in cancer prevention

Scientists divide the functions of vitamin D into skeletal (calciotropic) and extra-skeletal (noncalciotropic), which shows that it has pleiotropic effects. The skeletal functions refer mainly to the regulation of the level of calcium and phosphorus in the blood and consequently bone density. The extra-skeletal functions indicate the actions that are related to control of cell proliferation and differentiation, apoptosis, angiogenesis, and immunity (Reichel et al., 1989; Feldman et al., 2014). It is believed that these extra-skeletal actions are due to inactive form of vitamin D, 25-hydroxyvitamin D3 [25(OH)D or calcidiol], which is metabolized in different tissues and converted into the active metabolite, 1α,25-dihydroxyvitamin D3 (also known as calcitriol) (Schwartz et al., 1998; Zehnder et al., 2001; Tangpricha et al., 2002). Researchers reported that disrupted levels of vitamin D and its metabolites are involved in the pathogenesis of some diseases of skin (Umar et al., 2018), uterus (Ciebiera et al., 2018), liver (Abdel-Mohsen et al., 2018), and other organs (Holick and Chen, 2008). In addition, it has been found that vitamin D has an important role in the defense against cancer formation.

The protective role of vitamin D against cancer has attracted the interest of researchers across the globe since ancient times. The earliest attempts to investigate this role started during the early 80s of the last century. Two of these attempts were in vitro studies and demonstrated the inhibition of growth of cancer cells obtained from solid tumors (Frampton et al., 1983; Dokoh et al., 1984). Other studies were in vivo, and succeeded in documenting a reduction in size of cancer, or decreasing the metastasis of cancer cells, after administration of high doses of vitamin D (Sato et al., 1982; Eisman et al., 1987). The type of research work done to investigate the putative antitumor effect of vitamin D varies from epidemiological/geographical studies to dietary ones, or sometimes, by measuring serum level of vitamin D.

Accumulating evidence points to the relation of deficiency of vitamin D to the development of specific types of cancer, such as colorectal, prostate, and breast cancers as demonstrated in Fig. 15.4 and described below with the postulated mechanisms of the antitumor effects of vitamin D for these cancers. Fig. 15.5 summarizes the postulated antitumor effects of vitamin D on cells and tissues.

15.5.1 Vitamin D and breast cancer

Breast cancer is the most common type of cancer in females according to the American Cancer Society (Atlanta: American Cancer Society, 2019). Current literature strongly links between vitamin D and the protection against breast cancer (de La Puente-Yagüe et al., 2018). However, the interest in investigating this putative relationship between vitamin D and breast cancer started since long back (Eisman and Martin, 1989; Kaizer et al., 1989; Garland et al., 1990). The two studies by Gorham et al. (1989, 2007) described a significant relationship between reduction of exposure to sunlight (i.e., vitamin D deficiency) and increased mortality rate of breast cancer in Canada and the United States (US), whereas Kaizer et al. showed that consumption of fish oil (rich in vitamin D) decreased the incidence and mortality rate of breast cancer (Kaizer et al., 1989). The study conducted by Garland et al. confirmed these observations and conclusions by demonstrating the regional differences in the mortality rate of breast

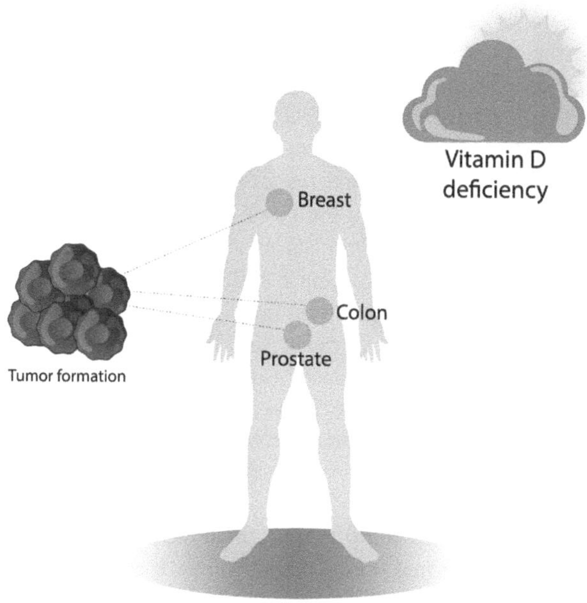

FIG. 15.4 Vitamin D deficiency is one of the leading factors for cancer formation, especially in breast, colon, and prostate.

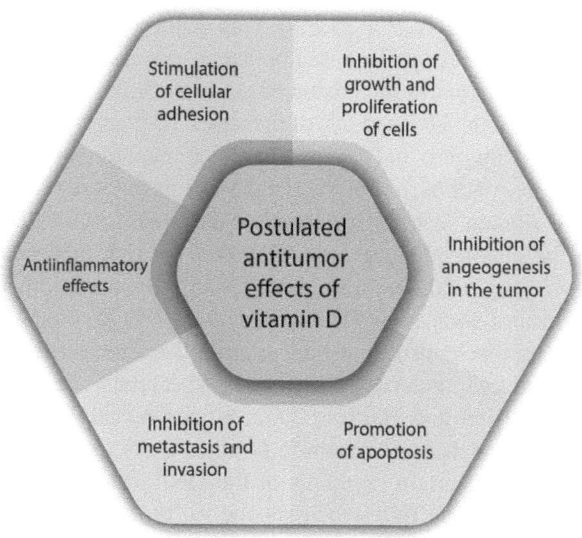

FIG. 15.5 Some of the postulated antitumor effects of vitamin D.

cancer in the United States, and this was explained by the variations in the solar radiation between these regions (Garland et al., 1990). Subsequent studies also confirmed this association (Caygill et al. 1996; Mohr et al. 2008) which included a large number of 24 and 107 countries, respectively. Regarding the reported protective levels of vitamin D, Garland et al. (2007) documented that females with serum level of 25(OH)D around 52 ng/mL were having 50% lower risk of developing breast cancer than those with levels lower than 13 ng/mL. According to another study, a daily intake of 400 IU of vitamin D and serum level of vitamin D of approximately 30 ng/mL is crucial for decreasing the risk of breast cancer (Hong et al., 2012). Some authors recommended a serum vitamin D level of 30–60 ng/mL as an optimal level for prevention of breast cancer (Stearns and Visvanathan, 2013). Despite this huge number of literature that documented this relation, Almquist et al. (2010) found only weak association between vitamin D and breast cancer and some authors found no association at all (Jiang et al., 2018). This discrepancy between the results is partly explained by variations in some individual factors like body mass index and alcohol intake (Deschasaux et al., 2016).

Some studies documented the presence of the nuclear vitamin D receptor (VDR) in normal and abnormal breast cells (Friedrich et al., 2002). It has been proposed that this expression of VDR could explain the antitumor effect of vitamin D in breast cancer (Garland et al., 2006). Some researchers investigated the genetic structure (genotype) of the VDR and postulated a role of the variations of this genotype in the susceptibility of women to breast cancer (Ruggiero et al., 1998). Ruggiero et al. (1998) examined the BsmI genotype of VDR in 167 healthy women, and found the following: 72% of women had Bb pattern (heterozygous), 16% had bb (homozygous recessive), and 12% had BB (homozygous dominant) (Ruggiero et al., 1998). This genotype pattern was not significantly different in the newly diagnosed breast cancer cases, but the distribution was significantly different in the advanced cases of breast cancer, when the bb and BB patterns were in 37% and 5% of the cases, respectively (Ruggiero et al., 1998). Therefore, Ruggiero and the coworkers concluded that women with homozygous recessive pattern (bb) of the BsmI VDR have more risk of developing metastasis than women with other patterns. Subsequent studies confirmed this link between the genotypic pattern of VDR and the risk of developing breast cancer (Ingles et al., 2000; Reimers et al., 2015). However, other studies debated the presence of such a link (Dunning et al., 1999; Xu et al., 2014).

The underlying mechanism by which vitamin D exerts its antitumor effect in the breast is still not yet understood. However, researchers are trying to unravel its complexity (Colston and Hansen, 2002; Krishnan and Feldman, 2011). In general, the active metabolite of vitamin D binds to its nuclear receptor VDR. This binding activates certain segments of the DNA strand, known as vitamin D response elements (VDREs), which encode for proteases or protease inhibitors (Álvarez-Díaz et al., 2010). Activation of VDREs has various effects on cell mitosis, apoptosis, and differentiation. Campbell et al. (1997) explained the antitumor effect of vitamin D in proposing that vitamin D inhibits mitosis of cells of the breast (Campbell et al., 1997). Some studies suggested that vitamin D induces apoptosis in these cells (Welsh, 1994; Narvaez and Welsh, 2001). In accordance to this, Mathiasen et al. (2002) concluded that vitamin D induces apoptosis by enhancing the release of calcium ions from the cells (Mathiasen et al., 2002). This was also supported by another study (Sergeev, 2012). Upregulation of cathepsin B (one of the proteases) (Simboli-Campbell et al., 1996) and inhibition of cathepsin L (Swami et al., 2003) were also suggested as possible mechanisms for the apoptosis and growth modulation in breast cancer cells. Reduction in the secretion of serine proteases (urokinase and tissue plasminogen activators) and the increase in their inhibitors were reported in breast cancer cells (Koli and Keski-Oja, 2000). This inhibition of the activity of the serine proteases interferes with the conversion of plasminogen to plasmin, thus preventing the breakdown of the extracellular matrix (Koli and Keski-Oja, 2000). Lowe et al. (2003) presented number of hypotheses and stated that "It has been found so far that 1,25$(OH)_2$D3 has an effect on the expression of certain cell cycle regulators and in this way can bring about G1 arrest." Evidence has also emerged that vitamin D compounds can also affect the growth-promoting pathways initiated by two important factors involved in breast cancer cell promotion and that these factors are insulin-like growth factor I (IGF-I) and estrogen-receptor (ER) pathways. Vitamin D compounds have also been implicated in promotion of apoptosis in breast cancer cells and evidence suggests that 1,25$(OH)_2$D3 and its synthetic analogs may potentiate responsiveness of breast cancer cells to conventional cytotoxic agents. It has been suggested that the antitumor effects of vitamin D in the breast are due to a balance between 2 enzymes, the 1α-hydroxylase (for synthesis of the active form of vitamin D) and 24-hydroxylase (for its degradation) (Lowe et al., 2003; Vuolo et al. 2012). In accordance to this notion, some studies found an increased expression of the enzyme that degrades the vitamin in tumor cells (Townsend et al., 2005). Upregulation of certain growth factors, such as keratinocyte growth factor, has also been suggested as a mediator of the antitumor effect of vitamin D (Lyakhovich et al., 2000).

Vitamin D has crucial role in regulating the apoptosis process through Bcl-2 down regulation in cancer cells. Bcl-2 and Bcl-xl are interconnected proteins and unregulated in cancer condition. Vitamin D effectively downregulates the antiapoptotic genes expression due to mitochondrial membrane inhibition and subsequent cytochrome C release. Also, it controls the activity of calcium fluxes connected to endoplasmic reticulum. It is yet to ascertain the protective effects of vitamin D on mitochondria through regulation of cytosolic calcium levels (Fedirko et al., 2009; Mathiasen et al., 2002; Pálmer et al., 2001).

Apoptotic effect of vitamin D in MCF-7 cells has been reported to deplete the level of intracellular calcium. Bcl-2 interference in inhibiting such activity of vitamin D and subsiding the apoptotic pathway mechanisms was elucidated. In addition, Bcl-2 involvement is reported in signaling cascade to release cytochrome C to cytosol from mitochondria. Cytochrome C release stimulates the caspase signaling pathway. In particular, procaspase 9 and associated cascades were stimulated by cytochrome C. It leads to inhibition of caspase downstream. However, vitamin D failed to stimulate caspases in breast cancer cell line (MCF-7 & T47D). Therefore, even though release of cytochrome C is exhibited, caspases activations are inhibited. Beside the protective effect of Bcl-2, the apoptotic pathway inhibition through caspase-independent route is possible (Fedirko et al., 2009; Mathiasen et al., 2002; Pálmer et al., 2001).

Anticancer drugs were shown to upregulate death receptors apoptosis antigen 1 (Fas or FasR) or p53 (tumor suppressor). Fas is actively involved in apoptosis by activating Fas-associated protein with death domain (FADD), TNFR1, and death receptor 3 (DR3)-related death pathways. However, vitamin D-induced apoptotic pathways are found to be independent with negative mutant of FADD and are not linked with such mediators. In addition, the role of tumor necrosis factor receptor (TNFR) is excluded due to the caspase-independent pathway. In case of T47D cell line, the apoptosis by vitamin D compounds (EB 1089, 1,25$(OH)_2D3$ or CB 1093), even in the absence of p53 functional receptor, shows the nonrelation of p53 in apoptotic pathway (Mathiasen et al., 1999). Therefore, such unique property of vitamin D to trigger apoptotic pathway independent of death receptors can be effectively used against drug-resistant tumors. In addition, inhibitors of apoptosis proteins, termed as IAP and heat shock protein (hsp 70), that play a key role as inhibitors in programmed cell death can be sensitive to vitamin D.

15.5.2 Vitamin D and colon cancer

Colorectal cancer (CRC) is caused by the genetic mutation in colon cells that leads to tumor condition. Colon cancer is regarded as the third most common type of cancer in both males and females (Atlanta: American Cancer Society, 2019). Epidemiological studies found that modification of diet, such as increase of consumption of vitamin D, or exposure to sunlight decrease the risk of colorectal cancer or improve its prognosis. This was first published in 1980, when the researchers noticed that the mortality rate of colon cancer patients was higher in areas of the United States with reduced solar radiation (Garland and Garland, 1980). This was also confirmed by a subsequent study, which documented an inverse relationship between vitamin D intake and the risk of colorectal cancer in 1954 men in the United States (Garland et al., 1985). Measuring the serum level of vitamin D and correlating this with the risk of developing colon cancer also confirmed this observation (Garland et al., 1989). In this latter study, Garland et al. reported that serum vitamin D level of 27–32 ng/mL led to 75% reduction in risk of colon cancer, whereas a level of 33–41 ng/mL reduced the risk by 80%. Other studies also supported these findings (Caygill and Hill, 1995; Feskanich et al., 2004; McCullough et al., 2019).

Calcitriol (1,25-dihydroxycholecalciferol), the active metabolite of vitamin D, containing hydroxyl groups is reported to exhibit anticancer activity against

CRC. Previous studies have reported that calcitriol plays a vital role in downregulation of cell proliferation, stimulating cell apoptosis, epithelial differentiation, cell metabolism, and antiangiogenesis effect. Vitamin D and CRC have inverse connection in tumor condition. Lack of vitamin D is linked to accelerate the uncontrolled cell growth (neoplasia) leading to tumor. Importantly, vitamin D plays an important role at the early stage of cancer in VDR expression and in CYP27B1 and CYP24A1 alterations of colorectal cancer. Calcitriol inhibits the uncontrolled CRC cells. In particular, G0/G1 phase upregulates the p21 and p27 family and inhibits the cyclin A and F in tumor condition. Cell cycle growth inhibition was associated with calcium sensing receptor, which was stimulated by calcitriol. In molecular mechanism, many cell proliferation genes (MYC, FOS, and JUN) are downregulated and apoptotic genes are upregulated when treated with calcitriol (Pereira et al., 2012).

However, there is no relation of vitamin D with colon cancer as reported previously (Peters et al., 1992; Ashmore et al., 2015). Some authors attributed these negative results to the inadequate intake of vitamin D and some other factors like concomitant intake of estrogen that interferes with the results of the experiments (Vuolo et al., 2012). Gorham et al. (2007) recommended a daily dose of 1000–2000 IU of vitamin D in order to reduce the risk of colon cancer (Gorham et al., 2007). A metaanalysis study reported a reduction of 59% and 22% in developing rectal and colon cancer, respectively, following an increase of serum level of $25(OH)_2D3$ by 20 ng/mL (Yin et al., 2009). Recently, the relation between vitamin D and colorectal cancer has been reviewed (Klampfer, 2014). This beneficial effect of vitamin D has also been found in decreasing the recurrence and improving the prognosis of patients with advanced stages of colon cancer (Fuchs et al., 2017).

The presence of the VDR in normal epithelial cells of colon has been reported (Wecksler et al., 1979; Delvin et al., 1996). An association between three variants of VDR gene [polyA (short), BsmI (BB), and TaqI (tt)] and reduced risk of colon cancer has been reported (Slatter et al., 2001). The frequency of allele of FokI variant of VDR was found to be associated with lower risk of colon cancer (Moossavi et al., 2018). However, Laczmanska et al. reported no association with the FokI variant, but a significant association was found with BsmI, TaqI, and ApaI genotypes (Laczmanska et al., 2014). A metaanalysis study reported an association of the BsmI VDR polymorphism with a lower risk of colorectal cancer (Touvier et al., 2011). Another metaanalysis study conducted on 14 studies concluded that there exists no correlation between TaqI VDR variant and the colorectal cancer risk (Sheng et al., 2017). The same observation was also made by Ashmore et al. (2015) as well as by Budhathoki et al. (2016). In the Japanese population, Takeshige and colleagues found association between ApaI genotype and reduced risk of colorectal cancer (Takeshige et al., 2015). In the Saudi population, the ApaI and BsmI variants were observed to be associated with risk of colorectal cancer in the elderly, and female patients, respectively (Alkhayal et al., 2016).

As the mechanism of antitumor effect of vitamin D in colon cancer is concerned, several hypotheses have been presented (González-Sancho et al., 2006; Ferrer-Mayorga et al., 2019). Some of these hypotheses refer to the inhibition of angiogenesis in the tumor (Majewski et al., 1996; Luan et al., 2017), promotion of the differentiation of the tumor cells (Pálmer et al., 2001), reduction of the cell proliferation of colon epithelial cells (Iseki et al., 1999), stimulation of adherence of cells (Pálmer et al., 2001), augmentation of the immune response against cancer cells, and enhancement of apoptosis (Fedirko et al., 2009). Interaction of the VDR with beta-catenin signaling pathway (a well-recognized step in the pathogenesis of colorectal cancer) was also suggested to be one of the mechanisms (Shah et al., 2006). Jung et al. (2014) suggested the host immunity as a factor in the mechanism of vitamin D for cancer protection. In accordance to this, Meeker et al. (2014) reported that vitamin D decreases the inflammatory reactions at the onset of neoplastic changes in colon. Recently, it has been found that vitamin D also acts on the stromal cells (fibroblasts) of colon cancer since these cells express the VDR gene (Ferrer-Mayorga et al., 2017). Another putative mechanism that is widely accepted nowadays is the induction of Cystatin D (an inhibitor of cysteine proteases) by vitamin D in colon cancer cells, which leads to the inhibition, proliferation, and migration of cells by interfering with the Wnt/beta-catenin signaling system (Alvarez-Díaz et al., 2009). Alvarez-Díaz et al. (2009) also suggested that vitamin D induces MicroRNA-22 and that this induction is responsible for the inhibition of migration and proliferation of cancer colon cells. Inhibition of the Wnt signaling system by vitamin D was also suggested by Klampfer (2014). A recent study reported that vitamin D action in colorectal cancer is mediated by cystatin D. Cystatin D is one of the targets of p53, the known tumor suppressor gene, and its induction enhances mesenchymal-epithelial transition (MET) (Hünten and Hermeking, 2015). Upregulation of number of genes, including protease M, has also been reported (Pálmer et al., 2003). Increased expression of plasminogen activator inhibitor-1 (a protease inhibitor) and modulation of the ubiquitin-proteasome system were observed in cultured human colon cancer cells (Álvarez-Díaz et al., 2010). Interestingly, researchers reported that vitamin D and its receptor are essential for the normal microbial balance and homeostasis of normal intestine. Any disruption of this would lead to dysbiosis and to increase the risk of cancer formation (Sun and Guo, 2017).

15.5.3 Vitamin D and prostate cancer

Prostate cancer (PCa) is the most common type of cancer in males. Researchers tried to investigate its etiology, and one of the earliest studies that pointed to the role of vitamin D deficiency in the pathogenesis of PCa was made in 1990 by Schwartz and Hulka, 1990). In this study, an association between increased mortality due to PCa and reduced exposure to sunlight (major source of vitamin D) was observed in the United States. This observation was supported by subsequent studies by various other authors (Corder et al., 1993; Schwartz and Hanchette, 2006). Corder et al. (1993) found that low-serum vitamin D level (especially 1α,25-dihydroxyvitamin D3) is associated with higher risk of developing PCa, especially in older men. Some studies noticed a relation between high consumption of fatty fish (rich in vitamin D) and reduction of risk of PCa (Augustsson et al., 2003). Robsahm et al. (2004) reported that PCa patients who had higher serum level of vitamin D had better prognosis than those with lower level (Robsahm et al., 2004). Despite this, number of investigators doubted the existence of this association between vitamin D and protection against PCa (Sawada et al., 2017; Jiang et al., 2018) or surprisingly reported a weak positive relation. Rather higher levels of vitamin D were found to be associated with increased risk of PCa (Gao et al., 2018). However, a recent large collaborative study concluded that vitamin D level is not associated with aggressive type of PCa, but positively with nonaggressive type (Travis et al., 2019). Kristal et al. (2014) suggested that the protective effect of vitamin D is obtained only when its level is neither high nor low (Kristal et al., 2014). Some studies attributed these discrepancies between studies to differences in race and/or BMI (Batai et al., 2017), variations in age, military service, and race (Stanaland et al., 2017). However, the association of vitamin D with PCa has been further complicated by suggesting a role of insulin-like growth factor in the ultimate effect of vitamin D on the risk of PCa (Miles et al., 2017). Grant (2014) recommended using serum level of vitamin D as a guide in the decision of ordering a biopsy for diagnosis of PCa. Some authors argued that the relationship between vitamin D level and incidence of PCa might not be a causal one, as some other factors like obesity or parathyroid dysfunction might contribute to the development of PCa. Therefore, caution should be practiced before supplementing patients with vitamin D as a treatment (Roca et al., 2016).

Just like colon and breast cancers, cells of prostate cancer possess VDR (Miller et al., 1995), and researchers assumed that there is an association between VDR polymorphism and the risk of PCa or the severity of the disease. The literature presented conflicting results: an association was reported in some studies (Hamasaki et al., 2001; Kambale et al., 2017) as opposed to some other studies (Atoum et al., 2015). Habuchi et al. (2000) found that only the Bsm I polymorphism had a role in the protection from PCa (Habuchi et al., 2000). In Asian population, the TaqI VDR polymorphism has been suggested to be associated with PCa (Fei et al., 2016), but not Bsm I (Kang et al., 2018). In a large metaanalysis study, some authors concluded that FokI variant is only associated with risk of PCa in Caucasian population (Kang et al., 2016). It is possible that racial differences are responsible about this inconsistency in the results, as some studies that reported an association were conducted on the Japanese (Hamasaki et al., 2001), Caucasian (Kang et al., 2016), or Indian populations (Kambale et al., 2017).

With regard to the mechanisms of this antitumor effect of vitamin D against PCa, several mechanisms have been postulated, such as inhibition of proliferation of cells, angiogenesis, metastasis, and promoting apoptosis and cell cycle arrest (Krishnan and Feldman, 2011; Ahn et al., 2016). One study suggested that the antiproliferative effect of vitamin D is due to its ability to decrease inflammation by reducing the level of active prostaglandins (PGs) (Moreno et al., 2005). This action is achieved by reducing the expression of cyclooxygenase-2 (COX-2) gene and inducting 15-prostaglandin dehydrogenase gene (15-PGDH) (Moreno et al., 2005), which are responsible for the synthesis and inactivation of PGs, respectively. The hypothesis of reducing the inflammation has also been suggested by some authors (Batai et al., 2016). It has been proposed that vitamin D is metabolized in the prostate gland and this is responsible for its action against cancer cells (Tuohimaa et al., 2001). They reported that vitamin D activates ERK-1 and ERK-2 (mitogen-activated kinases) and p38, and as well as induces keratinocyte growth factor and upregulates expression of androgen receptor. Another study led to a conclusion that vitamin D decreases the activity of certain groups of proteases that are involved in spread of cancer cells such as MMPs and cathepsins, and increases the activity of their inhibitors (Bao et al., 2006). Another study emphasizes the role of androgens in the antiproliferative effect of vitamin D through inhibition of citrate oxidation (Wang and Tenniswood, 2014).

15.5.4 Vitamin D and other types of cancer

Vitamin D also has protective effects against other types of cancer, like ovarian cancer (Lefkowitz and Garland, 1994), endometrial cancer (Terry et al., 2002), and skin cancer (Freedman et al., 2002), as well as lymphomas (Grant, 2003). Many more examples can be cited to emphasize the importance of vitamin D as an important factor for cancer prevention. Garland et al. (2006) recommended taking vitamin D supplements as a preventive measure against cancer. As per the National Academy of Sciences USA recommendation, the daily intake of vitamin D differs according to the age of the individual as 1–50 years (200 IU), 51–70 years (400 IU), and older than 71 years (600 IU). The aim is to achieve a serum of $25(OH)_2D3$ of the level of 30–150 ng/mL (Garland et al., 2006) (Garland et al., 2006).

15.6 Conclusions

Vitamin D can be an effective and safe approach for the treatment of cancers. There are three ways through which tumor progression can be inhibited by vitamin D and its analogs. First, calcitriol induces cell cycle arrest, differentiation, or apoptosis by inhibiting the cells of epithelial origin or the distal metastasis. Second, calcitriol reduces tumor metastasis through the regulation of proteases. Finally, calcitriol has been shown to inhibit angiogenesis of cancer cells by repressing metastatic invasion. Although there is a lack of data from clinical trials, a number of epidemiological studies, clinical and preclinical trials, and in vitro data strongly favor the hypothesis that the involvement of vitamin D in signaling pathways can be a promising approach for the prevention and treatment of various types of cancer. Therefore, various therapeutic interventions have been designed to target the dysregulation of vitamin D metabolism, or its activity has been examined and developed for cancer treatment (Giammanco et al., 2015). Unfortunately, there are some limitations that are associated with the vitamin D-based cancer chemotherapy, which should be taken into consideration in order to design suitable therapeutic strategies in best possible way (Mehta et al., 2013).

References

Abdel-Mohsen, M.A., El-Braky, A.A.-A., Ghazal, A.A.E.-R., Shamseya, M.M., 2018. Autophagy, apoptosis, vitamin D, and vitamin D receptor in hepatocellular carcinoma associated with hepatitis C virus. Medicine (Baltimore) 97, e0172.

Ahn, J., Park, S., Zuniga, B., Bera, A., Song, C.S., Chatterjee, B., 2016. Vitamin D in prostate. Cancer, 321–355.

Akhter, J., Chen, X., Bowrey, P., Bolton, E.J., Morris, D.L., 1997. Vitamin D3 analog, EB1089, inhibits growth of subcutaneous xenografts of the human colon cancer cell line, LoVo, in a nude mouse model. Dis. Colon Rectum 40, 317–321.

Alkhayal, K.A., Awadalia, Z.H., Vaali-Mohammed, M.-A., Al Obeed, O.A., Al Wesaimer, A., Halwani, R., et al., 2016. Association of vitamin D receptor gene polymorphisms with colorectal cancer in a Saudi Arabian population. PLoS One 11, e0155236.

Almquist, M., Bondeson, A.G., Bondeson, L., Malm, J., Manjer, J., 2010. Serum levels of vitamin D, PTH and calcium and breast cancer risk-a prospective nested case-control study. Int. J. Cancer 127 (9), 2159–2168.

Álvarez-Díaz, S., Larriba, M.J., López-Otín, C., Muñoz, A., 2010. Vitamin D: Proteases, protease inhibitors and cancer. Cell Cycle 9, 32–37.

Alvarez-Díaz, S., Valle, N., García, J.M., Peña, C., Freije, J.M.P., Quesada, V., et al., 2009. Cystatin D is a candidate tumor suppressor gene induced by vitamin D in human colon cancer cells. J. Clin. Invest. 119, 2343–2358.

Asano, L., Watanabe, M., Ryoden, Y., Usuda, K., Yamaguchi, T., Khambu, B., et al., 2017. Vitamin D metabolite, 25-hydroxyvitamin D, regulates lipid metabolism by inducing degradation of SREBP/SCAP. Cell Chem. Biol. 24, 207–217.

Ashmore, J.H., Gallagher, C.J., Lesko, S.M., Muscat, J.E., Hartman, T.J., Lazarus, P., 2015. No association between vitamin D intake, VDR polymorphisms, and colorectal cancer in a population-based case-control study. Cancer Epidemiol. Biomarkers Prev. 24, 1635–1637.

Atlanta: American Cancer Society, 2019. American Cancer Society. Cancer Facts & Figures 2019.

Atoum, M.F., AlKateeb, D., AlHaj Mahmoud, S.A., 2015. The Fok1 vitamin D receptor gene polymorphism and 25(OH) D serum levels and prostate cancer among Jordanian men. Asian Pac. J. Cancer Prev. 16, 2227–2230.

Augustsson, K., Michaud, D.S., Rimm, E.B., Leitzmann, M.F., Stampfer, M.J., Willett, W.C., et al., 2003. A prospective study of intake of fish and marine fatty acids and prostate cancer. Cancer Epidemiol. Biomarkers Prev. 12, 64–67.

Bao, B.-Y., Yeh, S.-D., Lee, Y.-F., 2006. 1α,25-dihydroxyvitamin D 3 inhibits prostate cancer cell invasion via modulation of selective proteases. Carcinogenesis 27, 32–42.

Batai, K., Murphy, A.B., Nonn, L., Kittles, R.A., 2016. Vitamin D and immune response: implications for prostate cancer in African Americans. Front. Immunol. 7. https://doi.org/10.3389/fimmu.2016.00053.

Batai, K., Murphy, A.B., Ruden, M., Newsome, J., Shah, E., Dixon, M.A., et al., 2017. Race and BMI modify associations of calcium and vitamin D intake with prostate cancer. BMC Cancer 17, 64.

Bessler, H., Djaldetti, M., 2012. 1α,25-dihydroxyvitamin D3 modulates the interaction between immune and colon cancer cells. Biomed. Pharmacother. 66, 428–432.

Brakta, S., Diamond, J.S., Al-Hendy, A., Diamond, M.P., Halder, S.K., 2015. Role of vitamin D in uterine fibroid biology. Fertil. Steril. 104, 698–706.

Budhathoki, S., Yamaji, T., Iwasaki, M., Sawada, N., Shimazu, T., Sasazuki, S., Yoshida, T., Tsugane, S., 2016. Vitamin D receptor gene polymorphism and the risk of colorectal cancer: a nested case-control study. PLoS One 11 (10), e0164648.

Caccamo, D., Ricca, S., Currò, M., Ientile, R., 2018. Health risks of hypovitaminosis D: a review of new molecular insights. Int. J. Mol. Sci. 19, 892.

Campbell, M.J., Elstner, E., Holden, S., Uskokovic, M., Koeffler, H.P., 1997. Inhibition of proliferation of prostate cancer cells by a 19-nor-hexafluoride vitamin D3 analogue involves the induction of p21waf1, p27kip1 and E-cadherin. J. Mol. Endocrinol. 19, 15–27.

Carlberg, C., Seuter, S., 2009. A genomic perspective on vitamin D signaling. Anticancer Res. 29, 3485–3493.

Caygill, C.P., Hill, M.J., 1995. Fish, n-3 fatty acids and human colorectal and breast cancer mortality. Eur. J. Cancer Prev. 4, 329–332.

Caygill, C.P., Charlett, A., Hill, M.J., 1996. Fat, fish, fish oil and cancer. Br. J. Cancer 74 (1), 159–164.

Chen, A., Davis, B.H., Sitrin, M.D., Brasitus, T.A., Bissonnette, M., 2002. Transforming growth factor-β1 signaling contributes to Caco-2 cell growth inhibition induced by 1,25(OH) 2 D 3. Am. J. Physiol. Liver Physiol. 283, G864–G874.

Chen, Y., Zhang, J., Ge, X., Du, J., Deb, D.K., Li, Y.C., 2013. Vitamin D receptor inhibits nuclear factor κB activation by interacting with IκB kinase β protein. J. Biol. Chem. 288, 19450–19458.

Chiang, K.-C., Chen, T.C., 2009. Vitamin D for the prevention and treatment of pancreatic cancer. World J. Gastroenterol. 15, 3349.

Ciebiera, M., Włodarczyk, M., Ciebiera, M., Zaręba, K., Łukaszuk, K., Jakiel, G., 2018. Vitamin D and uterine fibroids—review of the literature and novel concepts. Int. J. Mol. Sci. 19, 2051.

Colston, K.W., Hansen, C.M., 2002. Mechanisms implicated in the growth regulatory effects of vitamin D in breast cancer. Endocr. Relat. Cancer 9, 45–59.

Corder, E.H., Guess, H.A., Hulka, B.S., Friedman, G.D., Sadler, M., Vollmer, R.T., et al., 1993. Vitamin D and prostate cancer: a prediagnostic study with stored sera. Cancer Epidemiol. Biomarkers Prev. 2, 467–472.

Cordes, T., Hoellen, F., Dittmer, C., Salehin, D., Kümmel, S., Friedrich, M., et al., 2012. Correlation of prostaglandin metabolizing enzymes and serum PGE2 levels with vitamin D receptor and serum 25(OH)2D3 levels in breast and ovarian cancer. Anticancer Res. 32, 351–357.

Cui, N., Hu, M., Khalil, R.A., 2017. Biochemical and biological attributes of matrix metalloproteinases. Prog. Mol. Biol.Transl Sci. 147, 1–73.

Deeb, K.K., Trump, D.L., Johnson, C.S., 2007. Vitamin D signalling pathways in cancer: potential for anticancer therapeutics. Nat. Rev. Cancer 7, 684–700.

DeLuca, H.F., 2004. Overview of general physiologic features and functions of vitamin D. Am. J. Clin. Nutr. 80, 1689S–1696S.

Delvin, E.E., Lopez, V., Levy, E., Ménard, D., 1996. Developmental expression of calcitriol receptors, 9-kilodalton calcium-binding protein, and calcidiol 24-hydroxylase in human intestine. Pediatr. Res. 40, 664–670.

Deschasaux, M., Souberbielle, J.-C., Latino-Martel, P., Sutton, A., Charnaux, N., Druesne-Pecollo, N., et al., 2016. Weight status and alcohol intake modify the association between vitamin D and breast cancer risk. J. Nutr. 146, 576–585.

Díaz, G.D., Paraskeva, C., Thomas, M.G., Binderup, L., Hague, A., 2000. Apoptosis is induced by the active metabolite of vitamin D3 and its analogue EB1089 in colorectal adenoma and carcinoma cells: possible implications for prevention and therapy. Cancer Res. 60, 2304–2312.

Dokoh, S., Donaldson, C.A., Haussler, M.R., 1984. Influence of 1,25-dihydroxyvitamin D3 on cultured osteogenic sarcoma cells: correlation with the 1,25-dihydroxyvitamin D3 receptor. Cancer Res. 44, 2103–2109.

Dunning, A.M., Healey, C.S., Pharoah, P.D., Teare, M.D., Ponder, B.A., Easton, D.F., 1999. A systematic review of genetic polymorphisms and breast cancer risk. Cancer Epidemiol. Biomarkers Prev. 8, 843–854.

Eisman, J.A., Barkla, D.H., Tutton, P.J., 1987. Suppression of in vivo growth of human cancer solid tumor xenografts by 1,25-dihydroxyvitamin D3. Cancer Res. 47, 21–25.

Eisman, J.A., Martin, T.J., 1989. Vitamin D and breast cancer. Lancet (London, England) 1, 549–550.

Fedirko, V., Bostick, R.M., Flanders, W.D., Long, Q., Shaukat, A., Rutherford, R.E., et al., 2009. Effects of vitamin D and calcium supplementation on markers of apoptosis in normal colon mucosa: a randomized, double-blind, placebo-controlled clinical trial. Cancer Prev. Res. 2, 213–223.

Fedirko, V., Bostick, R.M., Long, Q., Flanders, W.D., McCullough, M.L., Sidelnikov, E., et al., 2010. Effects of supplemental vitamin D and calcium on oxidative DNA damage marker in normal colorectal mucosa: a randomized clinical trial. Cancer Epidemiol. Biomarkers Prev. 19, 280–291.

Fei, X., Shen, Y., Liu, N., Li, H., Guo, J., Wu, Z., 2016. Polymorphisms of vitamin D receptor gene TaqI susceptibility of prostate cancer: a meta-analysis. Onco. Targets. Ther. 1033.

Feldman, D., Krishnan, A.V., Swami, S., Giovannucci, E., Feldman, B.J., 2014. The role of vitamin D in reducing cancer risk and progression. Nat. Rev. Cancer 14, 342–357.

Ferrer-Mayorga, G., Gómez-López, G., Barbáchano, A., Fernández-Barral, A., Peña, C., Pisano, D.G., et al., 2017. Vitamin D receptor expression and associated gene signature in tumour stromal fibroblasts predict clinical outcome in colorectal cancer. Gut 66, 1449–1462.

Ferrer-Mayorga, G., Larriba, M.J., Crespo, P., Muñoz, A., 2019. Mechanisms of action of vitamin D in colon cancer. J. Steroid Biochem. Mol. Biol. 185, 1–6.

Feskanich, D., Ma, J., Fuchs, C.S., Kirkner, G.J., Hankinson, S.E., Hollis, B.W., et al., 2004. Plasma vitamin D metabolites and risk of colorectal cancer in women. Cancer Epidemiol. Biomarkers Prev. 13, 1502–1508.

Frampton, R.J., Omond, S.A., Eisman, J.A., 1983. Inhibition of human cancer cell growth by 1,25-dihydroxyvitamin D3 metabolites. Cancer Res. 43, 4443–4447.

Freedman, D.M., Dosemeci, M., McGlynn, K., 2002. Sunlight and mortality from breast, ovarian, colon, prostate, and non-melanoma skin cancer: a composite death certificate based case-control study. Occup. Environ. Med. 59, 257–262.

Friedrich, M., Axt-Fliedner, R., Villena-Heinsen, C., Tilgen, W., Schmidt, W., Reichrath, J., 2002. Analysis of vitamin D-receptor (VDR) and retinoid X-receptor alpha in breast cancer. Histochem. J. 34, 35–40.

Fuchs, M.A., Yuan, C., Sato, K., Niedzwiecki, D., Ye, X., Saltz, L.B., et al., 2017. Predicted vitamin D status and colon cancer recurrence and mortality in CALGB 89803 (Alliance). Ann. Oncol. 28, 1359–1367.

Gao, J., Wei, W., Wang, G., Zhou, H., Fu, Y., Liu, N., 2018. Circulating vitamin D concentration and risk of prostate cancer: a dose-response meta-analysis of prospective studies. Ther. Clin. Risk Manag. 14, 95–104.

Garland, C.F., Garland, F.C., 1980. Do sunlight and vitamin D reduce the likelihood of colon cancer? Int. J. Epidemiol. 9, 227–231.

Garland, C.F., Garland, F.C., Gorham, E.D., Lipkin, M., Newmark, H., Mohr, S.B., et al., 2006. The role of vitamin D in cancer prevention. Am. J. Public Health 96, 252–261.

Garland, F.C., Garland, C.F., Gorham, E.D., Young, J.F., 1990. Geographic variation in breast cancer mortality in the United States: a hypothesis involving exposure to solar radiation. Prev. Med. (Baltim). 19, 614–622.

Garland, C., Shekelle, R.B., Barrett-Connor, E., Criqui, M.H., Rossof, A.H., Paul, O., 1985. Dietary vitamin D and calcium and risk of colorectal cancer: a 19-year prospective study in men. Lancet (London, England) 1, 307–309.

Garland, C.F., Comstock, G.W., Garland, F.C., Helsing, K.J., Shaw, E.K., Gorham, E.D., 1989. Serum 25-hydroxyvitamin D and colon cancer: eight-year prospective study. Lancet 2 (8673), 1176–1178.

Garland, C.F., Gorham, E.D., Mohr, S.B., Grant, W.B., Giovannucci, E.L., Lipkin, M., Newmark, H., Holick, M.F., Garland, F.C., 2007. Vitamin D and prevention of breast cancer: pooled analysis. J. Steroid Biochem. Mol. Biol. 103 (3–5), 708–711.

Giammanco, M., et al., 2015. Vitamin D in cancer chemoprevention. Pharm. Biol. 53, 1399–1434.

González, E.A., Sachdeva, A., Oliver, D.A., Martin, K.J., 2004. Vitamin D insufficiency and deficiency in chronic kidney disease. Am. J. Nephrol. 24, 503–510.

González-Sancho, J.M., Larriba, M.J., Ordóñez-Morán, P., Pálmer, H.G., Muñoz, A., 2006. Effects of 1alpha,25-dihydroxyvitamin D3 in human colon cancer cells. Anticancer Res. 26, 2669–2681.

Gorham, E.D., Garland, C.F., Garland, F.C., 1989. Acid haze air pollution and breast and colon cancer mortality in 20 Canadian cities. Can. J. Public Health 80, 96–100.

Gorham, E.D., Garland, C.F., Garland, F.C., Grant, W.B., Mohr, S.B., Lipkin, M., et al., 2007. Optimal vitamin D status for colorectal cancer prevention. Am. J. Prev. Med. 32, 210–216.

Grant, W.B., 2003. Ecologic studies of solar UV-B radiation and cancer mortality rates. Rec. Results Cancer Res. 164, 371–377.

Grant, W.B., 2014. Vitamin D status: ready for guiding prostate cancer diagnosis and treatment? Clin. Cancer Res. 20 (9), 2241–2243.

Habuchi, T., Suzuki, T., Sasaki, R., Wang, L., Sato, K., Satoh, S., et al., 2000. Association of vitamin D receptor gene polymorphism with prostate cancer and benign prostatic hyperplasia in a Japanese population. Cancer Res. 60, 305–308.

Hamasaki, T., Inatomi, H., Katoh, T., Ikuyama, T., Matsumoto, T., 2001. Clinical and pathological significance of vitamin D receptor gene polymorphism for prostate cancer which is associated with a higher mortality in Japanese. Endocr. J. 48, 543–549.

Haverkamp, J., Charbonneau, B., Ratliff, T.L., 2008. Prostate inflammation and its potential impact on prostate cancer: a current review. J. Cell. Biochem. 103, 1344–1353.

Holick, M.F., 2004a. Sunlight and vitamin D for bone health and prevention of autoimmune diseases, cancers, and cardiovascular disease. Am. J. Clin. Nutr. 80, 1678S–1688S.

Holick, M.F., 2004b. Vitamin D: importance in the prevention of cancers, type 1 diabetes, heart disease, and osteoporosis. Am. J. Clin. Nutr. 79, 362–371.

Holick, M.F., Chen, T.C., 2008. Vitamin D deficiency: a worldwide problem with health consequences. Am. J. Clin. Nutr. 87, 1080S–1086S.

Hong, Z., Tian, C., Zhang, X., 2012. Dietary calcium intake, vitamin D levels, and breast cancer risk: a dose–response analysis of observational studies. Breast Cancer Res. Treat. 136, 309–312.

Hünten, S., Hermeking, H., 2015. p53 directly activates cystatin D/CST5 to mediate mesenchymal-epithelial transition: a possible link to tumor suppression by vitamin D3. Oncotarget 6, 15842–15856. https://doi.org/10.18632/oncotarget.4683.

Hussain, S., Zhang, Y., Galardy, P., 2009. DUBs and cancer: the role of deubiquitinating enzymes as oncogenes, non-oncogenes and tumor suppressors. Cell Cycle 8, 1688–1697.

Ingles, S.A., Garcia, D.G., Wang, W., Nieters, A., Henderson, B.E., Kolonel, L.N., et al., 2000. Vitamin D receptor genotype and breast cancer in Latinas (United States). Cancer Causes Control 11, 25–30.

Iseki, K., Tatsuta, M., Uehara, H., Iishi, H., Yano, H., Sakai, N., et al., 1999. Inhibition of angiogenesis as a mechanism for inhibition by 1alpha-hydroxyvitamin D3 and 1,25-dihydroxyvitamin D3 of colon carcinogenesis induced by azoxymethane in Wistar rats. Int. J. cancer 81, 730–733.

Jiang, X., Dimou, N.L., Al-Dabhani, K., Lewis, S.J., Martin, R.M., Haycock, P.C., et al., 2018. Circulating vitamin D concentrations and risk of breast and prostate cancer: a Mendelian randomization study. Int. J. Epidemiol. https://doi.org/10.1093/ije/dyy284.

Jiang, F., Li, P., Fornace, A.J., Nicosia, S.V., Bai, W., 2003. G 2 /M Arrest by 1,25-Dihydroxyvitamin D 3 in ovarian cancer cells mediated through the induction of GADD45 via an exonic enhancer. J. Biol. Chem. 278, 48030–48040.

Jung, S., Qian, Z.R., Yamauchi, M., Bertrand, K.A., Fitzgerald, K.C., Inamura, K., Kim, S.A., Mima, K., Sukawa, Y., Zhang, X., Wang, M., Smith-Warner, S.A., Wu, K., Fuchs, C.S., Chan, A.T., Giovannucci, E.L., Ng, K., Cho, E., Ogino, S., Nishihara, R., 2014. Predicted 25(OH)D score and colorectal cancer risk according to vitamin D receptor expression. Cancer Epidemiol. Biomarkers Prev. 23 (8), 1628–1637.

Kaizer, L., Boyd, N.F., Kriukov, V., Tritchler, D., 1989. Fish consumption and breast cancer risk: an ecological study. Nutr. Cancer 12, 61–68.

Kállay, E., Bareis, P., Bajna, E., Kriwanek, S., Bonner, E., Toyokuni, S., et al., 2002. Vitamin D receptor activity and prevention of colonic hyperproliferation and oxidative stress. Food Chem. Toxicol. 40, 1191–1196.

Kambale, P.R., Haldar, D., Kabi, B.C., Kambale, K.P., 2017. Study of vitamin D receptor gene polymorphism (FokI, TaqI and ApaI) among prostate cancer patients in North India. J. Clin. Diagnostic Res. 11, BC05–BC08. https://doi.org/10.7860/JCDR/2017/24290.9976.

Kang, S., Zhao, Y., Liu, J., Wang, L., Zhao, G., Chen, X., et al., 2016. Association of vitamin D receptor Fok I polymorphism with the risk of prostate cancer: a meta-analysis. Oncotarget 7. https://doi.org/10.18632/oncotarget.12837.

Kang, S., Zhao, Y., Wang, L., Liu, J., Chen, X., Liu, X., et al., 2018. Lack of association between the risk of prostate cancer and vitamin D receptor Bsm I polymorphism: a meta-analysis of 27 published studies. Cancer Manag. Res. 10, 2377–2387.

Keane, J., Elangovan, H., Stokes, R., Gunton, J., 2018. Vitamin D and the liver—correlation or cause? Nutrients 10, 496.

Klampfer, L., 2014. Vitamin D and colon cancer. World J. Gastrointest. Oncol. 6, 430.

Koli, K., Keski-Oja, J., 2000. 1alpha,25-dihydroxyvitamin D3 and its analogues down-regulate cell invasion-associated proteases in cultured malignant cells. Cell Growth Differ. 11, 221–229.

Krishnan, A.V., Feldman, D., 2010. Molecular pathways mediating the anti-inflammatory effects of calcitriol: implications for prostate cancer chemoprevention and treatment. Endocr. Relat. Cancer 17, R19–R38.

Krishnan, A.V., Feldman, D., 2011. Mechanisms of the anti-cancer and anti-inflammatory actions of Vitamin D. Annu. Rev. Pharmacol. Toxicol. 51, 311–336.
Krishnan, A.V., Peehl, D.M., Feldman, D., 2003. Inhibition of prostate cancer growth by vitamin D: regulation of target gene expression. J. Cell. Biochem. 88, 363–371.
Kristal, A.R., Till, C., Song, X., Tangen, C.M., Goodman, P.J., Neuhauser, M.L., et al., 2014. plasma vitamin D and prostate cancer risk: results from the selenium and vitamin E cancer prevention trial. Cancer Epidemiol. Biomarkers Prev. 23, 1494–1504.
de La Puente-Yagüe, M., Cuadrado-Cenzual, M.A., Ciudad-Cabañas, M.J., Hernández-Cabria, M., Collado-Yurrita, L., 2018. Vitamin D and its role in breast cancer. Kaohsiung J. Med. Sci. 34, 423–427.
Laczmanska, I., Laczmanski, L., Bebenek, M., Karpinski, P., Czemarmazowicz, H., Ramsey, D., et al., 2014. Vitamin D receptor gene polymorphisms in relation to the risk of colorectal cancer in the Polish population. Tumor Biol. 35, 12397–12401.
Larriba, M., González-Sancho, J., Barbáchano, A., Niell, N., Ferrer-Mayorga, G., Muñoz, A., 2013. Vitamin D is a multilevel repressor of Wnt/b-catenin signaling in cancer cells. Cancers (Basel). 5, 1242–1260.
Lefkowitz, E.S., Garland, C.F., 1994. Sunlight, vitamin D, and ovarian cancer mortality rates in US women. Int. J. Epidemiol. 23, 1133–1136.
Lisse, T.S., Liu, T., Irmler, M., Beckers, J., Chen, H., Adams, J.S., et al., 2011. Gene targeting by the vitamin D response element binding protein reveals a role for vitamin D in osteoblast mTOR signaling. FASEB J. 25, 937–947.
Lowe, L., Hansen, C.M., Senaratne, S., Colston, K.W., 2003. Mechanisms implicated in the growth regulatory effects of vitamin D compounds in breast cancer cells. Recent Results Cancer Res. 164, 99–110.
Luan, Z., Ma, Y., Xin, Y., Qian, J., Wang, H., 2017. Possible molecular mechanisms by which vitamin D prevents inflammatory bowel disease and colitis-associated colorectal cancer. Curr. Med. Chem. 24, 911–917.
Lyakhovich, A., Aksenov, N., Pennanen, P., Miettinen, S., Ahonen, M.H., Syvälä, H., et al., 2000. Vitamin D induced up-regulation of keratinocyte growth factor (FGF-7/KGF) in MCF-7 human breast cancer cells. Biochem. Biophys. Res. Commun. 273, 675–680.
Majewski, S., Skopinska, M., Marczak, M., Szmurlo, A., Bollag, W., Jablonska, S., 1996. Vitamin D3 is a potent inhibitor of tumor cell-induced angiogenesis. J. Investig. Dermatology. Symp. Proc. 1, 97–101.
Manna, P., Achari, A.E., Jain, S.K., 2017. Vitamin D supplementation inhibits oxidative stress and upregulate SIRT1/AMPK/GLUT4 cascade in high glucose-treated 3T3L1 adipocytes and in adipose tissue of high fat diet-fed diabetic mice. Arch. Biochem. Biophys. 615, 22–34.
Mathiasen, I.S., Lademann, U., Jäättelä, M., 1999. Apoptosis induced by vitamin D compounds in breast cancer cells is inhibited by Bcl-2 but does not involve known caspases or p53. Cancer Res. 59, 4848–4856.
Mathiasen, I.S., Sergeev, I.N., Bastholm, L., Elling, F., Norman, A.W., Jäättelä, M., 2002. Calcium and calpain as key mediators of apoptosis-like death induced by vitamin D compounds in breast cancer cells. J. Biol. Chem. 277, 30738–30745.
McCullough, M.L., Zoltick, E.S., Weinstein, S.J., Fedirko, V., Wang, M., Cook, N.R., et al., 2019. Circulating vitamin D and colorectal cancer risk: an international pooling project of 17 cohorts. JNCI. J. Natl. Cancer Inst. 111, 158–169.
Meeker, S., Seamons, A., Paik, J., Treuting, P.M., Brabb, T., Grady, W.M., Maggio-Price, L., 2014. Increased dietary vitamin D suppresses MAPK signaling, colitis, and colon cancer. Cancer Res. 74 (16), 4398–4408.

Mehta, R.G., Peng, X., Alimirah, F., Murillo, G., Mehta, R., 2013. Vitamin D and breast cancer: emerging concepts. Cancer Lett. 334, 95–100.

Miles, F., Goodman, P., Tangen, C., Torkko, K., Schenk, J., Song, X., et al., 2017. Interactions of the insulin-like growth factor axis and vitamin D in prostate cancer risk in the prostate cancer Prevention Trial. Nutrients 9, 378.

Miller, S., Coveney, C., Johnson, J., Farmaki, A.-E., Gupta, N., Tobin, M.D., et al., 2018. The vitamin D binding protein axis modifies disease severity in lymphangioleiomyomatosis. Eur. Respir. J. 52, 1800951.

Miller, G.J., Stapleton, G.E., Hedlund, T.E., Moffat, K.A., 1995. Vitamin D receptor expression, 24-hydroxylase activity, and inhibition of growth by 1alpha,25-dihydroxyvitamin D3 in seven human prostatic carcinoma cell lines. Clin. Cancer Res. 1, 997–1003.

Miyaura, C., Abe, E., Kuribayashi, T., Tanaka, H., Konno, K., Nishii, Y., et al., 1981. 1 alpha,25-Dihydroxyvitamin D3 induces differentiation of human myeloid leukemia cells. Biochem. Biophys. Res. Commun. 102, 937–943.

Mohr, S.B., Garland, C.F., Gorham, E.D., Grant, W.B., Garland, F.C., 2008. Relationship between low ultraviolet B irradiance and higher breast cancer risk in 107 countries. Breast J. 14, 255–260.

Moossavi, M., Parsamanesh, N., Mohammadoo-Khorasani, M., Moosavi, M., Tavakkoli, T., Fakharian, T., et al., 2018. Positive correlation between vitamin D receptor gene FokI polymorphism and colorectal cancer susceptibility in South-Khorasan of Iran. J. Cell. Biochem. 119, 8190–8194.

Moreno, J., Krishnan, A.V., Feldman, D., 2005. Molecular mechanisms mediating the antiproliferative effects of vitamin D in prostate cancer. J. Steroid Biochem. Mol. Biol. 97, 31–36.

Mulligan, M.L., Felton, S.K., Riek, A.E., Bernal-Mizrachi, C., 2010. Implications of vitamin D deficiency in pregnancy and lactation. Am. J. Obstet. Gynecol. 202, 429.e1–429.e9.

Nakai, K., Fujii, H., Kono, K., Goto, S., Kitazawa, R., Kitazawa, S., et al., 2014. Vitamin D activates the Nrf2-Keap1 antioxidant pathway and ameliorates nephropathy in diabetic rats. Am. J. Hypertens. 27, 586–595.

Narvaez, C.J., Welsh, J., 2001. Role of mitochondria and caspases in vitamin D-mediated apoptosis of MCF-7 breast cancer cells. J. Biol. Chem. 276, 9101–9107.

Nonn, L., Peng, L., Feldman, D., Peehl, D.M., 2006. Inhibition of p38 by vitamin D reduces interleukin-6 production in normal prostate cells via mitogen-activated protein kinase phosphatase 5: implications for prostate cancer prevention by vitamin D. Cancer Res. 66, 4516–4524.

Obiezu, C.V., Diamandis, E.P., 2005. Human tissue kallikrein gene family: applications in cancer. Cancer Lett. 224, 1–22.

Ordóñez-Morán, P., Larriba, M.J., Pálmer, H.G., Valero, R.A., Barbáchano, A., Duñach, M., et al., 2008. RhoA–ROCK and p38MAPK-MSK1 mediate vitamin D effects on gene expression, phenotype, and Wnt pathway in colon cancer cells. J. Cell Biol. 183, 697–710.

Paliouras, M., Borgono, C., Diamandis, E.P., 2007. Human tissue kallikreins: the cancer biomarker family. Cancer Lett. 249, 61–79.

Pálmer, H.G., González-Sancho, J.M., Espada, J., Berciano, M.T., Puig, I., Baulida, J., et al., 2001. Vitamin D 3 promotes the differentiation of colon carcinoma cells by the induction of E-cadherin and the inhibition of β-catenin signaling. J. Cell Biol. 154, 369–388.

Pálmer, H.G., Sánchez-Carbayo, M., Ordóñez-Morán, P., Larriba, M.J., Cordón-Cardó, C., Muñoz, A., 2003. Genetic signatures of differentiation induced by 1alpha,25-dihydroxyvitamin D3 in human colon cancer cells. Cancer Res. 63, 7799–7806.

Peehl, D.M., Shinghal, R., Nonn, L., Seto, E., Krishnan, A.V., Brooks, J.D., et al., 2004. Molecular activity of 1,25-dihydroxyvitamin D3 in primary cultures of human prostatic epithelial cells revealed by cDNA microarray analysis. J. Steroid Biochem. Mol. Biol. 92, 131–141.

Pendás-Franco, N., García, J.M., Peña, C., Valle, N., Pálmer, H.G., Heinäniemi, M., et al., 2008. DICKKOPF-4 is induced by TCF/β-catenin and upregulated in human colon cancer, promotes tumour cell invasion and angiogenesis and is repressed by 1α,25-dihydroxyvitamin D3. Oncogene 27, 4467–4477.

Pereira, F., Larriba, M.J., Muñoz, A., 2012. Vitamin D and colon cancer. Endocr. Relat. Cancer 19, R51–R71.

Peters, R.K., Pike, M.C., Garabrant, D., Mack, T.M., 1992. Diet and colon cancer in Los Angeles County, California. Cancer Causes Control 3, 457–473.

Pilz, S., Tomaschitz, A., Ritz, E., Pieber, T.R., 2009. Vitamin D status and arterial hypertension: a systematic review. Nat. Rev. Cardiol. 6, 621–630.

Reichel, H., Koeffler, H.P., Norman, A.W., 1989. The role of the vitamin D endocrine system in health and disease. N. Engl. J. Med. 320, 980–991.

Reimers, L.L., Crew, K.D., Bradshaw, P.T., Santella, R.M., Steck, S.E., Sirosh, I., et al., 2015. Vitamin D-related gene polymorphisms, plasma 25-hydroxyvitamin D, and breast cancer risk. Cancer Causes Control 26, 187–203.

Robsahm, T.E., Tretli, S., Dahlback, A., Moan, J., 2004. Vitamin D 3 from sunlight may improve the prognosis of breast-, colon- and prostate cancer (Norway). Cancer Causes Control 15, 149–158.

Roca, E., Valcamonico, F., Amoroso, V., Antonelli, A., Foroni, C., Simeone, C., et al., 2016. Serum vitamin D and prostate cancer prognosis: the story continues. J. Clin. Oncol. 34, 3709–3710.

Ruggiero, M., Pacini, S., Aterini, S., Fallai, C., Ruggiero, C., Pacini, P., 1998. Vitamin D receptor gene polymorphism is associated with metastatic breast cancer. Oncol. Res. 10, 43–46.

Sato, T., Takusagawa, K., Asoo, N., Konno, K., 1982. Antitumor effect of 1 alpha-hydroxyvitamin D3. Tohoku J. Exp. Med. 138, 445–446.

Sawada, N., Inoue, M., Iwasaki, M., Yamaji, T., Shimazu, T., Sasazuki, S., et al., 2017. Plasma 25-hydroxy vitamin D and subsequent prostate cancer risk in a nested case-control study in Japan: The JPHC study. Eur. J. Clin. Nutr. 71, 132–136.

Schwartz, G.G., Hanchette, C.L., 2006. UV, latitude, and spatial trends in prostate cancer mortality: all sunlight is not the same (United States). Cancer Causes Control 17, 1091–1101.

Schwartz, G.G., Hulka, B.S., 1990. Is vitamin D deficiency a risk factor for prostate cancer? (Hypothesis). Anticancer Res. 10, 1307–1311.

Schwartz, G.G., Whitlatch, L.W., Chen, T.C., Lokeshwar, B.L., Holick, M.F., 1998. Human prostate cells synthesize 1,25-dihydroxyvitamin D3 from 25-hydroxyvitamin D3. Cancer Epidemiol. Biomarkers Prev. 7, 391–395.

Sergeev, I.N., 2012. Vitamin D and cellular Ca2+ signaling in breast cancer. Anticancer Res. 32, 299–302.

Shah, S., Islam, M.N., Dakshanamurthy, S., Rizvi, I., Rao, M., Herrell, R., et al., 2006. The molecular basis of vitamin D receptor and β-catenin crossregulation. Mol. Cell 21, 799–809.

Sharma, K., Goehe, R.W., Di, X., Hicks, M.A., Torti, S.V., Torti, F.M., et al., 2014. A novel cytostatic form of autophagy in sensitization of non-small cell lung cancer cells to radiation by vitamin D and the vitamin D analog, EB 1089. Autophagy 10, 2346–2361.

Sheng, S., Chen, Y., Shen, Z., 2017. Correlation between polymorphism of vitamin D receptor TaqI and susceptibility to colorectal cancer. Medicine (Baltimore) 96, e7242.

Shrihari, T., 2018. Vitamin D role in prevention of cancer: overview. Indian J. Med. Paediatr. Oncol. 39, 75.

Simboli-Campbell, M., Narvaez, C.J., Tenniswood, M., Welsh, J., 1996. 1,25-dihydroxyvitamin D3 induces morphological and biochemical markers of apoptosis in MCF-7 breast cancer cells. J. Steroid Biochem. Mol. Biol. 58, 367–376.

Skowronski, R.J., Peehl, D.M., Feldman, D., 1993. Vitamin D and prostate cancer: 1,25 dihydroxyvitamin D3 receptors and actions in human prostate cancer cell lines. Endocrinology 132, 1952–1960.

Slatter, M.L., Yakumo, K., Hoffman, M., Neuhausen, S., 2001. Variants of the VDR gene and risk of colon cancer (United States). Cancer Causes Control 12, 359–364.

Slominski, A.T., Brożyna, A.A., Zmijewski, M.A., Jóźwicki, W., Jetten, A.M., Mason, R.S., et al., 2017. Vitamin D signaling and melanoma: role of vitamin D and its receptors in melanoma progression and management. Lab. Investig. 97, 706–724.

Slominski, A., Semak, I., Zjawiony, J., Wortsman, J., Li, W., Szczesniewski, A., et al., 2005. The cytochrome P450scc system opens an alternate pathway of vitamin D3 metabolism. FEBS J. 272, 4080–4090.

Stanaland, M., Jiroutek, M.R., Holland, M.A., 2017. Study of the association between serum vitamin D levels and prostate cancer. Mil. Med. 182, e1769–e1774.

Stearns, V., Visvanathan, K., 2013. Optimizing vitamin D concentrations for breast cancer risk reduction. Medicine (Baltimore) 92, 132–134.

Stewart, L.V., Weigel, N.L., 2004. Vitamin D and prostate cancer. Exp. Biol. Med. (Maywood) 229, 277–284.

Sun, M., Guo, B., 2017. Vitamin D and the epigenetic machinery in colon cancer. Curr. Med. Chem. 24, 888–897.

Swami, S., Raghavachari, N., Muller, U.R., Bao, Y.P., Feldman, D., 2003. Vitamin D growth inhibition of breast cancer cells: Gene expression patterns assessed by cDNA microarray. Breast Cancer Res. Treat. 80, 49–62.

Takeda, E., Yamamoto, H., Taketani, Y., Miyamoto, K.I., 1997. Vitamin D-dependent rickets type I and type II. Pediatr. Int. 39, 508–513.

Takeshige, N., Yin, G., Ohnaka, K., Kono, S., Ueki, T., Tanaka, M., et al., 2015. Associations between vitamin D receptor (VDR) gene polymorphisms and colorectal cancer risk and effect modifications of dietary calcium and vitamin D in a Japanese population. Asian Pac. J. Cancer Prev. 16, 2019–2026.

Tanaka, H., Abe, E., Miyaura, C., Kuribayashi, T., Konno, K., Nishii, Y., et al., 1982. 1α,25-Dihydroxycholecalciferol and a human myeloid leukaemia cell line (HL-60). Biochem. J. 204, 713–719.

Tangpricha, V., Pearce, E.N., Chen, T.C., Holick, M.F., 2002. Vitamin D insufficiency among free-living healthy young adults. Am. J. Med. 112, 659–662.

Tavera-Mendoza, L., Wang, T.-T., Lallemant, B., Zhang, R., Nagai, Y., Bourdeau, V., et al., 2006. Convergence of vitamin D and retinoic acid signalling at a common hormone response element. EMBO Rep. 7, 180–185.

Terry, P., Wolk, A., Vainio, H., Weiderpass, E., 2002. Fatty fish consumption lowers the risk of endometrial cancer: a nationwide case-control study in Sweden. Cancer Epidemiol. Biomarkers Prev. 11, 143–145.

Thakkar, A., Wang, B., Picon-Ruiz, M., Buchwald, P., Ince, T.A., 2016. Vitamin D and androgen receptor-targeted therapy for triple-negative breast cancer. Breast Cancer Res. Treat. 157, 77–90.

Ting, H.-J., Yasmin-Karim, S., Yan, S.-J., Hsu, J.-W., Lin, T.-H., Zeng, W., et al., 2012. A positive feedback signaling loop between ATM and the vitamin D receptor is critical for cancer chemoprevention by vitamin D. Cancer Res. 72, 958–968.

Touvier, M., Chan, D.S.M., Lau, R., Aune, D., Vieira, R., Greenwood, D.C., et al., 2011. Meta-analyses of vitamin D intake, 25-hydroxyvitamin D status, vitamin D receptor polymorphisms, and colorectal cancer risk. Cancer Epidemiol. Biomarkers Prev. 20, 1003–1016.

Townsend, K., Evans, K.N., Campbell, M.J., Colston, K.W., Adams, J.S., Hewison, M., 2005. Biological actions of extra-renal 25-hydroxyvitamin D-1α-hydroxylase and implications for chemoprevention and treatment. J. Steroid Biochem. Mol. Biol. 97, 103–109.
Travis, R.C., Perez-Cornago, A., Appleby, P.N., Albanes, D., Joshu, C.E., Lutsey, P.L., et al., 2019. A collaborative analysis of individual participant data from 19 prospective studies assesses circulating vitamin D and prostate cancer risk. Cancer Res. 79, 274–285.
Tuohimaa, P., Lyakhovich, A., Aksenov, N., Pennanen, P., Syvälä, H., Lou, Y.R., et al., 2001. Vitamin D and prostate cancer. J. Steroid Biochem. Mol. Biol. 76, 125–134.
Umar, M., Sastry, K.S., Al Ali, F., Al-Khulaifi, M., Wang, E., Chouchane, A.I., 2018. Vitamin D and the pathophysiology of inflammatory skin diseases. Skin Pharmacol. Physiol. 31, 74–86.
Vuolo, L., Di Somma, C., Faggiano, A., Colao, A., 2012. Vitamin D and cancer. Front. Endocrinol. (Lausanne). 3, 58. https://doi.org/10.3389/fendo.2012.00058.
Wang, W.-L.W., Tenniswood, M., 2014. Vitamin D, intermediary metabolism and prostate cancer tumor progression. Front. Physiol. 5. https://doi.org/10.3389/fphys.2014.00183.
Wecksler, W.R., Masont, R.S., Norman, A.W., 1979. Specific cytosol receptors for 1,25-dihydroxyvitamin d 3 in human intestine. J. Clin. Endocrinol. Metab. 48, 715–717.
Welsh, J., 1994. Induction of apoptosis in breast cancer cells in response to vitamin D and antiestrogens. Biochem. Cell Biol. 72, 537–545.
Wilson, E.N., Bristol, M.L., Di, X., Maltese, W.A., Koterba, K., Beckman, M.J., et al., 2011. A switch between cytoprotective and cytotoxic autophagy in the radiosensitization of breast tumor cells by chloroquine and vitamin D. Horm. Cancer 2, 272–285.
Wortsman, J., Matsuoka, L.Y., Chen, T.C., Lu, Z., Holick, M.F., 2000. Decreased bioavailability of vitamin D in obesity. Am. J. Clin. Nutr. 72, 690–693.
Xu, J., Li, H., Gu, L., Zhou, X., 2014. Association between vitamin D receptor poly(A) polymorphism and breast cancer risk: a meta-analysis. Tumor Biol. 35, 589–593.
Yang, L., Yang, J., Venkateswarlu, S., Ko, T., Brattain, M.G., 2001. Autocrine TGF? signaling mediates vitamin D3 analog-induced growth inhibition in breast cells. J. Cell. Physiol. 188, 383–393.
Yin, L., Grandi, N., Raum, E., Haug, U., Arndt, V., Brenner, H., 2009. Meta-analysis: longitudinal studies of serum vitamin D and colorectal cancer risk. Aliment. Pharmacol. Ther. 30, 113–125.
Yuan, L., Jiang, R., Yang, Y., DIng, S., Deng, H., 2012. 1,25-Dihydroxyvitamin D3 inhibits growth of the breast cancer cell line MCF-7 and downregulates cytochrome P4501B1 through the COX-2/PGE2 pathway. Oncol. Rep. 28, 2131–2137.
Zehnder, D., Bland, R., Williams, M.C., McNinch, R.W., Howie, A.J., Stewart, P.M., et al., 2001. Extrarenal expression of 25-hydroxyvitamin D 3-1α-hydroxylase 1. J. Clin. Endocrinol. Metab. 86, 888–894.
Zhang, Y., Leung, D.Y.M., Richers, B.N., Liu, Y., Remigio, L.K., Riches, D.W., et al., 2012. vitamin D inhibits monocyte/macrophage proinflammatory cytokine production by targeting MAPK phosphatase-1. J. Immunol. 188, 2127–2135.

Further reading

Shehzad, A., Khan, S., Shehzad, O., Lee, Y.S., 2010. Curcumin therapeutic promises and bioavailability in colorectal cancer. Drugs Today 46, 523–532.
Tommie, J.L., Pinney, S.M., Nommsen-Rivers, L.A., 2018. Serum vitamin D status and breast cancer risk by receptor status: a systematic review. Nutr. Cancer 70, 804–820.

Chapter 16

Molecular imaging of proteases in cancer

Ayesha Mahmood[a], Nadiah Zafar[a], Mohamad Tarhini[b], Abdelhamid Elaissari[b]

[a]*Faculty of Pharmacy, The University of Lahore, Lahore, Pakistan,* [b]*Univ Lyon, University Claude Bernard Lyon-1, CNRS, LAGEP-UMR 5007, Lyon, France*

16.1 Introduction

Cancer is the second leading cause of death around the world. World health organization (WHO) declared that approximately 9.6 million deaths occurred due to cancer. According to an estimate, cancer is responsible for 1 death out of 6 deaths globally (Niu and Chen, 2010). During last few decades, tremendous advances are witnessed in developing understanding of cancer pathogenesis and metastasis. The treatment modalities for cancer, such as surgery and radiotherapy, are successful in treatment, but only at early stages (primary cancers) while advanced and metastatic cancers show poor prognosis. Metastasis accounts for 90% of all cancer associated deaths worldwide but still this aspect of cancer is little understood. Metastasis is the spread of tumor cells from primary tumor to the surrounding cells and to distant organs (Yang et al., 2009). The spread from primary tumor cell is a sequential of multiple interrelated processes. The sequence of these steps as shown in Fig. 16.1 (Albritton and Miller, 2017) is as follows: Primary tumor cells invade the surrounding neighbor tissues, enter the microvasculature of lymphatic and circulatory system (intravasation), survive in these channels, then exit the microvasculature (extravasation) and enter into distant organs where these tumor cells adapt to the microenvironment and start growing and proliferating (colonization) to develop secondary tumors (Chaffer and Weinberg, 2011).

The life cycle of every cell requires synchronized turnover of essential regulatory proteins for programmed and timely degradation for progression through a number of stages and ultimately ends in apoptosis. Such degradation of proteins is regulated by proteases (McIntyre and Matrisian, 2003). Proteases are the group of enzymes which activate in response to the stimuli to regulate the cellular functions of cells such as gene expression, cell proliferation,

Cancer-Leading Proteases. https://doi.org/10.1016/B978-0-12-818168-3.00016-4

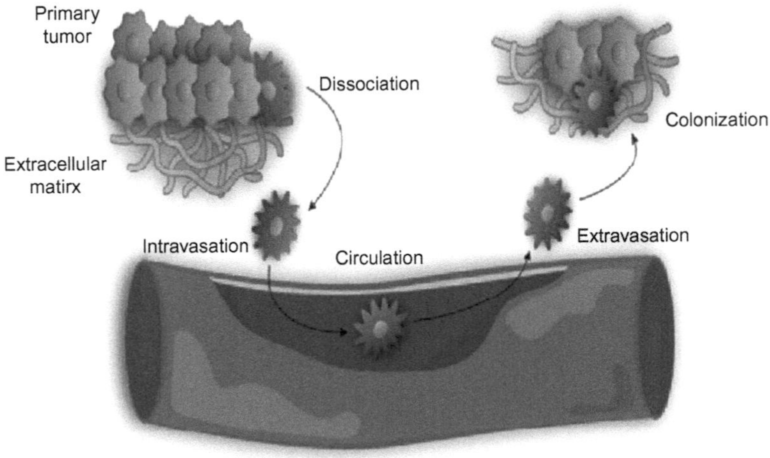

FIG. 16.1 Sequence of events during tumor metastasis. The primary tumor cells dissociate from their origin and then locally invade surrounding of primary tumor. The cells then intravasate into the blood vessels and small group of cells may then extravasate from endothelial cells to secondary sites. Then colonization and proliferation of secondary tumor cells takes place. *(Reproduced with permission from Albritton, J.L., Miller, J.S., 2017. 3D bioprinting: improving in vitro models of metastasis with heterogeneous tumor microenvironments. Dis. Model. Mech. Open access Publication.)*

differentiation, and cell death or apoptosis. The proteases are grouped in six sets based on their mechanism of action. These include serine, cysteine, threonine, glutamic acid, aspartate, and metalloproteases. The sites available for peptide bond cleavage may vary depending on the subtype of proteases. The catalytic site of cysteine proteases is a trio of cysteine, a histidine and asparagine residue are serine, cysteine and threonine residue (Olson and Joyce, 2015), while the cleavage site of matrix metalloproteases comprises of Zn^{2+} chelated by histidine and one cysteine residues and replacement of cysteine moiety with water results in matrix metalloproteases activation (Scherer et al., 2008a,b). Tumor cells require high oxygen and nutrition supply to grow which is stimulated by various proteases present in tumor cells and surrounding tissues. The concentration of these proteases is high in early stages of tumor progression and it is believed that these proteases play very significant role in angiogenesis, invasion, and dissemination (Fig. 16.2) (Rakashanda et al., 2012). The strategies to recognize the function of proteases in cancer pathogenesis and to identify tumor in early stages may be useful in achieving optimized therapeutic targeted drug delivery. To achieve better and improved cancer care, molecular imaging is gaining recognition.

Molecular imaging is a noninvasive imaging modality used for in vivo visualization, characterization, and measurement of specific biomolecules, molecular processes in biological and cellular processes in diseased cells. These imaging techniques make use of target-specific molecular probes engineered to

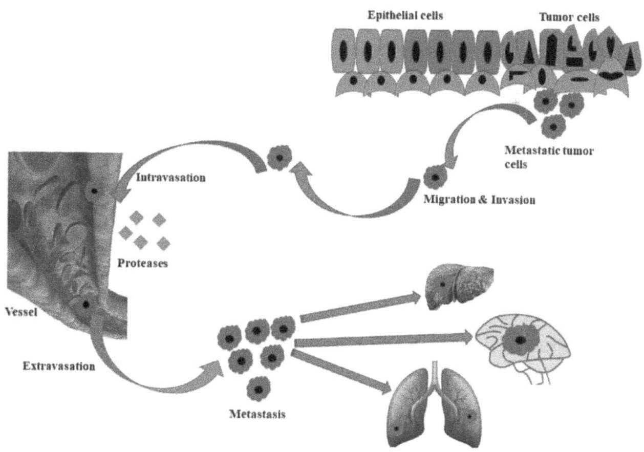

FIG. 16.2 Metastasis and colonization of tumor cells by proteases through activation and inactivation of other proteases pathways. *(Modified from Rakashanda, S., Rana, F., Rafiq, S., Masood, A., Amin, S., 2012. Role of proteases in cancer: a review. Biotechnol. Mol. Biol. Rev. 7, 90–101. Open Access Publication.)*

interact with key biomolecules involved in tumor development and to enhance image contrast. These target-specific probes have two components one is ligand for binding with endogenous molecule and the other is image label for image read-out (van Duijnhoven et al., 2015). In oncology, a number of molecular imaging techniques have been developed for protease imaging including nuclear strategies such as Magnetic Resonance Imaging (MRI), Single Photon Emission Computed Tomography (SPECT), Positron Emission Tomography (PET), and optical modalities such as fluorescence and bioluminescence. Molecular imaging can utilize either exogenous probes or endogenous information. Optical Imaging and Magnetic Resonance Spectroscopic Imaging (MRSI) make use of endogenous information. Intrinsic Raman Spectroscopy (nascent optical imaging technique) also uses endogenous information to identify the interaction of photons with the atomic bonds of molecules, to detect the photons with altered wavelength and subsequent characterization of diseased tissue. Most of the techniques use exogenous probes for molecular imaging. Probes used may be categorized into four groups: (1) *Phenotypic probes* that are used to detect the general physiological aspects of cancerous tissues, such as hypoxia, cell growth, metabolic events stimulated by malignancy, apoptosis and expressed receptors or antigens in tumor tissues, (2) *Targeted probes* that are used to identify specific biomolecules, such as proteins or antigen involved in particular tumor genesis. These targeted probes may require some inducible changes to get activated so that they can locate the enzymes, signal transducers, etc., (3) *Cell tracking probes* that are used to locate the movement of specific cell, significantly important for tumor development and sustainability (cancer cells, vascular endothelium, stromal cells, and stem cells). Tags such as radiotracer or supramagnetic tags or fluorescent dye may be used to label these cells (Kircher et al., 2003), and (4) *Reporter gene probes* that are used for evaluation of the actions of genes in tumor development. Protease activatable probe development had gained much recognition and acceptance in recent years. These probes are targeted toward active site of enzyme, causing cleavage and image probe activation. These probes also provide intensified signal, caused by continuous activation of image probe by the endogenous molecules (Funovics et al., 2003; Baruch et al., 2004; Blum, 2008).

Proteases, being significantly important enzymes involved in normal physiology and pathology, are the target for molecular imaging of a number of conditions such as cancer, neurological disorders, atherosclerosis, and myocardial infarction (Mahmood and Weissleder, 2003; Razgulin et al., 2011). Previously, the use of activatable molecular probes was confined only to Fluorescence Optical Imaging but now various other techniques have been developed including both optical and nuclear as already mentioned, e.g., PET, SPECT, and MRI. The molecular probes used in various modalities have specific rationale and nuclear imaging strategies are designed to retain and accumulate at specific site of action. The probes used in most of the techniques are targeted particularly toward enzymes' activity rather than toward enzymes levels. This chapter gives a good insight into different imaging modalities used for proteases in cancer. A brief mention of families of proteases and their members that may be responsible for cancer would not be out of place here, though they have been described in detail in some of other chapters.

16.2 Proteases

Proteases are the group of enzymes which impart proteolytic activity in the normal healthy cells needed for various biological processes. The protease activity is dependent on the balance between release of protease and antiprotease activity. Disturbance in equilibrium ends up in the form of diseases, such as cancer. Human degradome has at least 569 proteases of five classes (serine, metalloprotease, cysteine, aspartic acid, and threonine proteases), but all of them are not linked with cancer. Few studies revealed a positive correlation between some of the proteases and the cancer (Rakashanda et al., 2012). A brief description of all 5 classes of proteases and their roles in cancer are given below.

16.2.1 Matrix metalloproteases (MMPs)

Almost 40 years back, a protease, known as collagenase, considered to be involved in the tadpole tail desorption during morphogenetic changes, was discovered. Now this is known as matrix metalloproteinase (MMP), a family of extracellular zinc-dependent proteases capable of degradation of all elements of extracellular matrix. MMPs are the smart targets for many cancer imaging strategies. These degradative enzymes have clear links with tumor development/

malignancies. MMPs are over expressed by tumor as well as by proximal stromal cells. As soon as the tumor formation starts, various MMPs are induced in connective tissues, e.g., fibroblast and inflammatory cells which aggravate the invasion of epithelial tumor cells. It is believed that most of the MMPs are originated from the host stromal cells which may be overexpressed from tumor cells. Several MMPs are expressed in tumor malignant epithelium, which have transformed their anatomy from epithelial to mesenchymal type. MMP-2 is majorly involved in neo angiogenesis, invasion, and dissemination; MMP-9 shows substantially enhanced proteolytic activities in breast cancer and microvasculature in proximity (Rakashanda et al., 2012). MMP-7 is linked particularly with epithelial part of adenocarcinomas, whereas MMP-13 and MMP-14 are more significantly involved in other cancers such as breast, neck and, melanoma, lung (Salaün et al., 2015), and colorectal (Yan et al., 2015). The role of various MMPs is shown in Fig. 16.3 (Sagi and Gaffney, 2015).

The first ever molecular probe for MMP imaging was developed by incorporating peptide linker to the original protease sensing probe which may be cleaved by MMPs and few other proteases. The peptide substrate (GPLGVRGKC) added with cy5 dye label was reported to show self-quenching when in closeness. This sensing and imaging probe showed high signal to background ratio in MMP-2 positive tumor models (Achilefu et al., 2002). A study reported that protease sensing probe was developed by incorporating cell penetrating peptide and fluorescein/Cy5 label. MMP-2/9 causes the cleavage of probe and hence it enters into the cytosol of mammalian cells. This technique proves to be useful in targeting particular tumors and hence increased medicinal agent or imaging moiety retains within tumors or in close proximity of MMP-2/9 for longer durations providing efficient treatment or imaging (Bremer et al., 2001). A peptide (homotrimeric triple helical peptide) incorporated with type V collagen fragment was indicated by another study to be highly specific to MMP-2/9. Another target of molecular imaging is MMP-7 and dendrimer based fluorogenic substrate (RPLALWRS (Ahx)C) was developed for selective targeting of MMP-7 within tumor vasculature. This preparation was formulated for MMP-7 activity imaging (Scherer et al., 2008a,b). Gold nanoparticles with fluorescence dye (Cy5.5) based near infrared fluorescence (NIRF) probe with substrate sequence of PLGVR were also formulated for MMPs imaging. Satisfactory imaging was achieved in squamous cell carcinoma model (Lee et al., 2008). A fluorescence strategy was based on protein interaction for MMP-2 imaging and its activity with matrix metalloprotease inhibitors (MMPIs). Activatable quantum dots (QDs), which improve signal brightness and photo-stability with a great potential for several multiple imaging, are better alternatives of conventional strategies using fluorophores. QDs developed with substrate sequence of PLGVRG were reported to be taken up by tumors mediated by proteases specifically by MMP-2/7 (Yang et al., 2009).

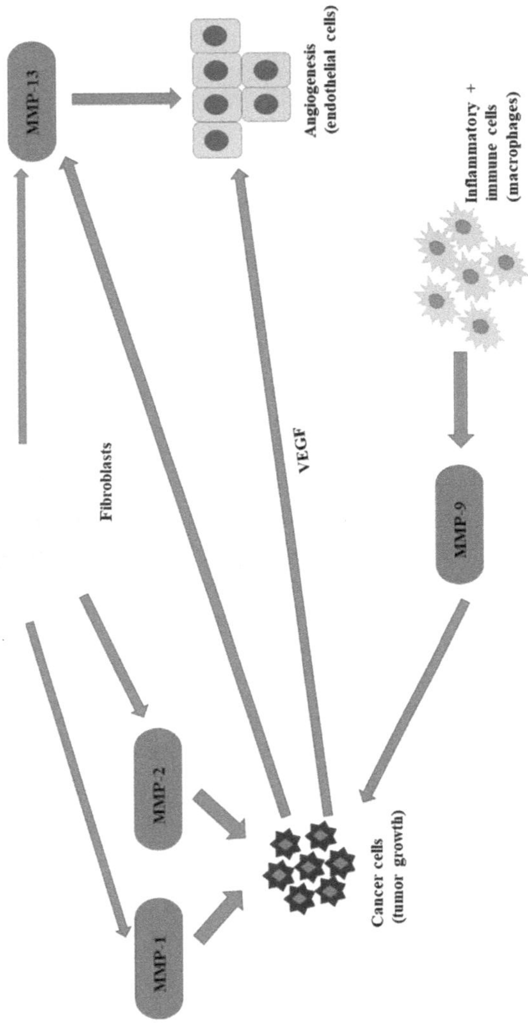

FIG. 16.3 A diagrammatic representation of the pathways adapted by MMPs to develop cancer.

16.2.2 Cysteine proteases

Cysteine proteases are the proteolytic degradative enzymes which may belong to three families i.e., caspase, calpain, and papain (Schwartz et al., 1999). Cathepsin B, C, F, H, L, O, S, V, W (Liaudet-Coopman et al., 2006); caspases; and bleomycin hydrolase are all included in Cysteine proteases, which are described below.

16.2.2.1 Cathepsins

Cathepsins are conserved endolysosomal peptidases present in macrophages lysosomes which may be of cysteine and aspartic acid type. The 11 cysteine cathepsins (cathepsins A, B, C, F, H, K, L, O, S, V, and W) found in humans belong to papain subfamily (Mohamed and Sloane, 2006). They are involved majorly in matrix degradation and hence in tumor advancement, progression, and metastasis. The equilibrium between the active forms of these cathepsins and their endogenous inhibitors is determinant of cathepsins actions. Cathepsins are useful biomarkers for identifying breast cancer, tongue carcinoma, pancreatic cancer, and colorectal cancers. Cysteine proteases act both as intracellular and extracellular proteases, such as cathepsin B (Cath-B) acts both as *endo*- and exopeptidase, but cathepsin L and S (Cath-L and -S) are endopeptidases. Cath-B and -L are major constitutively present cysteine proteases involved in protein turnover. These are primarily involved in various steps of tumor-stromal interaction, malignancy progression, neovascularization, and angiogenesis due to protein degradation within lysosome. Cath-B is overexpressed in laryngeal carcinoma and it is the ever first cathepsin that was reported to be majorly involved in breast cancer development. Cath-K is highly expressed in osteoclasts implicated in bone remodeling (Linnevers et al., 1997a,b), degrades bone matrix components in low pH extracellular milieu of tumor, a key component in tumor invasion and spread. Cath-S, -F, and -V are expressed in macrophages and dendritic cells and are concerned with antigen presentation (Riese and Chapman, 2000). Cath-L and -B both are implicated in human colorectal cancer (Segal et al., 2015). These are considered to be upregulated in tumor cells and surrounding host and stromal cells such as immune components like macrophages, lymphocytes, and neutrophils along with endothelial cells and fibroblasts. The Cath-L2 is the only member of cathepsin family which is absolutely expressed in cancerous tissues and is not only implicated in protein catabolism but also degrades nuclear transcription factor CDP/Cux and at high levels is upregulated in many tumor types, like endometrial cancer in particular (Skrzypczak et al., 2012). Cath-O has been reported to be highly expressed in colon cancer cells (Velasco et al., 1994). Cath-S is predominantly found in tumor cells as compared to host cells in its proximity, and implicated in lung tumor progress (Yang et al., 2009). Cath-W has been reported to be expressed specifically in CD8 and natural killer immune cells (Linnevers et al., 1997a,b).

16.2.2.2 Caspases

Caspases belong to cysteine protease family and are involved in programmed cell death (PCD). The members of caspase family include caspase-1, -2, -3, -6, -7, -8, -9, -10, and -11. Among these caspases, caspase-2, -8, -9, and -10 serve as initiators (apical) while caspase-3, -6, and -7 act as executioners (effectors) of apoptosis and induce cell changes as a consequence of their activation (Olsson and Zhivotovsky, 2011). The activated caspases induce cleavage of functional, structural, or DNA repair proteins which hamper the significant biological cellular mechanism and elicit cellular and other fundamental activities causing cell death. Caspase-1 is also called as interleukin -1β converting enzyme and serves as initiator (Thornberry et al., 1992). Caspase-1 is needed for programmed cell death of prostate cancer cells and a study reported that primary prostate cancer samples revealed 80% downregulation of caspase expression (Pasinelli et al., 2000). Caspase-3 is a classical executioner of programmed cell death (PCD) induced by the cleavage of functionally essential proteins and by mediating multiple steps in apoptotic signal transduction pathways. Caspase-8 acts as an initiator and causes activation of capsase-3. Recent studies reported that caspase-3 is a key and significantly important protease in cancer progression by implicating pro angiogenesis and regrowth of cancer cells after radiotherapy or after chemical exposure (Kurtova et al., 2015; Feng et al., 2017), and documented that low caspase-3 levels in colon cancer patients extended the duration of disease free survival.

16.2.2.3 Bleomycin hydrolase (Blmh)

Bleomycin hydrolase is a cytoplasmic neutral cysteine, placed in papain superfamily because of possessing a key amino acid moiety surrounding the cysteine residue of catalytic site. It is ubiquitously distributed in mammals with very low tissue specificity (Schwartz et al., 1999). The only known activity of this protease is inactivation of a Glycopeptide Bleomycin, an agent used in combination chemotherapeutic regimens. Bleomycin-resistant human tumors revealed high deamination activities due to overexpression of Blmh (Schwartz et al., 1999).

16.2.3 Serine proteases

Among serine proteases, the plasminogen activator (PA) system plays a vital role in many physiological actions related to tissue remodeling (Blasi and Sidenius, 2010). However, PA system also plays a vital role in diseases like atherosclerosis, thrombotic disorders, and stroke (Nicholl et al., 2006). The intensive research on PA system was initiated in 1960, when the serine protease, urokinase, was found in cancer patient (Riggenbach and von Kaulla 1961). The serine protease urokinase-type plasminogen activator (uPA), its glycosylphosphatidylinositol (GPI)-anchored cell membrane receptor (uPAR), the substrate plasminogen and the plasminogen activator inhibitors PAI-1 and PAI-2 are the

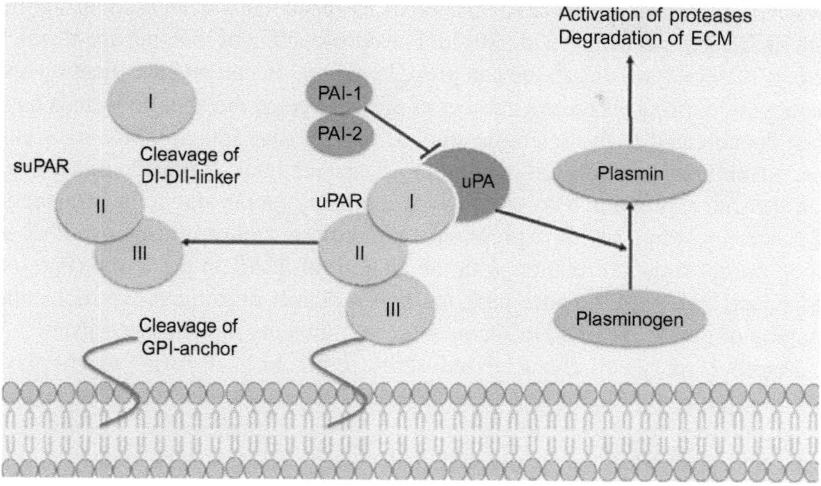

FIG. 16.4 Diagrammatic representation of uPA/uPAR system. *(Reproduced with permission from Skovgaard, D., Persson, M., Kjaer, A., 2017. Imaging of prostate cancer using urokinase-type plasminogen activator receptor PET. PET Clinics 12, 243–255. Copyright 2016 Elsevier.)*

essential components of PA system (Fig. 16.4) (Skovgaard et al., 2017). The uPAR was discovered in 1985 (Vassalli et al., 1985). Later, in 1988, uPA was identified as a prognostic marker for survival in a patient with breast cancer (Duffy et al., 1988). uPAR comprises of three domains, denoted as D1, D2, and D3. It is attached to cell membrane via GPI anchor. The binding of uPA to uPAR needs plasminogen to be converted into active plasmin which causes degradation of many extracellular proteins like fibrin, lamin, and fibronectin (Ploug et al., 1991, 1992; Andreasen et al., 1997). uPA also activates some matrix metalloproteinases (Lijnen et al., 1998), human growth factor, and vascular endothelial growth factor (Folkman, 1984).

The relation between uPAR and cancer was identified in 1991 (Ossowski et al., 1991) and since then studies have extensively indicated the importance of uPAR in cancer invasion and metastasis (Casslén et al., 1991; Pyke et al., 1993; Ganesh et al., 1994; Danø et al., 2005; Dass et al., 2008; Jacobsen and Ploug, 2008). Different Studies revealed that uPAR expresses itself in malignant epithelial cells and nonmalignant stromal cells in tumor region (Pyke et al., 1994; Hildenbrand et al., 2000). Plasma level of uPAR is an indirect indicator of expression level in the tumor. Also lack of correlation exists between tumor tissue uPAR expression and the level of secreted forms (D1 + D2 + D3). This fact complicates the information that can be obtained (De Witte et al., 2001). Optimal uPAR-based diagnostic and prognostic information require localized measurements in the tumor region. Various immuno-histo-chemistry studies on tumors showed that an increasing uPAR expression is found at the very front of the invasive tumors and due to this reason uPAR is marked as a potential local marker for invasive cancers. In relevance to this, uPAR has been recognized as quiet significant imaging target (Yang et al., 2011). The development of imaging agent which detects uPAR expressing tissue can prove beneficial in patient classification and therapy monitoring, as quiet a number of uPAR targeted therapeutic ligands have been documented in the scientific studies. Noninvasive imaging possesses evident advantages over conventional biopsy-based methods. It is difficult to represent the true expression level of uPAR through any biopsy due to heterogeneity of cancer including uPAR expression. Furthermore, cleaved forms of uPAR in blood do not show correlation with the amount of uPAR in the tissue (Persson and Kjaer, 2013). In the later part of chapter, details of noninvasive molecular imaging of uPAR classified in accordance with imaging modality are given.

Another very well-characterized serine protease is trypsin which plays role in digestion, blood coagulation and anticoagulation pathway, and also in blood pressure regulation. In earlier times it was considered as digestive enzyme produced from pancreatic cells but now its release from epithelial skin cells, lungs, kidneys, esophagus, stomach small intestine, and colon has been revealed. Trypsin is inhibited by pancreatic Secretory Trypsin Inhibitor (PSTI). Colorectal cancer is associated with upregulated trypsin. The invasion of basal cell membrane of tumor is mediated by type I collagen digestion by trypsin. It is also implicated in metastasis by coexpression with matrix metalloproteases (MMPs). MMP-2 and MMP-7 are coexpressed with trypsin, which together accelerate tumor growth, local tissue spread, neovasculature, and metastasis as shown in Fig. 16.5 (Rakashanda et al., 2012).

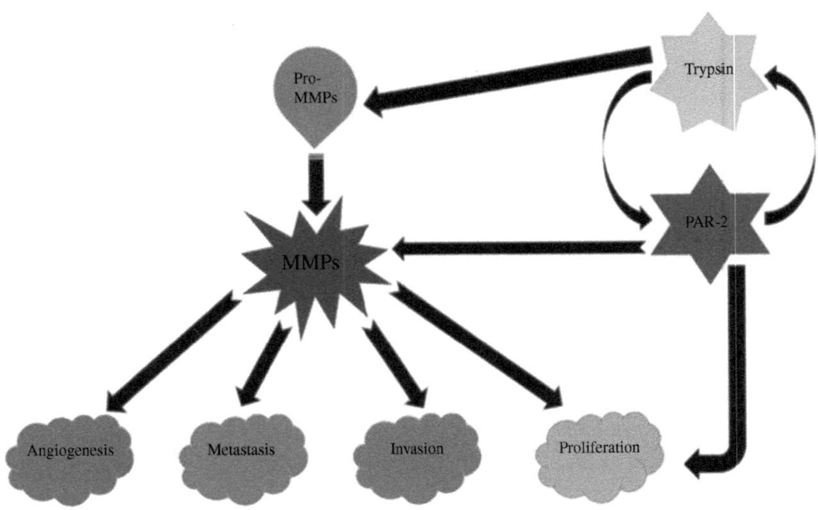

FIG. 16.5 Diagrammatic expression of trypsin interaction with proteinase activated receptors (PARs) and MMPs. *(Modified from Rakashanda, S., Rana, F., Rafiq, S., Masood, A., Amin, S., 2012. Role of proteases in cancer: a review. Biotechnol. Mol. Biol. Rev. 7, 90–101. Open access Publication.)*

16.2.4 Threonine proteases

The prototype members of this class of proteases are the catalytic subunits of the proteasome, a multisubunit enzyme complex that plays a central role in the regulation of proteins that control cell cycle progression and apoptosis, and has therefore become an important target for anticancer therapy. High levels of proteasome are indicated in a number of malignancies. Inhibition of proteasome activity has been evaluated for anticancer potential. Us FDA has approved 1st proteasome inhibitor for prognosis of multiple myeloma or relapsed multiple myeloma (Rakashanda et al., 2012).

16.2.5 Aspartate proteases

Aspartate proteases are comprised of Cath-D and Cath-E. Cath-D is lysosomal endopeptidase, mainly implicated in breast tumor progression and dissemination because of basement membrane degradation (Bremer et al., 2002). This proteolytic enzyme causes protein degradation in the acidic milieu of lysosomes. Cath-E is an intracellular nonlysosomal protease majorly implicated in carcinogenesis and various tumors such as pancreatic ductal adenocarcinoma (PDAC), cervical, intestinal, and gastric cancers.

16.3 Molecular imaging strategies

A number of imaging modalities have been developed which can identify very few number of tumor malignant cells and associated low levels of tumor/ cancer biomarkers levels on molecular basis. These techniques have gained importance not only in detecting cancer biomarkers but also in assessing the patients which can be benefited by a specific treatment and evaluating therapeutic response. Here we present the various imaging modalities applied to different proteases and their outcome.

16.3.1 Modalities for MMPs

The vast information about the pattern of MMPs expression in cancer and the epidemiological facts have made possible to use these proteases as prognostic agents in treating malignancies. The proteases used as molecular targets of imaging moiety in various imaging techniques have multiple folds benefits. The proteases are secreted from extracellular compartment so the imaging probe does not need to penetrate deep into intracellular environment. The proteases are physiologically active and functionally catalytic. Their catalytic activity promotes signal amplification.

Signal amplification cannot be achieved where imaging probe and target has one to one relation. There are a number of different strategies which have been employed since decades, for clinical identification and imaging of tumor masses at primary and metastatic stages. But utilizing MMPs in imaging techniques is a nascent field. A number of probes have been developed with different sequences to target MMPs. The commonly used imaging techniques for MMPs are Optical Imaging (OIM), Magnetic Resonance Imaging (MRI), Positron Emission Tomography (PET), and Single Photon Emission Computed Tomography (SPECT). Many molecular probes and techniques are in developing stages for MMPs imaging. These techniques and probes are thought to be useful not only for spatial and temporal resolution which reveals the advancement of tumor but also to assess the response to therapy.

16.3.1.1 Optical imaging (OIM) for MMPs

The OIM is a molecular imaging strategy used for detecting and visualizing various biological processes within living systems noninvasively with contrast agents. This requires fluorescent moieties to be accumulated at specific target site. The main principle is based on the capability of cells and tissues to induce measureable changes in the probe light preferably in visible and near infra-red regions. Imaging modalities for identification of biological pathways involved in cancer development and for assessing response to specific therapy have gained importance and a large number of molecular probes have been developed to achieve early cancer detection, diagnosis, decision-making for personalized molecular-based therapy, and to assess therapy response. The fluorescent probes (fluorescently labeled probes) have been developed for targeting particular receptor, specific enzyme distribution, gene modulation, and protein functions. These probes mostly emit in near-infrared (NIR) region where cell/tissue absorption is minimal.

A number of activatable probes are synthesized and frequently utilized for functional imaging of specific protease activity. These probes possess either identical or different chromophores joined together in proximity with protease (enzyme)-specific peptide linker as shown in Fig. 16.6 (Rao et al., 2007). The

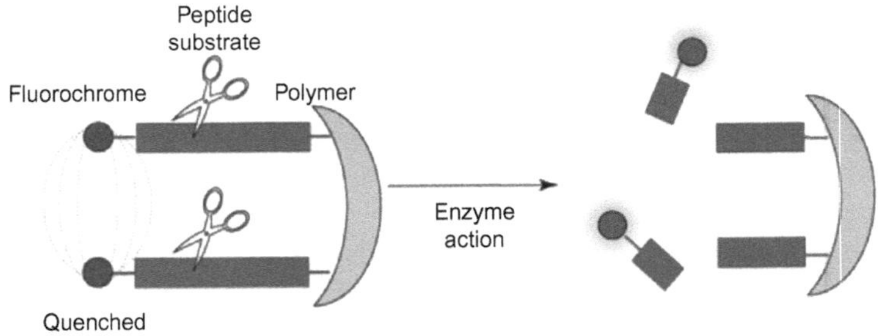

FIG. 16.6 A general scheme of enzyme activatable NIR fluorogenic probes. The fluorochrome is quenched *(brown colored; light gray in print version)* in absence of protease due to proximity of fluorochromes. Proteolytic cleavage of peptide substrate by specific protease, fluorochromes are set free resulting in fluorescence. *(Reproduced with permission from Rao, J., Dragulescu-Andrasi, A., Yao, H., 2007. Fluorescence imaging in vivo: recent advances. Curr. Opin. Biotechnol. 18, 17–25. Copyright 2006 Elsevier.)*

probes show no or little fluorescence and remain fundamentally dark (quenched) due to proximity of fluorophores or by Forster Resonance Energy Transfer (FRET). Cleavage of linker by specific protease results in release of chromophores and consequently amplified fluorescence emission. Self-quenched and FRET pair proteolytic beacons (PBs) have been designed for MMP-associated tumor imaging by utilizing modified substrates, specifically for MMPs working on/off and on fluorescent signal (Scherer et al., 2008a,b).

MMP-2 has been recognized as a major protease involved in tumor local invasion, dissemination, and neovasculature development. It indirectly affects basement membrane by degrading type IV collagen. The ever first probe for in vivo MMPs imaging by Bremer et al. (2001) was designed by adding peptide linker to original MMP sensing probe which is specifically cleaved by MMP-2 but not by other MMPs. By addition of a peptide linker to original MMP sensing probe, the sequence is cleaved selectively by MMP-2 but not by other MMPs. The cleavage site of the substrate (GPLG*VRGT (FITC) C-NH_2 was labeled with Cy5 Near infra-red fluorophores linked with amino terminal with principle depending on the quenching of proximal fluorophores. This specific probe has been helpful in evaluating the therapeutic response of matrix metalloprotease inhibitors (MMPIs) by detecting tumor-correlated activity of MMPs. The probe proved beneficial in sensing and imaging in vivo activity of MMPs. The limitation of this probe was its deficiency to quantifiably assess and determine specific activity of MMPs (Shalinsky et al., 1999).

For specific imaging of MMP-7 activity, the inadequacy of original reagent, a dendrimer-based fluorescent substrate ascribed as proteolytic beacon (PB), was developed by McIntyre et al. This dendrimer-based substrate (Fl(AHX) RPLA*LWRS (AHX)C–COOH, MMP-7 cleavage site is indicated by asterisk*) utilized a FRET pair and an inner assigned fluorophore. The core reference fluorophore associated with probe provides measurable assessment of cleaved and uncleaved substrate and hence a direct association between the specific MMP-7 activity and fluorescent signal is achieved (Scherer et al., 2008a,b). The substrate imparts specific targeting at MMP-7 compared to other subtypes of MMPs present in the tumor environment. The proteolytic beacon revealed distinct responses in MMP-7 positive and MMP negative xenograft tumors. A similar design with NIR and FRET pairs is recently developed to lower the absorption and scattering of the fluorescent signal and amplify the response of proteolytic beacon. By employing the precise targeting of MMP-7 and sensitivity of NIR-PB, this strategy can identify benign tumors of small size even of 0.11 cm in diameter (Jiang et al., 2004). Brian Wilson et al. developed another strategy for MMP-7 imaging by utilizing activatable quantum dots (QD) that provide better light stability, amplified vivid image, and capability to incorporate into multifunction reagent. The designed reagents have QD fluorescence silenced by FRET to a black hole quencher (BHQ-1) chromophore with absorption band overlapping the emission of QD. The MMP-7 cleavable peptide, GPLGLARK, is used for linking BHQ-1 with

QD. By altering the ratios of BHQ-1 to QD and the configuration of peptide, sensitivity and signal to background ratios can be mediated for optimized in vivo imaging and of MMP expression (Zheng et al., 2007).

For MMp-9 imaging, Yamamoto et al. (2012) designed a new probe based on adding fluorescein or CY5 tagged cell penetrating peptide (CPP), which is mainly cleaved by MMP-9 or MMP-2 and then transported into cytosol of mammalian cells. CPP assists the nonreceptor-mediated delivery of linked imaging or therapeutic moiety into the cells by a process of endocytosis and so that selective accumulation and aggregation occur in the proximity of MMPs in tumor cells. This idea of incorporating CPP was applied to xenograft of HT1080 cells and preferential uptake by tumor cells was achieved. The progress of disease along with response to clinical therapeutics may also be assessed by these activatable CPP (Lauer-Fields et al., 2007). Recently a homotrimeric triple helical peptide (THP) was developed by conjugating a fragment of collagen type V for specific targeting of MMP-9 and MMP-2. Achilefu et al. developed this architect by adding a pair of fluorophore combined with ε-amino groups of lysine adjoining the hydrolysis domain to self-quench and then fluorescence on MMP hydrolysis (Achilefu et al., 2002).

16.3.1.2 Bioluminescence imaging (BLI) for MMPs

Bioluminescence is a superior fluorescence strategy for in vivo detection and imaging of MMPs. This technique does not require any external light source for excitation so the background signals are almost negligible or nonexistent with good signal window. Enzymes, such as firefly luciferase, produce signal in visible range by inducing cleavage in substrate D-luciferin utilizing ATP and magnesium-dependent mechanisms. Various bioluminescence proteins have been extracted or modified to produce signal in the range of visible spectrum (400–700 nm). The major limitation of bioluminescence techniques for detection of MMPs is that they require residue in recognition site, as downstream residues of actively splitting bonds after cleavage can interfere with detection process and efficiency. The Promega Corporation recently provided solution of this limitation by introducing a technique of using circularly substituted luciferase enzyme developed by incorporation of protease peptide recognition sequence at the original ends of enzyme, thereby keeping the enzyme in its latent form. The conformational changes in protease substrate upon cleavage activate enzyme and make possible the detection of activity of MMPs in specific tissue (Scherer et al., 2008a,b). The same technique can be utilized for other protease activity imaging but with different peptide sequences. Early studies revealed bioluminescence as a highly sensitive technique for detecting in vivo activity of MMPs over a wide range. However, it proves to be ineffective for in vitro biological cell assays.

16.3.1.3 PET and SPECT imaging of MMPs

Positron Emission Tomography (PET) is a molecular imaging strategy important for quantitative assessment of radio-labeled tracer moiety within a biological system. The radioactive isotope, being short lived, deteriorates and emits positron on decaying. The emitted positron intercommunicates with the electron in its vicinity and annihilates by producing two 511 keV photons in opposite directions. For in vivo quantification, positron-producing radioactive isotopes are produced in cyclotron, conjugated with a tracer moiety and injected directly in blood stream through intravenous injection. The photons travel synchronously in a straight line and course of annihilation can be localized by using scintillation detectors. Hence PET is useful for in vivo molecular functional imaging by tracing radio labeled moiety.

Single Photon Emission Computed Tomography (SPECT) is also based on radio labeled principal but it utilizes gamma rays which have longer half-lives. Very low amounts of radio-labeled tracer can be injected, ingested, or inhaled for radioactivity administration. The collimator is used to allow the emitted photons to travel in a specific direction to be determined by a detector. SPECT may utilize gamma camera for determination of in vivo bio-distribution of small tracer molecules by generating two-dimensional images. The SPECT also provides three-dimensional images similar to other topographical techniques but its exceptional quality of imaging the slow kinetics makes it different from PET.

MMPs have been significantly important as a target for developing various anticancer drugs and for that purpose a number of MMPIs have been designed which cause reduction in proliferation of both primary and secondary tumors and also check the dissemination (Brown, 1999). As the MMPIs are directed toward active site of MMPs to inhibit their catalytic activity, they can differentiate active MMPs from latent MMPs and inhibited MMPs by tissue inhibitory metalloproteases (TIMPs). The conjugation of radio-labeled tracer with MMPIs serves to design an activity-based probe for in vivo catalysis of MMPs and develop agents which can recognize individual members of MMPs having unique active sites with improved selectivity. Earlier studies reported the unfruitful efforts in developing MMPIs due to nonspecific bio-distribution, but Furumoto et al. (2003) recently described the successful design of fluorine-18 labeled MMP-2 inhibitor, [18F]SAV03, a methyl ester derivative, as a pro-drug, [18F]SAV03M, and carboxylic acid based MMP-2 inhibitor with potentially increased uptake by tumor tissues or organs in comparison to normal tissues. The assessment of radioactivity in whole body tissues suggested that these radiotracers can be best studied by PET strategy. Furumoto et al. further evaluated the exact relationship of these radiotracers with MMP-2 activity. The novel radioiodinated metalloprotease inhibitors designed by modification of CGS 27023A, such as [123I]I- and [125I]I-CGS 27023A, HO-[123I]I- and HO-[125I]I-CGS 27023A, are reported to be used for in vivo imaging through SPECT. These iodinated CGS substrates proved to be significant attributable to their high affinity for MMP-2, MMP-9 and their quick clearance from plasma which support their use as radiotracer in MMP imaging (Scherer et al., 2008a,b). For selectively inhibiting MMP-2, Oltenfreiter et al. developed valine and tryptophane-based biphenylsulfonamide MMPIs (Oltenfreiter et al., 2005, 2006), but iv vivo imaging with agents in A549 lung tumor cells revealed poor uptake which made these agents not worthy of using as imaging contrast compounds. In vivo imaging also utilizes the endogenous metalloprotease inhibitors (TIMPs) as a probe for selective inhibition of MMPs. A substrate was developed by conjugating TIMP-2 with DTPA (diethylene triamine pentaacetic acid) and then labeled with 111In (111In-DTPA-N-TIMP-2) for imaging through SPECT. The membrane type 1 (MTI)-MMP, which is highly expressed in various malignancies being involved in regulation of cell transport and incursion, showed high affinity for 111In-DTPA-N-TIMP-2 and hence found valuable for in vivo imaging of MMPs' catalytic action (Seiki, 1999). MMP sense 680 probe has been utilized for early identification and assessment of colorectal adenomas by getting activated by a number of various MMPs and giving improved signal to background ratio in a period of almost 66 h (Clapper et al., 2011).

16.3.1.4 Magnetic resonance imaging (MRI) for MMPs

Magnetic resonance imaging is the most extensively used imaging modality in hospitals and clinical settings across the globe and highly suggestive for cancer imaging. This technique utilizes contrast agents for detecting tumor cells and evaluating their distinctiveness. The Gadolinium (Gd)-based contrast agents are most frequently used in MRI. The Gd is a paramagnetic ion which produces enhanced relaxation and reduced T1 in magnetic field due to presence of seven unpaired electron in its structure. The contrasting Gd-DTPA and Gd-DOTA readily distribute themselves in tumors through diffusion and are removed by renal clearance mechanisms. The traditionally contrasting agents do not have any attached biological ligand for imaging biological aspects of tumors and thus cannot work in functional imaging capacity. Recently designed contrasts are developed in which molecular substrates are attached for targeting specific overexpressed receptors in tumor tissues, and to alter the flexibility by enabling water to enter in paramagnetic atom Gd to improve signal intensity. Meade et al. reported the fabrication of a substrate where water access was primarily blocked and upon cleavage by beta-galactosidase, it was unlocked (Louie, 2000). Recent studies indicated the use of reagents which in acidic pH of microenvironment show diminished relaxation owing to acidification of tumor environment (Frullano et al., 2006; Blasi and Sidenius, 2010) and postulated that MRI contrasts can be cleaved by action of extracellular proteases and hence can assess and quantify the overexpressed proteases associated with primary or disseminated tumors. They developed a novel contrast agent which reveals reduced solubility once it is cleaved by MMP-7. These innovative protease-modulated contrast agents (PCAs) assess the in vivo protease activity by MRI based on switching solubility from hydrophilic to hydrophobic. PCA-7 is one of the novel agents used to detect MMP-7 activity in biological system. The minimization of MMP-7 activity was detected by PCA-7 switch in tumor bearing mice that were given MMPIs therapy. A study reported the design of a parallel agent PCA-2 used to detect MMP-2 activity in MMP-2 positive xenograft tumor by MRI. The association of PCA-2 with MMP-2 improves MRI contrast while estimated activity was reduced in treated tumor xenografts (Blasi and Sidenius, 2010).

16.3.2 Imaging modalities for cathepsins

Cathepsins are lysosomal proteases acting both as endopeptidases and exopeptidases. Cysteine proteases constitute the major class of cathepsins. The members of cathepsin family are A, B, C, D, E, F, G, H, L, K, O, V, and W and they may belong to different subfamilies and are expressed in different body tissues mediating their particular physiological constructive activities or may involve in tumor local invasion, dissemination by degrading extracellular matrix components and basement membrane, and angiogenesis. The various cathepsins with their family and site of expression are given in Table 16.1.

TABLE 16.1 Cathepsins, their expression tissues and main functions (Mohamed and Sloane, 2006, Olsson and Zhivotovsky, 2011; Tang and Han, 2013).

Cathepsins	Expression area	Functions
Subfamily: Serine		
A (endopeptidase)	Platelets, epididymis, and testis	Autophagy, platelet activation, fiber formation
G (Endopeptidase)	WBCs (Polymorphonuclear type)	Inflammation regulated by immune complexes, production of angiotensin II
Subfamily: Cysteine		
B (End/Exopeptidase)	Macrophages, hepatocytes, renal tubules	Protein breakdown, antigen, and hormones activation
C (Exopeptidase)	Wide body distribution	Hydrolyze amides, anilides, dipeptide esters, etc.
F (Endopeptidase)	Antigen presenting cells	Antigen presentation
H (Endopeptidase)	Ubiquitous in cells and tissues	Endopeptidase actions

Continued

TABLE 16.1 Cathepsins, their expression tissues and main functions (Mohamed and Sloane, 2006, Olsson and Zhivotovsky, 2011; Tang and Han, 2013)—cont'd

Cathepsins	Expression area	Functions
L (Endopeptidase)	Ubiquitously expression	Keratinocytes differentiation, protein turnover
K (Endopeptidase)	Heart, bones, ovaries, lungs, Placenta, small intestine, and colon	Bone adaptations and cartilage degradation
O (Endopeptidase)	Wide body distribution	Protein lysis and turnover
S (Endopeptidase)	Spleen, antigen presenting cells	Proteolysis of cartilage residing Link Proteins and aggrecan
V (Endopeptidase)	Thymus, testis, and corneal epithelium	Enkephalin and neuropeptide Y
W (Endopeptidase)	T lymphocytes	Cell regulated cytotoxicity
X (Endopeptidase)	Immune cells	Immune components regulation and phagocytosis
Z (Endopeptidase)	Wide distribution	Proteolysis
Subfamily: Aspartic acid		
D (Endopeptidase)	Sweat, synovial fluid of cartilage, lysosomes	Protein catabolism in acidic lysosomal medium.
E (Endopeptidase)	Immune system	Antigen presentation

16.3.2.1 Quenched fluorescent activity-based imaging of cathepsins

Activity-based probes (ABPs) use small molecules which attach with a specific target enzyme in an activity-based chemical process. These ABPs serve as indirect read-out of enzyme by utilizing techniques such as mass spectroscopy, fluorescence spectroscopy, or a biochemical reaction. These probes are of great significance in assessing the specific enzyme, their concentration, expression, and time of overexpression in tumor development and progression (Berger et al., 2004; Saghatelian and Cravatt, 2005). The ABPs have a reactive moiety to be attached with the target in enzymatically driven reaction and a reporter tag for proper imaging of the labeled proteins of probes as shown in Fig. 16.7 (Pasinelli et al., 2000).

The fluorescently labeled ABPs have been designed for the detection of various proteases including cysteine cathepsins (Papain class of cysteine proteases) (Greenbaum et al., 2002; Saghatelian et al., 2004). Cathepsins being potentially

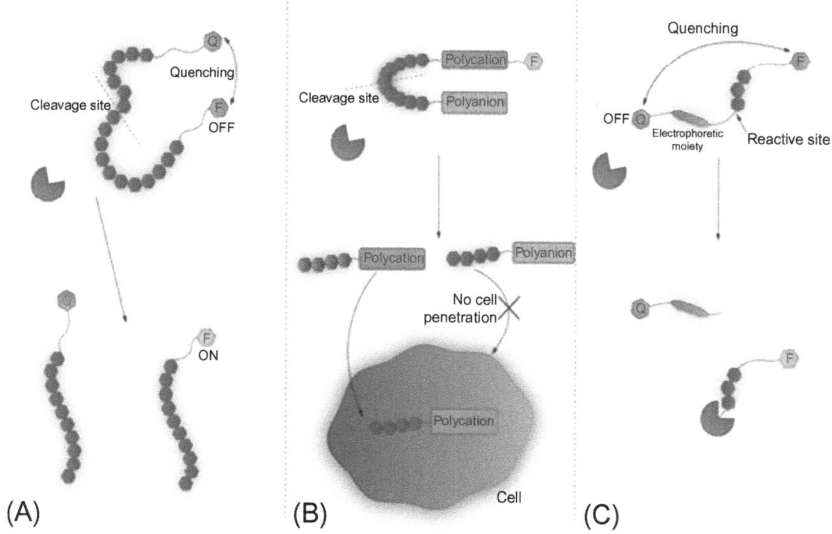

FIG. 16.7 Generic expression of activation mechanism of protease activatable probes: (A) FRET-based fluorescence quenching which restores after protease catalytic activity, (B) peptide hydrolysis as a driving force of fluorophores to cells after activation, and (C) quenched activity based probe by attaching with target enzyme loses its quencher and forms enzyme-fluorescent probe complex. *(Modified from Rao, J., Dragulescu-Andrasi, A., Yao, H., 2007. Fluorescence imaging in vivo: recent advances. Curr. Opin. Biotechnol. Open access Publication.)*

important in mediating various cellular processes and valuable biomarkers of a multitude of diseases are the targets for such small molecules. A direct relationship of cathepsins expressions with tumor proliferation and of local spread and tumor microvasculature development has been reported (Schwartz et al., 1999). The Cath-B and Cath-L are expressed in high amounts in various cancers such as mammary adenocarcinoma. The imaging probes serve as a tool to determine the enzyme activity of specific targets rather than assessing enzyme loads. Blum et al. (2007) and Bremer et al. (2002) reported the development of NIRF-ABPs such as unquenched GB 123, and GB137 designed by addition of fluorescent label and OAMK as "warhead and used to evaluate the cathepsin's activity in various cell lines but highest activity in mouse skeletal myoblast cell line C2C12/Hras1 cells was revealed. The study results showed quenched probes are promising clinical tools used for noninvasive imaging of cathepsins. Bremer et al. (2002) designed activatable molecular probes utilizing two fluorophores for investigating the cathepsins activity in two breast cancer cell lines i.e., highly aggressive breast cancer cell lines (DU4475) and well-differentiated breast cancer cell lines (BT20). The results revealed that aggressively invasive cancer cell lines DU4475 showed higher expression of Cath-B as compared to well differentiated breast cancer cell lines BT20 (Bremer et al., 2002).

Cathepsin D (Cath-D or CaD) belongs to aspartic proteases majorly accumulated in lysosomes. A 2- to 50-fold increase in Cath-D expression has been reported in mammalian breast cancers. The high Cath-D expression is associated with high probability of metastasis, invasion, angiogenesis, and basement membrane degradation. Tang and Han (2013) reported the development of NIRF probe (CY-CDF-PGC) for Cath-D with a synthetic graft copolymer (partially methoxypoly(ethylene glycol)-modified poly-L-lysine) with several fluorophores of near infra-red range. The NIR fluorophores get attached onto the graft copolymer with free lysine segment. The probe was formulated in a way that while in circulation it showed only minimal fluorescence and intense fluorescent signal was revealed when it enters the tumor site having optimum cath-D expressions. A peptide sequence specific for cath-D was added in the probe to act as a linker between the fluorochromes and graft copolymer. The sequence of Cathepsin fluorescein (CaF) peptide is Gly-Pro-Ile-Cys (ET)-Phe-Arg-Leu-Gly-Lys (FITC)-Cys-NH_2. The signal intensity is improved compared to background signal of quenched state due to large number of fluorochromes linked with backbone copolymer (Tung et al., 1999).

Cath-E is a nonlysosomal intracellular aspartic protease which is physiologically present in microglia, dendritic cells, human M-cells, and antigen-presenting lymphocytes as well as in gastric epithelial cells and osteoclasts (Sakai et al., 1989; Finzi et al., 1993; Sastradipura et al., 1998). In normal physiology, Cath-E is not expressed in pancreatic cells but high expression has been observed in cervical, intestinal, and gastric cancers (Tenti et al., 1994; Matsuo et al., 1996; Lin et al., 2001), pancreatic intraepithelial neoplasia (PaIN), and almost in all pancreatic ductal adenocarcinoma (PDAC) (Prasad et al., 2005). The elevated Cath-E levels in gastric juice serve as a diagnostic tool for PDAC identification and confirmation. So, Cath-E acts as biomarker and can be imaged by using Cathepsin activatable molecular probes for diagnosis and imaging. Both Cath-E and Cath-D have structural similarity and substrate specificity with hydrophobic moieties at the scission sites. Cruz-Monserrate et al. (2012) reported that no previous Cath-E specific substrate was ever developed till they designed Cath-E specific probe with fluorogenic peptide substrate, Ala-Gly-Phe-Ser-Leu-Pro-Ala-Lys-DArg-$CONH_2$, for in vitro Cath-E activity detection. This probe showed distinct and superior imaging of Cath-E. These authors also developed a specific Cath-E probe by a polymeric template, linking fluorescently labeled peptide substrate sequence, Ala-GLy-Phe-Ser-Leu-Pro-Ala-Gly-$CysCoNH_2$, with a polyethylene glycol protected grafted copolymer for assessment and imaging of Cath-E activity for localization to PDAC. The Cath-E activatable imaging probe having several proximally attached fluorochromes showed quenching behavior unless it reached a targeted tumor/cancer with high Cath-E levels which generate intense fluorescence due to attack by Cath-E. A previous study has shown the utilization of broad Cathepsin activatable fluorescence based probe for pancreatic cancer localization and imaging to detect the pancreatic intraepithelial lesions. A fluorescence probe (presence 680) is a commercially available probe which is specific for Cath-B/H/L/S and plasmin (von Burstin et al., 2008). Thus, cathepsin-specific fluorescent quenched probes are useful for localization and imaging of specific cathepsin positive tumors, directing and assisting surgical procedures, identifying cancer stages, and monitoring the effectiveness of therapy.

16.3.2.2 Magnetic resonance imaging (MRI) for cathepsins

Out of a variety of eleven Cathepsins Cath-B and Cath-L are primarily implicated in protein catabolism within lysosomes. Extensive research has been done to develop the noninvasive imaging modalities for in vivo protease activity assessment. But till recent years little success has been achieved. There has been no recognized high resolution, sensitive, noninvasive, and nonradioactive techniques other than near-infrared fluorescence (NIRF) optical imaging of Cath-B. The NIRF optical imaging is although very sensitive modality but it could not produce three-dimensional imaging, neither in higher animal nor in humans, because of lack of deep penetration (only up to few mm). Haris et al. (2014) first reported magnetic resonance imaging (MRI) for in vivo cathepsins' (Cath-B and Cath-L) activity and developed first MRI probe Poly-L-Glutamate (PLG) to get activated by proteolytic activity of specific proteases highly expressed in tumors. The mechanism underlying such imaging is chemical exchange saturation transfer (CEST) between the protons linked with nitrogen of amine moiety of PLG and the protons of bulk water. Under normal physiological conditions, the proton transfer is very slow from the amide linkages of PLG. Upon activation by proteolytic action of intra-lysosomal cathepsin, exceptionally good CEST was shown by individual Glu moieties and smaller peptide of glutamates produced by enzymatic activity because of very fast proton transfer from their amine residue (Haris et al., 2014). The study results revealed that brain tumors show positively high expression of Cath-B and that PLG-regulated CEST contrast depends on Cath-B levels. Thus PLG-based MRI probe assesses the in vivo changes in CEST contrast and proves to be helpful in quantification of Cathepsin expression in different types of tumors (Haris et al., 2014).

16.3.3 Imaging modalities for caspases

Caspase-1, also called as interleukin-1β-converting enzyme (ICE), is an initiator protease and it is believed that it generates active proinflammatory cytokine interleukin-1β by cleavage of inactive pro-interleukin-1β. The major setback in caspases imaging is that most of the caspase inhibitors also inhibit cathepsins. Irreversible inhibitors and active site-specific probes (Activity based probes) of caspases developed by Edgington et al. (2009) were selective over broad or narrow range within Caspase family and thus only optical imaging was found to be useful in case of caspases.

Messerli et al. (2004) reported development of an ICE-NIRF, optically quenched probe for detection and imaging of caspase-1 expression in relation to programmed cell death (PCD) induced by chemical, radiations, or any other agent. The designed caspase-1 activatable probe contains a selective peptide with sequence [Gly-Trp-Glu-Asp-Gly-Lys fluorescein isothiocyanate (FITC)-Cys-NH_2], a near infra-red fluorochrome Cy5.5, and fractionally PEGylated poly L-lysine as a delivery carrier (Folkman, 1984). The auto-quenching probe upon cleavage by caspase-1 produces fluorescence.

16.3.4 Molecular imaging of urokinase plasminogen activator (uPA) system

16.3.4.1 Optical imaging for uPA

Optical imaging was also found to be quite successful in case of urokinase plasminogen activator (uPA) system. Quite a few numbers of studies discussing optical imaging ligands for uPAR have been reported as shown in Table 16.2. Clinical application of uPAR show limited potential due to scarce number of available ligands. Moreover, optical imaging images only surface exposed tissues due to low penetration of light. Nonetheless, uPAR targeted optical imaging ligands present remarkable clinical potential in image guided surgery. The objective of any cancer curative surgery is the complete eradication of malignant tissue from the body. This entire delineation of cancerous area from normal tissue is usually complex and difficult. Since uPAR expression is mainly found at the front of invasive tumors, the uPAR of targeted ligands in imaging guided surgery would significantly help in reducing number of patients with postoperative relapse of cancer (Persson and Kjaer, 2013).

16.3.4.2 Magnetic resonance imaging for uPA

MRI has been reported to possess magnificent anatomical resolution but a very low sensitivity (James and Gambhir, 2012). Higher resolution helps in getting precise identification of invasive cancer. Due to limited sensitivity, generally higher amount of ligand is necessary to get sufficient signal in MRI. In contrast to SPECT and PET where lower amount of ligands are required, this factor poses a challenge as toxicity might occur at such high dose. uPAR-targeted ligands for MRI extensively employ paramagnetic iron oxide nanoparticles. Table 16.2 shows examples of few studies done using uPAR targeted MRI ligands (Persson and Kjaer, 2013).

16.3.4.3 SPECT and PET imaging for uPA

SPECT imaging has great clinical potential as its higher sensitivity can detect small micrometastatic lesions and invasive cancers. Another reason for considering SPECT imaging of uPAR as highly attractive is its low cost, availability of gamma cameras, and facile radiochemistry especially when using 99mTc. PET imaging may be considered the best imaging modality for uPAR as it carries

TABLE 16.2 A summary of few uPAR targeted imaging ligands in optical and MRI modalities (Persson and Kjaer, 2013).

Modality	Name	Ligand	Reference
Optical	uPAR mAb*Cy5.5	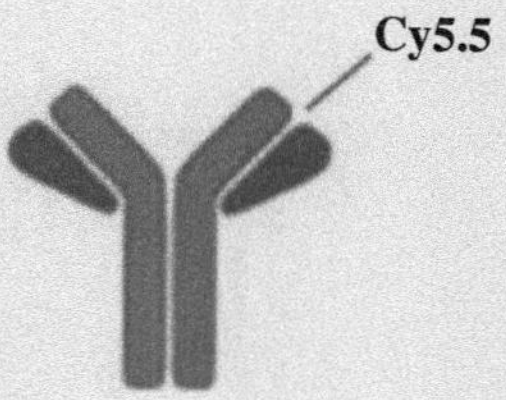	Dullin et al. (2009)
	U11	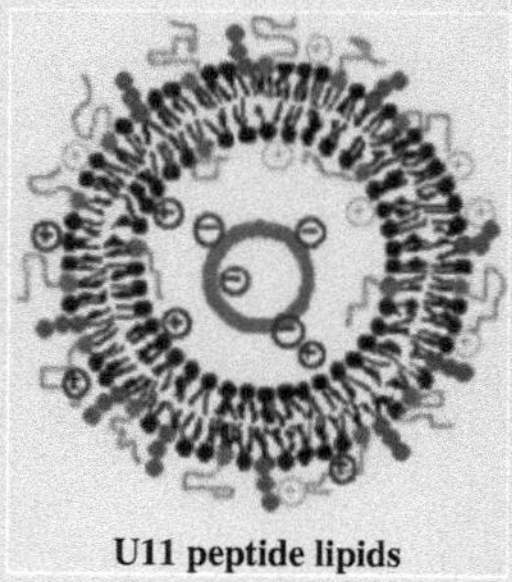	Wang et al. (2008)
	mATF-Cy5.5-IO	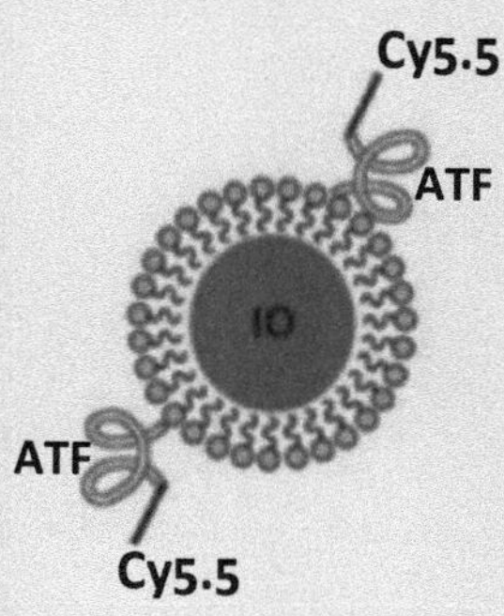	Yang et al. (2009)
	hATF-Cy5.5-IO-Nos	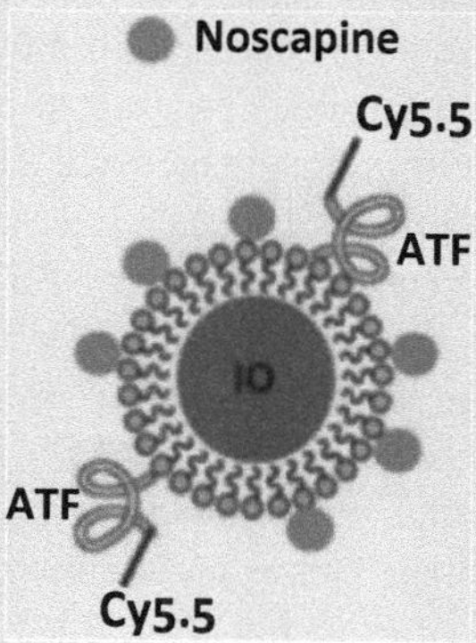	Abdalla et al. (2011)

Continued

TABLE 16.2 A summary of few uPAR targeted imaging ligands in optical and MRI modalities (Persson and Kjaer, 2013)—cont'd

Modality	Name	Ligand	Reference
	Zro2:Tb-hATF	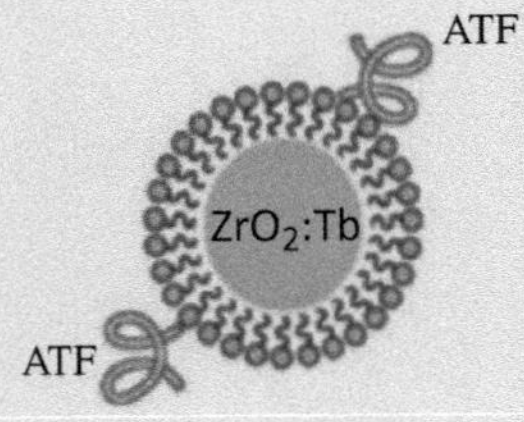	Liu et al. (2009)
MRI	mATF-Cy5.5-IO	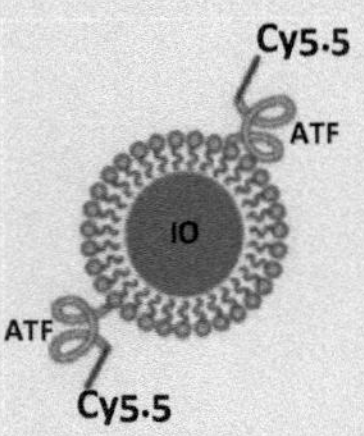	Yang et al. (2009)
	hATF-Cy5.5-IO-Nos	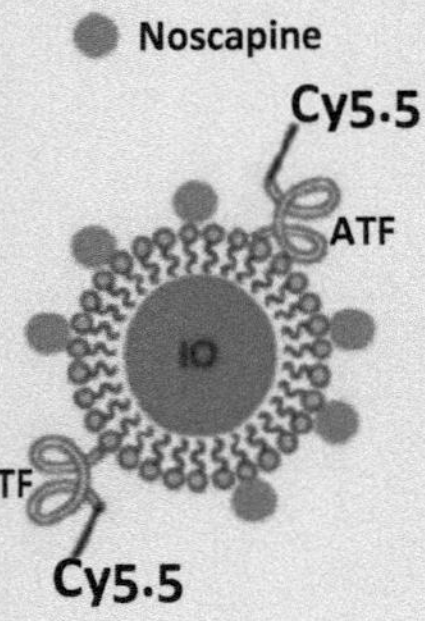	Abdalla et al. (2011)

high sensitivity combined with truly quantitative data. Moreover, majority of imaging studies have been conducted in PET area.

Advanced research studies relating to interaction between uPAR and uPA through Surface Plasmon Resonance and Radiograph Crystallography have encouraged the development of a chain of small peptides pertinent to noninvasive in vivo molecular imaging of uPAR by PET (Ploug, 2012; Persson and Kjaer, 2013). Majority of studies performed for progress in uPAR targeted imaging or therapy revolve around high affinity peptide AE105 and its derivatives. The sequence for this peptide is Asp1-Cha2-Phe3-Ser4-Arg5-Tyr6-Leu7-Trp8-Ser9. The chief feature which makes this peptide appropriate for PET imaging is Cha, cyclohexyl-(L)-alanine. This is an unnatural amino acid which makes the peptide quiet stable in serum (Li et al., 2013; Persson and Kjaer, 2013). In the first study related to uPAR-PET imaging (Li et al., 2008), a monomer type of AE120, denoted AE105, was conjugated with metal chelator DOTA at N-terminal and finally was labeled with ^{64}Cu (Ploug et al., 2001).

Though PET was found to be quite successful for uPAR imaging, ligands for uPAR imaging by SPECT were also investigated. Although uPA and PAI-1 are considered as prognostic biomarkers, noninvasive techniques to measure uPA activity are still insufficient. Vangestel et al. (2016) prepared Indium-111 (^{111}In)-labeled probe for in vivo uPA imaging through SPECT. DOTA was conjugated to uPA inhibitor and later it was radio-labeled with ^{111}In ([^{111}In] MICA-401) (Vangestel et al., 2016). Table 16.3 shows few examples of uPAR ligands for SPECT and PET Imaging (Persson and Kjaer, 2013). With SPECT imaging good tumor visualization was possible at 18 h post injection onward and marked radiotracer uptake was noticed in the rim of the tumor. Ideal tumor contrast was noted at 95 h post injection. Skin and lymph nodes also showed noticeable uptake.

In vivo SPECT images for [^{111}In]MICA-401 identified two tumors, namely MDA-MB-231 and HT-29. Further, SPECT images displayed remarkable uptake of [^{111}In]MICA-401 by skin, liver, and lymph nodes. In spite of these interesting results, major drawback of this type of probe for oncological application was the undesirable uptake of tracer in the noncancerous regions (Vangestel et al., 2016).

A new ^{64}Cu-DOTA-AE105 tracer for imaging uPAR through PET was prepared by Persson et al. (2014). This tracer was used to distinguish between indolent and aggressive cancers by performing PET studies in mice. In vivo biodistribution was estimated together with determination of human dosimetry of ^{64}Cu-DOTA-AE105. ^{64}Cu-DOTA-AE105 injection was delivered in the tail of the mice and PET images taken at 1 h, 4.5 h, and 22 h post injection showed that highest activity was found in liver followed next by the intestine (Persson et al., 2013) (Fig. 16.8).

Prostate cancer (PC) is considered as the most prevalent cancer in men of western countries. PC has markedly variable prognosis and few PCs are associated with great mortality rate (Almasi et al., 2011; Evangelista et al., 2016). Considerable limitations, e.g., sensitivity and specificity, are generally associated with conventional imaging techniques (MRI, contrast enhanced CT, ^{99m}Tc-methylene diphosphonate-bone scintigraphy). The heterogeneity of PC and these imaging-related constraints have forced scientists to focus toward creation of newer imaging techniques which should allow much better molecular visualization of malignant tissues in PC. These imaging methods include multiparametric MRI and PET, employing various radio-ligands, like choline (Evangelista et al., 2016). uPAR is being taken as favorable imaging target for PC. Several studies using immune histochemistry, biochemical assays, tissue microarrays, reverse transcriptase polymerase chain reactions performed on prostate cancer tissue have revealed that uPAR is extensively expressed in prostate cancerous cells, encircling tumor-based stromal cells and lymph node metastases (Gavrilov et al., 2001; Duffy, 2004; Riddick et al., 2005; Usher et al., 2005; Cozzi et al., 2006; Kumano et al., 2009). So, different radiopharmaceutical-based uPAR targeted

TABLE 16.3 Few examples of uPAR ligands for SPECT and PET imaging (Persson and Kjaer, 2013).

Imaging modality	Ligand	Name	In vitro data	In vivo data	Reference
SPECT	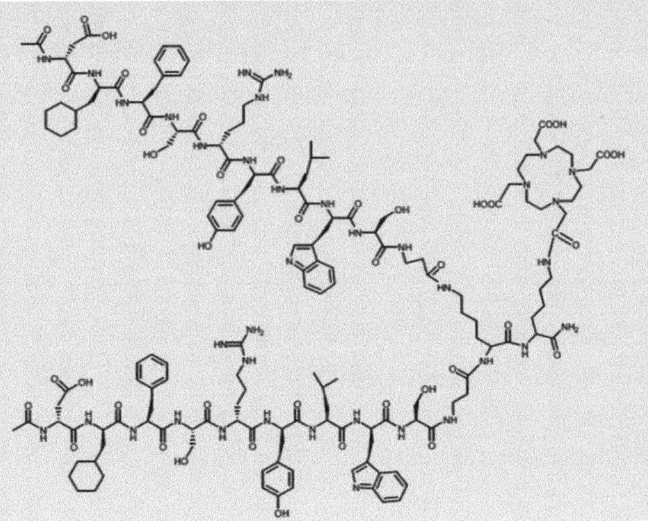	Nac-cD-Cha-F-dS-dR-Y-L-W-S-βAla-2-K-K(DOTA)-NH2	Yes	Yes	Liu et al. (2009)

PET	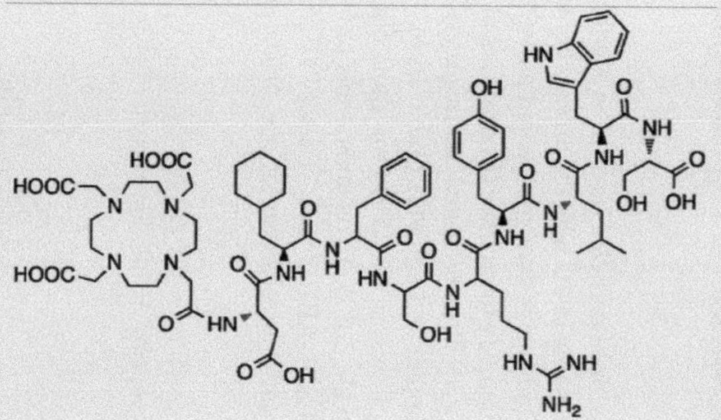	DOTA-AE105	Yes	Yes	Li et al. (2008)

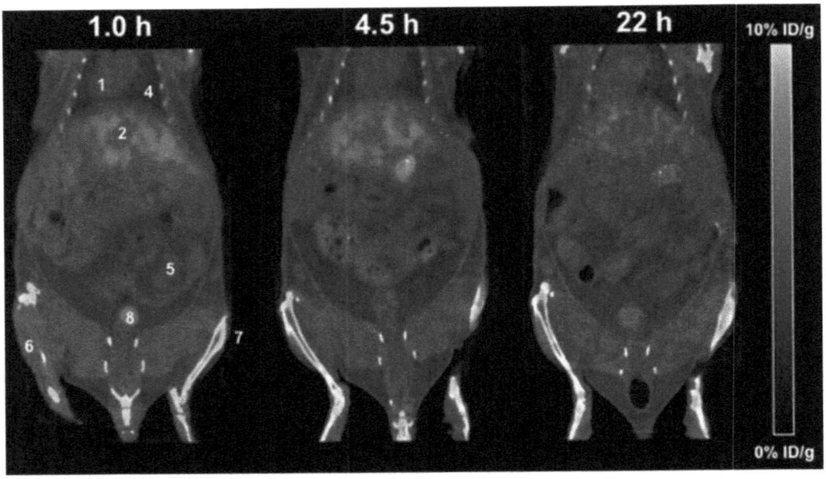

FIG. 16.8 PET/CT images of ^{64}Cu-DOTA-AE105 at 1 h, 4.5 h and 22 h post IV injection. The numbers indicate the ROI within the different organs. (1) Heart, (2) liver, (3) kidney (not displayed), (4) lung, (5) intestine, (6) muscle, (7) bone, (8) bladder. *(Reproduced with permission from Persson, M., El Ali, H.H., Tina, B., Pfeifer, A., Madsen, J., Rasmussen, P, Kjaer, A., et al., 2014. Dosimetry of 64Cu-DOTA-AE105, a PET tracer for uPAR imaging. Nucl. Med. Biol. 41, 290–295. Copyright 2014 Elsevier.)*

ligands using peptides, antibodies, proteins, nanoparticles have been studied well by researchers, as noninvasive uPAR mapping in PC with the probability to discriminate indolent tumors from invasive and aggressive types would prove to be an important diagnostic and prognostic imaging biomarker (Boonstra et al., 2011; Yang et al., 2011). Skovgaard et al. (2017) investigated various metal-binding chelators and isotopes for uPAR mapping through PET (Table 16.4).

The first tracer ^{64}Cu-DOTA-AE105 was, however, found to show quite high uptake in the liver (Fig. 16.9) (Skovgaard et al., 2017). To overcome this problem, two more tracers, namely ^{64}Cu-CB-TE2A-AE105 and ^{64}Cu-CB-TE2A-PA-AE105, were tested. Through in vitro and in vivo testing, it was observed

TABLE 16.4 Various PET ligands based on peptide AE105 (Skovgaard et al., 2017).

^{64}Cu	^{68}Cu	^{18}F
^{64}Cu-DOTA-AE105	^{68}Ga-DOTA-AE105	^{18}F-AIF-NOTA-AE105
^{64}CU-CB-TE2A-AE105	^{68}Ga-NODAGA-AE105	^{18}F-FB-AE105
^{64}Cu-CB-TE2A-AE105	^{68}Ga-NOTA-AE105	^{18}F-Click-AE105
^{64}Cu-NOTA-AE105		

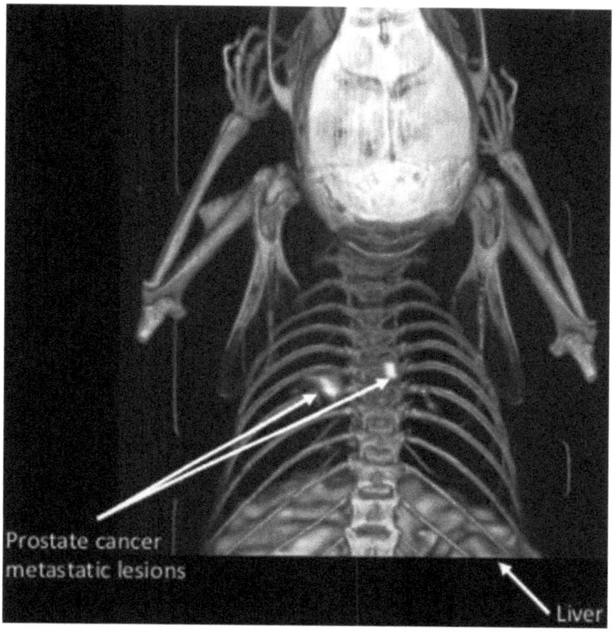

FIG. 16.9 ^{64}Cu-DOTA-AE105 based PET mapping of uPAR in a mouse model of disseminated human prostate cancer. *(Reproduced with permission from Skovgaard, D., Persson, M., Kjaer, A., 2017. Imaging of prostate cancer using urokinase-type plasminogen activator receptor PET. PET Clinics 12, 243–255. Copyright 2016 Elsevier.)*

that ^{64}Cu-CB-TE2A-PA-AE105 displayed better tumor-liver ratio. ^{68}Ga was used in place of Cu to reduce the uptake of biomarker by the noninvaded tissues (Persson and Kjaer, 2013).

^{68}Ga-DOTA-AE105-NH_2 (Fig. 16.10) and ^{68}Ga-NOGDA-AE105-NH_2 (Fig. 16.11) were the first gallium-68 labeled radiotracers used to image uPAR through PET scan. U87MG tumor cells displayed high uptake of both tracers (Fig. 16.12) (Persson and Kjaer, 2013).

The final studies were performed using ^{18}F-labeled uPAR PET ligand, ^{18}F-AlF-NOTA-AE105 (Fig. 16.13) (Persson et al., 2013). It displayed good visualization of tumor in mouse models with high tumor-to-background ratios (Persson et al., 2013). Tumor targeting by the tracer was evaluated in mice with subcutaneously inoculated PC-3 xenografts using small animal PET. uPAR binding specificity was also evaluated by co-injection of excess of uPAR antagonist peptide AE105 analog (AE152). Results showed a high specific uptake by the prostate tumor. uPAR binding specificity was showed by decreased uptake of the tracer after co-injection of a blocking dose of uPAR antagonist (Fig. 16.14).

The plasminogen activation system (PAS) is also a highly interesting target for biomarker based imaging strategy for castration resistant prostate cancer. In line with this, LeBeau et al. (2014) worked on human fragment antigen-binding

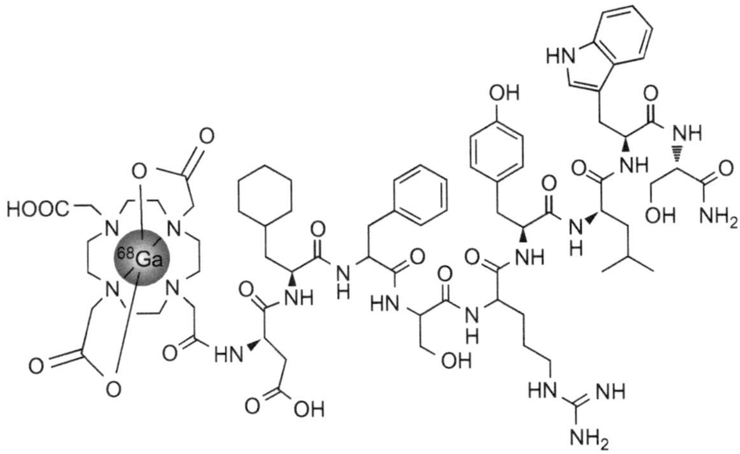

FIG. 16.10 Structure of ^{68}Ga-DOTA-AE105-NH_2. *(Reproduced with permission from Persson, M., Madsen, J., Ostergaard, S., Ploug, M., Kjaer, A., 2012. ^{68}Ga-labeling and in vivo evaluation of a uPAR binding DOTA- and NODAGA-conjugated peptide for PET imaging of invasive cancers. Nucl. Med. Biol. 39, 560–569. Copyright 2012 Elsevier.)*

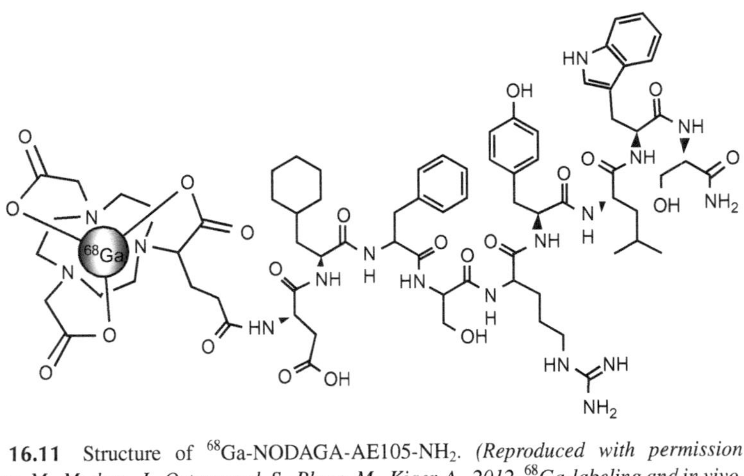

FIG. 16.11 Structure of ^{68}Ga-NODAGA-AE105-NH_2. *(Reproduced with permission from Persson, M., Madsen, J., Ostergaard, S., Ploug, M., Kjaer, A., 2012. ^{68}Ga-labeling and in vivo evaluation of a uPAR binding DOTA- and NODAGA-conjugated peptide for PET imaging of invasive cancers. Nucl. Med. Biol. 39, 560–569. Copyright 2012 Elsevier.)*

phage display library. They found that human antibody U33 displayed selective inhibition of uPA. Therefore, these authors used U33 IgG labeled with near-infrared fluorophores/radionuclides to image active uPA in PC xenograft models through optical and single photon emission computed tomography. ^{111}In labeled U33 Ig displayed significant tumor uptake of 43.2% at 72 h post injection. U33 IgG was labeled with Alexa Fluor 680 and used to detect uPA in vivo

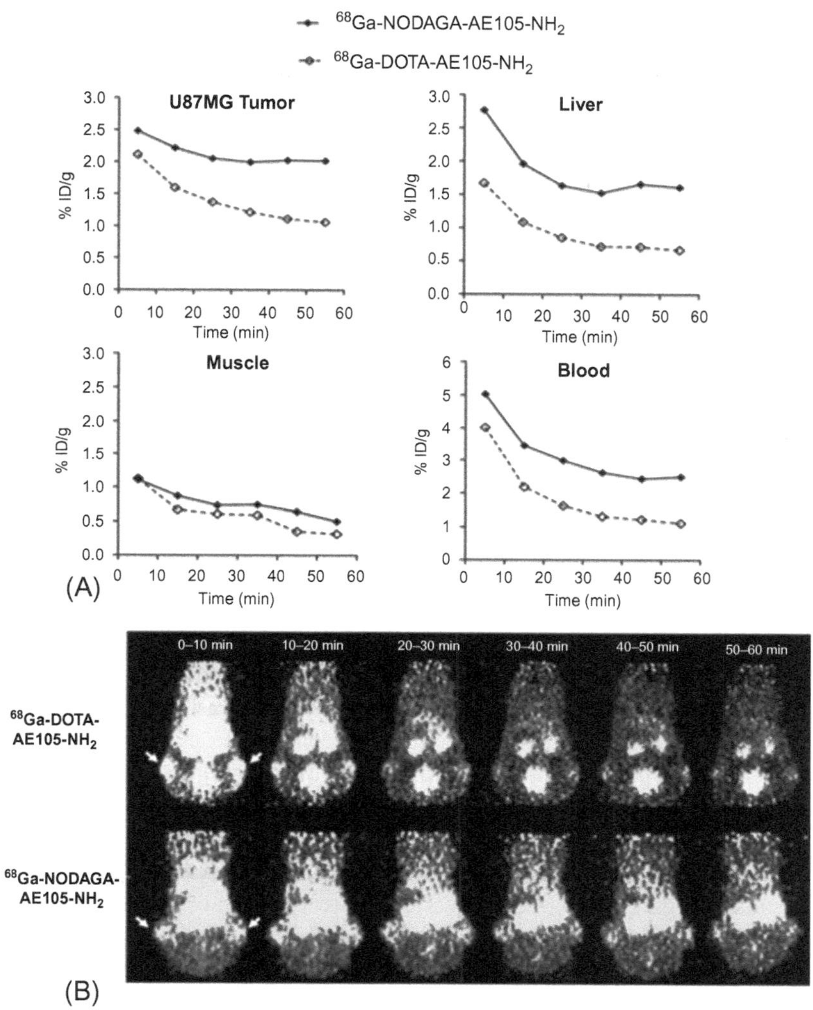

FIG. 16.12 (A) Quantitative results based on ROI analysis for the organ/tissue indicated during 1 h PET scan and (B) 10 min PET images taken during 1 h PET recording. White arrows indicate tumor. *(Reproduced with permission from Persson, M., Madsen, J., Ostergaard, S., Ploug, M., Kjaer, A., 2012. ^{68}Ga-labeling and in vivo evaluation of a uPAR binding DOTA- and NODAGA-conjugated peptide for PET imaging of invasive cancers. Nucl. Med. Biol. 39, 560–569. Copyright 2012 Elsevier.)*

through NIR optical imaging. However, PC3 xenograft showed highest uptake and retention, while DU145 xenograft demonstrated lower biomarker uptake and no uptake was shown by CWR22Rv1 xenograft. This kind of probe has an advantage of being an ideal candidate for radioimmunotherapy as well (LeBeau et al., 2014).

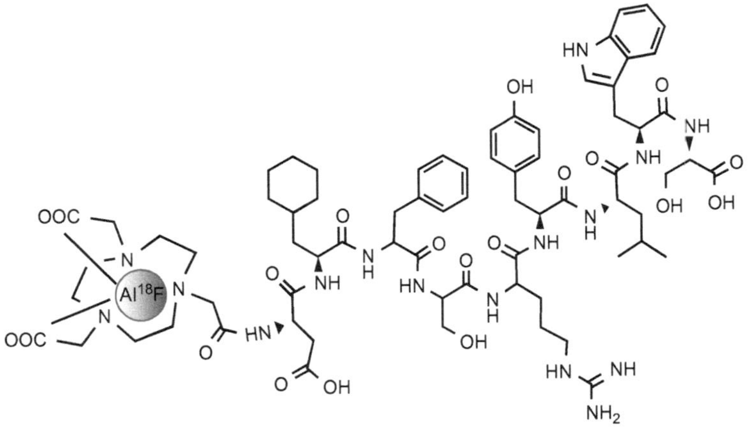

FIG. 16.13 Chemical structure of ^{18}F-AlF-NOTA-AE105. *(Reproduced with permission from Persson, M., Liu, H., Madsen, J., Cheng, Z., Kjaer, A., 2013. First 18F-labeled ligand for PET imaging of uPAR: In vivo studies in human prostate cancer xenografts. Nucl. Med. Biol. 40, 618–624. Copyright 2013 Elsevier.)*

16.4 Conclusions

Various proteases are present in tumor and its surrounding tissues which provide the high oxygen demand and nutrition supply required by the tumor region. Early stages of tumor progression display high concentration of these proteases; therefore, development in strategies to recognize these proteases might help in achieving optimized cancer therapy or control. Human degradome has at least 569 proteases of five classes (serine, metalloprotease, cysteine, aspartic acid, and threonine) but all of them are not linked with cancer. Different studies show that molecular imaging could play critical role in recognition of various proteases. It is noninvasive imaging modality used for in vivo visualization, characterization, and measurement of specific proteases. These imaging techniques employ target specific molecular probes which interact with key proteases involved in tumor development and help to enhance image contrast. Imaging protease has few advantages, for example, imaging probe does not need to penetrate deep into intracellular environment as proteases are secreted from extracellular compartments. Moreover, the proteases are physiologically active and functionally catalytic and this catalytic activity promotes signal amplification.

Protease imaging is performed by using nuclear strategies such as MRI, Single Photon Emission Computed Tomography (SPECT), Positron Emission Tomography (PET), and optical modalities such as fluorescence and bioluminescence.

Imaging MMPs is considered as a nascent field. A number of probes have been developed with different sequences to target MMPs. The commonly employed imaging techniques for MMPs include Optical Imaging (OIM),

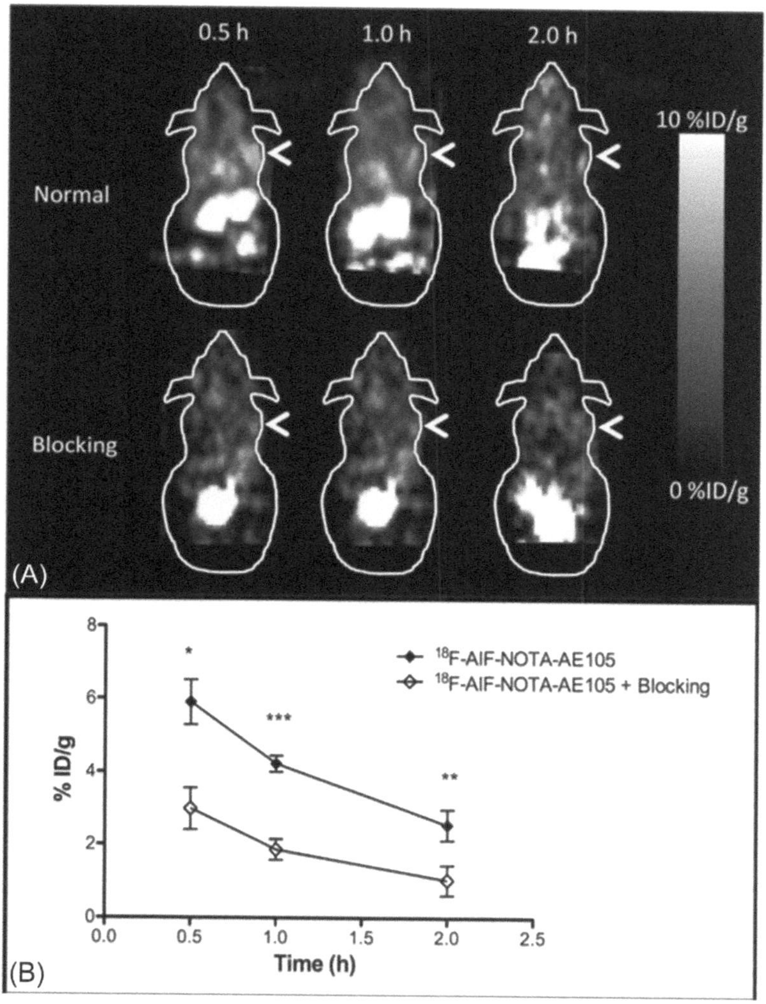

FIG. 16.14 (A) PET images after 0.5h, 1h, 2h post injection of ^{18}F-AIF-NOTA-AE105 and ^{18}F-AIF-NOTA-AE105 with blocking dose of AE152. Tumor indicated by white arrows and (B) Quantitative ROI analysis with tumor uptake values. Significantly higher uptake was observed in normal group as compared to that of blocking group. *(Reproduced with permission from Persson, M., Liu, H., Madsen, J., Cheng, Z., Kjaer, A., 2013. First 18F-labeled ligand for PET imaging of uPAR: In vivo studies in human prostate cancer xenografts. Nucl. Med. Biol. 40, 618–624. Copyright 2013 Elsevier.)*

Magnetic Resonance Imaging (MRI), Positron Emission Tomography (PET), and Single Photon Emission Computed Tomography (SPECT). Early studies showed bioluminescence as a highly sensitive technique for detecting in vivo MMPs activity over a wide range but it proved to be in effectual for in vitro biological cell assays.

MRI is the most extensively provided imaging modality in hospitals and clinical settings across the globe and highly suggestive for cancer imaging. MRI gives superb anatomical resolution but a very low sensitivity. Higher resolution assists in getting precise identification of invasive cancer but due to limited sensitivity, generally higher amount of ligand is necessary to get sufficient signal in MRI. In contrast to SPECT and PET where lower amount of ligands are needed, this factor presents a challenge as toxicity might occur at such high dose. The Gadolinium (Gd)-based contrast agents are most regularly deployed in MRI. The NIRF optical imaging is although very sensitive technique but it does not provide three-dimensional imaging neither in higher animal nor in humans because of lack of deep penetration.

Clinical applications of uPAR display restricted potential due to scarce number of available ligands. Optical imaging ligands for uPAR present remarkable clinical potential in image-guided surgery. Since uPAR is mostly expressed at the front of invasive tumors, uPAR targeted ligands utilization in imaging guided surgery would markedly aid in reduction of patients with postoperative relapse of cancer. SPECT imaging is considered as clinical important as its higher sensitivity detects small micro-metastatic lesions and invasive cancers. Another reason for considering SPECT imaging of uPAR as highly appealing is its low cost, availability of gamma cameras, and facile radiochemistry especially when using 99mTc. PET imaging is considered the best imaging modality for uPAR as it poses high sensitivity combined with truly quantitative data. Noninvasive uPAR imaging in prostate cancer, with the probability to distinguish indolent tumors from invasive and aggressive tumors, would prove to be a significant diagnostic and prognostic imaging biomarker.

References

Abdalla, M.O., Karna, P., Sajja, H.K., Mao, H., Yates, C., Turner, T., et al., 2011. Enhanced noscapine delivery using uPAR-targeted optical-MR imaging trackable nanoparticles for prostate cancer therapy. J. Control. Release 149, 314–322.

Achilefu, S., Jimenez, H.N., Dorshow, R.B., Bugaj, J.E., Webb, E.G., Wilhelm, R.R., et al., 2002. Synthesis, in vitro receptor binding, and in vivo evaluation of fluorescein and carbocyanine peptide-based optical contrast agents. J. Med. Chem. 45, 2003–2015.

Albritton, J.L., Miller, J.S., 2017. 3D bioprinting: improving in vitro models of metastasis with heterogeneous tumor microenvironments. Dis. Model. Mech. 10, 3–14.

Almasi, C.E., Brasso, K., Iversen, P., Pappot, H., Høyer-Hansen, G., Danø, K., et al., 2011. Prognostic and predictive value of intact and cleaved forms of the urokinase plasminogen activator receptor in metastatic prostate cancer. Prostate 71, 899–907.

Andreasen, P.A., Kjøller, L., Christensen, L., Duffy, M.J., 1997. The urokinase-type plasminogen activator system in cancer metastasis: a review. Int. J. Cancer 72, 1–22.

Baruch, A., Jeffery, D.A., Bogyo, M., 2004. Enzyme activity – it's all about image. Trends Cell Biol. 14, 29–35.

Berger, A.B., Vitorin, P.M., Bogyo, M., 2004. Activity-based protein profiling. Am. J. Pharmacogenomics 4, 371–381.

Blasi, F., Sidenius, N., 2010. The urokinase receptor: focused cell surface proteolysis, cell adhesion and signaling. FEBS Lett. 584, 1923–1930.

Blum, G., 2008. Use of fluorescent imaging to investigate pathological protease activity. Curr. Opin. Drug Discov. Dev. 11, 708–716.

Blum, G., Von Degenfeld, G., Merchant, M.J., Blau, H.M., Bogyo, M., 2007. Noninvasive optical imaging of cysteine protease activity using fluorescently quenched activity-based probes. Nat. Chem. Biol. 3, 668.

Boonstra, C.M., Verspaget, W.H., Ganesh, F.S., Kubben, J.G.M., Vahrmeijer, A.L., van de Velde, J.H.C., et al., 2011. Clinical applications of the urokinase receptor (uPAR) for cancer patients. Curr. Pharm. Des. 17, 1890–1910.

Bremer, C., Tung, C.-H., Weissleder, R., 2001. In vivo molecular target assessment of matrix metalloproteinase inhibition. Nat. Med. 7, 743.

Bremer, C., Tung, C.-H., Bogdanov Jr., A., Weissleder, R., 2002. Imaging of differential protease expression in breast cancers for detection of aggressive tumor phenotypes. Radiology 222, 814–818.

Brown, P.D., 1999. Clinical studies with matrix metalloproteinase inhibitors. APMIS 107, 174–180.

Casslén, B., Gustavsson, B., Åstedt, B., 1991. Cell membrane receptors for urokinase plasminogen activator are increased in malignant ovarian tumors. Eur. J. Cancer Clin. Oncol. 27, 1445–1448.

Chaffer, C.L., Weinberg, R.A., 2011. A perspective on cancer cell metastasis. Science 331, 1559–1564.

Clapper, M.L., Hensley, H.H., Chang, W.-C.L., Devarajan, K., Nguyen, M.T., Cooper, H.S., 2011. Detection of colorectal adenomas using a bioactivatable probe specific for matrix metalloproteinase activity. Neoplasia 13, 685–691.

Cozzi, P.J., Wang, J., Delprado, W., Madigan, M.C., Fairy, S., Russell, P.J., et al., 2006. Evaluation of urokinase plasminogen activator and its receptor in different grades of human prostate cancer. Hum. Pathol. 37, 1442–1451.

Cruz-Monserrate, Z., Abd-Elgaliel, W.R., Grote, T., Deng, D., Ji, B., Arumugam, T., et al., 2012. Detection of pancreatic cancer tumours and precursor lesions by cathepsin E activity in mouse models. Gut 61 (9), 1315–1322.

Danø, K., Behrendt, N., Høyer-Hansen, G., Johnsen, M., Lund, L.R., Ploug, M., et al., 2005. Plasminogen activation and cancer. Thromb. Haemost. 93, 676–681.

Dass, K., Ahmad, A., Azmi, A.S., Sarkar, S.H., Sarkar, F.H., 2008. Evolving role of uPA/uPAR system in human cancers. Cancer Treat. Rev. 34, 122–136.

De Witte, J., Foekens, J., Brünner, N., Heuvel, J., van Tienoven, T., Look, M., et al., 2001. Prognostic impact of urokinase-type plasminogen activator receptor (uPAR) in cytosols and pellet extracts derived from primary breast tumours. Br. J. Cancer 85, 85.

Duffy, M.J., 2004. The urokinase plasminogen activator system: role in malignancy. Curr. Pharm. Des. 10, 39–49.

Duffy, M.J., O'siorain, L., O'grady, P., Devaney, D., Fennelly, J.J., Lijnen, H.J., 1988. Urokinase-plasminogen activator, a marker for aggressive breast carcinomas. Cancer 62, 531–533.

Dullin, C., Zientkowska, M., Napp, J., Missbach-Guentner, J., Krell, H.-W., Muller, F., et al., 2009. Semiautomatic landmark-based two-dimensional–three-dimensional image fusion in living mice: correlation of near-infrared fluorescence imaging of Cy5.5-labeled antibodies with flat-panel volume computed tomography. Mol. Imaging 8 (1), 2–14.

Edgington, L.E., Berger, A.B., Blum, G., Albrow, V.E., Paulick, M.G., Lineberry, N., et al., 2009. Noninvasive optical imaging of apoptosis by caspase-targeted activity-based probes. Nat. Med. 15 (8), 967.

Evangelista, L., Briganti, A., Fanti, S., Joniau, S., Reske, S., Schiavina, R., Stief, C., Thalmann, G.N., Picchio, M., 2016. New clinical indications for 18F/11C-choline, new tracers for positron emission tomography and a promising hybrid device for prostate cancer staging: a systematic review of the literature. Eur. Urol. 70, 161–175.

Feng, X., Yu, Y., He, S., Cheng, J., Gong, Y., Zhang, Z., et al., 2017. Dying glioma cells establish a proangiogenic microenvironment through a caspase 3 dependent mechanism. Cancer Lett. 385, 12–20.

Finzi, G., Cornaggia, M., Capella, C., Fiocca, R., Bosi, F., Solcia, E., et al., 1993. Cathepsin E in follicle associated epithelium of intestine and tonsils: localization to M cells and possible role in antigen processing. Histochemistry 99, 201–211.

Folkman, J., 1984. Angiogenesis. In: Jaffe, E.A. (Ed.), Biology of Endothelial Cells, Developments in Cardiovascular Medicine. vol. 27.

Frullano, L., Tejerina, B., Meade, T.J., 2006. Synthesis and characterization of a doxorubicin-Gd (III) contrast agent conjugate: a new approach toward prodrug-procontrast complexes. Inorg. Chem. 45, 8489–8491.

Funovics, M., Weissleder, R., Tung, C.-H., 2003. Protease sensors for bioimaging. Anal. Bioanal. Chem. 377, 956–963.

Furumoto, S., Takashima, K., Kubota, K., Ido, T., Iwata, R., Fukuda, H., 2003. Tumor detection using 18F-labeled matrix metalloproteinase-2 inhibitor. Nucl. Med. Biol. 30 (2), 119–125.

Ganesh, S., Sier, C.M., Heerding, M., Griffioen, G., Lamers, C.H., Verspaget, H., 1994. Urokinase receptor and colorectal cancer survival. Lancet 344, 401–402.

Gavrilov, D., Kenzior, O., Evans, M., Calaluce, R., Folk, W., 2001. Expression of urokinase plasminogen activator and receptor in conjunction with the ets family and AP-1 complex transcription factors in high grade prostate cancers. Eur. J. Cancer 37, 1033–1040.

Greenbaum, D., Baruch, A., Hayrapetian, L., Darula, Z., Burlingame, A., Medzihradszky, K.F., et al., 2002. Chemical approaches for functionally probing the proteome. Mol. Cell. Proteomics 1, 60–68.

Haris, M., Singh, A., Mohammed, I., Ittyerah, R., Nath, K., Nanga, R.P.R., et al., 2014. In vivo magnetic resonance imaging of tumor protease activity. Sci. Rep. 4, 6081.

Hildenbrand, R., Leitz, M., Magdolen, V., Luther, T., Albrecht, S., Graeff, H., et al., 2000. Validation of immunolocalization of the urokinase receptor expression in ductal carcinoma in situ of the breast: comparison with detection by non-isotopic in-situ hybridization. Histopathology 36, 499–504.

Jacobsen, B., Ploug, M., 2008. The urokinase receptor and its structural homologue C4. 4A in human cancer: expression, prognosis and pharmacological inhibition. Curr. Med. Chem. 15, 2559–2573.

James, M.L., Gambhir, S.S., 2012. A molecular imaging primer: modalities, imaging agents, and applications. Physiol. Rev. 92, 897–965.

Jiang, T., Olson, E.S., Nguyen, Q.T., Roy, M., Jennings, P.A., Tsien, R.Y., 2004. Tumor imaging by means of proteolytic activation of cell-penetrating peptides. Proc. Natl. Acad. Sci. 101, 17867–17872.

Kircher, M.F., Allport, J.R., Graves, E.E., Love, V., Josephson, L., Lichtman, A.H., et al., 2003. In vivo high resolution three-dimensional imaging of antigen-specific cytotoxic T-lymphocyte trafficking to tumors. Cancer Res. 63, 6838–6846.

Kumano, M., Miyake, H., Muramaki, M., Furukawa, J., Takenaka, A., Fujisawa, M., 2009. Expression of urokinase-type plasminogen activator system in prostate cancer: correlation with clinicopathological outcomes in patients undergoing radical prostatectomy. Urol. Oncol. Semin. Ori. 27, 180–186.

Kurtova, A.V., Xiao, J., Mo, Q., Pazhanisamy, S., Krasnow, R., Lerner, S.P., et al., 2015. Blocking PGE 2-induced tumour repopulation abrogates bladder cancer chemoresistance. Nature 517, 209.

Lauer-Fields, J.L., Minond, D., Brew, K., Fields, G.B., 2007. Application of topologically constrained mini-proteins as ligands, substrates, and inhibitors. In: Fields, G.B. (Ed.), Peptide Characterization and Application Protocols.

LeBeau, A.M., Sevillano, N., King, M.L., Duriseti, S., Murphy, S.T., Craik, C.S., et al., 2014. Imaging the urokinase plasminogen activator receptor in preclinical breast cancer models of acquired drug resistance. Theranostics 4, 267–279.

Lee, S., Cha, E.J., Park, K., Lee, S.Y., Hong, J.K., Sun, I.C., et al., 2008. A near-infrared-fluorescence-quenched gold-nanoparticle imaging probe for in vivo drug screening and protease activity determination. Angew. Chem. 120, 2846–2849.

Li, D., Liu, S., Shan, H., Conti, P., Li, Z., 2013. Urokinase plasminogen activator receptor (uPAR) targeted nuclear imaging and radionuclide therapy. Theranostics 3, 507–515.

Li, Z.-B., Niu, G., Wang, H., He, L., Yang, L., Ploug, M., et al., 2008. Imaging of urokinase-type plasminogen activator receptor expression using a 64Cu-labeled linear peptide antagonist by microPET. Clin. Cancer Res. 14, 4758–4766.

Liaudet-Coopman, E., Beaujouin, M., Derocq, D., Garcia, M., Glondu-Lassis, M., Laurent-Matha, V., et al., 2006. Cathepsin D: newly discovered functions of a long-standing aspartic protease in cancer and apoptosis. Cancer Lett. 237, 167–179.

Lijnen, H., Silence, J., Lemmens, G., Frederix, L., Collen, D., 1998. Regulation of gelatinase activity in mice with targeted inactivation of components of the plasminogen/plasmin system. Thromb. Haemost. 79, 1171–1176.

Lin, C.-K., Lai, K.-H., Lo, G.-H., Cheng, J.-S., Hsu, P.-I., Mok, K.-T., et al., 2001. Cathepsin E and sub types of intestinal metaplasia in carcinogenesis of the Hu man stomach. Chin. Med. J. 64, 331–336.

Linnevers, C.J., Mcgrath, M.E., Armstrong, A., Mistry, F.R., Barnes, M.G., Klaus, J.L., et al., 1997b. Expression of human cathepsin K in Pichia pastoris and preliminary crystallographic studies of an inhibitor complex. Protein Sci. 6, 919–921.

Linnevers, C., Smeekens, S., Brömme, D., 1997a. Human cathepsin W, a putative cysteine protease predominantly expressed in CD8+ T-lymphocytes. FEBS Lett. 405, 253–259.

Liu, D., Overbey, D., Watkinson, L., Giblin, M.F., 2009. Synthesis and characterization of an (111) In-labeled peptide for the in vivo localization of human cancers expressing the urokinase-type plasminogen activator receptor (uPAR). Bioconjugate Chem. 20, 888–894.

Louie, A.Y., Huber, M.M., Ahrens, E.T., Rothbacher, U., Moats, R., Jacobs, R.E., et al., 2000. In vivo visualization of gene expression using magnetic resonance imaging. Nat. Biotechnol. (3), 321–325.

Mahmood, U., Weissleder, R., 2003. Near-infrared optical imaging of proteases in cancer. Mol. Cancer Ther. 2, 489–496.

Matsuo, K., Kobayashi, I., Tsukuba, T., Kiyoshima, T., Ishibashi, Y., Miyoshi, A., et al., 1996. Immunohistochemical localization of cathepsins D and E in human gastric cancer: a possible correlation with local invasive and metastatic activities of carcinoma cells. Hum. Pathol. 27, 184–190.

McIntyre, J.O., Matrisian, L.M., 2003. Molecular imaging of proteolytic activity in cancer. J. Cell. Biochem. 90, 1087–1097.

Messerli, S.M., Prabhakar, S., Tang, Y., Shah, K., Cortes, M.L., Murthy, V., et al., 2004. A novel method for imaging apoptosis using a caspase-1 near-infrared fluorescent probe. Neoplasia 6, 95–105.

Mohamed, M.M., Sloane, B.F., 2006. Cysteine cathepsins: multifunctional enzymes in cancer. Nat. Rev. Cancer 6, 764–775.

Nicholl, S.M., Roztocil, E., Davies, M.G., 2006. Plasminogen activator system and vascular disease. Curr. Vasc. Pharmacol. 4, 101–116.

Niu, G., Chen, X., 2010. Apoptosis imaging: beyond annexin V. J. Nucl. Med. 51, 1659–1662.

Olson, O.C., Joyce, J.A., 2015. Cysteine cathepsin proteases: regulators of cancer progression and therapeutic response. Nat. Rev. Cancer 15, 712–729.

Olsson, M., Zhivotovsky, B., 2011. Caspases and cancer. Cell Death Differ. 18, 1441–1449.

Oltenfreiter, R., Staelens, L., Kersemans, V., Cornelissen, B., Frankenne, F., Foidart, J.-M., et al., 2006. Valine-based biphenylsulphonamide matrix metalloproteinase inhibitors as tumor imaging agents. Appl. Radiat. Isot. 64, 677–685.

Oltenfreiter, R., Staelens, L., Labied, S., Kersemans, V., Frankenne, F., Noël, A., et al., 2005. Tryptophane-based biphenylsulfonamide matrix metalloproteinase inhibitors as tumor imaging agents. Cancer Biother. Radiopharm. 20, 639–647.

Ossowski, L., Clunie, G., Masucci, M., Blasi, F., 1991. In vivo paracrine interaction between urokinase and its receptor: effect on tumor cell invasion. J. Cell Biol. 115, 1107–1112.

Pasinelli, P., Houseweart, M.K., Brown, R.H., Cleveland, D.W., 2000. Caspase-1 and-3 are sequentially activated in motor neuron death in Cu, Zn superoxide dismutase-mediated familial amyotrophic lateral sclerosis. Proc. Natl. Acad. Sci. 97, 13901–13906.

Persson, M., El Ali, H.H., Tina, B., Pfeifer, A., Madsen, J., Rasmussen, P., Kjaer, A., et al., 2014. Dosimetry of 64Cu-DOTA-AE105, a PET tracer for uPAR imaging. Nucl. Med. Biol. 41, 290–295.

Persson, M., Kjaer, A., 2013. Urokinase-type plasminogen activator receptor (uPAR) as a promising new imaging target: potential clinical applications. Clin. Physiol. Funct. Imaging 33, 329–337.

Persson, M., Liu, H., Madsen, J., Cheng, Z., Kjaer, A., 2013. First 18F-labeled ligand for PET imaging of uPAR: In vivo studies in human prostate cancer xenografts. Nucl. Med. Biol. 40, 618–624.

Ploug, M., 2012. Structure-driven design of radionuclide tracers for non-invasive imaging of uPAR: the tale of a synthetic peptide antagonist. Theranostics 3, 467–476.

Ploug, M., Behrendt, N., Løber, D., Danø, K., 1991. Protein structure and membrane anchorage of the cellular receptor for urokinase-type plasminogen activator. Semin. Thromb. Hemost. 17, 183–193.

Ploug, M., Eriksen, J., Plesner, T., Hansen, N.E., Dano, K., 1992. A soluble form of the glycolipid-anchored receptor for urokinase-type plasminogen activator is secreted from peripheral blood leukocytes from patients with paroxysmal nocturnal hemoglobinuria. Eur. J. Biochem. 208, 397–404.

Ploug, M., Østergaard, S., Gårdsvoll, H., Kovalski, K., Holst-Hansen, C., Holm, A., et al., 2001. Peptide-derived antagonists of the urokinase receptor. Affinity maturation by combinatorial chemistry, identification of functional epitopes, and inhibitory effect on cancer cell intravasation. Biochemistry 40, 12157–12168.

Prasad, N.B., Biankin, A.V., Fukushima, N., Maitra, A., Dhara, S., Elkahloun, A.G., et al., 2005. Gene expression profiles in pancreatic intraepithelial neoplasia reflect the effects of Hedgehog signaling on pancreatic ductal epithelial cells. Cancer Res. 65, 1619–1626.

Pyke, C., Graem, N., Ralfkiaer, E., Rønne, E., Høyer-Hansen, G., Brünner, N., et al., 1993. Receptor for urokinase is present in tumor-associated macrophages in ductal breast carcinoma. Cancer Res. 53, 1911–1915.

Pyke, C., Ralfkiaer, E., Rønne, E., Høyer-Hansen, G., Kirkeby, L., Danø, K., 1994. Immunohistochemical detection of the receptor for urokinase plasminogen activator in human colon cancer. Histopathology 24, 131–138.

Rakashanda, S., Rana, F., Rafiq, S., Masood, A., Amin, S., 2012. Role of proteases in cancer: a review. Biotechnol. Mol. Biol. Rev. 7, 90–101.

Rao, J., Dragulescu-Andrasi, A., Yao, H., 2007. Fluorescence imaging in vivo: recent advances. Curr. Opin. Biotechnol. 18, 17–25.

Razgulin, A., Ma, N., Rao, J., 2011. Strategies for in vivo imaging of enzyme activity: an overview and recent advances. Chem. Soc. Rev. 40, 4186–4216.

Riddick, A., Shukla, C., Pennington, C., Bass, R., Nuttall, R., Hogan, A., et al., 2005. Identification of degradome components associated with prostate cancer progression by expression analysis of human prostatic tissues. Br. J. Cancer 92, 2171.

Riese, R.J., Chapman, H.A., 2000. Cathepsins and compartmentalization in antigen presentation. Curr. Opin. Immunol. 12, 107–113.

Riggenbach, N., von Kaulla, K.N., 1961. Urokinase excretion in patients with carcinoma. Cancer 14, 889–896.

Saghatelian, A., Cravatt, B.F., 2005. Assignment of protein function in the postgenomic era. Nat. Chem. Biol. 1, 130.

Saghatelian, A., Jessani, N., Joseph, A., Humphrey, M., Cravatt, B.F., 2004. Activity-based probes for the proteomic profiling of metalloproteases. Proc. Natl. Acad. Sci. 101, 10000–10005.

Sagi, I., Gaffney, J., 2015. Introduction to the MMP and TIMP families (structures, substrates) and an overview of diseases where MMPs have been incriminated. In: Sagi, I. (Ed.), Biology and Chemistry of Matrix Metalloproteinases (MMPs).

Sakai, H., Saku, T., Kato, Y., Yamamoto, K., 1989. Quantitation and immunohistochemical localization of cathepsins E and D in rat tissues and blood cells. BBA-Gen Subjects 991, 367–375.

Salaün, M., Peng, J., Hensley, H.H., Roder, N., Flieder, D.B., Houlle-Crépin, S., et al., 2015. MMP-13 in-vivo molecular imaging reveals early expression in lung adenocarcinoma. PLoS One 10, e0132960.

Sastradipura, D.F., Nakanishi, H., Tsukuba, T., Nishishita, K., Sakai, H., Kato, Y., et al., 1998. Identification of cellular compartments involved in processing of cathepsin E in primary cultures of rat microglia. J. Neurochem. 70, 2045–2056.

Scherer, R.L., McIntyre, J.O., Matrisian, L.M., 2008a. Imaging matrix metalloproteinases in cancer. Cancer Metastasis Rev. 27, 679.

Scherer, R.L., VanSaun, M.N., McIntyre, J.O., Matrisian, L.M., 2008b. Optical imaging of matrix metalloproteinase-7 activity in vivo using a proteolytic nanobeacon. Mol Imaging 7, 118–131.

Schwartz, D.R., Homanics, G.E., Hoyt, D.G., Klein, E., Abernethy, J., Lazo, J.S., 1999. The neutral cysteine protease bleomycin hydrolase is essential for epidermal integrity and bleomycin resistance. Proc. Natl. Acad. Sci. 96, 4680–4685.

Segal, E., Prestwood, T.R., van der Linden, W.A., Carmi, Y., Bhattacharya, N., Withana, N., et al., 2015. Detection of intestinal cancer by local, topical application of a quenched fluorescence probe for cysteine cathepsins. Chem. Biol. 22, 148–158.

Seiki, M., 1999. Membrane-type matrix metalloproteinases. Apmis 107, 137–143.

Shalinsky, D., Brekken, J., Zou, H., McDermott, C., Forsyth, P., Edwards, D., et al., 1999. Broad antitumor and antiangiogenic activities of AG3340, a potent and selective MMP inhibitor undergoing advanced oncology clinical trials. Ann. N. Y. Acad. Sci. 878, 236–270.

Skovgaard, D., Persson, M., Kjaer, A., 2017. Imaging of prostate cancer using urokinase-type plasminogen activator receptor PET. PET Clinics 12, 243–255.

Skrzypczak, M., Springwald, A., Lattrich, C., Häring, J., Schüler, S., Ortmann, O., Treeck, O., 2012. Expression of cysteine protease cathepsin L is increased in endometrial cancer and correlates with expression of growth regulatory genes. Cancer Investig. 30, 398–403.

Tang, L., Han, X., 2013. The urokinase plasminogen activator system in breast cancer invasion and metastasis. Biomed. Pharmacother. 67, 179–182.

Tenti, P., Romagnoli, S., Silini, E., Zappatore, R., Giunta, P., Stella, G., et al., 1994. Cervical adenocarcinomas express markers common to gastric, intestinal, and pancreatobiliary epithelial cells. Pathol. Res. Pract. 190, 342–349.

Thornberry, N.A., Bull, H.G., Calaycay, J.R., Chapman, K.T., Howard, A.D., Kostura, M.J., et al., 1992. A novel heterodimeric cysteine protease is required for interleukin-1βprocessing in monocytes. Nature 356, 768–774.

Tung, C.-H., Bredow, S., Mahmood, U., Weissleder, R., 1999. Preparation of a cathepsin D sensitive near-infrared fluorescence probe for imaging. Bioconjugate Chem. 10, 892–896.

Usher, P.A., Thomsen, O.F., Iversen, P., Johnsen, M., Brünner, N., Høyer-Hansen, G., 2005. Expression of urokinase plasminogen activator, its receptor and type-1 inhibitor in malignant and benign prostate tissue. Int. J. Cancer 113, 870–880.

van Duijnhoven, S.M., Robillard, M.S., Langereis, S., Grüll, H., 2015. Bioresponsive probes for molecular imaging: concepts and in vivo applications. Contrast Media Mol. Imaging 10, 282–308.

Vangestel, C., Thomae, D., Van Soom, J., Ides, J.L., Wyffels, P., Pauwels, S., et al., 2016. Preclinical evaluation of [111In] MICA-401, an activity-based probe for SPECT imaging of in vivo uPA activity. Contrast Media Mol. Imaging 11, 448–458.

Vassalli, J.-D., Baccino, D., Belin, D., 1985. A cellular binding site for the Mr. 55,000 form of the human plasminogen activator, urokinase. J. Cell Biol. 100, 86–92.

Velasco, G., Ferrando, A.A., Puente, X.S., Sánchez, L.M., López-Otín, C., 1994. Human cathepsin O. Molecular cloning from a breast carcinoma, production of the active enzyme in *Escherichia coli*, and expression analysis in human tissues. J. Biol. Chem. 269, 27136–27142.

von Burstin, J., Eser, S., Seidler, B., Meining, A., Bajbouj, M., Mages, J., et al., 2008. Highly sensitive detection of early-stage pancreatic cancer by multimodal near-infrared molecular imaging in living mice. Int. J. Cancer 123, 2138–2147.

Wang, M., Lowik, D.W., Miller, A.D., Thanou, M., 2008. Targeting the urokinase plasminogen activator receptor with synthetic self-assembly nanoparticles. Bioconjug. Chem. 20, 32–40.

Yamamoto, N., Bryce, N.S., Metzler-Nolte, N., Hambley, T.W., 2012. Effects of enzymatic activation on the distribution of fluorescently tagged MMP-2 cleavable peptides in cancer cells and spheroids. Bioconjugate Chem. 23, 1110–1118.

Yan, Q., Yuan, Y., Yankui, L., Jingjie, F., Linfang, J., Yong, P., et al., 2015. The expression and significance of CXCR5 and MMP-13 in colorectal cancer. Biochem. Biophys. 73, 253–259.

Yang, Y., Adelstein, S.J., Kassis, A.I., 2011. General approach to identifying potential targets for cancer imaging by integrated bioinformatics analysis of publicly available genomic profiles. Mol. Imaging 10, 123–134.

Yang, Y., Hong, H., Zhang, Y., Cai, W., 2009. Molecular imaging of proteases in cancer. Cancer Growth Metastasis 2, 13–27.

Zheng, G., Chen, J., Stefflova, K., Jarvi, M., Li, H., Wilson, B.C., 2007. Photodynamic molecular beacon as an activatable photosensitizer based on protease-controlled singlet oxygen quenching and activation. Proc. Natl. Acad. Sci. 104, 8989–8994.

Further reading

Persson, M., Madsen, J., Østergaard, S., Plouga, M., Kjaer, A., 2012. 68Ga-labeling and in vivo evaluation of a uPAR binding DOTA- and NODAGA-conjugated peptide for PET imaging of invasive cancers. Nucl. Med. Biol. 39, 560–569.

Pittayapruek, P., Meephanasan, J., Prapapan, O., Komine, M., Ohtsuki, M., 2016. Role of matrix metalloproteinases in photoaging and photocarcinogenesis. Int. J. Mol. Sci. 17, 868. https://doi.org/10.3390/ijms17060868.

Index

Note: Page numbers followed by *f* indicate figures and *t* indicate tables.

B

C

D

E

I

J

K

L

M

U

V

Kolibri 360 GmbH
Ferdinand-Jühlke-Straße 7
99095 Erfurt, Deutschland
produktsicherheit@kolibri360.de